Musici

Songwriters'

YEARBOOK

2008

Musicians' & Songwriters'
YEARBOOK
2008

Edited by Jonathan Little & Katie Chatburn

A & C Black • London

Second edition 2007
A & C Black Publishers Limited
38 Soho Square, London W1D 3HB
www.acblack.com

© 2007 A & C Black Publishers Limited

ISBN: 978-0-7136-8472-8

A CIP catalogue record for this book is available from the British Library.

This book is produced using paper that is made from wood grown in managed, sustainable forests. It is natural, renewable and recyclable. The logging and manufacturing processes conform to the environmental regulations of the country of origin.

Typeset by QPM from David Lewis XML Associates Ltd
Printed and bound in Great Britain by William Clowes Ltd, Beccles, Suffolk

Contents

Marketing, Management and Finance

Foreword

John Kennedy has headed record companies internationally and in the UK since the mid-1990s. Prior to becoming Chairman of IFPI – the music industry body which represents the recording industry worldwide – he was President and Chief Operating Officer of Universal Music International. Earlier in his 25-year music industry career, Kennedy was a successful entertainment lawyer, working with major artists, managers, and major and independent record labels. In the 1980s he played a leading role in the Band Aid and Live Aid projects, for which he was honoured with an OBE from the British government in 1985.

The value of creativity

A piece of music is a work of art that can live forever. Legend has it that 'Greensleeves' was written by Henry VIII for Anne Boleyn in the 1520s; more than 450 years later it was still being played – with American television producers using its stirring strains as the theme music for *Lassie*. As 'Greensleeves' now approaches its half-millennium, the tune is more widely known and appreciated than ever before.

Will any of the popular music generated today match the longevity of 'Greensleeves'? Some people think that modern pop music is ephemeral, and that therefore the answer is clearly, "No." Yet The Beatles' 'She Loves You' is already 44 years old, and it is still being played regularly.

How much do we value such creative works? In general, the answer is – disappointingly – not very much. I am always surprised when some people complain that the price of a legal music download, at around a dollar per track on most services, is too high. A work of art to own for life in exchange for half the price of a cup of coffee seems a bargain to me.

Of course, many people do not even pay that small amount of money. Billions of songs each year are downloaded illegally without the copyright-owner's consent. This is copyright infringement, and threatens to suck the life out of musical creativity – with the losers being the composers, artists and record producers who do not get a cent for their work.

No wonder investing in new music is a risky enterprise. Only one in ten new acts signed by record labels actually becomes a commercial success. It is the revenue from the sales generated by such acts that is ploughed back into investment in new talent as part of a 'virtuous cycle' at the heart of the music industry. Piracy threatens this whole business model.

The British government says that the creative industries are now a major force in the economy. They deliver four times the output of the agriculture, fisheries and forestry sectors combined, employ around five per cent of the UK's working population, and generate billions for the economy. Yet the sector remains vulnerable to piracy, and it should always be remembered that these creative industries could still be lost if we do not value creativity highly enough.

We must try to win the hearts and minds of the next generation, many of whom could well choose to work in the creative industries when they are older. The long-term consequences of piracy should be explained to everyone, and an appreciation of the concept of copyright firmly embedded within the school curriculum.

Once we recognise that copyright infringement is just plain theft and something that could damage all our future prospects, then we can begin to secure the creative sector, and enable

x Foreword

it truly to flourish. Musicians and songwriters must be able to earn a healthy living from their trade, so that consumers can continue to enjoy all manner of exciting new music – a proportion of which, in years to come, will surely achieve the longevity of songs like 'She Loves You', or even 'Greensleeves'.

John Kennedy, OBE
(Chairman and CEO, International Federation of the Phonographic Industry – www.ifpi.org)

About the editors

Consultant Editor

Dr Jonathan Little is a concert music composer whose works are published in Australia, and recorded in America on the ERM label. He holds a PhD in orchestration, and is a member of the Royal Philharmonic Society, the British Academy of Composers and Song-writers, and ASCAP in America. From 2001 to 2006 he was Principal of the Academy of Contemporary Music – Europe's largest school for rock and pop musicians. Also in 2001, he co-founded *Music Business Journal*, and was for five years its joint Managing Editor, while additionally writing on the future of the music and film industries for the Hudson Institute's prestigious *American Outlook* magazine. Jonathan is currently a music education consultant, Curriculum Advisor to the Brighton Institute of Modern Music, and Associate or Visiting Lecturer in Music at the Universities of Surrey and Chichester.

Assistant Editor

Katie Chatburn trained at the Royal Academy of Music as a media music composer. She currently works as a freelance composer and arranger on a variety of concert, educational and media music projects. She is Head of the Performance School at the Academy of Contemporary Music.

Contributing Editor

JoJo Gould is a UK-based lecturer, and was for five years joint Managing Editor of *Music Business Journal*. He lectures and consults on the European Degree in International Music Management, and holds a Master of Science degree in Business IT Systems. He was a co-founder and first Chairman of New Music in Scotland, and was previously Senior Lecturer in Music Industry Management at Buckinghamshire Chilterns University College.

Songwriting and composing
Introduction

For songwriters and composers (as, indeed, for performers and producers), a good demo tape is an essential calling card for your musical wares. Demo tapes (or 'demos') may need to be submitted to publishers, record companies, media companies, commissioners of new work, competitions, festivals, promoters and venue owners. It is best never to send in more than three songs or short tracks on one disc. Today the most likely format for such a demo is a CD (or a DVD – when it is sometimes more accurately termed a 'portfolio' or 'showreel', since it may include video footage). The disc itself should be clearly labelled as to order and duration of tracks, and copyright holder(s). An appropriate jewel case should also contain an insert clearly labelled with the same information. Always include your contact details on both CD and inserts (and/or those of your agent or manager).

While it is not necessary to spend hundreds of pounds on a demo, it is always a good idea to present material as professionally as possible, and to make the best of your resources at the time. Likewise, keep introductory letters short and to the point, enclosing a one-page bio sheet (biography), possibly with integral or separate photo if relevant, and perhaps including one or two short testimonials or reviews at the bottom of the page (ideally from independent third parties). Less is usually more when it comes to submitting material to music companies or industry professionals. Prior contact – or any previous dealings to establish the exact person to whom your submission should be sent – will be a great help, as this gives you an initial addressee who is expecting your work.

Simplicity and clarity are appreciated by music industry professionals, who often receive hundreds of submissions a week. Many experienced professionals are able to tell within the first five seconds of playing a track whether it may be suitable for their use at that particular time.

If you get a response, do try to evaluate objectively any feedback on your material. You may well learn something – either about your music, or about what the 'market' seems to require. Continue to refine the way in which you submit material, always improving the professionalism of your presentation. Try not to take knock-backs or lack of response personally; there is a niche, believe it or not, for most people with talent in the industry! But no matter how much talent you have, you must certainly steel yourself for the fact that you need an implacable will to persevere. You will also need to develop the ability to conduct your own research continually (often by trial and error initially), until it becomes clear where exactly your musical niche lies, and to establish, over time, your ideal music business partners: even a songwriter cannot work alone all day, and you will need to draw upon the creative or business talents of others for your mutual benefit. The musical world has today evolved into a giant interdependent mechanism, in which all sorts of extraordinary and gifted people fulfil specialist roles. Finding your own place in the profession is the challenge facing most new entrants to the industry.

Life as a songwriter or composer

Songwriter **Chris Bradford** explains the ups and downs of being a professional songwriter – and, more importantly, how to handle them!

"There is no great genius without an element of madness." – Aristotle

If Aristotle were around today, he could as well have been talking about songwriters, as any other artist or thinker. Undoubtedly, you have to be a little bit crazy to become a full-time professional songwriter or composer! As award-winning songwriter Rick Nowels once observed, "Only the obsessed need apply."

Songwriting is a wonderful yet demanding career choice. A songwriter will be faced with frequent rejection; inspiration may dry up at the very time when it is most needed; and the opportunities to get a 'cut' with an artist are, today, very few and far between. Even if you are fortunate enough to score a No.1 hit, it could be another five, ten or even 20 years before your next success.

At the same time, songwriting can be one of the most rewarding occupations in the entire music business. The songwriting community is a relatively small one, but it is arguably the most important within the music industry. In creating new music, a songwriter's work supports the careers of musicians, singers, music publishers, record companies and anyone else who works in the music business. Furthermore, the process of conceiving and crafting a song is a creative pleasure that few other activities can equal. Those moments when you hear your song performed live by an artist, played on a radio station, and even climbing the charts, are priceless. On top of all this, the fact that you are actually going to be paid for your success makes your Herculean songwriting efforts seem all the more worthwhile.

What it takes to be a professional songwriter

Assuming that you have some talent, your *attitude* to being a songwriter is what really counts. Songwriting should first and foremost be about enjoying oneself, and fulfilling one's creative potential. Writing should ideally be a pleasurable activity, with commercial success being merely a by-product of the creative process – never its overwhelming goal.

The business of songwriting is, of course, highly competitive: hundreds of thousands of songs are pitched each year to only a few hundred available acts. It is vital, therefore, that in view of such odds you accept 'rejection' as the norm (and not as some personal slur on your abilities). If you can maintain your enjoyment in songwriting through the inevitable rejection, then you will be capable of overcoming the 'lows' of being a professional songwriter.

This point leads on to the second key attribute of any successful songwriter: *perseverance*. As Lamont Dozier says in *Heart and Soul: Revealing the Craft of Songwriting*, "Don't listen when people say you can't do this thing, or you're wasting your time … You've got to be hard-headed, stubborn and driven. Be faithful to the music and the music will be faithful to you."

There are countless examples of songwriters who have stuck in the game long enough for their songs eventually to have risen to the top, and garnered them success, financial reward and accolades. "Never give up," should be your daily mantra. Despite knockbacks and criticism, you need to get up again each time, dust yourself off, re-examine your work honestly, and have the courage of your convictions. You have to remain confident in your own abilities as a songwriter.

This is where the third characteristic of the successful songwriter comes into play: *belief in yourself*. If you are willing to carry on writing, to develop your craft, and to persist in promoting your songs – all through thick and thin – then with the right material, success merely becomes a 'numbers game' ... and one which can be thrown in your favour, by developing your networking abilities.

Meeting the right people

For better or for worse, being a successful songwriter is no longer simply a matter of writing a great song. A writer cannot succeed within the vacuum of his or her own studio or bedroom. Success will be as much down to who you know, and who knows you, as to the song itself. All businesses rely on an element of networking, but none more so than the music industry. This is why the songs that get recorded and released may not always be the best! Rather, they will be the ones written by the best-connected songwriters, who by virtue of their 'network' find their songs in the right place, at the right time.

There is no great secret to networking. It simply lies in one's ability to relate to other people and maintain relationships. For some, this is a skill that comes instinctively; for others, there could be nothing worse than being presented with a room full of strangers with whom they need to converse. Yet there is no need for a personality transplant, or a confidence injection, to be able to network effectively. In any social or business situation, a professional attitude, honesty and politeness are often your most valuable tools. There are also basic methodologies that can be observed: always have a professional business card to hand; learn simple techniques to remember people's names; and follow up immediately on any contacts that you make, with an email or a phone call.

The networking process does not stop simply at meeting people. It is also about cultivating relationships, over time, for the mutual benefit of both parties. As a songwriter, you will need to work hard on being positive, genuine, approachable and proactive. Ensure that you develop your people skills, along with your musical abilities, because your charm and enthusiasm are tools of influence that are as valuable as your talents as a songwriter.

Writing with the right people

Such interpersonal skills apply equally when writing with others. While there is no rule stating that one should collaborate with another writer, working together has become a standard practice among most professional songwriters. There are many reasons for this, the most pertinent being economic and political: for an artist, involvement in the songwriting process means a share of much-needed income, as well as enhancing one's reputation as a 'credible' artist. Yet there are many other qualitative reasons for collaborating with a writing partner:

- The act of collaboration can itself result in increased output of songs.
- There is potential for a balancing of talents: for example, between a strong lyricist and a skilled musician.
- Writers have a more objective perspective when it comes to editing work, which often results in a far better song.
- There is an improved chance of success, as the number of potential opportunities to obtain a release necessarily increases.

Like any other kind of relationship, the key to a successful collaboration is communication. Aside from expressing your feelings, thoughts and ideas clearly and respectfully to one another, it is crucial that an agreement is reached regarding the ownership of copyright – and as early as possible in the collaborative process. Arguments over percentage splits in a joint composition have destroyed countless promising or successful writing partnerships over the years. Among all the possible problems a songwriter can face, this issue is the most damaging, yet one of the easiest to avoid.

In general, the professional songwriting community works on the principle of splitting the publishing income *equally* – based on whoever is in the room at the time the song is composed. Yet it is crucial not to take this assumption for granted when working with another writer: this principle is purely for guidance, and is not a rule. When a song becomes a success, the introduction of significant monetary reward has the regrettable tendency to distort people's perceptions of what actually occurred during a writing session! A simple written agreement detailing the title of the song, the name of the writers, and their respective shares in the copyright of the song (and who contributed to which elements) can prevent any such future disagreements. The British Academy of Composers and Songwriters offers useful advice on this important matter.

'Ninety-nine per cent perspiration'

Once such business elements have been settled, a songwriter is free to create without fear of future complications. This is where the real work begins. For a songwriter requires not only "an element of madness" to become a genius, but must also appreciate that genius is "one per cent inspiration, and ninety-nine per cent perspiration", as Thomas Edison famously maintained. Songwriting is an art *and* a craft. Like any great painting, sculpture or poem, after the genius of inspiration, what counts is the attention to detail, and the dedication to crafting it into a finished song. The songwriter Stephen Sondheim has commented, "it's not the writing; it's the re-writing". As demanding as indeed it may be, the ability to revisit your work with fresh ears, and the confidence to remove or rewrite any parts that sound weak, is a requisite skill of any true professional songwriter.

The crazy life

Life as a songwriter and composer therefore requires dedication, drive and talent. It is also a matter of persistence, of "being prepared to commit totally", as Ivor Novello Award-winning songwriter Pete Kirtley says – "to the point where you're going mad". But in the end, songwriting is about being creative, and enjoying that creativity.

Chris Bradford is a professional songwriter and author of *Heart and Soul: Revealing the Craft of Songwriting.* (Quotations are reproduced by kind permission of Sanctuary Publishing: ISBN 1860746411.) He is Lecturer in Composition and Arrangement at the Academy of Contemporary Music, Guildford, and Executive of the Songwriters' Committee, British Academy of Composers and Songwriters. For further information, visit **www.burningcandlemusic.co.uk**.

THE GREATEST, TOUGHEST JOB

"Being a professional songwriter is simply one of the greatest jobs you could ever have. The idea of being paid for putting pen to paper, or for playing a chord on the piano, is quite amazing. On top of this, there is the possibility that you can change a person's life through a song: even the simplest of lyrics can have the most profound effect on someone's outlook.

This reality, however, is tempered by the fact that this is also one of the toughest, most turbulent and inconsistent roles in the entire music business. The journey of a song – from conception through to success – can literally take years. You may write 300 songs before you get your first release; then another 300 before your second hit!

The dream of writing songs for a living is balanced by the need to put food on the table. We're now in a climate where people are downloading songs illegally without remorse or recrimination, and, as a result, record sales are at an all-time low. In such an environment, earning money is tough. Yet as we watch musical trends change, bands rise and fall, and piracy ebb and flow, one thing remains constant throughout: *the song*. There would simply be no 'music business' without songs. The songwriter is the lifeblood of this industry, and that is what still makes songwriting the greatest job to have."

Pete Kirtley is an Ivor Novello Award-winning songwriter and producer, who has written and produced tracks for artists including The Spice Girls, 5ive, Hear'say, Mis-teeq, Steven Gately, Aaron Carter, Gareth Gates and The Cheeky Girls. See **www.jiant.co.uk**.

GETTING A FOOT IN THE DOOR

"I am often asked, 'How do you get into the TV/film music business?' My answers used to start along the lines of, 'Just keep knocking on doors until one opens.' More recently, though, they have become a touch more flippant, and I am just as likely to reply, 'I haven't a clue, so when you find out, please let me know!'

The problem is that despite the low commissioning fees on offer, the tiny budgets for musicians, the nervous-breakdown-inducing deadlines, and the fact that most broadcasters will now want to acquire your publishing and buy out your mechanical rights (thereby halving your royalty income from broadcasting – removing any chance of you earning a penny from DVD sales, and so undercutting your profit and denying you a pension), the occupation is still seen as an attractive one (heavens, even I still want to give it a go!).

The competition is insanely intense. But if you are serious about the job of being a TV/film composer, the real answer remains to keep knocking on those doors. And when one opens, make sure that you can work to the highest standards, and that you do not sell yourself – or the craft – short. Hold on to your rights and join the British Academy of Composers and Songwriters. It's good to be among friends, in any business, but even more necessary in this business of music."

Mark Ayres is a composer and sound designer who has worked in TV and film, including *Rockcliffe's Babies*, *Casualty*, *Doctor Who*, and *The Innocent Sleep*. See **www.markayres.co.uk**.

A CAREER AS A MEDIA COMPOSER

"If you want any sort of career as a media composer, there is one thing you should always seek to do – solve more problems than you create!

Media composing is a collaborative effort, and consequently a complex process: the path is never as smooth as everyone would like. On a media project, things are guaranteed to go wrong.

So remain flexible – which means not being too precious about your music. Think quickly: time is money, and unsolved problems create increasingly embarrassing situations.

In particular, always be sensitive. If the producer has dropped an almighty clanger, you will get more Brownie points for quietly digging him out of a hole, than throwing your arms in the air and telling him what a klutz he is! At the time, it may feel like you have carried out a selfless and unrewarded act of rescue, but when the next commission comes in, it will be due in no small part to your measured response the last time – when the wheels appeared to be coming off."

Mark Fishlock is a songwriter, media composer and director of the British Academy of Composers and Songwriters.

THE SOUNDTRACK TO OUR LIVES

"Music has a purpose. It sounds obvious, but it's easy to forget what songs mean to non-musicians. We, as songwriters, provide the soundtrack to people's lives, and our music must reflect this in order to be commercially viable. And so it is that Nirvana speaks to disaffected and angst-ridden teenagers, while Whitney Houston can be said to speak to a generation of ice-cream-eating women who have just been dumped! If a writer is to communicate effectively with an audience, then the song he or she writes must reflect events relevant to people's lives. Just as advertising targets a specific demographic – well, so do songs. That sounds fairly calculated and cold, doesn't it? What it really means is that a writer should write from the perspective of experience: he or she should therefore try to experience as much of life as possible. If that means songwriters have to fill their lives full of incredible highs and depressing lows – then so be it; at least the music from within will then bear the hallmark of real experience."

Tim Hart is a songwriter for the highly successful UK production team, Jiant. He also writes for television and film in both the UK and the US.

THE NEED FOR AN UNDERSTANDING OF HARMONY

"Songwriting is an art. The greatest song moments are pure magic, and they aren't made by following rules. Songwriting, though, is also a craft – and mastery of the craft is important to becoming a good songwriter.

There are two main reasons why mastering technique can help your work. The first is that, as a general rule, inspiration is bounded by the limits of your capabilities. Technical expertise won't necessarily bring in inspiration, but it will expand your options as to how to use it.

The second reason is that technical understanding can help you when you know that something is wrong, but can't quite put your finger on what. A bit of informed analysis can save you hours of trial and error.

So it is a very good idea to learn some technique. But never forget that your heart, your mind, your gut feeling and – above all – your ear, are the true guides when writing."

David Stoll, a former Chairman of the British Academy of Composers and Songwriters, is a composer of concert, media and theatre music; he also wrote the DfES guide to teaching composing in primary schools.

A COMMUNITY OF SONGWRITERS

"Writing music can be a lonely activity. The archetypal image of the lone songwriter desperately wringing notes from a battered old piano or guitar still remains – augmented, perhaps, by a modern picture of the producer meticulously programming a music computer week after week, to produce just three minutes of glorious music.

Collaboration combats some of this voluntary solitary confinement, but still, to a new writer on the scene, the songwriting community can feel somewhat disjointed and unconnected. How do you meet other professional songwriters? How do you get that first foot in the door? And how do you avoid making the mistake of signing a poor deal?

The good news is that songwriters have a natural tendency to come together and help each other, because of our shared love of music and creativity. Whether we have a lifetime of writing behind us, or are just taking our first steps, it is this love which unites us above everything else. To many members of the British Academy, the most important thing the Academy does is to provide an opportunity to meet other writers, compare notes and establish friendships. It is through these means that new songwriters develop their career, improve their creative talents, and encounter writing opportunities."

Chris Green is Chief Executive of the British Academy of Composers and Songwriters. For further information on the Academy and how to join, see **www.britishacademy.com**.

LICENSED TO DREAM

"It was not an auspicious start. It was the hot summer of 1973 and Guy Fletcher and I were working in his study on an ancient Farfisa held together with gaffer tape! However, we soon found ourselves in that 'special place' which songwriters wish to inhabit – where the Muse checks in. Two verses and a great tune later, we had the makings of a splendid Gospel song. As one man, we both declared: 'Ray Charles'. Songwriters are licensed to dream: it is part of the profession.

The song was *Is There Anyone Out There?*, and a few months later we made our first visit to New York and Los Angeles, 'doing the rounds' of publishers and paving the way for the many fine things that followed. A little naive at the time, we decided to visit Tangerine Records – then Ray Charles' own record company in Watts. We met with the General Manager, Dee (*Do You Want To Swing On A Star?*) Irwin, who listened attentively, and said he would play it to Mr Charles.

We heard nothing. Nada. Zilch. Silence.

It was not until another five years later, when our catalogue of songs was taken up by a new professional manager at Irving/Almo in North America, that the song was given new life. The first we knew about it was a Telex saying that Ray Charles had a hold on the song, *Is There Anyone Out There?*. The man himself arranged, sang and produced it, and eventually Decca Records shipped over a white label of the recording. Guy and I sat down and listened to a sensational recording of our work, five years after it was first pitched. We were truly speechless.

It was Winston Churchill who said, 'Never give up, never give up, never ever give up.' This is sound advice for any songwriter, too. Hang on in there – you are licensed to dream."

Lyricist **Doug Flett**, together with long-time writing partner **Guy Fletcher**, was the first UK songwriter to be recorded by Elvis Presley. He has also written Top Ten hits for The Hollies, Cliff Richard, Ray Charles, Joe Cocker and Tom Jones.

24 HOURS TO WRITE …

"He phoned me up completely out of the blue, and said, 'Hello, this is Norman Cook. You have been recommended, and I would like you to sing some vocals on my new album.'

I was actually about to go to Stockholm, to do an international writing weekend with Zomba/BMG, but moved heaven and earth to squeeze in the session with Fatboy Slim before I went. Norman was extremely happy with the results, and on my return I found he had sent me a new track – this time for me to write on. Over the next couple of days I actually wrote two songs for the same track, just to improve my chances of something happening – but hadn't recorded them yet. About a week later, Norman called me and said he needed the songs by 5pm the next day!

So the deadline was extremely tight, and it was a bit of a panic to try to record the lead vocals, all the backing vox, and mix and master two songs within the specified timeframe.

It ended up being a 24-hour session. But that is what it sometimes takes if you want to be a professional songwriter."

Sharon Woolf is a professional songwriter and vocalist, who has worked with Fatboy Slim, Mousse T, Mike & The Mechanics, The Stereo MCs, Tin Tin Out, and Liberty X. For further information, see **www.sharonwoolf.com**.

Companies that commission songwriters and composers

ADVERTISING COMPANIES

1576 Advertising

1576 Advertising, 25 Rutland Square, Edinburgh, Lothian, Scotland
tel 0131-473 1576 *fax* 0131-473 1577
email info@1576.co.uk
website www.1576.co.uk
Joint Managing Directors David Reid, Gary Smith

Aims to fulfil all advertising campaign needs. Deals with TV, radio, online, direct mail, in press, sales promotion, outdoor and ambient solutions.

Andagi Productions

Old Search Lights, Runwick Lane, Farnham GU10 5EF
tel 0870-751 8012 *fax* 0870-751 8017
email david@andagi.co.uk
website www.andagi.co.uk
Contact David Perrelet

Specialises in visual media. Winner of the 'Late Lounge eDward' at eDIT|VES 2004 (the European Festival for Production & Visual Effects).

BBA Active

Studio 3, 62 Muswell Hill Road, London N10 3JR
tel 020-8883 7635
email bba@bbagenius.com
website www.bbagenius.com
Managing Director Stephen Benjamin *Creative Director* Lyn Lepard

Founded in 1981. Main areas of work include marketing, promotions, events and design. Specialises in corporate events, TV/radio advertising and product launches. Composers may make contact via email, fax, phone or weblink and should aim to provide a sample of work on DVD or CD.

BCMB Ltd

2 Brindley Road, Old Trafford, Manchester M16 9HQ
tel 0161-877 0521 *fax* 0161-877 7994
email mjs@bcmb.co.uk
website www.bcmb.co.uk
Chairman Morton Speyer

Established in 1989. Contains specialist division handling e-commerce and business-to-business clients. Deals with print, TV, radio, website development and interactive and new media, among other mediums. Clients include: Moben, Dolphins Bathrooms and Glyn Webb DIY.

CIB Communications

Bridge House, 27 Bridge Street, Leatherhead, Surrey KT22 8DD
tel (01372) 371800 *fax* (01372) 371801
email gavint@cibcommunications.co.uk
website www.cibcommunications.co.uk
Communications Officer Gavin Tadman

Provides advertising services to a range of major UK business-to-business sectors including construction, architecture, interiors, FM, healthcare, food, drinks and electronics.

The Clinic

32-38 Saffron Hill, London EC1N 8FH
tel 020-7421 9333 *fax* 020-7421 9334
email info@clinic.co.uk
website www.clinic.co.uk

Aims to develop and implement successful, impressive, innovative, outrageous, effective and creative strategies and concepts for brands large and small. Clients include: Virgin Retail, John Lewis and ITV Network.

The Design and Advertising Resource

7 Kings Wharf, 301 Kingsland Road, Hoxton E8 4DS
tel 020-7254 3191
email info@your-resource.co.uk
website www.your-resource.co.uk
Managing Director R Fearn

Founded in 1995. Clients include music/copyright organisations such as IFPI. Potential clients should make contact via the website.

Diabolical Liberties

1 Bayham Street, London NW1 0ER
tel 020-7916 5483 *fax* 020-7916 5482
email music@diabolical.co.uk
website www.diabolical.co.uk

Designs and implements campaigns for agency and brand clients. Services include: ideas generation, experimental and face-to-face marketing, creative and PR stunts, seeding and subliminal placement, street art and live event management.

DKA

87 New Cavendish Street, London W1W 6XD
tel 020-7467 7300 *fax* 020-7467 7350
email simon.hicks@dka.uk.com
email dannyquinlan@dka.uk.com
website www.dka.uk.com
New Business Director Simon Hicks *Creative Director* Danny Quinlan

Founded in 1980. Provides full-service advertising and design for a range of mediums including television and radio. The BBC, Morgan Stanley and Toshiba have featured among recent clients.

Doner Cardwell Hawkins
26-34 Emerald Street, London WC1N 3QA
tel 020-7400 1241
email aweeden@doner.co.uk
website www.doner.co.uk
Business Development Director Anne-Marie Weeden

Aims to make a demonstrable impact on clients' businesses, which is both immediate and sustainable. Clients have included: Big Yellow Storage, Blockbuster and Travelodge.

Emediates
Promise House, Stafford Road, Wolverhampton WV10 6AD
tel (01902) 378570 *fax* (01902) 378571
email info@emediates.co.uk
website www.emediates.co.uk
Managing Director Anil Varma

Aims to work hard and within budget to fully achieve clients' business objectives. Deals with web design, marketing strategy and creative design, among other mediums.

J Walter Thomson Co
1 Knightsbridge Green, London SW1X 7NW
tel 020-7656 7000
email chrissie.barker@jwt.com
website www.jwt.co.uk

Works with a wide range of businesses and a significant collection of famous brands. Aims to create a partnership, while challenging convention and committing to creating great ideas. Clients include: Allied Bakeries – Kingsmill, Rennie, Pro-plus, Sanatogen, Kellogg's Cornflakes range and Wilkinson's Sword.

Jupiter Advertising
Newton Silk Mill, Holyoak Street, Manchester M40 1HA
tel 0161-681 1500
email via website
website www.jupiterad.co.uk

Founded in 1992. Aims to produce branded, influential and occasionally controversial advertising within the recruitment sector. Deals with a range of media including video, cinema, digital television and radio.

Leo Burnett
Warwick Building, Kensington Village, Avonmore Road, London W14 8HQ
tel 020-7751 1800 *fax* 020-8348 3855
email laura.holme@leoburnett.co.uk
website www.leoburnett.co.uk
New Business Director Laura Holme

Chicago-based agency ranked as the 9th largest worldwide agency in 1998. Produces campaigns for major clients including McDonald's, Heinz, Nintendo and Samsung.

M & C Saatchi
36 Golden Square, London W1F 9EE
tel 020-7543 4500 *fax* 020-7543 4501
email london@mcsaatchi.com
website www.mcsaatchi.com

Major global advertising company with a pedigree of blue-chip clients from a range of industries including ITV, Foster's, Dixons, Lucozade and US Tourism board.

Martin Waxman Associates
56 St John Street, London EC1M 4HG
tel 020-7253 5500 *fax* 020-7490 2387
email info@waxman.co.uk
website www.waxman.co.uk
Director Ian Waxman

Aims to give clients shrewd strategic direction and stand-out creative and incisive media buying. Has assisted in formulating creative direction for companies such as Gameplay, PC World, Office Angels, Brother, Global Internet and The Performing Right Society.

Media Campaign Services
20 Orange Street, London WC2H 7EW
email via website
website www.mediacampaign.co.uk
Broadcast Director Steve Chapman

Established in 1975. Aims to search out and deliver the most salient and cost-effective solutions in order to achieve clients' objectives. Clients include: EMI, Virgin and Avent.

Radioville
143 Wardour Street, London W1F 8WA
tel 020-7534 5999
email stephen@radioville.co.uk
website www.radioville.co.uk
Creative Director Tim Craig

Specialist radio advertising agency making 10% of UK radio. Deals with brainstorming, writing, casting, producing, directing and distributing radio commercials from start to finish. Member of the IPA. Winner of 'Agency of the Year' at the 2007 Radio Advertising Awards.

Robson Brown Communico Ltd.
Digital World Centre, 1 Lowry Plaza, The Quays, Salford, Manchester M50 3UB
tel 0161-601 4900
email mikeg@robson-brown.co.uk
website www.robson-brown.co.uk
Group Account Director Mike Goundry

Deals with marketing services covering advertising, media planning, public relations, design and print.

Portfolio includes a wide range of national and international clients in diverse sectors from leisure to business.

Rowleys: London
One Port Hill, Hertford, Herts SG14 1PJ
tel (01992) 587350
email hello@rowleyslondon.com
website www.rowleyslondon.com
Managing Director Annie Rowley

Founded in 2001. Award-winning advertising agency specialising in creative marketing campaigns, merchandise production, launch parties and conferences. Clients include: Radiohead, Coldplay, Kylie Minogue, Parlophone, EMI, Sony BMG, Universal Music, Nokia, DreamWorks and Universal Pictures. Potential composers should make contact via email.

Saatchi & Saatchi plc
80 Charlotte Street, London W1A 1AQ
website www.saatchi-saatchi.com

Major advertising company with 134 offices in 84 countries. Aims to transform clients' businesses, brands and reputations through the power of ideas and the belief that nothing is impossible. Voted No. 1 Agency Network for global and regional new businesses, and in 1979 became the first agency to be appointed by a British political party to help win an election.

Small Japanese Soldier
32-38 Saffron Hill, Farringdon, London EC1N 8FH
tel 020-7421 9400 *fax* 020-7421 9380
email jungle@smalljapanesesoldier.com
website www.smalljapanesesoldier.com

Hip and eclectic agency dealing with a variety of media and campaigns. Clients have included Orange and *The Guardian*.

St Luke's Communications
22 Dukes Road, London WC1H 9PN
tel 020-7380 8888 *fax* 020-7380 8899
email info@stlukes.co.uk
website www.stlukes.co.uk

Aims to place creativity at the heart of the company. Clients include: Ikea, BT, Clarks, and Scottish and Newcastle. Voted *Sunday Times*' 'Best Company to Work For'; listed for 4 years.

TBWA London
85 Strand, London WCTR ODW
tel 020-7964 8200 *fax* 020-7964 0300
email nocorston@tbwa.com
website www.agency.com
Managing Director Jonathan Mildenhall

Large global advertising company boasting 258 offices worldwide and handling top-level advertising for some of the biggest names in industry – including

Apple, McDonald's, Playstation, Michelin, Nissan and Absolut Vodka.

Two: Design
Studio 37, Hampstead House, 176 Finchley Road, London NW3 6BT
tel 020-8275 8594
email studio@twodesign.net
website www.twodesign.net

Independent creative consultancy with 9 years' experience. Deals with a varied client base and delivers creative direction and brand consultancy. Specialises in working with clients in the entertainment, fashion and retail sectors at a national and international level.

TV COMPANIES

12 Yard Productions
10 Livonia Street, London W1F 8AF
tel 020-7432 2929 *fax* 020-7439 2037
email via website
website www.12yard.com

Leading television production company formed in 2001 by the team behind the BBC's *Weakest Link*, *Dog Eat Dog* and *Eggheads*. Specialises in game shows and reality TV shows.

Angel Eye Productions
9 Rudolf Place, Miles Street, London SW8 1RP
tel 0845-230 0062 *fax* 0845-230 9562
website www.angeleye.co.uk

Works in the genres of comedy, entertainment, documentary, education and drama. Recent productions have included: *The Last Chancers* and *Holy Offensive*. Clients include: BBC, Channel 4 and Five.

The Ashford Entertainment Corporation Ltd.
20 The Chase, Coulsdon, Surrey CR5 2EG
tel 020-8660 9609 *fax* 0870-166 4142
email info@ashford-entertainment.co.uk
website www.ashford-entertainment.co.uk
Managing Director Frazer Ashford

Founded in 1996. Aims to produce timeless television programming suitable for all audiences both in the UK and internationally. Mainly works with documentaries for which original music is often commissioned. Composers should make initial contact via email with small music file and CV.

At It Productions
68-70 Salusbury Road, Queens Park, London NW6 6NU
tel 020-7644 0000 *fax* 020-7644 0001
email enquiries@atitproductions.com
website www.atitproductions.com
Managing Director Martin Cunning

Established in 1997. Committed to realising television in a fresh and distinctive way. Aims to deliver demanding and highly innovative shows to tight deadlines and budgets, for mainstream audiences. Produces shows for C4, Five, BBC, ITV and Sky One.

Avalon

4a Exmoor Street, London W10 6BD UK
tel 020-7598 7333 *fax* 020-7598 7300
email promotions@avalonuk.com
website www.avalonuk.com

Established in 1993. Producers of comedy and light entertainment programmes in the UK. Supplies to all British terrestrial channels and some cable and satellite stations.

BBC

Wood Lane, Shepherd's Bush, London W12 7RJ
tel 020-8743 8000 *fax* 020-8749 7520
email info@bbc.ac.uk
website www.bbc.co.uk

Founded in 1922. A long-established British institution creating innovative, progressive and pioneering programmes that provide entertainment, education and information to millions of viewers through regional newstations across the country. Channels include: BBC 1, BBC 2, BBC 3, BBC 4, CBBC, CBeebies, BBC News 24 and BBC Parliament. Incorporates music as part of programmes and idents.

Brighter Pictures

10th Floor, Blue Star House,
234-244 Stockwell Road, London SW9 9SP
tel 020-7733 7333 *fax* 020-7733 6333
email via website
website www.brighter.co.uk

Established in 1992. Part of the Endemol group since 2001. Has a large portfolio of innovative and distinctive youth, music and reality shows. Productions include: *Big Brother* (since 2006), *Make me Perfect* and *All New Cosmetic Surgery Live.*

Celador Productions

39 Long Acre, London WC2E 9LG
tel 020-7240 8101 *fax* 020-7845 9541
website www.celador.co.uk
Joint Managing Directors Christian Colson (films), Danielle Lux (TV)

Channel 4

124 Horseferry Road, London SW1P 2TX
tel 020-7396 4444 *fax* 020-7306 8630
website www.channel4.com

Publicly owned corporation with a remit, as set out in Acts of Parliament, requiring it to be innovative, experimental and distinctive. Publishing and broadcasting company; does not produce its own programmes but commissions them from more than 300 UK independent production companies. The Channel 4 group also operates a variety of pay channels, including E4, E4+1, and 3 film channels. The Film 4 division produces and co-produces feature films for the UK and global markets. Also provides a wide variety of online and broadband services.

The Elstree Company

Shepperton Studios, Room 960, Studios Road, Shepperton TW17 0QD
tel (01932) 572680 *fax* (01932) 572682
email info@elstreefilmtv.com
website www.elsprod.com
Producer Greg Smith

Produces drama, entertainment and documentaries for TV. Credits include: award-winning productions of *Great Expectations* and *Porgy and Bess*, and BAFTA-nominated *Othello*.

Endemol UK plc

Shepherds Building Central, Charecroft Way, London W14 0EE
tel 020-8222 4299 *fax* 020-8222 4281
email amelia.hartley@endemoluk.com
website www.endemoluk.com
Music Supervisor Amelia Hartley

Large independent TV producer whose divisions include Initial, Brighter Pictures (see above) and Hawkshead. Typical productions involve live performance music events, documentaries and music-based drama. Incorporates music through original commissions, licensing and original commercially released songs. Potential composers should send CD/DVD showreels, or email CV.

Five

22 Long Acre, London WC2E 9LY
tel 020-7691 6610 *fax* 020 7691 6085
email via website
website www.five.tv

The UK's 5th terrestial channel. Hosts programmes such as *Extraordinary People*, *The Gadget Show* and *Home and Away*. Specialises in comedy, drama and sports programming.

FremantleMedia

1 Stephen Street, London W1T 1AL
tel 020-7691 6000 *fax* 020-7691 6100
website www.fremantlemedia.com

Leading producers of prime-time drama, serial drama, entertainment and factual entertainment, programming in around 43 territories. Runs production operations in more than 25 countries worldwide. Brands include: *Pop Idol*, *Grand Designs* and *Never Mind the Buzzcocks*.

Hat Trick Productions Ltd

10 Livonia Street, London W1F 8AF
tel 020-7434 2451 *fax* 020-7287 9791

email info@hattrick.com
website www.hattrick.com
Joint Managing Directors Denise O'Donoghue, Jimmy Mulville

Founded in 1986. Successful independent production company working in situation and drama comedy and light entertainment shows. Recent credits include: *The Kumars at No. 42, Worst Week of my Life, Have I Got News for You* and *Room 101.*

ITV Anglia

Anglia House, Norwich NR1 3JG
tel (01603) 615151 *fax* (01603) 631032
website www.itvregions.com/Anglia

Provides programmes for the East of England, daytime discussion programmes, documentaries and factual programmes for UK and international broadcasters. Does not produce any in-house drama.

ITV Border

The Television Centre, Carlisle CA1 3NT
tel (01228) 525101 *fax* (01228) 541384
email dutyoffice@itv.com
website www.itvregions.com/Border

Broadcasts to 3 different cultures: English, Scottish and Manx. Produces own regional programmes including history, wildlife and a variety of documentaries. Music incorporated as part of original productions, advertising and idents.

ITV Granada

Granada Television, Quay Street, Manchester M60 9EA
tel 0161-832 7211 *fax* 0161-827 2180
email dutyoffice@itv.com
website www.itvregions.com/Granada

Established in 1966. Produces internationally renowned programmes such as *Coronation Street, Brideshead Revisited, World In Action* and *I'm a Celebrity Get Me Out of Here!*.

ITV London

London Television Centre, Upper Ground, London SE1 9LT
tel 0870-600 6766 *fax* 020-7261 8163
email dutyoffice@itv.com
website www.itv.com

Part of ITV plc. Large commercial channel, watched on average by 45 million people every week. Consists of a network of 15 different regional licences, each with its own set of obligations and conditions designed to reflect the particular character of its region and the interests of its viewers. Also hosts 3 digital channels. Incorporates music as part of programmes and advertising.

ITV Meridian

Forum One, Solent Business Park, Whiteley, Hants PO15 7PA

tel (01489) 442000
website www.itvregions.com/Meridian

The ITV franchise-holder for the South and South East coast of England. Does not produce any in-house drama.

ITV Tyne Tees

Television House, The Watermark, Gateshead, Tyne and Wear NE11 9SZ
tel 0191-404 8700
email via website
website www.tynetees.tv

Established in 1955 and now part of ITV's Granada Media group. Production output includes: *After They Were Famous, Supergran, The Tube* and *Amazing Babies.*

ITV Wales

Television Centre, Culverhouse Cross, Cardiff CF5 6XJ
tel 029-2059 0590 *fax* 029-2059 9108
email e.owen@itvwales.com
website www.itcregions.com/wales
Programme Controller Elis Owen

Founded in 1968. ITV broadcaster for Wales. Produces and broadcasts 9.5 hours a week of programmes in English on ITV Wales and in Welsh for S4C. Potential composers should approach Elis Owen by post, including a showreel DVD.

ITV West

The Television Centre, Bristol BS4 3HG
tel 0117-972 2722 *fax* 0117-972 2400
email firstname.surname@itv.com
website www.itv.com/west

Provides programmes for the West of England. Productions include: *West Eye View, Coastal Ways* and *Vic Reeves Pirates.*

ITV West Country

Langage Science Park, Plymouth PL7 5BQ
tel (01752) 333333 *fax* (01752) 333444
website www.itvregions.com/west

Provides programmes for South West England. In-house production is mainly news, sport, and regional current affairs; other regional features are commissioned from independent producers.

ITV Yorkshire

Television Centre, Leeds, West Yorkshire LS3 1JS
tel 0113-243 8283 *fax* 0113-244 5107
website www.itvregions.com/Yorkshire

Established in 1968, now part of ITV Plc. Broadcasts to 5.7 million viewers in the ITV Yorkshire area. Production includes: *Heartbeat, A Touch of Frost, My Parents Are Aliens* and *Emmerdale.* Incorporates music as part of programmes and advertising.

Maya Vision International Ltd

43 New Oxford Street, London WC1A 1BH
tel 020-7836 1113 *fax* 020-7836 5169

email info@mayavisionint.com
website www.mayavisionint.com
Producer/Director Rebecca Dobbs

Founded in 1982. Film and TV production company. Produces features, TV dramas and documentaries, and arts programmes. Recent credits include: *In Search of Shakespeare* and *Conquistadors* (BBC); *Johnny Panic* (bfi); *Caught Looking* (Channel 4); *The World Turned Upside Down* (BBC2/Arts Council); and *The Story of India* (BBC/PBS).

Mendoza Productions

3-5 Barrett Street, London W1U 1AY
tel 020-7935 4674 *fax* 020-7935 4417
email office@mendozafilms.com
website www.mendozafilms.com
Managing Director Debby Mendoza

Founded in 1983. Specialises in producing TV commercials. Potential composers should email or phone.

Meridian

Forum One, Solent Business Park, Whiteley, Hants PO15 7PA
tel (01489) 442000
website www.itvregions.com/Meridian

The ITV franchise-holder for the South and South East coast of England. Does not produce any in-house drama.

MTV

Hawley Crescent, London NW1 OTT
tel 020-7284 7777 *fax* 020-7284 6466
website www.mtv.co.uk

MTV Network includes: MTV 2, MTV Base, MTV Hits, MTV Dance, TMF, VH1, VH2 and VH1 Classic. Produces a range of reality and entertainment shows including *The Osbournes, Jackass, Pimp My Ride* and *Southpark*.

Off The Radar TV

20-22 Rosebery Avenue, London EC1R 4SX
tel 020-7520 8340
email Patrick@offtheradar.tv
website www.offtheradar.tv
Commercial Manager Patrick Usmar

Delivers large-scale productions for agencies, broadcasters and global brands and produces a variety of TV shows, music promos, DVDs and corporate films. Aims to deliver slick, well-packaged productions and build key relationships with production partners. Specialises in advertiser-funded programming including productions for Pepsi, Mastercard, MSN and Volkswagen.

RTE (Radio-Telefis-Eireann)

Donnybrook, Dublin 4, Ireland
tel (00353) 1208 4502 *fax* (00353) 1208 3114
email boothj@rte.ie
website www.rte.ie
Head of Promotions Jim Booth

Founded in 1962. National broadcaster for Ireland. Incorporates music as part of promotions and station idents. Potential composers should submit material via email or CD.

S4C (Sianel Pedwar Cymru)

Parc Ty Glas, Llanishen, Cardiff, South Glamorgan CF4 5DU
tel 029-2074 7444
email via website
website www.s4c.co.uk

Primarily a Welsh-language channel commissioning, rather than producing, a range of documentary and entertainment programmes. Aims to make a dynamic contribution to the linguistic, cultural, social, economic and public life of Wales.

Sky Box Office

Sky Television, Unit 2, Grant Way, Isleworth, Middlesex TW7 5QD
tel 020-7805 8126 *fax* 020-7805 8130
website www.sky.com

Sky offers extensive culture and entertainment programming, blockbuster movies, international and foreign-language channels, educational and children's TV and non-subscription channels.

STV Central

The Television Centre, Craigshaw Business Park, West Tullos, Aberdeen AB12 3QH
tel (01224) 846846
email viewer.enquiries@stv.tv
website http://www.stv.tv

Central Scotland's ITV franchise, Scottish broadcasts a variety of national and local content.

STV North

Television Centre, Craigshaw Business Park, West Tullos, Aberdeen AB12 3QH
tel (01224) 848848
website www.stv.tv
Managing Director Derrick Thomson

Founded in 1961. Provides programmes for North Scotland.

True North

Television Centre, Kirkstall Road, Leeds LS3 1JS
tel 0113-222 7878 *fax* 0113-222 7637
email beckygoom@truenorthproductions.co.uk
website www.truenorthproductions.co.uk

Independent production company producing a range of programming from drama to documentaries. Productions include: *Getting Away with Murder, Animal 24:7* and *Crimefighters*.

UTV

Havelock House, Ormeau Road, Belfast, Co Antrim BT7 1EB
tel 028-9032 8122 *fax* 028-9024 6695

email info@utvplc.com
website www.u.tv

Major Irish television, radio and new media group. Part of ITV plc. Programmes include: *Gerry Meets, Home Sweet Home* and *Busker and Barney*.

FILM COMPANIES

Aardman Animations

Gas Ferry Road, Bristol BS1 6UN
tel 0117-984 8485 *fax* 0117-984 8486
email mail@aardman.com
website www.aardman.com
Director/Founder David Sproxton

Founded in 1976. Animation specialists famed for producing *Morph*, Peter Gabriels's *Sledgehammer* video, *Chicken Run*, *Creature Comforts* and Nick Park's *Wallace and Gromit* films. Also produces around 25-30 commercials each year.

APT Films

225A Brecknock Road, London N19 5AA
tel 020-7284 1695 *fax* 020-7482 1587
email admin@aptfilms.com
website www.aptfilms.com
Managing Director Jonny Persey *Director* Paul Morrison *Producer* Stewart Le Marechal

Young enterprise dedicated to development and production of feature films for national and international audiences. Also produces short films. Recent credits include: *Wondrous Oblivion* and *Solomon and Gaenor*.

Blue Wand Productions Ltd

2nd Floor, 12 Weltje Road, London W6 9TG
tel 020-8741 2038 or (07885) 528743
fax 020-8741 2038
email lino@bluewand.co.uk
Managing Director Lino Omoboni *Executive Producer* Paola Omobomi

Established in 1990. Works exclusively in feature film production. Recent credits include: *Camelot*.

British Lion Screen Entertainment Ltd

Pinewood Studios, Iver, Bucks SL0 0NH
tel (01753) 651700 *fax* (01753) 656844
website www.britishlionfilms.com
Contact Peter Snell

Founded in 1927. Responsible for classics such as *In Which We Serve*, *The Third Man*, *A Taste of Honey*, *The Entertainer* and *The Wicker Man*. Does not accept unsolicited material.

Carnival Film and Television Ltd

47 Marylebone Lane, London W1U 2NT
tel 020-7317 1370 *fax* 020-7317 1380
email info@carnivalfilms.co.uk
website www.carnivalfilms.co.uk
Managing Director Gareth Neame

Founded in 1978. Award-winning independent drama production company, producing more than 350 hours of popular drama for television, cinema and theatre. Commissioned by all the major UK broadcasters, including the BBC, ITV Network, Channel 4 and Sky, as well as US broadcasters such as NBC, HBO, TNT and the A&E Network. Productions range from returning series, such as *Hotel Babylon*, *As If*, *Poirot*, *Jeeves & Wooster*, *Rosemary and Thyme* and *Bugs*, to mini-series, including *Traffik*, *The Grid* and *Porterhouse Blue*, to feature films such as the multi-award-winning *Shadowlands*.

CC-Lab

5-6 Newman Passage, London W1T 1EH
tel 020-7580 8055 *fax* 020-7637 8350
email info@cc-lab.com
website www.cc-lab.com
Managing Director Jason Hocking

Production company and creative agency specialising in film and TV production, graphic design and brand communication. Also works closely with the music industry through live concert and promo film productions. Has filmed live footage for the Foo Fighters, The Prodigy and Coldplay.

Celador Films

39 Long Acre, London WC2E 9LG
tel 020-7240 8101 *fax* 020-7845 9541
website www.celadorfilms.co.uk
Joint Managing Director Christian Colson

Develops and produces high-quality, commercially viable feature films across all genres. All projects are commissioned and developed in-house. Output includes: *Dirty Pretty Things*, *The Descent* and *Dog Soldiers*.

Cosgrove Hall Films

8 Albany Road, Chorlton-Cum-Hardy, Manchester M21 0AW
tel 0161-882 2500 *fax* 0161-882 2555
email animation@chf.co.uk
website www.chf.co.uk
Founders Brian Cosgrove, Mark Hall

Founded in 1976. Animation-based studio and major producer of children's programming. Productions are shown in more than 80 countries.

Cowboy Films

34-35 Berwick Street, London W1F 8RP
tel 020-7758 4102 *fax* 020-7758 4108
email info@cowboyfilms.co.uk
email charles@cowboyfilms.co.uk
website www.cowboyfilms.co.uk
Managing Director Charles Steel

Works primarily with feature films. Recent productions include: *The Hole*, *Goodbye Charlie Bright* and the critically acclaimed *The Last King of Scotland*.

Ecosse Films

Brigade House, 8 Parsons Green, London SW6 4TN
tel 020-7371 0290 *fax* 020-7736 3436
email info@ecossefilms.com
website www.ecossefilms.com
Director Douglas Rae *Head of Drama* Robert
Bernstein

Founded in 1988. Feature film and TV production
company. Recent credits include: *Mrs Brown*,
Charlotte Gray, *Amnesia* and *Becoming Jane*.

Farnham Film Company Ltd

34 Burnt Hill Road, Lower Bourne,
Farnham GU10 3LZ
tel (01252) 710313 *fax* (01252) 725855
email info@farnfilm.com
website www.farnfilm.com

Produces television drama, documentaries and film.
Particularly interested in children's programmes –
drama, comedy and factual.

Film and General Productions Ltd

4 Bradbrook House, Studio Place, London SW1X 8EL
tel 020-7235 4495 *fax* 020-7245 9853
email cparsons@filmgen.co.uk
Producer Clive Parsons

Founded in 1971. Producer of high-quality feature
films and television drama. Potential composers
should email in the first instance.

Focus Films Ltd

The Rotunda Studios, rear of 116-118 Finchley Road,
London NW3 5HT
tel 020-7435 9004 *fax* 020-7431 3562
email focus@focusfilms.co.uk
website www.focusfilms.co.uk
Director David Pupkewitz *Project Co-ordinator*
Raimund Berens

Feature film production company founded in 1982.
Recent credits include: *51st State* with Robert Carlyle
and Samuel L Jackson; *Book of Eve* with Claire Bloom
and Julian Glover; and *Crimetime* with Stephen
Baldwin and Pete Postlethwaite.

Fragile Films/Ealing Studios Ltd

Ealing Green, London W5 5EP
tel 020-8567 6655 *fax* 020-8758 8658
email info@ealingstudios.com
website www.ealingstudios.co.uk
Managing Director James Spring

Among the world's oldest film studios, having
accommodated films such as *Star Wars – Episode 2*
and *Notting Hill*. Returned to filmmaking in 2002
with *The Importance of Being Earnest*; co-produced
the $40 million animated feature, *Valiant* and
released *I Want Candy* in 2007. Does not accept
unsolicited musical material.

Green Umbrella

4 The Links, Old Woking Road, Old Woking,
Surrey GU22 8BF

tel (01483) 726969 *fax* (01483) 721188
email jules@greenumbrella.co.uk
website www.greenumbrella.co.uk
Producers/Directors Steve Gammond, Mont
Tombleson, Bruce Vigar *Managing Director* Jules
Gammond

Icon Films

10 Redland Terrace, Redland, Bristol B56 6TD
tel 0117-970 6882 *fax* 0117-974 4971
email info@iconfilms.co.uk
website www.iconfilms.co.uk
Managing Director Laura Marshall
website Founded in 1990. Award-winning
independent company producing films for the
international market. Diverse interests ranging from
culture and religion to travel and natural history.
Uses music as an integral part of projects in order to
help illustrate, enhance and convey. The style of
music depends on the production and can be
anything from classical to contemporary. Potential
composers are advised to write to or email Laura –
laura.m@iconfilms.co.uk or Harry –
harry.m@iconfilms.co.uk, and to introduce
themselves.

Jim Henson Productions Ltd

30 Oval Road, Camden, London NW1 7DE
tel 020-742 84000

A prominent multimedia production company with
offices in London and headquarters in Hollywood.
Renowned as the creator of films such as: *The
Muppets*, *Dark Crystal*, *The Fraggles* and *Labyrinth*.

Kai Film and TV Productions

1 Ravenslea Road, London SW12 8SA
tel 020-8673 4550
email mwallington@btinternet.com

Established in 1987. Small independent company.
Credits include: *Walking on Water*, *Casino World* and
Big Hair.

Kelpie Films

227 St Andrews Road, Glasgow G41 1PD
tel (0871) 874 0328 *fax* (0871) 874 0329
email yearbook@kelpiefilms.com
website www.kelpiefilms.com

Independent production company that produces a
range of broadcast and corporate/commercial work,
from computer-animated children's programmes to
documentaries in the Middle East and low-budget
feature films. Credits include: BAFTA Nominated
Animation, *Cannonman*; Grierson Award-winning
documentary, *And So Goodbye*; and large-scale
corporate work for global clients such as Shell and
the UK Government.

Kismet Film Company

c/o The Works, 4 Great Portland Street,
London W1W 8QJ

tel 020-7281 7121

Michele Camarda's feature film production company. Credits include: *The River King* and *Born Romantic*.

Lagan Pictures Ltd

21 Tullaghbrow, Tullaghgarley, Ballymena, County Antrim BT42 2LY
tel 028-2563 9479 *mobile* (07798) 528797

Involved in the creation of features, drama and corporate films and videos.

Pathé Pictures

14-17 Kenthouse, Market Place, London W1W 8AR
tel 020-7323 5151 *fax* 020-7631 3568
website www.pathe.co.uk

Feature film production company. Recent productions include: *The Magic Roundabout* and *Mrs Henderson Presents*.

Picture Palace Films Ltd

13 Egbert Street, London NW1 8LJ
tel 020-7586 8763 *fax* 020-7586 9048
email info@picturepalace.com
website www.picturepalace.com
Producer & Chief Executive Malcom Craddock

Founded in 1972. Works mainly in feature films and TV drama production. Recent credits include: *Sharpe's Challenge, Frances Tuesday,* and *Extremely Dangerous* (all ITV); *Rebel Heart* (BBC); *A Life for a Life* (*The True Story of Stefan Kizko*); and the *Sharpe* series.

Prospero Films

1 Rook's Farm Road, Yelland, Barnstaple, Devon EX31 3EQ
tel (01271) 860294 *fax* (01271) 860294
email prosperofilms@aol.com
Head of Production Rob Price

Founded in 1997. Specialises in film drama for international distribution. Current projects include: *The Picture of Dorian Gray* (feature); *The Exmoor Saga* (series); and *Oppenheim Intrigues* (series of TV films). Interested in music with a strong 'classical' feel. Potential composers should post sample CD.

SilentSound Films Ltd

Cambridge Court, Cambridge Road, Frinton on Sea, Essex CO13 9HN
tel (01255) 676381 *fax* (01255) 676381
email thj@silentsoundfilms.co.uk
website www.silentsoundfilms.co.uk
Managing Director Timothy Foster

Established in 1998. Producers and co-producers of art house European features, having formerly presented classic silent movies with original orchestral music at the Royal Festival Hall and the Harwich Film Festival. No longer seeks composers for silent films, as concentrating on the development and co-development of feature productions. However, composers with specific experience writing for theatre or plays are welcome to send sample CDs and CVs by post only.

Spellbound Productions Ltd

90 Cowdenbeath Path, Islington, London N1 0LG
tel/fax 020-7713 8066
email phspellbound@hotmail.com
Producer Paul Harris

Produces feature film and drama productions. Current projects include: *Twist of Fate*, a romantic comedy in development with Columbia Pictures (LA); and *Chicane*. Potential composers may submit material on CD, by post.

Twentieth Century Fox Film Co

Twentieth Century House, 31-32 Soho Square, London W1D 3AP
tel 020-7437 7766 *fax* 020-7434 2170
website www.fox.co.uk

Major film production company with headquarters also in Los Angeles. Does not accept unsolicited material.

Walsh Bros Ltd

4 The Heights, London SE7 8JH
tel 020-8858 6870 *fax* 020-8854 5557
email info@walshbros.co.uk
website www.walshbros.co.uk
Producer/Director John Walsh

Founded in 1995. Creators of BAFTA-winning productions ranging from television series and dramas for BBC, Channel 4 and feature film productions. Works with both new and established composers on a variety of factual and drama work. Potential composers should post CDs as the first point of contact.

Warner Bros Entertainment

Warner House, 98 Theobald's Road, London WC1X 8WB
tel 020-7984 5000
website www.warnerbros.co.uk

Among the world's largest producers of film and television entertainment with headquarters in Burbank, California, USA. Includes several subsidiary companies, among them Warner Bros Studios, Warner Bros Pictures, WB Television, Warner Home Video, Castle Rock Entertainment, and Turner Entertainment. Will only consider material submitted through an agent.

Working Title Films Ltd

Oxford House, 76 Oxford Street, London W1D 1BS
tel 020-7307 3000 *fax* 020-7307 3001
email dan.shepherd@unistudios.com
website www.workingtitlefilms.com
Executive Tim Bevan

Founded in 1982. Recognised BAFTA-winning film company. Productions include: *Four Weddings and a Funeral*, *Bridget Jones's Diary*, *Love Actually* and most recently *Pride and Prejudice*.

COMPUTER GAMES COMPANIES

Atomic Planet Entertainment
72-80 Corporation Road, Middlesbrough TS1 2RF
tel (01642) 871100 *fax* (01642) 871080
email info@atomic-planet.com
website www.atomic-planet.co.uk
Managing Director Darren Falcus

Founded in 2000. Credits include: *Robin Hood: Defender of the Crown*; *Gametrak: Dark Wind*; *Jackie Chan Adventures*; and *The Mega Man Anniversary Collection*.

Bits Studio
112 Cricklewood Lane, Cricklewood,
London NW2 2DP
tel 020-8282 7200 *fax* 020-8450 9966
email contactus@bitscorp.com
website www.bitsstudios.com

Leading games developer. Has developed more than 30 titles published on multiple platforms including Nintendo's Game Boy Color, Game Boy, Super Nintendo & NES, Sega's Mega-Drive, Genesis, 32X, Game-Gear & Master System – PC & Online. At present developing titles for current generation consoles, including Sony's Playstation 2, Microsoft's XBox, and Nintendo's Gamecube and Gameboy Advance.

Broadsword Interactive
Unit 8C, Science Park, Cenfnllan, Aberyswyth,
Ceredigion SY23 3AH
tel (01970) 626299 *fax* (01970) 626291
email enquiries@broadsword.co.uk
website www.broadsword.co.uk
Managing Director David Rowe

Founded in 1991. Designs and produces computer software for the computer and console industry. Music showreels may be submitted via post or email.

Codemasters
Lower Farm, Stoneythorpe, Southam,
Warwickshire CV47 2DL
tel (01296) 914132 *fax* (01296) 810239
email licensing@codemasters.com
website www.codemasters.com
Head of Licensing Toby Heap

Founded in 1986. Videogame developer and publisher. Aims to incorporate music that will bring games to life. Potential composers and songwriters should contact the Head of Licensing via email.

Criterion
Westbury Court, Buryfields, Guildford,
Surrey GU2 4YZ
tel (01483) 406342 *fax* (01483) 406255
email rw-info@csl.com
website www.csl.com

Provides game development solutions through Renderware. Games published include: *Grand Theft Auto: San Andreas*; *Mortal Kombat Deception*; *Call of Duty: Finest Hour*; *Sonic Heroes*; and *Burnout 3: Takedown*.

Eurocom Entertainment Software
Eurocom House, Ashbourne Road, Mackworth,
Derby SE22 4NB
tel (01332) 825100 *fax* (01332) 824823
website www.eurocom.co.uk
Founder/Owner Mat Sneap

Founded in 1988. Develops games for all the major consoles and hand-helds across Sony, Microsoft, Nintendo platforms and PC. Big-selling titles include: *James Bond*, *Harry Potter*, *Buffy the Vampire Slayer*, *Crash Bandicoot*, *Spyro*, and *Tarzan*.

Fuse Games Ltd
The Old Brewery, Priory Lane, Burford,
Oxfordshire OX18 4SG
email info@fusegames.com
website www.fusegames.com
Co-founder Adrian Barritt

Founded in 2002. Devised *Mario Pinball* for Game Boy Advance. Specialises in hand-held games.

Konami Corporation of Europe BV
389 Chiswick High Road, London W4 4AL
tel 020-8987 5733 *fax* (01895) 200800
email enquiries@konami.co.uk
website www.konami.co.uk
Product Manager James Anderson

Established in 1984 as a wholly owned subsidary of the Konami Corporation, Japan. Games include: *Boktai*, *Castlevania* and *Pro Evolution Soccer*, available on a range of patforms including Playstation 2, Nintendo DS and XBox.

Kuju Entertainment Ltd
Unit 10, Woodside Park, Catteshall Lane,
Godalming, Surrey GU7 1LG
tel (01483) 414344 *fax* (01483) 414287
email kuju@kuju.com
website www.kuju.com

Independent games developer for console, PC and wireless platforms. Operates 6 studios in the UK. Output includes: *Eyetoy*, *Call of Duty* and *Battalion Wars*.

Lionhead Studios
1 Occam Court, Surrey Research Park, Guildford,
Surrey GU2 7YQ
tel (01483) 401000
email webmaster@lionhead.com
website www.lionhead.com

Aims to develop original, innovative yet commercially successful games in a creative, family-style environment. Games include: *Black & White*, *Fable The Lost Chapters*, and *The Movies*.

Namco Europe

Acton Park Estate, The Vale, London W3 7QE
Head of Business Development Pramesh Chauhan

Major games developer specialising in providing game and entertainment content on web-based and mobile platforms of all types.

Outerlight Ltd

Unit 10, Hardengreen Business Centre, Hardengreen Industrial Estate, Dalkeith, Midlothian EH22 5NX
tel 0131-654 1155 *fax* 0131-663 4628
email info@outerlight.com
website www.outerlight.com
Managing Director Chris Peck

Founded in 2002. First person shooter specialist inspired by games that broke the mould, such as *Counterstrike*, *Civilisation* and *Black & White*. Aims to keep good game design at the heart of all productions.

Real Time Worlds

1 Courthouse Square, Dundee DD1 1NH
tel (01382) 202821 *fax* (01382) 228188
email enquiries@realtimeworlds.com
website www.realtimeworlds.com

Software development company specialising in the entertainment sector. Output includes: *Lemmings* and *Grand Theft Auto*.

Rebellion

The Studio, Brewer Street, Oxford, Oxfordshire OX1 1QN
tel (01865) 792201 *fax* (01865) 792254
email kristien@rebellion.co.uk
website www.rebellion.co.uk
CEO Jason Kingsley

Founded in 1991. Computer games company that also works with low-budget movies. Games include: *Sniper Elite*, *Delta Force: Urban Warfare* and *Tiger Woods' PGA Tour Gold*. Recently announced plans to make new *Judge Dredd* movies with Shoreline Entertainment in the US.

Relentless Software

The Ironworks, Cheapside, Brighton BN1 4GD
tel (01273) 684499 *fax* (01273) 684285
email contact@relentless.co.uk
website www.relentlesssoftware.co.uk
Creative Director David Amor

Aims to design social and innovative games that everyone can enjoy. BAFTA-award-winning games include: *DJ: Decks & FX* on PlayStation2. *Buzz* and *The Music Quiz* are among forthcoming releases.

Slitherine Software UK

The White Cottage, 8 Westhill Avenue, Epsom, Surrey KT19 8LE
tel (01372) 812132 *fax* (01372) 817038
email jdm@slitherine.co.uk
website www.slitherine.com
Director JD McNeil

Games development company. Music should be presented via email.

Swordfish Studios

9th Floor Tricorn House, 51-53 Hagley Road, Edgbaston, Birmingham B16 8TP
email info@swordfishstudios.com
website www.swordfishstudios.com

Award-winning games developer. Games developed include: *Jonah Lomu Rugby*, *UEFA Striker* and *Hostile Waters (Anataeus Rising)*.

PRODUCTION AND LIBRARY MUSIC

Production and library-music listings can sometimes be difficult to categorise with accuracy, because the libraries themselves are also 'music publishers' (i.e. they not only own and deal in the phonographic rights in their recordings, but also the various other copyrights that subsist in their recordings). In order that listings do not appear twice – once under this present category and again under the 'Music publishers' section – the reader is advised that production and library-music companies do not appear separately under 'Music publishers' (unless they publish a substantial amount of work other than library music).

Active Music Library

PO Box 165, Shepperton, Middlesex TW17 9WT
UK Head of Marketing Paul Fitzgerald *Head of A&R* Neil Watson

Aims to provide quality musical composition and production for film, television and all media outlets. Specialises in providing background music for predominantly UK television broadcasters and corporate video companies. Potential composers should submit CDs of their music via post.

Arcadia Music Production (UK)

Greenlands, Payhembury, Devon EX14 3HY
tel (01404) 841601
email admin@arcadiamusic.tv
website www.arcadiamusic.tv
Proprietor John Brett

Founded in 1996. Library-music company dealing with all music genres.

Bandit Music Ltd

62 Slough Road, Iver, Bucks SL0 0DY
mobile (07973) 800370
fax (01753) 650164
email jonathanward@banditmusic.co.uk
website www.banditmusic.co.uk
Director Jonathan Ward

Founded in 1998. Provides library music for all forms of media. Potential composers should make contact by email or phone.

Big Life Music Ltd

15 Little Portland Street, London W1N 5DE
tel 020-7323 3888
email library@biglife.co.uk
website www.biglifemanagement.com

Provides a series of contemporary-sounding CDs suitable for use in film, radio and television (themed as dance, atmospheres, jingles, percussion, ancient voices, jazz, folk and roots, rhythms and grooves, etc.). A range of these sounds can be sampled online.

BMG Zomba Production Music

20 Fulham Broadway, London SW6 1AH
tel 020-7835 5300 *fax* 020-7835 5318
email musicresearch@bmgzomba.com
website www.bmgzomba.com
Head of Marketing Juliette Khan

Established in 1985. Provides music for film and TV; also supplies music for advertising and corporate use. Potential composers should submit music on CD.

Boosey Media

295 Regent Street, London W1B 2JH
tel 020-7054 7275
email booseymedia@boosey.com
website www.booseymedia.com
Media Manager Mike Shaw *Music Consultant* Annamarie Townsend

A one-stop shop representing several music libraries (BooseyTracks, Cavendish Music, Sonoton, PPM, Naxos, Dennis Music: ESCD series, Sanctuary Classics). Music may be auditioned online. Acts as a search, download and clearance facility, with music provided as a download or on CD.

Caritas Media Music

Achmore, Moss Road, Ullapool,
Ross & Cromarty IV26 2TF
tel/fax (01854) 612938
email media@caritas-music.co.uk
website www.caritas-music.co.uk
Managing Director James Douglas

Founded in 2000. Provides a production library service for the global audience. Potential composers should make contact in the first instance via email or

telephone – no unsolicited material. Also offers record company and music publishing services.

Countdown Production Music

2 Millward Road, Pevensey Bay,
East Sussex BN24 6BU
tel (01323) 761897 *fax* (01323) 461969
email jancolli@onetel.com
Director Jan Collins

Founded in 1981. Supplies CDs for radio and television companies in different countries. Potential clients should make contact by phone, fax or email.

EMI Production Music

127 Charing Cross Road, London WC2H 0QY
tel 020-7434 2131 *fax* 020-7434 3531
email firstinitiallastname@emimusicpub.com
website www.emimusicpub.com
Contact Nick Oakes

Offers a service to tailor music to any video sequence from EMI's extensive catalogue. Also supplies pre-recorded music through KPM (**www.playkpm.com**) and Music House (**www.playmusichouse.com**).

Focus Music Library

Studio 3, 166 Haverstock Hill, London NW3 2AT
tel 020-7722 3399
email info@focusmusic.com
website www.focusmusic.com
Manager Dean Mahoney

Founded in 1988. International music library based in media, film, TV and advertising. Deals with composing, recording, production and publishing. Composers should email for more information on submitting material.

Gung Ho Music Ltd

54 Crewys Road, London NW2 2AD
tel 020-8905 5955 *fax* 020-8905 5155
email info@gunghomusic.co.uk
Manager Paul West

Provides music for broadcasters, film and TV. Commissions music in a range of genres for use by the above. Accepts submissions in various formats.

KPM Music House

127 Charing Cross Road, London WC2H 0QY
tel 020-7412 9111 *fax* 020-7413 0061
email info@kpmmusichouse.com
website www.kpmmusichouse.com or
www.playkpmmusic.com
Director Peter Cox

Founded in 1955. Aims to commission and record high-quality production music for use in film and television productions throughout the world. Available to audition and download online. Potential composers should post showreel/audio CD with brief biography.

Latin Arts Group Productions

PO Box 14303, London SE26 4ZH
tel 020-8291 9236

email info@latinartsgroup.com
Director Hector Rosquete

Established in 1989. UK Latin entertainment specialist. Works with producers, composers and Latin artists to compile, produce and license tracks for commercial use. Predominantly supplies for artist release, corporate and film industry. Contact via post or email.

Media Pro Music

JMS Group Ltd, Hethersett, Norwich, Norfolk NR9 3DL
tel (01603) 811855 *fax* (01603) 812255
email carl@mediapromusic.com
website www.mediapromusic.com
Production Director Carl Goss

Founded in 1983. Library and bespoke production music company. Specialises in TV, radio and corporate video. Potential clients should make contact via post or email.

Melody First Music Library

Sovereign House, 12 Trewartha Road, Praa Sands, Penzance, Cornwall TR20 9ST
tel (01736) 762826 *fax* (01736) 763328
email panamus@aol.com
website www.panamamusic.co.uk
Managing Director Roderick Jones

Founded in 1990. Supplier and producer of recorded mood music and mood-music libraries to the television, radio, film, audio-visual, advertising and multimedia industries worldwide. Clients have included BBC and ITV television, BBC and independent radio and production companies. All genres covered. Potential composers should send a CD with short biog/background info and an sae. All submitted material must be clearly labelled.

North Star Music Publishing

PO Box 868, Cambridge CB21 4SJ
tel (01787) 278256 *fax* (01787) 279069
email info@northstarmusic.co.uk
website www.northstarmusic.co.uk
Managing Director Grahame Maclean *Label Manager* Brigitte Mwani

Works mainly within film and television – providing music of all styles. Also supplies music for Sony Warner BMG and large distributors worldwide. Potential composers should make contact by phone or send showreel by post.

Off the Shelf Music

51 Holmesdale Road, Teddington, Middlesex TW11 9LJ
tel 020-8977 3201 *fax* 0870-734 9363
email info@offtheshelfmusic.com
website www.offtheshelfmusic.com

Specialist library company with an extensive selection of online genres and catalogues of specific theme music which can be ordered from the website. The CD library is used by film companies, television and radio – nationally and internationally.

Panama Music Library

Sovereign House, 12 Trewartha Road, Praa Sands, Penzance, Cornwall TR20 9ST
tel (01736) 762826 *fax* (01736) 763328
email panamus@aol.com
website www.panamamusic.co.uk
Managing Director Roderick Jones

Founded in 1990. Supplier and producer of recorded mood music and mood music libraries to the television, radio, film, audio-visual, advertising and multimedia industries worldwide. Projects have included music for BBC and ITV television documentaries and advertisements. All genres covered. Potential composers should send a CD with short biog/background info and an sae. All submitted material must be clearly labelled.

Ronnie Bond Music

1 Woodchurch Road, London NW6 3PL
tel 020-7372 2229 *fax* 020-7372 3339
email rbm@easynet.co.uk
Managing Director Ronnie Bond

Founded in 1975. Provides a wide selection of library music, including songs, for advertising purposes.

SLIC

Canoltan Sain, Llandurog, Caermarton, Gwynedd LL54 5TG
tel (01286) 831111 *fax* (01286) 831497
email gwenan@sainwales.com
website www.sainwales.com
Director Gwenan Gibbard

Houses collection of original music – often with a Welsh emphasis or feel. Potential clients should contact via email.

Sony ATV

13 Great Marlborough Street, London W1F 7LP
tel 020-7911 8634 *fax* 020-7117 1098
email flash.taylor@sonymusic.com
website www.sonyatv.com
A&R Flash Taylor

Large catalogue of music of all genres from all eras of recorded music. Providing for a vast array of independent film companies. Offices and catalogues held in 40 countries around the world.

Soundtree Music Ltd

Unit 124 Canalot Studios, 222 Kensal Road, London W10 5BN
tel 020-8968 1449 *fax* 020-8968 1500
email info@soundtree.co.uk
website www.soundtree.co.uk
Manager Jay James

Established in 1997. Independent music and sound production company specialising in the creation and production of music to picture. Works within advertising and film, both creating new music and sourcing existing music. Also provides sound design, remixing, music editing and music research services. Works within fully equipped recording studio containing editing suite and extensive library of existing music.

Space City Music Ltd
77-79 Blythe Road, London W14 0HP
tel 020-7371 4000 *fax* 020-7371 4001
email info@spacecity.co.uk
website www.spacecity.co.uk
Chairman Victor Van Amerongen *Managing Director* Claire Rimmer

Founded in 1981. Specialises in commissioning and publishing original music for TV and radio commericals in the UK and Ireland. Potential composers may send CDs by post for consideration.

Standard Music Library
Onward House, 11 Uxbridge Street, London W8 7TQ
tel 020-7221 4275 *fax* 020-7229 6893
email info@bucksmusicgroup.co.uk
website www.bucksmusicgroup.com
Key Contact Catherine Joseph

Large established international and independent music library. Provides song search facility. Potential composers should submit 3-5 song demos.

Tom Dick and Debbie Productions
2 The Gallery, 54 Marston Street, Oxford OX4 1LF
tel (01865) 201564 *fax* (01865) 201935
email info@tomdickanddebbie.com
website www.tomdickanddebbie.com
Audio Producer/Studio Manager Rebecca Geall

Founded in 1999. Produces audio and music production for educational, corporate and broadcast clients. Specialises in good communications with clients and working with children and comedy. Only uses own in-house composer but audio engineers may approach for work. Also provides high-quality filming with sound engineers and houses 2 video edit suites.

Torchlight Music
34 Wycombe Gardens, London NW11 8AL
tel 020-8731 9858 *fax* 020-8731 9845
Director Tony Orchudesch

Founded in 1991. Provides a music and music consultation service. Works mainly within television commercials, television programmes, films and corporate films. Potential clients may make contact via phone or post.

Universal Music
website www.umplmusic.com

Provides production music from big-name artists across a range of genres. In-house composers include

high-profile names such as Freddie Ravel, Bruce Kulick and Steve Cole. Music has been placed in a variety of films and advertisements.

V – The Production Library
c/o Music 4 Ltd, Lower Ground,
41-42 Berners Street, London W1T 3NB
tel 020-7016 2010
email office@v-theproductionlibrary.com
website www.v-theproductionlibrary.com

A contemporary music library producing to commercial release standards. Holds 33 albums in the current series; each CD contains 9 compositions with an array of additional mixes and production tools.

Vivo Music Ltd
2 The Embankment, Twickenham,
Middlesex TW1 3DU
tel 020-8892 9236
website www.closetotheedge.biz
Owners Jon Astley

Production and library-music company.

Warner Chappell Music
The Warner Building, 28 Kensington Church Street, London W8 4EP
tel 020-7938 0000 *fax* 020-7368 2777
email info@warnerchappell.com
website www.warnerchappell.com

Has a commitment to make its music library (based on its catalogue of 1 million copyrights worldwide) available to music fans on as many devices and over as many platforms as possible. (Initially founded with the remit of providing music for films.)

DANCE COMPANIES

Amici Dance Theatre Company
Turtle Key Arts, Ladbroke Hall, 79 Barlby Road, London W10 6AZ
tel 020-8964 5060 *fax* 020-8964 4080
email info@amicidance.org
website www.amicidance.org
Artistic Director Wolfgang Stange

Dance theatre company integrating able-bodied and disabled artists and performers.

Anjali Dance Theatre Company
The Mill Arts Centre, Spiceball Park, Banbury, Oxfordshire OX16 8QE
tel/fax (01295) 251909
email info@anjali.co.uk or education@anjali.co.uk
website www.anjali.co.uk
Artistic Director Nicole Thomson *Admin Officer* Adrienn Szabo

Formed in 1993. Vibrant company comprising dancers with learning difficulties.

Ascendance Dance Company
75 Great George Street, Leeds LS1 3BR
tel 0113-217 7293 *fax* (07977) 110881

email info@ascendance.org.uk
website www.ascendance.org.uk
Artistic Director Rachel Wesson

Established in 1999. Known for its work in site-specific venues such as bookshops and railway stations. Has also undertaken 4 major UK tours and is involved in a variety of education projects.

Birmingham Royal Ballet
Thorp Street, Birmingham B5 4AU
website www.brb.org.uk

One of the UK's foremost touring companies. A mainly classic repertoire, with recent productions including *The Nutcracker*, *Giselle* and *Swan Lake*.

Blue Eyed Soul Dance Company
The Lantern, Meadow Farm Drive, Harlescott, Shrewsbury SY1 4NG
tel (01743) 210830
email admin@blueeyedsouldance.com
website www.blueeyedsouldance.com
Artistic Director Rachel Freeman

Produces dance/theatre for disabled and non-disabled participants. Aims to successfully combine authentic dance repertoire, education, outreach and training.

Carlson Dance Company
Chapter Arts Centre, Canton, Cardiff CF5 1QE
tel (01291) 635631 *fax* (01291) 635631
email emmacarlsonwales@hotmail.com
Co-Director Emma Carlson

Established in 1992. Aims to produce work that is fresh, focused and high-powered. Also involved in a range of community and education projects.

Curve Foundation
Ladywell Way, Musselburgh, East Lothian, Scotland EH21 6AA
tel/fax 0131-653 4211
email curve.foundation@btconnect.com
website www.curvefoundation.org
Artistic Director Ross Cooper

Established in 1996. Specialises in performing art and live dance performance.

Dance 4
PreSet, 3-9 Hockley, Nottingham NG1 1FH
tel 0115-941 0776 *fax* 0115-941 0776
email info@dance4.co.uk
website www.dance4.co.uk
Assitant Nicola Freeman

Aims to encourage the development of contemporary dance practice and to provide quality learning experiences for all. Strives to influence the continued development of the contemporary dance art form in the UK, through working with partners, artists and practitioners and by advocating the importance of research and the development of innovative practice. Main areas of work are 'Artistic' and 'Learning'.

CanDoco Dance Company
2T Leroy House, 436 Essex Road, London N1 3QP
tel 020-7704 6845 *fax* 020-7704 1645
email info@candoco.co.uk
website www.candoco.co.uk
Artistic Director Celeste Dandeker *Assistant Artistic Director* Claire Russ *Education Officer* Sarah Howard *Administrator* Verity Golding

Leading contemporary dance company of disabled and non-disabled artists.

English National Ballet
Markova House, 39 Jay Mews, London SW7 2ES
tel 020-7581 1245 *fax* 020-7225 0827
website www.ballet.org.uk

Aims to take classical ballet of the highest quality to the widest geographical audience, at a price everyone can afford. Repertoire moves from the cornerstones of classic works to new commissions in order to produce a popular repertoire for the nation.

Funkstylerz UK
23 The Clock Tower, Kings Road, Woking, Surrey GU21 5HU
tel/fax (01483) 834403
email info@funkstylerz.co.uk
website www.funkstylerz.co.uk
Director Rob Pountney

Leading breakdance, hip hop and funkstyle dance company. Works with events, film, television, commercials, live shows and theatre. Potential composers may make contact via email.

Green Candle Dance Company
Oxford House, Derbyshire Street, Bethnal Green, London E2 6HG
tel 020-7739 7722 *fax* 020-7729 8272
email info@greencandledance.com
website www.greencandledance.com
Artistic Director Fergus Early

Founded in 1987. Aims to take intelligent dance directly to those with least access to it in education, arts and community settings.

Henri Oguike Dance Company
LABAN, The Cottages, Office No. 2, Creekside, London SE8 3DZ
tel 020-8694 7444 *fax* 020-8694 3669
email info@henrioguikedance.co.uk
website www.henrioguikedance.co.uk
General Manager Isabel Tamen

Founded in 1999. Works with a variety of composers and musical styles from Baroque to contemporary. Recent works have involved composers such as Steve Martland and Pedro Carneiro. Tours for 5 months of the year in the UK.

LABAN Transitions Dance Company
LABAN, Creekside, London SE8 3DZ
tel 020-8691 8600 *fax* 020-8691 8400

email info@laban.org
website www.laban.org

Aims to bring together students, choreographers, designers, writers, researchers, artists, theatre practitioners and musicians in a range of contexts from new dance work to education and community projects.

Magpie Dance
tel 020-8509 1288
email info@magpiedance.wanadoo.co.uk
website www.magpiedance.org.uk
Artistic Director Avril Hitman *General Manager* Emma McFarland

Magpie is an inclusive community dance company for adults with and without learning disabilities; it has been based in Bromley since 1993. Also runs a mentoring project to support learning-disabled choreographers.

Northern Ballet Theatre
West Park Centre, Spen Lane, Leeds LS16 5BE
tel 0113-274 5355 *fax* 0113-274 5381
website www.northernballettheatre.co.uk
Artistic Director David Nixon

Vibrant and prestigous northern ballet company. Recent productions include: *Sleeping Beauty, The Three Musketeers* and *Romeo and Juliet*.

The Rambert Dance Company
94 Chiswick High Road, London W4 1SH
tel 020-8630 0641 *fax* 020-8747 8323
email ru@rambert.org.uk
email sslack@rambert.org.uk
website www.rambert.org.uk

Founded in 1926 – the oldest dance company in Britain. Produces a broad range of modern repertoire. Tours the UK annually with its associate orchestra, London Musici.

Random Dance
Sadler's Wells Theatre, Rosebery Avenue, London EC1R 4TN
tel 020-7278 6015 *fax* 020-7278 5469
email hazel@randomdance.org
website www.randomdance.org
General Manager Hazel Coggins

Founded by Wayne Macgregor in 1992; became resident dance company at Sadler's Wells in 2002. Renowned for its radical approach to new technology – incorporating 'virtual dancers', film and animation into its productions.

Richard Alston Dance Company
17 Duke's Road, London WC1H 9PY
tel 020-7121 1000 *fax* 020-7121 1142

Founded in 1994. Focuses on the choreography of major dance figure Richard Alston. Music is well

integrated into the performances and collaborations have involved esteemed composers such as Harrison Birtwistle and Steve Reich, alongside the more classic integration of music by Chopin, Rameau, Ravel and Monteverdi.

The Royal Ballet
Royal Opera House, Covent Garden, London WC2E 9DD
tel 020-7212 9712 *fax* 020-7212 9121
email webmaster@roh.org.uk
website www.roh.org.uk
Director Monica Mason OBE *Administrative Director* Anthony Russell-Roberts CBE

Founded in 1931. One of the great classical ballet companies of the world. Supported by the Arts Council of England. Aims to be accessible to all through a rich and varied repertory including the creation of new choreography, music and design. Provides a showcase for heritage repertory and endeavours to keep established classics relevant and exciting for today's audience. Outreach projects include work with young people and adults throughout the country. Potential composers should contact the director by letter.

Scottish Ballet
261 West Princes Street, Glasgow, Scotland G4 9EE
tel 0141-331 2931 *fax* 0141-331 2629
website www.scottishballet.co.uk

Founded in 1957. Performs across Scotland, the UK and abroad. Reguar educational activities bring together people of all ages and abilities. Presents a broad repertoire, ranging from new versions of the classics, through to 20th-century modern ballet repertoire and extending into signature pieces by living choreographers and new commissions.

StopGAP Dance Company
Farnham Maltings, Bridge Square, Farnham, Surrey GU9 7QR
tel (01252) 718664
email vicki@stopgap.uk.com
website www.stopgap.uk.com
Artistic Director Vicki Balaam

A vibrant integrated dance company that includes dancers with and without disabilities. It challenges traditional notions about dance by using each dancer's physical and intellectual potential as a starting point for creating new work. "We work from a philosophy of physical, psychological and social integration. In so doing, we recognise and celebrate individuality and the differences between people, while continually seeking artistic and technical excellence in all that we do."

Tabula Rasa Dance Company
Keepers Cottage, Amat, Ardgay, Sutherland IV24 3BS
tel (01863) 755315 *mobile* (07768) 172891

email tabularasadance@btinternet.com
Artistic Director Claire Pençak

Founded in 1999. Creates performances for both adults and children in theatre and non-theatre venues. Collaborates with a wide range of creative artists on a frequent basis.

Union Dance

Top Floor, 6 Charing Cross Road,
London WC2H 0HG
tel 020-7836 7837 *fax* 020-7836 7847
email info@uniondance.co.uk
website www.uniondance.co.uk
Company Manager Anthony Osbourne

Founded in 1985. Aims to 'explore and express an identity through dance that reflects the growing cultural fusion of contemporary society'. Collaborates with a range of composers and musicians.

THEATRE COMPANIES

Attic Theatre Company

New Wimbledon Theatre, The Broadway,
London SW19 1QG
tel 020-8543 7838
email info@attictheatre.com
website www.attictheatre.com
Artistic Director Jenny Lee

Formed in 1987 to produce high-quality theatre and develop audiences for new plays, musicals, reworked clasics and contemporary plays with a cutting edge. Work is presented at Wimbledon Studio Theatre and other venues, and the company tours on average 1 production each year. Tours up to 15 venues across the UK annually; these include arts centres, theatres, educational venues and community venues.

Big Telly Theatre Company

The Town Hall, The Crescent, Portstewart,
Co. Derry BT55 7AB
tel 028-7083 2588 *fax* 028-7083 2588
email info@big-telly.com
website www.big-telly.com
General Manager Louise Rossington *Artistic Director* Zoë Seaton

Established in 1987. Designs and delivers theatre productions, interactive workshop programmes and community creativity projects. Tours throughout Northern Ireland, the Republic of Ireland, the UK and internationally; concentrates on the visual potential of theatre through fusion with other art forms such as dance, music, magic and film to create a sense of spectacle. Aims to offer audiences entertainment that surprises, stimulates and ignites the imagination. Incorporation of music has included a series of Irish classics approached from a contemporary angle (music tends to be an accompaniment or used for specific sound effects),

and original scores for new work set outside traditional theatre spaces – such as its swimming pool production of *Little Mermaid*. Potential composers should email with CV and/or post letter with CDs of work.

Borderline Theatre Company

North Harbour Street, Ayr KA8 8AA
tel (01292) 281010 *fax* (01292) 263825
email enquiries@borderlinetheatre.co.uk
website www.borderlinetheatre.co.uk
Producer Edward Jackson

Founded in 1974. Stages 2-3 productions each year with an average annual total of 60-90 performances. Venues include arts centres and theatres across Scotland. Recent productions include: *Tally's Blood*, *Women on the Verge of HRT* and *Angel's Share*.

Cavalcade Theatre Company

57 Pelham Road, London SW19 1NW
tel 020-8540 3513 *fax* 020-8540 2243
Directors Graham Ashe, Kim Joyce, Carol Crowther

Founded in 1972. Stages an average of 5 productions each year – an annual total of around 200 performances. Tours approximately 20 venues per year, including arts centres, theatres, and outdoor, educational and community venues throughout the UK and Ireland. Also performs at conferences and exhibitions and covers publicity and PR events.

Cragrats Theatre

Cragrats Mill, Dunford Road, Holmfirth,
West Yorkshire HD9 2AR
tel (01484) 686451 *fax* (01484) 686212
email info@cragrats.com
website www.cragrats.com
Director Mark Greenop

Established in 1989. A theatrical communications company that uses performance to inspire learning. A values-driven creative organisation, offering an immense variety of work in TIE and corporate training, and in its in-house venue. 300+ productions per year are performed in educational venues, touring in the UK, France and the Middle East.

Creation Theatre Company Ltd

2nd Floor, Kennett House, 108-110 London Road,
Headington, Oxford OX3 9AW
tel (01865) 761393
email enquiry@creationtheatre.co.uk
website www.creationtheatre.co.uk
Artistic Director David Parrish

Oxford-based theatre company founded in 1996. Aims to produces theatre that is visually exciting and accessible by all ages and levels of understanding. Delivers plays in dramatic and intriguing open-air venues where audiences have exceeded 27,000. The company has a strong understanding of the importance of young people's interest in the theatre, and as such delivers regular educational workshops. Potential composers should contact the enquiry office, by letter or telephone in the first instance.

Frantic Theatre Company
32 Wood Lane, Falmouth TR11 4RF
tel (01326) 312985 *fax* (01326) 312985
email info@frantictheatre.com
website www.frantictheatre.com

Founded in 1990. Stages 2 productions annually, with around 1500 performances in 1500 venues throughout the UK and Ireland every year. Venues include: arts centres, village halls, theatres, outdoor venues, educational and community venues, private homes and hospitals.

Globe Theatre Company
21 New Globe Walk, Bankside, London SE1 9DT
tel 020-7902 1400 *fax* 020-7902 1401
email info@shakespearesglobe.com
website www.shakespeares-globe.org
Artistic Director Dominic Dromgoole

The brainchild of American actor/director Sam Wanamaker. The theatre incorporates a professional theatre company with international artists performing a summer season of plays. Has an education department working closely with students regarding the importance of Shakespeare's scripts and plays. An exhibition is also present, devoted to Shakespeare and his contemporaries and the theatre's history. Allows plays to be delivered in the original context in which they were written, including the accompaniment of incidental music by onstage musicians. Potential composers should contact the enquiry office via email, letter or telephone in the first instance.

Hull Truck Theatre Company
Hull Truck Theatre, Spring Street, Hull HU2 8RW
tel (01482) 224800 *fax* (01482) 581182
email admin@hulltruck.co.uk
website www.hulltruck.co.uk
Executive Director Joanne Gower

World-renowned small-cast touring company presenting popular and accessible theatre. Commissions up to 6 new plays each year. Produces plays in-house at Hull Truck Theatre as well as touring throughout the year to mid-, large- and small-scale venues. Also presents world premieres of the plays of John Godber.

Illyria
Cress Hill Farm, Barton Road, Welford-on-Avon, Warwickshire CV37 8HG
tel (01789) 751017
email illyriahq@btinternet.com
website www.Illyria.uk.com
Artistic Director Oliver Gray

Founded in 1991. Works the traditional path of Elizabethan players by delivering quality theatrical

performances with minimal actors, props and scenery in unusual and often stunning locations. Well-travelled throughout Europe and America, the company delivers enchanting adaptations of Shakespeare and modern plays to a family audience with humour, creativity and slick professionalism. Potential composers should make contact by email, letter or telephone in the first instance.

Improbable Theatre Company
4th Floor, 43 The Aldwych, London WC2B 4DN
tel 020-7240 4556
email office@improbable.co.uk
website www.improbable.co.uk
General Manager Kirstie McKenzie *Artistic Directors* Phelim McDermott, Julian Crouch, Lee Simpson

Formed in 1996. A history of 11 past productions which have toured all over the world and have won several notable awards, including the *Manchester Evening News* Award for Best Fringe Production. Stage ideas and costumes are rich and inventive, and performances dramatic and visually stunning. Potential composers should contact the enquiries office by email, letter or telephone in the first instance.

Mercury Theatre Company
Balkerne Gate, Colchester CO1 1PT
tel (01206) 245504
email info@mercurytheatre.co.uk
website www.mercurytheatre.co.uk

Founded in 1998 with a desire to create an ensemble company able to perform a strong classical repertoire with attention to detail and ensuring quality performance, direction and design. The company delivers a strong community programme, making theatre accessible to all ages and walks of life. 500 sessions were run last year to great acclaim. Potential composers should contact the enquiries office by email, letter or telephone in the first instance.

NTC Touring Theatre Company
The Playhouse, Bondgate Without, Alnwick, Northumberland NE66 1PQ
tel (01665) 602586 *fax* (01665) 605837
email admin@ntc-touringtheatre.co.uk
website www.ntc-touringtheatre.co.uk
Director Gillian Hambleton

Founded in 1978 as Northumberland Theatre Company. Small-scale touring theatre company performing at village halls, small theatres and community venues in predominantly rural areas. Main areas of work are new writing and ensemble physical theatre pieces. Stages 3-4 productions annually and gives more than 120 performances during the course of the year. Tours on average to 120 different venues nationally. Recent productions include: *Bedazzled*, *Great Expectations* and *Alex, The Warrior & The Winter Star*.

The Oxford Shakespeare Company

3 Gunter Grove, London SW10 0UN
tel 020-7351 5417
email info@oxfordshakespearecompany.co.uk
website www.oxfordshakespeare.company.co.uk
Directors Kevin Hosier, Charlotte Windmill, Nick Green

Founded in 2001. Took over from Bold and Saucy (established in 1992), staging Shakespeare plays in Wadham College Gardens, Oxford. Also has a residency at North Garden, Lincoln's Inn, London. Stages 3 productions with 90-100 performances during the course of the year. Tours have reached Oxford, London and Basingstoke. Recent productions include: *Merry Wives of Windsor* and *Macbeth*.

Paines Plough Theatre Company

4th Floor, 43 Aldwych, London WC2B 4DN
tel 020-7240 4533 *fax* 020-7240 4534
email office@painesplough.com
website www.painesplough.com
Artistic Director Roxana Silbert *General Manager* Ushi Bagga

Committed to producing and touring new plays. Commissions composers to write scores for new productions. Potential candidates should send a CV and CD to George Perrin for consideration.

The Royal Shakespeare Company

1 Earlham Street, London WC2H 9LL
tel 020-7845 0515 *fax* 020-7845 0505
website www.rsc.org.uk
Artistic Director Michael Boyd *Literary Manager* Jeanie O'Hare

One of the best-known theatre companies in the world, the RSC has been operating under its present name since 1961. The repertoire was widened at this time to include modern writing and classics other than Shakespeare. Formed around an ensemble of actors and core of associate actors who are committed to a "distinctive and unmissable approach to theatre". Stages approximately 15 productions each year. Recent productions include: *Hamlet*, *Beauty and the Beast*, *Macbeth* and *Romeo and Juliet*.

Scarlet Theatre Company

The Bull, 68 High Street, Barnet EN5 5SJ
tel 020-8441 9779 *fax* 020-8447 0075
email admin@scarlettheatre.co.uk
website www.scarlettheatre.co.uk
Artistic Director Gráinne Byrne

One of the country's foremost contemporary theatre companies. Produces highly innovative and stylistic productions that have taken on national and international tours to great critical acclaim. Has a very strong sense of training and education, particularly towards students of theatre studies. The company is constantly evolving and has made strong relationships with freelance contributors. Potential composers should contact the enquiries office by email, letter or telephone in the first instance.

Shared Experience

The Soho Laundry, 9 Dufour's Place, London W1F 7SJ
tel 020-7434 9248 *fax* 020-7287 8763
email admin@sharedexperience.org.uk
website www.sharedexperience.co.uk

An award-winning theatre company founded during the 1970s. Stages 2-3 productions annually and tours to different arts centres and theatres in the UK and abroad. Recent productions include: *After Mrs Rochester, Madame Bovary: Breakfast with Emma* and *A Passage to India*.

Theatre Alibi

Northcott Studio Theatre, Emmanuel Road, Exeter EX4 1EJ
tel/fax (01392) 217315
email info@theatrealibi.co.uk
website www.theatrealibi.co.uk
Artistic Director Nikki Sved

Founded in 1982. Contemporary storytellers producing theatre for both adults and children. Aims to create theatre that is physically and visually inventive and incorporates other art forms. Original live music is part of all productions. Potential composers should submit a CD or DVD.

Tinderbox Theatre Company

Imperial Buildings, 22 High Street, Belfast BT1 2BE
tel 028-9043 9313 *fax* 028-9032 9420
email info@tinderbox.org.uk
website www.tinderbox.org.uk
Artistic Director Michael Duke *General Manager* Kerry Woods

Established in 1988. Irish theatre company dedicated to new writing for the theatre, the playwrights who create it, and the environment in which it takes place. Works to develop, commission and produce dynamic new theatre plays that resonate strongly with audiences in Belfast, Northern Ireland and beyond. Provides professional expertise and innovative programmes to inspire, nurture and support both emerging and established playwrights. Offers a specialised and versatile outreach programme aimed at increasing the value of its plays and productions for the communities it serves. Original music is used as part of script or as background music during play. Potential composers should approach via email or post with CV and sample CD.

The Tricycle Theatre Company

Tricycle Theatre, 269 Kilburn High Road, London NW6 7JR
tel 020-7372 6611 *fax* 020-7328 0795
Contact Nicolas Kent

Established in 1980. Strives to produce a challenging and innovative programme of theatre, cinema and visual arts reflecting the cultural diversity of its neighbourhood – and in particular plays by Irish, African-Caribbean, Jewish and Asian writers – as well as responding to contemporary issues and events with its ground-breaking 'tribunal' plays. Stages 5 plays each year. Recent productions have included: the premières of Harold Pinter's *The Dwarfs* and Athol Fugard's *Sorrow and Rejoicings* and *10 Rounds* by Carlo Gebler; and a collaboration with the Royal National Theatre of Zinnie Harris's *Further than the Furthest Thing*.

Unlimited Theatre

Studio 11, Aire Street Workshops, 30-34 Aire Street, Leeds LS1 4HT
tel 0113-234 5400
email unlimited@unlimited.org.uk
website www.unlimited.org.uk
Artistic Director Jon Spooner

Founded in 1997. Aims to put 'marginalised voices centre stage'. Stages 1-2 productions annually, and gives 50-100 performances. Tours to 10-20 different venues each year including arts centres and theatres throughout the UK (including Glasgow, Edinburgh and Belfast) and overseas.

White Bear Theatre Club

138 Kennington Park Road, London SE11 4DJ
tel 020-7793 9193 *fax* 020-7793 9193

email www.whitebeartheatre.co.uk
Artistic Director Michael Kingsbury

Award-winning theatre, established in 1988 to focus on modern and new plays and a collection of lost classics. Renowned for its importance in allowing new playwrights and actors to take risks, its idea was to centralise on the nurture of new and developing talent. Has been host to 2 West End transfers: *Round the Horne ... Revisited* and *Viva Espana*. Potential composers should contact the enquiry office via the relevant section of the website, or by letter or telephone in the first instance.

Young Vic

66 The Cut, London SE1 8LZ
email info@youngvic.org
website www.youngvic.org
Artistic Director David Lan

Works with a strong belief that theatre should be a place of energy, intelligence and pleasure. One of the leading theatres for displaying the emerging talents of new young directors with a determination to reach out to new and diverse audiences. Runs many projects to develop a love of the theatre in young people. Around 100,000 people visit the Young Vic annually. Potential composers should approach via email or telephone in the first instance.

The evolving role of the music publisher

One hundred years ago, music publishers derived all of their income from selling sheet music or hiring out orchestral parts. They were the facilitating link between the music writer and the professional performer of musical works. Despite having to react to changing markets and new technology, **Keith Lowde** explains that the music publisher today still plays a vital role as promulgator of music within a fast-changing industry.

From the mid-19th century onwards, the formation of writer-publisher partnerships became the most crucial first step in facilitating sales of sheet music to an increasingly musically literate public. This was a time when – especially for the rising middle classes – the piano had not yet been threatened by the radio or gramophone as the primary source of entertainment in the home.

By 1900, performance of music in public places such as theatres, concert halls, restaurants and hotel lounges was generating huge public demand for music products: these were supplied by music publishers through a network of distributors and retail outlets. Then, in 1911, the Copyright Act conferred a newly defined *Performing Right* on composers. This required anyone who wished to perform music in a public place to seek the permission of the copyright owner, before doing so. However, leading publisher William Boosey initially argued against charging a fee for this new right, in the belief that it would result in fewer performances. In his view, fewer performances would reduce sales of sheet music, both to professional performers and to the wider public.

But, in the second decade of the 20th century, sales of sheet music had already started to slow down (for the first time in living memory). Furthermore, with a war in Europe about to reduce each family's disposable income, publishers were prompted to rethink their strategy. The *Performing Right* was, after all, an alternative source of income, and indeed the Music Publishers' Association was instrumental in forming The Performing Right Society (PRS) in 1914. The converted sceptic, William Boosey, was to become first chairman of the PRS.

There was also a new *Mechanical Right* defined within the 1911 Copyright Act, and this began producing income straight away. Anyone wishing to make a copy of music for a contrivance defined as mechanical (hence the name of the right) also needed permission of the copyright owner. In fact, the *Mechanical Right* was sometimes referred to as the *Musical Instrument Right* – since the bulk of income from this source was initially derived from the sale of piano rolls. These rolls of stiff paper were drawn over a cylinder in a specially adapted piano, which pumped air through perforations in the roll; this, in turn, forced hammers to sound against the appropriate strings. The player merely drove the process by pedalling.

Fortunately for music publishers, the definition of the *Mechanical Right* also covered sound recordings on wax cylinders and discs. Publishers could now target artists and record companies with their repertoire, as well as the producers of piano rolls. And it was not long before the gramophone overtook the piano roll as the primary source of mechanical income.

By 1930, film and broadcasting were becoming important new revenue sources. In the meantime, sheet music sales had declined severely. It was also firmly established that the piano was being replaced by the radio and the gramophone as the focus of family entertainment.

So, in the two decades between 1910 and 1930, the role of the music publisher underwent a complete transformation. The emphasis was now less on selling products directly 'to' the public, and more on the value of a 'use' of music in products or services created by others in the supply chain. Publishers had become experts in valuing the revenue potential of the various income streams that a musical work could generate. But they were still facilitators in the process of bringing music from the creator to the public, and they were skilled in bringing writers together in collaborative ventures – and matching the talents of music writers and performing artists. Publishers began to function as the industry's Artist and Repertoire (A&R) department.

Thirty years later, in the 1960s, the advent of the dedicated singer-songwriter would have a significant impact on popular music publishing. Prior to the 1960s, very few artists wrote their own material, but after this time the position was reversed. The majority of hit records were written by the featured artist, or the band, which also recorded them.

As record labels increasingly took on the A&R function, the publisher's role as facilitator diminished to some extent – at least for these new popular works, penned by the artists themselves. The artist with a record deal in place was no longer asking publishers or their writers for new material to record.

Of course, music publishers never entirely lost their original source of income: sheet music sales. Nor had they entirely divorced themselves from the facilitating role of bringing writing and performing talent together, because not every act wrote its own material. So the professional writer was still vital to some areas of the business.

However, hit records were a major source of income for publishers, and within a decade of the Beatles writing their first hit single, music publishers were forced once again to revise their strategy in order to offer more valid services for the writer-artist. For these dual skilled creators, the music publisher became an alternative source of initial finance.

Music publishers had ceased to be the primary investor in the writer's development, and knowing that a record label had signed the writer-artist to an album deal provided a level of certainty about future income. This then allowed the publisher to make an investment decision where the risk had been significantly reduced. The writer's advance now became the important financial bridge between the time of the original record deal being signed and the artist's royalties flowing from subsequent album sales. For this section of the business, at least, the publisher had become the financier.

In the second half of the 20th century, the process of creating popular music became increasingly dependent on synthesised sound and studio production. The writer-artist was now starting to experiment in a variety of sound textures, and in some genres it became common to use samples of other recordings in order to create a new work. As music publishers have always taken on the role of protector of their copyrights, sometimes this role has required them to take out an injunction against others to prevent them from copying or plagiarising their writer's repertoire – and they certainly try to uphold each creator's right in relation to the use of even the shortest of 'samples'. Sometimes, the effort to protect such rights has resulted in expensive court cases where the winner takes all, and the loser has to pay costs and/or damages.

The attitude of music publishers to sampling has today shifted from using the injunctive right to 'monetising the event'. Once it has been established that a sample has indeed been used (an issue which is seldom now left to opinion, given the ability of technology to match two sound streams digitally), music publishers will wish to share in the financial success of the new work. Negotiation usually produces a result that shares financial reward with both the sampler and the original copyright-owner.

The added technology and synthesised sounds in music production have somewhat reduced the opportunity for 'covers'. Revenue from new recordings of old songs has been a major source of income for music publishers and their writers. In the mid-20th century, music publishers were very active in trying to promote covers, but it is becoming increasingly hard to find acts that warrant the investment in this effort.

If a writer-artist is expecting less income from covers of their works, and they are generating much of their own income in performance and sales of their own recordings, then you may ask if finance is the only reason for doing a deal with a publisher. For some, the answer is an 'administration deal' – and not a 'publishing deal'. An administration deal does not usually involve an advance, and there is no obligation on the publisher to exploit the works; in addition, it takes advantage of the music publisher's understanding of the complex network of licensing bodies and procedures that operate in the different market segments and territories throughout the world.

In offering such a minimalist deal, the publisher expects a lower percentage share of the revenue, since there is no obligation on the part of the publisher to invest in exploitation on behalf of the writer.

Once again, therefore, it can be seen that the music publisher has adapted the service: not for reasons of technology here, but to meet the needs of the writer-artist who does not expect to expand their income though further exploitation.

In fact, adapting to market needs has been the outstanding feature of music publishing in the last hundred years. Printed music still produces revenue, but the music publisher's roles as facilitator, exploiter, protector, financier and administrator of music rights have developed to meet the ever-changing nature of the music industry in general, and of the writers in particular.

For the writer, the deals on offer today can be confusing, and undoubtedly a writer needs advice from someone who understands the commercial and legal implications of the various contracts with which they are likely to be confronted. Whether a writer wants to enter into a Single Song Assignment, Catalogue Deal, Exclusive Writer Agreement or Administration Deal, depends both on immediate individual circumstances, and on how the writer's career is expected to develop.

Can the writer do without a music publisher? Yes, it is indeed possible – but few do! For the majority of writers, the publisher has one or more useful services to offer. And could the industry as a whole operate without music publishers? Not yet, certainly. Indeed, rights management and administration will feature even more strongly in the future, and there is an argument that it is, in fact, the record industry which is 100 years behind music publishing in fully appreciating the value and the use of the rights they own.

With subscription services potentially giving consumers online access to the world's music repertoire, the record industry could well be faced with the death of the physical 'product' as its primary source of income. But that is exactly the position faced by music publishers, nearly a century ago!

Keith R D Lowde, FCA, is a former Deputy Chairman of the UK's Mechanical-Copyright Protection Society (MCPS). Today he runs his own company, which offers business solutions to the music, media and entertainment industries.

Music publishers

A List Music Ltd
500 Chiswick High Road, London W4 5RG
tel 020-8956 2615 *fax* 020-8956 2614
email mail@alistmusic.com
website www.alistmusic.com
Key Contact Deon Sharma

Looks after the rights of various artists and titles in all genres internationally. Provides a one-stop music solution for music partnerships. Writers include Wayne Pauli, James Berryman, Andy McGregor and Paul McGranaghan. Does not accept unsolicited demos.

Abacabe Music
10 Messaline Avenue, London W3 6JX
tel 020-8723 7376 *fax* 020-8723 7380
email fran@bluesinbritain.org
website www.bluesinbritain.org
Managing Director Fran Leslie *Artistic Director* Jon Taylor

Specialises in working with blues musicians and composers. Created as a medium for music promotion; also has a record label and produces *Blues in Britain* magazine. Potential artists should make contact by phone in the first instance.

Adventures in Music Publishing
PO Box 261, Wallingford, Oxon OX10 OXY
tel (01491) 832183
email info@adventuresin-music.com
website www.adventure-records.com
Managing Director Paul Conroy

Independent label and management company.

Air-Edel Associates Ltd
18 Rodmarton Street, London W1U 8BJ
tel 020-7486 6466 *fax* 020-7224 0344
email air-edel@air-edel.co.uk
website www.air-edel.co.uk
Business Manager Mark Lo

Established over 35 years ago, Air-Edel is a leading music company representing composers, arrangers, music editors and music supervisors worldwide. The company has offices based in LA and central London (including recording studios with picture sync facilities). Air-Edel offers full music supervision and production services for feature film, television and commercial projects, and works closely with the composer, director, producer, musicians and artists handling all aspects of music production – from the initial creative briefing to budgeting, booking of all musicians and recording studios, copyright clearance and negotiation of contracts, to final production of the music. It also acts as an agent. The group's activities also include a specialist publishing company, AE Copyrights, whose activities include administering both catalogue and individual works on behalf of composers working in the area of specially commissioned music for feature film, TV, radio, theatre, ballet and commercials.

Associated Music International Ltd
Studio House, 34 Salisbury Street, London NW8 8QE
tel 020-7402 9111 *fax* 020-7723 3064
email eliot@amimedia.co.uk
website www.amimedia.co.uk
Managing Director Eliot M Cohen

Based in central London, Associated Music International Ltd (AMI) is the new name for what was the Red Bus Group of Companies. It is run by the original founder, Eliot Cohen, who started Red Bus in 1970. AMI has a long and varied experience of the entertainment industry; the group's activities are divided into several sectors, covering: Music Publishing, Music Licensing, Music Recording (with 2 full automated studios at our London offices), Video and TV production, and Video and TV sales. AMI is a fast and efficient music consultancy service to clear recordings and compositions, producing original music from a team of talented and experienced writers, or specially commissioning writers from a database to best suit the creative and commercial needs of clients.

Bacon Empire
271 Royal College Street, London NW1 9LU
tel 020-7482 0115 *fax* 020-7267 1169
email info@baconempire.com
Director Maurice Bacon

Founded in 1980. Interested in an eclectic range of genres. Potential clients should email MP3s and include a link to website/any additional info.

BBC Music Publishing
Room A2040, BBC Worldwide, Woodlands, 80 Wood Lane, London W12 0TT
tel 020-8433 1723 *fax* 020-8433 1741
email victoria.watkins@bbc.co.uk
Catalogue Manager Victoria Watkins

Large catalogue of copyrighted music. Works with new and established composers creating music for a range of BBC programmes including drama, children's television and film, documentary and radio programmes. Composers should send music to the above address.

Big Life Music
67-69 Chalton Street, London NW1 1HY
tel 020-7554 2100 *fax* 020-7554 2101

email reception@biglifemanagement.com
website www.biglifemanagement.com
A&R Representatives Tim Parry, Paul Kennedy
General Manager Jackie Parkes *Head of Creative
Licencing and Synchs* Toby Slade-Baker

Established in 1986. Works in all genres. Clients
include: Badly Drawn Boy, The Futureheads and
Snow Patrol. Potential clients should submit a demo
by post.

Big World Publishing
9 Bloomsbury Place, East Hill, Wandsworth,
London SW18 2JB
email songs@bigworldpublishing.com
website www.bigworldpublishing.com

UK-based independent music publisher with a
worldwide network of sub-publisher partners. Works
with a range of genres including pop, rock, R&B and
classical crossover.

Blue Melon Publishing
240 High Road, Harrow Weald, Middlesex HA3 7BB
tel 020-8728 3810 *fax* 020-8863 2520
email info@bluemelon.co.uk
website www.bluemelon.co.uk
Directors Mark Albert, Steven Glen

Founded in 1994. Working within all genres.
Potential clients should submit material via email,
telephone or post.

Bluebeat Records c/o Express Music UK Ltd
Matlock, Brady Road, Lyminge, Kent CT18 8HA
tel/fax (01303) 863185
email s.jackson@expressmusic.uk.com
website www.bluebent.co.uk
Director Siggy Jackson

Founded in 1960. Music publishers and record
producers specialising in reggae, ska, bluebeat and
Irish music. Recent clients include: Laurel Aitken,
No. 1 Station and The Marvels. Potential clients
should submit material via post and must include an
sae.

Boosey Media
Aldwych House, 71-91 Aldwych,
London WC2B 4HN
tel 020-7054 7200 *fax* 020-7054 7293
website www.boosey.com

The largest classical publisher in the world. Home to
masters such as Rachmaninoff, Prokovief, and
Shostakovich as well as more contemporary
composers such as Karl Jenkins, Steve Reich and
Elena Kats Chernin. A global publisher, with offices
in New York, London and Berlin and a network of
agents in every major country. Boosey's
synchronisation department also represents more
contemporary works from indie labels such as

Labrador and Gronland as well as working with
young new media composers for bespoke work.
Recent sync successes include: *Children of Men* and
Hot Fuzz for films, and Lloyds TSB and American
Airlines for adverts.

Caritas Music Publishing
Achmore, Moss Road, Ullapool,
Ross & Cromarty IV26 2TF
tel/fax (01854) 612938
email caritas@caritas-music.co.uk
website www.caritas-music.co.uk
Proprietor Katharine H Douglas

Founded in 1998. Well-established classical music
publisher. Recent clients include: James Douglas and
Bedford Chambers. Does not accept unsolicited
material.

Carlin Music Corporation
Iron Bridge House, 3 Bridge Approach, Chalk Farm,
London NW1 8BD
tel 020-7734 3251 *fax* 020-7439 2391
email info@carlinmusic.com
website www.carlinmusic.com
CEO David Japp *A&R Manager* Simon Abbott

A major music catalogue founded in 1966. Covers all
genres. Clients have included: Elvis Presley, The
Kinks, Phil Spector and Aretha Franklin. Potential
clients should submit no more than 3 songs on CD.
Please do not chase.

Chrysalis Music Ltd
The Chrysalis Building, 13 Bramley Road,
London W10 6SP
tel 020-7221 2213 *fax* 020-7465 6178
email info@chrysalis.com
website www.chrysalis.com
Managing Director Alison Donald

Independent music publisher founded in the 1960s.

Demi Monde Records and Publishing
Llanfair Caereinion, Powys SY21 0DS
tel (01938) 810758 *fax* (01938) 810758
email demi.monde@dial.pipex.com
website www.demimonde.co.uk
Managing Director Dave Anderson

Publishing company with a niche back-catalogue of
experimental music spanning several decades. Clients
include: Van Der Graaf, Generator, Gong, Hawkwind
and Mr Quimby's Beard.

Edel Publishing
12 Oval Road, London NW1 7DH
tel 020-7482 9700 *fax* 020-7482 4846
email phil_hope@edel.com
website www.edel.com
Managing Director Phil Hope

One of Europe's leading independent music
companies specialising in several aspects of the

industry. Markets artists and products of all music genres to a worldwide audience through a network of partners and subsidiaries.

EMI Music Publishing Ltd
127 Charing Cross Road, London WC2H 0QY
tel 020-7434 2131 *fax* 020-7434 3531
email firstinitiallastname@emimusicpub.com
website www.emimusicpub.com
Managing Director Guy Moot

Major publishing company with roster including material by Justin Timberlake, Pink, Mutya, Jamiroquai and The Libertines.

Endomorph Music
29 St Michaels Road, Leeds LS6 3BG
tel 0113-274 2106 *fax* 0113-278 6291
email dave@bluescat.com
website www.bluescat.com
Proprietor Dave Foster *Assistant* Clio Bradbury

Established in 1986. Specialises in blues, jazz and ambient styles. Clients have included: Steve Phillips, Paul Lamb and Sam Payne. Potential clients should submit a CD and biography.

Eschenbach Editions
Achmore, Moss Road, Ullapool,
Ross & Cromarty IV26 2TF
tel/fax (01854) 612938
email eschenbach@caritas-music.co.uk
website www.caritas-music.co.uk
Managing Director James Douglas

Established in 1986. Classical music publishers. Clients represented include: James Douglas, Andreas Peterson and Bedford Chambers. Does not accept unsolicited material.

First Time Music Publishing (UK)
Sovereign House, 12 Trewartha Road, Praa Sands, Penzance, Cornwall TR20 9ST
tel (01736) 762826 *fax* (01736) 763328
email panamus@aol.com
website www.panamamusic.co.uk
Managing Director Roderick Jones

Founded in 1986. Works with songwriters and composers working in all styles. Potential acts and artists should post clearly labelled submissions including CD, biographies and sae.

Good Groove Songs Ltd
217 Buspace Studios, Conlan Street,
London W10 5AP
tel 020-7565 0050 *fax* 020-7565 0049
email tracey@goodgroove.co.uk
A&R Representative Tracey Fox

Founded in 1998. Works with all genres. Clients include: Tom Nichols, Steve Chrisanthou and John Beck. Potential clients should submit material on CD.

Grand Central Music Publishing Ltd
Habib House, 3rd Floor, 9 Stevenson Square,
Piccadilly, Manchester M1 1DB
tel 0161-238 8516 *fax* 0161-237 6717
email grandcentral01@btconnect.com
Key Contact Rudi Kidd

Established in 1998. Deals with all genres. Potential clients should submit a 3-song CD with biog by post.

Halcyon Music Ltd
233 Regents Park Road, Finchley, London N3 3LF
tel (07000) 783633 *fax* (07000) 783634
Managing Director Alan Williams

Founded in 1976. Main genres include: MOR, pop and rock. Clients include: The Rubettes and Alan Williams. Potential clients should post recorded material to the above address.

Haripa Music Publishing Ltd
282 Westbourne Park Road, London W11 1EH
tel 020-7985 0700 *fax* 020-7985 0701
email info@kickinmusic.com
website www.haripa.com
Head of Repertoire Alistair Wells

The publishing division of Kickin' Music Ltd, specialising in the publication of dance music. Offers a varied and strong catalogue. Services include: administration, worldwide registration and protection of works; also, contract assistance and assistance in prevention of the exploitation of works.

Heavenly Songs
47 Frith Street, London W1D 4SE
tel 020-7494 2998 *fax* 020-7437 3317
email info@heavenlyrecordings.com
website www.heavenly100.com
Managing Director Jeff Barrett

Part of the EMI group. Material published by artists such as The Doves, Ed Harcourt, The Magic Numbers and Pete Fowler.

Just Publishing
Hope House, 40 St Peters Road, London W6 9BD
tel 020-8741 6020 *fax* 020-8741 8362
email justmusic@justmusic.co.uk
Director Serena Benedict

Established in 1999. Aims to represent the best in cutting-edge, authentic music by working with artists and writers of integrity and talent. Typical clients include: Jon Hopkins, Honeyroot, Leo Abrahams, Dan Arborise, Laroca and Echaskech. Genres covered include: electronica, ambient, acoustic and downtempo chillout. Potential clients should submit material on CD.

Kevin King Music Publishing
16 Limetrees Avenue, Llangattock, Crickhowell, Powys NP8 1LB
tel (01873) 810142
email kevinkinggb@aol.com
website www.silverword.co.uk
Owner Kevin King

Established in 1983. Works with a variety of record companies and has enjoyed recent chart success. Aims to keep an open mind within a range of genres and looks for well-produced demos of good lyrics and melody. Potential clients should submit up to 3 songs via post or email. Please include sae and contact details on both CD and cover. Provides a proactive response to enquiries. Also offers distribution services via record company.

Kite Music Ltd

Binny Estate, Ecclesmachan, West Lothian EH52 6NL
tel (01506) 858885 *fax* (01506) 858155
email kitemusic@aol.com
website kitemusic@aol.com
Director Billy Russell

Founded in 1997. Specialises in R&B and pop genres. Potential clients should submit material via post. Also houses record label – Bluebeard Records.

Leopard Music Publishing

PO Box 45, Cleckheaton, West Yorks BD19 4YX
tel (05601) 480068 *fax* (01274) 879594
email info@leopardmusicgroup.com
website www.leopardmusicgroup.com
Managing Director Brian Williams

An independent publisher that is proactive in signing songs worldwide across most genres.

Music Sales Film & TV

14-15 Berners Street, London W1T 3LJ
tel 020-7612 7545 *fax* 020-7836 4874
email media@musicsales.co.uk
website www.musicsales.com/filmandtv
Head of Media John Boughtwood

Musicalities Ltd

Snows Ride Farm, Snows Ride, Windlesham, Surrey GU20 6LA
tel (01276) 474181 *fax* (01276) 452227
email info@musicalities.co.uk
website www.musicalities.co.uk
Managing Director Ivan Chandler

Founded in 1995. Deals with a wide variety of music including pop, indie, jazz, soul, ambient and film & TV scores. Potential composers must have an existing outlet for material – e.g. record deal, production deal, co-writing with recording artist(s). Also provides consultancy services to advise songwriters on copyright issues and music-business-related matters.

Native Songs

Unit 32, Ransomes Dock, 35-37 Parkgate Road, London SW11 4NP
tel 020-7801 1919 *fax* 020-7738 1819
email info@nativemanagement.com
website www.nativemanagement.com
Managing Director Peter Evans

The music publishing sister company to Native Management. Aims to publish the songs of some of the world's best and most successful songwriters.

Nervous Music Publishing

5 Sussex Crescent, Northolt, Middlesex UB5 4DL
tel 020-8423 7373 *fax* 020-8423 7773
website www.nervous.co.uk
Managing Director Roy Wiliams

Founded in 1979. Deals with rockabilly and psychobilly genres. Potential clients should make contact via the website.

Northstar Music Publishing

PO Box 868, Cambridge CB21 4SJ
tel (01787) 278256 *fax* (01787) 279069
email info@northstarmusic.co.uk
website www.northstarmusic.co.uk
Managing Director Grahame Maclean

Established in 1996. Aims to provide clients worldwide with music in all styles of the highest possible quality. Recent clients include: Universal, Warner and Sony BMG. Also supplies film and television music. Potential clients should make contact via email or post.

Nusong

Unit 105, Canalot Studio, 222 Kensal Road, London W10 5BN
tel 020-8964 4778 *fax* 020-8960 8907
email info@nu-song.com
website www.nu-song.com
Managing Director John MacLennan *A&R Manager* Ben Batson

Founded in 2005. Independent publisher aiming to be artist-friendly and proactive. Interested in quality, well-written songs in a range of genres. Potential clients should submit material to the A&R department via post.

P&P Songs Ltd

Hope House, 40 St Peters Road, Hammersmith, London W6 9BD
tel 020-8237 8400 *fax* 020-8741 0825
email firstname@panelpsongs.com
Managing Director Peter McCamley

Founded in 2005. Deals with a variety of clients in a range of genres. Recent clients have included: Craig David, Beyonce Knowles and Kings of Leon. Potential clients should post CD and include an sae.

Platinum Sound

Global House, Bridge Street, Guildford GU1 4SB
tel (01483) 501215 *fax* (01483) 501201
email Helen@platinumsound.co.uk
website www.platinumsound.co.uk
Contact Helen Gammons

A 'one stop shop' for any company looking for new music on a variety of multimedia platforms. Sources, produces and clears music for computer games companies. Currently supplying music to leading computer games companies including XBOX, XBOX

360, PS2, PC and PSP formats. Contains a digital imprint with Universal Music enabling music to be uploaded and sold through iTunes, Napster, 7Digital and other digital partners. Hosts a 'Song Search' facility enabling international TV and film companies to access music loaded onto the database.

Pogo Records Publishing

White House Farm, Pipe Gate, Market Drayton, Shropshire TF9 4HA
tel (01630) 647374 *fax* 020-7758 0222
A&R Manager Xavier Lee

Founded in 1969. Deals with all genres. Recent clients include: Daniel Boone, Orphan and Emmitt Till. Potential clients should make contact by post with audio/visual, biog and photo. Other services include RTL Music Publishing and POGO Publishing.

Proof Songs

PO Box 20242, London NW1 7FL
tel 020-7485 1113
email info@proofsongs.co.uk

Deals with a range of genres and mixture of artists signed to both major and independent labels. Potential clients should submit a clearly labelled 3-song CD.

Purple City Ltd

20 Woodlands Road, Bushey, Herts WD2 2LR
tel (01923) 244673 *fax* (01923) 244693
email barryblue@btconnect.com
website www.purplecitymusic.com
Press and PR Lynda West

Founded in 2004. Record and publishing company working with commercial releases, film, video and adverts. Contact via email.

Scamp Music Publishing

Sovereign House, 12 Trewartha Road, Praa Sands, Penzance, Cornwall TR20 9ST
tel (01736) 762826 *fax* (01736) 763328
email panamus@aol.com
website www.panamamusic.co.uk
Managing Director Roderick Jones

Founded in 1987. International publishing company working in all song styles. Potential acts and artists should post clearly labelled CD submissions with biographies, photos and sae.

Sony/ATV Music Publishing Ltd

13 Great Marlborough Street, London W1F 7LP
tel 020-7911 8868 *fax* 020-7911 8200
email flash_taylor@uk.sonymusic.com
website www.sonymusic.co.uk
Managing Director Rakesh Sanguvi *Senior Repertoire Manager* Simon Aldridge *A&R Manager* Flash Taylor

Long-established major publishers dealing with all genres. Clients have ranged from The Beatles to Katie Melua. Demos should be posted to the A&R department at the above address.

Stickysongs Ltd

33 Trewince road, West Wimbledon, London SW20 8RD
tel 020-8739 0928
email stickysongs@hotmail.com
Production Manager Pete Gosling

Television and library specialists working particularly with TV themes, commercials and songs. Potential clients should submit music via MP3. Also offers recording studio facilities.

Tairona Songs Ltd

PO Box 102, London E15 2HH
tel 020-8555 5423 *fax* 020-8519 6834
email tairona@moksha.co.uk
website www.moksha.co.uk
Managing Director Charles Cosh

Founded in 1985. Offers songwriters work registration/copyrighting, collection of fees and royalties, worldwide representation and licence uses including sychronisation licences. Genres covered include dance, urban and electronica. Members of Kosheen, The Shamen and Joi are amongst current clients. Potential clients should submit a CD and lyric sheets with details of any previous exploitation (if applicable).

Universal Music Publishing Group

136-144 New Kings Road, London SW6 4LZ
tel 020-8752 2600 *fax* 020-8752 2601
email firstname.lastname@umusic.com
website www.umusicpub.com
Managing Director Paul Connolly

Major publisher with roster including acts such as 50 Cent, Mariah Carey, Jack Johnson and Ludacris.

The Valentine Music Group

7 Garrick Street, London WC2E 9AR
tel 020-7240 1628 *fax* 020-7497 9242
email valentine@bandleader.co.uk
Band and Ensemble Sheet Music Manager Steve Storr

Supplies wind band music to bands worldwide and to examining boards, including the Associated Board. Specialises in wind, brass and swing band orchestrations. Also provides solo and ensemble music for woodwind, brass and percussion. Publishes and distributes on behalf of AV Music, Barclic Edition and Herald Music Company, among others. Also provides advice and research services on band music of a general and specialist nature, including locating rare and out-of-print publications.

Warner/Chappell Music Ltd

The Warner Building, 28 Kensington Church Street, London W8 4EP
tel 020-7938 0000 *fax* 020-7368 2777
email info@warnerchappell.com
website www.warnerchappell.com
Managing Director Richard Manners

Major publishing company hosting a wide variety of musical styles.

Womad Music Ltd

Mill Lane, Box, Corsham SN13 8PL
tel (01225) 743188 *fax* (01225) 744369

email publishing@realworld.co.uk
website www.relaworldmusic.com
Key Contact Rob Bozas

Specialises in world music publishing utilising good connections within the film and TV industries. Roster includes Stef Goodchild and Charlie Winston.

Courses

Academy of Contemporary Music

Rodboro Buildings, Bridge Street, Guildford,
Surrey GU1 4SB
tel (01483) 500800 *fax* (01483) 500801
email enquiries@acm.ac.uk
website www.acm.ac.uk

Established in 1996, and now at the forefront of
contemporary popular music education. Offers the 1-
year Diploma and Higher Diploma in Contemporary
Music, plus the groundbreaking 2-year BA (Hons)
Contemporary Popular Music Degree validated by
Middlesex University. Composition, arranging and
songwriting form an integral part of the performance
and production courses.

Qualifications: Diploma in Contemporary Popular
Music (Music Performance/Music Production);
Higher Diploma in Contemporary Popular Music
(Music Performance/Music Production); BA (Hons)
Degree in Contemporary Popular Music
(Performance/Production).

Barnsley College

Music Department, PO Box 766, Church Street,
Barnsley, South Yorkshire S70 TYW
tel (01776) 716716 *fax* (01776) 716553
email programme.enquiries@barnsley.ac.uk
website www.barnsley.ac.uk
CQL Music Richard Tolson

Offers a range of FE courses in performance and
music technology which incorporate study of
composition. Courses also contain units in
improvisation, production, Max NSP, synthesis
sampling, MIDI, electroacoustic music and live
sound. Houses a digidesign Pro Tools Centre with 4
recording studios and industry specialist staff.
Application through interview and audition.

Qualifications: NCFE Performance Skills; A Level
Music; A Level Music Technology; Digidesign
ProTools Courses; NCFE in Music Technology;
BTEC 1st Music; National Diploma in Music Practice
and National Diploma in Music Technology.

Bath Spa University

Department of Music, Newton Park, Bath BA2 9BN
tel (01225) 875875 *fax* (01225) 875505
website www.bathspamusic.com
website http://performance.bathspa.ac.uk
www.MAsongwriting.com www.myspace.com/
bathspamusic

Established in 1992; now has 350 full-time music
students. Hosts the UK Songwriting Festival every
August. The emphasis is on creativity through
composition (songwriting, classical and 'Sonic Art'),
although songwriters particularly are encouraged to
develop their music in a commercial context. The
undergraduate courses allow for composition
specialism after the first year. The MA in Creative
Music Technology programme is composition-based
and spans commercial and avant-garde styles with an
overall focus on a creative and experimental
approach. Also offers a unique Master's Degree in
Songwriting, supported by staff from ASCAP and the
Performing Right Society. Application through UCAS
for undergraduate programmes, or direct to the
University for Masters' programmes.

Qualifications: Foundation Degree (FdMus)
Commercial Music; BA (Hons) Commercial Music;
BA (Hons) Music; MA Creative Music Technology;
MA Songwriting.

Birmingham Conservatoire

UCE Birmingham, Paradise Place,
Birmingham B3 3HG
tel 0121-331 5901/2 *fax* 0121-331 5906
website www.conservatoire.uce.ac.uk
President Sir Simon Rattle CBE *Vice President* Peter
Donohoe *Principal* Prof George Caird *Vice-Principal*
Prof Mark Racz

An international conservatoire that is also a full
faculty of UCE Birmingham and a concert venue for
many of Birmingham's principal concert promoters
and organisations. Based in the city centre only a few
minutes' walk from Symphony Hall; facilities include
the renowned 520-seat Adrian Boult Hall, a state-of-
the-art Recital Hall customised for performance with
live electronics, 4 recording studios and a specialised
music library, recently rebuilt from the ground up. A
composition specialism is available at undergraduate
and Master's level. Units include: Techniques of
Instrumentation, Conducting, Orchestration,
Polyphonic Studies with additional optional
provision in Technology, Media Music, Non-Western
Idioms, Folk and Popular Music. The Postgraduate
programmes welcome composers working in music
technology, non-Western idioms and notated art
music. Provides a programme of masterclasses and
seminars by distinguished composers, critics and
performers.

Qualifications: BMus (Hons); BMus (Hons) Jazz;
GradDip Jazz; PgCert Music Performance; PgDip/
MMus Music; AdvPgDip (Professional Performance);
MPhil/PhD; Junior Conservatoire and collaborative
programmes.

Bournemouth University – The Media School

Weymouth House, Talbot Campus, Fern Barrow,
Poole, Dorset BH12 5BB

tel (01202) 524111
email media@bournemouth.ac.uk
website www.bournemouth.ac.uk/media

The Media School aims to combine the pursuit of academic excellence with thriving professional enterprise in an attempt to illuminate and enrich academic understanding.

The 1-year full-time Masters in Soundtrack Production (Composing) studies the conception, composition, recording and post production of music alongside studying how the business works, from seeking commissions to costing and managing production projects. Units include: Production Practices, Theory, Professional Development and Collaborative Projects. Applicants are most likely to have a music degree but may also have gained experience outside of studies in theatre or film for several years. Application forms can be downloaded from the website.

Qualification: MA Soundtrack Production.

Brighton Institute of Modern Music
7 Rock Place, Brighton, East Sussex BN2 1PF
tel (01273) 626666
email info@bimm.co.uk
website www.bimm.co.uk
Co-Founder Sarah Clayman

Specialises in contemporary popular genres. Aims to provide the facility for students to train to become the recording artists, songwriters, music teachers and session players of tomorrow. The songwriting courses are run alongside BMG Music Publishing Ltd and are designed for experienced writers, already working at a high level, who wish to write songs for a living. The BA (Hons) in Practical Musicianship also offers units in Songwriting.

Qualifications: Diploma and Higher Diploma in Songwriting; BA (Hons) in Practical Musicianship.

The BRIT School for Performing Arts and Technology
60 The Crescent, Croydon CR0 2HN
tel 020-8665 5242 *fax* 020-8665 8676
website www.brit.croydon.sch.uk
Principal Nick Williams

The UK's only non-fee-paying school for performing arts. Predominantly deals with contemporary popular styles. Specialises in recording, songwriting and performance with a very practical emphasis. Application details can be found on the website. Initial selection process on basic aptitude; successful applicants invited to audition.

Qualifications: GCSE Music; BTEC First Diploma in Music (years 10 and 11); BTEC National Diploma in Music Practice (years 12 and 13); AS/A2 Music (Edexcel); BTEC National Award in Music (Composing).

Brunel University
Uxbridge, Twickenham, Middlesex UB8 3PH
tel (01895) 274000 *fax* (01895) 232806
email admissions@brunel.ac.uk
website www.brunel.ac.uk
Head of School Steve Dixon

Offers study of composition within a variety of Degree and postgraduate courses – **see page 92.**

City University London
Music Department, City University London, Northampton Square, London EC1V 0HB
tel 020-7040 8284 *fax* 020-7040 8576
email music@city.ac.uk
website www.city.ac.uk/music
Departmental Administrator Louise Gordon

Founded in 1975. Provides units in the following areas at Undergraduate level: Performance (including lessons at the Guildhall School of Music), Music Technology, Western Music, Popular Music, Composition, Electro-Acoustic Composition, Sound Recording, Ethnomusicology, Music Business and Film Music. Opportunity to specialise in composition at Postgraduate level. Applicants for Undergraduate programmes should typically achieve BCC A level grades or 240 tariff points and a good First Degree result for MA.

Qualifications: BMus/BSc in Music; MA in Popular Music; Musicology; Composition MPhil/Phd; MMa/DMA (Doctor of Music Arts) joint with the Guildhall.

Coventry University
Priory Street, Coventry CV1 5FB
General: *tel* 024-7688 7688 Music: *tel* 024-7688 7446
email r.ramskill@coventry.ac.uk
website www.coventry.ac.uk
Senior Lecturer in Music Robert Ramskill

Music at Coventry aims to encourage experimentation, curiosity and investigation alongside a flexible and entrepreneurial approach.

The Music Composition and Professional Practice BA (Hons) Degree aims to provide diverse opportunites for composers, including experience in the fields of film, television, advertising and website music. Emphasises learning through practical assignments, including collaborations with the Dance, Theatre and Media courses, and through employing technology in creative ways. Students are also encouraged to experiment with a range of musical styles. Application through UCAS.

Qualification: BA (Hons) in Music Composition and Professional Practice.

Dartington College of Arts
Dartington Hall Estate, Totnes, Devon TQ9 6EJ
tel (01803) 862224 *fax* (01803) 861666
email enquiries@dartington.ac.uk
website www.dartington.ac.uk

Founded in 1961. Specialist arts college offering distinctive practice-led learning methods across contemporary arts practices. The music courses are aimed at dynamic, interactive musicians committed to exploring contemporary music styles, including contemporary classical/art music, jazz, pop, world and folk. Concerts are held regularly and the college is visited by a variety of visiting artists, residencies and more than 30 professional music tutors.

Offers specialist 3-year BA (Hons) (Composition), which is aimed at giving students substantial time to develop specialist skills while supported by a broad knowledge and understanding of contemporary music. Includes introductory sessions in a range of music/arts-based technologies. General 3-year BA (Hons) Music programme also includes study of composition alongside performance, musicianship and musicology.

The MA Contemporary Music programme is aimed at original, contemporary musicians and musicologists and allows for a composition focus.

Qualifications: BA (Hons) (Composition); BA (Hons), MA in Contemporary Music. (Also provides specialist music awards allowing for professional placement/exchange opportunities – see website.)

Guildhall School of Music and Drama

Silk Street, Barbican, London EC2Y 8DT
tel 020-7628 2571 *fax* 020-7256 9438
email registry@gsmd.ac.uk
email composition@gsmd.ac.uk
website www.gsmd.ac.uk
Director of Music Damian Cranmer

Founded in 1880. Composition specialisms available at Undergraduate and Postgraduate level – including study of composition for film and collaborations with the Drama school.

Qualifications: BMus (Composition); MMus (Composition).

Havering College

Ardleigh Green Road, Hornchurch, Essex RM11 2LL
tel (01708) 455011
email information@havering-college.ac.uk
website www.havering-college.ac.uk
Curriculum Manager (ND) Nigel Hooper *Curriculum Manager (HE)* David Wood

Offers a Diploma, HND and HNC level performance courses which incorporate Songwriting. The BA (Hons) in Music Practice and Technology combines study of composition with performance and music technology.

Qualifications: Level 3 National Diploma in Music Practice; Level 4 Higher Diploma Certificate in Music Performance; Higher National Diploma in Music Performance; BA (Hons) in Music Practice and Technology.

Kings College London

Department of Music, Kings College, Strand, London WC2R 2LS
tel 020-7848 2029 *fax* 020-7848 2319
email music@kcl.ac.uk
website www.kcl.ac.uk
Head of Department John Deathridge

Renowned centre of excellence working with strong belief in the central role of music in today's culture as a creative mode of self-expression. Aims to develop students' ability to deliver engaged and informed performances, vigorous historical writing, exciting new compositions and incisive analyses and criticism. The BMus and MMus programmes offer the opportunity to specialise in Composition.

Qualifications: BMus (Hons) – Dual Hons courses also available; MMus (Composition); MPhil/PhD.

Kingston University

School of Music, Coombehurst, Kingston Hill Centre, Kingston-upon-Thames, Surrey KT2 7LB
tel 020-8547 8624 *fax* 020-8547 7349
email s.winter@kingston.ac.uk
website www.kingston.ac.uk/music
Music Administrator Sarah Winter *Admissions Tutor* Tim Ewers

The music courses at Kingston aim to cover a broad spectrum: genres, from traditional to the cutting-edge; techniques, from composition to performance; and contexts from the history of music, to the role of music in education.

Offers specialisms in Composition at Undergraduate level and Composition and Composition for Film at Postgraduate level. Undergraduate applications are through UCAS; Postgraduate application forms can be downloaded from the website. All applicants may be called in for interview.

Qualifications: BMus (Hons); BA Joint Honours in Music; MA in Music; Research Degrees (PhD/MPhil), including composition.

Leeds College of Music

3 Quarry Hill, Leeds LS2 7PD
tel 0113-222 3400 *fax* 0113-243 8798
email enquiries@lcm.ac.uk
website www.lcm.ac.uk
Lecturer in Composition Dr Robert Wilsmore

The UK's largest specialist music college provides a creative and stimulating environment for study. Offers study of songwriting within Further Education courses, and specialisms in songwriting and composition at Undergraduate and Postgraduate level.

The BA and MA programmes encourage strong links with a range of performers, composers and other industry practitioners who offer students unique professional training through regular workshops, lectures and seminars. Also provides a specialist opportunity for the study of Indian and Latin American music, with internationally recognised artists lecturing in these fields. Study of composition is centred on learning to write in a variety of contemporary idioms for a variety of ensembles; there are opportunities for new work to be performed.

Qualifications: Music Foundation Programme (Performance); Access to Music; BTEC National Diploma in Music; BTEC National Diploma in Popular Music; BTEC National Diploma in Jazz; BA (Hons) Jazz Studies; BA (Hons) Music Studies; BA (Hons) Popular Music Studies; MA Jazz; MA Music.

Liverpool Institute for Performing Arts
Mount Street, Liverpool L1 9HF
tel 0151-330 3000 *fax* 0151-330 3131
email reception@lipa.ac.uk
website www.lipa.ac.uk
Principal Mark Featherstone-Witty

All LIPA qualifications work on the basis that to enjoy a long-term career in the contemporary and popular music field, musicians need to be versatile and to possess a wide range of abilities. Study of songwriting and composition is incorporated within the Degree programmes – **see page 95.**

Napier University
The Ian Tomlin School of Music, Craighouse Road, Edinburgh EH10 5LG
tel 0131-455 6200
email g.weir@napier.ac.uk
website www.napier.ac.uk
Acting Director of Music G Weir

The BA (Hons) degree gives students the opportunity to take principal study composition alongside a range of extra core and optional modules. These modules include History and Stylistic Studies, Jazz Improvisation, Acoustics for Musicians, Music Scoring Software, Keyboard Skills and MIDI Sequencing.

The Popular Music Degree also offers composition as principal study and focuses on developing versatility in the use of music technology and extending cultural, critical and creative abilities through a wide-ranging programme of study and practice. Units include: Recording Technology, The Business of Music, Elementary Acoustics for Musicians, Music Scoring Software, Music in the Community, Studio Techniques, and Introduction to Music Therapy.

Music facilities include 4 recording studios and fully networked MIDI suites, well-equipped teaching and rehearsal rooms as well as a recital area.

Qualifications: BA (Hons) in Music; BA (Hons) in Popular Music.

Perth College
Admissions Office, Perth College, Freepost, Perth PH1 2BR
tel 0845-270 1177 *tel* (01738) 877001

email pc.admissions@perth.uhi.ac.uk
website www.perth.ac.uk
Course Leader Lorenz Cairns

Leading Scottish HE institution providing a variety of popular music courses (established the UK's first full-time rock course in 1985). Includes aspects of songwriting and composition study within the full-time courses.

Qualifications: NQ Rock Music Studies; HNC Music; HND Music; BA in Popular Music Performance. (Students successfully competing the HND course may be able to progress directly to the 3rd year of the degree course) – **see page 96.**

Royal Academy of Music
Marylebone Road, London NW1 5HT
tel 020-7873 7373 *fax* 020-7873 7374
email go@ram.ac.uk
website www.ram.ac.uk
Comms Manager Peter Craik

Founded in 1822. Centre of musical excellence and Britain's senior conservatoire. The Undergraduate composition programme curriculum is designed to reflect the broad vistas and challenges faced by today's music creator. Teaching combines media and concert composition and takes place through individual tutorials, workshops, weekly composition and analysis seminars, electronic techniques and business studies, plus a variety of elective choices including conducting.

Postgraduate study includes extensive opportunities for performance of student works, including orchestral workshops and external collaborations.

Qualifications: BMus (Composition); MMus (Composition).

Royal College of Music
Prince Consort Road, London SW7 2BS
tel 020-7589 3643 *fax* 020-7589 7740
email info@rcm.ac.uk
website www.rcm.ac.uk

Established in 1882. Among the world's leading conservatoires. Aims to provide specialised musical education and professional training at the highest international level for performers and composers. Provides facility for students to develop musical skills, knowledge, understanding and resourcefulness, enabling them to contribute significantly to musical life in the UK and internationally.

The Graduate composition programmes provide 1:1 supervision, seminars in orchestration/creative transcription, and performance opportunities including visits from a professional ensemble specialising in contemporary performance.

Qualifications: BMus (Hons) (Composition); MMus (Composition and Composition for Screen); PGDip (Composition and Composition for Screen).

Royal Northern College of Music
124 Oxford Road, Manchester M13 9RD
tel 0161-907 5555

email helen.simms@rncm.ac.uk
website www.rncm.ac.uk
Admission Co-ordinator Helen Simms

Founded in 1973. Renowned centre of excellence for composers. Offers a range of composition-based Degree and Diploma courses at Undergraduate and Postgraduate levels, including an Undergraduate joint course run in collaboration with the University of Manchester. A collaborative arrangement with the Manchester Metropolitan University also exists at Postgraduate level.

Qualifications: BMus (Composition); MMus (Composition); PGDip (Composition).

Royal Scottish Academy of Music and Drama

100 Renfrew Street, Glasgow G2 3DB
tel 0141-332 4101 *fax* 0141-332 8901
email d.mccrory@rsamd.ac.uk
website www.rsamd.ac.uk
Director of Music Rita McAllister *Head of Composition* Gordon MacPherson

Provides high-quality musical education in a lively and friendly environment. Offers composition specialisms at Degree and Postgraduate level. Aims to broaden cultural horizons, while focusing heavily on individual talents and special interests. Has a strong vocational tradition; develops close links with international performers, professional companies and traditional musicians across Scotland.

Qualifications: BMus (Hons) (Composition); BA (Scottish Music) (Hons); MMus (Composition); PGDip (Composition).

Royal Welsh College of Music and Drama

Composition Study Area, Castle Grounds, Cathays Park, Cardiff CF10 3ER
tel 029-2039 1368 *fax* 029-2079 1304
email raymondtc@rwcmd.ac.uk
Head of Composition and Contemporary Music Timothy Raymond

Aims to provide thorough training in a broad spectrum of classical music, with a focus on 1:1 learning. Education and outreach projects are included as part of courses. Application forms may be obtained from the Admissions Officer; composition applications should include 3-4 original compositions with scores (plus recordings where possible).

Qualifications: BMus (Composition); MMus (Composition).

South Thames College

Wandsworth High Street, Wandsworth, London SW18 2PP
tel 020-8918 7189 *fax* 020-8918 7777
email tonybiola@south-thames.ac.uk
Course Leader Tony Biola

Supports over 20,000 students. Provides study of composition as part of a range of FE courses focusing on study of music technology. Facilities include fully equipped rehearsal, music studios and music technology suites – **see page 222.**

Qualifications: BTEC First Diploma in Music Technology (Level 2); National Award in Music Technology (Level 3); National Certificate in Music Technology (Level 3); Music Production National Award (Level 3); Foundation Degree in Music Technology.

Thames Valley University

LCMM Admissions Office, TC308, Thames Valley University, St Mary's Road, Ealing, London W5 5RF
tel 020-8231 2677
email music@tvu.ac.uk
website www.tvu.ac.uk
Head of Academic Studies Peter Rudnick

Founded in 1860 and with campuses in Ealing, Slough and Reading. TVU now runs music courses previously provided by the London College of Music and Media. The Composition department aims to place strong emphasis on frequent performance of student works by a variety of ensembles, from solo/ duo up to orchestral in size.

The 3-year music Degree course (specialising in composition) is based on developing students' specialist and supporting skills to a level enabling them to maintain a professional profile. Optional study units include: 19th Century Music, World Music Studies, Jazz Studies, Music Theatre Studies, Popular Music Studies, 20th/21st Century Performance Workshop, Desktop Music, and Orchestration and Arranging. The 3rd year culminates with a public concert displaying compositional achievements.

The MA in Composing Concert Music is designed for advanced composers and is studied through a range of individual tutorials, seminars and workshops. Students will learn to compose for a diverse range of instrumental, vocal and ensemble media and will benefit from collaboration with students on parallel pathways for film, television and theatre.

Qualifications: BA (Hons) in Music (Composition); MA in Composing Concert Music.

Trinity College of Music

Charles Court, Old Royal Naval College, Greenwich, London SE10 9JF
tel 020-8305 4444 *fax* 020-8305 9444
email enquiries@tcm.ac.uk
website www.tcm.ac.uk
Head of Composition Dominic Murcott

Renowned conservatoire based in an idyllic setting. The Composition faculty aims to be dynamic and adventurous, training composers for the diversity and realities of professional life. Individual and group tuition is underpinned by traditional techniques while providing the support needed to experiment with new ideas. Computer and technology-based composition techniques are fundamental to the programme. Composition students have recently written works for the following college ensembles: Bulldog Scholarship String Quartet, Early Music Ensemble, Small & Large Jazz Bands, and Trinity Symphony Orchestra.

Qualifications: BMus (Hons) (Composition); PG Dip (Composition); MMus (Composition).

University of Durham
University Office, Old Elvet, Durham DH1 3HP
tel 0191-334 3140 *fax* 0191-334 3141
email bennett.zon@durham.ac.uk
website www.dur.ac.uk/music
Head of Department Dr Bennett Zon

Established in 1832. Award-winning (voted University of the Year 2005 by the *Sunday Times*) university based in 2 locations: the City of Durham and Queen's Campus in Stockton.

Composition is a department specialism incorporated into the BA (Hons) and available for specialism at Masters level. Other department focuses include: historical musicology (particularly the 15th and 16th centuries), Haydn and Beethoven studies, British and Irish music of the 19th and early 20th centuries, sociology and music, popular music and theories of mass culture, electroacoustic music and music technology.

The Department has several active composers and performers of international standing. Facilities include: lecture rooms, concert room, recording collection and gamelan.

Qualifications: BA Hons and MA in Music (Composition).

University of Salford
School of Media, Music and Performance, University of Salford, Salford, Greater Manchester M5 4WT
tel 0161-295 5000 *fax* 0161-295 4704
email m.wilson@salford.ac.uk
website www.smmp.salford.ac.uk
Head of Compositional Studies Professor Mick Wilson

Provides facility for more than 400 students to study on 4 specialist degree music courses. Composition is incorporated into the Undergraduate programmes alongside study in Performance, Jazz, Analytical and Historial Studies and Music Technology. The Popular Music degree places emphasis on music business and the recording industry.

The Postgraduate programmes of study are intensive courses for composers and arrangers wishing to specialise in contemporary genres such as popular music, brass and wind bands, jazz and electro-acoustic music. Students are encouraged, through a variety of individual tutorials, seminars and workshops, to develop their compositional technique while pursuing their search for creativity and individuality.

Facilities include 24/48-track recording studios, video edit suites, music workshops, electro-acoustic, television and radio studios.

Qualifications: BA (Hons) Music; BA (Hons) Popular Music and Recording; MA/PG Dip in Music (Composition).

University of Surrey
Guildford, Surrey GU2 5XH
tel (01483) 686509 *fax* (01483) 686501
email music@surrey.ac.uk
website http://www.surrey.ac.uk/Music/Courses/
Editor Admissions Tutor Dr Stephen Downes

The degree course provides equal emphasis within performance, composition and academic study aimed at students wishing to pursue a career in any area of the music industry. Units offered include Western Art Music, Popular and non-Western Music, Music Technology, Film Music and Jazz. Students in their second and final years may specialise in composition.

Qualification: BMus.

University of York
Department of Music, Sir Jack Lyons Concert Hall, University of York, Heslington, York YO16 5DD
tel (01904) 432446 *fax* (01904) 432450
email music@york.ac.uk
website www.music.york.ac.uk
Head of Department Professor R Marsh *Admissions Tutor* Dr J Eaton

Founded in 1964. Undergraduate teaching is based on a 'project system' and practice-based learning with focuses including musicology, music technology and world music. Students may take specialist units in Composition. Supports a range of music types including early and contemporary, world, jazz and acoustic. MPhil/Phd in Composition provides students with an academic supervisor, weekly composing seminars and a wide opportunity for performance of works by a variety of university ensembles. All applicants are interviewed, including an instrumental audition for the Undergraduate programme.

Qualifications: BA (Hons) Music; MPhil/Phd (Composition).

Copyright, contracts and royalties

UK copyright law protects musicians' and songwriters' creative efforts – and, in fact, is the foundation for many of their income streams. **Ben Challis** explains the intricacies of how copyright law works to protect the 'creator'.

Copyright

Copyright is a law that exists to protect the creative effort: works of art, music, poems, plays, ballets, sculptures, films, photographs, and sound recordings – to name just a few. The law allows the owner of a copyright to protect their work, and then to benefit from the commercial exploitation of their work. The entire music industry is based upon the exploitation of copyrights, and anyone who is connected with the creative industries should have at least a basic understanding of how copyright works. In the United Kingdom, copyright laws are, for the most part, governed by an Act of Parliament called the *Copyright, Designs and Patents Act 1988* ('CDPA').

Section 1 of the CDPA states that copyright subsists (i.e. exists) in original literary, dramatic, artistic and musical works. Of particular importance here are musical works (i.e. the notes of a song) and literary works (which include the lyrics of a song). However, artistic copyright is also important as it will cover the ownership of photographs and artwork for a CD or a flyer. The next thing to note is that Section 1 of the CDPA also provides for the fact that there is a separate copyright in sound recordings. This means that there is the copyright in the song (written music and lyrics), and also a copyright in the recording of that song (aural version). So a new copyright will exist every time someone records a cover version of an existing song – but the copyright in the song, as first notated, will itself remain the same.

There is no hard and fast rule as to what can be copyrighted; nor (you may or may not be surprised to learn) is artistic merit important (or rather, it is irrelevant for legal purposes). What *is* important is that the work created should be 'original'. A single word cannot be copyrighted, but there can be a copyright in a short poem (the original arrangement of certain words). The definition of what can and cannot be copyrighted, and what can be protected by copyright, is particularly important when it comes to deciding if something has been copied; this is because a copyright is only infringed when a copy is made of a 'qualifying' work. Today, for example, this concept is very important with sampling (using snippets from the music of others). Sampling is commonplace in the music industry, and the law relating to music sampling is important to understand (described below).

Performers' rights

In addition to copyright protection, performers have, since 1996, had certain rights as well. This means that not only is the unauthorised recording of a concert illegal ('bootlegging' – or making pirate copies of a recording – is a criminal act), but also, recording a performance without the performer's consent constitutes an infringement of the performer's rights – and performers can take legal action to recover any losses they have suffered, or prevent the distribution of recordings.

Who owns a copyright?

The first owner of the copyright in a song is the person or people who wrote the music and the lyrics. Obviously, the copyright might be shared between two or more people.

When writing songs with other people, it is important to agree who wrote what, and what shares each writer has in the song. In a case involving the former members of Spandau Ballet, the court decided that in the absence of any written agreement, the copyright in all of Spandau Ballet's songs was owned by Gary Kemp – who wrote both melody and lyrics. Just contributing suggestions for songs was not enough to make the other band members co-writers.

Once an original work has been reduced to a permanent form (for example, 'fixed' as sheet music, a lyric sheet, or on a demo tape) then copyright automatically exists under UK law. Copyright in a song lasts for the lifetime of the writer(s) plus 70 years after the death of the writer(s) – or the death of the last co-writer. Unlike in the USA, there is no obligation to register copyrights; in fact, there isn't even a central copyright registry in the UK, as there is in the USA (the Library of Congress). However, because there is no central registration procedure in the UK, problems sometimes arise when it becomes difficult to prove when a song was created, and by whom. This is why people often post copies of their music or lyrics to themselves, or to their solicitor, in a sealed envelope: this doesn't create a copyright – that already exists; but the postmark does show when a work was first written.

Copyright infringements

If someone copies your work without permission, they usually 'infringe' your copyright. There are a variety of remedies available in the courts to prevent this from occurring, or to recompense a songwriter/s for any damage that he/she/they might suffer. The two main remedies are injunctions and damages. Injunctions are usually orders from the court to stop someone doing something – for example, courts can order a vendor to desist from selling records containing a copy of a song or a sound recording which has been used without the permission of the songwriter (or owner of the song, such as a music publisher), or owner of the sound recording. Ultimately, courts can order infringing copies to be destroyed or delivered up to the owner of the copyright. Damages are financial awards made by the courts to recompense the owner of a copyright for the losses they have suffered as a result of someone infringing their work. You should also note that infringing copyright can be a criminal act. Music piracy (such as bootlegging) can result in fines, and even imprisonment. We regularly hear of computer software, video, DVD and music pirates being imprisoned, some for a number of years. A three-and-a-half-year prison sentence was handed down to the defendant in R v Purseglove, in 2004, for large-scale music piracy and bootlegging which netted millions of pounds in profits. The defendant's house and other personal property were also seized.

Sampling

Sampling can be defined as placing a pre-existing lyric, melody or sound recording within another sound recording. While any use has to be 'substantial', recent US court cases involving the Beastie Boys and NWA have shown that using *any* part of a sound recording, and any recognisable part of a melody or lyrics, will result in the sampler being liable to legal action for copyright infringement if they do not obtain clearance from the owner in advance. There have been a number of cases where samplers have had to give away all of the income they received, and might receive in the future, from their recording – these monies being paid to the person or persons from whom they took the sample. It is always wise to get permission, and a proper licence, from the person or company who owns the original copyright in the song and the sound recording you want to use – to make sure you are not sued at a later date. If you make money from sampling the work of others without permission, the copyright owner usually finds out and may come knocking on your door!

Contracts and agreements

Once a copyright is established, the owner of that copyright can authorise other people to use it; or they can restrict other people from using it. Because of the complexities in managing the exploitation of songs worldwide, most songwriters use the services of one or more collection societies to act on their behalf. In the United Kingdom, the two main collection societies for songs are the PRS (Performing Right Society) and the MCPS (Mechanical-Copyright Collection Society). These are membership-controlled societies, which collect revenues on a domestic and worldwide basis from the use of songs on records, in downloads, on the radio, at live concerts, in films and on television (etc.). The songwriter will enter into an agreement with the collection society, allowing the society to manage the copyright(s) in the song(s). The collection society will take a commission (or sometimes fee) for acting on behalf of the songwriter, and collecting these monies. They will normally pay over any money due to the songwriter every three months.

Successful songwriters may utilise the services of a music publisher, which represents their work and in most cases takes an assignment of the copyright in the songs owned by the songwriter, so they become part-owner of these works. In return, the publisher guarantees that a royalty will be payable to the songwriter from any money the publisher collects from the use of the song.

A good publisher can make a big difference to an artist's career. Even when a band is writing music for themselves, publishers can generate additional money for the band – by helping to place their songs in films, television programmes or adverts, for example. A publisher will usually have the resources to manage the collection of income on a worldwide basis, and to protect the songwriter's copyrights – using the law where necessary. They can support and nurture a songwriting talent, and provide vital contacts with other parts of the music industry, such as the record labels.

Remember, if you are a performing artist you will also have a separate copyright in any sound recordings you make, and you may have performers' rights when you are filmed or recorded live in concert. These are not connected to the copyright in the songs you write.

Royalties

Most music publishers represent the works of a songwriter in return for a share of the income. They will take a certain share of the income, and pay the rest over to the songwriter on a regular basis as a 'royalty'. Some music publishers will pay a songwriter an 'advance': this is an advance payment of anticipated royalties, and it is recoupable from the artist's future income from songwriting. In effect, the publisher can collect what they have paid the songwriter as the advance from future income that would otherwise be payable to the songwriter. Royalties can also be paid directly to a songwriter from a collection society, such as the PRS (see above).

The main source of income for most songwriters is from the issuing of licences to record labels to enable them to record a performance of a song. The MCPS (see above) collects a fee equating to 8.5 per cent of the dealer price of a record on behalf of the songwriter (this is about 80p for a CD album; the sum would be divided between all of the songs on the album). However, royalties are also collected from radio plays; from television broadcasts; from 'synchronising' (or allowing the use of a song synchronised to a film or an advert); from the live performance of a song at a concert; from legal downloads over the Internet; and even from video games, mobile phone ringtones, plays on juke-boxes, and re-publishing lyrics in magazines.

Signing a contract

If you are presented with a music publishing contract, it is almost certain that you will need to take independent legal advice to make sure you understand what you are signing. This may be a very important document in your career. You could be signing an agreement which says you can only write songs for that publisher and no-one else for a given period of time, and you may be giving away ownership of your copyrights. Any contract should be a fair agreement for all parties, which provides the songwriter with support and long-term income from royalties – in proportion to the songwriter's success!

Ben Challis is a UK-based music lawyer, with the Glastonbury Festival among his top clients. He is a visiting lecturer at Buckinghamshire Chilterns University College, and a writer on music and entertainment industry law.

Societies

British Academy of Composers and Songwriters (BACS)
British Music House, 26 Berners Street,
London W1T 3LR
tel 020-7636 2929 *fax* 020-7636 2212
email info@britishacademy.com
website www.britishacademy.com
Membership Manager Fran Matthews

Founded in 1999. Main activites are political campaigning, showcasing composers and songwriters through the Ivor Novello and British Composer Awards, and the provision of varied members' services. Also aims to provide opportunities for social interaction and networking. Members receive the twice-yearly magazine *The Works*, and a newsletter – *FourFour* – 4 times a year; they can access a collaborative database; attend talks and workshops; and benefit from a range of discounted music services.

Within the academy, members tend to be grouped in 1 or more categories: Popular Songwriters, Media Composers and/or Concert Composers – each of which has its own Executive Committee. There are 2 membership levels: Professional (approx £115 annually) and Member (approx. £67.50 annually).

British Music Rights (BMR)
British Music House, 25-27 Berners Street,
London W1T 3LR
tel 020-7306 4446 *fax* 020-7306 4449
email britishmusic@bmr.org
website www.bmr.org

An umbrella organisation which promotes the interests of Britain's composers, songwriters and music publishers. Formed in 1996 by the British Academy of Composers & Songwriters (BACS), the Music Publishers Association (MPA), the Mechanical-Copyright Protection Society (MCPS) and the Performing Right Society (PRS), BMR strives to provide a consensus voice promoting the interests of creators and publishers of music at all levels. The BMR website has a useful Links page cross-referencing many other music industry and government organisations – explaining their acronyms and listing their websites.

The Guild of International Songwriters and Composers
Sovereign House, 12 Trewartha Road, Praa Sands,
Penzance, Cornwall TR20 9ST
tel (01736) 762826 *fax* (01736) 763328
email songmag@aol.com
website www.songwriters-guild.co.uk
General Secretary Carole A Jones

Established in 1938. An international organisation whose members include a variety of industry professionals. Offers advice, guidance, protection and a range of information about the music industry in general. Issues *Songwriting and Composing* magazine free to all members. Other services include: copyright and intellectual property witnessing registration, collaboration, song assessment and a range of legal and support services. Membership is £48 for UK residents and £55 for non-UK residents.

Incorporated Society of Musicians (ISM)
10 Stratford Place, London W1C 1AA
tel 020-7629 4413 *fax* 020-7408 1538
email membership@ism.org
website www.ism.org
Chief Executive Neil Hoyle *Marketing and Development Manager* Danny Whatmough

The UK's professional body for musicians, with separate sections for composers, performers and teachers/lecturers (most members tend to work in the field of classical/concert music). Has 46 regional centres throughout the United Kingdom.

Works to promote the art of music and the interests of professional musicians. Aims to raise standards in the profession, and gives its members practical advice on legal, professional and personal matters. Puts forward authoritative views on issues ranging from education to ethics, and from intellectual property to broadcasting. It has agreements with the BBC, links with education agencies, and contacts with government departments.

Releases a monthly *Music Journal* which reports the work of the society and its members, carries features on topics of professional interest, and summarises developments affecting musicians and their work. Publishes and maintains online, 3 separate registers: those of Professional Private Music Teachers, Performers and Composers, and Musicians in Education. There are 4 membership categories: Full (approx. £125 annually), Associate (approx. £56), Student (approx. £25) and also Corporate membership. There is an application form on the website which may be printed off and posted.

Mechanical-Copyright Protection Society (MCPS) and Performing Rights Society (PRS) Alliance
Copyright House, 29-33 Berners Street,
London W1T 3AB
tel 020-7580 5544
website www.mcps-prs-alliance.co.uk

The PRS collects and distributes licence fees for the public performance and broadcast of musical works. The MCPS collects and distributes 'mechanical' royalties generated from the recording of music onto many different formats. This income is distributed to their members – writers and publishers of music.

Writers should consult the website for full details regarding membership of one or both societies, and how to apply. The MCPS-PRS Alliance manages common activities, services both societies and is jointly owned by them. However, they remain separate societies in terms of income, constitution and guardianship of different rights.

For details regarding the MCPS in Scotland, contact: Duncan McCrone, 11 Sandyford Place, Glasgow G3 7NB. Tel: 0141-204 4030; Fax: 0141-204 4424; Email: duncan.mccrone@mcps.co.uk.

Musicians' Union (MU)

National Office, 60-62 Clapham Road, London SW9 0JJ
tel 020-7582 5566 *fax* 020-7582 9805
email info@musiciansunion.org.uk
website www.musiciansunion.org.uk
– see page 104.

Scottish Music Information Centre

City Hall, Candleriggs, Glasgow, Scotland G1 1NQ
tel 0141-552 5222
email info@scottishmusiccentre.com
website www.scottishmusiccentre.com
Managing Director Gill Maxwell *Information Manager* Alasdair Pettinger

Founded in 1968. Aims to provide information, contacts, resources and learning services to all aspects and genres of Scotland's music.

Society for Producers and Composers of Applied Music (PCAM)

Birchwood Hall, Storridge, Malvern, Worcs WR14 5EZ

tel (01886) 884204 *tel* Helpline 0906-895 0908
fax (01886) 884204
email bobfromer@onetel.com
website www.pcam.co.uk
Administrator Bob Fromer

A self-help association of composers and producers who work in commercials, television programmes, film, and across the spectrum of applied and media music. The PCAM executive can provide for help and guidance with members' projects. Other member benefits include: 4 issues of *The Bugle* per year; discounted rates to the PCAM annual seminar; discounted equipment purchasing; Associate Membership of BACS; and occasional social events. First year membership is approx. £85; in subsequent years, membership has stepped rates based on income. To join, contact the administrator.

Society for the Promotion of New Music (SPNM)

4th Floor, 18-20 Southwark Street, London SE1 1TJ
website www.spnm.org.uk

Founded in 1943. A membership organisation for anyone with an interest or involvement in new music. Aims to assist young composers and find them opportunities relating to their work; also promotes the creation, performance and appreciation of new music through a range of opportunities and services – including a membership card giving access to discounted concert tickets and merchandise at selected music shops. Issues a monthly magazine called *New Notes*, and an e-newsletter.

There are various membership rates: Ordinary (around £25); Junior/Concession (£10); Friend (£50); Patron (£150); University Department (£50); and School (£30). There is an application form on the website which may be printed off and posted.

Competitions

2 Agosto

Secretary's Office of the International Composing Competition '2 Agosto' via Oberdan 24 – 40126 Bologna, Italy
email info@concorso2agosto.it
website www.concorso2agosto.it

Open to musicians of all nationalities, who are no older than 41 on May 30, 2007. Submissions must be for cello, and/or electric bass and orchestra and must not last more than 10 minutes. Competitors may include various musical styles belonging to folk, jazz, blues and rock traditions, at their own discretion. All scores must be suitable for open-air performance (even if performed through appropriate amplification). Prizes are awarded as follows: 1st prize €5,000, 2nd prize €2,500 and 3rd prize €1,500.

The BOSAs

Bannon Productions, PO Box 4339,
Pittsburgh PA 15204
email info@thebosas.com
website www.thebosas.com

Songwriting competition now in its 7th year and created as a means of offering all songwriters of any ability and background the opportunity to gain recognition within the industry. The top songs within each category of the competition are compiled onto a showcase recording and are then considered by approximately 125 music industry professionals. Entry forms are available from the website.

Brandenburg Competition

Wallstraße 15, D-14770 Brandenburg an der Havel
tel +49-(0)3381-22 88 22 *fax* +49-(0)3381-22 88 66
email biennale@foerderverein-brandenburger-symphoniker.de
email mail@guentsch-brandenburg.de
website www.foerderverein-brandenburger-symphoniker.de
Chairperson of the Board Andrea-Carola Guntsch

Established in 1990. Aims to bring together composers of new music with the Brandenburg Symphony Orchestra to promote them both, and to bring new music to new listeners. Submission should consist of up to 3 scores of symphonic music not written before 1997, and recordings on CD. A CV of compositional professional achievements should also be submitted. There is no age limit. Participation fee is €10. There are 2 prizes as detailed below:

Brandenburg Composers' Prize:

The winner will receive a commission (€5,000) to compose an orchestral work for the Brandenburg Symphony Orchestra (classical structure with triple wind instruments) or the 1st performance of a not yet performed rendered composition. In both cases the work will receive its premiere performance in the Industrial Museum (former steelworks) during the summer of 2008.

Brandenburg Symphony Orchestra Prize:

The winner will get the invitation to compose an orchestral composition or the 1st performance of a not yet performed rendered composition to be premiered by the Brandenburg Symphony Orchestra (classical structure with triple wind instruments) during the season 2008/2009. In both cases the work will receive its premiere performance in the Concert Hall of the Brandenburg City Theater.

Typical submission dates: October 2007 to 31st of May 2008. See website for more details.

Cardiff International Festival of Musical Theatre

Market Chambers, 5/7 St Mary Street,
Cardiff CF10 1AT
tel 029-2034 6999
email enquiries@cardiffmusicals.com
website www.cardiffmusicals.com
Chief Executive Joanne Benjamin

Aims to provide opportunities for new musical theatre works to be developed and presented to the public and to theatre practitioners, with a view to bringing them to full professional production. Judging takes place in 3 rounds; in Round One, 5 songs and a synopsis will be judged; in Round Two, the full libretto and score will be judged; and in Round Three, the full score and libretto will go before the Grand Jury. Entries are welcome from all countries and at all levels of experience. Submissions may be in any length and any style, and on any subject.

Festival Pablo Casals de Prades

Service Concours, BP 24, 33 rue de l'Hospice,
F-66502 Prades Cedex 2
tel 0033 (0)468 963307 *fax* 0033 (0)468 965095
email contact@prades-festival-cassals.com
website www.prades-festival-casals.com
Communication Manager Karine Barreau

Composition competition for chamber music, taking place every 2 years. Works submitted should not have been performed professionally and must be unpublished. Works may employ forces ranging from trio to sextet, but must be some combination of the following instruments: violin, viola, cello (mandatory), flute, clarinet, oboe, bassoon, French horn and piano. Duration of the work should be around 15 minutes. Entry forms and scores (with biography) are usually due around mid-November onwards in a competition year (even-numbered years). The winning Laureate is currently awarded a prize worth €15,000.

Grawemeyer Award
c/o School of Music, University of Louisville, Louisville KY 40292
tel 502-852 6907 *fax* 502-852 0520
email grawmus@louisville.edu
website www.grawemeyer.org
Director Marc Satterwhite

Established in 1985. Aims to support excellence in contemporary classical music composition. Any genre that can reasonably be considered contemporary concert music is acceptable. Most winning pieces have been orchestral pieces or operas, with the exception of the 2007 winner (a piece of chamber music), and a few other exceptions. See website for a complete list of winners and titles.

Application to include: signed application form (available on the website); score; recording; letter of sponsorship; proof of date of premiere; programme notes; bio; photo and $40 processing fee. Prize consists of $200,000.00 – payable in 5 annual installments of $40,000.00. Deadline is next-to-last Monday in January.

International Songwriting Competition
1307 Eastland Avenue, Nashville TN37206 USA
tel 0161-5251 4441 *fax* 0161-5251 4442
email info@songwritingcompetition.com
website www.songwritingcompetition.com

This annual contest is open to established and budding songwriters and broken into many genre sections from instrumental, through to folk, hip hop, religious and world music. Entries are judged by an eclectic panel of established recording artists.

The John Lennon Songwriting Contest
180 Brighton Road Suite 801, Clifton NJ 07012
tel 1-888-884-JLSC (5572)
email info@jlsc.com
website www.jlsc.com
Executive Director Brian Rothschild

Established in 1997. International songwriting competition aimed at both amateur and professional songwriters. Songs may be entered in any of the following categories: rock, country, jazz, pop, world, R&B, hip hop, gospel/inspirational, latin, electronic, folk, and children's. Instrumental compositions are encouraged. Entries will be judged on originality, melody, composition, and where applicable, lyrics. Applicants should submit the following elements:

• 1 song of 5 minutes or less on MP3, CD or cassette
• A lyric sheet (no lyrics necessary for instrumental compositions)
• A payment of $30 per song
• A completed application form

Prizes are varied, from studio gear to publishing contracts and including a $20,000 'Song of the Year' cash prize.

Masterprize International Composers Competition
10 Barton Street, London SW1P 3NE
tel 020-7233 0111
email info@masterprize.com
website www.masterprize.com

Aims to encourage classical music enthusiasts to listen more to new music and to help living composers find a large international audience.

The Orchestre Symphonique de Montréal International Composition Prize
260 de Maisonneuve Blvd West, 2nd Floor, Montréal QC H2X 1Y9, Canada
tel +33 (0)3 8548 9441 *fax* +33 (0)3 8593 5820
email composition@osm.ca
website www.composition.osm.ca

Aims to encourage and promote musical creation whilst developing lasting ties between the OSM and the composers of today. This competition launched its 1st edition during the 2006/7 season and will run every 2 years. Open to all composers of all nationalities, aged 40 years and under. Works submitted should be orchestral. 3 prizes are awarded as follows: The Olivier Messiaen International Prize for 1st place; The Promise Prize for 2nd place; and The Claude Vivier National Prize for the best Canadian Work.

Orpheus Publications Composition Competition
PO Box 1363, Armidalensw 2350
tel/fax (02) 6772 2205
email info@orpheusmusic.com.au
website www.orpheusmusic.com.au

Aimed at increasing the Australian recorder music repertoire. The competition is split into the following sections:

Open:
• Work featuring solo recorder
• Recorder ensemble

18 years and under:
• Work featuring recorder

All work should have been written after 2000 and must not have been published or commercially recorded. Judging is based on originality, playability and appropriateness of recorder writing and general appeal. Prize would involve publication with Orpheus Music.

Queen Elisabeth International Competition for Composers
20 Rue aux Laines, B-1000 Bruxelles, 1000 Brussels, Belgium

tel +322 213 4050 *fax* +322 514 3297
email info@qeimc.be
website www.qeimc.be
Executive Assistant Patricia Breeus

Founded in 1951. An international composition competition aimed at composers under 40 years of age. The competition will be held in December 2008 and the work selected, for violin and either symphony orchestra or instrumental ensemble, will be performed during the finals of the violin competition. The prize is €10,000 as donated by SABAM; there will also be 12 live radio and television broadcasts and the work will be recorded on CD and/ or DVD. The composers of the other 4 works that reach the final will each receive €1,500. Interested musicians and composers can obtain further rules on the competition's website or by contacting its secretariat. The deadline for submitting an application is 7 November 2008.

Queen Marie Jose International Composition Prize

Secrétariat du Prix International de Composition Musicale Reine Marie José, Case Postale 102, 1237 Avully, Suisse
email prix@reinemariejose.ch
website www.reinemariejose.ch

Founded in 1958 by Her Majesty Queen Marie Jose of Savoy to encourage musical creation. Endowed with a prize of 15,000 Swiss Francs, the competition takes place every 2 years and aims to inspire new works of quality. The 2008 prize is for a work for a solo part (sung or instrumental) and electronics of any length and must be not yet performed. The contest is open to composers of all ages and nationalities.

The Royal Philharmonic Society Composition Prize

10 Stratford Place, London W1C 1BA
tel 020-7491 8110 *fax* 020-7493 7463
email admin@royalphilharmonicsociety.org.uk
website www.royalphilharmonicsociety.org.uk
General Administrator Rosemary Johnson

Established in 1813. Offers the opportunity for 2 professional composition performances alongside the possibility of grants/bursaries for further study. Deadlines are typically the end of March for the RPS Composition Prize and end of June for Susan Chilcott Scholarship.

The Singer/Songwriter Awards

email info@wearelistening.org
website www.wearelistening.org

Aimed at performing music artists of all genres and ability, both signed and unsigned. Entry of song or songs into the competition can be posted or uploaded through the website. International panel of judges

from various sectors of the music industry preside over the selection criteria and choose the winning songs on merits of lyrical content, melody and harmony composition and songwriting technique. Prizes include recording in a prestigious London Studio, mixing and mastering of work and promotion, etc. Entry forms available from website.

SongPrize1019

16th Avenue S Nashville, TN 37212
email info@songprize.com
website www.songprize.com

Online-based songwriting competition aiming to give successful applicants global exposure. Submission should be of a non-commerically released original song that is no more than 5 minutes in length. Songs will be judged on creativity, originality, structure, melody and lyrics. Offers a range of promotional prizes including the chance to be presented to major record labels such as Sony, Virgin, MCA, Arista, RCA, Capitol, Universal and more.

The Songwriters Academy

The British Academy of Composers & Songwriters, 26 Berners Street, London W1T 3LR
email hannah@britishacademy.com
website www.britishacademy.com/awards/songacademy

Founded in March 2006. Aims to discover future songwriters to present to the industry. Open to all – regardless of genre. The competition is split into 3 groups: 18s and under, solo writers, and groups. In 2006, finallists from each category experienced a 1-day intensive music industry masterclass. 1 winner from each category then had the chance to work with a hit songwriter on their material, receive airplay exposure, and win technology courtesy of Apple.

Tansman 2006 6th International Festival and Competition

Stowarzyszenie Promocji Kultury im. Aleksandra Tansmana, ul. Krzyżowa 14/51 91-457 Łódź, Polska
tel 0-601 295 495 *fax* 0-426 578 666
email wendland@tansman.lodz.pl
email jkruczkowska@poczta.onet.pl
website www.tansman.lodz.pl

The International Competition of Musical Personalities aims to select and promote the most outstanding musical personalities among composers, regardless of the styles they represent. The competition is held at the Academy of Music in Lodz in the concert hall of the Lodz Philharmonic. The competition is open to composers of all nationalities and has no age limits.

Submissions should consist of only original instrumental works that have not been awarded any 1st prizes at international competitions, and which have been written after or in the year 2000. Compositions should be for instrumental ensemble ranging from at least 14 instruments to a symphonic orchestra. The length of the composition may range from 10 to 20 minutes. Participants may submit any number of entries. An entry fee is required for each score. Jury includes prominent figures such as Krzysztof Penderecki (Poland), Michael Nyman (Great Britain) and Wing Wah Chan (Hong Kong).

4 prizes are awarded, with a 1st prize of $12,000.

Toru Takemitsu Composition Award

Tokyo Opera City Cultural Foundation 3-20-2 Nishi-Shinjuku, Shinjuku-ku, Tokyo 163-1403 JAPAN
tel +81 3 5353 0770 *fax* +81 3 5353 0771
email award@toccf.com
website www.operacity.jp

Founded in 1987. This international orchestral competition aims to maintain Takemitsu's principles of 'Prayer, Hope, Peace'. Open to all nationalities of composers born after 1972. Works must be written for ensemble (not concerto) and submitted by 31 August 2007. Steve Reich is the 2008 judge. Prize consists of a cash award – total sum of 3,000,000 Yen.

UK Songwriting Contest

website www.songwritingcontest.co.uk

International songwriting competition accepting entries from all in the following categories: pop, rock/indie, folk and country, jazz and blues, miscellaneous, dance, R&B/hip-hop/urban, christian/faith, lyrics only and instrumental. Prizes vary and include publishing deals, Gold Disc award, songwriting software from Sibelius and from Virtual Studio

Systems, and free Guild of International Songwriters and Composers membership. Candidates may submit by post or online. More information and mailing list sign-up available on website.

Unisong

Platt Avenue #729, West Hills, CA 91307-3218 USA
tel (213) 673-4067
email info@unisong.com
website www.unisong.com

Submissions may feature within any of the 18 specified genre categories. Songs may be of any length and should be submitted on CD, cassette or MP3. Applications are accepted online and by post. Prizes vary and include cash amounts and society memberships – 2006 competition grand prize involved no-expenses-spared Writers' Retreat package.

The USA Songwriting Competition

2881 East Oakland Park Blvd, Suite 414,
Fort Lauderdale, FL 33306, USA
info@songwriting.net
email www.songwriting.net

The 12th annual large-scale international songwriting competition. Songs are judged by a panel of high-profile music industry personalities. See the website for rules and regulations and how to submit songs for consideration. Overall grand prize is approximately $50,000 as well as merchandise, radio airplay and promotion. Entry forms are on the website.

Music and sound effects for games

Adi Winman gives us some essential background detail on a rapidly growing area of the music business, and outlines several important considerations for those wishing to try their hand at creating audio or musical content for games.

Introduction

With the videogame (or 'interactive entertainment industry') market already worth around US$30 billion in worldwide sales annually, the games business is booming, and the technology that supports it is getting ever more sophisticated. The so-called 'next gen' consoles such as the XBOX 360 and the PS3 are certainly pushing the boundaries of both visuals and audio, while the recent introduction of Nintendo's Wii console is giving the competition a run for its money in the game play stakes. Add to that the ever-popular PC market – as well as the growing mobile and handheld markets – and it seems that it couldn't be a better time to be a gamer, or someone considering embarking on a career in the games industry.

How music and effects are used

Music can take many forms within games, as there are huge variations in each game's style, genre and target market. In the heady days of Pong, PacMan and Jet-Set Willy, pretty much all audio was generated from internal synth algorithms, which emitted all manner of monophonic 'bleeps and bloops' – these were used simultaneously to represent both sound effects and music. Nowadays, music and effects are often treated separately, with 'real' sampled effects being triggered to play when a specific event occurs (such as a gun firing, or the revving of an engine). The music, by contrast, often plays along with the visual display to match the mood and so complement a particular scene or situation in the game.

Sound effects tend to be triggered in a similar way in all games, but the way in which the music is implemented to accompany the pictures does change quite drastically from game to game. For example, a high budget, third-person 'shooter' (such as *Ghost Recon*) may contain well-recorded and carefully structured orchestral music – created solely for that game – and include more or less the same theme throughout the various 'movements' corresponding to different stages of a game. By contrast, a car racing game (such as *Test Drive Unlimited*) can contain a series of random contemporary pre-made recordings, which vary drastically in style or genre, and can even be selected by the user (using a form of juke box, or radio station simulator). Such technology can now be taken a stage further, with the music being completely controlled by the user. The user can even play his or her own tracks – whether downloaded or copied from the console's hard drive (within the game). Indeed, there are now as many types of game music as there are games themselves, which means that the creation and implementation of the music also varies from project to project!

Incorporating music and effects into games

First, it's important to understand how a game is created. Each game is, essentially, nothing more than a series of instructions for controlling or changing the graphics, the user input, and, of course, the playback of audio. A game made from programming code (such as C++, C#, or Java, for example) will involve a huge team of programmers, artists and designers in its creation. Within such a creative team, there is also usually a dedicated 'audio team', which deals with how audio is created, processed and triggered. Indeed, each game may well have its own audio 'engine' that manages and plays back the audio. The role of the audio team programmers is to ensure that this engine triggers efficiently, and plays back audio in all manner of ways – using either their own bespoke audio tools, or those of a third party.

Audio tools allow the team to relate sounds to characters, objects, events and actions, as well as various sorts of audio parameters. Such parameters include: 3D (or 'Surround') Audio playback, obstructions, occlusions, exclusions, environment morphing, zoned Effects (such as Reverb), audio emitters, the Doppler effect, one-Shot/Looped audio, and randomisation – to name just a few! Add dialogue and music to this heady concoction, and you can see that there is a lot to consider when implementing any audio within a game!

Audio teams will also have to assign music to particular environments and situations in a game. Such a project can become extremely complicated when 'dynamic' music is used to highlight emotions and actions – such as tension, reward, health (or lack of it!), or the completion of a task. Dynamic music processes involve the 'composition' being literally sliced into several smaller musical and instrumental segments, so that a small movement, or section of the song or work, is triggered to play, if necessary, one on top of the other. This process is often randomised, so creating a more dynamic and unpredictable soundtrack, 'composed' of various smaller slices! Action Adventure, RPG, Third Person Shooters, and Strategy/Fantasy games tend to steer more towards this type of music, and often draw only upon the talents of one or two composers, although it is not unknown for a whole team of writers to be involved. Racing, Sports, Entertainment and Simulation games tend to have less use for this kind of music, because their game play is more 'linear'. Tracks licensed from third-party artists, or bespoke stylised music (created in-house), tend to appear in this latter type of game – but if dynamics or emotions are required, then at least some 'dynamic' music can still be employed.

Learning the skills

There are many areas of work even within the audio and music sectors of the games industry, ranging from those covered by freelance or in-house composers of bespoke music, to the roles fulfilled by in-house sound designers and audio programmers. Many 'stand-alone' composers or artists are just that – composers who create music for games, and don't necessarily have any formal training in game development. Although this might sound a little glamorous (and is probably a career goal to which some media-orientated composers aspire), it can be very difficult to find a way into such a career. With a bit of hard work, persistence, a decent showreel and some proverbial 'lateral thinking' (as well as useful contacts), you can at least, however, give yourself a chance.

Sending an unsolicited demo of your music to a games company is unlikely often to bear fruit, but if you aim it at the right people (and provide a few extras), it could make a difference to whether you will get a foot in the door. Creative Game Producers and Project Managers are good contacts to start with, as they (in consultation with others) make many of the creative and financial decisions. All major games companies have an audio department – and they usually contain an Audio Lead, Sound Designers/Composers, and a small team of audio programmers. Some of the big companies even have their own A&R and

Music Acquisition departments, so sending your 'package' to them may be a sensible approach. Or better still, send your submission to named contacts in both audio and A&R departments.

However, if your package is poorly produced, limited in content, badly labelled, or doesn't show examples of your music 'in situ', then it doesn't matter to whom you send it – it won't be considered! Sending any examples of your music used alongside some form of multimedia content (such as film/video/websites) would be helpful; but an example of your music being used in a non-linear interactive medium – such as a simple game – or a CD-ROM or website, would certainly be an advantage. Such a showreel would demonstrate that you understand the principles of interaction, story development, emotion and dynamics, not only in your music, but also in the medium of the game itself.

As a matter of course, your research and preparation should be supplemented by a detailed study of music and audio in the context of all sorts of games. Such study will help you understand the various *styles* of music used in games, and, of course, when *not* to use any music! But even if you have mastered all the above, the one additional quality that will really make you appeal to the games industry is the ability to 'program'.

Programming

Although potentially daunting, becoming *au fait* with a programming language (such as C++, C# or Java) can be of great benefit when applying for audio programming jobs, and could well show you to be a well-developed 'all rounder'. However, learning any programming language properly can take years to perfect! Game programming should be taken seriously, therefore, if you want a career in the business. If you are applying specifically for programming jobs, there are now plenty of games-orientated courses, although you will need to have a good background in Maths, Physics or Computer Science if you wish to enrol on one of the many Bachelors degree courses. But if serious game programming is not immediately appealing for you, then you could try the hobbyist approach – simply by building your own elementary games and adding your own audio using Microsoft's XNA Game Studio Express. That way, you will at the very least gain some sound design knowledge, and when united to the ability to write music, you will be much more attractive to a prospective employer.

Making your own game

XNA Game Studio Express is a new game development solution aimed at independent game developers and hobbyists. It's based on the C# programming language, Visual C# Express software, and allows users to create games for Windows and the XBOX 360. It is free, and can be downloaded from Microsoft's website. (However, you may be charged around US$99 if you want to join the XNA Creators Club – which allows you to develop, de-bug and play games for the XBOX 360.) Even if you create the simplest of games, you can quickly see how your music and audio could work alongside moving graphics and game play. This is probably a must for anyone wanting to get his or her music into a game, and should always be part of any games-orientated CV. But if this still sounds like it's not for you, then give programming a wide berth (as it can be very time-consuming) – and ask someone else to do the programming!

Once you have your music on a game

If your music is used in a game, you will usually have to sign a contract with the games publisher in the form of a 'non-exclusive sync licence' relating to that given track or tracks.

This means that you (or your music publisher) still own the rights to the material, and so can continue to exploit those rights in other ways. In some cases, of course, you may have a contract with a music publisher, and it is he or she who then licenses tracks on your behalf.

If you are contracted as a composer to write music for a major game, the chances are that you will be well paid – usually with a one-off fee, but in some cases, you could even command royalties. Such royalties can be calculated in the form of simple points (a small percentage of sales), or as a 'staggered' fee (where you are paid a further lump sum when an agreed sales figure is reached). As the budget for games music is usually quite small compared to the much larger sums spent on graphics, game development, QA and testing, whether or not you can earn a reasonable income as a games composer really depends on several other factors. Sharing the game music credits with 25 other 'artists' (as in a racing game) will certainly reduce your income, but especially so if a few of them are 'major' artists. Some deals, however, include what's called 'Favoured Nations', which is a clause ensuring that all parties involved will be paid the same. Money earned from any kind of 'points deal' will obviously depend on game sales (and the deal you've cut).

The larger and more lucrative deals are normally associated either with established bespoke games composers, or major artists (often 'pop' bands). But there are other ways of potentially making money, too. If the game soundtrack is also released separately – whether physically or digitally – then you could quite feasibly earn more money from the sales of CDs, or from MP3s downloaded from the Internet.

Final tips for creating bespoke music for games

- Get to know the genre and style of game for which you want to write music, and gather together a 'palette' of sounds that will suit the game
- Listen to the work of others, and build upon it (highly skilled games composers are chosen for a reason)
- If the game has a constant theme, try to stay within it, where applicable
- Vary your compositional methods and recording techniques, and experiment with sounds
- Always be aware that the music will have to be 'sliced' into sections, so that they can underline mood, storyline and user input (learning to use Excel will help you keep a record of the files used)
- Develop a process of composition with which you are comfortable (this includes consideration of the gear and environment)
- Immerse yourself in the game – live and breathe the project you are working on!

Adi Winman holds a Masters degree in Audio Engineering from Westminster University, and writes for leading games industry magazine *Develop*. Currently Adi is Music Supervisor and Project Manager for Platinum Sound Publishing – the supplier of music for many multi-award-winning games such as the *MOTO GP06* (XBOX 360) and *Juiced Eliminator* (PSP). He is also Creative Director and Audio Consultant at Dilute Recordings, which provides audio services for the games, music and multimedia industries. See **www.diluterecordings.com**.

Music synchronisation: how music licensing departments work

The granting of 'synchronisation licences' has now become an integral and increasingly lucrative part of the music industry. A 'sync' licence is so called because obtaining such a licence grants one the right to synchronise music with visual images. **Jen Moss** takes a closer look at the function of the well-oiled 'sync' mechanism within our increasingly 'visual' society.

The soundtrack

Music has always played a vital part as an accompaniment to moving images. Examples today might include the latest chart hit heard on the radio in the background of TV soap, *EastEnders* (aimed at keeping the feel of the programme 'contemporary'), or indeed the very pointed and dramatic use of the song, 'Stuck in the Middle with You', in cult film *Reservoir Dogs*. And when it comes to advertisements, think of pretty much any Levi's ad campaign aired in recent years, and you'll begin to realise how heavily such ads depend on their musical soundtrack (or perhaps the term 'soundscape' is more appropriate, as finished 'sync mixes' may often incorporate many layers of music and sound effects). In fact, try watching any ad with the sound turned off, and you should find its impact much diminished!

Clients: who needs a sync licence?

Any time that visuals are used together with music, a licence is needed (so ensuring that the composer gets paid!). The list of clients for music sync departments is, therefore, potentially a long *and* varied one: from clients who make training or promotional videos for small businesses, right through to big-budget filmmakers (and pretty much everyone else in between). Indeed, in order to attract larger fees, most major record labels and music publishing companies will understandably tend to concentrate on clients with bigger budgets – such as advertising agencies, film companies, video games companies, and some TV broadcasters. By contrast, the 'lower' end clients are usually handled by 'library music' departments, who can quickly fulfil a client's demands with off-the-shelf (i.e. ready-packaged and pre-recorded) music clips.

Fees

It is not unheard-of for advertising agencies to pay a small fortune (upwards of £100,000) for the 'right' music. However, this is the exception and not the rule, and large fees are only possible when a client can afford to use the music of a high-profile artist or band. Unlike 'library music', no fixed rate exists for most synchronisation licences, and consequently each case is assessed independently, taking into account various factors such as the popularity of the work, the client's budget, and the usage of the track (i.e. in what territories worldwide it may be broadcast, and the term – or time-length – of the contract, etc.).

How a sync department is run

It's worth remembering that just as with any other income-making music department, the main focus of a music synchronisation consultancy is to make money – by getting music tracks 'placed'!

Advertising agencies usually have access to the larger budgets, so these tend to be the clients on whom such a sync department will focus. If you think of the sheer number of ads that you see on TV, you can begin to imagine how many agencies behind them may be working daily to fulfil the potential music needs for similar future campaigns.

Once a synchronisation 'brief' comes in, the task is then to find the perfect piece of music amongst a music company's vast catalogues. (A 'sync brief' is a concisely documented summary of the type of music required for a particular visual use.) The ease with which a brief can be fulfilled is usually directly related to the precision (and sense!) of the original brief. Some clients will have a very clear idea of what they are looking for – even citing other similar tracks as examples of the type of music required. More often than not, though, the brief is incredibly vague, and refers only to a rough musical genre – or, worse still, refers just to an emotion or feeling (as for example, when a client says, "We're looking for a track that evokes a sense of guilty pleasure."). Some companies charge for music searches by the time and trouble involved, while some others base their fee on a successful placement (a mechanism which enables clients to explore all musical avenues, but sometimes leads them to change the brief several times before they feel happy with the result).

Indeed, before achieving the final 'placement', there can be as many as five or more different types of people needed to sign off a track for an advert: the music researcher, the director, the 'creatives' (usually a team of two who actually 'create' the ads – the 'copyrighter' who writes the script and the 'art director' who comes up with the visual concept), the TV producer, and, of course, the client. And with the matching of music to visual images being such a subjective matter, it can be very hard getting everyone to agree! But once a track has been chosen, the task is then to negotiate a suitable fee – based on many of the considerations already mentioned.

Film music is slightly different. Contrary to what one might imagine, fees for placing music in films can often be relatively small. Indeed, even the advantages to having a track feature prominently in a film are often more beneficial from a marketing/profile point of view than from a financial one. Film music briefs also tend to be a lot more specific than many of the briefs from ad agencies, as the director will usually have a clear idea in his or her head of what music s/he wants, and will then leave it up to the 'music supervisor' to find *either* the specific (sometimes high profile) track – if budget will allow it – *or* a similar-sounding track (for a smaller fee, often by a lesser-known composer or artist).

The synchronisation market is a highly competitive one, and so much of a synchronisation department's activities (aside from working on briefs) involves building and maintaining good relationships with existing and potential new clients. This is sometimes done by using traditional sales and marketing techniques, as well as by offering unique services, such as combined 'publishing and master rights' (allowing for a 'one-stop shop' service). Similarly attractive to clients will be a guaranteed 48-hour turn-around on composer approvals (or approvals by their estates, if the composer is deceased but the work still in copyright), or even ringtone and download possibilities for 'cross-collaterisation campaigns' (i.e. those aimed at maximising media exposure). It is the quality of the music itself that first attracts potential clients, but, in the end, as in any business, it is the quality of the synchronisation department's *services* that will keep clients coming back.

Bespoke work: media composers

Of course, not all music used is already published, pre-existing material. While there are many advantages to having a well-known piece of music attached to one's project (such as audience familiarity, and ease of access), many advertisers and broadcasters choose to have a piece of music specially tailored to their needs. This approach not only ensures that the music will perfectly fit the visuals (and to the exact specifications of the client), but it can also be a much cheaper alternative (and the 'bespoke' approach may not necessarily take any longer in music preparation or in the clearing of rights). In fact, many music 'writers' make a living full-time by writing bespoke pieces of music or in 'designing' sound for television and advertising. Although it is a very competitive industry, and incredibly difficult to enter by directly approaching TV, ad or film production companies, there are several media composer agencies (and some composer collectives), who have established firm relationships with many of the major media players. These agencies should be the first port of call for any young, aspiring media composer.

Conclusion

In the current climate of increasing financial uncertainty for music companies (at least in respect of traditional income streams), deriving income from 'synchronisation' is more than ever a priority for record labels and music publishers alike. The fees that sync departments can now command – alongside new and growing sync opportunities (from computer games, online licences, and the like) – has seen the sync industry grow considerably in importance over the past few years.

From a musician's point of view, having one's music placed in a high-profile ad or film still remains one of the quickest ways to gain access to a mainstream audience, and often results in a serious career boost. Although it may seem impossible for an unknown band or artist to have their music 'placed', it is true to say that more and more ad agencies (in particular) are shying away from big-name, mainstream acts in favour of 'discovering' the future sounds and stars of tomorrow, or quite simply unearthing some obscure, quirky gems with which to spice up their latest campaign. The advent of digital music, and community websites such as MySpace, has made it a little easier for music researchers to uncover such gems!

It may not be the easiest way of breaking into the music industry, but for those with the talent (and luck) to be successful, it is certainly one of the more glamorous ones. And, in this digital age, although the goal of having one's music 'placed' – or synchronised to images – takes a great deal of hard work and good fortune, it is, nevertheless, quite an achievable goal.

Jen Moss is a Music Consultant for the Boosey & Hawkes Synchronisation Department in London. She provides music searches and music-clearance services for film, TV and advertising. Previously, Jen helped promote up-and-coming bands and artists to the music industry.

Resources

BOOKS

Complete Guide to Film Scoring
Author Richard Davis
Publisher International Music Publications, 2000
ISBN 0634006363

A comprehensive guide to the business, process, and procedures for writing music for film or television (i.e. deals with the whole 'environment' of film composition, but not detailed compositional methods). Includes interviews with 19 film scoring professionals.

The Craft and Business of Songwriting (2nd edn)
Author John Braheny
Publisher Writers Digest, 2002
ISBN 1582970858

Promoted as 'a practical guide to creating and marketing artistically and commercially successful songs', the expanded 2nd edition of this title is a large-format book containing well-integrated exercises. It also provides a substantial amount of advice on business and commercial aspects of songwriting. Particular strengths are the chapters on lyric writing and song construction, which are then followed by detailed analyses, with examples drawn from both classic and recent songs. Also covered in a songwriting context is much-needed information on publishing, self-publishing, marketing, record deals and compiling demos.

Essential Dictionary of Orchestration
Authors Dave Black, Tom Gerou
Publisher Alfred Publishing, 1998
ISBN 0739000217

Compact pocket guide covering the ranges and technical characteristics of more than 150 instruments. Useful for composers, arrangers and orchestrators. Contains handy scoring tips, but is most useful because of its level of detail reminding the composer about the dynamic and tonal qualities of instruments in their various registers. The text is complemented by diagrams showing both the complete and practical ranges of instruments (with their transpositions, where relevant).

Film Music
Authors Mark Russell, James Young
Publisher Rotovision, 2000
ISBN 2880464412

Short introductory text in which film music composers discuss their craft in a series of interviews.

Focuses on the processes which led to the creation of musical themes in a selection of memorable films. Contributors include: Ennio Morricone, Zbignived Preisner, Gabriel Yared, Bernard Hermann, Elmer Bernstein, Maurice Jarre, Jerry Goldsmith, John Barry, Lalo Schifrin, Howard Shore, Danny Elfman, Ryuichi Sakamoto, Phillip Glass and Michael Nyman. Includes a CD with examples of various scores.

The Guide to MIDI Orchestration (3rd edn)
Author Paul Gilreath
Publisher MusicWorks Atlanta, 2004
ISBN 0964670534

Weighty tome concerning how to create realistic emulations of a symphony orchestra using samplers and computer recording techniques. Unusual in that it marries an explanation of the traditional art of orchestration with the latest technological innovations in order for composers to be able to produce vibrant new scores. Aimed at both traditional and new music composers, as well as arrangers, MIDI musicians, TV/film composers, game composers, teachers – and indeed anyone who may need to realise successful MIDI orchestrations.

Heart and Soul: Revealing the Craft of Songwriting
Editor Chris Bradford
Publisher Sanctuary, 2005
ISBN 1860746411

Written in association with the British Academy of Composers and Songwriters, this book offers a wealth of wide-ranging advice from some leading industry lights, each of whom explains their own personal experience of the process of songwriting. There are 3 main sections which reveal the craft, business and history of songwriting, and a final section of 'essential information' (comprising a guide to UK songwriting organisations, showcases, recommended reading, listening and websites, and a 'songwriter's glossary').

How to Write a Hit Song
Author Molly Anne Leikin
Publisher Omnibus Press, 2002
ISBN 0881888818

Concise, introductory text, explaining the technical components and structure of contemporary popular songs. The contents embrace the creation of melodies, harmonies, memorable lyrics (and their rhymes), as well as song craftsmanship and building textures, inspiration and writing environment, collaborating, selecting song titles, and how to work towards having your songs published and recorded.

On Track: A Contemporary Guide to Film Scoring (2nd edn)

Authors Fred Karlin, Rayburn Wright
Publisher Routledge, 2004
ISBN 0415941369

Comprehensive guide to scoring for film and television which covers various styles and genres. Takes a practical approach, and discusses timing, cuing, recording, and the need to balance the composer's musical vision with the precise demands of the film. Also contains interviews with noted composers.

Reading Lyrics

Editors Robert Gottlieb, Robert Kimball
Publisher Random House, 2000
ISBN 0375400818

A single-volume anthology which provides many excellent models of all sorts of lyrics, for songwriters to appreciate the art of lyric writing. Not a 'how to' guide (although the introductions are very informative), but a 'how it has best been done' sourcebook – which should serve to inspire all potential lyricists.

Rock, Jazz and Pop Arranging

Author Daryl Runswick
Publisher Faber, 2003
ISBN 0571511082

Presents an overview of many aspects of jazz, pop and rock-music arranging. The text is aimed at musicians and composers ranging in experience from entry to advanced levels.

The Technique of Orchestration (6th edn)

Authors Kent Kennan, Donald Grantham
Publisher Prentice Hall, 2004
ISBN 0130407712

Clear, practical, contemporary text which explains how to write for orchestral instruments. Examples are drawn from various periods and styles, and an accompanying audio CD contains selected examples. A companion practice Workbook is also available (ISBN 0130407720).

Writing Music for Television and Radio Commercials: A Manual for Composers and Students

Author Michael Zager
Publisher Scarecrow Press, 2003
ISBN 0810847221

Concise, but comprehensive and very clearly laid-out and illustrated guide to the processes involved in composing and arranging music for commercials in these 2 different media. Includes interviews with music professionals, and an audio CD of musical examples.

Performing
Introduction

It has been said that even if there were no audiences, music would continue to be performed as long as there are musicians who want to make music. But such a situation would never be entirely satisfying; the composer Benjamin Britten observed that there exists a 'Holy Trinity' between composer, performer and listener. Undoubtedly, music can move people's emotions powerfully by speaking directly from the heart of the creator to the heart of the listener (via the performer).

All performers certainly need to acquire the skill – or to refine their own natural gifts – for communicating as effectively as possible to any given audience. The longest and most successful performing careers belong to those artists who communicate through their art form with great honesty, and also with such passion that they imprint the experience indelibly upon a listener's mind. Ideally, every gig or concert should be capable of being remembered long after the performance itself has ended.

In terms of acquiring the skill of relating to an audience personally, a performer needs as much regular gigging experience as possible. A good relationship with venue owners or managers is therefore absolutely essential. There are as many types of venue as there are audiences, and all deserve to be respected: remember, even an audience of one individual is still an audience, and more often than not today, the camera – that impersonal eye – acts as an important vehicle for reaching thousands of individuals in their homes.

We can always learn something of the art of performing from watching established artists, but if there is one overriding truth regarding live music performance, it is the fact that at every single performance your audience will always be your best teacher. The finest performers always learn from, and respond to, their audiences. So find venues that suit your music, perform as regularly as possible, learn from everyone you can (especially your audience), and aim continually to refine your talent for communication through music. There is no greater fulfilment than communicating music to an understanding and appreciative audience.

THE IMPORTANCE OF LIVE PERFORMANCE

"The importance and rewards of live performance can never be overstated. As a songwriter, you tend to live in a creative vacuum. You mix influences, emotions, inspiration and your message with rhythm, harmony and melody, within the boundaries of your own creative world. But until someone – outside of this – hears the song and responds to it, you have only your instinct to guide you as to how effectively the song works.

Performing the song live to an audience provides you with a unique opportunity to gain instant feedback. If you are sufficiently astute and aware, you will be able to gauge quickly the impact of your music: whether the audience picks it up and understands it; whether some sections feel overlong or far too short; if the message of the lyric comes across; or if the melody is memorable enough for people to go home humming it. If things need 'tweaking' within a song, it's usually apparent after a live performance where the strengths and weaknesses of your creativity lie. People are always quick to praise something they really like, so you will be sure to know when you are on to something good."

Tony Moore, a singer-songwriter, performer and promoter *extraordinaire*, was the driving force behind the legendary Kashmir Klub. He now promotes an even more successful live acoustic club, The Bedford. In 2004, Tony was inducted into the Music Managers Forum Roll of Honour for 'outstanding contribution to the music industry'. See **www.tony-moore.com**.

IDENTITY

"Confidence, hunger and self-belief are the three personality traits I look for in any artist with whom I work. I also look to see if they have a game plan.

Many artists come through my studio who have incredible talent, but who honestly do not know what they want to do, or why they are doing it – they lack *artistic identity*. This identity is ultimately what sells an artist, sets them apart from the competition – and is, in fact, why identity should come from the artist, and not from the record label.

An identity cannot be falsified. When I get an artist who knows why, what and where, there is no time wasted pinpointing their musical direction. These are the elements every producer should try to identify in the acts with whom they work."

Colin Emmanuel is a versatile writer-producer who has worked with Mary J Blige, D'Angelo, En Vogue and Beverly Knight. He was the productive force behind Jamelia's platinum-selling *Superstar* album. For further information, visit **www.record-producers.com**.

Booking fees and contractual arrangements: a performer's perspective

Len Bendel unravels the mysteries relating to the contractual obligations upon those working in the field of live music performance: the performers themselves, promoters, and other 'third parties'.

The basics of contract law

Every time you enter into an agreement – with an agent, promoter or venue – to undertake a live performance, you are committing yourself to a legally binding contract.

An agreement requires some sort of offer to be made, and accepted. The offer can either be made orally or in writing. Acceptance occurs legally at the point at which the person receiving the offer communicates his/her agreement back to the person who has made the offer. Importantly, the acceptance must *exactly* match the terms of the offer. So if, for example, a promoter offers your band a gig for £100, and you say that you will accept the gig for £150, you have, in fact, made a counter-offer. This constitutes a rejection of the original offer. The promoter can in turn choose either to accept or reject your counter-offer: if it is rejected, you may not then go back and accept the original offer without the promoter's agreement. The original offer is taken to have expired, and so the promoter is under no obligation to you.

Whether written or oral, the offer must be clear and the terms reasonably certain, so that both parties understand what is being offered. Otherwise, it can be argued that no contract is in place. There must be also 'consideration' for the contract: this is a legal phrase which can be summarised thus – 'I will do something for you, if you in return do something for me.' The consideration need not be financial, but must have some *value*. There must also be an intention by both sides to enter into a contract.

A contract comes into existence when all of the above has taken place; it can be valid whether oral or written. Even if you never sign a piece of paper, you can still have entered into an agreement. However, the best advice is still, 'Get it in writing.' The reason for doing this is so that when a dispute occurs (and sooner or later a dispute will occur, if money is involved), you have some evidence of what was agreed. An exchange of emails or a letter or fax can constitute that evidence – you don't need the formalities of a 'signed contract', although this is often preferable.

What should be in the contract?

The contractual terms will, to a large extent, depend upon the nature of the gig. Is it for a local band at a local venue? Is it for a function band at a wedding? Or is it for an international band, as part of a tour?

The fee

For many, the most important term is the fee. How much will you be getting? Will it be a share of the door receipts, a flat fee, or a combination of both – and in cash or as a cheque?

Some smaller venues will require you to guarantee a minimum number of people at the door (so if no-one comes, how much will this cost you – and is it worth it to you?). If you will be paid a share of the door receipts, how can this be checked? And *when* will you be paid (will you get any money upfront, or all of it at the end of the night)? Your individual circumstances clearly have a bearing on all of these factors.

Other terms

Other common and important terms are (in no particular order):
- The date, time and place of the gig and the soundcheck, and the duration of the performance.
- Your technical requirements (stage size, number of microphones, dressing room, etc.).
- Will you be sharing equipment with other bands – and, if so, will it be theirs or yours? What happens if the equipment gets damaged?
- Will there be food or refreshments provided?
- If the gig is for a function band, how many sets will you be required to play over the evening (and are there any particular song requests)?
- How many musicians will be required? Who will book them? Will there be a dress code? Then, depending upon the size and the importance of the gig, the parties may wish to clarify more points, and make further binding warranties or promises to each other. For example, the artist will often be obliged to agree that he/she (or, of course, they) will: appear and perform to the best of their ability; provide a list of personnel, staff and crew, and will be responsible for them; guarantee that any replacement of band members will not harm the band's commercial attraction; allow the promoter to use his/her name and likeness in promoting the gig.

There will also commonly be more 'legal' warranties – such as an assurance that the artist can enter into the agreement, and will not be breaching any other agreement by doing so; that no part of the performance will breach any third party's rights; and that the artist will not make defamatory comments about anyone.

The promoter's obligations

The promoter's obligations and warranties commonly include terms outlining that they will: agree to pay the fee; comply with Inland Revenue and Withholding Tax regulations; provide the required equipment; and ensure that the venue is licensed, safe, and that it and all persons in it are appropriately insured. The promoter will also provide staff and security and access for the artist and crew.

For more established bands, there will also be significant financial and accounting clauses. These clauses will relate to such things as:
- How much the artist will want as a deposit.
- If the artist is to be paid a percentage of receipts, whether this will be on net or gross receipts: if net, what are the allowable expenses, and who will check these on the artist's behalf?
- Will there be a charge by the venue for the artist to sell merchandising?
- Will the promoter provide staff and security for this?

The venue should also be registered with the Performing Right Society (PRS) – which is very important if the artist is to collect further revenue from the performance of his or her own songs – and the appropriate cue sheets should be provided. The promoter should also use all reasonable endeavours to ensure that there are no unauthorised recordings of the concert.

Performing abroad

If you are performing abroad, a number of other questions and matters arise:
- Should any agreement you make with foreign promoters be subject to English, or local, law and jurisdiction? (English law and jurisdiction is generally preferable for English- or UK-based artists, as English-based lawyers are rarely able to advise on foreign law.)
- Will you require a work permit or visa to play in a particular country (or will your crew)?
- Will the local promoter provide local accommodation?
- Will you and your equipment be insured?
- Will there be local taxes?

You should be aware of all of these factors when considering playing outside the UK.

TV appearances and recordings

If you are contracted for a one-off TV appearance, a number of other issues arise. The TV production company will probably want to own the copyright in the recordings of the TV appearance, so you will need to consider:
- How they will be exploited.
- What your remuneration will be from each method of exploitation.
- Whether the appearance is for a one-off programme, or whether it is possible that it may be included on a commercial DVD of the programme.
- Whether the programme is to be sold to other TV stations or countries.
- Whether the audio recording of the performance will be made available for sale, and/or for radio broadcast.

Depending on the proposed exploitation, you may want a royalty-based percentage of the sale price, or a fee (or possibly a combination of the two). In any event, you should make sure that your compositions and recordings are registered with the PRS and PPL (Phonographic Performance Limited), so that you don't lose income from broadcasts of your works.

It is likely that the TV production company will want a number of warranties from you (confirming that your performances don't infringe the rights of any third parties, and aren't obscene or defamatory, etc.). Such terms are quite standard.

Similarly, if a concert at which you are performing is to be recorded, who will *own* that recording? The Copyright Designs and Patents Act 1988 states that first ownership of the copyright of a sound recording belongs to the 'producer '– i.e., the one who made the necessary arrangements for the creation of the sound recording. This is most commonly the record label (as they generally provide the money to fund the recording), but you should ensure that contractually, the venue owner, promoter and recording engineers do not have any share of ownership of the sound recordings, or share of income from those recordings (unless it is otherwise agreed with them). Could you do a webcast of the concert? If you are bringing extra equipment to a venue to record or stream a performance, you should clear this in advance with the venue, as there will be additional power and space requirements.

What if the contract is breached?

For various reasons, it is not uncommon in the music industry for contracts to be breached. So having a clear, written agreement with the promoter, or venue, is essential. In order to claim successfully for damages, or for money in compensation against someone, you will need evidence of what they were supposed to do, and what they subsequently failed to do.

For simple claims relating to amounts of money under £5000, you can now make a claim online through the Court Service website (**www.hmcourts-services.gov.uk**). You should, however, note the general rule in litigation that a defendant has the right to be heard in his or her local court.

Professional advice

If it seems likely that you will have to issue legal proceedings on any complicated or high-cost matters, you would be wise to seek professional legal advice. You should definitely seek professional specialist legal advice when entering into *any* contractual arrangement in the music industry, whether with a tour agent, a promoter, directly with a venue, with a TV production company, or for a management, recording or publishing agreement.

Len Bendel is a music lawyer and bass player. He advises clients such as performing artists, record labels, and management companies. He also lectures on music law.

Venues

LONDON

12 Bar

22-23 Denmark Place, off Denmark Street,
London WC2H 8NL
tel 020-7240 2120
(Box Office) *tel* 020-7240 2622 (Enquiries)
email 12barclub@btconnect.com
website www.12barclub.com
Promoter Andy Lowe

Small, intimate venue staging 4 acts a night, 7 nights
a week. Features a variety of solo performers and full
bands with an emphasis on good songwriting. Also
has restaurant (open 9am – 9pm). *Opening Hours*:
Mon to Thur: 7.30pm – 1am; Fri to Sat: 7.30pm –
3am; Sun: 7pm – 12.30pm.

100 Club

100 Oxford Street, London W1D 1LL
tel 020-7636 0933 *fax* 020-7436 1950
email info@the100club.co.uk
website www.100club.co.uk

Central London venue with The Rolling Stones and
The Kinks as past performers. Hosts jazz and indie
bands and attracts a varied crowd. Also available for
hire. Opening times and ticket prices vary according
to event.

Alexandra Palace

Alexandra Palace Way, Wood Green,
London N22 7AY
tel 020-8365 2121 *fax* 020-8883 3999
email sales@alexandrapalace.com
website www.alexandrapalace.com

Established in 1878 as The People's Palace. Stylish
and versatile venue hosting a range of events
including exhibitions and conferences, alongside
musical events. Provides a variety of additional
services including venue managers. Acts have
included: Placebo, Kaiser Chiefs and Morrissey.

Astoria

157 Charing Cross Road, London WC2 8EN
tel 020-7434 9592
email astoria@meanfiddler.com
website www.meanfiddler.com

Part of the Mean Fiddler promotions group;
renowned live venue. Recent acts have included:
Graham Coxon, Stiff Little Fingers, Primal Scream
and Dirty Pretty Things. Has developed strong
associations with Radio 1 and Steve Lamacq. Phone
for booking information.

Barbican Centre

Barbican Centre, Silk Street, London EC2Y 8DS
tel 020-7638 4141
email info@barbican.org.uk
website www.barbican.org.uk
Head of Music Robert van Leer

Established in 1982. Performing arts complex
including 1949-seat concert hall, 1168-seat theatre,
180-seat studio theatre, 3 cinemas and 2 art galleries.
Presents a diverse programme encompassing all
forms of classical and contemporary music alongside
dance, theatre, art, film and education events. The
centre is home to the London Symphony Orchestra
and works closely with associates the BBC Symphony
Orchestra and Serious. Promotions include the Great
Performers classical series and the Mostly Mozart
festival alongside jazz, world and rock promotions.
The concert hall is also available for hire.

Barfly – Camden

49 Chalk Farm Road, London NW1 8AN
tel 020-7691 4244 *fax* 020-7691 4245
email london.info@barflyclub.com
website www.barflyclub.com
Head Promoter Terry Kirby

Established in 1997. Aims to support and showcase
the world's best new music. Acts have included:
Coldplay, Franz Ferdinand and The Editors. Tickets
£8. Capacity of 200 upstairs. Potential new acts
should send demos to the Head Offices at Barfly
Bookings, Zeppelin Building, 59-61 Farringdon Road,
London EC1M 3JB. Venue can be used for private
hire on request. *Opening Hours*: Mon to Sat: 7.30pm,
until late.

The Bedford

77 Bedford Hill, London SW12 9HD
tel 020-8682 8941 *fax* 020-8882 8959
email info@thebedford.co.uk
website www.thebedford.co.uk
Music Manager Tony Moore

Established in 2002. Renowned music venue hosting
a wide variety of music performances on a regular
basis – typically 4 nights a week. Also offers full bar
and food. Potential acts should post a demo
addressed to 'The Booking Team'. Free entry and
capacity of 180. *Opening Hours*: Mon to Wed: 7.30 –
11pm; Thurs: 7.30 – 12pm.

The Betsey Trotwood

56 Farringdon Road, London EC1R 3BL
tel 020-7336 7326 *tel* 020-7253 4285
email via website
website www.betseytrotwood.com
Assistant Manager Sarah Thirtle

Established in 2002. Intimate unsigned showcase
venue also hosting private-label showcases and

comedy nights. Hosted early shows from The Magic Numbers, KT Tunstall, Simple Kid, New Rhodes, Hot Chip and The Subways. Ticket prices and opening hours vary according to event. Capacity of 60. Potential acts should see website for more details regarding music policy before submitting demos to: Plum Promotions, 56b Farringdon Rd, London EC1R 3BL.

Borderline
16 Manette Street, London W1D 4JB
tel 020-7434 9592 *fax* 020-7434 2698
email borderline@meanfiddler.co.uk
website www.meanfiddler.com

Part of the Mean Fiddler promotions group. Hosts an eclectic variety of up-and-coming acts and world music. Renowned for showcasing new indie groups and appreciated for its diversity and atmosphere. Standing capacity of 275. Those wishing to book should send a demo to: The Borderline Promoter's Office, 157 Charing Cross Road, London WC2H 0EN, or call as above. *Opening Hours*: Mon to Sat: 10am – 6pm (Box Office).

Bull & Gate
389 Kentish Town Road, London NW5 2TJ
tel 020-7093 4820
email info@bullandgate.co.uk
website www.bullandgate.co.uk
Promoters Andy Clarke, Phil Avey

Renowned unsigned band venue hosting all original styles of music. Provides in-house PA, sound engineer and promoter. Capacity of 150. Potential acts should email or post material to Bull & Gate Promotions, Building A, Trinity Buoy Wharf, 64 Orchard Place, London E14 0JW. Ticket prices range from £4 – £6. *Opening Hours*: 8pm – 12am (pub open all day).

Cargo
83 Rivington Street, Shoreditch, London EC2A 3AY
tel 020-7613 7732 or
020-7613 7743 (Bookings) *fax* 020-7613 7790
website www.cargo-london.com
Press Officer Joe Roberts

Established in 2001. Large, popular club and live-music venue hosting a wide variety of music all nights of the week – from rock to jazz and electro to folk. Acts range from big names such as the Dandy Warhols and Paul Weller to special nights for unsigned acts. Tickets prices range from £4 – £10. Capacity of 500. For music and event bookings, contact Chris Wheeler on the Bookings telephone number. *Opening Hours*: Mon to Thurs: 7 – 1pm; Fri and Sat: 8pm – 3am; Sun: 6 – 12pm.

Carling Academy Brixton
211 Stockwell Road, London SW9 9SL
tel 0870-771 2000 (Box Office)
or *tel* 020-7771 3000 (Enquiries) *fax* 020-7738 4427

email mail@brixton-academy.co.uk
website www.brixton-academy.co.uk
General Manager Nigel Downs

Built in 1929 – elaborate, art deco venue. Winner of Best Live Venue in NME Awards 2005. Recent acts include: Incubus, Tool, Kaiser Chiefs and N.E.R.D. Full capacity of 4291 (2391 seated and 3760 downstairs). Contains 9 bar areas. Ticket prices and opening hours vary.

Carling Academy Islington
N1 Centre, 16 Parkfield Street, Islington, London N1 0PS
tel 0870-771 2000
(Box Office) or 020-7288 4400 (Enquiries)
email mail@islington-academy.co.uk
website www.islington-academy.co.uk
General Manager Lucinda Brown

Established in 2003. Acts have included: Muse, Craig David, Athlete and the Lost Prophets. Hosts regular events such as the recent VH1's *Bands Reunited* featuring ABC and Haircut 100; shows for Nordoff-Robbins Music Therapy by The Cure; and Carling's New Kings of Rock & Roll. Capacity of 800. Ticket prices and opening hours vary.

Cecil Sharp House
Cecil Sharp House, 2 Regent's Park Road, London NW1 7AY
tel 020-7485 2206 *fax* 020-7284 0534
email hire@efdss.org
website www.efdss.org
Hirings Administrator Pat Knight

Established in 1930. Listed building close to Camden Town; 3 halls with sprung floors and natural light. Home of the English Folk Dance and Song Society (EFDSS) and the Vaughan Williams Memorial Library. The EFDSS hosts many events celebrating traditional song and dance. Bar, cafe, basic PA, tables, chairs and staging also available. Tickets vary from £5 per night for folk classes to £12 for special concerts and seasonal events. Capacities of 500, 150 and 50 plus 2 smaller 30-capacity rooms. *Opening Hours*: (Office) Mon to Fri: 9.30am – 5.30pm.

Dublin Castle
94 Parkway, Camden Town, London NW1 7AN
tel 020-7485 1773
Proprietor Tony Gleed

Small and intimate stage hosting up-and-coming acts. Popular stop-off point for rock celebrities; has a shrine to Camden band Madness. Capacity of 250. *Opening Hours*: Mon to Sat: open until 1am; Sun: open until 12pm.

Earls Court
Warwick Road, London SW5 9TA
tel 020-7385 1200
email info@eco.co.uk
website www.eco.co.uk

Primarily an exhibition centre. Also hosts big-name acts; past names have included: The Red Hot Chili Peppers, Phil Collins and Dire Straits.

English National Opera
St Martin's Lane, London WC2N 4ES
tel 020-7845 9347 *fax* 020-7845 9277
email music@eno.org
website www.eno.org
Head of Music Martin Fitzpatrick

Home to the English National Opera (ENO), a world-class company famous for groundbreaking modern opera settings. Currently stages around 20 productions a year with an annual audience of approx. 450,000.

The Forum (Kentish Town)
9-17 Highgate Road, Kentish Town,
London NW5 1JY
tel 020-7284 1001
email ebownes@meanfiddler.co.uk
website www.meanfiddler.co.uk

Part of the Mean Fiddler promotions group. Acts have included: Snow Patrol, Yeah, Yeah, Yeahs, Manic Street Preachers, Neds Atomic Dustbin, Teenage Fanclub, and Iron and Wine. Aims to showcase the cutting edge of indie and world music. Potential acts should forward an outline of the event, including the proposed line-up, ticket prices, audience attendance, running times, details of similar events that may have been promoted in the past, and planned dates for the show. Proposals will then receive a quote for venue hire (the venue rental fee is inclusive of venue and PA hire).

The Garage
20-22 Highbury Corner, London N5 1RD
tel 020-7607 1818
website www.meanfiddler.com
Booker Joady Thornton

Established in 1993; part of the Mean Fiddler promotions group. Renowned indie rock venue. Hosted early gigs for Dinosaur Jnr, Radiohead, Placebo and Supergrass. Also houses smaller venue – The Minibar. Potential acts should email marie@meanfiddler.co.uk with a link to website or myspace page containing downloadable tracks. Alternatively, demos may be posted to Marie McPartlin, Mean Fiddler Music Group, 16 High Street, Harlesden, London NW10 4LX. Include a biography, photograph, gig history and reviews where available. Allow up to 3 weeks for demos to be heard.

Grey Horse
46 Richmond Road, Kingston, London KT2 5EE
tel 020-8541 4328
email rfandjh@aol.com
website www.grey-horse.co.uk
Proprietor Richard Fletcher

Established in 1850. Hosts blues, indie and tribute bands. Tickets £3 – £8. Capacity of 100. Potential clients should post a demo and biog. *Opening Hours:* 11am – 12pm.

Hackney Empire
291 Mare Street, London E8 1EJ
email hadrian.garrard@hackneyempire.co.uk
Programming Manager Hadrian Garrard

Split into 3 areas: the Marie Lloyd Bar, the Main House and the Studio Theatre – capacities of 250, 1600 and 150 respectively; all host a wide variety of music genres. Kitchen area provided. Potential clients should post CD or email MP3s. Tickets are free in bar area and range from £8 – £25 in theatre. *Opening Hours*: 7pm – 1am.

Halfmoon Putney
93 Lower Richmond Road, Putney,
London SW15 1EU
tel 020-8780 9383 *fax* 020-8789 7863
email office@halfmoon.co.uk
website www.halfmoon.co.uk
Bookings and Promotions Managers James Harris, Kirk Barclay

Long-running and well-established live music venue. Has hosted The Rolling Stones, The Who, Kate Bush, U2 and more recently Kasabian. Hosts a 7-nights-per-week programme with an eclectic range of genres including rock, indie, folk and americana, including acoustic nights. Offers full professional in-house PA and engineers. Potential acts should book through agent or, if unrepresented, should visit the website for more details. Ticket prices and opening hours vary according to event and artist. Tickets available online. Capacity of 200.

Hammersmith Apollo
Queen Caroline Street, London W6 9QH
tel 0870-606 3400

Well-established rock venue now part of the Carling group. Has staged AC/DC, Black Sabbath, The Who and Queen, and more recently Sigur Ros, Sugababes and Tool. Capacity of 5039 standing and 3532 sitting.

Hope & Anchor
207 Upper Street, Islington, London N1 1BZ
tel 020-7354 1312 (Enquiries)

Recognised as one of the best places in London to spot new musical talent, this trendy pub boasts a downstairs music venue with different live bands (mostly indie) and DJs every night. Also hosts Open Mic and Unplugged nights. Phone for booking information.

Jazz Cafe
5 Parkway, Camden Town, London NW1 7PG
tel 020-8963 0940

website www.meanfiddler.com

Part of the Mean Fiddler group. Hosts a wide range of musical styles – not exclusively jazz. *Opening Hours:* Mon to Sun: 7pm – 2am.

London Astoria
157 Charing Cross Road, London WC2H 0EL
tel 020-7434 9592 *fax* 020-7437 1781
email calexander@londonastoria.co.uk
website www.meanfiddler.com
Venue Booker Chris Alexander

Hosts various gigs including rock, indie and pop. Ticket prices vary according to event. Capacity of 2000. Potential acts should contact the venue booker or post demos. *Opening Hours:* 7 – 11pm for gigs.

The Marquee Club
1 Leicester Square, London WC2H 7NA
email live@themarqueeclub.co.uk
website www.themarqueeclub.net
Owner and Main Booker Allan North

Established in 1958. Famous for hosting British rhythm and blues bands during the 1960s, including The Rolling Stones, The Yardbirds and The Animals. Also staged Jimi Hendrix, Cream and Led Zeppelin. Recently relocated in Leicester Square. Capacity of 550 in the main area and 320 in the balcony. Potential acts should send demos to the above address.

Mean Fiddler
165 Charing Cross Road, London WC2H 0EL
tel 020-7434 9592 *fax* 020-7437 1781
email calexander@londonastoria.co.uk
website www.meanfiddler.com
Venue Booker Chris Alexander

Part of the Mean Fiddler Group. Previously the LA2. Hosts various gigs (mainly rock, pop and indie). Recent acts have included: Wishbone Ash, Reuben and Pendragon. Ticket prices vary according to event. Capacity of 1000. Potential acts should contact the venue booker or post demos. *Opening Hours:* Club Nights: 11pm – 4am.

The Pleasure Unit
359 Bethnal Green Road, London E2 6LG
tel 020-7729 0167
email info@pleasureunitbar.com
website www.pleasureunitbar.com

Founded in 2001. Welcomes a variety of styles including indie, retro, funk, punk and electro. Offers PA, backline, sound engineer and decks for DJs. Potential acts should send demo to venue address with short biog, photo and contact email/mobile. Ticket prices vary. Capacity of 150. *Opening Hours:* Sun to Thurs: 6pm – 12pm; Fri and Sat: 6pm – 2am.

Ram Jam Club
46 Richmond Road, Kingston, London KT2 5EE
tel 020-8541 4328

email rfandjh@aol.com
website www.grey-horse.co.uk
Proprietor Richard Fletcher

Hosts acoustic, jazz and folk acts. Tickets £3 – £8. Capacity of 60. Potential clients should post a demo and biog. Also contains restaurant and comedy club. *Opening Hours:* 11am – 12pm.

Riverside Studios
Crisp Road, Hammersmith, London W6 9RL
tel 020-8237 1000 *fax* 020-8237 1001
email alexbowley@riverstudios.co.uk
website www.riversidestudios.co.uk
Programming Manager Alex Bowley

Multimedia centre incorporating music, theatre, TV, cinema and a restaurant. Recent shows include: The Ukelele Orchestra of Great Britain; The Magnets; The Exonerated; and Ed Byrne. Capacity of approx. 400. Potential acts should email the programming manager with a detailed proposal. *Opening Hours:* 9am – 11pm.

Ronnie Scott's
47 Firth Street, London W1D 4HT
tel 020-7439 0747
email ronniescotts@ronniescotts.co.uk
website www.ronniescotts.co.uk
Founders Pete King, Ronnie Scott

Founded in 1959. Renowned and historically important jazz venue hosting international jazz artists. Past guests have included: Stan Getz, Benny Golson and Bill Evans. Admission for 2 sets is £20 Mondays to Thursdays, and £25 Fridays and Saturdays. *Opening Hours:* 7 nights a week: 8.30pm – 3am.

Royal Albert Hall
Kensington Gore, London NG1 5ND
tel 020-7589 3203
website www.royalalberthall.com
Director James Ashworth

Famous classical and popular music venue. Hosts the annual BBC Proms concerts; home of the Royal Philharmonic Orchestra. Strong association with popular headlining artists such as Sting, Eric Clapton and Elton John, as well opera favourites Pavarotti, Carreras and Domingo. Available for hire by event organisers and commercial promoters and offers a package of facilities and services aimed at ensuring that each event meets its full potential. For booking information, contact the business and marketing team by phone.

The Royal Opera House
Bow Street, Covent Garden, London WC2E 9DD
tel 020-7304 4000 *fax* 020-7240 1200
email info@theroyaloperahouse.org
website www.theroyaloperahouse.org

Landmark venue containing 2 performing spaces in addition to the recently refurbished historic main auditorium. Hosts a variety of major classical and popular music events. The Linbury room has a capacity of 400 and is a major mid-scale public theatre, hosting events such as chamber opera and educational activities. Home to the Royal Opera House orchestra.

Shepherd's Bush Empire

Shepherd's Bush Green, London W12 8TT
tel 0870-771 2000 (Box Office) or 020-8354 3300 (Enquiries) *fax* 020-8743 5384
email mail@shepherds-bush-empire.co.uk
website www.shepherds-bush-empire.co.uk
General Manager Bill Marshall

Well-established London live-music landmark. Acts have included: Bob Dylan, Patti Smith, Radiohead, The Smashing Pumpkins and Iggy Pop. Also hosts dance artists with performers such as Faithless, Air, Death In Vegas, Tricky, Moloko and Groove Armada. Full capacity of 2000; all-seated, 1278. Ticket prices and opening hours vary.

Sound

Swiss Centre, 10 Wardour Street, London W1V 3HG
tel 0871-075 1739
website www.soundlondon.com

Large club divided over 2 floors and 3 bars. Very professional sound systems and visual projections. Often used for high-profile events.

The Spice of Life

6 Moor Street, London W1V 5LJ
tel 020-7437-7013 *fax* 020-7437-7013
email info@spiceoflifesoho.com
website www.spice oflifesoho.com

Built in 1898. Maintained a strong association with live music through the 1960s and 1970s and was also a popular venue for folk musicians such as Bob Dylan, Paul Simon, Cat Stevens, Bert Jansch, The Strawbs and Sandy Denny. Soon became a popular punk venue, staging bands such as The Sex Pistols. Incorporates a recognised Jazz Club which has played host to Jamie Callum and Soweto Kinch among others. Presents live music every night in The Backstage Bar, ranging across worldwide blues, jazz, acoustic and electric acts. For bookings, call the above telephone number or email.

St James's Church Piccadilly

197 Piccadilly, London W1J NLL
tel 020-7301 0441 *fax* 020-7734 7449
email boxoffice@lfo.co.uk
website www.st-james-piccadilly.org
Concerts Manager Sarah Baxter

Built in 1684. Quiet and atmospheric church staging a range of music events. Lunchtime concerts Mon, Wed and Fri: 1.10pm (suggested donation of £3); evening concert times and prices vary.

St John's Smith Square

St John's Smith Square, London SW1P 3HA
tel 020-7222 1061

website www.sjss.org.uk

Built in 1728. Famous classical venue, valued for its excellent acoustics. Presents a varied programme of classical music involving symphony orchestras, choirs and solo recitals. *Opening Hours*: (Box Office) Mon to Fri: 10am – 5pm; 6pm on concert days.

St Martin-in-the-Fields

Trafalgar Square, London WC2
tel 020-7839 8362
website www.stmartin-in-the-fields.org

Stages regular popular classical concerts with lunchtime and evening performances. The renowned Concerts by Candlelight take place on Tuesdays and every Thursday, Friday and Saturday at 7.30pm: these include Early and Baroque Music, piano and song recitals, and chamber and world music. Tickets cost between £6 and £22. Lunchtime concerts provide opportunity for talented young classical musicians to play in a professional environment. For tickets for lunchtime concerts, a donation of £3.50 is suggested.

The Swan

215 Clapham Road, London SW9 9BE
tel 020-7978 9778 *fax* 020-7738 6722
email info@theswanstockwell.co.uk
website www.theswanstockwell.co.uk
Entertainment Manager Bronwyn Silva

Founded in 1960. Hosts a variety of live music events. Tickets typically £6. Capacity of 700. Potential acts should post a proposal. *Opening Hours*: Fri: 7pm – late; Sat: 8pm – late; Sun: 7pm – late.

The Telegraph

228 Brixton Hill, London SW2 1HE
tel 020-8678 0777 *fax* 020-8678 9066
email info@thebrixtontelegraph.co.uk
website www.thebrixtontelegraph.co.uk
Contact Simon Hooper

Historic music venue (the venue that first hosted The Clash and Joe Strummer) combining a bar and club. Open all week. Capacity 600. Potential acts should contact the above address sending a demo on CD.

The Southbank Centre

Southbank Centre, Belvedere Road, London SE1 8XX
tel 0871-663 2501
website www.southbankcentre.co.uk

Venues comprising Royal Festival Hall, The Hayward, Queen Elizabeth Hall and Purcell Room. Iconic arts and cultural venue hosting the world's finest artists across all genres of music, dance, the visual arts and the spoken word. Resident orchestras are the London Philharmonic Orchestra, the Philharmonia, the London Sinfonietta and the Orchestra of the Age of Enlightenment. Associate artists include the Takacs Quartet, the Sixteen, George Benjamin, Vladimir Jurowski, Oliver Knussen, Nitin Sawhney and Sir Willard White.

ULU (University of London Union)

Malet Street, London WC1E 7HY
tel 020-7664 2022 *fax* 020-7436 4606
email entsinfo@ulu.lon.ac.uk
website www.ulucube.com
Venue Manager Laurie Pegg

Versatile and busy venue which has played host to the following acts: Soulwax, The Delays, Death Cab for Cutie, and The Strokes.

The Underworld

174 Camden High Street, London NW1 0NE
tel 020-7482 1932 *fax* 020-7482 1955
email contact@theunderworldcamden.co.uk
website www.theunderworldcamden.co.uk
Booking Manager Jon Vyner

Well-established live music venue hosting a selection of rock, indie, and metal and acoustic artists and bands including J Masics, Queens of the Stone Age, Radiohead, Placebo, Soundgarden and KT Tunstall. Capacity 500. Supports the Wildplum Network for viewing and listening to prospective bands, media, news clippings and demo tracks. Information about Wildplum can be viewed at **www.wildplum.co.uk**.

The Water Rats

Venue: 328 Grays Inn Road, Kings Cross, London WC1X 9BZ
tel 020-7336 7326
email via website
Office: Plum Promotions, 56b Farringdon Road, London EC1R 3BL
website www.plummusic.com
Assistant Manager Sarah Thirtle

Part of the Plum Promotions Group. Renowned showcase venue for unsigned indie bands. Hosted early shows by Keane, Muse, The Doves, The Hives, and Black Rebel Motorcycle Club – as well as low-key 'secret' gigs by Feeder, The Breeders, Alanis Morissette and Ash. Ticket prices vary. Capacity of 200. Potential acts should consult the website for more details regarding music policy before submitting demos. *Opening Hours*: Vary according to event.

The Watershed

267 Broadway, Wimbledon, London SW19 1SD
tel 020-8540 0080
email info@the-watershed.com
website www.the-watershed.com
Manager Richard Amon

Established in 1995. Live music Wed and Thurs. Has 2 separate rooms, PA and lights, and all support staff. Tickets £4 – £10. Capacity of 330. Potential acts should make contact via email or post. *Opening Hours*: Wed and Thurs: 9pm - 2am; Fri: 7.30pm - 2.30am; Sat: 9pm - 2.30am.

Wembley Arena

Arena Square, Middlesex HA9 0DW
tel 0870-060 0870

email contact@wembley.co.uk
website www.wembley.co.uk

Established in 1934. Seated/part-standing venue catering for large-scale pop and rock concerts, sports and entertainment events and location filming. Recent acts include: Beyonce, The Stereophonics, and Gwen Stefani. Potential acts should contact the sales team via telephone or email. New promoters/shows will be required to complete an event profile before availability is discussed. Hospitality facilities and support staff are provided. Average ticket prices are £35. Capacity of 12,200 fully seated. *Opening Hours*: Various as required; Box Office open Mon to Fri: 10am – 4.30pm.

Wembley Stadium

Wembley, London HA9 0WS
tel 020-8795 9000 *fax* 020-8795 5050
email contacts@wembley.co.uk
website www.wembleystadium.com

Newly built for 2007. Epic seated/part-standing venue catering for large-scale pop and rock concerts, sports and entertainments events and location filming. Recent acts have included: Muse and George Michael. Potential acts should contact the sales team via telephone or email. New promoters/shows will be required to complete an event profile before availability is discussed. Hospitality facilities and support staff are provided. Average ticket prices of £40. *Opening Hours*: Various as required.

West One Four

3 North End Crescent, North End Road, West Kensington, London W14 8TG
tel 020-7603 7006
website www.westonefour.com

Hosts a variety of events including unsigned showcases. Ticket prices and opening hours vary according to event.

Wigmore Hall

36 Wigmore Street, London W1U 2BP
tel 020-7258 8200 *fax* 020-7258 820 1
email info@wigmore-hall.org.uk
website www.wigmore-hall.org.uk
Director Jon Gilhooly

Built in 1901 by the Bechstein piano company. Regarded as a major great recital hall, attracting leading classical musicians and supporting international chamber music and song. Aims to support new classical talent. The programming also features an innovative Community & Education programme.

UK OUTSIDE LONDON

1 in 12 Club

21-23 Albion Street, Bradford, West Yorkshire BD1 2LY

tel (01274) 734160 *tel* 0845 345 8628
email info@1in12.com
email pete@1in12.com
website www.1in12.com
Joint Co-ordinator Pete Chapman

Founded in 1981. Gig space is rented out at £60 (including membership) with acts keeping the door takings. All types of music/events welcome. Tickets priced according to promoters. Capacity 100. Potential acts should make contact via email or post; demo CDs are helpful to allow for radio play (has 2 local shows). 2K rig, lights and engineer all in-house.*Opening Hours*: 7 – 11pm

Aberystwyth Arts Centre
Aberystwyth University, Aberystwyth, Ceredigion SY23 3DE
tel (01970) 622882 *tel* (01483) 623232 (Box Office)
fax (01970) 622883
email aeh@aber.ac.uk
website www.aber.ac.uk/artscentre
Director Alan Hewson *Deputy Director* Louise Amery

Founded in 1970. Aberystwyth Arts Centre is the main regional arts centre for Mid and West Wales and a major centre for arts development throughout Wales. Presents a variety of events across all art forms in numerous auditoria – including theatre, concert hall, studio and foyer space. Tickets range from £5 – £30 depending on act. According to setting/format, capacities are from 250 up to 1200 in Concert Hall; Theatre: 312; Studio: 60 – 80; Foyer spaces between 250 – 300. The following services are available in-house: catering, bars, tech team, front of house, marketing and admin.

Adelphi
Vicarage Road, Sheffield S9 3RH
Director D Maloney

Club venue hosting hard dance, trance, psychedelic and ska, among other genres. Also provides catering, event staff, security service, publicity and marketing services. Tickets typically priced at £10. Capacity of 600. Potential acts should write explaining what gap in the market they are representing. *Opening Hours*: Fri and Sat: 9pm – 8am; Sun to Thurs: 4pm – 4am.

The Anvil
Churchill Way, Basingstoke, Hampshire RG21 7QR
tel (01256) 844244 (Box Office) or (01256) 819797 (Enquiries) *fax* (01256) 331733
email firstname.secondname@theanvil.org.uk
website www.theanvil.org.uk
Programme Manager Ann Dickson

Founded in 1994. Concert hall; also houses smaller venue (The Forge). Hosts all genres of music and provides in-house technical support. Ticket prices vary widely. Capacities: The Anvil at 1400, and The Forge at 94 maximum. Potential acts should make contact via post or email.

Assembly Room and Guildhall Theatre
Market Place, Derby DE1 3AH
tel (01332) 255440 *fax* (01332) 255788
email assemblyrooms@derby.co.uk
website www.assemblyrooms-derby.co.uk
Programme Manager Sarah-Jane Leyden *General Manager* Peter J Ireson

Founded in 1977. Multi-purpose entertainment venues hosting a full range of theatrical, lyrical and musical acts. House appropriate technical and catering facilities and resources. Capacity of 1500 seated and 2000 standing (Assembly Room), and 242 (Guildhall Theatre). Potential acts should contact the Programme Manager. *Opening Hours*: 24 hours as required.

The Attick
15 Free Lane, Leicester LE1 1JX
tel 0116-222 3800
email mail@the-attik.co.uk
website www.the-attik.co.uk
Proprietor Paul Matts

Founded in 2001. Hosts all underground live and dance music. Provides acts with backstage area and full PA on both floors. Ticket prices typically £3 – £5. Capacity of 177. Potential applicants should make contact via the website and include a brief biography and demo. *Opening Hours*: Typically 8pm – 2am.

Auntie Annie's Porter House
44 Dublin Road, Belfast BT2 7HN
tel 028-9050 1660
website www.the-limelight.co.uk

Pub-style venue promoting a variety of music genres and hosting live nights, open mic nights and singer/songwriter sessions. Telephone for booking information.

Barfly – Birmingham
78 Digbeth High Street, Birmingham B5 6DY
tel 0870-907 0999 (Box Office) or 0121-633 8311 (Enquiries) *fax* 0121-633 8344
email carlo@barflyclub.com
website www.barflyclub.com

– see entry under Barfly – Camden. Potential acts for Barfly – Birmingham should send demos to Barfly Bookings, c/o The Sanctuary, 78 Digbeth High Street, Birmingham B5 6DY. Include contact information, biography and any press coverage of the band. For feedback on the demo, email paul.muller@barflyclub.com, 2 weeks after the demo was sent. Ticket prices and opening hours vary.

Barfly – Cardiff
Kingsway, Cardiff CF10 3FD
tel 0870-907 0999 (Box Office) or 029-239 6589 (Enquiries)
email cardiff.info@barflyclub.com
website www.barflyclub.com

– see entry under Barfly – Camden. Potential acts for Barfly – Cardiff should post clearly labelled demos to the above address. Include contact information, ages, biography, any press coverage of the band, and some information about proposed promotional techniques. For feedback on the demo, make contact by phone 2-3 weeks after sending. Ticket prices and opening hours vary.

Barfly – Glasgow

Riverside House, 260 Clyde Street, Glasgow, Lanarkshire G1 4JH
tel 0870-907 0999 (Box Office) or 0141-204 5700 (Enquiries)
email glasgow.info@barflyclub.com
website www.barflyclub.com

– see entry under Barfly – Camden. Potential acts for Barfly – Glasgow should post demos to the above address. Include a brief biography with details of where the band has played before, and when they want to play. Phone 1 week after posting demo. Ticket prices and opening hours vary.

Barfly – Liverpool

90 Seel Street, Liverpool L1 4BH
tel 0870 -907 0999 (Box Office) or 0151-707 6171 (Enquiries)
email lyndsey@barflyclub.com
website www.barflyclub.com

– see entry under Barfly – Camden. Potential acts for Barfly – Liverpool should post a clearly labelled 2-track demo for the attention of Chris Wareing at the above address. After posting demo, send an email to chris.wareing@barflyclub.com stating the band name, where the band is based, when the demo was posted, biography of band, preferred dates and what kind of following the band expects to be present. If no reply is received after 4 weeks, email again – or phone. *Opening Hours*: (Office) Mon to Fri: 10am – 6pm.

Barfly – York (Fibbers)

Stonebow House, The Stonebow, York YO1 7NP
tel (01904) 651250
email fibbers@fibbers.co.uk
website www.fibbers.co.uk
Founders Tim Hornsby, Michelle Hodgen

Founded in 1992. Recently runners-up in *Freehouse of the Year* and *Small Business of the Year*. Hosts live music of every type, 7 nights a week including local and national circuit acts. Acts have included: Shed Seven, Electric 6, and The Seahorses. Hosts annual 'battle of the bands' competition. In the first instance, potential acts should email details to the above address. Also contains restaurant. Available for private hire. Ticket prices and opening hours vary.

Barrowland

244 Gallowgate, Glasgow G4 0TS
tel 0141-552 4601 *fax* 0141-552 4997
email manager@glasgow-barrowland.com
website www.glasgow-barrowlands.com

Voted the second-best small venue in Europe, and awarded the best venue in Great Britain by 60 bands in a Radio 1 poll. Incredibly popular live venue hosting a wide range of indie and rock bands of high calibre, including: Razorlight, Royksopp, The Darkness and The Doves. Opening times and ticket prices vary according to artist: for information, check the website. Promoters should also check the website or telephone the above contact.

Bedford Corn Exchange

St Paul's Square, Bedford MK40 1SL
tel (01234) 344813 *fax* (01234) 325258
email cornexchange@bedford.gov.uk
website www.bedfordcornexchange.co.uk
Venue Manager Carl Amos

Multi-purpose venue comprising 2 main performance spaces – main auditorium and the Civic Theatre (with smaller spaces also available). Hosts bands, including tribute acts, alongside a residency from the Philharmonia Orchestra. Also provides catering, technical support staff, recording facilities and is available for hire. Capacity of up to 800 in Main Auditorium and 285 in Civic Theatre. Potential acts should email with proposal. *Opening Hours*: (Box Office) Mon to Thurs: 9.30am – 5.30pm; Fri: 9.30am – 5pm; Sat: 10am – 2pm.

The Bell

103 Walcot Street, Bath BA1 5BW
tel (01225) 460426
email steve@bathfringe.co.uk
website www.welcotstreet.com
Proprietor Steve Henwood

Pub venue but does not book 'pub bands'. Will consider ethnic, folk, acoustic blues, old-style R&B, jazz and the utterly unclassifiable. Open mic on Thursdays. Accepts submissions by email or post; will reply if interested. Free entry and capacity of 200. *Opening Hours*: 12 – 11pm, with gigs on Monday and Wednesday evenings and Sunday lunchtimes.

Blackpool Winter Gardens

Winter Gardens & Opera House, 97 Church Street, Blackpool, Lancashire FY1 1HL
tel (01253) 625252
email events@leisure-parcs.co.uk
website www.wintergardensblackpool.co.uk

Established in 1878. Comprises The Opera House, Empress Ballroom, The Arena, Pavilion Theatre, Olympia and Spanish Hall. The Empress Ballroom has hosted a wide variety of music artists such as Paul Weller, Status Quo, Heather Small, and James. Full food and beverage facilities available throughout performances. Ticket prices vary according to event. Capacity of up to 3500. Contact via promoter. *Opening Hours*: Vary according to event.

Blue Cat Bar

17 Shaw Road, Heaton Moor, Stockport, Lancashire SK4 4A9
tel 0161-432 2117
email danny@bluecatcafe.co.uk
website www.bluecatcafe.co.uk
Owner Danny Donnelly

Established in 1996. Hosts all types of original music including unsigned acts. Free entry and capacity of 100. Potential acts may make contact by phone, email or post. Provides lights and PA and also contains in-house recording studio. *Opening Hours*: Mon to Sun: 7 – 12pm.

Bongo Club

37 Holyrood Road, Edinburgh EH8 8BA
tel 0131-558 8844 *fax* 0131-558 7604
email ally@thebongoclub.co.uk
website www.thebongoclub.co.uk
Venue Manager Ally Hill

Specialises in live music, covering all styles from jazz to heavy metal, reggae to electro and everything else in-between. Does not promote – venue hire only; make contact by phone or email. Full technical support available. Tickets priced from £2 – £10. Capacity of 450; Arts cafe upstairs. *Opening Hours*: Licensed until 3am; cafe open from 11am weekdays and 12.30pm at weekends.

The Bridgewater Hall

Lower Mosley Street, Manchester M2 3WS
tel 0161-950 0000 *fax* 0161-950 0001
email admin@bridgewater-hall.co.uk or georgina@bridgewater-hall.co.uk
website www.bridgewater-hall.co.uk
Programming Manager Georgina Williamson

Founded in 1996. International concert hall hosting and co-promoting classical, jazz, world, blues and folk events. In-house PA and catering available. Ticket prices vary. Capacity of 2341. Applications for hall usage should be addressed to the Programming Manager. *Opening Hours*: 10am – 8pm on concert nights.

Brighton Centre

Brighton Centre, Kings Road, Brighton, Sussex BN1 2GR
tel (01273) 292642 *fax* (01273) 779980
email penny.parker@bighton-hove.gov.uk
Manager Penny Parker

Established in 1977. Entertainment and conference complex. Tickets average at £23. Capacity can vary from 50 to 5000. Potential acts should make contact by phone or email. *Opening Hours*: 24 hours a day, 7 days a week.

Cambridge Corn Exchange

3 Parsons Court, Wheeler Street, Cambridge CB2 3QE
tel (01223) 357851 *fax* (01223) 329074
website www.cornex.co.uk

Multi-purpose venue. Recent music acts hosted include: Arctic Monkeys, Jose Gonzalez, Craig David, and The Zutons. Ticket prices and opening hours vary.

Cardiff International Arena

Mary Ann Street, Cardiff CF10 2EQ
tel 029-2022 4488
Event Manager Graham Walters

Hosts a wide variety of events, from concerts and ice shows to dance and comedy. Also a convention centre hosting exhibitions and conferences. Typical music events include: Il Divo, MacFly, Shirley Bassey, and *X Factor Live*. Ticket prices vary. Capacity of 7500. *Opening Hours*: (Box Office) Mon to Sat: 10am – 6pm.

Carling Academy Birmingham

52-54 Dale End, Birmingham B4 7LS
tel 0121-262 3000 *fax* 0121-236 2241
email mail@birmingham-academy.co.uk
website www.birmingham-academy.co.uk
General Manager Carl Bathgate

Established in 2000. Major live-music venue voted Best Live Venue 2004 by NME readers. Recent acts include: Snow Patrol, Motorhead, Maroon 5, Goldie Lookin' Chain, The Hives, Joss Stone and Groove Armada. Capacity of 2700. Also has secondary room, Carling Academy 2, hosting more intimate sets (capacity 400-600) and Bar Academy (292). Ticket prices and opening hours vary.

Carling Academy Bristol

Frogmore Street, Bristol BS1 5NA
tel 0870-771 2000
(Box Office) or 0117-927 922 (Enquiries)
email mail@bristol-academy.co.uk
website www.bristol-academy.co.uk
General Manager Helen Spillane

Founded in 2001. Hosts a range of internationally acclaimed artists, recently including: Massive Attack, Portishead, PJ Harvey, Thin Lizzy, Basement Jaxx and Sugababes. Full capacity for gigs is 1600. Also has 1 smaller venue – Star Bar (220 capacity). Ticket prices and opening hours vary.

Carling Academy Glasgow

121 Eglinton Street, Glasgow G5 9NT
tel 0870-771 2000 (Box Office) or 0141-418 3000
fax 0141-418 3001
email boxoffice@glasgow-academy.co.uk
website www.glasgow-academy.co.uk
General Manager David Laing

Established in 2002. Built in the 1920s and still retains art deco features. Artists have included: Sugababes,

Prodigy, Travis and Basement Jaxx. Capacity of 2500. Ticket prices and opening hours vary.

Carling Academy Liverpool

11-13 Hotham Street, Liverpool L3 5UF
tel 0870-771 2000 (Box Office) or 0151-707 3200
(Enquiries) *fax* 0141-707 3201
email boxoffice@liverpool-academy.co.uk
website www.liverpool-academy.co.uk
General Manager Steve Hoyland

Hosts a range of major acts, which have included: The Thrills, Lamb, Electric Soft Parade and Robert Plant. Aims to showcase new material within 2nd venue (CA2) as part of Project 47. Main room has capacity for 1200 and CA2, for 500. Ticket prices and opening hours vary.

Carling Academy Newcastle

Westgate Road, Newcastle upon Tyne NE1 1SW
tel 0870-771 2000 (Box Office) or 0191-260 2020
(Enquiries) *fax* 0191-260 4650
email boxoffice@newcastle-academy.co.uk
website www.newcastle-academy.co.uk
General Manager Polly Woodbridge

Established in April 2005. Acts have included: Goldfrapp, Supergrass, The Bravery, Athlete, My Chemical Romance, and Ian Brown. Contains option to become fully seated. Also contains CA2 venue primarily hosting new local talent and breaking new acts. Main venue capacity of approx. 2000. Ticket prices and opening hours vary.

Carling Apollo Manchester

Stockport Road, Ardwick Green,
Manchester M12 6AP
tel 0161-273 6921 *fax* 0870-749 0779
email manchester.apollo@LiveNation.co.uk
website www.LiveNation.co.uk
General Manager Phil Sheeran

Founded in 1930. Art deco cinema/variety hall. Hosts all styles of live music and comedy. Available for hire. Ticket prices range from £5 – £140. Capacity of 2693 (fully seated), or 3500 (part-standing, part-seated). Potential clients should email with contact details, a brief overview of event, and proposed date/s. Alternatively contact Laura Taylor at Live Nation venue bookings on 020-7009 3465. *Opening Hours*: 9.30am – 11.00pm (late licence available).

The Cavern Club

10 Mathew Street, Liverpool L2 6RE
tel 0151-236 1965
email cavernnow@gmail.com
website www.cavern-liverpool.co.uk

Founded in 1957. Originally famous for supporting early beat music and gigs for The Beatles. Currently hosts a variety of local and touring bands. Potential acts should email contact details and band biography. *Opening Hours*: Mon to Wed: 11am – 6pm; Thurs: 11 – 2am; Fri and Sat: 11 – 2.30am; Sun: 11 – 12.30am.

De Montford Hall

Granville Road, Leicester LE1 7RU
tel 0116-233 3111 *fax* 0116-233 3182
email www.demontforthall.co.uk
Manager Richard Haswell

Versatile venue hosting a range of diverse performances from West End musicals, gospel choirs and classical ensembles to touring rock, pop and indie bands and artists. Has a variety of rooms for private functions.

The Forum

Fonthill, The Common, Tunbridge Wells,
Kent TN4 8YU
tel (08712) 777101
email twforum@globalnet.co.uk
website www.twforum.co.uk
Publicity Manager Mark Randall

Established in 1993. Small independent music and arts centre hosting national touring acts, acoustic lounge and independent promotors during the week for local bands. Recent acts have included: The Libertines, Bloc Party and The Ordinary Boys. All genres welcome. In-house engineer and production team. Tickets priced from £4 – £7. Capacity of 250. Potential acts should make contact by email or phone. Also provides daytime rehearsal space. *Opening Hours*: 7.30pm – 1am.

Glasgow Royal Concert Hall

2 Sauchiehall Street, Glasgow, Lanarkshire G2 3NY
tel 0141-353 8080 *fax* 0141-353 8001
email colinhynd@glasgowculturalenterprises.com
website www.grch.com
Head of Events Karen Taylor

Auditorium seats 2000; typically hosts orchestral concerts and touring bands. Ticket prices determined by promoter. Also houses conference facilities, catering and equipment hire. Potential artists should contact Colin at address above.

Grand Opera House

Great Victoria Street, Belfast, Co Antrim BT2 7HR
tel 028-9024 0411 *fax* 028-9023 6842
email info@goh.co.uk
website www.goh.co.uk

Established in 1895. Presents a variety of music and theatrical performances. Past performers have included: Van Morrison and Luciano Pavarotti. Ticket prices and opening hours vary according to event.

Hallam FM Arena Sheffield

Broughton Lane, Sheffield, South Yorkshire S9 2DF
tel 0114-256 5656
email lynda.cliffe@livenation.co.uk (Hire Enquiries)
website www.hallamfmarena.co.uk

Part of the Live Nation (Venues) UK company. Large and award-winning arena. Has staged a wide

selection of stadium bands from Sting to Westlife and
BB King to Iron Maiden. Capacity of 12,500 seated.
Opening Hours: (Office) Mon to Sat: 10am – 6pm.
Occasional Sunday opening.

Hull Arena
Kingston Park, Kingston Street, Hull HU1 2DZ
tel (01482) 325252 *fax* (01482) 216066
email sharon.bingham@hullcc.gov.uk

Established in 1988. Large and versatile venue. Has
hosted a wide range of successful events, including:
Robbie Williams, Jamiroquai, Blur, and Oasis. Large
seating and standing capacity.

The Joiners Arms
141 St Mary Street, Southampton SO14 1NS
tel/fax (02350) 225612
email info@joinerslive.co.uk
website www.joinerslive.co.uk
Manager/Promoter Kai Harris

Founded in 1969. Hosts a wide range of musical
styles including rock, dance, funk, metal and hip hop.
Ticket prices vary from £4.50 – £10. Full PA, engineer
and doorstaff provided. Capacity of 150 in venue and
50 in bar. Potential acts should post CD and
information, or register online. *Opening Hours*: Sun
to Tues: 7.30 – 11.30pm; Wed and Thurs: 7.30pm –
1am; Fri and Sat: 7.30pm – 2am.

King Georges Hall
Northgate, Blackburn, Lancashire BB2 1AA
tel (01254) 582582 (Box Office) or (01254) 582579
fax (01254) 667277
email dave.cooper.hughes@blackburn.gov.uk
website www.kinggeorgeshall.com
Promotions Manager Geoff Peake

Presents a variety of musical and theatrical
productions across classical and rock/pop genres.
Capacity of 2000 (1807 seats, 2000 seating &
standing). See website for hire details.

King Tut's Wah Wah Hut
272a St Vincent Street, Glasgow G2 5RL
tel 0141-248 515 *fax* 0141-566 4998
email kingtuts@dfconcerts.co.uk
website www.kingtuts.co.uk
Promoter Dave McGeachlan

Founded in 1990. Covers all genres. Recent acts have
included: The Killers, Keane, The Magic Numbers
and the Arctic Monkeys. Catering provided at lunch
and dinner times. Tickets typically priced £5 – £15.
Capacity of 300 standing. Potential acts should post a
CD demo of 2-3 tracks to above address and follow
up within 1 month by email. *Opening Hours*: 12pm –
12am.

The Leadmill
6 Leadmill Road, Sheffield, South Yorkshire S1 4SE
tel 0114-2212 860 *fax* 0114-2212 848

email rupert@leadmill.co.uk
website www.leadmill.co.uk
Live Promoter Rupert Dell

Founded in 1980. Hosts a variety of genres from
unsigned bands to club nights. Tickets typically
priced at £5 – £15. Capacity of 900. Potential acts
should send demos to the above address. *Opening
Hours*: Sat and Sun: 7 – 11pm (gigs) and 10pm – 3am
(club nights).

Limelight
17 Ormeau Avenue, Belfast, Co Antrim BT2 8HD
tel 028-9066 5771 *fax* 028-9066 8811
Venue Manager Eamonn McCann

Prominent Northern Irish live-music venue with a
busy schedule of gigs by well-known acts including:
Oasis, The Strokes, The Hives, Interpol, The Arctic
Monkeys and The Magic Numbers.

Limelight Club
Hightown, Crewe, Cheshire CW1 2BP
mobile (07967) 579666
email social2@btinternet.com
Promoter Martin Bentley

Founded in 1995. Hosts a variety of genres and
groups, including original unsigned acts. In-house
engineer, door staff and ticket collectors available.
Potential acts should call and book a slot. Ticket
prices vary. Concert room has a capacity of 400; cafe
bar has a capacity of 150. Typically gigs are on a
Tuesday in the concert room and Saturday in the cafe
bar. *Opening Hours*: Mon to Sat: 12pm – 1am.

Liverpool Philharmonic Hall
Philharmonic Hall, Hope Street, Liverpool L1 9BP
tel 0151-210 2895 *fax* 0151-210 2902
email simon.glinn@liverpoolphil.com
website www.liverpoolphil.com
Executive Director Simon Glinn

1930s art deco concert hall. Home to the Royal
Liverpool Philharmonic Orchestra and also hosting
rock, pop, jazz, blues and world music concerts. Has
in-house restaurant and cafe bar. Maximum capacity
of 1803. Potential acts/artists should contact Simon
Glinn by email. Ticket prices range from £10 – £50
depending on event. *Opening Hours*: (Office) 8am –
6pm.

Manchester Academy and University
University of Manchester Student Union,
Oxford Road, Manchester M13 9PR
tel 0161-275 2930 *fax* 0161-275 2980
email maximum@umu.man.ac.uk
website www.manchesteracademy.net
Events Manager Sean Morgan

Founded in 1990. Has 4 venues with capacities
ranging from 400 to 1800; caters for all genres but
specialises in rock, metal and indie. Recent artists
have included: Dinosaur Jr, Zero 7, Imogen Heap,

and Funeral for a Friend. Most events are hired by promoters but unsigned nights are run in conjunction with MCR:Music (please see website for more details, or contact Lee Donnelly on 0161-907 0028). Tickets typically priced at £10. *Opening Hours*: 7.30pm – 11pm for most gigs; 7pm – 10.30pm on Sundays.

Manchester Evening News Arena

Victoria Station, Manchester M3 1AR
tel 0871-226 5000
email event.marketing@men-arena.com
website www.men-arena.com
General Manager John Knight

Established in 1995. Multi-purpose arena. Music events have included: The Rolling Stones, Paul McCartney, Kylie Minogue, U2 and Pavarotti. Capacity of 21,000. *Opening Hours*: (Office) Mon to Fri: 9am – 5pm.

Moles

14 George Street, Bath BA1 2EN
tel (01225) 404445
email info@moles.co.uk
website www.moles.co.uk
Manager Michelle Cain

Established in 1978. Prides itself on a professional sound rig. Potential acts should send a good-length sample of music, plus a little additional information (such as line-up of musicians, info on whether you have a record deal, reviews of gigs you've played) and a photo of the band. Send info for the attention of Kath or Sarah to the above address. Thursday Indie nights are run by Pulp Promotions – see **http://www.myspace.com/pulp_promotions**.

Motherwell Concert Hall and Theatre

Civic Centre, Motherwell,
North Lanarkshire ML1 1TW
tel (01698) 302991 *fax* (01698) 268806
email motherwellconcerthall@northlan.gov.uk
website www.northlan.gov.uk
Venues Manager Nick Parr

Founded in 1967. Multi-purpose concert hall with a capacity of 1008 (plus theatre, capacity 395). Part-refurbished in 2006. All genres of music covered. Ticket prices typically £15. Contact as above with regard to use of the Bellshill Cultural Centre (capacity 150) and Sir John Wilson Town Hall (capacity 666).

The Musician

Clyde Street, Leicester LE1 2DE
tel 0115-2510080 *mobile* (07970) 529760
email rideout@stayfree.co.uk
website www.themusicianspub.co.uk
Manager/Booker Darren Nockles

Founded in 2000. Hosts a range of roots styles including blues, americana, funk, soul and jazz. PA, engineers and door staff available. Tickets priced

between £5 and £15. Capacity of 220. Potential acts should post demos, or email. *Opening Hours*: 7 nights a week, 8pm – 12pm.

The National Bowl

c/o BS Group plc, Abbey Stadium, Lady Lane, Swindon, Wiltshire SW2 4DW
tel 0117-952 0600 *fax* 0117-952 5500
email info@thenationalbowl.net
website www.thenationalbowl.net
Contact Gordon Cockhill

Major UK rock and pop venue. Capacity of 65,000.

NEC Arena

The NEC Group, Birmingham B40 1NT
tel 0121-780 4141
email feedback@necgroup.co.uk
website www.necgroup.co.uk

Large-scale versatile stadium complex showcasing classical, rock and pop music. A popular venue for orchestral performances and large stage set-ups.

New Theatre Oxford

George Street, Oxford OX1 2AG
tel (01865) 243041
Manager Louise Clifford

Formerly The Apollo Theatre. Typically hosts bands, musicals and opera. Recent events have included: The Drifters, Jethro Tull, and Jose Gonzalez. *Opening Hours*: (Box Office) Mon to Fri: 10am – 6pm.

Newport Centre

Kingsway, Newport, Gwent NP20 1UH
tel (01633) 662663 *fax* (01633) 662675
email roger.broome@newport.gov.uk
Event Manager Roger Broome

Large multi-purpose venue. Recent acts staged include: The Arctic Monkeys, Fall Out Boy, and The Beautiful South. Capacity of 2024 in main hall. *Opening Hours*: (Box Office) Mon to Sat: 10am – 6pm.

Night and Day Cafe

26 Oldham Street, Manchester M1 1JN
tel 0161-236 4397 *fax* 0161-236 1822
email jay@nightnday.org
website www.nightnday.org
Managing Director Jay Taylor

Established in 1991. Will consider original rock n' roll bands in all forms – no cover bands please. Accepts submissions by post or email. Capacity of 250 and ticket prices from £5. Also provides in-house PA, lights, press, PR, mailing list, poster and flyer designers, gallery space and full catering. *Opening Hours*: Mon to Sat: 10 – 2am; Sun: 10am – 10.30pm.

Pavillion Theatre

Union Place, Worthing, West Sussex BN11 1LG
tel (01903) 231799 *fax* (01903) 215337

email theatres@worthing.gov.uk
website www.worthingtheatres.co.uk
Theatre Manager Peter Bailey

Part of 3 multi-purpose theatres hosting popular music, comedy, musicals and exhibitions. Ticket prices and opening hours vary according to event. Capacity of 850. Potential acts should make contact by letter in the first instance.

The Point Arena and Theatre

East Link Bridge, Dublin 1, Rep of Ireland
tel (00353) 1836 6777 *fax* (00353) 1836 6422
website www.thepoint.ie
General Manager Cormac Rennick

Established in 1988. Hosts a variety of national and international acts. Potential acts may make contact via phone. Tickets range from £40 – £60; capacity of 8500. *Opening Hours*: (Office) Mon to Fri: 9am – 5.30pm.

The Roadhouse

8 Newton Street, Piccadilly, Manchester M1 2AN
tel 0161-237 9789 *fax* 0161-236 9289
email info@theroadhouselive.co.uk
website www.theroadhouselive.co.uk
Bookings Manager Kris Reid

Well-established small Manchester venue presenting a variety of touring and up-and-coming bands. Has staged Coldplay, Idlewild, Mogwai, The Chemical Brothers and Muse. Potential acts should send demos to the above address. *Opening Hours*: (Office) Mon to Fri: 12 – 6pm.

Rock City

8 Talbot Street, Nottingham NN1 5GG
tel 0115-958 8484 (Box Office) or 0115-941 2544 (Enquiries) *fax* 0115-941 8438
email kim@alt-tickets.co.uk or amy@rock-city.co.uk
website www.rock-city.co.uk
Promoter George Atkins

Rock-orientated club-style venue. Acts staged have included: A Perfect Circle, Nightmares on Wax, Jane's Addiction and Lost Prophets. Unsigned acts should contact Amy at the above email address.

The Snooty Fox

1 Brunswick Street, Kirkgate, Wakefield WF1 4PW
tel (01924) 37445 or (07989) 508693
email Enquiries@SnootyFoxLive.com
website www.snootyfoxlive.com

Large pub venue with live music each night. Provides professional stage set-up including air-conditioning, mixing desk, and audio and video recording facilities. Showcases local talent and touring unsigned bands. Bands wishing to book the venue should contact the above address for further information. Ticket prices and opening hours vary.

South Hill Parks Arts Centre

South Hill Park, Ringmead, Bracknell RG12 7PA
tel (01344) 484858 *fax* (01344) 411427

email music@southhillpark.org.uk
website www.southhillpark.org.uk
Music Officer William Trevelyan

Founded in 1973. Multi-purpose arts venue equipped with 5 different music venues, including The Recital Room, Cellar Bar and Wilde Theatre, and The Atrium – plus the grounds of the centre, which are used for festivals and outside performances. All styles of music are covered, including classical, innovative new world music, jazz, experimental indie and folk. Runs a number of unsigned events, including an acoustic indie night run by Josaka (**www.josaka.co.uk**), a web-based promotions company; an acoustic night called The Platform (**www.parkstudio.co.uk**); and a regular, all-encompassing local-bands night on Tuesdays and Sundays (**www.the-cellar-bar.co.uk**). Typical ticket prices are £13.50 – £15. Capacities are: Cellar Bar, 110; Wilde Theatre, 330 sitting and 470 in full flat floor; and Recital Room, 85. Full catering is available. Potential artists are advised to send a full pack including a band biography with CD and covering letter explaining what venue they would like to play. Emails will be answered; phone calls are not welcome.

St George's Bristol

Great George Street, Bristol BS1 5RR
tel 0117-929 4929 *fax* 0117-927 6537
email administration@stgeorgesbristol.co.uk
Events Manager Jillian Wilson

Founded in 1976. Concert venue specialising in classical, folk, jazz and world music. Aims to attract high-profile world-leading musicians. On-site cafe. Capacity of 562. Potential acts should make contact via email. Tickets typically priced between £12 and £30. *Opening Hours*: (Office) Mon to Fri: 9am – 5.30pm.

Star & Garter

18-20 Fairfield Street, Manchester M1 2QF
tel 0161-273 6726 *fax* 0161-272 8704
email enquries@starandgarter.co.uk
website www.starandgarter.co.uk

Founded in 1877. Pub-style venue presenting a range of genres including rock, pop, indie, ska, americana and artschool. Ticket prices from £3 – £5 and capacity of 100. Opening hours vary, including late-night opening.

The Studio

Tower Street, Hartlepool TS24 7HQ
tel (01429) 424440 *fax* (01429) 424441
email studiohartlepool@btinternet.com
website www.studiohartlepool.com
Manager Liz Carter

Founded in 1998. Welcomes all genres of live music. Bands/acts should make contact via post, sending CD and biography. Capacity of 180. Has in-house PA.

Also offers rehearsal space, recording studio, and music technology training courses. *Opening Hours*: Mon to Sun: 8pm – 12pm.

TJ's

16-18 Clarence Place, Newport,
South Wales NP19 UAE
tel (01633) 216608
website www.tjs-newport.demon.co.uk
Proprietor J A Sicolo

Welcomes bands with original material, and occasionally tribute bands. Ticket prices typically £2 – £14. Capacity 500.

Tumbledown Dick

Victoria Bikers Rock Pub

Whitwick Road, Coalville, Leicestershire LE67 3FA
tel (01530) 814718
email vicbikerspub@btconnect.com
website www.vicbikerspub.co.uk
Proprietor John Commons

Popular bikers' and live music pub with 4 stages – 1 main stage and support stage (and the same outside in the summer). Hosts up to 4 indie rock bands on a Friday night (including unsigned acts) and covers bands on a Saturday night. Also hosts a couple of 1-day festivals (The Hard Drive Rock Fest in July and The Moxsters of Rock in June). Contains 3 PA systems with engineer and effects lighting. Regularly updates newsletter (see website) and info also provided via myspace (**www.myspace.com/vicbikerspub**). Provides hot food inside and as part of garden BBQ. Admission varies. Capacity of 200 in function room and 150 outside. Potential acts should make first contact via email. *Opening Hours*: Weekdays: 7pm – 12pm and weekends: 12pm – 1am.

Victoria Theatre

Wards End, Halifax, West Yorkshire HX1 1BU
tel (01422) 351156 *fax* (01422) 320552
email alison.metcalfe@calderdale.gov.uk
website www.victoriatheatre.co.uk
Deputy Theatre Manager Alison Metcalfe

Founded in 1901. Multi-purpose venue with removable stalls-seating for standing concerts. Typical genres include rock, pop, opera and orchestral. Ticket prices vary from £6.50 – £28.50, depending upon performance. Capacity of 1568 seated or 1860

standing. Potential clients should make contact by email or phone. *Opening Hours*: Dependant upon performance, but licensed until 2am Mon to Sat.

Wakefield Theatre Royal and Arts Centre

Drury Lane, Wakefield, West Yorks WF1 2TE
tel (01924) 215531 *fax* (01924) 215531
email mail@wakefieldtheatres.co.uk
website www.wakefieldtheatres.co.uk
Executive Director Murray Edwards

Established in 1894. A 2-theatre complex offering a mixed repertoire of events to appeal to a wide variety of ages and tastes. More than 35 productions presented across both venues each season, including stand-up comedy, drama, music, ballet and pantomime. Potential acts should make contact via post or email. Tickets range from £9 – £17. Capacity 499. *Opening Hours*: Mon to Sat: 9am – 6pm; to 8pm on performance days.

West End Centre

Queens Road, Aldershot, Hampshire GU11 3JD
tel (01252) 408040 *fax* (01252) 408041
email westendcentre@hants.gov.uk
website www.westendcentre.co.uk
Centre Director Barney Jeavons

Founded in 1975. Arts centre hosting rock, indie, hip hop, blues and world-music concerts. Tickets vary from £6 – £12. Capacity of 200 standing and 140 seated. Potential acts should make contact via email. *Opening Hours*: 10am – 11pm.

The Zodiac

190 Cowley Road, Oxford OX4 1UE
tel (01865) 420042
email info@the-zodiac.co.uk
website www.the-zodiac.co.uk
Owner Nick Morrbath

Established (as The Venue) in 1989. Locally renowned live venue. Stages a range of acts aiming to support the local scene (has presented gigs for local successes Radiohead and Supergrass). Acts have also included: The Killers, The Scissor Sisters and Arctic Monkeys. Most acts are booked through agencies; however, demos may be sent to The Club That Cannot be Named for consideration: see **www.theclubthat.com**.

Music festivals

Ashton Court Festival

1 Ninetree Hill, Stokes Croft, Bristol BS1 3SB
tel 0117-904 2275 *fax* 0117-904 2276
email info@ashtoncourtfestival.com
website www.ashtoncourtfestival.com

Annual July festival with 2 outdoor stages presenting local and national headline bands. Accommodates around 100,000. Tickets £5 – £6. Large-name acts have included: Roni Size, Lemonjelly and Super Furry Animals. Also has an acoustic marquee, performing arts area and 150 stalls selling foods and crafts, 3 bars and fairground rides. No camping available on site. Potential acts should send a demo to the above address.

Bath International Music Festival

Bath Festivals, 3rd Floor, Abbey Chambers, Kingston Buildings, Bath BA1 1NT
tel (01225) 462231 *fax* (01225) 445551
email info@bathfestivals.org.uk
website www.bathmusicfest.org.uk
Artistic Director Joanna MacGregor

Established in 1948. Aims to bring a diverse mixture of the finest in classical, jazz, folk and electronica to Bath. Takes place between mid-May and early June. Tickets priced between £7 – £25. Audience sizes vary according to event. Potential acts should make contact via email; see website for more information.

BBC Proms

BBC Proms, Box Office, Royal Albert Hall, London SW7 2AP
tel 020-7589 8212
Proposals: The Artistic Administrator, BBC Proms, Room 330, Henry Wood House, 3-6 Langham Place, London W1B 3DF
website www.bbc.co.uk/proms

Founded in 1895 by Henry Wood. Annual summer series of around 70 main concerts culminating in the renowned Last Night. Presents international symphonic and operatic ensembles and soloists with a focus on the best of the British music scene. Also hosts 5 Proms in the Park concerts across the UK. Ticket prices vary. Popular 'Promming' tickets are available for discounted prices on the day.

Big Green Gathering

PO Box 3423, Glastonbury BA6 9ZN
tel (01458) 830281 or (01458) 834629 (Information)
email Tickets: bggshop@speakingtree.co.uk or info@big-green-gathering.com
website www.big-green-gathering.com

Established in 1994. 5-day camping event focused on Green issues. Aimed at people who care about issues

such as health, the environment, sustainability and our children's future. Previous acts include: Damien Rice, Nizlopi and The Egg. Full tickets priced at around £85. Hosts audiences of 15,000 – 20,000.

Bloodstock

54 Arundel Drive, Spondon, Derby DE21 7QW
tel (01332) 665834
email paul@bloodstock.uk.com
website www.bloodstock.uk.com
Director Vince Brotheridge

Founded in 2000. Aims to create a European-style independent heavy-metal festival organised 'by fans for fans'. Hosts around 40 bands of which approximately 15 are unsigned. Outdoor festival takes place in July and indoor festival in September. Tickets typically £50 for 2 days. Capacity outdoors of 10,000 and indoors of 2500. Potential acts should email their website details.

The Cambridge Music Festival

10 Gurney Way, Cambridge CB4 2ED
tel (01223) 350544
email director@cammusic.co.uk
website www.cammusic.co.uk

Classical music festival held over several weeks. Aims to provide music for and by anyone who lives, works, studies, or shops in Cambridge. Audiences average at around 15,000; more than 1500 local musicians involved. Programme features international artists alongside local choirs and orchestras. Takes place in November, for 2-3 weeks, with over 60 events in each. For tickets and further information about events, check the website.

Canterbury Festival

Festival Office, Christ Church Gate, The Precincts, Canterbury, Kent CT1 2EE
tel (01227) 452853 *fax* (01227) 781830
email info@canterburyfestival.co.uk
website www.canterburyfestival.co.uk
Festival Director Rosie Turner

Founded in 1984 and held annually in October, Kent's international arts festival showcases the best local and international talent across the art forms. Average audience of 700. Interested applicants should send promotional material to Rosie Turner at the given address.

Castle Rock

9 High Street, Launceston, Cornwall PL15 8ER
tel (01566) 772774
email info@itscastlerock.co.uk
website www.itscastlerock.co.uk
Festival Organiser Chris Parsons

Established in 1989. Takes place end of July. Aims to support local bands as well as bringing new acts to the area. Recent acts include: Reuben. Capacity of 1500 with typical ticket prices of £10. Provides food and drink on site and camping nearby.

Coventry Festival

Robin Hood Road, Willenhall, Coventry CV3 3AN
email jackie@coventryfestival.com
website www.coventryfestival.com

Free festival aiming to give unsigned artists the opportunity to play on a professional concert stage. Prizes are awarded; these include recording-studio time, a professional studio photoshoot and a promotional video. Sponsored by Kerrang with backline provided by Marshall.

Creamfields

Cream Group Nation, Wolstenholme Square,
1-3 Parr Street, Liverpool L1 4JJ
tel 0151-707 1309 *fax* 0151-707 1761
email info@cream.co.uk
website www.cream.co.uk
Head of Press and PR Gill Nightingale

Founded in 1998. Major UK festival hosting high-profile dance acts. Recently welcomed: The Prodigy, The Chemical Brothers, Kelis, Groove Armada, Beck, Scissor Sisters, and Massive Attack. Takes place on the Saturday of August bank-holiday weekend. Tickets typically priced at £49.50. Capacity of 40,000.

D Percussion

c/o Ear to the Ground, 2nd Floor, 24 Lever Street, Northern Quarter, Manchester M1 1DW
tel 0161-237 9786 *fax* 0161-237 9503
email info@dpercussion.com
website www.dpercussion.com
Event Organiser David Norris

Started in 1997, in response to the IRA bomb of 1996, in order to encourage people back into the town centre. Hosts a range of genres including dance, hip hop, rock, indie and D&B on 10 stages. Free entry, 50,000 capacity. Potential acts should send demos or weblinks.

Download Festival

Festival Site: Donnington Park, Leicestershire
tel 020-7009 3333 *fax* 020-7009 3213
email andy.copping@livenation.co.uk
Festival Enquiries: 19-25 Argyll Street, London W1F 7TS
website www.downloadfestival.co.uk
Festival Booker/Promoter Andy Copping

Founded in 2002. Annual rock festival covering all rock, alternative, metal, punk and emo genres. Takes place early June. Tickets priced at £50 per day and £120 for the weekend. Capacity of 60,000. Potential acts should make contact via agent (occasionally accepts demos or recommendation).

Glastonbury Festival

Glastonbury Festival Office, 28 Northload Street, Glastonbury, Somerset BA6 9JJ
tel (01458) 834 596 *fax* (01458) 833 235
email office@glastonburyfestivals.co.uk or infoman@glastonburyfestivals.co.uk
website www.glastonburyfestivals.co.uk
Festival Manager Dick Vernon

Established in 1970. Highly renowned 3-day arts festival aiming to encourage youth culture from around the world in all its forms, including pop music, dance music, jazz, folk, fringe theatre, mime, circus, cinema, poetry and art & design. Hosts large mainstream acts as well as providing smaller unsigned opportunities across 7 stages. Tickets approx. £140.

The Green Man Festival

Festival Site: Glanusk Park Estate, Brecon Beacons National Park
tel (08700) 667799
email info@thegreenmanfestival.co.uk
Enquiries: PO Box 42, Brecon LD3 8YX
website www.thegreenmanfestival.co.uk

Provides 3 stages of music over 3 full days. Also contains DJ tent, cinema and children's entertainment. Named as the 'hippest' festival in the UK by the *Guardian*. Weekend adult tickets approx. £98 including camping; free for under-12s.

Greenbelt Festival

tel 020-7374 2760 *fax* 020-7374 2731
email info@greenbelt.org.uk
website www.greenbelt.org.uk

Faith-based festival founded in the 1970s. Takes place annually for 4 days in August. Aims to help people see every area of life as moulded by the Gospel. Proposed line-up for 2007 includes: Billy Bragg, Coldcut, and Soweto Kinch. Tickets approx. £70. Potential acts should submit demos.

Guilfest

54 Haydon Place, Guildford, Surrey GU1 4NE
tel (01483) 536270 *fax* (01483) 306551
email info@guilfest.co.uk
website www.guilfest.co.uk
Festival Organiser Tony Scott

Family-friendly 3-day festival with 6 stages of music, comedy tent, kidzone, art/craft stalls and caterers from around the world. Takes place mid-July. Tickets at £35 for a day ticket, £75 for the weekend and £85 with camping. Capacity of 17,500 per day. Potential acts should contact Tony by phone.

HiFi (North and South)

HiFi North Site: Matfen Estate, Newcastle
tel 0870-042 2006
email info@hififestival.com
HiFi South Site: Matterley Bowl, Winchester, Hampshire

website www.hififestival.com

HiFi aims to bridge the gap between dance and rock music. Held across 2 sites in Newcastle (1 day) and Hampshire (2 days including camping). Both events feature 5 arenas. Bands run from 2pm until 4am. Capacity of 25,000 on both sites. HiFi South tickets priced at approx. £99 and HiFi North, approx. £52.

Huddersfield Contemporary Music Festival

Department of Music, University of Huddersfield, Huddersfield, West Yorkshire HD1 3DH
tel (01484) 472957 *fax* (01484) 472103
email info@hcmf.co.uk
website www.hcmf.co.uk
Festival Manager Nikki Cassidy

Established in 1978. Leading new and experimental music festival hosting more than 50 events in 11 days. Features recognised international artists and composers alongside new talents. Takes place at the end of November as a series of concerts, recitals, workshops and films; includes a featured composer. Capacity varies from 80 to 700, depending on venue. Tickets prices vary from £3.50 – £16 (some events free of charge). Potential acts should check the website for suitability then submit proposal to the Artistic Director at the above address.

International Guitar Festival

IGF, Bath Spa University, Newton Park, Newton St Loe, Bath BA2 9BN
tel (01225) 875522 *fax* (01225) 875495
email emmanuelle@igf.org.uk
website www.igf.org.uk
Bookings Administration Emmanuelle Ginn

Europe's largest festival of its kind. Recent artists have included: Antonio Forcione, Tuck and Patti, John Williams, Paulo Bellinati, Dominic Williams and Eric Roche. Takes place during July and August annually.

Isle of Wight Festival

Festival Site: Fairlee Rd, Newport, Isle of Wight
tel (08705) 321321
website www.isleofwightfestival.com

Established in 1968. Famous for the 1970s appearances of acts such as Jimi Hendrix, Bob Dylan, The Doors and Leonard Cohen, and for hosting a record-breaking half-a-million-strong audience in 1970. After more than 30 years' absence the festival returned in 2002 in a new format, involving a variety of different events including rock concerts, beach parties, and jamming sessions. Capacity 35,000. Tickets approx. £100.

JezFest

Play and Youth Service, East Area Team, Heaton Complex, Trewhitt Road, Newcastle upon Tyne NE5 6DY
tel 0191-276 4264
email bill.ely@newcastle.gov.uk
website www.jezfest.com
Founder Bill Ely

Established in 1999. A 1-day free August music festival for local bands and unsigned talent. Provides the opportunity for younger, newer groups to experience playing to a large crowd.

Larmer Tree Festival

Festival site: Larmer Tree Gardens, Tollard Royal, Salisbury
email info@larmertreefestival.co.uk or james@larmertreefestival.co.uk
website www.larmertreefestival.co.uk

Founded in 1990, a 5-day family-friendly festival set in idyllic Victorian gardens. 70 bands on 5 stages from a range of genres including world, folk, roots, Americana, reggae, jazz, blues. Typical ticket (3-day): adult £105, youth £85, child £65. 4-day, 5-day and 1-day tickets also available. Capacity 4000. Takes place mid-July. Potential acts should email James, including website or myspace address – please do not send demo until requested.

Latitude

tel 0870-060 3775
website www.meanfiddler.com

Festival of music, drama, poetry and cabaret taking place on Henham Park Estate in Southwold, Suffolk. Tickets £45 for the day or £112 for the weekend.

Leeds Festival

Festival Site: Bramham Park, Wetherby (nr Leeds), West Yorkshire
tel 020-8961 5490 or 0870-060 3777 (Box Office)
fax 020-8961 9238
Festival Enquiries: Mean Fiddler Music Group plc, 16 High Street, Harlesden, London NW10 4LX
website www.leedsfestival.com

Major UK rock festival run by Carling Group and Mean Fiddler. Takes place over 3 days in August with acts beginning at 11.30am each day. Tickets approx. £140 for 3 days and £60 for 1 day. Camping available.

Leicester International Music Festival

New Walk Museum, 53 New Walk, Leicester LE1 7EA
tel 0116-225 4916
email musictest@btconnect.com
website www.musicfestival.co.uk
Chair of the Board of Trustees Peter Baker *Artistic Director* Nicholas Daniel

Founded in 1988. Classical chamber-music festival also featuring some world music and jazz. Attracts Europe's leading soloists, and showcases resident composer. Provides catering, bar and support staff. Takes place mid-June. Capacity of 200. Tickets typically priced between £6 and £18. Potential acts should make contact by phone, email or post.

Morecombe Punk Festival

Wasted Festivals, 14 Prior Street, Hereford HR4 9LB
email info@wastedfestivals.com
website www.wastedfestivals.com
Promoters Darren or Jennie Russell-Smith

Established in 1996. Punk/alternative family-friendly
festival hosting a range of older and present-day
bands. Also provides merchandise stalls and DJs.
Takes place mid-August with tickets typically priced
at £55 – £75 for weekends and £30 per day. Capacity
of 4000. Potential acts should email initially with a
brief biography.

Off the Tracks Festival

Festival Site: Donnington Park Farmhouse Hotel,
Isley Walton, Castle Donnington Nr JCT.24 M1
tel (01332) 384518 or (07899) 826955
email info@offthetracks.co.uk (put 'off the tracks' in
the subject line or your email will be rejected)
Festival Enquiries: PO Box 68, Derby DE1 3XY
website www.offthetracks.co.uk

Popular 3-day family-orientated festival held twice
yearly in spring and early autumn. Offers an eclectic
range of music on 2 stages in an atmospheric orchard
setting. Also stages acoustic sessions and jam sessions.
Camping facilities provided. Tickets can be bought
online at the website or via telephone for approx.
£45.

Reading Festival

Little Johns Farm, Richfield Avenue, Reading,
Berkshire RG1 8EQ
tel 0870-060 3777 (Box Office) or 020-8961 5490
(Enquiries) *fax* 020-8961 9238
website www.readingfestival.com

Major UK rock festival run by Carling Group and
Mean Fiddler. Takes place over 3 days in August with
acts beginning at 11.30am each day. Tickets approx.
£140 for 3 days and £60 for 1 day. Camping available.

Rise Festival

Festival Site: Finsbury Park, London
tel 020-7983 6554 *fax* 020-7983 4706
email info@risefestival.org
Office: 4th Floor, Greater London Authority, City
Hall, The Queen's Walk, London SE1 2AA
website www.risefestival.org

Established in 2000. Free anti-racist music festival
presenting a mix of hip hop, indie, pop, jazz and
reggae. Aims to bring together the diverse
communities across London. Takes place in July. Rise
2005 hosted 80,000 attendees.

Rockinbeerfest

Festival Site: The Kings Bush Centre,
Godmanchester, Huntingdon, Cambs PE29 2NH
tel 0845-299 0845
email info@rockinbeerfest.co.uk or
bands@rockinbeerfest.co.uk

Festival Enquiries: Hop Row, Haddenham, Ely,
Cambs CB6 3SR
website www.rockinbeerfest.co.uk
Festival Organiser Dave Roberts

Rock festival based within 50 acres and including an
indoor arena. Takes place over 3 days in August.
Stages both unsigned bands and well-established acts,
including: The Stranglers, The Blockheads, Hugh
Cornwell, Pete Brown, and Wishbone Ash. Capacity
of 3000. Weekend tickets approx. £65. Potential acts
should post demos or email band address above for
more information.

Summer Sundae

De Montfort Hall, Granville Road, Leicester LE1 7RU
tel 0116-233 3111 (Box Office) or 0116-233 3113
(Enquiries) *fax* 0116-233 3182
email dmh.office@leicester.gov.uk
website www.demontforthall.co.uk
Marketing Officer Claire Ward

Weekend festival held around August with 4 stages
(indoor and outdoor), more than 70 acts and 2
campsites. Voted 2nd in the Best Small Festival
category. Previous bands have included: Idlewild, KT
Tunstall and Mylo. In addition to the main Outdoor
and Indoor stages there are the Musician Acoustic
and Rising stages, which feature local and up-and-
coming artists. Weekend adult ticket approx. £75 and
children under 16 approx. £20. Camping approx. £2
per tent.

T in the Park

Festival Site: Balado, Nr Kinross, Scotland
Enquiries: Concerts, PO Box 25241, Glasgow G2 5X
website www.tinthepark.com

Founded in 1994. Scotland's largest music festival and
one of the most critically acclaimed in Europe.
Presents a variety of indie, rock and pop bands across
9 stages. Attracts A-list acts and also supports
unsigned bands of the moment. Capacity 69,000.
Tickets can be obtained through
www.ticketmaster.co.uk.

UK Songwriting Festival

Bath Spa University, Newton Park Campus,
Newton St Loe, Bath BA2 9BN
tel (01225) 875875 (Box Office) or (01225) 875522
(Enquiries) *fax* (01225) 875444
email www.uksongwritingfestival.com

Founded in 2004. Takes place annually in mid-
August in the form of a 6-day residential course.
Welcomes contributions from songwriters, artists,
producers and representatives of the UK music
industry who will take part in a series of lectures and
workshops.

V Festival

Festival Site: Weston Park, Staffordshire (North),
Hylands Park, Chelmsford (South)

tel 0870-060 3778 (Box Office)

Festival Enquiries: Cake Media, 10 Stephen Mews, London W1T 1AG
website www.vfestival.com

Popular large-scale festival usually held over 2 days at 2 different venues in the north and the south. Attracts big-name bands and large crowds, with tickets selling out quickly. More than 80 bands play 4 stages in the venue area over the 2 days, with the acts rotating between the 2 different venues. Bands have included: Coldplay, Kaiser Chiefs and Dido. Tickets are priced at approx. £120 for both days with camping, £100 for both days with no camping, or £58.50 for either day.

Whitby MusicPort

The Port Hole, 16 Skinner Street, Whitby YO21 3AJ
tel (01947) 603475 *fax* (01947) 603475
email info@whitbymusicport.com
website tickets@whitbymusicport.com or artistes@whitbymusicport.com
Festival Organiser Jim McLaughlin

World/folk music festival held over 2 days in October in a variety of venues. Acts have included: Daby Balde, Fueye Tango, Apache Indian & The Reggae Revolution, Eliza Carthy & The Ratcatchers, and Desmond Dekker & The Aces. Tickets priced at approx. £62.

The Wickerman Festival

Festival Office: Algo Business Centre, 24 Glenearn Road, Perth PH2 0NJ
tel (01738) 450442 *fax* (01738) 449431
email info@thewickermanfestival.co.uk
Festival Site: East Kirkcarswell, Dundrennan, Kirkcudbright
website www.thewickermanfestival.co.uk
Festival Co-ordinator Audrey Fenton

Founded in 2001. Aims to celebrate the diversity of music culture by catering for all kinds of music lover, including punks, travellers, scooterists and folkies.

Brings cult music and cult cinema together in an attempt to recreate a 'counter culture' vibe. 2008 Festival will be held Friday 18 and Saturday 20 July. Tickets available for weekend with camping (2007 price £65 + bf), and Saturday only with camping Saturday night (2007 price £45 + bf). No Friday only tickets available. Car parking extra. Children 12 years and under go free. Capacity in excess of 15,000.

Womad

Mill Lane, Box, Corsham SN13 8PN
tel (01225) 743188 *fax* (01225) 743481
email info@womad.org
website www.womad.org
Artistic Director Thomas Brooman

Established in 1982. The World of Music, Arts and Dance festival aims to bring together and celebrate many forms of music, arts and dance drawn from a range of countries and cultures all over the world. A variety of festivals are staged, including annual events in Adelaide in March, Caceres (Spain) in May, Taormina (Sicily) in July, Rivermead (UK) in July, and Singapore in August. Ticket prices and capacities vary. Potential artists should send a demo and additional information to 'WOMAD demo' at the above address between 1 September and 31 December each year.

York Early Music Festival

The National Centre for Early Music, St Margaret's Church, Walmgate, York YO1 9TL
tel (01904) 632220 *fax* (01904) 612631
email boxoffice@ncem.co.uk
website www.ncem.co.uk
Festival Organiser Dr Delam Tomlin

Established in 1977. Takes place in July hosting an audience of up to 1600. Acknowledged as a premier British festival of early music. Takes place in a wide variety of historic churches in the City of York, including York Minster and the recently restored church of St Margaret's. Offers a mix of concerts, workshops, and performance opportunities.

Dealing with agents and intermediaries

Drummer/band leader/label boss **Bill Bruford** gives us an insider's view into people management.

It is sometimes said that, in order to get one artist onstage, you need about 12 characters *off*stage. An incomplete list of those characters would include a manager, a tour manager, a booking agent and an accountant, in addition to the local promoter, technical crew, and several record-company personnel (such as a record producer, product manager, and press). As a group or band leader, you might speak to all of these people within a single day, so closely related are their functions. In the music industry you can deal with these people contractually in a variety of ways. Here, though, we are more interested in how to deal with them personally, rather than as business entities – because the music business is a *people business*.

As *de facto* band leader (and for the purposes of this article we'll assume that you're the guy – or girl – who makes the calls), you're trying to co-ordinate a number of functions into one harmonious whole. In other words, you're the ship's captain: you can see where you are trying to get to; you may even have agreement from nearly everyone as to the best way to get there ... but you find that not everyone wants to pull together. Why, for instance, has your agent booked you on a tour of Kurdistan just when the CD is being launched in London? Why does the record company want a tenth re-mix, with the tambourine louder in the chorus? (On the ninth re-mix they wanted it quieter!) And why doesn't the local promoter return your calls when you went down a storm on your last gig in Skegness?

The main reason why people make such disparate demands is usually a lack of communication: they are not talking to each other, or to you. Additionally, they are probably putting their own short-term interests over and above the long-term health of the whole project (even though long-term considerations tend ultimately to benefit all parties far more). To find out why such demands are being made, and to get all the pieces of the personnel jigsaw-puzzle to fit snugly together (so that everyone remains friends), you may need to consider things from the respective points of view of each of the parties involved.

What does the record company want?

Funnily enough, the record company wants the same thing that you do: a successful record. The best way to achieve this is through communication. Labels are sometimes guilty of the same tactic as the prospective bride: well, he's the best I can do for now; a bit rough around the edges, but I'll change him after we're married! You (the groom) are rough and gritty, and like things done in a certain way, but the label needs to smarten you up for market. Differing expectations can sometimes lead to a mountain of trouble. But if you can understand the other person's point of view, and even see that certain compromises may have to be made, you'll have a better chance of rubbing along. Yes, the music is your baby, but there is no sense in paying a lot for these record-company people if you don't listen to their advice. They've probably done (and seen) it all before.

There was a time when the musician played directly to his/her audience, without a record label as intermediary – and that time may well come round again. No-one is indispensable. But the song comes first: no song, no record company. So, want a tip? At the very first dinner with the label, *you* pay the bill. It's a strong indicator that you refuse to be an indentured servant, and that this is about to be a partnership of equals.

What does the agent want?

The agent wants you out on the road, earning commission. If he/she is a poor agent, it's any road, anywhere! The band is usually 'grateful' for the work – until they realise that they are going around in expensive circles and overplaying the same venues and cities. You, along with your manager, will be conveying a much longer-term strategy to the agent: one that looks at release dates, the potential loss that may be made on gigs, label tour support (or lack thereof), and any number of other related issues. Rather than spread yourself thinly over several countries, it might be better to concentrate on one region – in the UK, perhaps the north-east? – and to build up a head of steam there, which allows you then to flow naturally into the next-door region. Each gig should be played for sound strategic reasons, and reasons on which all parties agree, rather than as an exercise in throwing darts at the map. The agent, like others whom you're working with, may be asked to delay instant gratification for the good of the long-term plan.

What does the local promoter want?

The local promoter wants a full house and a happy bartender, and a modest profit at the end of the night. The audience are your customers; whether you deal with them directly, or through your agent, you must always treat them well. Be honest, fair, and reasonable. Any old fool can put an audience in a building once, but to get them to come back in increasing numbers is much, much harder. And to do just that, you'll need not only a cracking stage performance, but also a good local promoter who will work *for* and *with* you. So the ticket pricing of your group is a very delicate thing: a little too high and the promoter will lose money. If you lose him just £10, he'll never forget … but equally, if you make him £10 profit, he'll never forget. First time in town, he's going to pay you next to nothing, but he'll have you back if you keep his customers satisfied. I've worked with a champion local promoter in Birmingham, who knows his local audience like the back of his hand. Over five appearances in seven years we have trebled the audience, and trebled the band's fee. That is what you are hoping to do in perhaps 200 similar markets all over the western world.

What does the manager want?

The manager probably wants too many things, but he'll certainly want an incentive! When you are starting out, he won't be able to live on the meagre income you generate for him, so to avoid him spending all his time on other artists, or other interests, the deal you strike with him will need to have a built-in incentive. If you are openly hostile to every record company or publishing house he suggests, for example, he'll tire pretty quickly; and that's because your signature on a contract with either of those two entities will be his first good payday.

So, you are trying to understand the other person's needs and point of view, in order that you may co-operate more effectively, and steer around potential disasters. If you are in a state of continual conflict with someone, or if he/she – or their organisation – is unreliable (or promises unrealistic things), it's probably best to stop things right there. Everyone is buying or selling, and sometimes you can be in a strong position to go elsewhere. If someone wants to be your manager, and they are tempting you backstage with all the fabulous things they can do for you, make them commit to realising a shortlist of them by Christmas – after which, and only after which, you'll sign something. That tends to separate the men from the boys.

If you keep to the following four guidelines in respect of your own behaviour, and your plan for world domination ultimately fails, then it will not, at least, be your people skills that were to blame.

1. Be honest – and by implication, be accurate.

Do it when you said you would do it, and pay it when you agreed to pay it. Only then can you expect people to treat you the same way. If you are hiring musicians for a night or a tour, pay them before you pay anyone else. Be honest and accurate with yourself and your colleagues about exactly how talented you are, what you have for sale, and what it's worth. As with any business, know your product, and know your customer.

2. Be nice to people on the way up, and they'll take your call on the way down.

A former colleague of mine was – shall we say – less than a gentleman on his way up to the first million sales; consequently, when the bubble burst and he could have used some help on the way down, it was no surprise that there was no-one around. And *everything* that goes up will sooner or later come down! If you are a musician and you have to leave a band leader in the lurch at short notice, even with good reason, then find him a replacement.

3. Keep your eyes on the bigger picture.

As much as any of the above, this is just plain common sense. But it's an easy trap – don't get lost in the small print of your daily life as a musician. The music game is not about the fine detail; it's very much about the broad brushstroke. No-one else in the band cares about your personal feud with the guitarist, or whether your aural exciter is on the blink … so just get over it! Your continual fussing about minutiae could be holding up progress in the broader sense. Not everything is going to be neat and tidy – it's a messy business. And with instrumentalists, a good idea poorly executed is much better than a perfect rendition of the same old, tired stuff.

4. Remember, they *are* (usually) on your side.

There are far fewer people out there trying to 'rip you off' than you think. Generally, people want success for themselves, and everyone else around. Anyway, there's no point in trying to rip you off until they've helped you make some money in the first place.

Bill Bruford has been one of the country's best-known drummers/composers/band leaders for the past 35 years. He has run the jazz quartet Earthworks internationally for 20 years, and recently started Summerfold and Winterfold Records, to cater for – among other things – his own voluminous back-catalogue. See **www.billbruford.com**.

Courses

Academy of Contemporary Music
Rodboro Buildings, Bridge Street, Guildford,
Surrey GU1 4SB
tel (01483) 500800 fax (01483) 500801
email enquiries@acm.ac.uk
website www.acm.ac.uk

Europe's leading school for rock and pop musicians.
Offers contemporary popular music programmes in
guitar, bass, drums and vocals, giving students
extensive performance experience and enabling them
to achieve the professional standards which the
modern music industry expects. There is great
emphasis on practical performance skills: all
performance courses offer practical rehearsals,
showcase opportunities and live performance
workshops which help to equip students for
professional performance situations.

Qualifications: Diploma in Contemporary Popular
Music (Music Performance); Higher Diploma in
Contemporary Popular Music (Music Performance);
BA (Hons) Degree in Contemporary Popular Music
(Performance).

Barnsley College
Old Mill Lane site, Church Street, Barnsley Street,
Barnsley S70 2AX
tel (01776) 716716 fax (01776) 716553
email programme.enquiries@barnsley.ac.uk
website www.barnsley.ac.uk

Offers a range of FE courses based in performance.
Courses also include study of improvisation,
composition and production. Houses a digidesign
Pro Tools Centre with 4 recording studios and
industry specialist staff. Application through
interview and audition.

Qualifications: NCFE Performance Skills; A Level
Music; BTEC 1st Music; National Diploma in Music
Practice.

Basstech, Drumtech, Guitar X, Vocaltech and Keyboardtech
76 Stanley Gardens, London W3 7SZ
tel 020-8749 3131 fax 020-8740 8422
email darren@guitar-x.co.uk
website www.guitar-x.co.uk
Founder and Director Francis Seriau

Aims to provide a unique atmosphere with spirit,
drive and energy in order for students to network,
play and perform together. Courses are available for
bass, drums, guitar, vocals and keyboard (keyboard –
Degree only). The 1-year Diploma includes units in
Live Performance Workshop and Rhythm Section
Skills. The Master Performance Course studies units

such as composition, arrangement, programming and
business studies. The 2-year Dip HE is suited for
those who wish to enter higher education but do not
possess all the necessary qualifications to start at
degree level – students will learn to play to a
professional standard and will develop arranging,
programming, and composition skills. The Degree
programme provides advanced study and includes
units in Sight Reading, Music Theory and Aural
Training, Keyboard Skills, 20th Century Popular
Music History, Applied Rock Studies and Specialised
Playing Styles.

Qualifications: Diploma; Master Performance; Dip
HE; BA (Hons).

Bath Spa University
Department of Music, Newton Park, Bath BA2 9BN
tel (01225) 875875 fax (01225) 875505
website www.bathspamusic.com or
http://performance.bathspa.ac.uk
www.myspace.com/bathspamusic
Head of Music Department Joe Bennett

Established in 1992 and now with 350 full-time music
students. Offers study of music performance within
either popular or classical music genres as part of the
Degree courses. All Commercial Music and BA Music
students receive 1:1 instrumental tuition.
Performance opportunities include Bath Guildhall,
Bath Abbey, Assembly Rooms, Moles club, etc.
Commercial Music students undertake a national
tour in year 2. Creative Music Technology (BA &
MA) includes opportunities to perform
contemporary Sonic Art using digital media. The
department has a 120-strong choir, 90-piece
orchestra, a Big Band and a Javanese Gamelan, plus
various small ensembles and 30 gigging bands.
Students perform an annual opera at the University's
concert venue, the Michael Tippett Centre.
Application through UCAS for undergraduate
programmes, or direct to the University for Masters'
programmes.

Qualifications: Foundation Degree (FdMus)
Commercial Music; BA (Hons) Music (main
campus); Foundation Degree (FdA) Popular Music
(at local partner colleges).

Birmingham Conservatoire
UCE Birmingham, Paradise Place,
Birmingham B3 3HG
tel 0121-331 5901/2 fax 0121-331 5906
website www.conservatoire.uce.ac.uk
President Sir Simon Rattle CBE Vice President Peter
Donohoe Principal Prof George Caird Vice-Principal
Prof Mark Racz

An international conservatoire that is also a full faculty of UCE Birmingham, and a concert venue for many of Birmingham's principal concert promoters and organisations. Based in the city centre only a few minutes' walk from Symphony Hall. Facilities include the renowned 520-seat Adrian Boult Hall, a state-of-the-art Recital Hall customised for performance with live electronics, 4 recording studios and a specialised music library – recently rebuilt from the ground up. Performance specialisms are available at all levels for a range of disciplines.

Qualifications: BMus (Hons); BMus (Hons) Jazz; GradDip Jazz; PgCert Music Performance; PgDip/MMus Music; AdvPgDip Professional Performance; MPhil/PhD; Junior Conservatoire and collaborative programmes.

Bournemouth and Poole College

Knighton Heath Music Centre, 855 Ringwood Road, Bournemouth BH11 8NE
tel (01202) 582192 *fax* (01202) 582192
email jacobsj@bpc.ac.uk or skinnerh@bpc.ac.uk
website www.thecollege.co.uk
Head of Music Martin Outhwaite

Established in delivering music courses for 15 years. Aims to create a well-resourced and professional environment. Offers Diploma specialisms in music performance. Potential students should phone for application pack.

Qualifications: NC and ND Music Practice, and FDA Popular Music.

Brighton Insitute of Modern Music

7 Rock Place, Brighton, East Sussex BN2 1PF
tel (01273) 626666
email info@bimm.co.uk
website www.bimm.co.uk
Co-Founder Sarah Clayman

Specialises in contemporary popular genres. Aims to provide the facility for students to train to become the recording artists, songwriters, music teachers and session players of tomorrow. The performance courses are available for bass, drums, guitar and vocals.

Qualifications: Certificate in Modern Music; Diploma in Modern Music; Higher Diploma in Modern Music; BA Hons in Professional Musicianship.

The BRIT School for Performing Arts and Technology

60 The Crescent, Croydon CR0 2HN
tel 020-8665 5242 *fax* 020-8665 8676
website www.brit.croydon.sch.uk
Principal Nick Williams

The UK's only non-fee-paying school for performing arts. Predominantly deals with contemporary popular styles. Specialises in performing, recording and songwriting with a very practical emphasis.

Application details can be found on the website. Initial selection process on basic aptitude; successful applicants invited to audition.

Qualifications: GCSE Music; BTEC First Diploma in Music (years 10 and 11); BTEC National Diploma in Music Practice (years 12 and 13); AS/A2 Music (Edexcel).

Brunel University

Uxbridge, Twickenham, Middlesex UB8 3PH
tel (01895) 274000 *fax* (01895) 232806
email admissions@brunel.ac.uk
website www.brunel.ac.uk
Head of School Steve Dixon

Provides modern music courses enabling students to develop knowledge of a broad range of musical styles; particular emphasis on 20th-century music. Focuses on exploring the rich diversity of musical cultures (past and present, improvising and interpreting, traditional and avant-garde) through performing, composing and the study of musical technique. Access is available to a range of performance and recording spaces, and practical activities such as orchestra, choirs, big bands and rock/pop bands can be accredited as part of the course.

The MMus course aims to take full advantage of the range of specialisms from the teaching staff, including study of improvisation, music and dance, and world music.

Qualifications: Music BA (also combined study with Drama, English and Film and Television available); Contemporary Music MMus.

City Literary Institute

Keeley Street, Covent Garden, London WC2B 4BA
tel 020-7492 2630 *fax* 020-7492 2735
email music@citylit.ac.uk
website www.citylit.ac.uk
Head of Music Janet Obi-Keller

Established in 1919. Provides part-time courses for adults in Central London from beginner to professional levels. Offers study in a variety of disciplines and genres including classical, popular, jazz and world music. Specialist instrumental training available alongside ear training, harmony, musicianship, music appreciation and choral singing.

Qualifications: ATCL; LTCL; Music Foundation Levels 1, 2 and 3.

City University London

Music Department, City University London, Northampton Square, London EC1V 0HB
tel 020-7040 8284 *fax* 020-7040 8576
email music@city.ac.uk
website www.city.ac.uk/music
Departmental Administrator Louise Gordon

Founded in 1975. Undergraduate study includes units in the following areas: Performance (including lessons at the Guildhall School of Music), Music Technology, Western Music, Popular Music, Composition, Electro-Acoustic Composition, Sound Recording, Ethnomusicology, Music Business, and Film Music. Applicants for Undergraduate programmes should typically achieve BCC A level grades or 240 tariff points and a good First Degree result for MA.

Qualifications: BMus and MA in Popular Music, Musicology or Performance.

Coventry University
Priory Street, Coventry CV1 5FB
tel 024-7688 7688
email info.rao@coventry.ac.uk
website www.coventry.ac.uk

Music at Coventry aims to encourage experimentation, curiosity and investigation alongside a flexible and entrepreneurial approach. The Performance Undergraduate Degree provides training to allow performers to be flexible and diverse in their abilities; also provides study of performance technique through practical assignments and by exploring uses of technology, arranging and 'real world' skills, including opportunities for collaborations.

The Postgraduate Media Arts Degree focuses on experimentation within the framework of contemporary performance. It encourages students to develop analytical study with a view to developing student progression into doctoral study and business development ideas.

Qualifications: Music and Professional Practice BA Honours Degree; Performance and Media Arts MA Degree.

Dartington College of Arts
Dartington Hall Estate, Totnes, Devon TQ9 6EJ
tel (01803) 862224 *fax* (01803) 861666
email enquiries@dartington.ac.uk
website www.dartington.ac.uk

Founded in 1961. Specialist arts college offering distinctive practice-led learning methods across contemporary arts practices. The music courses are targeted towards dynamic, interactive musicians committed to exploring contemporary music styles, including contemporary classical/art music, jazz, pop, world and folk. Concerts are held regularly and the college is visited by a variety of artists and more than 30 professional music tutors.

The 3-year BA (Hons) Performance course aims to allow students to develop practical skills through individual and group performance work, while developing their knowledge and understanding of contemporary music and its cultural role in society. Also offers opportunity for performance study as part of 3-year BA (Hons), including study of composition, musicianship, musicology and ensemble skills. The

MA Contemporary Music programme is aimed at original, contemporary musicians and musicologists, and allows for a performance focus.

Qualifications: BA (Hons) Music (Performance); BA (Hons) Music; MA in Contemporary Music. Also provides specialist music awards allowing for professional placement/exchange opportunities – see website.

Doncaster College
High Melton Site, Doncaster, South Yorkshire
tel (01302) 553553 *fax* (01302) 553559
email infocentre@don.ac.uk or david.collins@don.ac.uk
website www.don.ac.uk
Head of Intermedia and Performance Arts Dr David Collins

Successful Institute of Further and Higher Education. Aims to nurture a reputation for giving individual attention to students' needs, while developing close links with industry. Undergraduate performance study opportunities exist within the Music and Digital New Media degrees.

Qualifications: BA (Hons) Music and Digital Media.

East Berkshire College
Langley Centre Campus, Station Road, Langley, Berkshire SL3 8BY
tel (01753) 793000 *fax* (01753) 793316
email info@eastberks.ac.uk
website www.eastberks.ac.uk
Music Lecturers Adrian Oxaal, Dion Connelly

College of Further Education with courses specialising in popular music performance. See website for application processes. All applicants are interviewed and perform at audition.

Qualifications: BTEC First Diploma in Music Practice; BTEC National Diploma in Music Practice.

Guildhall School of Music and Drama
Silk Street, Barbican, London EC2Y 8DT
tel 020-7628 2571 *fax* 020-7256 9438
email registry@gsmd.ac.uk
website www.gsmd.ac.uk
Director of Music Damian Cranmer

Founded in 1880. Prinicipal Study lies at the heart of Guildhall performance study. Optional study units at Undergraduate level include Advanced Ensemble, Advanced Principal Study, Conducting, Composition for Film, TV & Radio, Electronic Studio Techniques, Interpretation through Improvisation, Jazz Arranging and Music History.

Qualifications: BMus (Performance, Jazz); MMus (Performance, Jazz, Early Music, Orchestral Training, Leadership and Opera).

Guitar Institute
35 Warple Way, London W3 0RX
tel 020-8740 1031 *fax* 020-8749 0892

email enquiries@guitarinstitute.com
website www.guitarinstitute.com

Offers a range of courses for students in guitar, bass, drums and vocals. The FE courses focus on 4 main areas: performance, core curriculum (aural skills, theory, arranging and transcribing), sight reading, and stylistic studies. Regular live performance workshop sessions are provided.

Qualifications: Certificate in Popular Music Performance (Level 1 Diploma); Diploma in Popular Music Performance.

Havering College

Ardleigh Green Road, Hornchurch, Essex RM11 2LL
tel (01708) 455011
email information@havering-college.ac.uk
website www.havering-college.ac.uk
Curriculum Manager (ND) Nigel Hooper *Curriculum Manager (HE)* David Wood

Offers a Diploma-level performance course incorporating units in Musical Interpretation, Improvisation and Songwriting, and HNC and HND courses with an ensemble and band-studies focus. The BA (Hons) in Music Practice and Technology combines study of performance with composition and music technology; the Media and Music Degree course offers study of music performance in relation to video and radio production, multimedia and production.

Qualifications: Level 3 National Diploma in Music Practice; Level 4 Higher Diploma Certificate in Music Performance; Higher National Diploma in Music Performance; BA (Hons) in Music Practice and Technology; BA (Hons) in Media and Music.

The Institute of Contemporary Music Performance

1a Dyne Road, London NW6 7XG
tel 020-7328 0222 *fax* 020-7372 4603
email enquiries@icmp.uk.com
website www.icmp.uk.com
Marketing Executive Sarah Warburton

Established in 1986 as the Guitar Institute; now known as the Institute of Contemporary Music Performance. Offers full- and part-time study in bass, drums, guitar and vocals at all levels from beginner to degree level.

Qualifications: BMus in Popular Music Performance; Dip and Dip HE in Popular Music Performance. Part-time certificates include Live Performance Workshop and Acoustic Guitar Studies.

Jewel and Esk Valley College

24 Milton Road East, Edinburgh EH15 2PP
tel 0131-660 1010 *fax* 0131-657 2276
email info@jevc.ac.uk
website www.jevc.ac.uk
Curriculum Leader (Performance) Althea Duff

Performance specialisms available in bass, drums, guitar, voice and keyboards. Applications via website.

Qualifications: NQ Access Level; NQ Higher Level (SQA) Certificate Programmes; HNC/D Music. All validated by SQA.

Keele University

Keele, Staffordshire ST5 5BG
tel (01782) 583295 *fax* (01782) 583295
email a.jackson@mus.keele.ac.uk
website www.keele.ac.uk
Director of Music Dr Barbara Kelly

Aims to provide a lively musical environment, within and beyond the academic curriculum. Individual lessons are provided as part of the strong performing tradition; also based in a range of orchestras and smaller ensembles. The Dual Honours Music Degree allows students to study performance, composition and musicology in the 1st year, enabling specialisms in the 2nd and 3rd years. Optional units include: Popular Music, Film Music, Theory, Analysis and Dissertation. Music must be combined with another principal study as part of Keele's distinctive double-honours scheme.

Qualifications: BA (Dual Hons) Music (a range of combined subjects available, including Music Technology).

Kings College London

Department of Music, King's College, Strand, London WC2R 2LS
tel 020-7848 2029 *fax* 020-7848 2319
email music@kcl.ac.uk
website www.kcl.ac.uk
Head of Department John Deathridge

Renowned centre of excellence working with strong belief in the central role of music in today's culture as a creative mode of self-expression. Aims to develop students' ability to deliver engaged and informed performances, vigorous historical writing, exciting new compositions, and incisive analyses and criticism.

Initial study on the BMus programme offers limited choices, with the opportunity to specialise during the 2nd and 3rd years with options such as Music History, Performance and Aural Training, Free Composition and Musical Analysis. Module collaborations are available at the School of African and Oriental Studies and at the Royal Academy of Music. The MMus programme aims to nurture leaders in the fields of historical and analytical musicology, performance practice and composition.

Qualifications: BMus (Hons – Dual Hons courses also available); MMus; MPhil/PhD.

Kingston University

School of Music, Coombehurst,
Kingston Hill Centre, Kingston-upon-Thames,
Surrey KT2 7LB

tel 020-8547 8624 *fax* 020-8547 7349
email s.winter@kingston.ac.uk
website www.kingston.ac.uk/music
Music Administrator Sarah Winter *Admissions Tutor* Tim Ewers

The music courses at Kingston aim to cover a broad spectrum: genres, from traditional to the cutting-edge; techniques, from composition to performance; and contexts, from the history of music to the role of music in education. Undergraduate and Postgraduate specialisms are available in Performance. Undergraduate applications are through UCAS; Postgraduate application forms can be downloaded from the website. All applicants may be called in for interview.

Qualifications: BMus (Hons); BA Joint Honours in Music; MA in Music.

Leeds College of Music
3 Quarry Hill, Leeds LS2 7PD
tel 0113-222 3400 *fax* 0113 243 8798
email enquiries@lcm.ac.uk or d.smith at lcm.ac.uk
website www.lcm.ac.uk
Head of Music Darren Sproston

The UK's largest specialist music college provides a creative and stimulating environment for study. Offers performance specialisms within a range of Further Education, Degree and Postgraduate level courses. The Undergraduate and Postgraduate programmes encourage strong links with a range of performers, composers and other industry practitioners who offer students unique professional training via regular workshops, lectures and seminars. Provides a specialist opportunity for the study of Indian and Latin American music, with internationally recognised artists lecturing in these fields. All performance study centres around a variety of ensembles and study of rehearsal techniques, improvisation and musical direction.

Qualifications: Music Foundation Programme (Performance); Access to Music; BTEC National Diploma in Music; BTEC National Diploma in Popular Music; BTEC National Diploma in Jazz; BTEC National Award Performance (Classical) Music; BA (Hons) Jazz Studies; BA (Hons) Music Studies; BA (Hons) Popular Music Studies; MA Jazz; MA Music; Postgraduate Cert in Advanced Piano Performance.

Liverpool Institute for Performing Arts
Mount Street, Liverpool L1 9HF
tel 0151-330 3000 *fax* 0151-330 3131
email reception@lipa.ac.uk
website www.lipa.ac.uk
Principal Mark Featherstone-Witty

All LIPA qualifications work on the basis that to enjoy a long-term career in the contemporary and popular music field, musicians need to be versatile and to possess a wide range of abilities. The Music Degree focuses on creative, production, performance, music business and contextual skills.

The Performing Arts Music Degree aims to develop a repertoire of skills relating to musical performance, including songwriting, composition, singing as performance, movement and dance, and musical theatre across a wide range of musical genres. Performance facilities include 5 large-sized and 6 medium-sized band rehearsal rooms, all fully equipped, plus 7 smaller instrumental practice rooms.

Qualifications: LIPA Diploma in Performing Arts (Song); BA (Hons) in Music; BA (Hons) in Performing Arts (Music).

The London Centre of Contemporary Music
50-52 Union Street, Southwark, London SE1 1TD
tel 020-7378 7458 *fax* 020-7407 2819
email contact@lccm.org.uk
website www.lccm.org.uk

Independent specialist music school. Offers performance courses in trumpet, guitar, studio production, saxophone, bass, drums, voice, piano and trombone. Specialisms include funk, jazz, rock, soul and electronica.

The Professional Diploma includes units in Career Development, Performance and Improvisation, Ear Training, Roots of Modern Music, Applied Harmony, Instrument Technique, Music Production and Recording, and Composition and Arranging. The Higher National Diploma will create the opportunity for students to perform live and in the studio at the highest technical level, while studying modern composition, audio technology, harmony, and arranging and writing music for film and a wide combination of ensembles.

Qualifications: Professional Diploma in Music Performance and Production (Level 4 – 1 year full-time); Higher National Diploma in Music Performance and Production (2 years full-time).

The London Music School
41 Spelman Street, London E1 5LQ
tel 020-7247 1311
email jo@londonmusicschool.com
website www.tlms.co.uk
General Manager Jo Kemp

Provides a range of 6-month and 1-year courses in music performance and production. Performance courses are available for the following disciplines: bass, drums, guitar, vocals, sax, and keyboard. Courses are available to all, aged 16 years upwards – no audition process. Enrolment form available for download from the website.

Miskin Music
North West Kent College, Oakfield Lane, Kent DA1 2JT

tel (01322) 629561 *fax* (01322) 629400
email miskinrecords@yahoo.co.uk
website www.miskintheatre.co.uk or
www.myspace.com/miskinrecords
Head Producer Matt Power

Founded in 1992. Aims to provide a springboard for those interested either in pursuing a career within the music industry, or in furthering their knowledge at university. Students are encouraged and supported to play at a number of outside venues. Applicants are required to audition and/or interview. To receive a prospectus and/or application form, please make contact by phone.

Qualifications: BTEC First Diploma in Performing Arts (Music); BTEC National; BTEC National Diploma in Music Performance; BTEC National Award in Performance.

Napier University

The Ian Tomlin School of Music, Craighouse Road, Edinburgh EH10 5LG
tel 0131-455 6200
email g.weir@napier.ac.uk
website www.napier.ac.uk
Acting Director of Music G Weir

The BA (Hons) Degree gives students the opportunity to take principal study performance alongside a range of extra core and optional modules. These modules include History and Stylistic Studies, Jazz Improvisation, Acoustics for Musicians, Music Scoring Software, and Keyboard Skills – culminating in Public Recital.

The Popular Music Degree also offers performance (bass, drums, guitar and vocals) as principal study and is aimed at students who want to study performance with regard to the wider musical community. The programme focuses on developing versatility in the use of music technology and extending cultural, critical and creative abilities through a wide-ranging programme of study and practice. Units include Art of Teaching, The Business of Music, Elementary Acoustics for Musicians, Music Scoring Software, Music in the Community, Studio Techniques, and Introduction to Music Therapy.

Music facilities include well-equipped teaching and rehearsal rooms, 4 recording studios and fully networked MIDI suites, as well as a recital area.

Qualifications: BA (Hons) in Music; BA (Hons) in Popular Music.

North Downs & Ards Institute of Further Education

Castle Park Road, Bangor, Co Down, N Ireland BT20 4TF
tel 028-9127 6600 *fax* 028-9127 6601
email gcaffrey@ndai.ac.uk
website www.ndai.ac.uk
Senior Lecturer Dr Greg Caffrey

Leading educational establishment in N Ireland for the delivery of BTEC qualifications. Currently has approximately 250 music and performing arts students. The music department aims to deliver its variety of qualifications in a very practical environment. For an application form, make contact by phone.

Qualifications: First Diploma Performing Arts (Music); National Diploma Music; Higher National Diploma Music Performance.

North Glasgow College

110 Flemington Street, Glasgow G21 4BX
tel 0141-558 9001 *fax* 0141-558 9905
email cowens@north-gla.ac.uk
website www.north-gla.ac.uk
Senior Lecturer Campbell Owens

FE College offering a range of courses. Application online or by post.

Qualification: HND Music.

Perth College

Admissions Office, Perth College, Freepost, Perth PH1 2BR
tel 0845-270 1177 or (01738) 877001
email pc.admissions@perth.uhi.ac.uk
website www.perth.ac.uk
Course Leader Lorenz Cairns

Leading Scottish HE institution providing a variety of popular music courses (established the UK's first full-time rock course in 1985). The NQ in Rock Studies is aimed at providing the opportunity for students to gain experience of live performance and recording; to learn about theory and history of music; and to develop skills in their chosen instrument. The NQ provides a good foundation for the HNC, which has more of a focus on versatility, reading music, improvisation, stage performance and studio work – as well as looking at the development of professional etiquette. The HND builds on the HNC and involves the skills being applied to specialist situations such as cameo performance and songwriting, more advanced music reading, and critical analysis.

The BA in Popular Music Performance aims to produce talented graduates who can sustain a career in the growing music industry. It covers all aspects of study for the modern musician and is suitable for those serious about a career in performance, production and management. Chosen instruments for all levels may be guitar, vocals, drums, bass, keyboard, trumpet, trombone or saxophone.

Qualifications: NQ Rock Music Studies; HNC Music; HND Music; BA in Popular Music Performance. (Students successfully competing the HND course may be able to progress directly to the 3rd year of the Degree course.)

Royal Academy of Music

Marylebone Road, London NW1 5HT
tel 020-7873 7373 *fax* 020-7873 7374

email go@ram.ac.uk
website www.ram.ac.uk
Communications Manager Peter Craik

Founded in 1822. Britain's senior conservatoire aims to prepare students for careers in music according to the constantly evolving demands of the profession. Specialisms include: classical performance, composition, jazz, musical theatre and opera. Entry by audition; applications due by autumn of year prior to entry.

Qualifications: BMus (Performance); MMus (Performance); PG Dip (Performance).

Royal College of Music

Prince Consort Road, London SW7 2BS
tel 020-7589 3643 *fax* 020-7589 7740
email info@rcm.ac.uk

Established in 1882 as one of the world's leading conservatoires. Aims to provide specialised musical education and professional training at the highest international level for performers and composers. Provides facility for students to develop musical skills, knowledge, understanding and resourcefulness, enabling them to contribute significantly to musical life in the UK and internationally.

Qualifications: BMus (Hons) (Performance); MMus (Performance); PG Dip (Performance).

Royal Northern College of Music

124 Oxford Road, Manchester M13 9RD
tel 0161-907 5555
email helen.simms@rncm.ac.uk
website www.rncm.ac.uk
Admission Co-ordinator Helen Simms

Founded in 1973. Recognised centre of excellence for performers and composers. Offers a range of degree and diploma courses at Undergraduate and Postgraduate levels, including an Undergraduate joint course run in collaboration with the University of Manchester. A collaborative arrangement with the Manchester Metropolitan University also exists at Postgraduate level.

Qualifications: BMus (Performance); MMus (Performance); PGDip (Performance).

Royal Scottish Academy of Music and Drama

100 Renfrew Street, Glasgow G2 3DB
tel 0141-332 4101 *fax* 0141-332 8901
email d.mccrory@rsamd.ac.uk
website www.rsamd.ac.uk
Director of Music Rita McAllister

Provides high-quality musical education in a lively and friendly environment. Degree courses available based on performance, composition or education. Aims to broaden students' cultural horizons, while focusing heavily on their individual talents and special interests. Provides a strong vocational tradition, developing close links with international performers, professional companies and traditional musicians across Scotland.

Qualifications: BMus (Hons) (Performance); BA (Scottish Music/Scottish Music – Piping) with Honours; Mmus and PGDip (Performance).

Royal Welsh College of Music and Drama

Castle Grounds, Cathays Park, Cardiff CF10 3ER
tel 029-2034 2854 *fax* 029-2039 1304
email music.admissions@rwcmd.ac.uk
website www.rwcmd.ac.uk
Music Admissions Officer Jeni Gray

Founded in 1949 as the national conservatoire of Wales. Provides specialist practical and performance-based training that enables students to enter and influence the music industry. Students total 550 (two-thirds musicians; one-third drama students). Presents 300 public performances every year, including concerts and guest recitals, opera, musical theatre and a range of drama productions. Performances take place at the college's theatre and recital spaces and a variety of external venues.

Qualifications: BMus (Hons) (Performance); HND in Music Performance (Popular Music); BA (Hons) in Performance (Popular Music); Postgraduate Diploma, MMus (Performance); MPhil/PHD and Postgraduate Diploma in Music Performance; MA in Music Therapy. Applications through CUKAS (Conservatoires' UK Admissions Service).

South Thames College

Wandsworth High Street, Wandsworth, London SW18 2PP
tel 020-8918 7189 *fax* 020-8918 7777
email tonybiola@south-thames.ac.uk
Course Leader Tony Biola

Supports over 20,000 students. Provides facility for a double-award intensive performance and production course. Study includes analysing recording styles, musicianship and keyboard classes, rehearsal sessions and performances. Students will gain technical expertise on their chosen instrument/voice through small group workshops, culminating in their taking original songs out on a tour of local schools. Facilities include fully equipped rehearsal and music studios and music technology suites.

Qualifications: Diploma in Music Production and Performance (Level 3).

Sussex Downs College

Mountfield Road, Lewes, East Sussex BN7 2XH
tel (01273) 402328 *fax* (01273) 488974
email international@sussexdowns.ac.uk
website www.sussexdowns.ac.uk/international.asp
Curriculum Manager Mark Allen *Admissions Officer* Catherine Tucker

Founded in 1994. FE College with 4500 students. Offers support to its large international department including an 'English Plus Music' – specifically designed for international students who wish to combine the study of English and preparation for English Language exams alongside the study of music performance.

Qualifications: Internal certification only.

Thames Valley University

Thames Valley University, St Mary's Road, Ealing, London W5 5RF
tel 020-8231 2677
email music@tvu.ac.uk
website www.tvu.ac.uk
Head of Academic Studies Peter Rudnick

Founded in 1860 and with campuses in Ealing, Slough and Reading. TVU now runs music courses previously provided by the London College of Music and Media. The 3-year BA Performance Degree course is based on developing students' specialist and supporting skills to a level enabling them to maintain a professional profile. Optional study units include: 19th Century Music, World Music Studies, Jazz Studies, Music Theatre Studies, Popular Music Studies, 20th/21st Century Performance Workshop, Desktop Music, and Orchestration and Arranging. The 3rd year culminates in a public concert displaying performance achievements. It is possible to combine study with a range of subjects including Music Technology, World Music and Media.

The new Popular Music performance Degree is aimed specifically at contemporary popular guitarists, drummers, bass players, vocalists and keyboard players. Conceived by and associated with Drumtech, Vocaltech and Guitar-X, the course is tied strongly to a deep understanding of the needs of the business and aims to fall in line with industry expectations – delivering strong, versatile and employable musicians.

Qualifications: BA (Hons) in Music (Performance) (Ealing and Slough campus); BMus (Hons) in Popular Music Performance (Acton campus).

Trinity College of Music

Charles Court, Old Royal Naval College, Greenwich, London SE10 9JF
tel 020-8305 4444 *fax* 020-8305 9444
email enquiries@tcm.ac.uk
website www.tcm.ac.uk
Head of Performance Sean Farrell

Well-established conservatoire based in an idyllic setting. The Performance programmes are designed to train students to respond creatively to the demands of a rapidly changing profession. Particular focus is given to public performance including solo and chamber recitals, professionally coached chamber music ranging from duos up to large ensembles, and collaborations with composers and other art forms.

Qualifications: BMus (Hons) (Performance); PG Dip (Performance); MMus (Performance).

University College of Ripon and York St John

Lord Mayors Walk, York YO31 7EX
tel (01904) 624624 *fax* (01904) 612512
email admissions@yorksj.ac.uk
website www.yorksj.ac.uk
Head of Music David Lancaster

Offers music courses in combination with other subjects. Aims to create a contemporary and relevant approach to music education, including strong industry and community links. Includes units within the fields of composition, music technology and recording, world music, music in the community and popular music. Application through UCAS.

Qualifications: BA (Performance); BA QTS Music and Education; MA Professional Performance Practice; BA Joint Honours with either Art, Design, Film, Education, Communication, Theology or Literature.

University of Chichester

Bishop Otter Campus, College Lane, Chichester, West Sussex PO19 6PE
tel (01243) 812083 *fax* (01243) 816080
email admissions@chi.ac.uk
website www.chi.ac.uk
Head of Music Ben Hall

A small and friendly university containing a large and vibrant music department. Focuses on music as an applied art – from improvisation, composition, and professional performance, to music therapy and community music, as well as the traditional music analysis and critical theory (with a suitably wide variety of module choices). Also specialises in preparing graduates for employment as peripatetic music teachers within schools or in private practice.

Qualifications: BA (Hons) Music, Foundation Degree Instrumental or Vocal Teaching; Foundation Degree in Commercial Music (Platform One, Isle of Wight); BA (Hons) Music with Instrumental or Vocal Teaching; MA Music Performance; MA Choral Studies.

University of Durham

University Office, Old Elvet, Durham DH1 3HP
tel 0191-3343140 *fax* 0191-3343141
email bennett.zon@durham.ac.uk
website www.dur.ac.uk/music
Head of Department Dr Bennett Zon

Established in 1832. Award-winning (voted University of the Year 2005 by *The Sunday Times*) university based in 2 locations: the city of Durham and Queen's Campus in Stockton. Department specialisms include: historical musicology (particularly the 15th and 16th centuries), Haydn and Beethoven studies, British and Irish music of the 19th and early 20th centuries, sociology and music, popular music and theories of mass culture, composition, electroacoustic music and music technology. The Department has several active composers and performers of international standing. Facilities include lecture rooms, concert room, recording collection and gamelan.

Qualifications: BA (Hons) and MA in Music (Performance).

University of Salford

School of Media, Music and Performance, University of Salford, Salford, Greater Manchester M5 4WT
tel 0161-295 5000 *fax* 0161-295 4704
email d.king@salford.ac.uk
website www.smmp.salford.ac.uk
Head of Music Professor David King

Provides facility for more than 400 students to study on 4 specialist Degree music courses. Performance is at the centre of the Undergraduate programmes alongside study in Performance, Jazz, Analytical and Historial Studies and Music Technology. 1:1 instrumental tutorials are given; the various bands and other ensembles – including the school's own Aspects Theatre Company, Big Band, Wind Band and Choir – give over 300 public performances annually. The Popular Music Degree offers a 'Studio Performer' pathway and focuses on popular music and technology with emphasis on music business and the recording industry.

The Postgraduate programmes of study are intensive courses for performers wishing to specialise in contemporary genres such as popular music, brass and wind bands, and jazz. Emphasis is placed on repertoire, interpretation and musical and performing style through a variety of individual tutorials, seminars and workshops. The courses culminate in a public recital/concert performance.

Qualifications: BA (Hons) Music; BA (Hons) Popular Music and Recording; MA/PG Dip in Music (Performance).

University of Surrey

Guildford, Surrey GU2 5XH
tel (01483) 686509 *fax* (01483) 686501
email music@surrey.ac.uk
website http://www.surrey.ac.uk/Music/Courses/
Admissions Tutor Dr Stephen Downes

The Degree course provides equal emphasis within performance, composition and academic study aimed at students wishing to pursue a career in any area of the music industry. Units offered include: Western Art Music, Popular and Non-Western Music, Music Technology, Film Music, and Jazz. Students in their 2nd and final years may specialise in performance.

Qualifications: BMus.

University of York

Department of Music, Sir Jack Lyons Concert Hall, University of York, Heslington, York YO16 5DD
tel (01904) 432446 *fax* (01904) 432450
email music@york.ac.uk
website www.music.york.ac.uk
Head of Department Professor R Marsh *Admissions Tutor* Dr J Eato

Founded in 1964. The department of music aims to put performance at the heart of learning. Teaching is through a 'project system' and practice-based learning with focuses including musicology, music technology and world music. Other specialisms include: Composition, Early Music, Vocal Music, Computer Music, Community Music, and Ethnomusicology. Applications through UCAS. All applicants are interviewed, including an instrumental audition.

Qualifications: BA (Music); MA (Music); MPhil/PhD Diploma in Music Technology.

The Vocal Athlete

tel 0870-803 4778
email info@vocalathlete.com
website www.vocalathlete.com
Director Ana Gracey

Provides a range of unique 1-day, weekend and 5-day workshops and courses using training methods based on the latest vocal research. Specialises in equipping vocalists with the ability to perform the music of today with power, intensity, passion and magnetism alongside retaining optimum vocal health. Private tuition also available.

Health & Safety in the live performing industry

Iain Hill explains why every performer, and every individual considering staging a live music event, should consider thoroughly all the potential hazards involved in giving any kind of musical performance. Indeed, only by thorough planning can an enjoyable and safe concert be guaranteed.

Health & Safety issues quite rightly pervade the whole of the live performing industry. Any social event which involves people gathering at a particular location necessarily gives rise to a number of potential dangers. Such possible safety threats require careful consideration if injuries are to be avoided. And in the case of a musical performance – which is usually given from a raised platform, and more often than not involves the use of musical instruments powered and/or amplified by electricity – the dangers are obviously multiplied. From the performers' perspective alone, there are particular dangers. Is the electricity supply safe? Are the stage you are standing on, and the lighting system suspended over your head, sure not to collapse? And are those flashy pyrotechnics – which are due to explode (just a few feet away from you) at the end of the performance – completely safe?

Health & Safety in the venue

Many of the legal guidelines regarding Health & Safety apply to performing venues in exactly the same way that they apply to any place of work. There is a clear obligation on the part of the venue owner to provide an environment that is safe in which to work. The Health & Safety at Work Act 1974, and the Occupiers' Liabilities Act of 1957, aim to provide legal guidelines to establish an environment that is safe both for performers and for their entourage or road-crew, as well as for the venue staff and the promoter's technical staff. The Licensing procedure further prescribes the conditions for a safe and comfortable environment for public, performers and staff alike. Additional guidelines for the safe management of concerts are provided in *The Event Safety Guide*, published by HMSO.

Health & Safety and touring

The modern touring band is set up and run like a small industry in itself. Performers employ travelling 'crews' of specialised staff, with the objective of making their working environment as comfortable and easy as possible. A legal 'rider' – which specifies the technical requirements needed to stage the show – forms part of the contract with the promoter of the show, or of the tour. This part of the overall agreement seeks to ensure that what is often a highly complex stage-set can be erected and broken down in such time as to allow for a performance to take place on a daily basis – in different cities, or even in different countries. And there are many well-established rules and regulations that now govern this process.

Firstly, the routing of the tour is determined by the distances that the trucks which transport the band's equipment can legally travel in the prescribed time. International legislation covering the amount of time that drivers can work in any 24-hour period should ensure that shows are booked in such a way that the safety of the driver (and the general public) is not compromised: a driver is not legally allowed to travel huge distances with no respite. Then, there is the question of the band's own stage-set and equipment. All drapes and backdrop material need a relevant fire-proofing certificate – and one that is recognised internationally. All electrical equipment needs to be wired correctly, and to international specifications. Any riggers employed will need a licence that permits them to work at heights, in order to comply with local Health & Safety regulations.

In seeking to establish the working environment for the travelling 'crew', the 'performer' (and here we define the performer as the employer) has a responsibility to make this environment as safe as possible. All crew members employed on a tour need to be fully qualified for the work that they are asked to undertake – and they should never be asked to undertake tasks for which they have not received adequate training. You cannot, for example, ask a guitar technician to climb up and fix something on the lighting truss!

Where goods and services are contracted locally, the management team that the performer employs (usually consisting of the manager, the tour manager and the production manager) have a duty to ensure that the conditions set out in the rider to the contract are properly enforced. A production manager has every right to cancel a concert if the stage that has been supplied by a local promoter is not safe to work on; s/he has a responsibility to the crew and to the performer not to put them at risk by allowing a concert to go ahead where there is the remote possibility of a stage collapsing.

'Advancing' the show

The corollary of such responsibility lays a parallel obligation on the touring management team not to include on paper in their rider, or in their hardware as part of their own equipment, anything which would produce a danger to the local promoter's crew, the venue staff, or the audience; and to ensure that local Health & Safety regulations have all been incorporated into the working procedures of the show. A harmonious agreement is usually achieved by the well-established process of 'advancing' the show – whereby the performer's production manager, and the local promoter's production representative (and often a representative from the venue management – particularly where the venue is the holder of the Public Entertainment Licence) liaise thoroughly in advance to ensure that sufficient information is given to all parties, in order to provide a safe working environment. One single, tragic incident, when this process was not followed, has now become infamous in the live performing industry. The failure properly to advance a show in Newport, Rhode Island (USA) in 2001 led to the performers' pyrotechnic display setting fire to the ceiling of a club in which the concert was being held – leading directly (and very quickly) to the deaths of 105 people, including one of the performers.

The performer and the audience

The obligation to provide a safe environment for the public usually lies with the promoter, and with the venue management; the process is commonly governed by the licensing procedure, which ensures the correct application of relevant Health & Safety legislation. This legislation provides rulings on the legal capacity of the venue, the amount of emergency exits that need to be provided, the means of controlling ingress and egress, and the provision of adequate toilet facilities and crowd barriers in front of the stage. While it is not unknown for the tour manager of a band to enforce the cancellation of a show if s/he sees that there is a clear and obvious danger to the public (lack of any crowd barrier, for instance), the process is more often enforced by the local licensing authorities, or by the venue management.

Nevertheless, one aspect of the performer's relationship with the audience remains critical: the question of the extent to which the performance itself either excites, or incites, the crowd towards a state where people are put in danger of injury or death from crowd surges, crushes, or possible platform or equipment collapse. It should be a matter of common sense that a performer should not incite the crowd towards actions which could endanger their own safety. But the rise in popularity among certain audiences of what is termed 'anti-social crowd behaviour' – which encompasses activities such as crowd surfing and 'moshing' (surging) – has given rise to a dilemma among both performers and promoters of certain concerts with regard to the behaviour of the crowd, and what steps they can take to control it. In the case of the tragic events that led to nine deaths at the Roskilde Festival in Denmark in 2000, the initial response of the Danish police was to attribute blame to the band Pearl Jam, as performers, for failing to take sufficient measures to control the crowd. The subsequent inquiry in fact exonerated Pearl Jam, and pointed to a lack of communication between the various management teams and the emergency services at the show, as a contributory factor in the tragedy. This incident highlights the potential pitfalls that face any performer in the course of entertaining a large audience – particularly in an outdoor festival environment. If any performer were to be found responsible for inciting a crowd to behave in a way that leads to death or injury, they would then be open to prosecution for criminal negligence – as well as liable for enormous claims for damages. It must be said that the same dilemma confronts the promoter of the show, and the reaction of many event organisers is to make it clear to the public that any behaviour of the type described could lead to expulsion from the venue. The means by which they enforce this, however, is another question.

Show-stop procedure

The fact remains that, even today, the live entertainment industry has many issues to address in terms of the management of large crowds. Show-stop procedure is one of the issues requiring the most pressing attention. To what extent should the performer intervene to stop a show, when the audience is at risk, or when an incident has occurred requiring immediate resolution? While it would be normal to expect a 'human' reaction – whereby any performer confronted with visible evidence of an audience in distress would immediately stop the show, and do everything they could to assist – it must be remembered that the performers themselves are often in a state of high excitement and cannot (indeed *should not*) be expected to have the wherewithal to take an objective decision as to when exactly it becomes necessary to stop a show. In fact, much of the crowd-management industry is now calling for a clear show-stop procedure that is universally accepted by all parties concerned.

Good practice versus litigation

The seriousness with which some performers take this aspect of crowd safety is exemplified by the British band, Oasis. Oasis employs a crowd safety expert, who has the specific remit of monitoring the behaviour of the crowd throughout the show. This consultant has the authority to request the band to stop playing, and to address the crowd, in an attempt to control any behaviour which s/he deems to be potentially dangerous. Many crowd-safety management experts feel that this type of initiative by performers is essential to break through the inertia that inevitably arises out of the current situation – where different bands, and different promoters (as well as different local authorities), all approach the question of crowd control from varying perspectives.

Government authorities only tend to become involved when situations are not competently self-governed by the industry. This sometimes leads to the withdrawal of licences – such as occurred at the Glastonbury Festival in the year 2001, where local police opposed the granting of the licence, on the basis that they (correctly) felt that the organisers had lost control of certain aspects of the security of the festival. Government can also become involved by legislating to curtail the size of concert audiences, or to control the way in which large open-air concerts are mounted. But if government legislation were to become too pervasive, this would have a very detrimental effect on the enjoyment of the concert by the audience, potentially leading to a significant lowering of audience numbers – and in turn making many concerts economically unviable.

So the performer will always have an important part to play in the evolution of live-performance safety procedures: indeed, a central role, guaranteed by the fact that society has always tended to increase the extent to which concerns over all aspects of Health & Safety are dealt with, by increased legislation. The implementation of universally accepted 'good practice' in the live performing industry is the only way by which over-regulation – through excessive legislation – will be avoided. The difference in attitude over the last few decades, from the more happy-go-lucky 1960s through to the thorough and careful practices quite recently adopted by Oasis, show that this evolutionary process is well advanced. While the live performing industry is still, in some respects, a fairly young industry, considerable confidence should nonetheless be placed in modern live-performing safety procedures – provided they are followed to the letter, and in detail.

Iain Hill is Lecturer in Music Industry Management at Buckinghamshire Chilterns University College (UK), and specialises in issues within the live music industry. Reference: *The Event Safety Guide* (see latest available edition), HMSO. Further information can be found at the ILMC's official website: **www.ilmc.com**.

Societies

Bandname.com
website www.bandname.com

Established in 1977, the *World Wide Band and Artist Directory* exists both online and as a 3-volume reference work. (The former *National Band Register* – **Bandreg.com** – has now merged with **Bandname.com**.) Member services include registration of name, and access to business tools developed for the benefit of members. These features are accessible via an account page upon completion of registration. A dated certificate is sent out which confirms your registration. **Bandname.com** has an online search facility. There is a one-off, lifetime registration fee of approx. US$12 (£6.90; 10.23 Euro).

Incorporated Society of Musicians (ISM)
10 Stratford Place, London W1C 1AA
tel 020-7629 4413 *fax* 020-7400 1538
email membership@ism.org
website www.ism.org
Chief Executive Neil Hoyle *Marketing and Development Manager* Danny Whatmough

Founded in 1882. Professional musicians' organisation offering a wide range of benefits to members. Services include: public liability insurance, legal expenses insurance, 24-hour legal and tax advice, Inland Revenue enquiry insurance, copyright advice, free publications and a range of discounts. Different styles of membership available. Approx. £130 for full membership.

Irish Music Rights Organisation/Eagras Um Chearta Cheolta (IMRO)
Copyright House, Pembroke Row,
Lower Baggot Street, Dublin 2, Republic of Ireland
tel (00353) 1661 4844 *fax* (00353) 1676 3125
email info@imro.ie
website www.imro.ie

A non-profit national organisation that administers the performing rights in copyright music in Ireland on behalf of its members – songwriters, composers and music publishers – and on behalf of the members of the international overseas societies affiliated to it. IMRO's function is to collect and distribute royalties arising from the public performance of copyright works. Also prominently involved in the sponsorship and promotion of music in Ireland. Every year it sponsors a large number of song contests, music festivals, seminars, workshops, research projects and showcase performances. Membership is free for songwriters, composers, music publishers or arrangers of public domain works, whose compositions have been commercially recorded, broadcast or performed live in public. Completing the online enquiring form leads to an officer of the membership department contacting you regarding joining the society.

Music for Youth (MfY)
102 Point Pleasant, London SW18 1PP
tel 020-8870 9624 *fax* 020-8870 9935
email mfy@mfy.org.uk
website www.mfy.org.uk
Executive Director Larry Westland

An educational charity and 'grassroots' musical organisation providing free access for young people to perform before live audiences at regional and national level through its annual programme of festivals and concerts. MfY is notable for having provided many children with their first ever music-making experiences. Over 2 million 4 to 18 year olds have taken part in MfY events since 1971.

The calendar comprises 3 major events: the Regional Festival Series, the National Festival, and the Schools Proms. Groups enter these events at the beginning of the academic year (September) and are then invited to take part in a local Regional Festival in the spring. Up to 300 groups are then invited to perform at the National Festival in July. Following the National Festival, a further 30 groups are invited to appear at the Schools Proms at the Royal Albert Hall in November. MfY runs other events as well – such as the Primary Prom, and a Singposium (a choral training day held each year during the National Choral Festival of Music for Youth). There is an online application process, divided into 4 steps: read the special application notes (including information on how to submit recorded entries); decide which Regional Festival you would like to attend; decide which category your groups/ensembles should enter; and register in the Online Entry section (submitting your group for the Regional Festival Series).

Musicians' Union (MU)
National Office, 60-62 Clapham Road,
London SW9 0JJ
tel 020-7582 5566 *fax* 020-7582 9805
email info@musiciansunion.org.uk
website www.musiciansunion.org.uk

The Musicians' Union represents over 30,000 musicians working in all sectors and genres of the music business. As well as negotiating on behalf of musicians with major employers in the industry, MU offers a range of services tailored for the self-employed – including assistance for full-time and part-time professional and student musicians of all ages. Specialist officials tackle issues raised by musicians working in the live arena, the recording studio, or when writing and composing. Such issues can range from copyright protection to contractual advice, recovery of unpaid fees, and Health & Safety advice. Benefits of MU membership include: careers and business advice; legal assistance and contract advice; exclusive insurance schemes; networking opportunities; rights protection; media and session specialists; public liability cover; industry lists and leaflets; partnership advice; courses, seminars and workshops; and teacher services. MU has a regional structure, with offices in London, Cardiff, Birmingham, Manchester and Glasgow, staffed by full-time officials and administrative support. To contact MU, see the website, then select from 1 of 6 Regional Offices: London, Midlands, East & SE England, Wales & SW England, North of England, Scotland & Northern Ireland. Annual subscription rates are based on gross earnings from music: £240pa where you earn more than £15,000 from music; £120pa if less than £15,000; £60 if under 21 or a student in full-time education.

New Music in Scotland (NEMIS)
2nd Floor, 22 Jamaica Street, Glasgow G1 4QD
tel 0141-221 6660 *fax* 0141-427 5755
email alec@nemis.org
website www.nemis.org
New Music Development Officer Alec Downie
– see page 228.

Northern Ireland Music Industry Commission
Unit 2, Northern Whig House, Bridge Street, Belfast BT1 1LU
tel (02890) 923488
email info@nimusic.com
website www.nimusic.com
CEO Ross Graham *Communications* Sandra Gourley

Founded in 2001. Works to accelerate the creative and business development of the Northern Ireland music industry, and to promote the sector nationally and internationally. Membership is free of charge and includes marketing and promotional support, showcasing opportunities regionally and internationally, advice, guidance/mentoring, and seminars/workshops in creative and business skills development.

Performing Artists Media Rights Association (PAMRA)
PAMRA (3rd Floor), 161 Borough High Street, London SE1 1HR

tel 020-7940 0413 *fax* 020-7407 2008
email office@pamra.org.uk
website www.pamra.org.uk

A non-profit-making organisation run by performers for performers. PAMRA is the largest performers' collecting society in the UK and represents all performers – featured and non-featured – across all genres of music. It administers the performers' right to receive payments for the exploitation of their commercially published sound recordings. Also promotes performers' rights and aims to ensure that all musicians and singers receive their maximum income-entitlement from the UK and overseas.

Performers who can register are divided into 3 categories for the purposes of distribution. (1) Non-Featured Performer ('N' – commonly known as session musician or singer) – a performer who has been engaged for a fixed period of time, specifically to make 1 or more recorded backing performances which subsequently are included in the sound recording *or* whose performance is included in a sampled sound recording. (All performers who do not fall within the 'N' category as described here are treated as Featured Performers. The distribution scheme provides for 2 categories as follows.) (2) Contracted Performer ('C') – a Featured Performer who is bound by an exclusive agreement entered into directly or indirectly with the record company producing a recording, to perform on it but excluding agreements to do session work. (3) Other Featured Performer ('O') – a Non-Featured or Contracted Performer; guest artists or non-contracted members of a featured band or artist may fall into this category. Performers who fit into one of the above 3 categories may register for an application form online.

Performing Right Society (PRS)
Copyright House, 29-33 Berners Street, London W1T 3AB
tel 020-7580 5544
website www.mcps-prs-alliance.co.uk

The UK collecting society which licenses broadcast and public performance of musical works **– see page 48.**

Rehearsal studios

Attic Studios
Unit 2A, Longford Street Industrial estate,
Longford Street, Warrington WA2 7PG
mobile (07876) 52155
website www.myspace.com/atticwarrington

Offers 1 rehearsal room equipped with 3KW PA, 2
vocal mics, guitar amp and 5-piece drum kit. Also
provides music tuition, recording and live sound
reinforcement.

Backfeed Rehearsal Studios
Black Dyke Mills, Queensbury, Bradford,
West Yorkshire BD13 1QA
tel (01274) 817817 *mobile* (07769) 972537
website www.backfeed.co.uk

A complex of 4 rehearsal studios, all acoustically
tempered, ranging from 600 sq. ft. to 1100 sq. ft. for
large piece bands. Covered loading area gives direct
access to studios. Secure storage available.

Backline Recording and Rehearsal Studios
1-2 The Archways, Guildford Park Road,
Guildford GU2 5NP
tel (01483) 533876
email mail@backlinestudios.co.uk
website http://home.btconnect.com/backlinestudios/
index.html

Intimate rehearsal complex sometimes hosting gigs in
larger room (containing small stage). Competitive
rates include a range of equipment hire.

Big City Studios
159-161 Balls Pond Road, London N1 4BG
tel 020-7241 6655 *fax* 020-7241 3006
email pineapple.agency@btconnect.com
website www.pineappleagency.com

Contains 2 studios of 50ft x 27ft and 25ft x 21ft. Each
contains piano, PA, air-conditioning, sprung floors
and mirrors.

Bonafide Recording and Rehearsal Studio
Burbage House, 83-85 Curtain Road, London EC2
tel 020-7684 5350/1 *fax* 020-7729 7935
email findus@bonafidestudio.co.uk
website www.bonafidestudio.co.uk
Owner/Producer Deanna Gardner

Rehearsal complex consisting of 3 differently sized,
fully soundproofed studios. Full backline is available,
including: Marshall, Fender and Trace Elliot amps as
well as Pearl and Ludwig Drums. Also provides:
recording; production; mixing and mastering;
programming; and sound engineering and song-
building tutorials.

The Boom Boom Rooms
Beehive Mill, Jersey Street, Ancoats,
Manchester M4 6JG
tel 0161-950 4250 *fax* 0161-228 0357
email rich@bigfishcorporation.com
website www.bigfishcorporation.com

A complex of rehearsal rooms including a showcase
studio, PA and bass/guitar backline. Offers
instrument and backline hire.

Burst Studios
Unit 8, Bilting Farm Business Centre,
Canterbury Road, Bilting, Ashford, Kent TN25 4HF
tel (01233) 663148
email info@burststudios.com

New rehearsal facility offering 2 air-conditioned
rooms each with quality PA, full backline and drum
kit. Also provides a comfortable relaxation area with
free refreshments.

Bush Studios
152 Macfarlane Road, London W12
tel 020-8740 1740
email info@bushstudios.co.uk
website www.bushstudios.co.uk

Rehearsal studios situated next door to Shepherds
Bush tube station. Provides 350-750 sq. ft.
acoustically tempered rooms with comprehensive
PAs, amplification and drum kits. Also offers storage,
air conditioning, free parking and digital recording
facilities.

Cybersound
Unit C102, Faircharm Trading Estate,
8-12 Creekside, London SE8 3DX
tel 020-8694 9484 *fax* 020-8694 9466
email studio@cyber-sound.co.uk
website www.cyber-sound.co.uk

Contains 4 air-conditioned rehearsal studios, ranging
from 4-piece band suitability, up to much larger
bands and showcases. Clients have included:
Kasabian, Placebo and Paulo Nutini. Has free parking
facilities and easy access for public transport. Also
contains storage facilities and a small shop stocked
with refreshments and accessories.

Downs Sounds Rehearsal Studio
Units 3-4 Lower Park Road,
New Southgate Industrial Estate, London N11 1QD
tel 020-8211 3656
email info@downssounds.co.uk
website www.downssounds.co.uk or
www.myspace.com/downssounds

Offers 5 modern rehearsal rooms – each equipped with PA, backline amplification and drum kits for hire. Free on-site car parking.

G2

1st Floor, Wellington House, Pollard Street East, Ancoats, Manchester M40 7FS
tel 0161-275 9211 *fax* 0161-273 3931
email info@ghstudios.co.uk
website www.ghsstudios.co.uk

Offers well-equipped rehearsal rooms and equipment hire. Storage also available.

Gracelands

East Acton Lane, East Acton, London W3 7HD
tel 020-8740 8922 *fax* 020-8740 8922
email paul@gracelandsstudios.co.uk
website www.gracelandsstudios.co.uk

Contains 3 rehearsal rooms offering various levels of quality backline. Also offers an onsite shop selling strings, straps and drumsticks, etc.

The Greenhouse

Unit 16, Brighton Road Industrial Estate, Brighton Road, Heaton Norris, Stockport SK4 2BC
tel 0161-431 4127 *fax* 0161-442 8796
email info@ghstudios.co.uk
website www.ghsstudios.co.uk

Offers well-equipped rehearsal rooms and showcase studios. Equipment hire and storage also available.

Groove Tunnel

Eldin Industrial Estate, Loanhead, Edinburgh EH20 9QX
tel (0131) 448 2170
email rodspark@groovetunnel.com
website www.groovetunnel.com

A 4-rehearsal studio complex offering PA, bass/guitar backline, mics and drum kit. Also contains a recording studio. Additional equipment, including a Hammond Organ and Fender Rhodes, can be hired. Open 7 days a week from 10am until midnight. Ample free parking.

Ground Zero Studios

43-45 Coombe Terrace, Brighton BN2 4AD
tel (01273) 819617
email studio@g-zero.co.uk

Studio complex offering 3 rehearsal rooms with full backline. Also offers 8 resident rooms, 2 recording studios and refreshments. Cheap slots available on daytime weekdays, and discounts on block bookings.

Harbour Sound

Unit C3, JKS Workshop, Clydebank, Glasgow G81 1ND
tel 0141-941 2654
email info@harboursound.net
website www.harboursound.net

Well-equipped and acoustically tempered rehearsal rooms. Equipment available includes Pearl Masters, Marshall DSL and custom built PAs. Also offers music tuition.

Henry Wood Hall

Trinity Church Square, London SE1 4HU
tel 020-7403 0118 *fax* 020-7378 8294
email bookings@hwh.co.uk
website www.hwh.co.uk

A former church, converted in the early 1970s to become a classically recognised rehearsal and recording hall. Large dimensions – 33mx20mx10m high on several levels. Ample space for seating. Also contains 2 recording control rooms, one of which is acoustically treated. The crypt of the hall contains a restaurant.

Imp Hut

9 Melrose's Yard, Walmgate, York YO1 9XF
tel (01904) 642828
email jan@imp-hut.co.uk
website www.imphut.co.uk

Studio offers 3 air-conditioned rehearsal rooms each fitted with a PA system. Bass and guitar backline and drum kits can be hired. Rehearsal and recording facilities also available.

Impact Studios

14 Wokingham Road, Reading, Berkshire RG6 1JG
tel 0118-935 1479
email mail@impactstudios.co.uk
website www.impactstudios.co.uk

Comprises 4 air-conditioned rehearsal rooms. Each is equipped with PA, bass/guitar backline, mics and drum kit. Additional equipment hire and onsite shop also available.

JJM Studios

20 Pool Street, Walsall WS1 2EN
tel (01922) 629700
email info@jjmstudios.co.uk
website www.jjmstudios.co.uk

Offers 6 rehearsal studios, each with raised drum stage offering PA, bass/guitar backline, mics and drum kit. Additional equipment can be hired. Also offers tuition and a recording studio.

John Henry's

16-24 Brewery Road, London N7 9NH
tel 020-7609 9181 *fax* 020-7700 7040
email info@johnhenrys.com
website www.johnhenrys.com
Studio Bookings Manager Andrea Westwood

Contains 6 professional studios of varying size, all acoustically tempered. Equipment includes: Soundcraft SM12 console and extensive monitoring system; cassette deck; equalisation and digital reverb/delay. Accessories and spares can be bought from the onsite Pro Shop. Qualified audio engineers are at hand to handle equipment needs. Has onsite Canteen; also offers transport and event crew, event production, staging, set design and flightcases.

Loz Vegas Music

Unit 39, Silicone Business Centre,
28 Wadsworth Road, Perivale, Middlesex UB6 7JZ
tel 020-8998 9122 *fax* 020-8991 2661
email matt@vegassoundhouse
website www.lozvegasmusic.co.uk

Contains 3 rehearsal studios with PA, backline and drum kit included in room hire. Additional equipment hire/purchase available. Ample free parking.

Madhouse

41 Hampton Street, Hockley, Birmingham B19 3LS
tel (0121) 233 1109 *fax* (0121) 233 1286
website www.madhouserehearsals.com

Contains 11 rehearsal studios offering PA, bass/guitar backline, mics, drum kit and lighting rigs. Additional equipment can be hired. Also offers a recording studio and a bar/music venue.

Magnet Studios

Unit 2 South, Davisella House, Newark Street,
Sneinton, Nottingham NG2 4PP
tel (0115) 9243324
email rob@magnetstudios.co.uk
website www.magnetstudios.co.uk

Contains 4 good-sized rehearsal rooms that are modern, well presented and acoustically treated. Each room offers a 6-input, 300-watt Fender mixer amp and Shure SM58 mics. Secure storage facilities and a chillout area with refreshments available. Also offers extensive PA and equipment hire, including band transport.

Mushroom Rehearsal Studios

Hullbridge Road, Rayleigh, Essex
tel (01268) 784599 *mobile* (07833) 104822
email mushroomstudio@aol.com

Contains 7 rehearsal rooms, each with PA and backline for bass/guitar and drum kit. A shop is provided within the studio for standard spares.

Music Room

Unit 121 Lydney Industrial Estate, Harbour Road,
Lydney, Forest of Dean
tel (01594) 841851 *mobile* (07834) 812205
email info@musicstudio.org.uk
website www.musicstudio.org.uk

Includes 2 soundproofed studios with drum kit, 6-channel 600W PA, guitar/bass amps and chillout room.

National Opera Studios

2 Chapel Yard, off Wandsworth High Street,
London SW18 4HZ
tel 020-8874 8811
email a.konkka@nationaloperastudio.org.uk
website www.nationaloperastudio.org.uk

Large rehearsal studio offering seating for 70 people. Also contains a Yamaha grand piano and simple lighting rig.

Planet Sounds

The Arches, 40 Terminus Terrace, Southampton,
Hants SO14 3FE
tel (02380) 334040 *mobile* (07989) 259217
email planet-sounds@btconnect.com
website www.redrockstudios.co.uk

Rehearsal complex consisting of 5 rooms of varied size for solo, small or larger group rehearsals. Rooms contain PA and basic drum kit. Recording facilities are also available.

Playback System

Unit 1B South, New England House,
New England Street, Brighton BN1 4GH
tel (01273) 671297 *fax* (01273) 275768
email info@playbacksystems.com
website www.playbacksystems.com

A large rehearsal space (approx. 500 sq. ft.). This includes 1 9KW Funktion PA system with in-house technical engineers on hand, a large storage space and loading bay access. Also offers a professional recording studio with editing room.

Polestar

Uptin House, Stepney Road, Shieldfield,
Newcastle Upon Tyne NE2 1TZ
tel 0191-230 1831
email info@polestarstudios.co.uk
website http://loversofoutrage.com/polestar/contact.htm

Contains 3 rehearsal rooms fitted with PA equipment. Further equipment hire available. Also offers recording studio and free parking.

Practice Pad

Unit 5A, St Margaret's Park, Pengam Road,
Aberbargoed CF81 9FW
tel (01443) 838484
email enquiry@thepracticepad.co.uk
website www.thepracticepad.co.uk
Manager Glen Speary

Contains 4 rehearsal rooms fully equipped with 2 guitar amps, 1 bass amp, a Sonor drum kit, 2 microphones and a quality PA system. Also offers guitar, bass and drum tuition and hosts a music shop onsite. Open 7 days a week.

The Premises

209 Hackney Road, London E2 8JL
tel 020-7729 7593
email info@premisesstudios.com
website www.premisesstudios.com
CEO Viv Broughton *Studio Director* Nathan Hale

Founded in 1985. Contains high-spec/low-cost complex of 14 recording and rehearsal studios. Recent clients have included: Bloc Party, Lily Allen, Jamie Cullum and Klaxons. *Rates*: From £9.75 p.h.

Pulse Studios

Unit K, Blackhorse Mews, Blackhorse Lane, London E17 5HB
tel 020-8527 0440 *mobile* (07793) 251399
email pulsestudiose17@hotmail.com
website www.pulsestudiose17.co.uk

Comprises 4 fully equipped rehearsal rooms including drum kit, PA, mics and guitar/bass amps. Secure storage available.

Redrock Studios

Unit D3, Britannia Enterprise Centre, Pengam Road, Blackwood, Gwent NP12 3SP
tel (01443) 879222 *mobile* (07817) 894483
email info@redrockstudios.co.uk
website www.redrockstudios.co.uk
Engineer Lyn Price

Offers relaxed, modern rehearsal space in 2 rooms. Each room incorporates Mapex/Pearl drum kits, Marshall, Laney and Hughes and Kettner guitar amps and Behringer and Laney Bass Amps. Also offers 24 Track recording studio facilities.

The Rehearsal Rooms

4 St Andrews Street South, Bury St Edmunds, Suffolk IP33 3PH
tel (01284) 700353
email neil@therehearsalrooms.co.uk or ken@therehearalrooms.co.uk
website www.therehearsalrooms.co.uk

Comprises 2 well-laid-out rooms, 1 containing a 200W Wharfedale PA system and the other a Behringer 500W PA. Rooms also come with 2 mics and stands. Additional equipment can be hired, including a Pearl EX Export drum kit, a Marshall and Line 6 guitar amp and Hartke bass amp. Seated lounge areas, musical spares and car parking all available.

Robanna's Studios

Robanna House, Cleveland Street, Birmingham B19 3SN
tel 0121-333 3201 *fax* 0121-359 3071
email robannas.studios@btinternet.com
website www.robannas-studios.co.uk

Several rehearsal rooms, each offering PA, drum kits, bass/guitar backline, mics and further equipment hire. Storage, lockouts, private studios and recording studio also available.

Stage 2000

Taybridge Station, Riverside Drive, Tayside, Dundee DD1 4DB
tel (01382) 223332

email info@stage2000.co.uk
website www.stage2000.co.uk

Complex containing 5 rehearsal studios offering PA, bass/guitar backline, mics and drum kit. Basic recording facilities are fitted in 2 of the studios. Additional equipment can be hired. Also offers tuition and workshops.

Station Studios

Station Forecourt, Station Road, New Southgate, London N11 3BL
tel 020-8361 8114
email info@stationstudios.co.uk
website www.stationstudios.co.uk

Contains 3 rooms of varying size equipped with full PA and backline. A drum kit can be provided for a small extra cost. The chillout reception area includes TV and kettle. Parking is free and local shops and pubs are close by. Day, evening and weekend hourly rates available.

Sync City Media Ltd (Sync City Studio)

16-18 Millmead Business Center, Millmead Industrial Estate, Millmead Lane, Tottenham
tel 020-8808 0472
email info@ballystudios.co.uk
website www.synccity.co.uk

Several rooms equipped with full PA; basic cassette tape recording facility, raised stage, and 1 large room with a balcony chillout area. Amps and drum kit available for hire.

Terminal Studios

4-10 Lamb Walk, London Bridge, London SE1 3TT
tel 020-7403 3050 *fax* 020-7407 6123
email info@terminal.co.uk
website www.terminal.co.uk

Large-scale and well-equipped rehearsal room complex offering equipment hire, storage and equipment repair. All studios come with a comprehensive setup of PA, mixing desks, backline, lighting rigs and monitors.

The Toilets

4 Hill Street, Stoke on Trent, Staffordshire ST4 1NL
tel (01782) 503084 *mobile* (07973) 253542
email karenhbs@hotmail.co.uk
website www.toiletsrehearsalstudios.com

Contains 2 rooms, complete with vocal PA and 3 mics. Additional backline can be hired, including Laney, Marshall and Crate guitar amplification, a Hartke bass amp and cabinet and a Sonor drum kit. Easy access into the rooms.

The Tollhouse

First Floor, 10 Possil Road, Glasgow G4 9SY
mobile (07809) 650345
email tollhousestudio@googlemail.com
website www.tollhousestudio.co.uk

Newly opened dedicated rehearsal rooms incorporating high-spec equipment in acoustically tempered spaces. Also offers recording facilities and equipment hire.

Tweeters 2 Studios

Unit C1, Business Park 7, Brook Way, Leatherhead, Surrey KT22 7NA
tel (01372) 386592
email info@tweeters2studios.co.uk
website www.tweeters2studios.co.uk

Contains 5 sound-proofed studios all including full PA systems and drum/equipment risers. Also has recording facilities and 'off premises' equipment hire.

Unit 9 Rehearsal Studios

Unit 9 Rehearsal Studios,
Unit 9 Zennor Road Industrial Estate, Balham, London SW12 OPS
tel 020-8675 9666
website www.unit9rehearsals.com

Comprises 8 rehearsal rooms. Each is equipped with 2 guitar amps, a bass amp, drum kit, PA and 3 microphones.

Unit 25 – Mill Hill Music Complex

Bunns Lane Works, Bunns Lane, London NW7 2AJ
tel 020-8906 9991
email enquiries@millhillmusic.co.uk
website www.millhillmusic.co.uk

Large complex consisting of 12 rehearsal rooms. Each offers PA, mics, backline for bass/guitars and drum kit. Instrument hire and recording studio also available.

Voodoo Rooms

Bishop's Stortford, Herts
tel (01279) 460222
website www.voodoorooms.com

Rehearsal studios with backline hire and live 'two track' recording facilities. Drum lessons also available.

Water Rat Music Studio

Unit 2, Monument Way East,
Woking Surrey GU21 5LY

tel (01483) 764444 *mobile* 07889 375126
email jayne@waterrat.co.uk
website www.waterrat.co.uk
Manager Jayne Wallis

Westbourne Rehearsal Studios

The Rear Basement, 92-98 Bourne Terrace, Little Venice, London W2 5TH
tel 020-7289 8142 *fax* 020-7289 8142

Large, air-conditioned, mirrored studios with acoustically conditioned rooms and full PA and backline. Refreshments and storage shop. Free parking.

Yellow Arch Studios

30-36 Burton Road, Sheffield,
South Yorkshire IP33 3PH
tel 0114-273 0800
email mail@yellowarch.com
website www.yellowarch.com

Complex of 4 rooms, 3 of ample size and 1 very large room for touring bands and large-piece bands. All studios come equipped with PA and full quality backline. Additional gear can be hired. Ample secure storage. The studios also incorporate a recording facility, chillout room, shop and offsite equipment hire.

Zed One

Camden, London
tel 020-7482 3500
email rehearsals@zed-one-studios.co.uk
website www.zed-one-studios.co.uk

Contains 4 air-conditioned rehearsal studios available with facilities for storage and equipment hire. Rooms available for around £25 per hour. Also includes 24-track recording studio available from £150 per day with large live music area, Pro Tools and live music specialists.

FAQs: The role of the musical director

What does a musical director do?

Some bands work as a unit and make decisions by 'committee' about direction and material, and about arrangements and sound. Sometimes, however, this very democratic approach can lead to endless disagreements, which can ultimately result in that famous musical euphemism, 'artistic differences' (the reason given for the break-up of many famous groups over the years). To prevent possible discord, and to keep the tasks well coordinated, many bands prefer to have a Musical Director (MD) – someone who is ultimately responsible for the artistic direction of the band. In some instances, that person emerges from the performing body of the group itself, to become the key songwriter and driver of artistic style (such as Pete Townsend of The Who). In other instances, an MD may be chosen because he or she is clearly, from the outset, the person who has the major musical input to the band – often the band's writer, arranger and producer (such as Babydaddy of the Scissor Sisters).

Solo acts or boy/girl bands very often have an MD, who is responsible for writing, collecting or suggesting material that s/he will then arrange or orchestrate. This person may also play in the backing band, and conduct or lead the band from his or her instrument. While the Musical Director is often a keyboard player, it is not unknown for a guitarist or even a drummer to be an MD.

How do I find the right Musical Director?

So, if you are a solo performer, how do you choose your MD? Certainly, s/he should be someone who is:

- supportive;
- understands your musical style;
- has a flair for instinctively hearing the sort of arrangement that will work best for your songs;
- can play an instrument (and/or operate a mixing desk);
- knows how to make *tactful* suggestions for improvement, without causing offence.

What do I do to become a Musical Director?

MDs work in all fields of the music industry – from pop and rock to TV and theatre – so there are many kinds. In all cases they should be able to play an instrument (ideally including keyboard), and, if necessary (especially if the act requires a large orchestra), be able to arrange, orchestrate and conduct. In the case of theatre work, they should have a well-developed ability to read music at sight.

An MD also needs good 'people skills', in order to communicate with musicians as well as non-musicians (including business people) – besides sound engineers, producers, and, of course, the artists themselves. Dealing with every single one of these types of people may require a different approach! If you want to become a theatre MD, you will have to understand the needs of *all* the performers (including dancers, actors and singers). You should

112 Performing

also be able to hold auditions, teach the music (even to non-musicians), and be prepared to conduct or play the show eight times a week, with the same enthusiasm and freshness as if it were the first night every night.

David Beer has conducted many West End shows, and is well-known as a Musical Director and vocal coach in both theatre and popular music. He is currently Musical Supervisor of all UK productions of *FAME*. He worked with Roger Waters in Berlin on Pink Floyd's *The Wall*, and his recording work includes several *Original Cast* albums and Sarah Brightman's album, *The Songs That Got Away*. He has also made many TV and radio appearances as conductor and pianist. Between 2001-2004, David was Director of Music at the BRIT School for Performing Arts – where his students included Katie Melua and Leona Lewis.

How to approach a performance

Stefan Redtenbacher, one of Europe's leading bass players and a frequent stage performer, passes on his accumulated wisdom on the subject of live performance.

Having a clear goal

Knowing *exactly* what you want to achieve is fundamental to the successful outcome of any type of musical performance. Should, for example, your music form a pleasant background to your audience's social interaction in a restaurant? Do you want them to listen attentively in a prestigious concert hall? Or do you, perhaps, want them to revere you as a demi-god at a stadium rock concert?

Performing only seems complete when the performers and audience 'become one' – sharing a mutual experience. So try to find yourself a performing *credo* which suggests how you might measure your own success. For instance, Count Basie (in his inimitable style) said: "If you play a tune and a person don't tap their feet, don't play the tune."

Ego, trust and performance

Too much personal focus can stand in the way of musicians achieving their highest level of performance. Comments such as "the music swept me away" and "being in the zone" are strong indicators that the best performances transport a person into an almost mystical, 'trance-like' state. This intensity can only be achieved with plenty of personal and group practice, because the skills required have to be so deep and ingrained that the performer does not have to think about the technical aspects of their playing – only the musical and emotional aspects.

Trust in one's own musical capabilities, and those of one's fellow musicians, is a vital element in performance. *Preparation* is therefore essential, so that 'what to perform' can be forgotten (or sublimated), and 'how to perform' can emerge as the main focus.

Preparation before the gig

With ample preparation it is possible to focus on the performance, blending out any irrelevant or unhelpful 'noises' – both inside and outside one's head. Some performers refrain from spending time alone before a performance, in order to avoid thinking themselves into a state of distress. Indeed, it is generally good advice to show up early, avoid distractions, take time to 'still' the mind, and focus calmly on the task ahead. Warming up can be a perfect tool to achieve the necessary level of single-minded concentration.

Team mentality

Making music is often a social activity. In a small group it is advisable to have a moment together before stepping on stage; this helps to boost morale, and to instill team confidence. Whether an audience has acute listening skills, trained ears, or no musical knowledge whatsoever, it will pick up on the 'energy' of the performer/s. Therefore, it is best to leave all distracting thoughts aside and focus entirely on the shared experience with the audience. If your music has both energy and depth, you will give a lasting and meaningful experience to a wide range of audiences. Perhaps the best unifying statement relating to a personal musical philosophy was recorded by composer and arranger, Charles Brent, about the famous bassist, Jaco Pastorius: "Write it, orchestrate it, give a performance with a huge intensity level and perform it yourself; what else is there but heaven after that ..."

Stefan Redtenbacher is Head of Bass Studies at the Academy of Contemporary Music in Guildford. He is an alumni of the Vienna Conservatory, and Berklee College of Music in America. His recording and performing credits include Steve Winwood, Amy Winehouse, Sam Brown and Herb Alpert. The 'RB Funkestra' is Stefan's own band – which has recorded with funk legends such as Fred Wesley, and 'Doc' Kupka (Tower of Power).

How vocal performers communicate

Penelope Appleyard unravels some of the mysteries behind the singer's unique role in the business of audience communication. She reveals just how vital to the singer's art are such obscure factors as musical interpretation and performance 'delivery'.

"Music is the most profound, magical form of communication there is." – Lesley Garrett
As a vocalist, you are in the business of communication – more so, perhaps, than any other musician. Your chief currency is words; your instrument is yourself. In fact, singer-songwriter Alanis Morissette once described her body as "an instrument, rather than an ornament". Singing certainly seems to be the most 'human' method of music-making that there is, and your performance is a personal display drawing on inbuilt powers of expression and gesture.

This 'personal touch' has an immense and often underestimated influence on a performance. Personal input can enhance considerably the powers of communication between you – the performer – and your audience. Yet both of these parties should, in effect, be treated as equal in importance. You might even define the audience as the other 'half' of any musical conversation. American pop singer Meredith Brooks once claimed that she liked her lyrics "to feel conversational and truthful, as if we're having real talk". It is vital, therefore, to establish a two-way relationship with your audience. After all, you can't communicate something if there's no-one there to hear it!

So what are the main ingredients of an effective performance? The following equation might neatly summarise the situation:
The *material* itself (M) + the *personal* touch (P) = the *meaning communicated* (MC).
Indeed, the type of performance that you give depends very much on the way these first two elements work together. Your personal touch can influence the given material, as much as the musical material can influence your particular approach. Also consider the ratio of *your own input* to the *song itself*, and try to achieve a reasonable balance.

The raw material
The music itself partially dictates (often subconsciously) the way in which a performance will be given. And this, in turn, will vary with the style of the music you are singing. Let's look at this with regard to the song itself.

Genre
The expectations that each genre (or style of singing) carries with it are important to your performance style. You can choose how to adapt your performance to these expectations. There are, perhaps, greater restrictions in interpretation with certain genres than others. In a broad sense, it might be argued that there is less scope for individuality in some classical music (in the performance of a well-known Puccini opera aria, for instance) – due to long-established traditions, 'masterpiece' associations, and the almost sacred status of certain composers. So while new and individual voices are encouraged, traditional methods of performance and interpretation are, in reality, often fiercely 'protected'.

Sometimes a fine balance is struck, in order to make any new musical 'product' inoffensive to the widest possible audience (an aim which usually helps guarantee record sales). Take the group G4, for example. Their boy-band addition to the 'popera' genre – combining both pop and classical favourites – has appealed to a reasonably broad cross-section of the public, received a good deal of air-time, and started them on successful performance careers.

As a performer in the 'popular', as opposed to 'classical', genre, you will sometimes feel yourself to have greater status alongside the writer (and you may, in fact, even be the songwriter yourself) – so having more scope for individuality, particularly in original but also in 'cover' songs. Indeed, with an effective method of delivery in the pop genre, you can usually make it appear as if you, in fact, wrote the song, irrespective of whether or not you actually did!

Then again, jazz encourages quite a unique approach, with its tradition of (and emphasis on) improvisation. This heartfelt, 'spur-of-the-moment' genre positively encourages an intimate and personal style. As legendary jazz icon Ella Fitzgerald once put it, "I sing like I feel." This approach was clearly important to her own success, for as Broadway composer Richard Rogers commented, "Whatever she does to my songs, she always makes them sound better."

Musical content

The music itself carries an inherent style and mood – and, of course, its own meaning and complexity. You can build upon all of these factors in an individual way. In fact, how you understand and interpret the music is ultimately essential to how credible a performance actually is. Furthermore, the music will have an inextricable relationship with the lyrics.

Lyrics

The delivery of the lyrics is the vital 'something extra' that distinguishes you – as a vocalist – from instrumental performers; it allows for a personal quality in both timbre and meaning, and is therefore worth conveying as effectively as possible. Singer-songwriter Vanessa Carlton once described her songs as being "a direct route into my brain and my heart". No matter what the genre, the lyrics are crucial in the process of communicating the song's core sentiment – the contents of that brain and heart.

History

A song's 'history' is also worth considering. It may be a brand new song (allowing perhaps for greater creative freedom), or you may be providing an updated version of a work which is already well-established. If the song is considered to be a 'classic', it may need to be handled with much more care when adding the second element of our equation – the 'personal touch'.

The personal touch

After familiarising yourself with all the musical and lyrical material, next comes the task of communicating it to an audience. The process is a delicate one, even for someone as accomplished as soprano Sarah Brightman, who for this reason admits to "a love-hate relationship with performing".

In general terms, a performance can go one of two ways: it might be said to be either 'open' or 'closed' to the audience. In other words, some singers have an open style that immediately acknowledges the audience. This tends to reinforce the fact that these are indeed *performances* – not attempting to create the illusion of the situation conjured up by the lyrics (in which the audience has no part).

Take, for example, the style of any flamboyant cabaret performer, or perhaps someone as extrovert as the multi-platinum-selling Robbie Williams (the 'great entertainer'). Through both musical and physical means, Robbie Williams communicates directly and openly with his audience at a live show. On the other hand, some performances do not seem to recognise the presence of the audience at all, appearing rather to let them be witness to a private moment in the life of the vocalist. This 'closed' style is sometimes employed by singer-songwriters in order to help create intensity, and often results in an effective, if indirect, form of communication. But in either case, in order for the material to carry meaning, your own personal interpretation of it remains fundamental. So it is worth explaining more about the two major components to delivering an interpretation: aspects both *musical* and *physical*.

Musical aspects

The musical aspects of communication revolve around how you use your individual voice to make the best of the material, in a memorable way. This is a matter of stylistic judgment, and often depends upon the level of your natural musicality. Your distinctive sound is important here, and can add the vital ingredient which makes your audience sit up and listen. A recognisable tune sung by Country & Western singer Dolly Parton, for instance, is never quite what you expect. The way she exploits the natural agility of her voice is unmistakable as *her*, and – as well as having a pleasant and captivating vocal sound – it also constitutes an instantly recognisable marketing tool! Likewise, Demis Roussos provides a good example of a singer whose tone-quality is memorable for its immediate 'recognisability'.

Other musical aspects which influence the effectiveness of a performance might include, for example, the way in which you express the meaning of the lyrics through vocal style, diction and emphasis, in order to make them sound genuine. This air of sincerity is particularly valuable. Take a musical theatre singer like Michael Ball, who has described himself as "an interpreter of songs". While acting as a character in any given role, the apparent sincerity of his lyrics is what endears him to audiences. As Ball once explained, "You can move an audience, you can talk to an audience, you can capture an audience far more with music than with anything else."

Creating well-placed dynamics, and responding to the music's own inner drama (when modulations or key changes occur, for example), also aids communication, and can greatly enhance an emotional atmosphere. You might notice how key-shifts are sometimes exploited by pop singers to reinforce penultimate lyrical phrases. And in any performance, even if you are not yet confident enough to be a great 'showman', even minor physical gestures can enhance the musical aspects of a performance.

Physical factors

Physical aspects of delivery are highly significant in defining your performance as being either 'inclusive' or 'exclusive' to your audience. Take physical position, for example. A boy-band such as Westlife will very often work to a formula that involves sitting during the opening verses of a ballad, then rising at the key change to walk forwards. Within one song, they demonstrate both inclusive and exclusive performance styles, and how both are able to aid communication. After the key change, they will openly recognise the audience. Before it, however, they usually 'internalise' the song much more – a powerful technique (which is often used subconsciously by more accomplished and experienced performers, who are able quickly to 'read' their audience).

Then of course, there are more subtle physical aspects, such as facial expression. Facial expressions almost always directly reflect your response to the music, again with the aim of enhancing its credibility. In the world of classical song and opera, mezzo-soprano Cecilia Bartoli provides an example of how clear facial expressions can help build rapport with an audience. Despite language barriers, her expressions convey the essential meaning of the lyrics. Indeed, she is well known for displaying vivid emotion while singing, and she herself insists upon the necessity of believing in what you are singing about. Otherwise, she argues, "it will never work".

The eyes are probably the most expressive facial feature, and can further enhance the communication of meaning. If this seems obvious, then it's also worth considering for a moment the opposite phenomenon: that of the singer-songwriter who likes sometimes to perform with eyes closed, as if almost to force listeners into that private, deeply felt world, which they seem at the time to be inhabiting. This technique is more prominent in slow-tempo songs, which generally call for greater emotional intensity (and therefore a more 'exclusive' performance style). The theory is that by closing the eyes – although in one sense you are shutting out your audience – you are in fact drawing the audience much closer into your 'inner world'.

So choreographed routines, large physical gestures, small hand movements, and subtle facial gestures can all have an impact on communication. Likewise, the acknowledgement of other performers – or even objects such as microphones – will help indicate that there are wider concepts to consider than just you and your song. Even the smallest of actions may greatly influence the 'interpretation' which the audience takes home with them – so make sure it is the interpretation you intended! Simply separating a microphone from its stand can open up a performance within the most intimate of ballads. It also suggests that you have become more conscious of your surroundings (and therefore the audience) at that point.

The audience is, crucially, the reason for all this communication, and in order to ensure a successful performance, the audience should always remain at the forefront of a singer's concept of how to convey musical meaning. As jazz vocalist Diana Krall once pointed out, "It's their experience, not yours."

The power of vocal communication

As a vocalist, you are communicating a song's meaning through a highly personalised musical process. And as a performer, you communicate not only with your *audience*, but you also commune with the *music* itself. It is a mark of high artistry when the relationship between you and your material is completely believable (as in the case of that seemingly unlikely star, Edith Piaf, who captured the hearts of millions with her passionate, intimate style, and extraordinary tone).

During a performance there are, in fact, any number of communicative channels that can be opened simultaneously: you with the music, you with the audience, you with the ensemble, the audience with the music, and so on. Furthermore, if you can add a unique, heartfelt and personal touch to the music, you have a chance to communicate something powerful, fresh and memorable.

Penelope Appleyard holds Bachelors and Masters Degrees in English and Music Performance. Besides experience in songwriting, she has performed in a variety of genres and settings, and currently specialises in singing baroque and classical repertoire.

Logistics and the freelance percussionist

Graham Bradley gives us an insight into the world of moving percussion equipment around various venues, in order to ensure that all manner of exotic instruments – large and small – arrive where they are supposed to, when they are supposed to!

Being organised

As a freelance percussionist (effectively a 'drummer for hire' – but so much more besides) the concept of 'logistics' is probably a more important concern than for any other musician. You might be providing percussion instruments just for yourself, or for an entire percussion section. And the only way to survive is by being organised! Freelance playing can range from bookings for TV, Radio, and CD recordings, to scratch dates, theatrical shows and choral concerts. One recent personal gig, for example, saw me recording the music for *Dr Who* with the BBC National Orchestra of Wales. Because the work is potentially so varied, you do have to be flexible – and generally if the 'fixer' (the person who books and coordinates all the players for a gig) wants, then the fixer gets!

A fixer might choose to book not only a percussion player, but also a percussionist whom they know will bring along all the right gear. Or they may book one principal percussionist whom they know will, in turn, organise to bring an entire section of players (if a large work) *together with* all the appropriate instruments. Offering such a 'complete' service (organising both personnel and instruments) can help you to become the first point of call for many a fixer. Together with building up a percussion-hire business, this is one effective strategy for survival as a freelance.

So where do you start when the call comes in?

The equipment

The first requirement is to know what instruments you need. The fixer will either give you a list of the repertoire (which means you have to do the work), or will give you a list of instruments.

If the fixer gives you a list of repertoire, then you will have to determine the instrumentation. Sometimes this can be quite difficult, but there are several helpful resources available, giving you equipment lists for a wide selection of repertoire – such as the *Percussion Orchestrations* website, and Maggie Cotton's *Percussion Work Book* (further information can be found at: **www.elitepercussion.com**). Sources like these are very good, but they are not always perfect ... or indeed entirely accurate for every purpose. So you must also do your own homework, especially as people will have different preferences.

If the fixer gives you a list of instruments, then it is advisable to check if the music is in the standard 'rep' – or repertoire – and ideally try to get a paper copy of this list from the fixer (in order to cover yourself in case there is any subsequent confusion). One or two conductors over the years have asked me questions such as, "Where is the whip?" – and when you reply that it is 150 miles away, they are not usually too pleased! But if the information you are given is not correct, then all you can do is busk as well as you can.

If you are playing a new work, then (if possible) try to contact the composer to check the instrument list, and maybe chat to them about what they actually had in mind. And if you are providing timpani, and do not know the repertoire, then it is often a good idea to ask for the music well in advance, so that you can take the drum sizes that are most suitable.

Sorting your gear

The only way to make sure you turn up with all the right equipment is by *using lists*. If you are providing percussion instruments for a whole section (for works such as Carl Orff's *Carmina Burana*), then you have to make sure you have three glockenspiels *and* three stands. When I write out my lists, I will jot down, "instrument plus stand"; and if it is something like tubular bells or tam-tam (which have special beaters), then I will write, "instrument plus mallets". Little things like that do help! And when you put in music stands, make sure you have enough of them, and always carry enough sticks for the whole section. A small bag of 'spares', and a couple of tools, can also help to prevent a crisis!

Packing

If you need a van for the gig, then make sure it is booked well in advance – and check it is big enough! Tick off the gear against your list as you load, and then check your list again. I always make sure I have plenty of time to get set up before the session starts. Being late annoys any fixer, but when you have a load of instruments to bring in and set up, it is so much worse!

The venue

Getting into concert halls is normally fine, and muddy field-dates largely speak for themselve – but the seemingly innocuous local-church booking can be the one that is most fraught with danger. If you are playing in a church (usually for the local choral society), the doors into the venue can sometimes be smaller than you might expect!

Normally, two standard timpani are fine, but if you are taking a large 32-inch timp, then it might be advisable to check if there is a wide enough double-door into the premises. The most frustrating experience of all is to be greeted by the sight of a promisingly large front door, only to realise that it leads on to much smaller internal doors. This situation often results in having to leave large timpani outside – and in the subsequent concert, pedalling furiously on smaller instruments (including the odd unwelcome glissando) in order to hit all the notes! For safety's sake, I normally take Adams universal timpani to a gig in a church where I have not played before, as these *do* usually fit through the doors.

Packing up

Although you might want to be the first at the bar after the show, it rarely happens on a freelance date. The saying, "First to arrive, last to leave" is a fact of musical life, and you just have to accept that as part of being a percussionist. What is more annoying, though, is the astonishing number of people after a show who can't wait to say to you, "I'll bet you wished you played the piccolo!" Aaaaargh! When this happens at the end of a long day, and you are tired and irritable, there is an overwhelming desire to retort, "No, if I *wanted* to play the piccolo then I *would*!" (Or possibly you might consider saying something a bit stronger …)

It could be argued that the greatest test of your character as a musician and a freelance percussionist, is – after an arduous day of music-making and when confronted with such a question – whether you can still smile sweetly, and politely wish the enquirer goodnight.

Graham Bradley is a freelance percussionist based in South Wales, who undertakes regular orchestral, radio, TV and session work. He studied at the Welsh College of Music and Drama, followed by postgraduate studies at the Royal College of Music. He also runs a percussion case manufacturing company, and a percussion hire business. See www.gbzperc.co.uk.

New artistic projects: some methods of proceeding

Based on the experience of mounting successful concerts, producing records, providing the blueprints for new music courses, and even helping design purpose-built facilities for music, **Jonathan Little** codifies the main points to be considered when co-ordinating a new music-based project.

Initial thoughts

In developing any new artistic project, try first to determine if/how that particular project fits into a broader, long-term (e.g. three- to five-year) growth strategy for the individual or organisation concerned. (This strategy may have as its aim simply the goal of increasing 'prestige', or reputation – though it may also be considerably more complex and ambitious than that.) If, on reflection, the project does not seem to contribute substantially to the development of the relevant individual or organisation, then determine exactly *why* you are doing it: perhaps there may be an alternative, more productive project that you could undertake.

Early stages in the process of developing a new 'project'

● Consider if a certain project/angle might be more likely than others to gain the attention of press, audiences, record companies, promoters, etc. What is unique, different, or striking about this particular project? Try to articulate the answer in one short phrase or sentence.

● Agree upon a project that inspires most of the parties involved – especially the audience. Is the project 'audience-facing' (i.e. customer-facing)? Not all are, and almost all should be. You ignore your potential audience's needs at your peril!

● Try to work with other organisations/individuals during their 'career growth' phase, and/or with the will and resources to help you develop.

● Is the *aim* of your project clear, and do all parties understand this? Are they in agreement with your aim, or are there any internal organisational contradictions to be overcome/ resolved?

● Opening the path

● Begin to document/refine your ideas and related opportunities in writing. Ask those with experience in the relevant field to comment upon your ideas.

● Undertake thorough research, and consult fully with all interested parties. The research phase may initially be a slow process, but remember the tortoise and the hare; it is vital to future success. Don't miss or ignore any aspects of detail; find out what the various potential parties/partners really want, or need, to achieve – and remember that this may not be necessarily what they first think or say. *Don't* assume that you know!

● Find out exactly who needs to be involved in the project in order to maximise success. And find out who ultimately has the authority to make relevant crucial decisions each step of the way. Then, talk to these people in person, and try to establish a good relationship with them.

● Try to canvass support from any interested or influential parties, and indeed 'sponsors' of all types (not necessarily just commercial sponsors) before the project officially goes forward, or is launched.

- Build an economic case to justify the project, and also compile a budget. Present two or more cost options – more and less expensive – and work from there.

When all of the above has been achieved, only then should you present a firm proposal that has had prior approval, at least in principle, from all the interested parties – and one which is unique, and worthwhile for all. Ideally, something truly inspirational.

Making it happen

Be honest in making sure that there are benefits for all parties involved in the project. Try clearly to address everyone's needs; you may need to be gently persistent in pursuing the parties who are contributing to the project, and in making the proposal so attractive that they themselves want to push ahead with it. Try to gain an understanding of the needs of the conductor, Musical Director or band leader, performers, audience/supporters, sponsors, agents, venue managers, promoters, and official music bodies. If you are to succeed, they must be happy.

When meeting the various representatives as the project takes shape, take/show hard evidence of previous or related high-quality work. Always present your track record in the best possible light! You can volunteer to assist other parties/organisations, through your own participation in the very stimulating programme or project you have developed. Show that your reputation and contribution will be a considerable asset to all concerned.

Timeline and clarity

Be clear about what will happen,and when, at every stage of the process towards achieving your project goal. Set small, step-by-step 'targets', and uncover the various minor hurdles that must be overcome on the way to your major goal.

Plan your campaign and actions in as much detail as possible, taking into account your initial research as well as the needs and strengths of all parties. If, however, an outstanding opportunity arises unexpectedly, be prepared to seize on it at once if it helps to secure your goal (i.e. don't develop a plan that is so inflexible that it takes no account of change or opportunity – but do keep everyone informed all the way).

Finally, be sure to delivery a quality product on time, and with the least possible fuss. Once your project is complete, endeavour to remain on the best of terms with all parties involved – if only for the sake of developing increasingly strong partnerships in the future, and fostering further opportunities. And be slightly more ambitious with every exciting new project!

Jonathan Little was Principal of the Academy of Contemporary Music during its dramatic growth phase (2001-2006). He also helped to establish the first contemporary music degree course in Italy. He was previously Senior Lecturer at Buckinghamshire University College on their innovative Music Industry Management course (the first such degree course in Europe), where he specialised in the workings of the British and international recording industry, and taught songwriting analysis.

Performing and teaching

Many performers and other musicians supplement their income – at least at some stage in their career – by teaching privately, or in institutions of various types. Indeed, many musicians find teaching so fulfilling that they choose to pursue it as a full-time vocation. **Louise Jackson** outlines what is involved in various present-day music teaching roles.

The importance of music education

A truly creative teacher may be the main inspiration behind the choice to follow a career in music. And sometimes, the opposite can also be the case. If someone has a bad experience with music or music education, it may cause them to dislike music! A very few musicians are self-taught, but for anyone with a deep and abiding interest in the music, the value of a good music teacher to one's creativity and general well-being cannot be overestimated.

There is a common misconception that you can't both teach and follow a career as a musician. The reality of the relationship between teaching and performing is that it is not, in fact, mutually exclusive, and most musicians will at some point in their lives teach music. The importance of music education was felt so strongly by the virtuoso violinist Yehudi Menuhin that he established a specialist school for musically gifted children in Surrey. Menuhin provides us with an example of a musician who certainly had no need to supplement his income through teaching. Rather, he taught because of his love of music and overwhelming need to encourage others in their own enjoyment of music – a discipline which he also insisted had a profound and civilising influence on society.

Why do musicians teach?

Besides providing regular income, there is great personal satisfaction to be gained from hearing someone write his or her first song, play that really difficult piece well, or perform in front of an audience. Looked at in this light, a music teacher is effectively paid to talk about something they love – and how many people can actually say that about their job?

A teacher may potentially get more holidays, and the working conditions generally tend to be better than in many other jobs. However, it is important to take the task of educating students seriously. It won't be a success if students (who are instinctively perceptive) feel that you regard them as a meal ticket! Your pupils will be relying on you to open up the whole world of music to them. Try to be patient with them, and don't neglect areas you don't particularly like yourself.

Before embarking on any form of teaching, it is worth thinking about a music teacher who particularly inspired you, and considering how they did it. What qualities did *they* have that really made you admire them? If you have never had formal music training, consider from what advice you might have benefited.

Routes into teaching

Generally, the routes into various types of teaching could be said to be similar. Teaching privately relies heavily on reputation and word of mouth, and in post-compulsory education you have to get yourself known – either by a strong professional reputation, or by having networked with the local educational providers. Any educational provider (whether school, college, or university) will require you to have some form of qualification and/or professional experience.

Private teaching: instrumental and theory

To teach privately, you are not currently required to have any qualifications at all; you set your own hourly fee, and this, generally, is how most musicians begin teaching (in order to bolster their income). Private teaching is ruled by the law of customer demand: it is up to your student (and/or their parents) to decide if you have the capability to teach! Usually, some ads in the local shop and nearby music shops will start you off, and if you're working from home, you can get a free single line in the *Yellow Pages* (which is usually well worth it).

There are many online music teacher directories, and to advertise or be listed in these is often free. By law, you are required to have some form of Public Liability Insurance – in case anyone has an accident on your property, or on the property where you choose to teach. This insurance can be expensive, but if you join an organisation such as the Incorporated Society of Musicians (ISM), then you are automatically covered by their insurance (and entitled to legal and financial advice as well).

You may have to provide instruction on your chosen instrument or instruments at various levels – from beginner to advanced level; and you may also decide to teach music theory or tutor GCSE music. While you can choose the style of music you teach, again you may have to be flexible and respect the requirements of each individual student (by tailoring your teaching to fit their needs). It is quite usual for a private teacher to enter students for Grade and Diploma examinations, but this is done at your discretion. You don't have to if you don't want to.

A possible downside to teaching privately is potentially not being paid should a student fail to turn up for their lesson. This situation can be avoided if you draw up a general contract between yourself and the student, stating that you reserve the right to charge for any missed lessons (unless adequate notice is given), and that you require payment in advance: monthly, half-termly or termly payments are usual. You must ensure that you keep a record of payments so you can submit an accurate tax return. As you will be classed as Self-Employed, it is important to keep thorough records, and unless you are experienced with numbers, paperwork, and all the legal requirements (not the strength of most musicians!), it is well worth drawing upon the services of an accountant. An accountant will often save you much time, worry, and perhaps a hefty fine if your tax return is late or just plain wrong.

You can also feel quite isolated as a private teacher, but networking with other local teachers can help avoid this, besides providing you with a platform to discuss ideas. Also, putting yourself forward for one of the many qualifications the music exam boards now offer can help keep you up-to-date with methods and repertoire, and enhance your teaching methods.

School teaching: peripatetic instrumental and vocal teaching

'Peris' can be employed either directly by a school, or by the local area Music Service. (The word 'peripatetic' derives from a Greek word referring to wandering scholars: Aristotle's students would learn their lessons while following him as he talked and strolled around the shady garden groves of the Lyceum.) You don't always need to be a qualified teacher to be a 'peri' – but you often need some form of degree or diploma (although this may be at the discretion of the school or music service). However, you will have to agree to the school or music service carrying out a police Criminal Records Bureau (CRB) check. It is now a legal requirement that this be done before you are allowed to work with children. Local Music Services will tend to accept unsolicited CVs – which they may choose to keep on file – and schools also tend to advertise in the local paper when they need to recruit an instrumental or vocal teacher.

The role of a peripatetic teacher varies greatly from school to school, and from region to region: such variability is often a result of regional differences in funding. You may find yourself teaching individuals or small groups on your instrument in rapid succession (for sometimes as little as 15 minutes each, though more usually for 20-30 minutes). The constraints of teaching for so short a time require careful planning of lessons, in order to maximise the students' experience.

The requirements of peripatetic teaching tend to be very similar to that of private instrumental or vocal teaching, except that you will often find yourself preparing students for school concerts and shows, writing reports on student progress, and having to enter students for an exam at least once a year. Schools and Music Services tend to organise in-house career development for all teaching staff, and you may be salaried, or paid automatically by the number of students per hour, or given an hourly rate to claim periodically on a time sheet. This sounds confusing, but it represents the difference between having to fill in a time sheet once a month, or receiving a pre-agreed amount of money per month. The time sheet is not generally a problem, provided you remember to keep a record of who has and hasn't turned up for lessons.

School teaching: in the classroom

Classroom teaching offers the security of a regular salary, but will not leave you much time to pursue outside musical interests. To become a primary or secondary music teacher you will need a degree in music and a Postgraduate Certificate in Secondary Education (PGCE), or to have completed a Graduate Training Programme (GTP) or a degree in teacher education that gives you Qualified Teacher Status (QTS).

As a primary level teacher (4 to 11 years old) you are required to teach a general curriculum, including English, Maths and Science; Music forms only part of that curriculum. Teaching at a secondary school involves specialist teaching, and working within National Curriculum guidelines relating to what students are supposed to be learning. You prepare students for Key Stage 3 and GCSE exams, and teach performing, composing and listening. You might find yourself spending your evenings preparing arrangements of pop songs for the school orchestra to play, arranging and organising student concerts, and timetabling instrumental lessons, as well as preparing your own individual lessons. You become in a sense a 'jack-of-all-trades', in a contemporary climate where there is now some pressure for students to achieve their best possible academic grades. Although there has been some recent government investment in music, there is still a general shortage of people going into school music teaching, or primary teachers who are qualified in music.

Teaching in post-compulsory education

Education beyond secondary level can be divided into Further Education (FE) and Higher Education (HE). FE Colleges deal with A/AS-Levels, BTECS and Higher National Diploma (HND) qualifications in music – in areas such as music technology, sound production, and performing arts. HE embraces undergraduate to postgraduate qualifications. Your level of expertise is expected to be greater at this level of teaching, and a postgraduate qualification is very useful in order to move into FE teaching. In fact, a postgraduate degree is usually a minimum requirement in order to teach in HE. In FE teaching, you may find yourself either in the classroom, delivering lessons related to the syllabus, or teaching one-to-one instrumental or vocal lessons. The types of teaching roles in FE are fairly similar to those in school teaching, but a greater depth of knowledge is required.

In HE, you tend to teach in your own specialist area – which could be anything from 'contrapuntal harmony' to 'wave synthesis' – depending on your background, the course and the department! You may find yourself writing new modules as part of an undergraduate degree, and also pushing back the boundaries of knowledge in your specialist field(s). You are often expected to publish articles and essays, or to continue working in some professional capacity, which may include giving recitals or composing music. Again, there are opportunities for instrumental and vocal teachers within HE, but you will need an impressive professional CV to be contracted to undertake such prestigious work.

Music examiner

Being an examiner is one of the more peculiar jobs in music teaching. Many teachers will have spent hours preparing students to sit a grade exam ... but imagine being on the other side of the table. There are usually quite strict procedures for employing an examiner, and you must be able to demonstrate a high level of musical understanding. To become an examiner, you often need to undertake rigorous training with whichever exam board has hired you. You are required to possess some keyboard and computer skills in order to implement supplementary tasks in the exam, especially as the traditionally illegible hand-writing of examiners – like that of doctors – is increasingly being frowned upon!

Making a difference

The world of music education can be as diverse and entertaining as music itself. Although the job can frequently be demanding on time and energies, harnessing or cultivating the raw talent of students can be the most satisfying and stimulating experience a musician can have. It is important to remember, too, that there are many more areas of music education than have already been mentioned – including Music Therapy and Community Music Projects. Teaching not only provides a source of income for musicians, but enables them to help different people gain some enjoyment out of music. Perhaps *you* may even be the one to inspire a pupil to pursue an enriching and rewarding career in music.

Louise Jackson, BA (Hons), MA (Sussex), is an Associate Lecturer in Music at the University of Chichester – an institution with a distinguished history as a teacher training institution. She has taught piano, singing and music theory in private schools, in state schools, and at Sixth Form Colleges, and also run a music teacher agency. Besides lecturing on theory and musicology, she composes music for theatre and dance companies.

Resources

Choral Performance: A Guide to Historical Practice
Author Steven Plank
Publisher Scarecrow Press, 2004
ISBN 0810851415

A concise starting point for understanding various aspects of historical choral performance practice – especially as they relate to liturgical styles of the Renaissance. Issues of timbre, tempo, ensemble, ornamentation, and pitch are discussed in this work intended to broaden the understanding of both contemporary choral performers and conductors.

The Gigging Musician: How to Get, Keep and Play the Gig
Author Billy Mitchell
Publisher Backbeat, 2001
ISBN 0879306343

A highly practical overview of the considerations necessary in order to initiate and build a career as a gigging musician.

The Historical Performance of Music: An Introduction
Authors Colin Lawson, Robin Stowell
Publisher Cambridge University Press, 1999
ISBN 0521627389

A concise overview of historical performance, which emphasises practical considerations relating to early instrumental and vocal treatises, and also mainstream classical repertory. Historical bases for artistic decision-making are examined – with the aim of re-creating performances as closely as possible to the composer's original conception. Relates many of the issues discussed to major works by Bach, Mozart, Berlioz and Brahms, composed around 1700 to 1900. (A 'parent' volume for the series, *Cambridge Handbooks to the Historical Performance of Music*.)

Mastering the Art of Performance: A Primer for Musicians
Author Stewart Gordon
Publisher Oxford University Press, 2006

ISBN 0195177436

An introductory book of advice and exercises for musicians on conquering the demands of music performance, from planning and preparatory stages through to actual performance, evaluation, and cultivation of a life devoted to performance.

The Performance of Popular Music: History, Place and Time
Editor Ian Inglis
Publisher Ashgate, 2006
ISBN 0754640574

A historical/contextual examination of selected popular musical performances that became hugely influential in the way they shaped the subsequent development of popular music – introducing new styles, confronting existing practices, and shifting accepted definitions. International scholars examine how it is often through the interaction between performer and audience that patterns of musical change and innovation are recognised. Ranges through the Beatles and Bob Dylan to Michael Jackson and Madonna, from Woodstock and Monterey to Altamont and Live Aid.

Singing and the Actor (2nd edn)
Author Gillyanne Kayes
Publisher A&C Black, 2004
ISBN 0713668237

Well-regarded and well-rounded introduction to theatrical and popular music vocal performance, following the author's specially created, structured training programme for the 'singing actor and dancer'. Pitching, registers and breath management, the communication of sung text and the production of belt, twang and speech qualities are covered. Initial chapters cover the nature of the vocal instrument. Also incorporates exercises on each topic.

DJs
Introduction

The role and profile of the DJ have evolved enormously over the last few decades. The most gifted of DJs have set important trends, and even influenced the way in which music is created and heard. DJ-ing today has its own special environment and terminology – and, of course, as a new 'musical discipline' it embraces a whole realm of cutting-edge technological and business factors. Clearly, it's no longer just about playing records! The DJ's world often sits on the cusp of the latest musical trends, and therefore a DJ needs to be at the heart of a local community's musical tastes. What is 'hot' one month may not be the next, so all DJs need the capacity to change gear, venue, city, or even country if need be, as fashion dictates.

As for staying abreast of developments, magazines like *DJ* and *Mixmag* have now passed their 15th birthdays, and so are well-established today. (Both started out as newsletters which provided basic information and general industry updates for DJs.) *DJ* and *IDJ* are read regularly by many budding and professional DJs; *Music Week* magazine places the whole industry in its business context; and *Sound on Sound* covers most of the production issues likely to be of relevance to DJs – as well as, naturally, being of great use to producers and music technologists.

The DJ market is certainly highly competitive: as with any performer, you need some special quality to justify your place in the musical world. Increasingly, discerning audiences are expecting innovation and novelty of sound, as well as depth of musical knowledge. It is no longer enough to be able to mix well, even if this skill is allied to a talent for generating excitement in a crowd.

Many specialist club DJs may well have gained vital early experience by obtaining radio slots, and compiling programmes for different audiences. All opportunities to learn the craft of turntablism should be seized. For some DJs, success in the field of radio leads to a resident show or other job – although the fact that a job in radio is often the exception, rather than the rule, in the world of the contemporary DJ does demonstrate how much the industry has changed. Today's DJ fulfils a role that can range from live performer in front of dozens of people every night, to that of highly respected producer of specialist dance records.

As for any performing musician, the concept of having a clearly defined 'image' is crucial. In name, and in look, a DJ needs to appear as cool (if not cooler) than the coolest musician; image is a vital ingredient in commanding the audience's 'respect'. And besides a very overt public image, every DJ should have the backing of a strong biography. A typical bio sheet might be headed with your contact details (name, address, email and contact numbers), then include a few lines on your background, your style (in music, as well as what particularly characterises you as a DJ), highlights about the most important club nights or events at which you play/have played (including a current Top 20 of your favourite tracks), and perhaps a line or two of quotes from respected independent commentators. And – of course – you need to include a striking showreel: the best mix CD you currently possess, labelled with your full contact details.

A DJ capable of innovative programming and of mixing well can earn a good living. The mark of a good DJ might be said to be that of possessing the skill for presenting consistently – every night – a good mix or set.

Yet just staying on top of new technology can be a challenge. Indeed, the DJ industry was founded upon the ability of enterprising individuals to take existing technology, then to develop and use it for their own particular creative ends. The turntable and the sampler, for instance, were never specifically intended for use by DJs, but they are today essential tools in the armoury of any DJ.

As with all other music industry roles, it is imperative to socialise with and learn from as many well-respected, working DJs as possible (and indeed other music industry professionals). Networking is vital. A DJ needs to self-promote as much as anyone else in the music profession, in order to obtain those vital bookings. As part of making a name in the industry, it's often a good idea to start your own night (ensuring that everything about it is very much *your own*) – whether in a club, bar or house party. Drive, determination, and the ability to create a special musical 'aura' are essential qualities for the DJ – who must necessarily get out into the thick of things night after night, displaying brilliant technical skills and the ability to read a crowd like some new musical gladiator.

Equipment manufacturers, retailers and distributors

Ableton

Ableton, Schönhauser Allee 6-7, D-10119 Berlin, Germany
tel +49 030-288 7630 *fax* +49 030-288 763 11
email contact@ableton.com
website www.ableton.com

Established in 1999 and put live on the market in 2001. Developers, manufacturers and sellers of the multi-award-winning Live Production software, which allows DJs and musicians to create, produce and perform their music. The majority of the software developers are also DJs and musicians.

AC Lighting (Audio Division)

Hawksworth Commercial Centre, Elder Road, Leeds LS13 4AT
tel 0113-256 7666 *fax* 0113-255 7676
email audiosales@aclighting.com
website www.aclighting.com
Audio Sales Manager Peter Butler

Established in 1970. Stocks hundreds of leading-brand audio products and accessories. Will provide custom-assembled audio racks and all types of system cabling to suit specific requirements. Items stocked include: amplifiers, cable and stage boxes, in-ear monitoring systems, loudspeakers, recording equipment, microphones and mixers.

Akai

Unit 9, The Christie Estate, Ivy Road, Aldershot GU12 4TX
tel (01252) 341400 *fax* (01252) 353810
email support@akaipro.com
website www.akaipro.com

Established in 1984. Renowned for achievements in the manufacture of digital sampling equipment, pad controllers for drum and percussion sampling, MIDI sequencing and recording equipment.

Alesis

Unit 9, The Christie Estate, Ivy Road, Aldershot GU12 4TX
tel (01252) 341400 *fax* (01252) 353810
email nbutcher@alesis.com
website www.alesis.com
Sales Manager N Butcher

Founded in 1998. Manufactures professional audio and musical instrument products. Production includes: keyboards, hard disk recorders, mixers, signal processors, effects units, electronic drums, amplifiers, synthesisers and speakers.

Audio Technica Ltd

Technica House, Royal London Industrial Estate, Old Lane, Leeds, West Yorkshire LS11 8AG
tel 0113-277 1441 *fax* 0113-270 4836
email sales@audiotechnica.co.uk
website www.audio-technica.co.uk
Managing Director Adrian Rooke *Sales Director* Tony Cooper

Founded in 1978. UK and European distributor of Audio-Technica products such as microphones, headphones, audio accessories, styluses and cartridges. Also provides warranty and non-warranty repairs, after-sales support and technical advice for all Audio Technica products.

Audio Visual

3 Grange Way Business Park, Grange Way, Colchester, Essex CO2 8HF
tel (01206) 798000
email info@getinthemix.co.uk
website www.getinthemix.co.uk

Retailer founded circa 1993. Stocks a range of specialist DJ equipment including CD and deck mixers, speakers, lighting, turntables and mics. Brands stocked include: Alesis, Numark and Technics. Offers next working day delivery. *Opening Hours*: Mon to Sat: 10am – 5.30pm (shop); 7 days a week, 10am – 10pm (order online).

Behringer

Behringer International GmbH, Hanns-Martin-Schleyer-Str, 36-38 47877 Willich
tel +49 2154 9206 *fax* +49 2154 9206 4199
email via website
website www.behringer.com

Manufacturers of professional DJ mixers, DJ effects modules and headphones. The company was founded in 1989 in Germany and currently has offices in 10 countries.

Celestion

Claydon Business Park, Great Blakenham, Ipswich, Suffolk IP6 0NL
tel (01473) 835300
email info@celestion.com
website www.celestion.com
Contact Kevin Shove

Global manufacturer of professional loudspeakers to the music industry, DJs, recording studios and musicians.

Citronic

c/o SkyTronic Ltd, Containerbase, Barton Dock Road, Manchester M41 7BQ

email via website
website www.citonic.co.uk

Has 30 years' of experience supplying the professional DJ market. UK manufacturer of DJ turntables, amplifiers, rack-mounted/desk mixers, crossfaders, domestic/rehearsal loudspeakers, performance loudspeakers, CD players, gooseneck lights, microphones, headphones and a range of lighting units.

db Technologies

AEB Srl, Via Brodolini 8, 40056 Crespellano (Bo), Italy
tel 0039 051 969870 *fax* 0039 051 969725
email info@dbtechnologies-aeb.com
website www.dbtechnologies-aeb.com

Established more than 25 years ago; manufactures professional stereo amplifiers, active and passive speakers for studio, performance and recreation, and large-scale professional public address systems for performance and in-situ practice areas, etc. Also produces receivers and in-ear headphones.

Denon

D&M Professional, Americas,
1100 Maplewood Drive, Itasca, IL 60143
tel 001-866 405 2154 or (01753) 680023
email techsupport@d-mpro.eu.com
website www.denondj.com

Design and manufacture of industry-specific DJ turntables, faders, analogue/digital mixers, headphones, and effects units. Manufacturer to the professional, mobile and occasional DJ.

DJ Box

119 Dartford Road, Dartford, Kent DA1 3EN
tel (01322) 288938 *fax* (01322) 223447
email sales@djbox.co.uk
website www.thedjbox.com

Online shop selling DJ sound lighting and accessories alongside music mix CDs. Contains large stock with brands including Behringer, Pioneer, Denon and Stanton.

DJ Gear

734-736 Oxford Road, Reading RG30 1EH
tel 0118-950 9696 *fax* 0118-950 7072
email sales@djgear.co.uk (Sales) or
docdjgear@djgear.co.uk (Technical Support)
website www.djgear.co.uk

Online store stocking all types of DJ equipment from mixers, turntables and speakers to lighting and even clothing. Brands include: Alesis, Ion, Behringer, Mackie, and db Technologies. Offers discounted mixer and CD-player packages. *Opening Hours*: Mon to Fri: 10am – 6.30pm; Sat: 9am – 6pm (phonelines).

DJ Kit

37 Bartholomew Street, Newbury,
Berkshire RG14 5LL

tel (01635) 580448 *tel* (0845) 458 4434
email sales@djkit.co.uk
website www.djkit.co.uk

Showroom and online store stocking a variety of equipment including CD players, turntables, speakers, microphones and lighting. Brands stocked include: Technics, Vestax, Numark and Pioneer. Also provides online tuition documents. *Opening Hours*: Mon to Fri: 9am – 5pm; Sat: 10am – 4pm.

DJ Superstore

Unit 5, Airborne Industrial Estate,
A127 Arterial Road, Leigh on Sea, Essex SS9 4EX
tel (01702) 520020 *fax* (01702) 520030
email MailDesk@DJSuperstore.co.uk
website www.superstore.co.uk

Established in 1988. Provides full showroom facilities complete with live demonstrations and free parking, alongside online sales. Offers a selection of equipment including decks, mixers, stands and amps. Stocks Numark, Gemini and Stanton among others. *Opening Hours*: Mon, Tues and Thurs: 9am – 9pm; Wed, Fri and Sat: 9am – 6pm.

The DJ Warehouse

Unit 10, Neath Business Park, Neath Abbey,
Neath SA10 7D
tel (08700) 555830
website www.ukdjequipment.co.uk

The DJ Warehouse is the webtrading name for Ent UK Ltd – Internet DJ equipment retailer. Provides a range of speakers, mixers, amps, lighting and turntables. Brands stocked include: Numark, Sennheiser, Alesis and Behringer. *Opening Hours*: (phonelines) Mon, Wed, Thur and Fri: 11am – 6pm; Sat: 11am – 4pm.

Ecler

Miltec (UK) Ltd, Unit 1, Laddingford Farm,
Darman Lane, Laddingford, Maidstone,
Kent ME18 6BL
tel (01622) 873378
email david.faulkes@miltec.org.uk
website www.eclerdjdivision.com or
www.miltec.org.uk
Contact Mr David Faulkes

Manufacturer of specialist DJ mixing consoles.

Exclusive Distribution

Fostex

SCV London, 40 Chigwell Lane,
Oakwood Hill Industrial Estate, Loughton,
Essex IG10 3NY
tel 020-8418-0778 *fax* 020-8418-0624
email fostex@scvlondon.co.uk
website www.fostexinternational.com

Manufacturer of digital/analogue multi-trackers, digital effects units, DAT recorders, DVD-RAM, field recorders, studio monitors and performance speakers, PA speakers, microphones, headphones, headphone amps and speaker components.

Gemini

Gemini Sound Products Ltd,
Unit C4 Hazelton Industrial Estate,
Waterlooville PO8 9JU
tel 011-44-87-087-00880 *fax* 011-44-87-087-00990
email sales@geminidj.co.uk
website www.geminidj.com

Established in 1974 and possessing many dealer outlets. Manufacturer of comprehensive and specific DJ systems including mixers, CD/MP3 players/recorders, turntables, road cases, headphones and performance amplifiers, rehearsal and recording speakers/bass units. Specialises in replacement cartridges and styluses.

Guildford Sound and Light

Moorfield Road, Slyfield Green, Guildford,
Surrey GU1 1RB
tel (01483) 502121 *fax* (01483) 301314
email sales@guildfordsl.com
website www.djdeals.co.uk

Founded in 1994. Showroom and online store providing a wide collection of DJ sound and lighting equipment. Offers discounted packages on Technics CD and deck packs. Brands stocked include: Alesis, Vestax, Gemini and Numark. *Opening Hours:* (showroom) Mon to Fri: 10am – 6pm; Sat: 10am – 5pm.

Hard to Find Records

Vinyl House, 10 Upper Gough Street,
Birmingham B1 1JG
tel 0121-687 7777 *fax* 0121-687 7774
email sales@htfr.com
website www.htfr.com
General Manager John MacDonald

Founded in 1991. Offers a wide range of equipment including turntables, mixers, amplifier and music production equipment and software. Technics, Vestax, Stanton, Pioneer, Sony and Sennheiser are among many brands stocked. Also supplies a record-finding agency, compilation album consultancy and DJ training courses.

Ion

1536 West Twenty Fifth Street #333 San Pedro,
CA 90732
tel 001-310 832 9100
email info@ions.com
website www.ions.com

American manufacturer of a range of professional DJ-ing equipment including turntables, DJ MP3/CD units, CD duplicators, headphones, microphones, PA systems for performance and studio, turntable cartridges and hard cases for records, CDs and hardware.

JB's Music

108-110 St James Road, Tunbridge Wells,
Kent TH1 2HH
tel (01892) 515007 *fax* (01892) 515602
email info@jbsmusic.co.uk
website www.jbsmusic.com

Stocks DJ amps, decks and mixers alongside musical instrument beginners' packs and accessories, recording equipment and music software. Brands stocked include: Numark, Alesis, Technics, Pioneer, Stanton, and Ministry of Sound.

Kam

Lamba plc, Unit 1, Southfields Road, Dunstable,
Bedfordshire LU6 3EJ
tel (01582) 690600 *fax* (01582) 690400
email info@kam.co.uk or sales@kam.co.uk
website www.kam.co.uk

Specialist manufacturer of professional mixing units – rack- and desk-mounted, rehearsal and performance turntables, CD players/mixers, speakers and amplifiers, rack-mounted processors, microphones and flight cases for records and hardware, etc. Kam is designed, manufactured and distributed by Lamba plc; the company does not sell direct to the public. Check website for resellers and dealers.

Lightstorm Trading

14 Forest Hill Business Centre, Clyde Vale,
London SE23 3JF
tel 020-8699 6788 *fax* 020-8699 5056
email sales@lightstormtrading.co.uk
website www.lightstormtrading.co.uk
Director Rod Bartholomeusz

Founded in 1996. Provides lighting for the entertainment industry. Stocks and distributes most major brands of lighting equipment products, including: Celco, Anytronics, CCT, Ceep, Clay Paky, Doughty, Pulsar, Optikinetics and Philips.

Mackie

2 Blenheim Court, Hurricane Way, Wickford,
Essex SS11 8YT
tel (01268) 571212 *fax* (01268) 570809
email lesley.honeywood@mackie.com
website www.mackie.com
Contact Lesley Honeywood

American manufacturer of a range of professional DJ-ing equipment, including digital recording and mixing equipment, analogue/digital mixing desks and performance mixers, studio and on-stage mixers and effects modules, amplifiers, rehearsal and performance speaker units, studio monitors. Also redistributes DJ and recording software.

Numark

Unit 9, The Christie Estate, Ivy Road,
Aldershot GU1 24TX
tel (01252) 341400 *fax* (01252) 353810

email info@numark.com
website www.numark.com

Over 30 years' industry experience. Utilises the experience of professional DJs to design turntables, etc. Manufactures the following professional DJ equipment: turntables, cartridge units, portable and desk mixers, amplifiers, CD/MP3 players, hard drives, microphones, headphones, recording and sampling software, and comprehensive DJ packages for students.

Pioneer

Hollybush Hill, Stoke Poges, Slough, Buckinghamshire SL2 4QP
tel (01753) 789789
email via website
website www.pioneerprodj.com

Manufacturer of digital vinyl turntables, DVD turntables, digital media players, dual CD players, headphones, flat-panel portable performance speakers, mixers, and DJ accessories and performance-ready Pro DJ Systems.

RANE

Rane Corporation, 10802 47th Avenue West, Mukilteo, WA 98275
tel 001-425 355-6000 *fax* 001-425 347 7757
email info@rane.com
website www.rane.com

Manufacturer of professional equipment including compressors, limiters, gates, crossovers, delays, amplifiers, graphic equalisers, parametric equalisers, DJ mixers, microphone pre-amps, headphone amplifiers, loudspeaker amplifiers and accessories.

Sapphires Sound and Light

Burlington Parade, Edgware Road, Cricklewood NW2 6QG
tel 020-8960 8989 *fax* 020-8960 8990
email info@decks.co.uk
website www.decks.co.uk

Shop trader established circa 1991 and operating under the webtrading name of Decks. Also offers a variety of specialist DJ equipment, including discounted packages. Stocks Mackie, Korg, Stanton, Technics, Alesis, Numark and Pioneer.

Sennheiser Ltd

3 Century Point, Halifax Road, High Wycombe, Bucks HP12 3SL
tel (01494) 551551 *fax* (01494) 551550
email via website
website www.sennheiser.co.uk

Manufacturer of sound-recording and professional audio-performance equipment, including headphones and headsets, conference and information systems, public address systems, microphones for public address and professional studio microphones for recording, and wireless communication systems.

Shure Distribution

167-171 Willoughby Lane, London N17 0SB
tel 020-8808 2222 *fax* 020-8808 5599
website www.shure.com

Manufacturer of wired microphones for the entertainment industry and recording studios, wireless performance systems, mixers and digital signal processors for studio, performance and in-the-field, earphones and headphones, DJ record styluses and Hi-Fi/turntable cartridges and professional cabling.

Shuttlesound

4 The Willow Centre, Willow Lane, Mitcham, Surrey CR4 4NX
tel 020-8646 7114 *fax* 020-8254 5666
website www.shuttlesound.com
Sales Director Sean Maxwell

Founded in 1979. Retailer of Pro Audio equipment including speakers, amplifiers and microphones. ElectroVoice, Midas and Klark Teknik are among main brands stocked.

Skytronic

Unit 11 HiTech Village, Superior Close, Midrand, South Africa
tel 011-805 9910 *fax* 011-805 9930
website www.skytronic.co.za

South African manufacturer of DJ turntables, DJ CD players, smoke machines, lighting units, mixers and lighting controllers, loud speakers and public address systems.

Stageline

Stageline Electronics, Bochumer Landstrasse 121, D-45276 Essen, Germany
tel +49 201 500 933 *fax* +49 201 501 171
website www.stageline.de
Contact Martin Gödde

German manufacturer of event lighting units, strobe lighting and professional industrial lighting for concert venues, etc.

Stanton

tel (01494) 416326
email ukservice@stantonmagnetics.co.uk
website www.stantondj.com

Founded in 1946. Manufacturer of rack-mounted, desk and portable mixers, cross-faders, turntables, cartridges, CD players, headphones, DJ packages, accessories and DJ software.

Stirling Trading (UK) Ltd

Unit 5, The Chase Centre, 8 Chase Road, London NW10 6QD
tel 020-8963 4790 *fax* 020-8963 4799
email info@stirlingtrading.com
website www.stirlingtrading.com
Managing Director Andrew Stirling

Provides a comprehensive range of software and hardware for studio and live applications. Distributor and exclusive supplier for Aphex, Audient, Audix, Avantone, Bricasti, Enhanced Audio, ETA Systems, Hear Technologies, iZ, Metric Halo, NHT, Otari, Pro Booth, Sanken, SPL, Summit and Taytrix. Offers a part-exchange programme on certain products and holds a 'used gear' stock which can be viewed on the website.

Tannoy

Coatbridge, North Lanarkshire ML5 4TF
tel (01236) 420199 *fax* (01236) 428230
website www.tannoy.com

Founded in 1930. Manufacturer of specialist and commercial loudspeaker systems and PA announcing systems, studio monitors, amplifiers, subwoofers and arena sound systems.

Tascam

TEAC UK Ltd, Units 19 & 20, The Courtyards, Hatterslane, Watford, Hertfordshire WD18 8TE
tel 0845-130 2511 or (01923) 236290
website www.tascam.de

Global manufacturer of professional audio equipment and DJ equipment, including stereo recording/playback equipment, mobile mixers, DJ CD players, headphone amplifiers, studio monitors, hard-disk multitrack recorders, and high-definition mastering equipment.

Technics

tel (08705) 357357
website www.panasonic.co.uk

Celebrating 30 years of successful manufacturing in Europe. Manufacturer of professional DJ turntables, cartridges, DJ headphones, monitor headphones, mixers, and CD DJ turntables.

Total Sounds

50 Station Hill, Reading RG1 1NF
tel 0118-951 0050
email sales@totalsounds.co.uk
website www.totalsounds.co.uk

Online and shop showroom sales. Stocks a wide range of DJ equipment and goods for beginners through to experienced professionals; bestsellers include: Stanton, Vestax, Numark and Kam products. *Opening Hours*: (shop) Mon to Fri: 10am – 6pm; Wed: closed; Sat: 10am – 5:30pm; Sun: closed.

Turnkey

114-116 Charing Cross Road, London WC2H 0JR
email barry.smyth@turnkey.co.uk
website www.turnkey.co.uk
Sales Manager Barry Smyth

Landmark store founded in 1978. Aims to help the recording musician get the best results by delivering the latest equipment with great service and advice. Provides a range of DJ and recording equipment alongside musical instruments and computer software. Stocks Behringer, Pioneer, Numark and Vestax brands among many others. *Opening Hours*: Mon to Wed: 10am – 6pm; Thurs: 10am – 7pm; Fri to Sat: 10am – 6pm.

UDG

UDG/Ultimate DJ Gear,
Van Oldenbarneveldtstraat 109, 6827 AM, Arnhem, The Netherlands
tel +31 (0)26 370 60 74
email info@ultimate-dj-gear.com
website www.ultimate-dj-gear.com

Manufacturer of hardware carry bags (CD player/turntable, etc.), CD and record wallets, cases, courier bags, sling bags and record boxes.

Vestax

Vestax Europe Ltd, Unit 5, Riverway Industrial Park, Alton, Hampshire GU34 2QL
tel (01420) 83000 *fax* (01420) 83040
email info@vestax.com
website www.vestax.com

Manufacturer of rack-mounted/desk and portable DJ and studio mixers, CD players, turntables, hybrid musical-instrument controllers, digital controllers, rack effects units, DJ turntable racks, cases, bags, recorders and speakers.

WestendDJ.com

10/12 Hanway Street (off Tottenham Court Road), London W1T 1UB
tel 020-7637 3293 or 020-7636 2179
fax 020-7637 1398
email info@westenddj.com
website www.westenddj.com

Specialises in DJ equipment including carts and styluses, effects and DJ software alongside mixers, amps and decks. Stocks Ableton, Akai, Alesis, Pioneer, Stanton and Vestax among others. Offers good deals on delivery costs. *Opening Hours*: Mon to Sat: 9:30am – 6:30pm; Sun: 11am – 5pm.

DJ agencies

a51 DJ Management
email contact@a51djs.com
website www.a51djs.com

Online booking agency for house, progressive, breaks and techno DJs. DJs represented play regular spots in prestigious clubs such as Bedrock, Spundae, Renaissance, Pacha, Tribal Sessions and Space. Website gives gig updates and MP3 mix downloads from all DJs. Email for membership information.

BPM (Booking Promotion Management)
Unit 205, Saga Centre, 326 Kensal Road,
London W10 5BZ
email bela.molnar@bpmagency.co.uk
website www.bpmagency.co.uk

Roster includes: Anthony Pappa, Quivver and Rowan Blades.

Coda
2nd Floor, 81 Rivington Street, London EC2A 3AY
tel 020-7012 1555 *fax* 020-7012 1566
email agents@codaagency.com
website www.codaagency.com
Agent Phil Banfield

Founded in 2002 following the merging of the MPI and Concert Clinic agencies. DJ roster features names such as David Holmes, Marky, Mr Scruff, Boy George and Roni Size.

Coffee Artists Ltd
5 Weyhill Close, Maidstone, Kent ME14 5SQ
tel (01622) 222222 *fax* (01622) 222223
email admin@coffeeartists.com
website www.coffeeartists.com
Head of DJ Roster Gelli Graham

Part of the Coffee Arts and Media Company. Represents DJs working in the dance, ambient and urban genres. Professional and dedicated DJs working in these genres may post a clearly labelled demo and biography/CV.

Concorde International Artistes Ltd
Concorde House, 101 Shepherd's Bush Road,
Hammersmith, London W6 7AP
tel 020-7602 8822 *fax* 020-7603 2352
email cia@cia.uk.com
website www.cia.uk.com
Directors Soloman Parker, Paul Fitzgerald

Founded circa 1978. Represents musicans in the pop, urban and dance genres. Commission is variable but a standard 10% is taken on all exclusively represented artists. Potential clients should make contact (with showcases/showreels) through management.

Electronic PM
Unit 204, The Saga Centre, 326 Kensal Road,
London W10 5BZ
tel 020-8964 4900 *fax* 020-8964 3600
email oliver@electronicpm.co.uk
website www.electronicpm.co.uk
Partner Oliver Way

Established in 2001. Typically works with techno, electro and house genres. Clients include: DJ Hell, Underground Resistance, and Rob Hood. Booking fee of 15% on top of artist fee. Accepts mix CDs. Aims to work also with producers, not just performers.

Elite Music Management
PO Box 3261, Brighton, East Sussex BN2 4WA
tel (01273) 621999 *fax* (01273) 623999
email info@elitemm.co.uk
website www.elitemm.co.uk
Artist Manager Paul Wells

Founded in 1999. Represents DJs worldwide. Specialises in house music. Commission charged at 15% (plus VAT where applicable). Potential clients may approach via email.

Excession Agency
242 Acklam Road, London W10 5JJ
tel 020-7524 7676 *fax* 020-7524 7677
email joe@excession.co.uk
website www.excession.co.uk
Artist Agent Joe Christie

Founded in 1998. Represents a mixture of 10 leading and break-thru house-tech-progressive genre DJs. Hybrid, James Zabiela, Jan Carbon and Sasha are amongst clients.

Femaledjs.com
Hindol House, Beadles Lane, Oxted, Surrey RH8 9JJ
email info@femaledjs.com
website www.femaledjs.com
Booking Agent Niki Potterton

Works with female DJs worldwide in a range of genres on a subscription basis. If a placement is offered, members pay a subscription of £99 for 1 year. Applicants should send demo and DJ-ing details to Suzie Miller at the above address.

Gremlin UK Ltd
70 Dalnabay, Silverglades, Aviemore,
Highlands PH21 1RG
tel 0870-7487 078 *mobile* (07092) 197823
email enquiries@gremlinuk.com
website www.gremlinuk.com

Represents DJs who work in nightclubs, in venues and at functions across the world. Aims to provide

DJs who cover a range of music genres from hip hop to trance to suit many venues and functions. Lisa Lashes, Miss Roberta, Ryan Morales and DJ Scratch are amongst acts. Accepts applications from top-quality DJs with good reviews and positive DJ-ing history, who have played at major clubs. Members get 24-hour telephone help, free email address and webspace. Potential DJs should email for more information.

International Management Division Ltd
Unit 4C, Bannon Court, 54 Michael Road,
London SW6 2EF
tel 020-7371 0995 *fax* 020-7751 3095
email rachel@imd-info.com
website www.imd-info.com
Director Rachel Birchwood-Gordon

Founded in 1999. Offers support in all areas of artist management such as DJ bookings, production and remix management and press, radio and TV promotions worldwide. Has strong international media contacts and is able to offer PR support for festivals, events and brands worldwide. DJ roster features: Pete Tong, Jeff Mills, Danny Howells and Sandy Rivera, among other high-profile acts. Potential clients should send mixes by post; all other enquiries by email.

MN2S Management
4-7 The Vineyard, Sanctuary Street, London SE1 1QL
tel 020-7378 7321 *fax* 020-7378 6575
email info@mn2s.com
website www.mn2s.com
Director Sharron Elkabas

DJ agency that also houses a record label and event organisation facility. Commission is typically 10-20%. Potential clients should make contact via email.

Most Wanted
PO Box 305, Hayes, London UB4 9SZ
tel (08707) 454940
email lee@mostwanteduk.com
website www.mostwanteddjs.com
Agent Lee Bridle

Clients have included Anne Savage, Blank & Jones, John 00 Fleming, and Robbie Riviera.

Pure DJs
2 Whiting Street, Sheffield, South Yorkshire S8 9QR
tel (01142) 555768 *fax* (01142) 812788
email paul@puredjs.com
website www.puredjs.com
Director Paul Grayson

Founded in 1995. Aims to provide DJs from most genres to clubs and festivals throughout the world. Clients range from independent promotors to corporate and plc companies. Commission charged at 10-18% depending on client. Potential acts should make contact via telephone or email initially.

Represents Artists Management
Office 3, Bannon Court, 54-58 Michael Road,
London SW6 2EF
tel 020-7384 2080 *fax* 020-7384 2055
email vanessa@represents.co.uk
website www.represents.co.uk
Director Vanessa Fontaine

International agency that deals with promoters, record labels and event organisers. Organises bookings for the renowned club night 'Type', internationally. Also supplies management services. Commission is added on top of artist fee. Make contact by email or phone.

Serious Artist Management
website www.seriousworld.com
Promotions Manager Sacha

DJ agency and promotions company. Aims to provide a highly professional service to DJs and their industry. Commission charged at 10%.

Supersexy DJ Agency
email SuperSexy@SuperSexyPromotions.co.uk
website www.supersexypromotions.co.uk

Represents DJs worldwide specialising in funky and tribal house, club classics and trance. Provides a free service to promoters. Website divided into genre-specific sections.

TrusttheDJ.com
White Horse Yard, 78 Liverpool Yard,
London N1 0QD
tel 020-7288 9814 *fax* 020-7288 9817
email contact@trustthedj.com
website www.trustthedj.com

Annie Nightingale, Carl Cox and Dave Angel are amongst clients.

UKDJs
email NewDjs@uk-djs.net
website www.uk-djs.net

Aims to provide club promoters with the ultimate resource for direct booking of talented up-and-coming UK-based DJs. Accepts applications from new DJs (aged 18 to 31) with club and bar experience. Specialisms accepted include house, trance, breaks, techno or club classics. Interested applicants should email at the above address.

Ultra DJ Management
42 City Business Centre, Lower Road,
London SE16 2XB
tel 020-7740 2119 *fax* 020-7394 1139
email info@ultradj.co.uk
website www.ultradj.co.uk
Contact Catherine Mackenzie

Brandon Bloc, Lisa Loud, Leeroy Thornhill, Benny Benassi, Alex P and Sonique are amongst clients.

Making a living as a DJ

Jim Jomoa explains that modern DJ-ing isn't simply about playing records, and getting paid to do it. Today, it is a complex career requiring consistent hard work, diligence, focus and – above all – knowledge. Knowledge is what makes the difference between long-term success and failure in a DJ's career.

The following article is intended to give you an insight into the world of the dance music DJ – the type of DJ who works primarily in clubs. Although we'll touch upon the role of the radio DJ (the term 'disc jockey' originated in radio, of course), we are assuming that you mainly want to earn a living from club nights, and not as the stereotypical Radio 1 DJ – who is effectively a 'behind-the-scenes' presenter.

Ten years ago, this article would have been very much more straightforward in its advice. That was the time – in the mid-1990s – when dance music DJ-ing was at its height. The primary source of work for DJs was club work, and with a worldwide market eager for their skills, DJs could command fees of £1000 and upwards – often for just two hours' work. The other main source of income would be mobile work. Mobile work would involve the DJ having their own sound and lighting equipment, and being able to provide entertainment for anything from weddings to children's parties.

But today the role of the DJ has evolved to become much more complex. Inevitably, technology has had some part to play in this, but the natural evolution of a relatively new and competitive industry, and the need to forge ahead with vital innovations, have been the main drivers of change. So the modern DJ is not only a performing DJ, but also a music producer and businessman (or entrepreneur). Being able to fuse these three roles is key for any individual wanting to succeed as a DJ.

One of the best examples of the new role of the DJ is New York artist Eric Morillio. Having been a successful recording artist, Morillio then set up a record label called Subliminal so that he was able to DJ, produce music, and build a global brand that has included tour merchandising and playing to audiences of 10,000 people in American stadiums. Morillio is able to generate his own work, staying firmly in control of his own destiny. Even on a more modest scale, this is precisely what all professional DJs should aspire towards.

Nightclub work

Nightclub work – or 'club' work, as it is known – remains the mainstay of the DJ's income. There are thousands of clubs in the UK and many more around the world. Looked at from this perspective, you might think that there should be plenty of work for anyone wishing to become a DJ. Unfortunately, this is not really the case. With most clubs, people will turn up with no real interest in who is actually playing the music; as long as it is reasonably good, and they can dance and drink the night away, they are happy. So some clubs may not even feel the need to hire a professional DJ.

Dance clubs, however, work in quite a different way. There, the DJ *is* the attraction, and thousands of 'clubbers' will go to a venue simply because their favourite DJ is playing. Some professional DJs can play 'sets', at different times during a single evening, in up to five clubs – up and down the country – thanks in part to today's more relaxed licensing laws. But to reach these heights, there must first come a lot of hard work and many industry contacts. Frankly, it usually takes about ten years to get there.

The ease with which dance records can be produced makes the high-profile DJ phenomenon a little easier, but becoming a 'Superstar DJ' remains every young DJ's dream. As for pop stars, the dream is only realised by about 5 per cent of professional DJs worldwide.

So how, realistically, are *you* actually going to make a living?

Mobile work

For a young DJ, this is not the most glamorous side of the business. But get it right, and it can lead to a very stable income. There is, of course, some initial outlay; you have to invest in a mobile set-up. A basic mobile set-up will include: decks (CD or vinyl – though CD is now preferred), a PA system, an amplifier, and lights. Initially, you can expect to lay out up to £5000; this also includes money for business cards, a website, and some local advertising. It sounds a lot, but when you consider that for a wedding you can charge £500 once you know what you are doing, you will soon see that this can easily be recouped in a year.

This type of mobile work is often taken up by the older DJ, aged 35 years and upwards (mainly due to the type of music you have to know and play). It is favoured by the DJ who has knowledge of at least two decades of music, and who probably likes to get out at the weekends – perhaps re-living those wild, younger days!

If you are just starting out, mobile work won't be an ideal choice. But if, after 20 years as a DJ, you find that the stock of vinyl in your garage now holds the equivalent in value of a luxury one-bedroom flat, it might be time to consider it as an option and try to get back some of your investment.

Agency work

There are two types of DJ 'agent'. First we'll deal with the kind who will also act as your manager, booking flights and hotels around the world for you as well as arranging your press, and driving you to gigs. These agents are associated with the 'Superstar DJ' (see above): they look after stars like Carl Cox, Sasha, and Danny Rampling. One of the leading agents of this kind is Cosmack, set up by CJ Macintosh and Lyn Cosgrove.

Unless you are an established name, it is very hard to get onto this type of DJ agent's books. This is not because they do not respect your talent; it is simply a matter of business. Such agents charge 15 or 20 per cent of a DJ's fees, so only where a DJ earns at least £2000 a booking and works four or five nights a week does this become a viable proposition. If you are a new DJ who will earn £250 a night a couple of times a month, you are not in a position to warrant this type of agent. Nevertheless, some of these agents do take on 'up and coming' DJs, where they recognise youthful talent and potential. There are two main ways in which you can get recognised:

- *DJ competitions.* It may seem obvious, but only about 15 per cent of young DJs who are trying to get a break actually enter competitions. These can be national or local, and are often run by magazines, clubs, radio or sponsors.
- *Create a name for yourself.* Pester DJ agents; make a record. Whether or not you are successful at competitions, by creating your own publicity you will greatly increase your chances of getting known.

The other main type of agency work is that of the commercial DJ. A huge number of clubs and bars exist in the UK, and a good many of them use DJs. But often these establishments

140 DJs

are nationally based, and form part of quite large corporations, so they don't take on the individual DJs themselves – they use an agent to book them.

As a newcomer to this type of business, you may start by just playing the warm-up set (the first one or two hours when the bar or club has just opened, and the night is yet young). Don't expect too much in your pay packet at this stage: between £25 and £30 is the norm. But if you prove successful at this, you can soon move up to wages of between £300 and £500 a night. I trust this gives you some hope!

Radio

Radio is an industry in itself, and can, for the most part, be seen as a very separate activity from club DJ-ing. It's simply a definition of roles. Modern DJ-ing is primarily about playing records, whereas radio is always more about presentation. The main skill required for radio is in presenting and speaking. In actual fact – and perhaps sad to say – the majority of radio stations now use computers for the selection of music.

So to get into radio, where do you start? Well, local radio or hospital radio stations are best; many a Radio 1 DJ started there. You can approach any hospital or local radio station, and express an interest in being a radio DJ. You will almost certainly be asked to submit a 'showreel' – a demo not only of you playing records, but also of you talking. It is the talking, or the 'link', that will be of most interest to potential employers. The way that you introduce records will be examined – but you might also want to do a news or a weather link, and you may want to create a competition, or create your own 'jingles'.

Creativity is the name of the game in radio; and, again, it is suitable only for a certain proportion of the DJ community. The shy DJ (the DJ who doesn't want to be seen so much, or play live in front of an audience) can, ironically, often find a niche in radio.

Record producer/artist

Most successful DJs eventually want to make their own records. Why? Well, with experience, a DJ comes to know what makes people dance, what type of records they like, and what makes a good record stand out from a bad one. A DJ also learns to be quite creative in the way in which s/he mixes. A good DJ is not simply playing one record after another – they are, in fact, creating a 'third' record, somewhere in the transition.

So a DJ develops convictions about the kind of records that people like to hear, and often then begins to start thinking about becoming a dance-music producer. The quickest and most fruitful way to do this is to link up with a production partner who has engineering skills, while you take on the producer role.

If you are to survive in the long term as a DJ, the production side of the business will be important, as this new revenue stream will not only bring in money from your own productions (typically, an advance of about £1000 per track), but will also then generate remix work (£1000 to £5000 per remix). Finally, the exposure that your record gets is likely to secure you additional DJ work.

A successful record can increase your DJ-ing fee from £500 to £2000 – since you are no longer just a DJ, but a recording artist as well.

Record-label owner

As more people are now making their own dance music, it has become harder to get record labels to agree to take on such records. Within the last few years, dance music has gone from about 100 releases a week to an average today of 300-400. The market is, in fact, becoming saturated. So record companies are spoilt for choice, and often don't need to take a risk on new artists and new material.

The solution, in this case, is simple: set up your own record label! A small vinyl label can be set up for as little as £1500: £650 for pressings, £650 for promotion, and £200 for artwork. But you will need to find a good distribution company to make this option work.

Even better, with the evolution of digital distribution, a small dance label can now be set up for about £250. Most of this fee would be used for artwork, and you would simply upload your tracks to music websites, for sale around the world. Anyone with a broadband connection and a computer can now sell their music worldwide, with very little outlay.

Entrepreneur

The best DJs are highly creative and motivated people, and their obsessive and goal-driven nature allows them to achieve success in other, related areas.

I often get asked, "Do I really need to be able to run my own business to be a DJ?" The simple answer is, "Yes." As a DJ, you are self-employed, and therefore necessarily have to organise your own tax and accounts. Work is never guaranteed, and you will probably have to work tirelessly to maintain a steady, long-term income, and to build your business.

You may have quite a lot of non-performing time on your hands as a DJ, as you tend only to work at the weekends and in the evenings. So use this time to start making your own music: set up a record label and/or DJ agency, or perhaps a record shop, or a management company, or even a promotions company – indeed, any other music-related business, where your skills and contacts are relevant. This is vital to generating future income.

Summary

The way in which a DJ makes a living has changed markedly over the past ten years. What started out as a part-time hobby for music enthusiasts has now turned into a multimillion-pound global business.

If you wish to create a long-term and successful future for yourself in the DJ business, you have to understand how the business has evolved, and learn both the hands-on and the business skills that the job now requires.

Jim Jomoa has been a professional DJ for the past 18 years. He has played alongside Sasha and Carl Cox, produced more than 75 dance tracks, and DJ-ed in over 21 countries. For the last ten years he has worked in DJ education, setting up the pioneering DJ Course at the School of Audio Engineering, in 1995. He is former Head of DJ Studies at the UK's Academy of Contemporary Music.

Club venues

LONDON

93 Feet East
150 Brick Lane, London E1 6QN
tel 020-7247 3293 *fax* 020-7247 5980
email neil@93feeteast.co.uk or sean@93feeteast.co.uk
website www.93feeteast.co.uk
Technical Contact Neil Abrahams

Contains 3 main areas including a large main hall with a stage, lighting and PA. Open 7 days a week. Cutting-edge DJ sets from established names and up-and-coming unsigned DJs. Hosts the Encompass Festival in May, which features a workshop for aspiring musicians. Chris Duckienfield, Chris Bones and John Power have all played this venue. Free entry before 9pm; £5 after. *Opening Hours:* Mon to Thurs: 5pm – 11pm; Fri: 5pm – 1am; Sat: 12pm – 1am; Sun: 12pm – 10.30pm.

Aquarium
256-264 Old Street, London EC1 V9DD
tel 020-7253 3558 *mobile* (07838) 360990
fax 020-7253 9885
email liga@clubaquarium.co.uk
website www.clubaquarium.co.uk
Contact Liga Mezmale

Established in 1995. Popular London venue split between a club with a swimming pool and a bar, with live DJs and music. Regular large club evenings featuring renowned DJs and club acts. Home to many prestigious events, concerts and video shoots. Opening times and ticket prices vary.

Babalou
The Crypt, St Matthews Church, Brixton Hill, London SW2 1JF
tel 020-7738 3366
email info@babalou.net
website www.babalou.net
Office Manager Lesley Ellard

Founded in 2005. Bar, restaurant and club hosting DJs Fri and Sat in soulful house genres. Ethnic-chic decor in church crypt. Admission £8 after 11pm Fri and Sat, with concessions for members. Capacity of 450. *Opening Hours:* Wed, Thurs and Sun: 5pm – 1am; Fri and Sat: 5pm – 5am. Available for private hire Mon and Tues.

Barrumba
36 Shaftesbury Avenue, London W1V 7DD
tel 020-7287 6933 *fax* 020-7287 2714
email barrumba@thebreakfastgroup.co.uk
website www.barrumba.co.uk

Launched by The Breakfast Group in 1993. A large number of renowned DJs have performed here, playing a selection of house, garage, funk, trance and urban hits. Boasts a world-class sound system by SLR.

Bed
33 London Road, Sheffield S2 4LA
tel 0114-276 6777 (Venue) or 0114-252 6107 (Information) *fax* 0114-252 6111
Venue Contact Lisa Barraclough

A venue with a long history of entertainment, situated on the outskirts of the city centre. Resident DJs include Corey Mahoney. Check website for a comprehensive list of events and for ticket booking. Event times and prices vary.

Cafe de Paris
3 Coventry Street, London W1V 7FL
tel 020-7734 7700
email reception@cafedeparis.com
website www.cafedeparis.com
Venue Contact Jack Westhead

Established in 1924 and regarded as one of Europe's premier clubs. A busy venue and a landmark of the London club scene. For information on events and opening times, check the website or call the above contact number. DJs should send a demo to Stefan at 9 King Street, London WC2 8HN.

Cargo
83 Rivington Street, Shoreditch, London EC2A 3AY
tel 020-7613 7732 or 020-7613 7743 (Bookings)
fax 020-7613 7790
website www.cargo-london.com
Press Officer Joe Roberts

Established in 2001. Large and popular club and live-music venue hosting a wide variety of music all nights of the week – from rock to jazz and electro to folk. Club night currently has a respected regular DJ: Andy Smith (Portishead, The Document). Admission ranges from £4 – £10. Capacity of 500. For music and event bookings, contact Chris Wheeler on the Bookings telephone number. *Opening Hours:* Mon to Thurs: 7 – 1pm; Fri and Sat: 8pm – 3am; Sun: 6 – 12pm.

Cirque at the Hippodrome
10-14 Cranbourn Street, London WC2H 7JH
tel 020-7437 4311 *fax* 020-7434 4225
email charmaine@cirquehippodrome.com
website www.cirquehippodrome.com
Director Charmaine Haig *Venue Contact* Jeremy Hartley

Established in 2006. Private hire and corporate venue specialising in album launches, film premier after-parties and conferences. Potential clients should submit proposal by post and await email. Capacity of 1855. DJs wishing to send in a demo should first contact Jeremy Hartley on the above telephone number or email address. Opening hours vary.

Club 414
414 Coldharbour Lane, Brixton, London SW9 8LF
tel 020-7924 9322
email info@club414ent.co.uk
website www.club414ent.co.uk
Director Louise Barron

Founded in 1991. Long-standing supporter of the underground house scene, also playing all varieties of trance, techno and house music. Has hosted DJs such as Fabio, Grooverider, Colin Dale and The Liberators in their early days. Provides 5K sound system, security and laser and lighting rig. Admission typically £8 – £10. Capacity of 150. Potential acts should visit website and email. *Opening Hours*: Fri: 10pm – 6am; Sat (after-parties): 6.30am – 1pm; Sat (evenings): 10pm – 6am; Sun: 10pm – 6am.

Colosseum
1 Nine Elms Lane, Vauxhall, London SW8 5NQ
tel 020-7720 3609 *fax* 020-7627 1284
email info@clubcolosseum.com
website www.clubcolosseum.com

Award-winning venue, winning the World's Best Club Award in 1999. 4 rooms, 3 dance floors and 3 DJ booths. Has hosted many prominent dance events. Expensive digital sound system. Capacity 1200. DJs should send a demo to the above address.

Cross
Kings Cross Goods Yard, York Way, London N1 0UZ
tel 020-7837 0828
email info@the-cross.co.uk
website www.the-cross.co.uk

Built within 6 disused railway arches. Hosts renowned DJs such as Seb Fontaine and Malcolm Duffy on a regular basis. DJs interested in booking the venue should contact Blonde Productions on 020-7833 4212, or email info@blondeproductions.co.uk.

Cube – London
135 Finchley Road, Swiss Cottage, London NW3
tel 020-7483 2393

Former bank spread over 3 levels. The ground floor contains a large square room with DJ booth – hosting regular DJ slots for resident and guest DJs alike. Prospective DJs should also contact the above telephone number.

Egg
5-13 Vale Royal, London N7 9EX
tel 020-7609 8364 *fax* 020-7619 6189
email egg@evmlondon.com
website www.egglondon.net
Venue Contact Laurence Malice

Opened in 2003. Winner of the BEDA award for Best London Club. Set over 3 floors and including a terrace and private garden. Playing a wide range of club music attracting big name DJs such as Robert Owens, now a resident DJ. Prospective DJs should send a demo to Laurence Malice at the above address.

Elbow Room – Bayswater
103 Westbourne Grove, Bayswater, London W2 4UW
tel 020-7221 5211 *fax* 020-7221 5512
email info@theelbowroom.co.uk
website www.theelbowroom.co.uk

Established in 1995. Part of the chain of Elbow Room clubs – recognised music venues co-owned by legendary music producer and DJ, Arthur Baker. Enjoys a wide range of popular acts and DJs including: Soulwax, Norman Jay, Boy George and Shaun Ryder, and Radio 1's Zane Lowe. Primarily set up as a Pool Lounge. Awards won range from Best Bar BEDA Awards 2002, to Best Use of Technology and Theme Awards 2000. Information on a selection of events across all its venues can be found on the website. DJs interested in playing any of the venues should contact Head Office at 89-91 Chapel Market, Islington, London N1 9EX. Telephone: 020-7833 4392 or email as above.

Elbow Room – Islington
89 Chapel Market, Islington, London N1 9EX
tel 020-7278 3244 *fax* 020-7278 3266
email Islington@theelbowroom.co.uk
website www.theelbowroom.co.uk
Venue Contact: Joe Ward

For comprehensive details of this chain of clubs – **see page 143.**

Elbow Room – Shoreditch
97-113 Curtain Road, Shoreditch, London EC2
tel 020-7613 1316 *fax* 020-7613 1336
email Shoreditch@theelbowroom.co.uk
website www.theelbowroom.co.uk

For comprehensive details of this chain of clubs – **see entry under page 143.**

The End
18 West Central Street, London WC1A 1JJ
tel 020-7419 9199 *fax* 020-7419 9099
email info@endclub.com
website www.endclub.com
Venue Contact Kate Everest

Busy and vibrant venue offering plenty of established and up-and-coming national and international DJs and acts most nights of the week. Critically acclaimed resident DJs, including Fabio, Darren Emerson and Mr C of the Shamen. High standard of technical equipment and an option to hire the venue.

Escape – London
8-10 Brewer Street, London W1R 3FP
tel 0871-332 4026

Venue Contact Vince Carr

Small but popular dance venue with 2 distinct floors, playing a mix of dance anthems and cutting-edge house, garage and funk.

Fabric

77A Charterhouse Street, London EC1 6HJ
tel 020-7336 8898
website www.fabriclondon.com
Promotions Manager Judy Griffith

Renowned East London club venue with an impressive volume of guest DJs and live acts, recently including Craig Richards, Luciano and the Scratch Perverts. Friday nights regularly host breaks, hip hop and D&B, while Saturdays tend to specialise in house and techno. Entry £12 – £15. Capacity of 1500. *Opening Hours*: Midweek: varies; Fri: 9.30pm – 5am; Sat: 10pm – 7am.

Fridge Bar

1 Town Hall Parade, Brixton Hill, London SW2 1RJ
tel 020-7326 5100 *fax* 020-7274 2879
email Bianca@allthingsorange.com
website www.fridgerocks.com

Established in 1985. Hosts large club nights including themed parties in a grand and slightly unusual setting. Has recently undergone an expensive overhaul to both interior and sound system. Admission approx. £5 before 11pm and £8 after. Capacity 1600. *Opening Hours*: (Main Bar) Mon to Thurs: 6pm – 2am; Fri: 7pm – 4am; Sat: 8pm – 3am; (Chill Out Bar) Sat and Sun: 5.30pm – 11am.

Gramaphonic

60-62 Commercial Street, London E1 6LT
Promotions Manager Emily Miller

Hosts funky accessible acts including hip hop, house, R&B, reggae and raregroove genres. Over 2 floors; specialises in cocktails and Mediterranean cuisine. Free entry. Capacity of 300. Potential acts should post CDs, biographies and proposals to Alex Ling at above address. *Opening Hours*: 11am – 1am daily.

Heaven

The Arches, Villiers Street, London WC2N 6NG
tel 020-7930 2020 *fax* 020-7930 8306
email info@heaven-london.com
website www.heaven-london.com
Events Co-ordinator Sarah Libretto

Established in 1979. Hosts all types of club event and private bookings. Admission ranges from £6 – £20. Capacity of 1625. Potential acts should make contact via email. *Opening Hours*: Varies depending on day of the week; generally 10pm – 6am.

Herbal

10-14 Kingsland Road, London E2 8DA
tel 020-7613 4462 *fax* 020-7117 3048
email someone@herbaluk.net
website www.herbaluk.net
Contact Spencer Carroll

Popular venue with connections to well-established artists and DJs, including Shy FX hosting Digital Soundboy fortnightly. Hosts regular nightly sets by guest and in-house DJs. Admission £3 – £6 (after 10.30pm Wed, Thurs; after 10pm Fri, Sat). Potential DJs should telephone on the above number. *Opening Hours*: Tues: 8pm – 2am; Wed to Sun: 9pm – 2am.

Hidden

101 Tinworth Street, Vauxhall, London SE11 5EQ
tel 020-7820 0788 or (07788) 456530
email amanda@hiddenclub.co.uk or chloe@hiddenclub.co.uk
website www.hiddenclub.co.uk
Contact Louis Young

Versatile venue comprising 3 rooms with expensive sound systems, lighting rigs and an outdoor courtyard. Has hosted big name acts such as Eric Pooley and Aaron Ross. Plays an eclectic mix of hard house, soulful house, deep house and classic soul and funk.

Madame Jo Jo's

8-10 Brewer Street, Soho, London W1F OSE
tel 020-7734 3040
email events@madamejojos.com
website www.madamejojos.com
General Manager Paajoe Gaskin

Internationally renowned venue. Plays a range of genres including electronica, hip hop, rock, disco and funk; also hosts burlesque performances, comedy nights and artist showcases. Ticket prices vary between £4 – £12; capacity of 180. Potential clients should make contact via telephone or email. *Opening Hours*: until 3am, with the exception of 2am Wed (and closed Mon).

Mass

St Matthews Church, Brixton, London SW2 IJF
tel 020-7738 7875 *fax* 020-7788 5772
website www.mass-club.co.uk
Manager Mike Kellas

Established in 2000. Large club hosting a range of dance-music styles from house to jungle. Admission is typically £5 – £10. Potential acts should make contact by phone. *Opening Hours*: 10pm – 3am weekdays; 10pm – 5am weekends.

Ministry of Sound

103 Gaunt Street, London SE1 6DP
tel 0870-060 0010 *fax* 020-7403 5348
email arnie@ministryofsound.com
website www.ministryofsound.com
Private Hire and Special Events Manager Hadley Newman

Well-established club playing house, garage and funky beats and hosting world-renowned DJs. Contains 4 bars, 3 dance floors and 3 DJ boxes. Capacity of 1500. *Opening Hours*: Fri: 10.30pm – 5am; Sat: 11pm – 7am.

Moonlight
32 Railway Approach, Harrow, London HA3 5AA
tel 0871-332 3662
Contact Sonia Mihaylova

Contains 1 main dancing area and plays a selection of club and chart anthems. Capacity of 400.

Pacha
Terminus Place, Victoria, London SW1V 1JR
tel 020-7833 3139
website www.pachalondon.com

Part of the world-renowned Pacha franchise. Hosts regular and extensive sets from world-class DJs including Brandon Block, Meck, Hoxton Whores, Sasha and Judge Jules. Plays a selection of funky house, garage and urban classics.

Rhythm Factory
Ground and Basement, 16-18 Whitechapel Road, Aldgate East, London E1 1EW
tel 020-7375 3774 *fax* 020-7375 2771
email info@rhythmfactory.co.uk
website www.rhythmfactory.co.uk
Promotions Co-ordinator Alex Ling

Founded in 1999. DJ venue hosting a range of styles including hip hop, funk, soul and D&B. Also houses live acts in a wide variety of genres including specific unsigned-band and open-mic nights. Admission is typically £3 – £10. Capacity of 400. Catering 12 – 8pm. Live acts should send demo CD or DVD to promotions office with contact details written clearly on CD. DJs should enquire by email. *Opening Hours*: Mon to Thurs: 11am – 12pm; Fri: 11 – 3am; Sat: 9pm – 3am.

SeOne London
41-43 St Thomas Street, London Bridge, London SE1 3QX
tel 020-7407 1617 *fax* 020-7378 7463
email info@seonelondon.com
website www.seonelondon.com
Bookings Manager Marcus Kay

Founded in 2002. Large dedicated dance venue. Capacity of 3000; 5 rooms and impressive sound and light facilities. Potential clients should contact venue via email – see website for more details. Ticket prices from £10 – £20.

The Telegraph – Liquification Ltd
The Telegraph, 228 Brixton Hill, London SW2 1HE
tel 020-8678 0777 *fax* 020-8678 9066
email info@thebrixtontelegraph.co.uk
website www.thebrixtontelegraph.co.uk
Owner Simon Hooper

Established in 2001. Hosts Liquification playing hip hop, house, funk, D&B, reggae and dub styles. Admission is £7 – £10. Capacity of 650. Potential acts should make contact by phone. Rehearsal studio also available. *Opening Hours*: Mon and Sun: 12.30pm – 2.30am; Fri: 12.30pm – 4am; Sat: 12.30pm – 6am.

Turnmills
63B Clerkenwell Road, London EC1M 5NP
tel 020-7324 3388 *fax* 020-7250 1046
email stix@turnmills.co.uk
website www.turnmills.co.uk
Contact Paul Stix

Large Mediterranean-style venue with acid-house feel. Hosts a range of large club nights and artists, including Roni Size, Justin Robertson, Stereo MCs, Mr C, and club nights 'Together' and 'Release Yourself'. Tapas restaurant attached. Admission £12 – £15. Capacity of 1000. *Opening Hours*: Fri: 10.30pm – 7.30am; Sat: 10pm – 6am.

Vibe Bar
91-95 Brick Lane, London E1 6QL
tel 020-7247 3479 *fax* 020-7426 0641
email muck@vibe-bar.co.uk
website www.vibe-bar.co.uk
Venue Booker Chris McMuck

Founded in 1995. Club/live venue situated in the Truman Brewery and playing diverse and eclectic sounds from soul, jazz and hip hop to rock, punk and dance. Free admission. Capacity of 300. Potential acts should post CD/promo pack only (no cold calling). *Opening Hours*: Sun to Thurs: 11am – 11.30pm; Fri and Sat: 11am – 11am.

The Watershed
267 Broadway, Wimbledon, London SW19 1SD
tel 020-8540 0080
email info@the-watershed.com
website www.the-watershed.com
Contact John Tyman

Largest club venue in Wimbledon, comprising 2 rooms and playing the latest club tunes with a mix of trance, funky soul and R&B. Hosts 2 well-received nights, 'Furtive' (Friday) and 'Sauce' (Saturday), playing a selection of club classics, soul, funk and disco until 3am. Capacity 330.

UK OUTSIDE LONDON

9eleven
9-11 Walker Street, Sheffield S3 8GZ
tel 0114-233 8239
Contact Andy Usher

Formerly the Arches. Popular club on 2 floors staging big nights, including 'Planet Zogg' (2nd Friday), 'Pressure' (3rd Friday) and 'Headcharge' (last Friday). Plays a mixture of R&B, hip hop, breaks, hard trance and techno. Prospective DJs should telephone for further details.

Above Audio
10 Marine Parade, Brighton BN2 1TL
tel (01273) 606906 or (01273) 697775
fax (01273) 620440

email info@audiobrighton.com
website www.audiobrighton.com
Contact Oli Hyde

Popular club venue that builds on strong collaborations with Juice FM radio station. Has hosted renowned DJs, Jack Johnson, Coldcut and Mula. Opening times and ticket prices vary.

Air

49 Heath Mill Lane, Digbeth, Birmingham B9 4AR
tel 0871-425 5555
Contact Andy Tatum

Popular club and venue, featuring 3 large rooms of music and hosting one of the largest and best-known DJ Club nights, 'Godskitchen', on a Friday – featuring sets by the cream of UK and international DJs. Tim Westwood has regularly performed sets. Capacity of 2000. Opening times and ticket prices vary.

Arch 9 Manchester

Arch 9, Deansgate Lock, Manchester M1 5LH
tel 0161-833 4222 *fax* 0161-833 4750
email arch9-manchester@luminar.co.uk
website www.arch9.com
Manager Mat Carden

Founded in 2002. Accommodates dance events, promotions and gigs. Multimedia and food available if pre-booked. Potential acts should send a demo by post. Admission approx. £3; capacity of 720. *Opening Hours*: Mon to Wed: 12pm – 12am; Thurs to Sat: 12pm – 2am; Sun: 12pm – 1am.

Arches – Glasgow

253 Argyle Street, Glasgow G2 8DL
tel 0141-565 1009 *fax* 0141-565 1001
email joe@thearches.co.uk
Music Programme Manager Joe Splain

Established in 1991. Multi-functional venue hosting techno and house nights alongside a diverse live-music programme. Holds 3 of the UK's biggest club nights featuring artists such as Pete Tong, Judge Jules and Mylo. Provides 15K PA. Has cafe bar and catering. Admission £6 – £25. Overall club capacity of 2500. Potential acts should phone or email for more info, or post demos. *Opening Hours*: 11pm – 3am.

Atrium

6-9 The Grand Arcade, Leeds LS1 6PG
tel 0113-242 6116
email supertee@atrium2000.fsnet.co.uk
website www.atrium-leeds.co.uk
Manager Georgina Wellett

Established in 1999. Contains 3 floors of music, catering for a wide variety of genres. Hosts live bands and DJs. Equipment includes 8-channel mixer, outboard EQ and decks. In-house engineer available on request. Potential acts should contact promoter at **www.rockingfish.com**. Venue also available for hire.

Admission typically £2 – £15. Capacity of 660 (220 per floor). *Opening Hours*: Mon to Thurs: 9pm – 2am; Fri and Sat: 9pm – 3am.

The Baa Bar

Arches 9 and 10, Deansgate Lock,
Manchester M1 5LH
tel 0161-832 4446
email info@baabar.co.uk
website www.baabar.co.uk
Contact Marcus Riedisperger

Part of the Baa Bar chain with venues in Manchester, Liverpool and Wigan. Popular club playing a selection of club music with regular hosted DJs.

Baby Blue

Edward Pavillion, Albert Dock, Liverpool L3 4AF
tel 0151-702 5831
email suzanne.watson@jientertainment.co.uk
website www.lyceumgroup.co.uk/babyblue
Marketing Manager Suzanne Watson

Popular, well-presented club with 3 nights of music playing an eclectic blend of new and classic funk, R&B and disco. Admission £5 before 11pm, £10 after. For bookings, contact the Marketing Manager. *Opening Hours*: Fri to Sun: 11pm until late.

Beach

171-181 Kings Road Arches, Brighton BN1 1AL
tel (01273) 722272

Popular club venue presenting a diverse range of music. Ticket prices and opening hours vary. Telephone for more information.

Blueprint

509 Alfreton Road, Nottingham NG1 2ED
tel 0115-942 2050
email finbarbryson@amserve.com
website www.blueprintclub.co.uk
Contact Finbar Bryson

The venue site has been a club of some kind since WWII, and during the Acid House phase of the late 80s and early 90s was know as The Skyy Club – home to the renowned DIY Soundsystem held every Tuesday. Has been Blueprint since 2000. Acts hosted have included: Massive Attack, Portishead and Asian Dub Foundation. Plays an eclectic selection of underground house, vibe and garage alongside well-known anthems and popular hits. A wide selection of resident DJs play regularly; guest DJs and MCs play each month.

Chapel

Milford Street, Salisbury SP1 2AP
tel (01722) 504255 *fax* (01722) 502630
email info@thechapelnightclub.co.uk
website www.thechapelnightclub.co.uk

Award-winning club (BEDA UK Nightclub Of The Year Award 2000) catering for most musical tastes within 4 rooms. Hosts regular guest DJs. Capacity of 1200. Times and entry prices should be checked on the website or via the above telephone number. DJ demos can be sent to the above address.

City Edinburgh

1A Market Street, Edinburgh EH1 1DE
tel 0131-226 9560 *fax* 0131-226 9561
email enquiries@citypeople.info
website www.citypeople.info
Venue Contact Amanda Gerlach

Large club belonging to the City group. Popular resident DJs include Tokyo Blu and DJ Filthee. Capacity of 2100.

Claire's Night Club

41 Torwood Street, Torquay TQ1 1DZ
tel (01803) 292079 *fax* (01803) 200605
email info@clairesnight.co.uk
website www.clairesnightclub.co.uk
Director Ann McGowan

Established in 1994. Hosts DJs in 2 rooms – a house room and a funky/R&B room. Guest DJs have included: Lisa Lashes, Judge Jules, Ronnie Herel. Hosts special events such as Old Skool and Hardcore nights. Admission typically £5 – £6. Capacity of 1000. Potential acts should contact by email, or post CDs and biogs. *Opening Hours*: 9.30pm – 4am.

Concorde 2

Madeira Drive, Brighton BN2 1EN
tel (01273) 673311 *fax* (01273) 696157
email info@concorde2.co.uk
website www.concorde2.co.uk
Events Manager Alison Hildyard

Nightclub and live-music venue. Potential acts should make contact via email or phone. Ticket prices vary according to event; capacity of 540. *Opening Hours*: Vary according to events; office hours are Mon to Fri: 10am – 7pm; Sat: 10am – 5pm.

Creation – Brighton

78 West Street, Brighton BN1 2AL
tel (01273) 321628
website www.creationbrighton.com
Venue Contact Emma Flaherty

Popular venue playing a mixture of club tunes from house and garage to chart. Events most evenings. Potential DJs can fill in an online form with their details.

Creation – Bristol

13-21 Baldwin Street, Bristol BS1 1NA
tel 0117-922 7177
Venue Contact Alistair Paul

Large nightclub showcasing some of the UK's best DJs, including Judge Jules, Lisa Lashes and Sonique. Plays popular and commercial dance music on Saturdays. State-of-the-art sound system. Capacity 1400.

Creation – Leicester

97 Church Gate, Leicester LE1 3AN
tel 0116-262 9720
website www.creation-leicester.co.uk
Venue Contact Clive Davis

Popular venue playing a mix of club tunes from house and garage to chart. Events most evenings. Potential DJs can fill in an online form with their details.

Cuba Norte

17 John Street, Glasgow G1 1HP
tel 0141-552 3505
email enquiries@favelaglasgow.com
website www.favelaglasgow.com
Manager Emma-Jane Bell

Restaurant containing piano bar and downstairs club. Hosts live acts regularly, usually funk and salsa. Capacity of 400 and ticket prices from £3 – £10. Potential clients should make contact via email or phone. *Opening Hours*: Sun to Thurs: 10am – 12pm; Fri to Sat: 10am – 3pm.

Dance Academy

121-123 Union Street, Plymouth PL1 3NB
tel (01752) 220055
website www.danceacademy.co.uk
Venue Contact Tom Costelloe

Popular venue hosting the best local, national and international DJs. Favourably regarded by *Mixmag*. Plays an eclectic selection of house, trance and underground. Past DJs include: Simon Patterson, Alex Kidd, Marc Vedo. Website has online contact page for mailing listings and for prospective DJs.

The Drink

Onslow Street, Guildford GU1 4SQ
tel (01483) 440900

Houses 2 adjoining rooms playing a mix of house, funk, soul and R&B. Recent acts have included: The Sunset Strippers and United Nations.

Elbow Room – Bristol

64 Park Street, Bristol BS1 5JN
tel 0117-930 0242 *fax* 0117-930 0243
email bristol@theelbowroom.co.uk
website www.theelbowroom.co.uk

For comprehensive details of this chain of clubs
– see entry under page 143.

Elbow Room – Leeds

64 Call Lane, Leeds LS1 6DT
tel (01132) 457011 *fax* (01132) 457022
email leeds@theelbowroom.co.uk
website www.theelbowroom.co.uk
Venue Contact Lee Toomes

For comprehensive details of this chain of clubs
– see entry under page 143.

Elemental – Leeds

Corn Exchange, Leeds LS1 7BR
tel 0113-244 3906 *fax* 0113-244 3910
email elemental.leeds@virgin.net
Venue Manager Lee Deakin

Situated in the Old Corn Exchange, Bar Elemental plays a wide range of tunes throughout the week, from resident and guest DJs. Prospective DJs should contact the above number, or email.

Enigma

10 Ship Street, Brighton BN1 1AD
tel (01273) 328439
Venue Manager Ross Barnes

Small but popular club based in the city centre. Mainly attracts a student clientele. Plays a selection of popular house, dance and hip hop. Hosts one of Brighton's most popular nights – Phonic Hoop. Capacity of 300. Prospective DJs should contact the above number, or email.

Escape – Swansea

Northampton Lane, Swansea SA1 3EH
tel (01792) 470000
email enquiries@escapegroup.com
website www.escapegroup.com
Venue Contact Laura Campbell

Popular venue playing house, club and garage. Hosts well-established nights by Hed Kandi and Godskitchen. An array of well-known national and international DJs have played this venue, including Trevor Nelson, Judge Jules and Norman Jay. Organiser of the 'Escape into the Park' outdoor event. In the first instance prospective DJs should contact the club via the above telephone number.

Essential

8 Minshull Street, Manchester M1 3EF
tel 0161-236 0077
email info@essentialmanchester.com
website www.essentialmanchester.com
Venue Contact John Barnes

Hosts 3 floors of current and classic club music, including the critically acclaimed night, 'Flip and Sabbath'. Additional information for prospective DJs and acts can be had by calling the above telephone number.

Fez – Bristol

26 St Nicholas Street, Clifton, Bristol BS1 1UB
tel (01179) 259200 *fax* (01779) 259500
email info@bristolfez.com
website www.ponana.com

Unusual underground venue with hidden alcoves. Plays a selection of street soul and house. Aims to showcase a high calibre of national and local DJs. Capacity 300. DJs should post demos. *Opening Hours*: Open until 2am; Sat: until 3am.

Funky Buddha Lounge

169 Kings Road Arches, Brighton BN1 1NB
tel (01273) 725541
website www.funkybuddha.co.uk

Popular Brighton club with New York style décor, playing a selection of modern club music. Friday night is very popular, with local DJs Stompa Phunk delivering tech-house sets. Admission £3 – £10. *Opening Hours*: Mon to Thurs: 10pm – 2am; Fri to Sat: 10pm – 3am.

Hippodrome – Colchester

131 High Street, Colchester CO1 1SP
tel (01206) 762555
Contact Glen Freeman

Plays a selection of popular/commercial dance music, UK garage anthems and R&B. A venue popular with touring DJs, including Dave Pearce, and hosting a good selection of resident DJs. Potential DJs should telephone the above contact in the first instance.

Honey Club

214 Kings Road Arches, Brighton BN1 1NB
tel (07000) 446639
email info@thehoneyclub.co.uk
Office Address: Central Entertainments Ltd, PO Box 3333, Brighton, East Sussex BN2 9HJ
website www.thehoneyclub.co.uk
Contact Joy Kenny

Large venue with 5 rooms and 2 beach-front terraces playing an eclectic selection of house, funk, garage, vibe and party anthems. Recently rebuilt and refurbished. Hosts well-known events such as Hed Kandi. The 2nd room now hosts some of the UK's best promotions, such as Dusted, Formula, Pukka Up, Bliss & Sedition. Potential DJs should telephone the above contact. *Opening Hours*: (Office) Mon to Fri: 10am – 5pm.

Junction

Clifton Road, Cambridge CB1 7GX
tel (01223) 511511 (Box Office) or (01223) 578000 (Admin)
email info@junction.co.uk
website www.junction.co.uk
Contact Gary Woolley

Hosts a varied array of musical acts and big dance nights featuring acclaimed DJs such as Judge Jools, Scott Mac, Scratch Perverts, Goldie and Fabio. Plays the latest selection of garage, house, trance and vibe. Capacity of 1050.

K1 Bar and Klub

K-House, Terrace Road, Bournemouth BH2 5NN
tel (01202) 317070/317818
email info@k1experience.com
website www.k1experience.com
Directors Martyn Harris, Nic Mcavoy

A 4-room venue with capacity of 860; welcomes all genres of music. Contact M Harris directly for more information. Every proposal is taken into consideration. Ticket prices typically £5 – £8. *Opening Hours*: Mon and Tues: private hire; Wed and Thurs: 8pm – 2am; Fri: 11am – 2am; Sat: 12pm – 2am; Sun: 12pm – 12am. Restaurant also available.

The Leadmill
59 Tylney Road, Sheffield S2 2RX
tel 0114-221 2828
email rob@leadmill.co.uk
website www.leadmill.co.uk
Contact Shane O' Connor

Popular music venue hosting weekly club nights with 3 rooms – 1 offering sets from guest DJs. Each room plays a mix of R&B, vocal house, funky soul and popular anthems. Potential DJs should phone or email.

Level 4
39 Sheep Street, Northampton NN1 2NE
(Recorded Event Listing Service): *tel* 0906-470 0867
(service available 9am – 6pm Mon to Sat)
Contact Asa Ashton

A stylish, intimate club with 4 bars/rooms set over 3 different levels. The top floor contains a chillout and relax area playing mellow tunes; the basement is the dance floor playing a selection of club anthems, garage and house. Capacity of 400.

Liquid
Brook Street, Wrexham LL13 7LH
tel (01978) 310580 *fax* (01978) 312479
email wrexham@liquidnightclub.co.uk
website www.liquidnightclub.co.uk

Part of the Liquid chain of clubs and nights. Recently spent £1m on light and sound in an attempt to turn venue into a super-club. Hosts selection of in-house DJs including DJ Kuta (Ministry of Sound) and founder member of chart act N-Trance. Also, DJs Spoons, Bone and Dee. Plays a selection of house, dance, trance and club music.

The Liquidroom
9C Victoria Street, Edinburgh EH1 2HE
tel 0131-225 2564 *fax* 0131-225 2574
email kath@liquidroom.com
website www.liquidroom.com
Director Katherine MacKenzie

Established in 1995. Hosts DJs and live music of a variety of genres. Provides full security and technical staff. Admission £10 – £14. Capacity of 1000. Potential acts should post demos. *Opening Hours*: Office: 10am – 4pm; Club: 10.30pm – 3am.

Lizard Lounge
4th Floor, 26-30 Stoney Street, Nottingham NG1 3NL
tel 0115-952 3264
Contact Danny Webster-Clamp

Popular club with 3 floors. Plays a whole range of music from garage to disco; hosts in-house DJs.

Capacity 360. Open 3 nights a week: Thurs, Fri and Sat.

Maymies
Hemlock Way, Cannock WS11 3DR
tel (01543) 466467 *fax* (01543) 467337
email contact@maymies.net
website www.maymies.net

Hosts the club night 'Ice' on a Friday and 'Fire' on a Saturday, playing club anthems, popular R&B and house. A good mix of guest DJs have played the venue, including Caroline Banx, Steve Arnold and Gaz James. Potential DJs should phone or email.

Maze
270 North Sherwood Street, Nottingham NG1 4EN
tel 0115-947 5650 *fax* 0115-947 5650
Contact Marion Atkinson

Live music and club venue featuring guest DJs and acts. For further information on upcoming events and ticket prices, etc. call the above telephone number. Capacity of 200.

Milk Bar
Tomb Street, Belfast BT1 3AS
tel 028-9027 8876
email info@clubmilk.com
website www.clubmilk.com

Plays big club tunes by Mobo Award-winning DJ, DJ Shortee Blitz, and established resident DJ, DJ Hix.

Moles
14 George Street, Bath BA1 2EN
tel (01225) 404445
email info@moles.co.uk
website www.moles.co.uk
Manager Michelle Cain

Established in 1978. Live and DJ venue. Hosts regular dance night on a Friday – 'Elixir'. Potential DJs should contact Doug McGregor by emailing doug@moles.co.uk or steve@moles.co.uk.

Sanctuary – Birmingham
78 Digbeth High Street, Birmingham B5 6DY
tel 0121-246 1010 *fax* 0121-240 1020
Contact Jon Eaton

Popular student club playing a selection of club anthems, chart dance, funk and R&B within 2 rooms. Presents big nights including Godskitchen, Slinky and Sundissential. Hosts big-name DJs most weeks; past DJs include: Lisa Lashes, Anne Savage, and Jez and Charlie. Prospective DJs should phone for more information. *Opening Hours*: Fri and Sat: 9pm – 4am.

Sanctuary – Swansea
85 Kingsway, Swansea SA1 5JE
tel (01792) 459027 (Enquiries) or (01792) 459027 (Box Office)

This venue has 2 rooms and 1 large dance floor, playing a selection of chart anthems and a mixture of house, vibe and garage. Prospective DJs should phone the Enquiries number. Capacity of 750.

Sands

17-20 Road, Weston Super Mare BS23 1SY
tel (01934) 414414 *fax* (01934) 414417

Central venue playing a mixture of popular and chart club hits.

Sea

Neptune House, Close, Newcastle NE1 3RQ
tel 0191-230 1813
email sea@ultimateleisure.com
website www.ultimateleisure.com/sea
Contact Mark Whitaker

Opened in 2000. Popular venue situated in a converted old shipping building on the banks of the Tyne. Plays a varied selection of music from chart house to R&B and funky house. Hosts 'Silk' on a Tuesday. Resident DJ, DJ Slik Fingaz; also presents names such as Phatts and Small. Capacity 1000.

Society

64 Duke Street, Liverpool L1
website www.societyuk.com
Contact Les Calvert

Popular and flamboyant club venue hosting big-name nights (Jubilee, Cirque Du Societe and Scent – each Friday) and renowned DJs. Regular DJs include: Mike Di Scala, Dave Whelan and Colin Airey, playing a diverse range of funky house, club and chart anthems.

Sound Exchange

49-50 High Street, Banbury OX16 0LA
tel (01295) 275057 *fax* (01295) 259982
email info@sound-exchange.co.uk
website www.sound-exchange.co.uk
Contact Russell Manning

Over 2 floors; hosts a range of styles from house, garage and funk to popular chart and club anthems. The main dance floor is very large, covering 11,000 sq. ft. Potential DJs should make contact by phone.

Squires

Market Street, Preston PR1 2ES
tel (01772) 251074 *fax* (01772) 886962
email squires-preston@luminar.co.uk
website www.squiresnightclub.co.uk
General Manager David Beveridge

Twin venue hosting a range of genres including chart, party, dance, R&B, funk and northern soul. Catering facilities available. Capacity of 1200. Potential acts should email, post demo or phone. Admission £3 – £8. *Opening Hours*: Mon: 10pm – 2am; Fri and Sat: 10pm – 3.30am.

Stageworks Worldwide Productions

525 Ocean Boulevard, Blackpool FY4 1EZ
tel (01253) 342426/7 *fax* (01253) 407715

email info@stageworkshop.com
website www.stageworkshop.com
Creative Director Antony Johns *Entertainment, Sales and Marketing Director* Phil McCandlish

Large venue encompassing a range of performance spaces. Capacities are as follows: Arena – 2200; Globe – 1100; Paradise Room – 700 seated; Horseshoe – 400; White Tower – 100 seated. Will consider unsigned acts. Send promotional material via post for application. Also provides technical staff and catering services.

Stereo Central

Sandygate, The Quayside,
Newcastle upon Tyne NE1 2AG
tel 0191-230 0303
email info@stereocorp.co.uk
website www.stereocorp.co.uk
Contact Aaron Mellor

Popular venue in view of the Millennium Bridge. Awards won for Best New Bar. Host to a weekly night by the Hed Kandi DJs. Popular as a warm-up venue for some of the city's bigger clubs. Potential DJs should email or phone.

The Sub Club

22 Jamaica Street, Glasgow G1 4QD
tel 0141-248 4600 *fax* 0141-847 0657
email info@subclub.co.uk
website www.subclub.co.uk
Manager Mike Donald

Founded in 1986. Small basement music venue attracting international and local DJs. All underground music genres covered. Offers Martin Audio backline sound system, flexible staging and lighting rigs, and full tech support. Also available for hire. Admission typically £5 – £12 and capacity of 420. Potential clients should email with information. *Opening Hours*: 4 nights a week: 11pm – 3am.

Sugar House

Sugar House Alley, Lancaster LA1 1NW
tel (01524) 63508
email amdavies@lancaster.ac.uk
website www.thesugarhouse.co.uk
Contact Louise Davies

Owned and operated by the Lancaster University Student Union. Hosts the 'Scandalous' night, which plays a mix of R&B, hip hop and club chart anthems along with the once-a-month club-night Juicy. Capacity 1150.

Telegraph

228 Brixton Hill, London SW2 1HE
tel 020-8678 0777 *fax* 020-8678 9066
email info@thebrixtontelegraph.co.uk
website www.thebrixtontelegraph.co.uk
Contact Simon Hooper

Historic music club venue (the venue that first hosted The Clash and Joe Strummer), combining a bar and

Thai restaurant with 2 dance floors playing nights of house, techno and trance. Presents plenty of touring DJs, including Chad Jackson and Mike Duffy; acts have included the Basement Jaxx. Open all week. Capacity 600. Potential DJs should contact the above address, sending a demo on CD.

Thursdays

Drayton House, Drayton, Chichester PO19 8EL
tel (01243) 786170
email info@thursdays.co.uk
website www.thursday.co.uk
Contact Richard Nye

Plays a selection of popular club chart anthems, funky house, R&B, hip hop, D&B and old skool. Open Tuesdays, Fridays and Saturdays.

Toast

25 North Road, Lancaster LA1 1NS
tel (01524) 842444
Contact Oliver Bennet

Busy club with an active events listing. Presents a mix of resident and guest DJs playing a selection of supa-funk, funky house, northern soul and urban grooves. Winner of BEDA Bar of the Year 2003. Prospective DJs should phone for further information.

Toffs

3-5 Toft Green, York YO1 6JT
tel (01904) 620203 *fax* (01904) 613592
email toffs-york@luminar.co.uk
website www.ukcn.com/clubs
Contact Nick Westwell

Busy city-centre club hosting a variety of nights playing a mix of club chart anthems, funk, soul and R&B. Large dance area. Mixture of resident and guest DJs.

Toucan

95-97 St Mary Street, Cardiff CF10 1DW
tel 029-2049 1061 or (07850) 461684
email simon@toucanclub.co.uk
website www.toucanclub.co.uk

Celebrated for its diversity and promotion of funk, world beats, hip hop, live acts and DJs. Welcomes contact from new DJs and acts; requests contact via the above email address in the first instance.

Tramps

Angel Place, Worcester WR1 3QN
website www.night-clubber.com/tramps
Contact Dean Hill

Recently refurbished venue with a big emphasis on light and sound systems. Contains 2 dance floors with resident DJs playing a range of club, chart and house tunes. The Lounge Room plays R&B and relaxed vibes. Hosts popular night 'Funked-Up Fridays'. Open Thursday, Friday and Saturday each week.

Tunnel

84 Mitchell Street, Glasgow G1 3NA
tel 0141-204 1000 *fax* 0141-248 6803
email enquiries@cplweb.com
Contact Simon Morrison

Popular city-centre venue hosting large club nights. Presents a spectrum of urban, street, R&B, hip hop and soul music from a mixture of resident and guest DJs. Saturday 'Basenight' hosts resident DJ, DJ Sketch playing the latest R&B and hip hop. Prospective DJs should telephone the above contact number for further information.

Tuxedo Royale

Hill Gate Quay, Tynebridge, Newcastle NE8 2QS
tel 0191-477 8899
Contact George Elliot

Unique 'club on a ship' venue. Contains many different themed rooms and is complete with a revolving dance floor. Hosts Planet Earth club night. Resident and guest DJs play a mix of club chart tunes along with funk, soul, R&B and hip hop.

Waterfront

139-141 King Street, Norwich NR1 1QH
tel (01603) 632717 *fax* (01603) 615463
email pingleby@uea.ac.uk
website www.ueaticketbookings.co.uk
Proprietor Paul Ingleby

Founded in 1993. Ex-brewery warehouse conversion over 2 floors with good live facilities. Plays alternative, indie, rock and hip hop. Admission varies between £4.50 – £15. Capacity of 700. Local acts should make contact via email. *Opening Hours*: Fri to Sat: 10pm – 2am; Midweek: 7.30pm – 11am.

XS

West Walls, Carlisle C83 8UB
tel (01228) 544282
email via website
website www.club-xs.com

Well-equipped club venue with 3 dance floors. Open 7 days a week and offering a variety of nights from northern soul to club-chart anthems.

Zap

189-192 Kings Road Arches, Brighton BN1 1NB
Contact Rich Chidlow

Popular club often attracting big-name DJs and acts. Comprises 2 main rooms and dance areas. Hosts the well-received 'Chopper Choons' night combining club and disco anthems with modern R&B, funk and hip hop. Has hosted guest appearances from Tim Westwood. Capacity 600.

Courses

Confetti School of Recording Technology

6-10 Convent Street, Nottingham NG1 3LL
tel 0115-952 2075
website www.confettistudios.com
Student Adviser Cate Johnson

A custom designed facility, housing a progressive learning institute alongside commercial recording studios and a film company. Aims to create a modern, influential learning environment, inspirational staff and creative, vocational courses in order to give students a head start in the creative industries, as well as to develop invaluable life skills, gain confidence and think positively about their future.

Qualifications: NCFE Level 2 Certificate in Music Technology (Mix DJ Skills).

DJ Academy Organisation

1 Damaskfield, Worcester WR4 0HY
tel/fax (01905) 22551
email office@djacademy.org.uk
website www.djacademy.org.uk
Managing Director Andy King

Founded in 2000. Offers 1-day and 8-week courses. Provides training in all aspects of a DJ's career towards real job opportunities. Delivered in a 'hands-on' way and operated by award-winning professional DJs with many years of experience within the nightclub industry. Takes place at locations all over the UK, including Birmingham, Bristol, Cardiff, Exeter, Edinburgh, Glasgow, Nottingham;, Swindon and Worcester. Potential applicants must fill out an application form and send it back to the Academy along with a small deposit of £75 to reserve a place the following term.

Qualifications: Internal Certificate of Excellence.

Manchester MIDI School

Bexley Chambers, 1 Bexley Square M36DB
tel 0161-833 4722
email mail@midischool.com
website www.midischool.com
Course Manager Jonny Miller

Founded in 1997. Specialises in DJ training, including study of Reason and Music Business. The 10-week Basement DJ course covers all aspects of DJ-ing and is for beginner and intermediate DJs. Units covered include: Equipment Set-up and Calibration, Beat Mixing (turntable and mixer operation), Cueing and Pitching Techniques, Music Theory (BPMs, bars and sections), EQ within DJ-ing, Creative DJ-ing, Scratching Basics, Acapellas and CD Mixing Techniques. The 4-week Scratch Lab studies basic and/or advanced scratching techniques and turntablism, and offers the chance to record and master a DJ demo.

Qualifications: MMS Certificate.

Online Studios

Unit 9, Croydon House Business Centre, No 1 Peall Road, Croydon CR0 3EX
tel 020-8287 8585 *mobile* (07789) 635325
email info@onlinestudios.co.uk
website www.onlinestudios.co.uk
Studio Manager Rob Pearson

Established circa 1997. Provides 1:1 training and short courses including DJ training. Students learn how to mix with vinyl, CDs and MP3s. Offers 2-day or 3-day courses (costs approx. £280 – £375).

Point Blank

23-28 Penn Street, London N1 5DL
tel 020-7729 4884 or 0870-600 4884
fax 020-7729 8789
email studio@pointblanklondon.com
62 Brown Street, Sheffield S1 2BS
website www.pointblanklondon.com
Head of Music College Dave Pine

Offers award-winning courses in DJ skills, based in 2 premises. Courses range from beginner to intermediate and advanced and can take place over a weekend or 1, 2 or 3 months. Also provides online distance learning. DJ courses accredited to 1 LOCN (London Open College Network) credit.

School of Audio Engineering Institute (SAE)

United House, North Road, London N7 9DP
tel 020-7609 2653 *fax* 020-7609 6944
email saelondon@sae.edu
website www.saeuk.edu
Founder Tom Misner

Runs courses in sites across the world. London college offers an Electronic Music Production Certificate (6 months), which is designed for DJs who enjoy experimenting with music technology and wish to be able to remix more effectively.

Qualifications: Electronic Music Production Certificate.

Sub Bass DJ Academy

Unit 104, 24-28A Hatton Wall, London EC1N 8JH
tel 020-7404 7080
email info@subbassdj.com
website www.subbassdj.com
Tutor Graeme Lloyd

Aims to provide high-quality tuition as provided by professional and successful DJs. Offers a 3-month Full DJ course that begins with basic pitch matching and moves to drop mixing and use of Ableton Live. The 1-month Basic DJ course offers the basics for those with little or no experience of the decks, with study of basic pitch matching and mixing and EQs. The Weekend Advanced DJ course is for those who wish to hone and broaden their skills. It involves learning EQ tricks, advanced mixing board techniques, acapella mixing and 3 channel mixing – among other techniques. Also offers weekend courses such as the Weekend Crash Course, the Digital DJ Course, Turntablism Weekend and Urban Weekend.

Technics DJ Academy
65-69 Downing Street, Manchester M1 7JE
tel 0161-276 2100 (General) or 0161-276 2111 (Admissions) *fax* 0161-272 7242
website www.s-s-r.com

Technics DJ Academy is the DJ arm of the School of Sound Recording. The DJ Courses offer a comprehensive range of learning from the basics of DJ skills to advanced technique, for mixers, for scratchers and for the digital DJ. They also offer training in promotions and events, electronic music production, Reason, CDJs, Serato and Ableton.

Glossary of DJ terms

Acapella: A term derived from the Latin, meaning 'with the voice (alone)'. To DJs, this indicates a vocal line without any music – a very effective tool for creating new remixes live.

Acetate: A one-off pressing, made from an acetate (soft vinyl) material. These are prized possessions of DJs, as they are often available to play up to six months before the record actually gets released. (They are also very expensive, and only last for a limited number of plays.)

Amplifier: An active device used to amplify audio signals for effective playback. The amplifier is connected between the speakers and the output of the mixer.

Anti-skating: A device on a turntable arm that helps to apply downward force on the cartridge. It is essential that this is set up properly to prevent the record from skipping while it is being played.

Baby scratch: The most basic form of scratch there is, and usually the first scratch that a DJ learns. It involves gently moving the record back and forth over the scratch point. It requires no crossfader control in the beginning.

Balance control: A control on a stereo amplifier or mixer that is used to adjust the balance between left and right of the stereo programme. DJs sometimes use this to enhance their effects while playing in a club environment.

Bass: The lower frequency range (up to 250Hz). In DJ terms, the kick drum and bass sounds are normally associated with bass. The bass sound represents a significant part of all dance music genres.

Beat: Usually a kick drum on a record. It is this that a DJ uses as a guide to mix records.

Beat juggling: A DJ turntablist technique that involves mixing and scratching two copies of the same record. DJs use this technique to create their own drum patterns. It is a difficult technique to master, but when done properly, is impressive to watch.

Beat mixing: The most fundamental form of DJ mixing. This involves ensuring that the beats and BPMs (beats per minute – see below) on each record in the mix accurately match together.

Beatmatch: Speeding up and slowing down an incoming music track so that it plays at the same speed as the outgoing track. A DJ usually has to use his/her hands to manipulate and control the record, since it can be very difficult to get one record to match exactly the speed of the other.

Beats per minute (BPM): The measure used to count the tempo of vinyl. A vital piece of information for all DJs, this can aid quick and professional mixing.

Beltdrive turntable: A basic form of turntable often bought by new 'bedroom' DJs. They are cheap and have basic pitch controls. The drive is literally driven by a belt system. While fine for basic mixing, the start delay on the turntable and the friction caused when holding the platter make it ineffective for professional use.

Cartridge: This is the stylus pickup assembly mounted on the turntable tonearm, and allows the playback of sound from the vinyl.

CD: The abbreviation for Compact Disc – a small optical laser disc encoded with digital information. This is fast becoming the format of choice for DJs in the digital age.

Clipping: This refers to a type of distortion that occurs when an amplifier is overdriven. The sound becomes hard and edgy (often liked by many DJs). Hard clipping is the most frequent cause of 'burned out' tweeters. This is why a low-powered amplifier driven into clipping can damage high-powered speakers.

Crab: A complicated turntablist technique that involves tapping the crossfader with each finger to create a stacatto transformer effect. It was best demonstrated by DMC World Champion, DJ A-Trak.

Crossfader: This is the switch between the left and right channel on a mixer. It allows the DJ to blend or mix both sound-sources to create a new sound, which is a combination of the two records.

Crossfader curve: Describes the way in which the volume changes when a fader moves on a mixer. It is often switchable, depending on the type of use you desire. If you are simply mixing, you have a long curve; if you are scratching, you have a sharp curve. Vestax are best known for introducing this feature onto modern mixers.

Cue: Can either mean PFL (Pre-Fade Listen), or to have a CD or record ready in the right place for instant playback, scratch or mix.

Decibel (dB): A measure of sound or volume – or a scale of relative loudness (to give it the correct definition). A difference of approx. 1dB is the minimum perceptible change in volume. The lowest threshold of hearing is 0dB, while the normal speaking voice is 65-70dB. A live rock concert is around 120dB+, and the pain threshold of hearing is 130dB. One of the loudest sounds known to man is a jet aircraft, at 140-180dB.

Delay: An audio circuit which suspends the output of an audio signal, and mixes it with the original audio-source to create a fuller sound.

Dial input fader: A rotary fader or pot control, used for adjusting the signal level of an input for music on a DJ mixer. The type of mixers using rotary faders are often referred to as 'New York' style faders, and are the mixers of choice for some of America's top House DJs.

Direct track access: The controls on a CD or DVD player that allow easy access to a track on the disc, without having to keep pressing the skip button.

Dynamic: The most common type of microphone used in live situations.

Echo: A type of effect used in DJ-ing with acapellas (see above). It is mostly used with vocals to enhance their sound using delay, repeat and vocal reverberations.

Equaliser: An electronic set of filters used to boost or emphasise certain frequencies.

Feedback: One of the DJ's worst fears, feedback often makes a performer look unprofessional – as well as potentially damaging the audience's ears! Feedback is a howling noise caused by a microphone picking up sound from the speakers.

Filter: Similar to kill-switches (that cut off bass, mid and treble), but a filter sweeps through the frequencies. When turning a filter switch, the first thing to be heard will usually be the bass, then mid, then treble. Resonance can be added to give a more dramatic effect.

Frequency response: The range of frequencies that a speaker, microphone or audio device can reproduce.

Garage: A form of house music that came from the 1970s disco clubs. Its name originated in the Paradise Garage, where Larry Levan DJ-ed.

Groove: The long microscopic indentations on a piece of vinyl which contain audio sources enabling the playback of audio from a record.

Hamster switch: A feature mainly on Vestax DJ mixers that reverses the direction of the crossfader. This gives left-handed DJs more control, and also allows a more complex range of scratch techniques to be performed.

Hum: Audio electronic noise that has a steady, low-frequency pitch.

Kill switch: A switch on a DJ mixer that will completely remove a certain set of frequencies (all the low or bass frequencies, for example). It allows a smoother and more professional mix, by cutting out unwanted frequencies.

Microphone: Device for converting sound waves to an electrical signal. Microphones come in many forms for different applications (recording, studio, PA, etc.). There are also different formats (hand-held, headworn, etc.) and they may have a fixed cable, or be wireless (requiring a radio transmitter). The most common type for PA live vocals must be robust, good at rejecting feedback, and have a frequency response tailored to the vocal range.

Mid-bass: Mid-frequency bass – usually frequencies just above the sub-bass range, from around 100-400Hz.

Mid-range: The middle range of frequencies. A mid-range speaker is sometimes combined with a woofer for low frequencies, and a tweeter for high frequencies, to form a complete, full-range system.

Mixer: A device that combines sound from microphones, CD players, and other devices. It allows you to alter the volume – and in some cases, the sound itself – and then send the mixed signal to an amplifier. (See also Pre-amplifier.)

MP3: MP3 players are the latest innovation in DJ-ing and music, thanks in part to the Apple iPod. Tracks can be downloaded from the Internet onto a computer, or to an MP3 player, or be burnt onto a CD. DJs have utilised this technology to be able to access new music quickly, and carry more music to a venue. It has also increased the use of CDs in clubs.

Output: This term can have various meanings – most commonly referring to the sound level produced by a loudspeaker, or to the sockets where the signal leaves a piece of hardware (e.g. video output, speaker output, mixer output, etc.).

PA (Public Address System): Usually the main front-of-house sound system for the audience.

Peak music power (or PMPO – Peak Music Power Output): A method of rating the output power of an amplifier – or the power which a speaker can handle. Peak music power is roughly four times the RMS rating, so an amplifier or speaker rated at 100w PMPO corresponds to one rated at 25w RMS.

Phono: Phono-connectors are the most common type of connections used between turntables/CD players/tuners/mixers/amplifiers, to link stereo audio products together (i.e. the red and white sockets on the back of all CD players). A single (yellow) socket is also used for the main video output on a CDG or DVD player, to take the signal to a TV video input.

Pitch control: A slider on a turntable that changes the tempo (speed) of the music.

Power amplifier (or Power-amp/Slave-amp): A device that takes the signal from a mixer or Pre-amp, increases the signal level, and passes it on to the speakers.

Pre-amplifier (or Pre-amp): A device that takes a source signal – such as from a turntable, tape deck or CD player – and passes this signal on to one or more power amplifiers. The pre-amp may have controls, such as source-selector switches, balance, volume and tone controls.

Scratching: A turntable mix technique that involves moving the record back and forth by hand, with the cartridge on the record, thus creating a variety of rhythmic sound patterns (depending on the type of movement used).

Slider: An electronic control that moves up and down. The ones on DJ mixers that control sound-volume are known as 'faders'. The most notable slider that is not a fader is the 'pitch control slider' on turntables, and some CD players. This makes it possible to change the speed of the record or CD – which is very important when trying to beatmatch.

Slip cue: A record cue technique that involves rocking the record back and forth by hand to locate the desired position. Once this position is found, the record is then released on cue, to achieve near-instant start-up.

Slipmat: A circular piece of felt, exactly the same size as a 12-inch vinyl record. It replaces the rubber mat on the turntable, allowing a DJ to stop the record without stopping the motor on the turntable.

Timbre: The quality of a sound that distinguishes it from other sounds of the same pitch and volume (the distinctive tone of an instrument, or a singing voice).

Tone control: Usually a single control that boosts either the bass or the treble. Use of the plural – tone controls – often implies that there will be separate controls for bass and treble.

Turntablism: The art of using a record player's turntable as a musical instrument, by making new sounds emerge from records.

Tweeter: A speaker (driver) used to reproduce the higher range of frequencies. To form a full-range system, a tweeter needs to be combined with a woofer (in a 2-way system), or a woofer and mid-range (in a 3-way system).

Woofer: A speaker (driver) used for low-frequency sound reproduction (bass), which is larger and heavier than a mid-range or tweeter.

FAQs: Becoming a DJ

Who can become a DJ?

Anyone with a keen interest in music can become a DJ. It is like learning any musical instrument: some people may have enough natural talent and ability to learn initially from books, while others may need to go on a course. As with everything we learn, there will be those who find they are naturally good at it, and others who will have to train hard to reach the same standard.

If you become fairly good at DJ-ing, then this is sufficient for an enjoyable hobby. It is however only the truly accomplished DJs that can turn this skill into a career.

How much might I be paid as a professional DJ?

A small club or wine bar is likely to pay you about £50 a night when you are first starting out. If you are able to impress the manager of the venue, and hold a crowd, this could rise to around £150 a night. Professional Commercial Club DJs can expect to receive a maximum of £250 to £300 a night. In order to earn more, you need to venture into the lucrative Dance Music market. In London, a DJ with a good reputation can expect to earn £500 a night playing a two-hour set.

To achieve higher earnings than £500 you would need to have put out a successful record, or have remixed a mainstream artist; this could earn you £1000 a night for a two-hour set in the UK, and £2000 internationally. A hit dance record and a number of successful remixes could even push your price up to £10,000 and above, around the world.

How do I get started as a professional DJ?

Once you have perfected your skills as a bedroom DJ, you should start by organising your own parties – or letting your friends know you can do parties for them. This is a great way to learn to play in front of a crowd (who are usually forgiving if you make the odd mistake while you build up your confidence!).

You should then approach local venues such as pubs, or small clubs, to see if they will let you do a warm-up set in their venue. They will require a mixtape of your skills before they allow you to do this, but you should have perfected the art of making mixtapes during your practice at home. Be persistent, and if you are turned down, offer to play on one of their quiet nights and make sure all your friends turn up to support you. This could either lead to your own night, or a local residency; once you have this achievement under your belt, it is time to start venturing further afield.

What is the ideal equipment set-up?

DJ-ing can be an expensive hobby. It is important to build up your equipment list as you receive more work – but bear in mine that you don't always need the latest equipment to be the best DJ!

An ideal Club or mobile set-up would be:

- 2 x Pioneer DVJ 1000 Mk 3
- 1 x Pioneer DJM 800 DJ Mixer
- 1 Laptop 1 x Final Scratch
- 2 x Mackie powered monitors

- 1 x Mackie amplifier

This is a good contemporary set-up, as the DVJ 1000 will allow you to play DVDs as well as MP3s. The laptop allows storage of your music collection, and could be played via the DVJ desks using the Final Scratch programme. It all comes at a cost, of course, and in total could set you back around £6000.

How can I promote myself as a DJ?

You should aim to do about four mixtapes a year. Make sure that these are professionally presented, with appropriate artwork and all your contact details. Make about 50 to 150 copies (you may have to call upon the services of a company that specialises in this field), and distribute them to friends, clubs and bars – both locally and nationally.

Try to enter at least four or five DJ competitions a year. Competitions can really help build your profile and enhance your performance skills.

You should have your own My Space site and ideally a website with downloadable mixes, together with suitable information on your background. These sites can be used effectively to build up your fanbase, while additionally providing a place for prospective venue managers to view your information. Podcasts can also be a very good way of developing your audience, but ideally you should develop some microphone skills to do this effectively.

Jim Jomoa has been a professional DJ for the past 18 years. He has played alongside Sasha and Carl Cox, produced over 75 dance tracks, and DJ'd in over 21 countries. For the last ten years he has worked in DJ education.

How the role of the DJ developed

From the earliest experiments at the start of the 20th century, the role of the DJ has developed positively and symbiotically with the evolution of new technology. Today, the DJ's art has become a complex and varied one, as **Venetia Allan** explains.

The beginnings

There is some debate over who was the very first Disc Jockey. American electrical engineer, Lee De Forest, played the *William Tell* Overture on the radio in 1907. A little earlier, on Christmas Eve in 1906, Canadian Reginald Fessenden played 'O Holy Night' on an Edison cylinder as part of a short broadcast to ships in the Atlantic Ocean. Yet no matter what the precise details, whoever played the first music to an audience over the airwaves can lay claim to being called the very first DJ. Since that time, the role of the DJ has evolved unceasingly (through many an incarnation), and today continues to develop as rapidly as ever.

The whole concept of having a radio DJ was, at first, opposed by many musicians, who felt that music should always be heard 'live'. By contrast, the role of the DJ was widely accepted by listeners by the time commercial radio was launched in America in the 1920s. In the UK, the BBC launched music radio in 1927. On both sides of the Atlantic, radio's power and influence – both in the promotion of music, and for the transmission of information – was quickly acknowledged, it would be many years before those playing records would be viewed as 'performers' in their own right, or DJ-ing itself be considered an art form. Radio DJs act in a sense as 'musical editors'; they can perhaps be viewed as 'filters' through which the best music of the day is selected (from the plethora of available recordings), and then passed on to a specific audience. This is a role that radio DJs have fulfilled from the very first broadcast until the present day.

Initial experiments

Even in the early part of the 20th century, avant-garde composers started experimenting with using new sound sources, and by 1937 recognised that this could include sound generated by record decks. Musical iconoclast John Cage proposed just such a concept in a lecture that same year, later published as *The Future of Music: Credo*. In 1948, the French composer Pierre Schaeffer employed record turntables to play and manipulate sounds from records. He did so by adjusting the volume, altering the playback speed, and playing some of the sounds backwards.

After the Second World War, however, another branch of DJ-ing developed, whereby a DJ might play records to a live audience. The development of the DJ as a 'solo performer' is inextricably linked with the development of technology, as this new role could only become viable with the invention of the turntable – and, of course, decent amplification.

In the England of the 1940s, the role of the DJ took an evolutionary leap forwards, thanks partly to the efforts of Jimmy Savile – a later TV presenter and true eccentric, not afraid to innovate. Savile is said to have been the first in England to stage a party at which the soundtrack was provided by records (and not by live bands). As his career in the running of venues developed, he rolled out this idea of 'bandless' dance parties. Of course, such an approach had the benefit of saving money by not employing live musicians –

something naturally opposed by musicians' representatives. But it did allow his club to feature the very best of the music recorded throughout the world, and not simply that of a local band, with their potentially limited repertoire. Furthermore, Savile was the first to use two record turntables, and also to talk between playing records. In addition, he was instrumental in the development of the equipment needed to play records to a large group of party-goers, using friends to design and build the more robust system that the DJ would need to play such records.

In 1947, the liberated and swinging city of Paris opened the very first 'discotheque' – the infamous Whiskey-a-Go-Go club – proving irrefutably that people were even then happy to spend wild nights out dancing to records in dingy basements!

DJs as pioneers

During the 20th century, many revolutions in commercial music could be argued to have been DJ-led. Even today, DJs on pirate radio still bring music from the fringes to a larger audience, and DJs in small clubs break new sounds, too.

The dawn of rock 'n' roll was ushered in on radio by DJs who brought black-influenced music to a white audience. Later, disco was developed in clubs by DJs adapting their record collection to generate the most excitement from a dancing crowd. And reggae was developed by DJs for sound systems, becoming popular in Jamaica from the mid 1950s onwards. By the late 1960s, DJs such as King Tubby were cutting dub-plates of tunes for their own use – essentially creating their own version of records, and pressing these one-off edits onto vinyl. Such DJs were adapting technology for their own ends, using any tool they could to improve their DJ sets.

Sound systems had a big influence on the development of hip-hop in New York in the late 1970s and 1980s. Underground sounds sometimes cross over into the mainstream, and each of the styles previously mentioned has had a lasting impact on popular music. DJs can therefore be viewed as trendsetters in this process, and they can also educate an audience as to what new music is appearing. They are the ones who can get the work of new musicians to an audience – a vital role for any aspiring producer or musician.

By the time DJs had adopted technology to create entirely new sounds, and to perform these sounds to a live audience, they could finally be considered 'performers' in their own right. However, it took another few decades before the DJ would be given much credit for providing this service. If good performance can be defined as good communication, then an accomplished DJ is just as capable a performer as an instrumentalist. This leap could not, however, have occurred until record deck technology reached a certain level of complexity. It was in 1979 – with the release of the Technics SL1200 MK2 direct-drive turntable – that the technology became available to permit the next stage of DJ evolution. The deck featured a 'pitch control', which allowed the DJ to change the speed of the record. Two records of different speed could be matched together and blended seamlessly without a break in the beat. This technique is a staple skill of most DJs, and is called mixing or 'beatmatching'.

There were many advantages to 'decks' over traditional instruments. Decks – capable of playing all kinds of music – were incredibly versatile and did not need years of study before they could produce powerful results. Creative people then began to appropriate this technology for their own purposes.

DJs as musical creators

Hip hop is often described by its protagonists as being made with 'two turntables and a microphone'. It was during the 1970s that DJs from the New York Bronx started to exploit this new advancement in deck technology, and develop DJ-ing into a 'solo performance' in its own right.

Kool Herc was the first to play 'breakbeats'. By taking the percussive sections from funk and soul records, and playing these sections in a sequence, he created musical 'collages' of other people's records. The drum breaks of a record were the bits to which people loved to dance the most, and this eventually led to the coining of the term, 'break dancing'. Kool Herc also added Masters of Ceremonies (MCs) into the mixture – a nod to his Jamaican roots. As this style of DJ-ing became more popular, employing a good MC or rapper was an excellent way for a DJ to set himself apart from the crowd, and very quickly 'rap' turned into an art form in its own right.

Another DJ, Grandmaster Flash, further expanded the breakbeat style by experimenting with sound and equipment in a 'scientific' way. He tried to inject greater precision into his approach, in order to get the switching between records tighter, more continuous, and more accurate – all in the interests of encouraging dancing. He even developed his own equipment. At this point, hip hop emerged as truly a new form of music, rather than just blending other people's records. Vinyl became a tool for the DJ to create new music.

The other widely acknowledged member of the 'Big Three' founders of hip hop was Afrika Bambaataa. He could not compete with Kool Herc's powerful sound system, nor with Grandmaster Flash's technical skill, but he was immensely popular because of his *choice* of music: he would play anything that enhanced the party atmosphere. As the founder of Zulu Nation (hip hop's oldest and largest 'international awareness' group), he also showed that a DJ can fulfil a role of sociological importance.

An important aspect of the role of DJ is that of 'pleasure dispenser'. DJs can be conduits for celebration – truly the life and soul of the party. But DJs like the Big Three are also craftsmen and technicians: techniques that they used included mixing and chopping between records, and using two copies of the same record to rearrange tracks on the fly. Grandmaster Flash, in particular, developed more complex techniques. He would use the decks to make manual samples and to loop small segments of music. Such techniques were slow to catch on, but by 1976 Grandmaster Flash and his MCs – the Furious 5 – were hugely popular, and this 'cut-and-paste' approach became the basis of a whole style of musical creation (which later became mainstream with the advent of digital sampling). Flash was also the first DJ to do body tricks (spinning and jumping around whilst playing, for example).

In 1977, the next phase of development in DJ history took place – by accident. Grand Wizard Theodore invented the 'scratch'. As a kid, Grand Wizard Theodore had played with Grandmaster Flash, often standing on a box to reach the decks. Apparently, the 14-year-old Theodore was playing records when his mother came into the bedroom to talk to him (purportedly to tell him to keep the noise down). Preoccupied, the young Grand Wizard stopped the record with his fingers to listen, but kept moving the record back and forth over one drumbeat. This proved an interesting sound effect, and scratching has been part of DJ-ing ever since!

1981 saw the release of 'Adventures of Grandmaster Flash on the Wheels of Steel' – a seven-minute mash-up of current big tunes, recorded live with several decks and a mixer. This was the first record to demonstrate hip-hop DJ-ing skills, and the post-modern collage was a huge hit in clubs in both the United States and in Europe.

Using turntables as 'instruments' became mainstream in 1983 with the release of Herbie Hancock's 'Rockit'. Music fans throughout the world watched in fascination as Grandmaster DST scratched a record in time to the beat of the song. The scratching functioned both melodically and rhythmically. Teamed with a great video, the song became an MTV hit and helped to break the 'no black music' policy which the network was implementing at the time.

This style of DJ-ing – scratching and rapping – spread throughout the 1980s. Many 'systems' working in a small area helped a battle culture to develop, where different crews at local parties came up against each other to fight for territory. The theatrical style that Grandmaster Flash had pioneered caught on, as competitive DJs vied with one another to be the fastest and most creative, while still maintaining the rhythm. They competed in volume, spectacle, tunes and skills. These performances were often astonishingly gymnastic and daring, and sometimes featured a cash prize.

As the performances became more and more complex, the decks took on a life of their own. DJ-ing developed into more of an art form: into what became known as 'turntablism'. The term was first used in 1994 by DJ Supreme to describe the difference between a DJ who merely plays records, and one who actually 'performs' – by using decks as instruments to manipulate tiny slices of sound, thus creating new music. Hip-hop turntablist DJs combined the early techniques, such as beat matching and scratching, and also took things further with beat juggling – using individual drum hits as sound source material. Some turntablists today seek to be recognised as legitimate musicians: they argue that effective performance is just as important in DJ-ing as in playing traditional instruments. In 1987, the Disco Mix Club (DMC) held their first turntablist championship, and these battles still continue today.

In the late 1980s the music industry saw the potential of hip hop as a marketable genre of music, and it was easier to create stars of rappers than of DJs. DJ-ing and turntablism went back underground – where it continued to thrive amongst its truly devoted fans.

Digital technology was the next big influence on the evolution of DJ-ing and turntablism. In 1992, Denon Electronics launched the DN-2000F – a dual rack-mount CD player with a featured pitch control (as on a vinyl deck). This player became the industry standard for the next five years. It meant that a track made using this technology could make the journey from studio to dance floor in a matter of minutes. These days, it would be very rare to find a club that does not have CD decks, and some of these decks have features that far outstrip the capabilities of a vinyl deck.

The superstar DJ

In the UK in the late 1980s it was the explosion of 'Acid House' that turned the DJ from supplier of background music to the focus of attention for a whole generation.

During the 1980s, the first wave of influence arrived from American hip-hoppers Grandmaster Flash, Kool Herc, Afrika Baambaataa, and others. The second wave was 'House' and 'Techno' music from Detroit, and particularly Chicago – futurist music featuring the TB 303, providing squelches, bleeps and other-worldly weirdness!

DJs like Pete Tong and Danny Rampling were inspired by the sounds heard at house pioneer club, Delirium, in London. In 1987, Paul Oakenfold, Johnny Walker, Nicky Holloway and Danny Rampling took a holiday in Ibiza. For some time, the drug 'Ecstasy' had been popular in this established hippy island, and aspiring DJs were wowed by the club culture they found on the island. They vowed to start their own nights in London where the soundtrack would be house music, and the new drug MDMA – or 'E' – the 'catalyst'.

These new clubs became an oasis for 'blissed-up' dancers. Ecstasy and house music made a pretty heady combination, and the strong empathetic feelings invoked by E gave the clubbers a feeling of unity and love. Philosophers since Plato have seen the danger inherent in young people (especially intoxicated ones) gathering in large groups and dancing – and this new phenomenon was also at odds with the prevalent Thatcherite values of consumerism and individualism.

Restrictive nightclub licensing laws in the UK meant that promoters began to stage events outdoors, outside London, and outside of licensed venues. These events attracted thousands of people, and they were soon slated in the tabloid newspapers, which were only too happy to assist in generating moral panic. The 'evils of acid house' were discussed in all the papers, and seemingly overnight thousands more young people liked the sound of it, and joined in! By 1988, the whole country knew about it.

The heightened feelings in clubs were naturally directed towards DJs. As the provider of the soundtrack to a novel and ecstatic experience (and with no live bands), DJs became the 'shaman' stars. This perception represented a huge shift in the nation's culture, and the DJ led the way – truly the leader of the dance.

The UK Government began to legislate against the phenomenon of acid house, and at the same time relaxed club licensing laws. 'Raving' was getting more difficult, but clubbing easier, a factor which led to the next stage of life for the DJ. Big-name DJs would attract large crowds, and large crowds meant big profits. Many US dance record producers were brought over to the UK as guest DJs. People would travel miles just to hear a particular DJ, and quite soon big names were playing several sets in different clubs each night. These DJs could command huge fees – and in some cases they achieved near god-like status. In February 1994, dance culture magazine *Mixmag* featured Sasha in a prayer pose, with the headline, 'Son of God?'

The DJ had to be an entertainer. Clubbers paying large sums for entry into a club expected value for money. And, of course, there were plenty of other clubs they could choose to go to if they weren't happy.

Production and DJ-ing in these styles of music were inextricably linked. The best DJs instinctively knew which tunes worked on dance floors, and successful producers whose names were instantly recognisable by crowds could fill a club if their names appeared on a line-up.

But the music industry had not yet worked out how to exploit the figure of the DJ as a profitable artist. Dance records were signed as singles, not albums, and artists often remained faceless. Early forays into marketing DJs as album artists did not work well. However, the 1990s saw the rise of the 'superclubs' – such as Ministry of Sound, and Cream. They released mix CDs, often selling hundreds of thousands of copies. The DJ whose name would appear on the cover might be paid tens of thousands of pounds – yet he or she may not even have been involved in the mixing! The mixes would often be put together by engineers in a studio. A DJ resident at a club also became an ambassador for a venue or clubnight, and/or the record label to which they were signed. DJ 'brands' began to travel the world, and – as club culture spread – DJs were paid large fees to play abroad.

An entire industry built up around the DJs, involving promoters, managers, press, radio pluggers, flyer designers, drivers – and many others, too, lived off the 'club culture'.

The lifestyle of the superstar DJ was a huge draw for youngsters. There appeared to be lots of cash, glamour, travel, and (especially for men who might not otherwise seem so appealing) the chance of attracting the opposite sex! In any 'glamorous' industry, there will naturally be competition, and this meant that it became quite normal for a fledgling DJ to have also to be a marketer, promoter, label manager, probably a producer, and a good many other things to boot – just to get noticed!

Present and future

A competent DJ has always had to be something of a mind-reader – able to empathise with the audience, and instinctively determine what they would like to hear. He or she must also tread the fine line between entertaining and educating in order to keep an audience's interest.

DJs also act as 'librarians' – archiving our musical history, especially as new ways of music 'consumption' appear to be pointing towards more personal choice in music programming. Internet streaming of music allows listeners to choose their favourite style. There is so much music around now, in fact, that it makes sense that these experts should act as musical filters. DJs, therefore, can be programmers and determiners of future music consumption, as well as fulfilling an important social function.

DJs have always seen technology as something to be exploited, not feared. Many are 'tech heads', and enjoy developing new ways of performing music. In the present day, the development of technology is increasing at an astonishing rate, and DJs can be seen using CDs, MP3s, mixing software, and more complex programs which allow for 'live remixing'. With programs such as Ableton, a DJ can now edit, reconstruct and adapt any piece of music within a live performance. This fact leads logically to the point where a DJ can be considered a truly creative musician.

Digital technology has given us much more control over the *means* of music production. Studios where professional tracks can be produced now cost a fraction of what they did even ten years ago. And the rise of the Internet gives independent musicians control over the means of distribution, too. Such factors must necessarily have a huge impact on the future of music, and how DJs must consequently work.

DJ-ing has always been the epitome of post-modern culture. Cutting and pasting musical information, and creating new music and meanings through the consumption of the music of others, is about as 'post modern' as you can get! So what's next, then: where does the future lie? Technology is now so fast-moving that this is incredibly difficult to predict. The best method of spotting new musical trends is still to go down to a reputable club, and see what the most cutting-edge DJ is doing; or else trawl the web for DJs' sets and videos. DJs continue to sculpt their role in society with each passing year, and there is every likelihood that the evolution of the role of the DJ will, in future, prove as revolutionary and fascinating as it has done in the past.

Venetia Allan holds a degree in Commercial Music from Westminster University. She has been a DJ with a residency at Turnmills, and played at venues including Fabric, The Boutique, The End and Eden in Ibiza. She formerly ran record label Pear Music, and produced for it with support from the likes of Roger Sanchez, Erick Morillo and Danny Rampling. She also helped develop Pear Press – a promotions company specialising in dance music. Now a solo artist, she currently lectures in Music Technology at the University of Chichester.

The basics of DJ technique

DJ equipment

In terms of traditional DJ-ing (involving the use of turntables), the following equipment might be recommended:

- 2 x Technics Sl-1200 Turntables
- A DJ mixer (ideally with four channels)
- 2 x speakers (ideally, powered speakers)
- 1 x stereo amplifier
- Headphones
- Cartridges
- 2 x slipmats
- 1 x deck stand
- Some records!

An estimate for start-up costs would total around £1000 – £1500.

Basic techniques
Setting up the equipment

The deck (or turntable) stand provides you with a tailor-made unit on which to put your expensive equipment. Such a stand will also have dedicated space for your speakers, records and amplifier.

Place one turntable carefully on the left on the deck stand, and the other on the right-hand side. The DJ mixer should be placed in the centre. The turntables are connected to the DJ mixer using two red and white 'phono' switches. The leads are already connected to the turntables, and you simply need to plug them into the back of the mixer at the connection marked 'phono'; a ground connection is also used to earth the equipment, and prevent hum.

The speakers are connected to the amplifier using speaker wires, and the amplifier connects to the mixer by means of a phono cable connected to the back of the mixer.

The cartridges are placed on each turntable arm, with slipmats on the turntables themselves to protect your records.

Controlling the vinyl

The first basic technique that a new DJ must master is that of controlling the vinyl.

It's often best for new DJs to start off using two copies of the same record. The art of DJ-ing is to 'beatmatch': learn to use the natural symmetry of the body by splitting the listening between your left and right ears.

Place identical copies of a record of your choice on both turntables (choose a record you like, or are familiar with). Small stickers can be used to mark the '12 o'clock' point on the record. This will make your task easier from a visual perspective. To find the '12 o'clock' point, you need to place the needle on the record, and use your middle finger in the centre of the vinyl to spin round the record, until you hear sound. (At this stage, play the music through the main speakers and leave the headphones off for now.) You should then rewind the record back to mark the 'First Beat'.

Stop the turntable and place your sticker at the top of the record. Do this for both records. Then hold the edge of the vinyl on the right turntable with your left hand, as you switch on the turntable with your right hand. This prevents the vinyl moving on from this point. (You will need to do this gently). The Technics direct-drive turntable has enough power to drive the turntable round, while the slipmat enables you to hold the record still. Now take your right hand, spread your fingers out as far as you can (your thumb will provide balance), and bring your middle finger down onto the vinyl. You should place your hand in a position on the record directly opposite the turntable arm.

You should now be controlling the vinyl with the platter spinning freely underneath. It may take a few attempts as you adjust your pressure on the record, and you may also need to wet your finger slightly, to give you more grip.

Cueing the record

Keep your hand in the position described above, but this time move the record forwards and backwards over the first beat. The mark at 12 o'clock should help you identify where this is. As you build up your confidence, speed up this motion until it can be done with a flick of the wrist.

Pull the record back about an inch, and flick your wrist to the right (into the beat), counting '1' as you do so. This will take a while to perfect, but once you have done it, repeat the action, and count '1, 2, 3, 4.' Here you are cueing the record in time, and creating a one-bar intro in which to release the record.

Let the record play for four to eight bars, while you listen to and ascertain the tempo of the record. Place your middle finger in the centre of the record (where the label is), and press hard as you rewind the record back to just behind its starting point. Repeat the process, keeping in time with the speed and tempo of your record.

The first mix

Two copies of the same record are used to make it easier to identify when your cueing is at fault. Play the record on the left deck, and practise placing the first beat on the right deck exactly on top of the beat playing. This will take five or ten minutes to master.

This time you will count in phrases, '1, 2, 3, 4', '1, 2, 3, 4', '1, 2, 3, 4', '1, 2, 3, 4'. Then release the record. It will take a few adjustments and attempts, but this technique will enable you to achieve your first mix.

Split cue

Now it is time to introduce the headphones. All modern DJ mixers have a 'split cue' feature, which allows you to feed the sound of each record to a different ear (left or right) on your earphones.

There are two techniques that can be employed here. You can complete a mix with your headphones on (both ears) and the split cue activated – although this is often best left until later. Alternatively, you can place one side of the headphones on one ear, and listen to the sound of the other record playing through the speakers.

It is here that a good pair of professional headphones will prove their worth.

Crossfader control

Place both records at the start, make sure that your 'two line' faders are up fully, and move the 'crossfader' completely to the right-hand side.

Play the record on the left deck, and cue your right-hand record in your headphones. Count four bars as above, and release the record. You will find that this is difficult at first, as you will previously have done it through speakers, so your ears will need to adjust to the difference in sound.

When the beats are matched slowly, move the crossfader from the right-hand side into the middle (try to do this over four bars), then take another four bars to move the crossfader from the middle to the left-hand side. Again, it will take a few attempts, but this process will allow you to complete your first mix.

- There are a number of ways to improve your technique:
- Practise for only 1-2 hours at a time.
- Ensure that the pitch control on both records is at 0 or the 'quartz lock' position.
- Make sure you have a good-quality pair of headphones.
- Practise using headphones and also working without headphones.
- Adjust the volume controls on the mixer and on the headphones.
- Record your first practice sessions, so you can listen back in order to see where you are going wrong.
- Try to find two records that start with a strong kick drum (house records are highly recommended for all trainee DJs).

Once you have completed your mix, return the record to the beginning, and repeat the process. You should try to create a smooth loop that effectively sounds like one record playing continuously. You will need to time your mixes using the counting method, so that you have always completed your mix by the time the intro of the record has finished (usually 16 or 32 bars).

Now you are ready to move on to two *different* records!

BPM-ing your records

The first thing to establish is the 'BPM' (Beats Per Minute) of both records. Use one of the records you have started with for familiarity.

Before modern mixers (like the Pioneer DJM 600 or the DJM 800) came to market with built-in beat counters, the only way to establish BPM was by using a stop-watch, and counting the beats in 15 seconds, and then multiplying by four. You would next mark the BPM of each record using white stickers on the record and its sleeve.

When starting to mix two records of different BPM, make sure that the records are within two to six BPM of each other. The closer the BPM, the easier it will be to mix the records. So, one record at, say, 120 BPM, and the other at 123 BPM, would be an ideal start.

Pitch control

The 'pitch control' is situated on the right side of each turntable, and goes from -8 to +8. (Make sure you start your original record at 0.) If this first record is the one at 120 BPM, move the pitch control of the other record to +2. Repeat the steps in cueing the record, but listen carefully as the records start to go out of sync, and adjust the pitch faster, or slower, as necessary. You will also find it easier if you re-cue the record every second or third attempt.

This is an area many new DJs find difficult. You have to ensure you have perfected your cueing technique, and that it is accurate. Timing is very important. You also have to split your hearing between your left and right ears, and use the natural symmetry of your brain in order to match the sounds together. It can take some time and practice, but you will normally achieve it after two or three sessions.

You should try to minimise using your hands on the record once it is cued. By squeezing the pitch control gently between your thumb and first finger, you gain control of the groove of the record in order to match the beats.

Jim Jomoa has been a professional DJ for the past 18 years. He has played alongside Sasha and Carl Cox, produced over 75 dance tracks, and DJ-d in more than 21 countries. For the last ten years he has worked in DJ education.

Resources

BOOKS

DJ Cookbook: Business Start-Up Guide
Author Dan Titus
Publisher Venture Marketing, 2002
ISBN 1582911088

Most DJs work on a self-employed basis. Therefore, careful consideration of the business and commercial aspects of life as a DJ – just as much as a focus on technique and artistry – is absolutely essential for economic survival. This book is currently one of the few texts to tackle this issue directly. Foreword by Dave Kreiner.

DJ Culture
Author Ulf Poschardt
Publisher Quartet Books, 2000
ISBN 0704380986

Looks outside technical considerations to the wider context in which the DJ operates. The whole environment which revolves around, and is reliant upon, the DJ, is examined in social terms – and significant trends and fashions explored.

The DJ Handbook (2nd edn)
Author Charles Slaney
Publisher PC Publishing, 2005
ISBN 1870775996

Slim, useful volume which covers topics relating to mobile and club DJs, the art of mixing, how to obtain the best sound, equipment set-up, troubleshooting and sample DJ business contracts.

DJ Techniques
Authors Tom Frederikse, David Sloly
Publisher Sanctuary, 2003
ISBN 1844920275

With supporting CD, many helpful diagrams and other useful tips, this large-format book is a clear, teach-yourself course for would-be turntablists.

How to Be a DJ
Author Chuck Fresh
Publisher Thomson Course Technology PTR, 2004
ISBN 1592005098

Clear, practical and more comprehensive than most DJ guides. Subtitled, 'Your guide to becoming a radio, nightclub or private party disc jockey'.

How to DJ: The Definitive Guide to Success on the Decks
Authors Tom Frederikse, Phil Benedictus
Publisher Piatkus/Point Blank, 2002

ISBN 0749923253
Written by industry professionals, this book concisely demonstrates concepts ranging from basic DJ technical skills to explaining the role of the contemporary DJ/Producer, while also putting the whole art of DJ-ing into its business and commercial context.

How to DJ (Properly): The Art and Science of Playing Records
Authors Frank Broughton, Bill Brewster
Publisher Bantam Press, 2002
ISBN 0593049667

Highly regarded introduction to the world of DJ-ing, of value to the novice and also to more experienced DJs, thanks to its range of illustrated tutorials from basic to advanced. Presents a balanced view of the DJ's world by explaining the often tough realities behind the dance music industry, while at the same time revealing its rewards. Mixing techniques and styles are covered, as are tips on buying the right equipment and records, and creating your own tracks. Includes advice from superstar DJs.

Last Night a DJ Saved My Life: 100 Years of the Disc Jockey
Authors Frank Broughton, Bill Brewster
Publisher Headline Book Publishing, 2006
ISBN 0755313984

An expanded and updated version of this classic account of the history of the disc jockey, issued to celebrate what is now said to mark 100 years of DJ-ing: an art form born on Christmas Eve, 1906, when Reginald Fessenden first played a record over the radio. The story of how, from humble 'talking jukebox' origins, DJs today have evolved into mainstays (even superstars) of the music industry, is the stuff of a fascinating and turbulent legend.

The Live Sound Manual
Author Ben Duncan
Publisher Backbeat Books, 2002
ISBN 0879306998

A comprehensive introductory handbook written for sound engineers, musicians and DJs, and including a technical glossary. Covers setting up and using microphones, DI boxes, mixers, EQ, compressors, crossovers, power amps and speakers. With tips on mic placement, EQ-ing, stopping feedback, plus monitoring, troubleshooting and equipment maintenance.

Music Industry Manual (MIM)
Editor James Robertson
Publisher Ampire Publications (Annual)

ISBN 0954361431

Subtitled as the 'DJ, Nightclub, Promoter Handbook', this comprehensive directory focuses on the DJ/VJ market (not the music industry as a whole, but with all related DJ industry contacts), and contains more than 30 editorial/feature articles. Within its 90 or more categories, this annual publication lists everything from top DJs to small underground clubs and esoteric record labels. Listings are all UK-centred (although there is an international appendix). Formerly promoted as the 'Dance Music Bible'. Includes a CD-ROM and online access. See **www.mim.dj**.

Pump Up the Volume: A History of House Music

Author Sean Bidder
Publisher Channel 4 Books, 2001
ISBN 0752219863

Explains the roots of house music in Chicago, where it grew out of the ashes of disco to become the soundtrack of modern popular culture. The story moves from Chicago and New York via Ibiza to Britain, and involves key players on both sides of the Atlantic (Paul Oakenfold, Carl Cox, and the people behind the superclubs like Ministry of Sound and Cream). The importance of house within the music of leading mainstream artists is also examined, as it is said to have influenced more people than any style since rock 'n' roll. (Written to accompany the TV series.)

Sound and Recording: An Introduction (5th edn)

Authors Francis Rumsey, Tim McCormick
Publisher Focal Press, 2005
ISBN 0240519965

A comprehensive, easy-to-read reference manual for those at the outset of their careers. Covers basic acoustics, auditory perception, mixing-console layout and functions, mixer automation, analogue and digital recording, noise reduction, MIDI, timecode synchronisation, microphone principles and loudspeaker systems.

Turntable Technique: The Art of the DJ

Author Stephen Webber
Publisher Berklee Press Publications, 2000
ISBN 0876390106

Step-by-step tutorial guide for the beginner/amateur that covers scratching, beatmatching, mixing, crossfader techniques, stabs and other DJ techniques. Includes 2 practice vinyls.

The Virgin Encyclopedia of Dance Music

Editor Colin Larkin
Publisher Virgin, 1999
ISBN 0753502526

Documents essential facts relating to the diverse dance-music scene from the early 1980s to the end of the 1990s – including bands, producers, labels and remixers. Also incorporates otherwise hard-to-find dates, career bios and discographies, and an exposition of the prime movers and shakers in the business.

MAGAZINES

DJ (DJ Magazine)

Editor Lesley Wright
Publisher Future Publishing

Monthly magazine which includes news and features, updates on the clubbing scene, Ibiza, the latest charts, new DJ technology and record reviews. See **www.djmag.com**.

IDJ (International DJ)

Editor Russell Deeks
Publisher Headrush Media

Monthly magazine with regular/special features on the international DJ scene, and covering DJ gear, techniques and tunes, as well as containing major interviews. See **www.i-dj.co.uk**.

Mixmag

Editor Andrew Harrison
Publisher Development Hell Limited

Monthly dance music magazine launched in 1982, and then re-launched in April 2006 with a renewed commitment to new music – from electronica to house and urban and beyond. Also intended to help plan nights out in the UK and elsewhere. Includes a free cover CD mixed by high-profile DJs. See **www.mixmag.net**.

Music Week

Editor Martin Talbot
Publisher CMP Information: United Business Media
ISSN 0265-1548

The UK's main music business weekly aimed at those involved or interested in all aspects of the business side of the music industry. Contains current news, technology and business developments, and chart information. See **www.musicweek.com**.

Recording and production
Introduction

Our present recording technology bears little relation to that famously used by Thomas Edison when he recorded 'Mary Had a Little Lamb' onto a tinfoil cylinder, nearly 130 years ago. However, in spite of such progress, most of the business structures of the traditional music industry were established before the Great War, and only now – around a century later – are they set to change. At that time (a century or so ago), live music performances and printed music sales were major sources of income for performers and composers, and before the age of recordings and radio it was sheet music, with its attractive covers, that – in terms of popularity and ease of use – acted as the equivalent of today's CD.

Nowadays, recorded music forms a huge part of the worldwide music market; globally it is worth over 30 billion US dollars a year. The British recorded music market is the third largest in the world – after the USA and Japan – and comprises a vital part of our economic and cultural life.

Broadcasting created the first mass audience for music (from the 1920s and 30s onwards), replacing previous historical periods that could be said to be defined by their more limited means of communication. Now, following further technological evolution, the 21st century is set to emerge as an era of 'unlimited channel space'. So distribution of recorded music should, in future, become ever more efficient and lucrative.

Remembering that customer loyalty is of paramount importance to artists, and sometimes to composers, all those needing to have their music recorded should set up strategic partnerships. The composer and the artist should form an alliance, for example, and they, in turn, need to work in partnership with producers and record labels/distributors (and, likely as not, also with agents and promoters).

In an environment where traditional music industry roles are beginning to change, record companies – and especially the major labels – seem increasingly to be acting as distributors of finished product, superseding their long-standing role as investors in developing artists and repertoire (A&R). This A&R function is now often absorbed by smaller, independent labels (or artist management companies), and even some very astute and well-organised artists themselves. The implications of this trend are threefold:

1) Music which professional artists or songwriters/composers need recorded has increasingly to be prepared, even in demo form, as closely as possible to a polished 'master' recording. Some songwriting partnerships today also form their own production companies to achieve this goal – thereby also benefiting financially from the additional income due from production royalties. Their musical product can often be licensed to major labels, or used for 'synchronisation' purposes (in TV, film, games, or other forms of media).

2) Artists, songwriters and producers need to do all they can to give themselves a head start in the industry by developing as far as possible their own careers, and building up a strong, unique profile (all the while also helping those to whom their fortunes may be linked).

3) As a corollary of the previous situation, artists, songwriters/composers and producers need to be prepared to market-test their own 'product' (ideally in more than one national

market), so that they can show evidence of real earning potential, in hard numbers. If they can demonstrate to record companies or other clients a solid profit through sales of their music on a small scale, such companies won't fail to take notice as they calculate the potential profit on a larger scale.

In recent years, we have seen many traditional recording studios having to adapt to survive, as the old 'rent out the studio' business model increasingly fails to generate sufficient revenue – unless, of course, those studios happen to be ultra-specialists in their field. The large studios of old are being replaced by more compact facilities, and their huge recording consoles by virtual desks and other powerful new computer equipment. Music technologists and producers also have to operate in a world of increasing convergence of all forms of media.

However, irrespective of the pace of change, the art of networking remains vital in such a potentially isolating profession as that of the music producer. Keeping up-to-date with the latest hardware and software is made possible by reading publications like *Sound on Sound*, as well as selected music technology texts (and, of course, it is always useful to develop an expertise in absorbing the contents of music software manuals). Undoubtedly, new entrants to the field of music technology will find the sheer array of equipment potentially bewildering. But the principles that have always applied to music recordings remain the same. Artists and songwriters need the best possible recordings that money can buy (and technology can deliver), in order to be able to showcase their talents, and make progress within the industry. New formats certainly need also to be embraced: the impact of fine music played by great musicians, and recorded on SACD or in Surround Sound, for example, can be extraordinarily impressive.

Recording studios

2 kHz Studios
97A Scrubs Lane, London NW10 6QU
tel 020-8960 1331
email info@2kHzstudios.co.uk
website www.2kHzstudios.co.uk
Studio Manager Mike Nelson *Key Producers/Engineers*
Ian Grimble, Richard Matthews, Adrian Newton

Founded in 2001. Recording and mixing studio with
vintage equipment including Trident series 80 desk
and Studer 2" tape machine (full equipment list
available from website). Recent clients include: The
Futureheads, Babyshambles, Franz Ferdinand and
The Darkness.

Rates: Studio 1: approx. £600 per day; Studio 2:
approx. £250 per day.

Abbey Road Studios
3 Abbey Road, London NW8 9AY
tel 020-7266 7000 *fax* 020-7266 7250
email bookings@abbeyroad.com
website www.abbeyroad.com
Studio Manager Colette Barber

Opened in 1931. Became famous for its large
orchestral recording sessions. Hosts technically
advanced recording and mixing, stereo and surround
mastering and remastering, interactive design and a
digital video service. Contains 3 studio spaces: Studio
1 uses a 72 channel Neve 88RS with full surround;
Studio 2, a Neve VRP 60 channel; and Studio 3, a SSL
9000J series 96 channel.

Air-Edel Recording Studios
18 Rodmarton Street, London W1U 8BJ
tel 020-7486 6466 *fax* 020-7224 0344
email tbest@air-edel.co.uk
website www.air-edel.co.uk
Studio Manager Trevor Best

Established in 1990 and recognised for its sound-to-
picture facility. Contains 3 studios: Studio 1 can
accommodate approx. 30 musicians and has a
Steinway 'B' grand piano; Studio 2 is suited to smaller
line-ups and voice-over recordings; and Studio 3
offers digital editing facilities and is often used for
sound-effect dubbing.

Air Studios (Lyndhurst)
Lyndhurst Hall, Lyndhurst Road, Hampstead,
London NW3 5NG
tel 020-7794 0660 *fax* 020-7794 8518
email info@airstudios.com
website www.airstudios.com
Bookings Manager Alison Burton

Opened in 1992 by founder George Martin.
Especially popular for large-scale film music and
classical recording. Contains 3 studios, and Lyndhurst
Hall itself: Studio 1 has Custom Neve 72ch; Studio 2,
80 channel SSL 8000G; and Studio 3 uses 4x48 stereo
path AMS Neve Logic console. Lyndhurst Hall
utilises a Neve 88R 96 channel, contains a Steinway
'D' concert grand piano and is suitable for symphony
or chamber orchestra and large choir recording.

Angel Recording Studios
311 Upper Street, Islington, London N1 2TU
tel 020-7354 2525 *fax* 020-7226 9624
email angel@angelstudios.co.uk
website www.angelstudios.co.uk
Studio Manager Lucy Jones *Key Producers/Engineers*
Gary Thomas, Steve Price, Niall Acott

Founded in 1980. Renowned 3-studio complex.
Clients have included: George Fenton, Guy
Chambers, Debbie Wiseman. Studio 1 contains Neve
88R; Studio 2, Euphonix Systems; and Studio 3, Neve
VXS60. Phone the studio manager for current rates
information.

Ape Studios
15 Quayside, Little Neston, Neston,
Cheshire CH64 0TB
tel 0151-336 1098
email info@apestudios.com
website www.apestudios.com
Studio Manager Coz Littler

A vintage analogue studio that aims to bring out the
classic, big-sounding production of the past.
Equipment includes Vintage Helios, Neumann desk
and Pro Tools.

Appletree Studios
Glebe Farm, Piddington Road, Ludgershall,
Aylesbury, Buckinghamshire HP18 9PL
tel (01844) 237916
email info@appletreestudios.co.uk
website www.appletrestudios.com

Records using a Tascam MSR 16 analogue reel to
reel, Tascam 2424 digital recorder and Soundcraft
Ghost 32 (72 channel) mixer. Also provides location
recording facilities.

B and B Studios
280 Park Avenue, Kingston Upon Hull,
East Yorkshire HU5 4DA
mobile (07092) 087573
email info@bandb-group.com
website www.bandb-group.com
Contact Dave Bradfield

Recording studio also offering post-production and
mastering. Uses an array of modern and professional

standard equipment. Houses a self-contained duplicating factory, duplicating CD and vinyl. In-house digital artwork design and creation.

Blueprint Studios

Elizabeth House, 39 Queen Street, Salford M3 7DQ
tel (08700) 112760 *fax* (08700) 112780
email tim@blueprint-studios.com
website www.blueprint-studios.com
Studio Manager Tim Thomas

Mixes analogue and digital technology. Studio 1 contains a Neve VR Legend 36, and Studio 2 uses Digidesign D Command (24 channel).

BonaFide Studio

Burbage House, 83-85 Curtain Road,
London EC2A 3BS
tel 020-7684 5350/5351 *fax* 020-7729 9935
email info@bonafidestudio.co.uk
website www.bonafidestudio.co.uk
Studio Director Deanna Vukovic *Key Producer/
Engineer* Brian Bogdanovic

Founded in 1999. Works with a range of clients from unsigned acts to established artists on a variety of projects, from demos and singles to radio plays and interactive CDs. Specialises in the production and development of new and original musical ideas in an attempt to provide top-quality but affordable recording. Both analogue and digital recording techniques are utilised.

Rates: From only £12.50 per hour.

Boomtown Studio

Valetta Road, London W3 7TG
tel 020-8723 9548
email info@boomtownstudio.co.uk
website www.boomtownstudio.co.uk
Proprietor Simon Wilkinson

Founded in 1995. Specialises in recording and producing singer/songwriters. Clients have included: Peter Andre, Sonia Jones and Peter Darbyshire. Works with Pro Tools 24bit system, RatisaDA7 desk and Genezec monitoring alongside a range of software synths and samplers. Also provides production music services for film and TV companies worldwide.

Rates: From £30 per hour.

Brighton Electric Recording Co

43-45 Coombe Terrace, Lewes Road,
Brighton BN2 4AD
tel (01273) 819617
email info@g-zero.co.uk
website www.brightonelectric.co.uk
Studio Manager Luke Joyce

Founded in 1999. Large studio complex incorporating cinema, cafe, 7 rehearsal rooms and 3 recording studios. Recent clients include: Jonny

Truant, The Others, Charlottefield and Elle Milano. Recording takes place with 2 inch 24 track tape, 96 track Pro Tools, neve and API outboard, PRE's Sony DMX and 400FT2 hardwood liveroom.

Britannia Row Studios

3 Bridge Studios, 318 Wandsworth Bridge Road,
Fulham, London SW6 2TZ
tel 020-7371 5872 *fax* 020-7371 8641
email info@britanniarowstudios.co.uk
website www.britanniarowstudios.co.uk
Director Jamie Lane *Key Producers/Engineers* Dave Eringa, Youth, Guy Massey, Craig Silvie

Founded in 1976. Aims to combine state-of-the-art digital recording with classic analogue equipment. Recent clients include: Snow Patrol, Westlife and Embrace. Works with Pro Tools HD3 Accel and Vintage Neve console. Rooms available for long-term rental.

Bush Studios

The Arches, 152 Macfarlane Road, Sheperds Bush,
London W12 7LA
tel/fax 020-8740 1740
email info@bushstudios.co.uk
website www.bushstudios.co.uk
Contact Malcolm Ford

Digital recording studio. Clients have included: the BBC and Universal and Island Records. Utilises a Mackie 24-8 Bus mixing desk.

The Cowshed Recording Studio

125 Myddleton Road, London N22 8NG
tel 020-8881 2288
email enquiries@cowshedstudio.com
website www.cowshedstudio.com
Studio Manager Biba Leach

Contains 2 live rooms and a combination of analogue and digital equipment, including Amek Angela 38/24/8/2 (90 inputs) and Otari MX80 2in 24tk recorders. Clients have included: Jamie Cullum, Charlotte Church and Gwyneth Herbert.

Creekside Studios

Units C102 & C104 Faircharm Trading Estate,
8-12 Creekside, London SE8 3DX
tel 020-694 9484 *fax* 020-8694 9466
email studio@creeksidestudios.co.uk
Studio Manager Steve Unterberger

Services include digital editing, mastering of DAT, CDR, Wav, Aif, MP3, Minidisc and CD copying, cross fading in or out and digital editing within a well-equipped studio using: TC Electronic Finalizer Plus, 5 band parametric EQ, delay processor, compressor, limiter, expander, Noise Gate, pitch control de-click/de-noise and Red Book CD writing.

CTS & Lansdowne Recording Studios

Lansdowne House, Lansdowne Road,
London W11 3LP

tel 020-7727 0041 *fax* 020-7792 8904
email info@cts-lansdowne.co.uk
website www.cts-lansdowne.co.uk
Studio Manager Chris Dibble *Key Producers/Engineers*
Chris Dibble, Steve Pellvet

Founded in 1958. Sony BMG, Mercury and V2 are
among clients. Specialises in film soundtrack
recording. Equipment includes 72 channel AMS-
NEVE VX-S with flying faders, recall and 8 channel
film monitoring panel, Pro Tools MD and ATC
SCM200 monitoring.

The Cutting Rooms

Abraham Moss Centre, Crescent Road,
Manchester M8 6UF
tel 0161-740 9438
email cuttingrooms@hotmail.com
website www.citycol.com/cuttingrooms
Assistant Managers Tom Winstanley, Damien
McCarthy *Key Producers/Engineers* Adam Speakman,
Chris Hughes, Colin Dunkerley

Founded in 1987. Works mainly with local guitar
bands; however, projects have ranged from spoken
word to D&B, bhangra to heavy metal, and include
work for the BBC Commonwealth Games. Studio is
part of City College Manchester and can offer simple
demos to fully mastered albums within 3 studio
complexes. Equipment includes: Pro Tools HD3 with
Apogee converters, Sony plug-ins, Duende, Native
Instruments Komplete and Mackie Pro Control. Also
contains large live room including use of a grand
piano, Hammond organ and Leslie cabinet.

Rates: Vary according to nature of project, but start at
£15 per hour including engineer.

The Dairy Ltd

43-45 Tunstall Road, London SW9 8BZ
tel 020-7738 7777 *fax* 020-7738 7007
email info@thedairy.co.uk
website www.thedairy.co.uk
Studio Manager Emily Taylor

Launched in 1995. Recently upgraded significantly
with the inclusion of a second studio and 4
production rooms. Provides a professional selection
of modern and vintage equipment. ADSL lines in all
rooms to allow swift digital data transfer from studios
to production rooms.

Delta Recording Studio

Deanery Farm, Bolts Hill, Chartham, Kent CT4 7LD
tel (01227) 732140
email deltastudios@btconnect.com
website www.deltastudios.co.uk
Studio Manager Julian Whitfield

Founded in 1997. Deals with all types of recording in
a Pro Tools based studio.

Earth Terminal Studios

The Hop Kiln, Hillside, Odiham, Hook,
Hants RG29 1HX

tel/fax (01256) 704043
email studio@earthterminal.co.uk
website www.earthterminal.co.uk
Studio Manager Lewis Childs

Based in a 300-year-old Oast House. Utilises a
combination of analogue and digital recording
equipment featuring a Saturn Research 824 24 track
2" and Digital 24 track MOTU 2408 mkIII.

Eastcote Studios

249 Kensal Road, London W10 5DB
tel 020-8969 3739 *fax* 020-8960 1836
email info@eastcotestudios.co.uk
website www.eastcotestudios.co.uk
Manager Phillip Bagenal

Established in 1979. Aims to encourage chemistry
between musicians wanting to make music together.
Recent clients include: Kevin Ayers, Placebo and Plan
B. Equipment includes Pro Tools HD3, 2" 16 track
analogue, vintage outboard and eclectic collection of
microphones.

Rates: Studio 1: approx. £550 per day; Studio 2:
approx. £350 per day.

Eden Studios

20-24 Beaumont Road, Chiswick, London W4 5AP
tel 020-8995 5432 *fax* 020-8747 1931
email eden@edenstudios.com
website www.edenstudios.com
Studio Manager Natalie Horton

Established in 1967. Offers 4 studios, and facilities
ranging from live-in accommodation to well-
qualified in-house engineers. Contains industry
leading equipment and a client list boasting Coldplay,
Dave Matthews, Elbow, The Killers, Soulwax and
Kaiser Chiefs.

Fairview Studios

Cavewood Grange Farm, Common Lane,
North Cave, East Yorkshire HU15 2PE
tel (0800) 0181482 or (01430) 425546
fax (01430) 425547
email info@fairviewstudios.co.uk
website www.fairviewstudios.co.uk
Studio Manager Andrew Newlove *Head Engineer* John
Spence

Recording studio and duplication service. Clients
include: *Sound on Sound* Magazine, Mercury Records
and Sincere Management. Equipment includes a
Radar II and Soundcraft Seris desk. Also provides
video post production services.

Full Stack Recording Studio

Albert Mill, St Hubert's Street, Great Harwood,
Blackburn, Lancashire BB6 7BE
mobile (07816) 263593
email fullstackstudio@hotmail.co.uk
website www.fullstackstudio.fusivenet.co.uk
Studio Manager/Engineer Matt Richardson

Small studio catering for local and not-so-local bands (minimal residential facilities included). Specialises in rock, metal, indie, punk, hardcore, etc., although all styles of music can easily be catered for. Clients include: Apes Fight Back (indie rock), Bastard Of The Skies (metal), False Negative (jazz/funk), and Glass (indie). Equipment includes Tascam 32 channel desk and Alesis Hd-24 (24 track)recorder integrated with a G5 Apple Mac for 32/48 track recording. Full mic selection and backline available. Contact via phone or email.

Rates: Weekend (3 days): approx. £250 including recording/mixing/mastering; weekly deals and hourly rates available.

Gateway Studios

Kingston Hill Centre, Kingston, Surrey KT2 7LB
tel 020-8547 8167 *fax* 020-8547 8167
email studio@gsr.org.uk
website www.gsr.org.uk
Studio Manager Jason Edge

Part of the Gateway Sound Education Trust with extensive facilities including 4 studios, live rooms, programming suites, 3 mastering rooms and a wide selection of digital and analogue equipment. Industry standard software – Cubase, Pro Tools, Reaktor and Final Cut Pro on both PC and Mac platforms.

Goodge Street Studios

7 Goodge Place, London W1T 4SF
tel 020-7436 6487
email info@aczintermedia.com
website www.goodgestreetstudios.com

Offers recording, mixing and editing services within a central London location. Facilities include 3 live rooms, grand piano, digital Pro Tools suite HD3TDM and analogue 24 track.

Rates: From £50 per hour plus VAT.

Gracieland

382 Edenfield Road, Rochdale, Lancs OL12 7NH
tel (01706) 648829 *fax* (01706) 658052
email info@gracieland.co.uk
website www.gracieland.co.uk
Co-owner Ian Devaney

Recording equipment includes Otari MTR90 Mk2 – 2" analogue, Ampex ATR102 half-inch analogue and Studer B67 – quarter-inch analogue. Also, Alesis ADAT (x4) and Pro Tools Digidesign 888 interface. Clients have included: New Order, The Charlatans and Black Grape.

Greystoke Studios

39 Greystoke Park, London W5 1JL
tel 020-8998 5529 *fax* 020-8566 7885
email andy@greystokeproductions.co.uk
website www.greystokeproductions.co.uk
Key Producers/Engineers Andy Whitmore

Founded in 1990. Specialises in production led by chart-topping keyboard player and writer, Andy

Whitmore. Equipment includes Mackie D8B desk, Yamaha Motif ES6, Mini Moog VC53 and Hammond C3. Production and writing credits include: Lemar ('Time to Grow') and Lisa Scott-Lee ('Get It On').

Rates: Studio plus engineer: approx. £150; studio plus producer (Andy Whitmore) and engineer: approx. £300.

Grouse Lodge

Rosemount, County West Meath
tel +353 (09064) 36175 *fax* +353 (09064) 36131
email info@grouselodge.com
website www.grouselodge.com
Contact Tom Skerrit

Established in July 2002. Contains 2 world-class studios located as part of a Georgian estate. Studio 1 contains a Neve VR60 console (40in-40out), 24 track analogue and Pro Tools HD3 Core System. Studio 2 features a 36 channel Neve v series console and Pro Tools HD2. Complex contains a health spa featuring swimming pool, sauna, jacuzzi and gym.

Iguana Studio

Iguana Studio, Unit 1, 88A Acre Lane, Brixton, London SW2 5QN
tel 020-7924 0496 *mobile* (07966) 665349
email info@iguanastudio.co.uk
website www.iguanastudio.co.uk
Contact Andrea or Tom

Recording studio also offering post-production, mastering, recompilation and duplication services. A selection of the following equipment is available: Mackie d8b console (72 tracks), Mackie and Yamaha monitors, Logic Pro software, Focusrite and Mackie preamps, Roland, Lexicon and Akai outboards.

Intimate Studios

The Smokehouse, 120 Pennington Street, London E1 9BB
tel 020-7702 0789 *mobile* (07860) 109612
email p.madden47@ntlworld.com
website www.intimatestudios.com
Studio Manager Paul Madden

Founded in 1982. Recent clients include: Jah Wobble, John Cameron, The White Stripes. Equipment features a classic 1970s Harrison Console, Pro Tools and Radar, 2" and 1/2" analogue, and large live area with Yamaha grand piano and Hammond organ.

Jaba Recording Studios

Weeke Barton, North Tawton, Devon EX20 2AB
tel (01837) 82294
email info@jaba.co.uk
website www.jaba.co.uk
Managing Director Ben Roberts

Set in an idyllic location in the Devonshire countryside. Records with Pro Tools mix 24 and Logic Pro; mixes with Yamaha 02R.

Jacobs Studios Ltd
Ridgeway House, Dippenhall, Nr Farnham,
Surrey GU10 5EE
tel (01252) 715546 *fax* (01252) 712846
email andy@jacobs-studios.co.uk
website www.jacobs-studios.co.uk

Comprises 2 studios housed within an impressive
Georgian country residence. Studio 1 equipment
includes a NEVE VR60, Pro Tools HD, 2 x Otari
MTR, 24 track 2" or 16 track 2". Studio 2 utilises SSL
4064E 64 input (48 mono 8 stereo), Pro Tools HD
and 2 x Otari MTR 90, 24 track 2" and 16 track 2".
Recent clients have included: Bloc Party, Ordinary
Boys, Portishead, and Queen Adreena.

JellyJam Studios
21 Tannery Lane, Penketh, Warrington,
Cheshire WA5 2UD
tel (01928) 577944 *mobile* (07747) 046764
email info@jellyjam.co.uk
website www.jellyjam.co.uk
Key Producer/Engineer Pete Coleman

Provides recording and mixing services in facilities
utilising AMS Neve 1081R/1073 Mic Pres, TC
Electronic mainframe, Eventide H8000's and Lexicon
960L.

The Levels Recording Studio
Pincombe House, Woodhill, Stoke St Gregory,
Taunton, Somerset TA3 6EW
tel (01823) 490151
email record@levelsound.com
website www.levelsound.com
Studio Manager Robin Brown

Established in 1999. Employs use of analogue and
digital hardware including Allen and Heath GL3300
32 channel desk, Yamaha O3D with ADAT card,
Cubase and Spirit Folio utility mixer.

Rates: Full day hire (10am – 8pm): approx. £300
inclusive (with engineer).

Lighthouse Studios
20-22 West Harbour Road, Edinburgh EH5 1PN
tel 0131-551 5788 *fax* 0131-551 5787
email via website
website www.lighthousestudios.org

Offers 96 kHz, 24 bit digital recording with Logic Pro
7.1 audio editing, Yamaha monitoring, Dual G5
Apple Macintosh, Neumann mics, and an extensive
sample library. Clients have included: The Beta Band,
BBC, Idlewild, and Turin Breaks.

Rates: Approx. £30 per hour inclusive (with
engineer).

Livingston Studios
Brook Road (off Mayes Road), London N22 6TR
tel 020-8889 6588 *fax* 020-8888 2698
email jerry@livingstonstudios.co.uk
website www.livingstonstudios.co.uk

Contains 2 studios set in a Victorian chapel. Studio 1
has a recently renovated classic SSL 56 channel E/G
series; Studio 2 hosts a 40/80 channel Amek
Rembrandt. Recording for both is on a choice of Pro
Tools, analogue 2" Dolby SR or Radar-II. Clients
have included: Placebo, Muse, Coldcut, and Feeder.

MAP Music
46 Grafton Road, London NW5 3DU
tel 020-7916 0544
email info@mapmusic.net
website www.mapmusic.net
Director Chris Townsend

Established in 1992. Studio facility also incorporating
CD duplication and record label. Clients have
included: Dawn Penn, Tyman Dogg, Private Lives
and Jimmy Screech.

Rates: £35 per hour.

Mayfair Recording Studios
11A Sharpleshall Street, Primrose Hill,
London NW1 8YN
tel 020-7586 7746 *fax* 020-7586 9721
email bookings@mayfair-studios.co.uk
website www.mayfair-studios.co.uk

Well-established studio with Kylie Minogue, Robbie
Williams and U2 among clientele. Utilises SSL
XL9000K and Neve VR60 consoles along with
numerous vintage outboards.

Metropolis Studios
The Power House, 70 Chiswick High Road,
London W4 1SY
tel 020-8742 1111 *fax* 020-8742 2626
email hello@metropolis-group.co.uk
website www.metropolis-group.co.uk
Studio Bookings Alison Hussey

Caters for a range of ensembles from bands up to 26-
piece string sessions. Works in 5 studios with a wide
variety of equipment, including Pro Tools and SSL
and Neve consoles. Michael Jackson, U2 and Sting
feature among clients.

The Mews Recording Studio Ltd
219 Bow Road, London E3 2SJ
tel 020-8980 9745
email themewsstudios@aol.com
website www.themewsrecordingstudios.com
Founder Dave Clarke

Pro Tools (V5.1.3) and Logic Platinum (V7.01)
recording, programming and production suite. Also
utilises an analogue 56 channel Mackie. Clients have
included: The Prodigy, Sade, Jet Johnson, Out with
Mummy.

Mill Hill Recording Company Ltd
Unit 7, Bunns Lane Works, Bunns Lane, Mill Hill,
London NW7 2AJ
tel 020-8906 9991 *fax* 020-8906 9991

email rogertichborne@btinternet.co.uk
website www.millhillmusiccomplex.co.uk
Manager Jeanette Aubury *Key Producers/Engineers*
Jeanette Aubury, Fillipe Ross

Established in 1983. Works with Logic 6, 2 x 24 track
analogue desks and plenty of outboard effects. Recent
clients include: 2 Kings, Zoe Bonham, Hewi Lloyd
Langton.

Rates: Demo and engineer: £20 per hour. Minimum
fee £100.

Mojo Sound Studios

The Old Coach House, St Lukes Road, Torquay,
Devon TQ2 5NX
tel (01803) 290074
email info@mojostudio.co.uk
website www.mojostudios.co.uk
Contact Leo Brown

Equipment includes an Otari Radar II, Ampex
MMI200 2" 24 track, and a Sony MXP3036 80 input
analogue.

Rates: Approx. £25 per hour (minimum of 4 hours).

Moles Studio

Moles Studio, 14 George Street, Bath BA1 2EN
tel (01225) 404445 *fax* (01225) 404447
email paul@moles.co.uk
website www.moles.co.uk

Located on the 1st and 2nd floors of a 5-storey 18th-
century Georgian house in central Bath. Equipment
includes SSL 4056 E Series and 2 x Otari MTR 90's
series II. Artists recorded include: Blur, Manic Street
Preachers, and Catherine Wheel.

Rates: 12-hour day: approx. £900.

Music Room

116-118 New Cross Road, London SE14 5BA
tel 020-7252 8271 *fax* 020-7252 8252
email sales@musicroomsolutions.com
website www.musicroomsolutions.com
Co-Director Gordon Gapper *Key Producer/Engineer*
Dean Gaisburgh-Watkyn

Established in 1985. Large rehearsal facility with a
range of new and vintage stock. Primarily deals with
live band and artist recording from folk to rock.
Caters for complete projects, but will also help to
complete home projects. Equipment includes small-
format analogue/ADAT digital, range of mikes,
Lexicon and KRK monitors.

Rates: 8-hour day: £150 (plus media costs).

NAM Recording Studios

4-7 Forewoods Common, Holt, Trowbridge,
Wilts BA14 6PJ
tel/fax (01225) 782281
email namanage@aol.com
website www.namrecording.com
Owner Nick Allen

Fully residential studio. Equipment includes
MTA990, Soundcraft 2", MKIII and Pro Tools.
Clients have included: Julian Cope, Robert Plant and
KT Tunstall.

NuCool Studios

34 Beaumont Road, London W4 5AP
tel 020-8248 2157
email r.niles@richardniles.com
website www.richardniles.com
Director Richard Niles *Key Producers/Engineers*
Richard Niles, Peter Dace

Founded in 1989. Works with live bands within pop
and jazz genres providing a recording, mixing and
mastering service. Kylie Minogue, Bo Selecta and Jim
Mullen have been among recent clients. Equipment
includes Mackie D8B, Motu Digital Performer and
Yamaha C3 Piano.

Rates: £35 per hour; minimum 4 hours.

Olympic Studios

117 Church Road, Barnes, London SW13 9HL
tel 020-8286 8600 *fax* 020-8286 8625
email siobhan@olympicstudios.co.uk
website www.olympicstudios.co.uk
Manager Siobhan Paine

Well-established studio that has played host to artists
such as The Rolling Stones, Jimi Hendrix and Led
Zeppelin. Specialises in audio recording using 4 x SSL
consoles alongside a range of other equipment within
3 studios and a mix suite.

Online Studios

Unit 18-19 Croydon House, 1 Peall Road, Croydon,
Surrey CR0 3EB
tel 020-8287 8585
email info@onlinestudios.co.uk
website www.onlinestudios.co.uk
Director Rob Pearson *Key Producers/Engineers* Rob
Pearson, Neil Jones

Founded in 1995. Specialists in dance and urban
music production and recording. Also works with
voice overs and DJ recording. Recent clients include:
Group 4 Security, BBC, Sony and So Solid Crew. See
website for equipment details.

Rates: £200 including engineer. Hourly rate: £30.

Parkgate Studio

Catsfield, Battle, East Sussex TN33 9DT
tel (01424) 774088 *fax* (01424) 774088
email parkgatestudio@hotmail.com
website www.parkgatestudio.co.uk

Fully residential studio with a variety of extra facilities
available. Equipment includes Neve VR60 and Pro
Tools. Clients have included: The Cure, Blur and
Terrorvision.

Rates: Approx. £1200 per day with discounts for
block booking.

ecording studios 181

Pig Hut Studios
Unit 3B, Acaster Industrial Estate, Acaster Malbis,
York YO23 2TX
tel (01904) 706440
email info@pighutstudios.co.uk
website www.pighutstudios.co.uk

Offers 24 tracks of digital audio and a variety of both
digital and analogue processing techniques. Also
provides duplication services.

Rates: Approx. £20 per hour, or full 8-hour session
from £150.

The Premises
209 Hackney Road, London E2 8JL
tel 020-7729 7593
email info@premisesstudios.com
website www.premisesstudios.com
CEO Viv Broughton Studio Director Nathan Hale

Founded in 1985. Contains high-spec/low-cost
complex of 14 recording studios. Recent clients have
included: Bloc Party, Lily Allen, Jamie Cullum, and
Klaxons. Equipment includes SSL AWS900 console
with Pro Tools HD and ATC main monitoring.

Rates: From £350 per day.

Propagation House Studios
East Lodge, Ogbeare, North Tamerton, Holsworthy,
Devon EX22 6SE
tel (01409) 271111
email info@propagationhouse.com
website www.propagationhouse.com
Studio Owner Mark Ellis

Residential studios with full facilities. Works with
Digidesign Pro Tools and Logic platinum, Mackie 32/
8/2 and Spirit Folio.

Rates: Approx. £25 per hour, with day and weekly
discounts available.

Quince Recording Studios
62A Balcombe Street, Marylebone,
London NW1 6NE
tel (07810) 752765 fax 020-7723 1010
email info@quincestudios.co.uk
website www.quincestudios.co.uk
Studio Manager Matt Walters

Founded in 2000; works on a wide variety of projects.
Specialises in pop, rock, indie, nu metal and dance
genres. Recent clients include: Andy Hayman (All
Saints, Blue and Joe O' Meara), Mig Ayesa (INXS and
We Will Rock You) and Rosie Ribbons (Telstar, Pop
Idol). Full equipment list available online. Also works
with creating advertisements for radio, TV and film.

Rates: From £25 per hour; call for more details.

Quo-Vadis Recording and Rehearsals
Unit 1, Morrison Yard, 551A High Road,
London N17 6SB

email quovadis_2002@yahoo.co.uk
Owner Don Mackenzie

A Pro Tools HD2 TDM recording studio with a wide
variety of output.

Rates: Approx. £25 per hour.

RAK Studios
42-48 Charlbert Street, London NW8 7BU
tel 020-7586 2012 fax 020-7722 5843
email trisha@rakstudios.co.uk
website www.rakstudios.co.uk
Studio Manager Trisha Wegg Key Producers/Engineers
Richard Woodcraft, Raj Das

Established in 1978. Son of Dork, Jamie Cullum and
Gomez are among recent clients. Equipment includes
2 X API, 1 X Neve and 1 X SSL 4056G desks, Pro
Tools and Studer A800 multi-tracks. Phone for
quotes.

Real World Studios
Box Mill, Mill Lane, Box, Corsham, Wilts SN13 8PL
tel (01225) 743188 fax (01225) 743787
email owenl@realworld.co.uk
website www.realworld.on.net/studios
Key Producers/Engineers Marco Migliari, Ben Findlay

Utilises SSL 4080G 72 Channel G Series Console, SSL
4052E 48 Channel Console, Studer A820 tape
machines, Neve BCM-10 console, Pro Tools and
Logic alongside a wide range of other facilities across
2 studios. Kylie Minogue, Beautiful South, Midge Ure
and Stereophonics feature among clients.

Red Bus Recording Studios
Studio House, 34 Salisbury Street, London NW8 8QE
tel 020-7402 9111 fax 020-723 3064
email eliot@animedia.co.uk
website www.redbusstudios.com
Managing Director Eliot M Cohen

Established in 1979. Diverse range of clients from
Culture Club to The Cheeky Girls. Also provides
record label service.

RMS Studios
43-45 Clifton Road, London SE25 6PX
tel 020-8653 4965
email studiosrms@aol.com
website www.rms-studios.co.uk

Over 25 years' experience. Offers 2 studios, 1
including grand piano. Records with RADAR II 24
track digital hard disk system, Studer A80 16 track,
Pro Tools and Sadie.

Rates: Approx. £220 per 10-hour day.

Rockfield Studios
Amberley Court, Rockfield Road, Monmouth,
Gwent NP25 5ST
tel (01600) 712449
email lisaward@rockfieldstudios.com
website www.rockfieldstudios.com
Contact Lisa Ward

Residential studios founded in the 1960s. Recording facilities are available in 2 areas: Quadrangle (inc. MCI 500 series console, Mackie d8B and Studer A820 24 track recorder) and Coach House (inc. customised 48 channel NEVE 8128 and Studer A820 24 track tape recorder). Queen, Black Sabbath, Mike Oldfield and Motorhead were among earlier clients; more recently Coldplay, Manic Street Preachers, Oasis and Annie Lennox.

Roll Over Studios

29 Beethoven Street, London W10 4LG
tel 020-8969 0299 *fax* 020-8968 1047
email via website
website www.rollover.co.uk
Director Phillip Jacobs *Key Producers/Engineers* Ollie J, P McMahon

Founded in 1983. A 7-studio complex providing in-house production for a range of music projects. The Prodigy, Raghav, Sly and Robbie, and Vega 4 are among recent clients. Equipment includes a 24 track 2 inch, Pro Tools, Radar, Logic and Soundtracs Jade.

Sanctuary Town House Studios

150 Goldhawk Road, London W12 8HH
tel 020-8932 3200 *fax* 020-8932 3207
email recording@sanctuary studios.co.uk
website www.sanctuarystudios.co.uk
Studio Manager Nikki Affleck

Well-established studio – part of Sanctuary group. Recording takes place over 3 studios and a Pro Tools Suite running Pro Tools and Logic. Studio equipment includes SSL 4000G, SSL 8072G and SSL 4000E. Also specialises in location audio recording for TV, DVD and radio.

Sawmills Residential Recording

Golant Fowey, Cornwall PL23 1LW
tel (01726) 833338 *fax* (01726) 832015
email office@sawmills.co.uk
website www.sawmills.co.uk
Studio Manager Ruth Taylor

Based in a 17th-century water mill. Equipment includes Trident customised Series 80B with 82 channels on remix, Soundscape 64-track Hard Disk Recorder and Otari MTR-90 MkII 24-track. The Stone Roses, Oasis, Feeder and Razorlight feature among clients.

Sensible Music Ltd

90-96 Brewery Road, London N7 9NT
tel 020-7700 9900 *fax* 020-7700 4802
email studio@sensible-music.co.uk
website www.sensible-music.co.uk
Managing Director Jeff Allen *Key Producer/Engineer* Jon Moon

Founded in 1975. Specialises in recording (inc. live recording), mixing, rehearsing, rentals and production suites. Lemar, Kings of Leon, George

Michael and Miss Dynamite have featured among recent clients. Equipment includes Euphonix C5300, PMC monitors, Pro Tools HD3 Accel, Fairchild and Massenburg compressors and a Apogee AD800 converter. Rates vary according to requirements; email for more information.

Soho Recording Studio

The Heals Building, 22-24 Torrington Place, London WC1E 7HJ
tel 020-7419 2444 *fax* 020-7419 2333
email dominic@sohostudios.co.uk
website www.sohostudios.co.uk
Studio Manager Dominic Sanders *Key Producers/Engineers* Joe Fields, Dominic Katsav

Houses 2 studios with equipment including Sony 3348, Otari MTR 90, 48 track Pro Tools and Yamaha 02R96 and SSL desks.

Soleil

Buspace Studios, Unit 10, Conlan Street, London W10 5AP
tel 020-7460 2117 *fax* 020-7460 3164
email soleil@trwuk.com
Key Engineer/Producer Jose Gross

Founded in 1989. Offers a complete support service including multitrack tape and Pro Tools recording, MIDI sequencing, live drums and arranging. Clients work in a range of styles from urban dance to voice overs. Equipment includes 16 track reel to reel, Pro Tools 48 track, Tannoy monitors, 24:16 analogue desk, Logic Pro and Cubase.

Rates: Approx. £32 per hour.

Sound Recording Technology

Audio House, Edison Road, St Ives, Cambridgeshire PE27 3LF
London: *tel* 020-8446 3218
Cambridge: *tel* (01480) 461880 *fax* (01480) 496100
email sales@soundrecordingtechnology.co.uk
website www.soundrecordingtechnology.com

A 6-studio complex also offering location facilities. Offers use of Steinway Grand; specialises in classical music production, editing and voice over.

The Sound Suite

92 Camden Mews, London NW1 9AG
tel 020-7485 4881
email peter@thesoundsuite.co.uk
website www. thesoundsuite.co.uk
Owner Peter Rackham *Key Producers/Engineers* Peter Rackham, Ben Amesbury and Andy Parker

Founded in 1976. Mainly works with voice-over recording, sound to picture/Foleys and live bands. Equipment used includes: Pro Tools HD3, Accel; Protools; Logic Audio and an Amek 40 channel Hendrix Analogue console.

Rates: From £180 per day.

Southern Studios

10 Myddleton Road, Wood Green, London N22 8NS
tel 020-8888 8949 *fax* 020-8889 8036
email studio@southern.com
website www.southern.com/studio.com
Studio Manager Harvey Birrell

Specialises in recording bands that want to sound live
and real. Aims to help the artists achieve their
ultimate recording goals. The Buzzcocks, Crass,
Therapy?, and Jesus and Mary Chain have featured
among clients. Equipment includes a 24 track
analogue 2" Studer A870, Pro Tools, Vintage Desk
and range of effects boards.

Rates: Basic rate approx. £300 (plus VAT) per day.

Strongroom

120-124 Curtain Road, London EC2A 3SQ
tel 020-7426 5100 *fax* 020-7426 5102
email mix@strongroom.com
website www.strongroom.com
General Manager Nina Mistry *Studio Booker* Linda
Dixon *Key Producers/Engineers* Ken Thomas, Mike
Nielson

Founded in 1984. Recent clients include: Son of
Dork, Goldfrapp, The Prodigy, and Kaiser Chiefs.
Uses Neve VREO, SSL Gt, ProControl, Pro Tools HD
and MixPlus, 2" and 1/2" machines. Contact via
phone or email for information.

Westpoint Studio

Unit GA, 39-40 Westpoint, Warple Way,
London W3 0RG
tel 020-8740 1616 *fax* 020-8740 4488
email info@westpointstudio.co.uk
Studio Manager Ian Sherwin *Key Producers/
Engineers:*Brendan Lynch, Max Heyes, Matt Howe
and Ian Sherwin

Established in 1994. Aims to combine the comfort of
a private studio with professional standards. Hosts a
vast collection of vintage instruments, backline,
outboard and microphones along with the latest
modern technology. Recent clients include: The
Rakes, Primal Scream, Rooster, Serena Maneesh,
Brinkman and Jack Penate. Equipment includes

1970s Vintage Neve console, Pro Tools, 24 Track
Analogue, and ATC monitoring. Call for rates
information.

Wolf Studios

83 Brixton Water Lane, London SW2 1PH
tel 020-7733 8088 *fax* 020-7326 4016
email brethes@mac.com
website www.wolfstudios.co.uk
Director Dominique Brethes *Key Producers/Engineers*
Dominique Brethes, Alex Balzama

Established in 1984. Specialises in mixing and
mastering with the use of Pro Tools. Recent clients
have included: Steven Severin, Alex Wilson and Ska
Cubano. Works with Pro Tools HD3, Studer 2",
ADAT and Amek Angela.

Rates: From £35 per hour inc. VAT.

Yellow Shark Recording Studio

121 Promenade, Cheltenham,
Gloucestershire GL50 1NW
tel (01242) 515160 *fax* (01242) 242120
email music@yellow-shark.co.uk
website www.yellow-shark.co.uk
Key Producer/Engineer Gareth Williams

Offers analogue and digital recording with equipment
including RADAR 24 (48 track), Studer A827 Dolby
XP 24 SR, Pro Tools 6 and Soundtracs Jade-S 48.

Zed One Studios

225A Camden Road, London NW1 9AA
tel 020-7482 3500
email info@zed-one-studios.co.uk
website www.zed-one-studios.co.uk
Key Producers Pete Lyons, Colin Leggett and Jaime
Gomez

Founded in 2000. An independent recording studio
and rehearsal complex specialising in guitar bands
and 'live' music production. Clients include: EMI
Music, Sony, Atlantic Records, and Universal. Studio
equipment includes: Pro Tools, Soundcraft and
DC2000 with flying faders. See website for current
special rates and deals.

Contemporary recording processes

Antony Greaves provides a thorough overview of the technology needed to undertake a recording.

Technology seems to advance at an alarming rate. This is true of just about everything you can think of: cars now 'know' when you're going to crash and apply the brakes for you; computer games allow you to browse through realistic 'virtual worlds' with infinite possibilities; and the mobile telephone – once at the pinnacle of audio communication technology – is now pushing forward the boundaries of visual imaging technology.

Music technology has also advanced at an astonishing rate. Manufacturers are developing increasingly advanced gear to make sound recording easier, more accessible, and of higher quality.

Nevertheless, there is a lot to be said for the technologies of the past. Many sound engineers still believe that older gear is better. Even though maintenance costs are often more expensive (and the equipment hard to come by), many modern engineers insist that the investment is worth the difference in sound quality that this 'vintage' gear can provide.

So let's go through the basic equipment needed in order to make a recording – and how you can adapt your set-up to achieve the best possible result for your budget.

Recording bands

Establishing yourself in the world of sound engineering can be like stepping off a curb, or stepping off a cliff! It all depends how far you want to go to achieve your desired result.

The most basic recording studio could be set up simply with a Dictaphone or Walkman, and would cost you next to nothing. However, it would be very difficult indeed to make it sound like it was recorded at Abbey Road.

No matter how modest your budget, there will always remain two fundamental things that affect the quality of recordings:

1. The source – the music

The source is clearly the most important element. The Beatles would not have made all the classic recordings they did if they had been unable to play their instruments reasonably well. As the producer in your home studio, you need to keep a level head and decide whether instructing someone else to play or sing on your recording will achieve a better result. It's very easy to let your ego get the better of you – but think about how great it will sound with someone who can *really* sing.

2. Ambience

The room you are in has a huge influence on the sound that you hear, and therefore on what gets recorded. The sound from an instrument bounces off the walls, floor and ceiling, and combines to create what your ears finally hear, and what the microphone hears.

When next in your bathroom, clap your hands and think about how it sounds. Then go into your bedroom and do the same thing. It will sound different because of the different furnishings and wall-surfaces in the two rooms. A bathroom sounds very 'bright' – or sometimes 'harsh' – because bathrooms are generally covered in waterproof tiles. These hard, shiny surfaces allow a lot of the sound to bounce back to your ears. The soft furnishings of your bedroom (your bed, for example) absorb a lot of the sound, rather than reflecting it. This makes the room sound 'duller'.

The acoustic properties of various environments clearly differ, but this fact doesn't mean that one environment is always better than another: it just depends on what you want to record. Recording an acoustic guitar in a bedroom and a bathroom will result in two different types of sound – one of which will be closer to how you *want* it to sound.

You can easily experiment in a particular room, by moving the furnishings around. Try moving a duvet near the microphone if things sound a little bright, or try putting a mirror near the mic if things sound a little dull.

In addition to the shape of the room and interior furnishings, another thing to consider is the amount of noise you are planning to make. (Bear in mind that what *you* think is beautiful music might be unwanted noise to those around you!) This is where sound-proofing comes in. You can easily spend thousands of pounds making a room almost completely acoustically isolated from the outside world. But in the real world, you can reduce the problem of extraneous noise either by not playing so loud in the first place, or simply by making sure that doors and windows are closed. (Also, remember that in the middle of summer, closed windows may mean it gets a little hot – particularly if you have equipment such as guitar amps that generate heat.)

The world's top studios undertake significant investment to isolate and treat the walls of a room to make the room sound great. The result is worth the investment, as countless Top 10 hits testify.

The gear
Mixing desk

The mixing desk is the control centre of the recording studio, and might be the most expensive single item in your studio. The mixer combines your different recorded tracks together so that you can hear them all at once.

Creating a good mix is widely acknowledged as an art form in itself. The top mix engineers (such as Bob Clearmountain and John Hudson) are paid well for their mixes, simply because they know how to get it right, and will do so time after time. Their clients will keep coming back to them in the same way that a good studio's clients will keep coming back to that studio.

Every recording studio in the world has some form of mixing desk. Depending on your budget, this could vary from something built into your computer as part of your soundcard and software package, or – if budget allows – you might opt for an SSL or Neve console, which could set you back in the region of £500,000. Mixing desks, as with most other technology, follow the rule that you get what you pay for: this might consist of extra functionality or extra quality, and both of these can vary considerably.

If you're using a computer-based recording system, such as Pro Tools, Logic Audio, or Cubase, the easiest and cheapest method of mixing is achieved by using the software's built-in mixer. This will generally give good results (if done well) – and, if your computer has a CD burner built into it, you have the advantage of being able to mix and burn the CD all from the same machine.

If you are using a dedicated hardware recording device, such as a tape machine or hard disk recorder, you will need a hardware mixer.

There is a huge selection of hardware available to buy, any of which will offer different features and qualities. The cheaper ones may give you limited facilities (such as fewer channels), and will probably be noisier or give you less dynamic range than the more expensive models.

As a general rule, when looking at mixing desks, buy the one that offers you the closest specification to what you require, for the price you can afford. Although the mixer is possibly the most expensive thing in your studio, do not spend so much on it that you can't afford any other good gear to connect to it!

Computers

If you own a computer, there are some huge advantages to using it as your recording device. The multitrack software sequencers now available give you a huge range of editing options for compiling the best takes – such as the option to 'undo' if you make a mistake, and a whole host of effects plug-ins to change the way your recording sounds.

Computers are fast becoming the preferred method of recording for most sound engineers. Perhaps their most useful function to an amateur engineer is the ability to correct your mistakes. If you are recording on to tape, you are committed to making a certain decision that you can never reverse: as soon as you hit the record button on a tape machine, what was there before will be erased – and if that happens to be Kylie's best vocal take, she's not going to be happy!

Tape machines

Tape machines are still widely acknowledged to have a particularly good sound when used to record rock music. This is due to the way the tape reacts when loud signals are recorded on to it. Many engineers describe it as 'warm', and the crackle or 'tape hiss' that goes with tape recording is said to lend character rather than pose a problem. However, hiss can sometimes be a problem, and you need to be able to minimise it as much as possible.

When recording onto any sort of recording device, you should aim to get the signal recorded as loudly as possible without it distorting. This will maximise the 'signal to noise ratio', which is absolutely critical when recording to a noisy medium such as tape, and is almost as vital when recording digitally (in order to maximise the dynamic range).

The DAW

You may have heard of the DAW – or Digital Audio Workstation. This can refer to a computer-based (digital) recording system, or to a dedicated hardware device that incorporates a recording system with a hardware mixer. DAWs have grown in popularity over the last few years, and are basically a development of the cassette multitrack of yesteryear.

The original cassette multitracks were 4-track (i.e., they recorded four different tracks, or recordings, on a standard cassette), with four faders for adjusting the relative levels of each track. They were fairly primitive, but invaluable to amateur sound engineers or musicians, as they opened up the world of multitrack recording – which was only otherwise available at professional and costly studios.

Nowadays, we have digital versions of these multitracks, which record onto hard disks, or even portable media – such as the flash cards used in digital cameras. They also have faders for every track, and make available as many as 32 tracks – something that wouldn't have been possible on the humble cassette.

Many of the modern, dedicated DAWs include additional functionality, such as a built-in drum machine, effects (such as reverb), and even screens for editing and metering.

Microphones

The quality of microphone you use can make a huge difference to the final quality of your recording. For the big boys in the industry, microphone choice is a key decision, and can sometimes prove the difference between a hit record and an expensive miss.

However, there is little point spending thousands of pounds on an exceptional microphone if you don't know what to do with it! Microphones can only reproduce what they are 'hearing', so putting them in the right place makes a much bigger difference to the overall quality of a recording than using the right one in the first place.

If your budget will only allow for a £20 microphone, then you will need to work quite hard to find the 'sweet spot' where it sounds best. Even if you have a big budget when you start out, it may still be worth buying one cheap microphone, to push yourself to the limit when learning where these sweet spots are. Then, when you do use a good microphone, you will already have that knowledge under your belt.

Microphones come in three basic constructions:

- Dynamic
- Condenser
- Ribbon

Each of these has different characteristics, and each is appropriate for recording particular things. For example, a dynamic microphone is fairly robust and can deal with very high volume levels – so would be appropriate to put in a kick drum, or next to a loud guitar amplifier. As a condenser microphone is a little more fragile – yet capable of picking up a lot more detail than a dynamic microphone – it is perfect for vocals or acoustic guitar. A ribbon microphone has a small 'ribbon' of metal which vibrates when it is hit by a sound, generating an electrical signal at the microphone's output. The technology is similar to that of the dynamic microphone, but it is much more sensitive (like a condenser microphone). Ribbon microphones are, in fact, extremely delicate, and so are mainly used just in professional studios.

Microphones range in price from £20 to several thousand pounds. A good all-round microphone is the Shure SM58. This will cost you in the region of £80, and will give you generally good quality; it is also incredibly robust. If your budget is considerably larger, and you feel you could get the most from it, one of the best professional microphones is the Neumann U87 condenser – but this will set you back about £1500.

If possible, try to budget for at least one good dynamic and one good condenser mic. A reasonable quality condenser mic will cost between £200 and £400, and can be used on many different instruments; the biggest difference you will notice, however, will be in the quality of your vocal recordings.

Monitor speakers

The next vital thing to think about is how you are going to listen to what you have recorded.

If your studio is based in the bedroom of your Mum and Dad's house, then they might not be too pleased if you've got loudspeakers blasting out music until the small hours – in which case a practical option would be headphones. There are many pairs of headphones available, at vastly differing prices (and again, you get what you pay for).

I recommend opting for the 'closed' headphone design rather than the 'open' alternative. Closed headphones are designed to keep what you are hearing to yourself – and, more importantly, to keep external sounds out. Closed headphones often have a much better frequency response, which means they can reproduce all the different frequencies from low bass to high treble.

If sound levels aren't a problem, then you may wish to opt for a set of monitor speakers. These come as either passive, active or powered.

Passive speakers are similar to those which typically come with a domestic Hi-Fi. You use speaker wire to connect an amplifier (in the Hi-Fi) to the back of the speaker.

Powered speakers are similar to passive speakers, except that the speaker has the amplifier built in to it. While being more convenient, powered speakers are considerably more expensive than their passive equivalents.

Active speakers work on the same principle as powered speakers, but offer the additional benefit of having an 'active' crossover. The crossover is the electrical circuit that splits the treble and bass and sends it to the relevant speaker cone; by powering that circuit the crossover can be more accurate in reproducing the different frequencies.

Cabling – the hidden cost!

The last item that is absolutely vital, and often overlooked, is cabling.

Now that you have all this equipment, you will need to connect it together. The number of cables involved can be huge – and therefore costly. It can be hard to justify spending your hard-earned money on something that doesn't make a noise, but without cabling, nothing will make a sound!

To give you an idea of the costs involved, I recently designed a 24-track studio at a well-known music technology college, where the cost of cabling was approximately £3000 – and it could easily have been more than that, with a few more options.

That isn't to say that your home studio needs nearly as much cable as that, and you will find that as your studio grows, you will collect more and more cabling, thus spreading the cost. The important thing to do is to consider how you plan to use your equipment before you buy the cabling. Then you will only buy the cables you need.

Buying cables off the shelf can be very expensive; a cheaper alternative is to solder the cables yourself, by buying cable and connectors separately from a studio supplies shop. This could easily halve the cost of the cables, and is fairly easy to do: just ensure you have someone initially to show you what to do, and how to operate a soldering iron safely.

All professional studios install something called a 'patchbay'. This is a series of sockets that can be joined together by patch cables, to connect different pieces of equipment. You may have seen something similar in old newsreels showing telephone operators connecting calls. Every input and output on every device will be available on the patchbay, making it easy to connect things together. This saves you reaching around behind your equipment every time you want to connect something. It can be expensive to set up a patchbay, so it is only something you should consider doing if you *need* this flexibility.

Optional extras

FX

Now you've got the right gear to record as you would want, there are a number of optional items which will help you to achieve a 'professional' result.

Certainly, it is easy to buy more and more equipment to make a better sounding recording, but it is far more important that you understand what you are doing. Don't buy more gear until you feel you are getting the most from what you have already.

Optional items include 'FX' or 'effects'. These are dedicated boxes or plugins that either add to or change the original sound that you put through them. For example, 'reverb' will make things sound like they were recorded in a room of particular shape, and 'delay' will add an echo effect. There are hundreds of different FX available, and many come as multi-effects units. These are units that have a multitude of different effects in the one box, and can range in price from just £50 to several thousand pounds.

When starting out in sound engineering, it can be very difficult to hear the difference in quality between these units, but as your hearing develops you will begin to appreciate subtle differences in effects.

Dynamics

In addition to FX, another key option is dynamics – consisting most commonly of compression, expansion and gating. These dedicated units alter the way in which the sound changes volume over time, and are much more subtle than FX. It may take you some time to hear these subtle differences, and it can be very easy to ruin a good recording if such techniques are used inappropriately.

Compression is used to even out the level of a recording. For example, if you have a vocal recording where the singer is singing louder at one point than at another, compression can be used to reduce the difference between the loudest and quietest points (reducing the 'dynamic range').

Compression is widely accepted as making a big difference to the quality of a mix. The top studio engineers and producers will insist on using certain brands and models of compressor, such as the Urei 1176, Fairchild 660, Teletronix LA2a, or others regarded as classics. Modern compressors from manufacturers such as Manley, Focusrite, and Avalon, are also highly regarded but very costly.

To give you an idea of the cost of these items, a decent budget compressor can range in price between £150 and £300. An original Urei 1176 costs in the region of £1700, and a Fairchild 660 nearer £50,000 – so only the top engineers tend to use them!

Expansion and gating are used to minimise unwanted sound, which can occur in between your desired sounds. For example, you may have a vocal recording that sounds reasonably good, but with some traffic noise, or even 'spill' from the headphones, that ruins the recording. A gate or expander will remove or reduce this noise, and if used well, will not affect the sound of the vocal line.

As a general rule, it is wise to avoid using dynamic processing at the recording stage, because once you have committed this to your recording you are unable to correct it at the mix stage. However, once you are happy that you can hear what compression is doing, and can adjust the settings correctly, then you might want to use compression when recording to try to maximise the dynamic range of your recording medium.

Always remember, you can't fix everything in the mix! It is imperative to get things right at the recording stage. This applies equally for dynamics, recording level, and – of course – microphone placement.

Computer recording
Mac vs. PC

More and more sound engineers are now turning to computers for their recordings, as computers open up a huge world of possibilities – such as visual editing, undo history, and multiple takes per track. So which computer should you buy?

There is a lot of apparent rivalry between Apple Macintosh users and PC users. I started out using a PC, as it was the cheaper option – plus it meant I could easily build the machine myself. Having said that, as soon as I started working with other sound engineers, it became apparent to me that I needed to be using the same system as them for compatibility reasons, so I bought a Mac. There is a lot to be said for going with what you are comfortable with, so – if possible – try both before deciding.

Sound cards

Once you have bought your computer, the next challenge is getting audio in and out of it. Most PCs and Macs come with a basic stereo output – such as a headphone connector on the motherboard, which is fine if you're purely using pre-recorded samples from sample CDs. But this output will become quite restrictive if you want to record something into the computer.

As always, you get what you pay for, and the more expensive sound cards offer higher quality and/or more inputs and outputs. As this technology is constantly changing, it may be best to speak to your local retailer or an experienced friend for advice on particular makes and models of sound card.

RAM/processor

The specifications of computers vary, so as a general rule buy the fastest processor with as much RAM (Random Access Memory) as you can afford.

As your recordings get more complex, you will be using more tracks of audio, and using many more plugins and making more edits. All this puts additional strain on the computer's processor (its 'brain'). Having more RAM means that the computer can remember more things at once while it is calculating with the processor.

If you already have a computer, and you are finding that you are running out of processing power, the most cost-efficient upgrade would be to add more RAM. Upgrading the processor can be very complicated, and may involve upgrading the motherboard, which may then involve buying new format RAM and potentially causing several other software conflicts.

All computer components vary in price, but RAM and processors vary the most due to the volatile nature of the silicone market. If you are looking to upgrade the RAM in your machine, check what format the RAM is, as there are several different speeds available. Ask your retailer which is appropriate to your machine.

Hard drives

The hard drive is the device in a computer that stores your data, even when the computer is turned off.

Generally, you will have at least one hard drive in your computer that runs the operating system, and stores all your programs. I recommend buying an additional drive onto which to record your audio. This will make a huge difference to the performance of your computer, in terms of how many audio tracks you can run, and how many edits you can perform.

You could opt either to install a second internal hard drive – generally an IDE (Integrated Drive Electronics) format – which is the cheapest option, or you could take the slightly more flexible, but more expensive option of an external drive that connects to the computer via a dedicated cable.

Hard drives come in several different speeds – such as 5400rpm, 7200rpm and 10,000rpm. As a rule, buy the fastest you can afford. The number connected with your hard drive is the speed at which the disc in it can spin (in revolutions per minute): the faster the disc can spin, the faster the data can be read.

The fastest of these drives tend to be SCSI (Small Computer System Interface), which is a communication protocol that is fast becoming superseded by the more user-friendly USB and Firewire formats. If deciding on a USB external hard drive, be sure to opt for a USB2 version, as USB1 will probably not be fast enough when your sessions come to incorporate more and more audio. Firewire also comes in two formats: either Firewire400 or Firewire800 (being either 400 or 800 megabits per second). Firewire 800 is recommended. However, the format you choose will depend on which your computer is capable of connecting to – and, of course, the difference in cost.

Software

When it comes to which software package to use, there are several options to choose between, depending on how you want to work and the budget you have available.

The three most popular software packages are:

Steinberg Cubase

Cubase is the most popular option for PC users. It is relatively easy to use once you understand the basic principles involved.

Apple Logic

Logic is easily the most popular software package for Apple Mac users. A German company called Emagic (who were bought out by Apple) originally produced Logic. Logic will only now run on Apple computers. There are two versions available: Logic Pro (approximately £700 retail) and Logic Express (around £200 retail). The most significant difference between these two versions is that Logic Pro comes with a huge number of Apple branded plugins (effects) and software instruments (such as pianos, drum machines and samplers) which would otherwise cost you over £1000.

Digidesign Pro Tools

Pro Tools is the most popular software package for professional sound engineers. Pro Tools is a very logical system for recording rock bands (and all sorts of other musical groups as well), because it is largely based around the old analogue tape recording concept. So engineers identify with it closely.

It is an extremely powerful piece of software, but some users will find it lacks the additional elements of Logic and Cubase (such as the included virtual instruments and plugins).

Historically, Pro Tools was a very expensive system, and the high-end TDM (Time Division Multiplex) systems would set you back at least £5000. These set-ups use dedicated hardware cards in the computer to do all the processing, meaning that the computer's own processing can be left to cope with more menial tasks.

But, in recent years, Digidesign have launched two budget systems aimed at the home studio engineer: these are Pro Tools LE and Pro Tools M Powered (the latter designed to work on M-audio hardware, a company recently acquired by Digidesign's parent company, Avid).

There are a number of other software applications available that run on different platforms and function differently. If you decide against the Big Three, then a brief conversation with your local retailer, or a browse through some magazine articles, should give you an idea what to choose.

Conclusion
Costs
You may have noticed throughout this article the following dictum: you get what you pay for, so spend as much as you can afford! This doesn't mean spend too much, so that you can't afford to buy your next meal. It means work out how much money you have to spend, and once you have set your budget, stick to it. A great variety of gear is available (from a huge range of manufacturers), so it should be possible to find something that fits your budget.

Also, shop around. Your local dealer may be convenient, and they may be friendly and give good advice, but you might be able to find the same gear a lot cheaper elsewhere. There is the option of buying second-hand goods privately, but this is always going to have an element of risk – so, if possible, ask the seller to show you the item working. If they are reluctant to do so, then walk away.

All the gear, but no idea
Now you've got all the gear you ever wanted, the question is, can you use it to good effect? There are a number of ways you can develop your knowledge and skills as a recording engineer or producer:

● *Get a job in a studio.* This is easier said than done, but undoubtedly the best way to learn the trade. You will probably have to put up with making lots of tea for the first few months, but if you are keen, polite, do what you are told and generally fit in, then you will be at the heart of the studio and learning from experienced engineers while they are actually working on real jobs. It is quite likely you won't be paid very well (if at all) when you first start out, but that is sometimes the price you pay for doing a job you love …

● *Do a course.* There are many courses available throughout the world. All are slightly different, and will incur varying costs. A good way to start might be to do a part-time course in the evenings or at weekends. This will not only give you a basic education, but will also give you the opportunity to meet like-minded people who share your interests. If you are more serious, there are also full-time courses lasting one, two or three years. Many will lead to a formal qualification.

● *Read a book/watch a DVD.* If you go into your local musical instrument retailer, you will no doubt find a huge selection of books, DVDs, videos and CDs that will help you teach yourself to be a studio engineer, producer, guitarist, singer – or pretty much anything else musical. These are a great way of furthering your education in your own time, and are best used in conjunction with other ways of learning, particularly when starting out. The main advantage here is that you can be reading a book when you're on the train or bus, rather than having to be in your studio.

A final word …
One thing is always true, whichever way you learn. You must try something before you know if you can do it. If you get it wrong, then get it right next time. Even if you're making tea in a major recording studio, if you get the order wrong the first time, you'll get told to do it again. But if you get it right, you will remember it. This principle applies equally when you get your hands on the gear. The key thing is to make all your mistakes when it doesn't matter (i.e., in studio 'down time'). You certainly don't want to be making mistakes when Robbie Williams is on the other side of the glass!

Whichever route you take into the recording industry, be sure to enjoy it. If you don't enjoy recording music, then you're in the wrong business. It can be hard work, and require long hours, so you need to enjoy it to be able to cope with it. Nevertheless, it is extremely satisfying to be involved in a project from start to finish, and your knowledge will increase the more you are involved.

Antony Greaves trained at Kingston University, then worked as a freelance Pro Tools engineer and music video editor. He subsequently joined Mayfair Studios in London, where he maintained their Neve and SSL consoles, and made important contacts with high-profile artists such as Travis, Coldplay and Robbie Williams. He now lectures full-time on recording and music technology subjects.

PITCHING SONGS PROPERLY

"If you are a songwriter pitching songs to artistes and producers, the key thing to remember is to present *the song*. In other words, don't fill the track with unnecessary overdubs. Most good producers with good ears – myself included – prefer to have a simple arrangement that showcases the song: a good song will always shine through. The worst scenario is where a great song gets lost in a bad arrangement, or in a dated or unoriginal production.

When presenting any material, ensure that you provide it on a quality CD with all the information on the disc. Invariably, the cover will get separated from the package and your contact details will get lost. Most producers receive hundreds of CDs a year, so it's easy to lose such contact details. The next step is to follow up with an email – but don't hassle, since that puts people off!

If you are pitching for a gig as a producer to an artiste, maybe showcase the original song and give an example of how you would develop the track from a production point of view. Depending on the musical genre, there is often a very fine line between production and songwriting. So if you suggest to the artiste that the song needs a new middle-eight, for example, and you co-write that bit with them, make sure you agree a royalty split in writing there and then. If you leave such negotiations until the end of the record, you are guaranteed to get shafted."

Steve Levine is a Grammy Award-winning producer and songwriter, who has worked with acts as diverse as Culture Club, the Beach Boys, Deniece Williams, Louise, Mystique and The Honeyz. See **www.stevelevine.co.uk**.

MIRACLES CAN HAPPEN

"These days it's harder than ever for non-performing songwriters to get their material cut by major artists (or even minor ones) – let alone get it heard by their A&R person, producer or manager. But with a bit of research, and a lot of luck, miracles can still happen, often with unexpected results.

Here's a true story. Some time ago, an independent writer/producer took out a subscription to *SongLink*, received his first issue of leads (a monthly list of artists looking for songs), and sent off his first pitch to the great soul diva, Oleta Adams, who was working on a new project. A couple of days later, he received a call from her A&R manager, saying they loved the song – which was recorded for the album, and eventually went on to receive a prestigious Grammy nomination.

The writer called me straight away to ask, 'Does this happen every time?' Well, no. But the point is that it all starts with the song, and always has done. Provided that you have a great demo, and do your homework, the sky's still the limit. You just have to make your own luck in this business."

David Stark is the Editor/Publisher of *SongLink International*. See **www.songlink.com**.

Glossary of terms used in recording

AFL: An acronym for After Fade Listen – used to solo a channel after the fader (as opposed to before the fader, with PFL).

Attenuate: To make quieter.

Aux: See Auxiliary.

Auxiliary: This refers to the function on a mixing desk of sending part of a signal in a channel to an additional output or destination. Most commonly used for sending a varying amount of signal to a reverb, or other effect.

Balanced: A type of connection between two devices, most commonly using either XLR, 1/4" Jack, or bantam connectors. It offers excellent rejection of external interference using phase cancellation.

Bandwidth: The width of frequencies allowed to pass with no significant loss at any contained frequency.

Bus: An internal connection in a mixing desk that carries the signal from one place to another.

Cannon: A type of connection, identical to XLR.

Cardioid: A polar pattern of microphone. Cardioid pattern mics are most sensitive to sounds in front of the mic.

Channel: One functional path of a mixing desk. Generally the signal will come into a channel input and be routed to a bus from the channel's output.

Clipping: When an audio signal is too loud within a circuit, causing distortion. Digital clipping sounds significantly worse than analogue clipping, and should be avoided at all costs!

Condenser: A type of microphone that uses a capacitor to function. Capacitor mics are generally more sensitive than dynamic mics, and require a power source to operate, in the form of 'phantom power' from a mixing desk or an internal battery.

Console: Also known as mixing desk, the device that combines all the different sound sources into the final mix.

dB: See Decibel (dB).

Decibel (dB): The measurement of sound level. A high number of decibels means a sound is quite loud compared to the reference level.

Delay: In the studio, this refers to an echo for special-effect purposes, or the time it takes for a signal to go through a circuit from input to output.

Dry: Without any effects added.

Dynamic: A type of microphone that uses a moving diaphragm in a magnet to generate an electrical signal.

Dynamic range: The difference in decibels between the quietest point and the loudest point.

Echo: In real life, this is a sound bouncing off a surface and into your ears. This echo arrives at your ears later than the original sound. 'Delay' effects are used to simulate this in the studio, making things recorded in a small studio seem like they were recorded in a larger space.

Effects: Used to add something to a recorded signal – such as reverb, delays, chorus, flange, phasing, and more.

EQ: See Equalisation.

Equalisation (EQ): Used to change the tonal balance of a sound. Bass and treble are the most basic forms (generally found on a home Hi-Fi). Mixing desks can have much more complex EQ – capable of adjusting several different specified frequencies of a signal at the same time. This may be used to correct problems when recording or mixing, or used for special effect to make a sound seem like it is in a certain location, or from a different source. EQ can, for example, be used to make a normally recorded voice sound like it is coming through a megaphone.

Fader: The part of a mixing desk that controls the output level of a channel.

Filter: A type of equaliser that removes certain frequencies, depending on the type of filter.

Frequency: How often something repeats in one second. In sound terms, the higher the frequency of a sound wave, the higher the pitch that we hear.

Gain: How much an amplifier circuit increases the signal level (you increase the gain to make a signal louder).

Ground loop: A hum caused by having two or more pieces of equipment connect with a clear path from the earth of one to the earth of another. While this can be cured by removing the earth connection in one of the mains plugs, such a course of action can be highly dangerous, and is not recommended! There are several other ways of curing ground loops (which vary depending on the system in question).

Hertz (Hz): The unit of frequency per second.

Hum loop: See Ground loop.

Knee: How severely the dynamics of a signal are affected when they exceed the threshold of a compressor or expander.

Level: The volume of a signal in an electrical circuit.

Line input: Used for connecting to the output of a line level device – such as a keyboard or synthesiser.

Master: Generally refers to the overall volume control on a mixing desk – normally a stereo fader labelled Mix, L+R, or Master.

Mic level: The signal level or volume output by a microphone. A microphone should be connected to a Mic Level input on a mixing desk, to make the best use of the signal.

Mic pre-amp: The first amplifier that a microphone signal goes through when entering a mic level input, and normally consisting of a variable gain control.

Microphone: A device that converts sound into electrical signal – technically known as a transducer.

Monitor: In a recording studio, the monitors are the speakers used for 'monitoring' the recording. (Monitor can also relate to a computer screen.)

Mono: One channel that can be heard equally by both ears.

Noise: Signal in a recording that we don't want to be there – such as distortion, or tape hiss.

Pan: Used to position the sound in a channel at a variable point between the left and right speakers. There is normally a detent at the dead-centre position.

Parametric EQ: Uses three variable controls to change the equalisation of a signal. These are Gain (how much Boost or Cut applied); Frequency (which frequency this effects); and Q, or Quality (meaning how large the area of frequencies affected is).

PFL: Pre Fade Listen, or listening to a single channel before it goes through the fader.

Phantom power: Used to supply power to condenser microphones from the mixing desk.

Q: Relates to the Quality control in a parametric EQ. This determines how wide the range of frequencies the parametric EQ band affects.

RCA phono: A type of connection found on modestly priced equipment. This is an unbalanced connection that consists of a male plug and female jack (and most commonly found on consumer HiFi equipment).

Reverb: See Reverberation.

Reverberation: When we hear a sound in a room, the sound is picked up by our ears almost immediately. However, sound travels in every direction, and bounces from surface to surface, until it reaches our ears again. This delayed sound is reverb, and this gives us a sense of the space we are in. When recording, we don't necessarily have the ability to record in a huge church, or at the Grand Canyon, so we use dedicated effects processors that can simulate such environments.

RMS: Root Mean Square. A way of measuring an average of varying signal level.

Send: Generally refers to an additional output in the signal chain (for example, an Auxiliary send or Insert send).

Shelving: A type of equaliser curve that affects all frequencies above a given frequency. The treble and bass controls on a home HiFi are High and Low Shelf EQs.

Slapback: One echo shortly after the original sound.

Solo: A control on a mixing desk that makes it possible to hear just one element of a mix (for example, a particular channel or Auxiliary bus).

Stereo: A recording that provides separate signals for the left and right speakers. Stereo has an advantage over mono because it creates a much more believable simulation of the original recording.

Tinnitus: A ringing in the ears caused by exposure to prolonged high volume levels. There is no way of curing tinnitus, and so exposure to sustained high levels of sound should be avoided at all costs.

Trim: A gain control – such as the pre-amp gain, or channel fader.

TRS: Tip Ring Sleeve. The type of connection commonly used on stereo consumer headphones. This can be situated on a mini-jack or a 1/4" jack, and also on more professional connections such as bantams; it can provide either a stereo connection or a balanced connection, depending on the equipment it is connecting.

TS (Tip Sleeve – see TRS above): This misses out the ring element of the connection, and is used on mono headphones, and unbalanced connections, such as guitar leads.

Wet: With effects added (such as reverb). Most effects processors have a Wet/Dry control, which varies the amount of effect added to the signal.

XLR connector: A type of connection that uses three pins from a male inserted into a female. This is the professional standard for microphone connections, and is a balanced connection.

Production companies

Aardvark Sound Ltd

32/34 Great Marlborough Street, London W1F 7JD
tel 020-7292 9969 *fax* 020-7292 9960
email bridget@aardvarksound.co.uk
website www.aardvarksound.co.uk
Senior Producer Bridget Sapiano

Established in 2001. Specialises in composition and
sound design for TV commercials, including idents
and sonic branding. Clients have included:
Landrover, Smirnoff, Lenor, Shell and Ford. Based in
client-friendly studios in Soho.

Adage Music

Hill Lodge, Warren Wood Drive, High Wycombe,
Bucks HP11 1DY
tel (07973) 295113
email dobs@adagemusic.co.uk
website www.adagemusic.com
Director Dobs Vye

Specialises in the composition and production of title
music packages and music branding. Recent clients
include: BBCTV – *Real Story with Fiona Bruce*;
Hardspell; *Do Something Different*; Endemol – *The
Games*; and BSky – *Sky News*. Also co-writer and co-
producer of *Public Symphony* ('A Pink Floyd for the
Coldplay generation'). Works in fully digital studio.

Air-Edel Associates

18 Rodmarton Street, London W1U 8BJ
tel 020-7486 6466 *fax* 020-7224 0344
email air-edel@air-edel.co.uk
website www.air-edel.co.uk
Roster Supervisor Mark Lo

Established in 1969. Offers full music supervision,
production services and composer representation for
feature film, television and commercial projects. Also
provides specialist music publishing, copyright
clearance and recording studios. Does not accept
unsolicited showreel material.

Amadeus Music

50 Leicester Road, London N2 9EA
tel 020-8883 0813 *fax* 020-8712 514089
email info@amadeusmedia.com
website www.amadeusmedia.com
Managing Director Ivo Fiorenza

Founded in London during 2004, with second office
and recording studio established in Milan in 2005.
Provides music for TV, films and commercials. Also
deals with music licensing, sound design and music
consultancy and research. Recent output includes:
Gordon's Gin, and Sky documentary commercials.

Apollo Sound

32 Ellerdale Road, London NW3 6BB
tel 020-8830 6103

website www.apollosound.com
Director Toby Herschmann

Founded in 1968. Specialises in media music. Recent
clients include: BBC TV (*Auf Wiedersehen Pet*),
Channel 5, AMR and Landor. Rates as for PCAM
standards.

Be Nice to Gracie

31 Madrid Road, Guildford, Surrey GU2 7NU
mobile (07875) 263322
email info@benicetogracie.com
website www.benicetogracie.com
Director Justin Clark

Young and innovative production company
specialising in music for film, TV, radio and
advertising. Features conservatoire-trained composers
working in a range of styles. Projects undertaken have
involved multimedia and documentary music for the
BBC, Channel 4 and Televisa Radio. Rates are
project-orientated and competitive. Make contact via
email in the first instance.

Bent Ear

PO Box 148, Manchester M20 2BE
tel 0161-445 8304
email info@bentear.co.uk
website www.bentear.co.uk
Directors Simeon Davies, Sean Mortimer

Founded in 1999. Provides music, sound design and
voice over for TV, advertising, radio, film and theatre.
Recent clients have included: Umbro Evolution,
Yorkshire Building Society, and Dettol.

Big George and Sons

PO Box 7094, Kiln Farm MK11 1LL
tel (01908) 566453
email big.george@btinternet.com
website www.biggeorge.co.uk
Director George Webley

Established in 1987. Provides music for film, TV and
radio in-house. Styles include hip hop, rock and
funk, but specialises in 'crash, bang, wallop!'.
Successes include: TV themes for *Have I Got News for
You* and *The Office*, alongside a range of radio jingles.

Candle

44 Southern Row, London W10 5AN
tel 020-8960 0111 *fax* 020-8968 7008
email tony@candle.org.uk or charlie@candle.co.uk
website www.candle.org.uk
Executive Composer Charlie Spencer

Founded in 1979. Specialises in composing, recording
and producing music for TV, radio and cinema
commercials worldwide. Also works with music

searches, conference music and film soundtracks. Equipment includes HD Pro Tools digital studio, fast ftp site and media 100 video suite.

Crocodile Music
35 Gresse Street, London W1T 1QY
tel 020-7580 0080 *fax* 020-7637 0097
email info@crododilemusic.com
website www.crocodilemusic.com
Manager Ray Tattle

Established in 1980. Specialist music company, writing and producing original music for national and international advertising campaigns and TV programmes. Also provides audio branding and soundscaping, aiming to keep pace with the new technological advances and challenges in the world of sound. Clients include: Channel 4, ITV and the BBC. Potential composers should approach via the website.

De Wolfe Ltd
Shropshire House, 2nd Floor East,
11-20 Capper Street, London WC1E 6JA
tel 020-7631 3600 *fax* 020-7631 3700
email info@dewolfemusic.co.uk
website www.dewolfemusic.co.uk
Manager W De Wolfe

Provides specially composed music for films, television programmes and commercials, library music and worldwide distribution (other libraries include Hudson Music Co Ltd and Rouge Music Ltd). Also owns and runs Angel Recording Studios. Potential composers may send showreels by post.

Final Touch
4 The Oaks, Uxbridge Road, Hanworth,
Middlesex TW13 5EF
tel 0870-844 4422
email mail@finaltouch.co.uk
website www.finaltouch.co.uk
Head of Production Chris Smith

Specialises in composing and producing music to picture for advertising, TV, film and interactive media. Also deals with songwriting and production, including 5.1 recording and mixing. Clients have included: Guerilla Films, CC3 Amsterdam, Karen David, and KPM. Works with a range of equipment including a Mac G4 Dual Processor, Mackie D8D, Genelec 1032A, Fender Deluxe Lexicon PCM 9, and Logic Platinum. Available for commissions of original scores, music research and clearance, and song production and recording.

Finger Music
59 Rupert Street, London W1D 7PN
tel 020-7287 8733 *fax* 020-7287 8751
email john@fingermusic.tv
website www.fingermusic.tv
Managing Director John Murrell

Founded in 2002. Creators of bespoke music composition and production for TV and film. Recent

clients include: AMV BBDO, Saatchi & Saatchi, HHCL and M & C Saatchi.

Grand Central Music
Grand Central Sound Studios,
51-53 Great Marlborough Street, London W1F 7JT.
tel 020-7306 5600 *fax* 020-7306 5616
email james@grand-central-studios.com
website www.grand-central-studios.com
Producer James Cooper

Specialises in composition, negotiation, search and sound design. Recent clients have included: Saatchi & Saatchi, DCKW and JWT. Works with Pro Tools and Logic. Also delivers radio commercial production.

HUM
31 Oval Road, London NW1 7EA
tel 020-7482 2345 *fax* 020-7482 6242
email info@hum.co.uk
website www.hum.co.uk
Principal Composer Joe Glasman

Founded in 1989. Creates music for global commercials campaigns featuring leading brands, TV on-screen identities and worldwide news stations, alongside incidental TV and film music. Works in a range of genres but specialises in abstract textures and world music.

Instant Music
14 Moorend Crescent, Cheltenham,
Gloustershire GL53 0EL
mobile (07957) 355630
fax (01242) 523304
email martin@instantmusic.co.uk
website www.instantmusic.co.uk
Managing Director Martin Mitchell

Founded in 1975. Provides composition services for multimedia. Also provides mastering services.

Jeff Wayne Music Group
97 Mortimer Street, London W1W 7SU
tel 020-7927 8300 *fax* 020-7927 8364
email info@jeffwaynemusic.com
website www.jeffwaynemusic.com
Head of Licensing Jane Jones *Head of Production* Mandy Hughes

Established in 1968. Provides original music composition, re-mixes, re-recordings, creative music research, licensing for existing copyright recordings and clearances in both recording and publishing. Clients include all major advertising agencies, production companies, feature film and TV companies.

Jonathan Goldstein
41 Castelnau Mansions, Barnes, London SW13 9QU
tel/fax 020-8563 8589
email jonathan@jgmusic.com
website www.jgmusic.com
Director Jonathan Goldstein

Founded in 1989. Classically trained composer working with commercials, film, TV and theatre. Clients include: Saatchi & Saatchi, Publicis (London and New York), and The Royal National Theatre.

Lime Street Sound
3 Lime Court, Lime Street, Dublin 2, Ireland
tel 00353 1 6717271 *fax* 00353 1 6707639
email via website
website www.limesound.com

Offers recording, mixing, editing, dubbing and sound design services for television, radio, multimedia, film and advertising.

Loriana Music
PO Box 2731, Romford RM7 1AD
tel (01708) 750185
email info@lorianamusic.com
website lorianamusic.com
Owner Jean-Louis Fargier

Founded in 1995. Specialises in downtempo electronic music – from cinematic lounge to chilled pop and house. Works with the mainstream music market (CD and DVD sales) and film and TV market. Also runs independent record label. Potential composers should submit material on CD or DVD.

Lotown
60A Golborne Road, London W10 5PR
tel 020-8969 8412
email lotown@btconnect.com
website www.lotown.com
Manager Toby Andersen

Established in 1989. Specialises in music for television commercials. Clients have included: Orange, Party Poker, Volvic and Direct Line. Utilises Pro Tools and Logic.

Lounge Productions
1st Floor, 7 Poland Street, London W1F 8PU
tel 020-7734 7822
email studio@lounger.co.uk
website www.lounger.co.uk
Founder and Director Dominic Shovelton *Producers* Laurence Glover, Suki Kang

Established in 2003. Specialises in composition and production of music to picture for film, TV and advertising, corporate film and events. Clients have included: Nokia, 118 118, Churchill, Chevrolet, Prudential, HSBC, Saab, Shell, IBM and Toyota.

Mammoth Music
43 Bath Road, Chiswick, London W4 1LJ
tel 020-8994 6995 *mobile* (07770) 791091
email julian@mammothmusic.co.uk
website www.mammothmusic.co.uk
Composer Julian Ronnie

Established in 2002. Aims to provide high-quality music on time and on budget – either live or

recorded. Past work has included: TV programmes such as *Skins*, and advertising campaigns for Famous Grouse, Pepsi and Sainsburys.

Mcasso Music Production
34 Great Marlborough Street, London W1F 7JB
tel 020-7734 3664 *fax* 020-7439 2375
email info@mcasso.com
website www.mcasso.com

Formed in 1984 and employing 4 full-time composers who compose, produce and arrange music worldwide, including the following: TV themes and incidental music, commercials and film scores. Clients have included: Guinness, ITV, Pepsi Cola, Ericsson and the BBC.

Milk Music
47 Oakdale Road, Streatham, London SW16 2HL
tel 020-8769 2848
email info@milk-music.com
website www.milk-music.com
Director Simon Dehany

Established in 2003. Music supervision and consultancy service for media and business. Clients include: Saatchi & Saatchi, Ogilvy & Mather, 12Foot6, DX3 and Monkey Kingdom.

Mollusc Music
83 Great Titchfield Street, London WIW 6RH
tel 020-7580 8928
email mollusc@btconnect.com
website www.molluscmusic.co.uk
Key Contacts Anthony Smith, Jonathan Maris

Established in 1993. Supplies music and sound design for television, film, radio and advertising. Recent clients include: Grand Designs, National Geographic and BBC World Service. Equipment includes Mac G5 running Logic.

Montagu Music
306 Canalot Studios, 222 Kensal Road, London W10 5BN
tel 020-8960 1965
email info@montagubourcier.com
website www.montagubourcier.com
Director Damian Montagu

Provides music and sound design for a range of high-profile clients in areas including advertising and film.

Myers Maggs Music
The Flint Barn, Holt Road, Thornage, Holt, Norfolk NR25 7QB
tel (01263) 715840
email justin@myersmaggs.demon.co.uk
Partner Justin Myers

Founded in 1988. Provides a broad range of musical styles for TV, commercials, station idents and library albums among others. Works in a digital studio including picture sync with Cubase. Recent clients include: BBC (*National Lottery Jetset*), J Walter Thompson (B&Q), and Viasat.

Panama Productions

Sovereign House, 12 Trewartha Road, Praa Sands, Penzance, Cornwall TR20 9ST
tel (01736) 762826 *fax* (01736) 763328
email panamaus@aol.com
website www.panamamusic.co.uk
Managing Director Roderick Jones

Founded in 1990. Multi-faceted company writing for songwriters and artistes alongside composing music for the fields of television, radio, film, advertising and multimedia worldwide. Potential composers/songwriters should post showreels, biogs and CV. Also provides studio and production facilities.

Propetik

15 Lower Cookham Road, Maidenhead, Berks SL6 8JN
mobile (07967) 328152
email info@propetik.co.uk
website www.propetik.co.uk
Composer Adrian Lloyd

Founded in 1998. Creates bespoke original music for all production types. Clients have included: National Geographic, Zomba, and Focus. Works with full audio production facilities. MCPS rate card applies.

Quince Productions

62A Balcombe Street, Marylebone, London NW1 6NE
tel (07810) 752765 *fax* 020-7723 1010
email info@quincestudios.co.uk
website www.quincestudios.co.uk
Producer Matt Walters

Founded in 2000. Production house aiming to offer the very latest in production styles. Works with all genres and project types. Specialises in creating advertisements and working on film and TV projects. Potential clients should make contact by phone or email. Potential composers should send showreels.

Radford Music Productions

22A Buer Road, Fulham, London SW6 4LA
tel (07958) 578576
email info@radfordmusic.com
website www.radfordmusic.com
Composer James Radford

Founded in 2000. Specialises in the production of music in a wide range of styles for use in commercials and on TV. Recent advertisement campaigns have included: Polo 'Guardian Angel' for DDB London; American Airlines; and a range of other campaigns for major UK and US advertising agencies. Uses Logic Pro, Cubase and all current VST instruments. Has access to Fairlight Mews studios (c/o Private and Confidential Music) for live recordings. Works by PCAM rates.

RBM Composers

1 Woodchurch Road, London NW6 3PL
tel 020-7372 2229 *fax* 020-7372 3339
email rbm@easynet.co.uk
Managing Director Ronnie Bond

Founded in 1975. Provides music for advertising. Clients have included: Kellogg's, Cadbury's, Kwikfit and Horlicks. Works in Digital 40 track studio.

Shriek

39 Margaret Street, London W1G 0JQ
tel 020-7499 7778
email info@shriek-music.com or tim@shriek-music.com
website www.shriek-music.com
Producer Tim Rabjohns

Founded in 1993. Specialises in creating music and sound design for the television and advertising industries. Also provides track-searching and licensing services. Recent clients include: Red Bee Media, Nickelodeon and the BBC. Equipment includes Mackie monitors, Cubase, Native instruments and Propellerhead software.

Sound Dimensions

9 Boleyn Way, New Barnet, Herts EN5 5LH
tel/fax 020-8440 6583
email info@sounddimensionsmusic.com
website www.sounddimensionsmusic.com
Company Director Alan Danson

Founded in 2001. Specialises in composition, arrangements, ochestrations, consultancy and musical directing. Recent work has included arrangements for London Fashion Week and a variety of TV commericials and productions. Works with electronic/sampled sounds within in-house studio facility, including Logic and Sonar.

Rates: According to PCAM for commercial work; Musicians' Union for fixing, etc.; commissioned work negotiable.

The Sound House (N1) Ltd

The Strand, 156 Holywood Road, Belfast, Co Antrim BT4 1NY
tel (02890) 656769 *fax* (02890) 673771
email steve@thesoundhouseni.tv
website www.thesoundhouseni.tv
Managing Director Steve Martin

Originally Jingle Jangle studios. Specialises in the production of commercials, sound beds, music beds and jingles for radio and television. Contains complete production facilities including 2 sound suites, 3 editing suites and a graphics and animation department. Potential clients should submit showreels.

Spiral Music

Unit 5B, 101 Farm Lane, Fulham, London SW6 1QJ
tel 020-7386 0386 *fax* 020-7386 8878

email cliff@spiral-music.com
website www.spiral-music.com
Writer/Producer Cliff Charles

Established in 2000. Areas of work include writing, producing, arranging and recording original music to picture. Operates with Pro Tools, Logic and a 48 channel analogue desk. Studio available for hire at approx. £250 per 10-hour day. Also works with artist development.

Sublime Music
211 Piccadilly, London W1J 9HF
tel 020-7917 2948
website www.sublime-music.co.uk
Managing Director Nick Grant

Founded in 1998. Provides music for TV, adverts, films and trailers. Specialises in 'jazzy-funk' styles. Clients have included: Siemens, Warner Bros, Dreamworks and Fox TV.

Sumthink Productions
13 East Walk, East Barnet, Herts EN4 8JX
tel (07932) 064101
email james.sumthink@gmail.com
website www.sumthinkproductions.co.uk
Director James E McCluskey

Founded in 2001. Dance music specialists aiming to produce infectious music with a professional and classy edge for dance floors and television. Specialises in remix work. Recent output includes: compilations for Sony and Beechwood Music, and 'Give it to 'Em' – a download chart-topping breakbeat release. Works within a fully equipped 32 channel analogue, digital recording studio using a Mac G5 and Logic 6. Email for rate details. Television fees as standard.

Synesthesia
91 Saffron Hill, London EC1N 8PT
tel 020-7242 4362
website www.synesthesia.net
Director/Composer Paul Thompson

Established in 2000. Aims to provide creative and unique solutions for music to picture and record production. Recent clients include: McDonalds, Heineken, Mercedes and Virgin Atlantic. Facilities contain Pro Tools HD3/192K, 8 networked PCs, vintage mics and outboard, marshall amps and a range of plug-ins.

Tamborine Productions
14 Livonia Street, Soho, London W1F 8AG
tel 020-7434 181 *fax* 020-7434 1813

email tim@tamborine.co.uk
website www.tamborine.co.uk/music
Managing Director Mark Blackledge *Composers* Tim Dodd, Nick Harris

Founded in 1993. Provides music for feature film, drama and children's TV, including animation, alongside pop song production and writing for new artists. Clients have included: the BBC, Third Rock, Granada and Endemol. Works within 3-studio Soho complex with Soundscape hard disc editing and recording, Cubase, Korg and voice booths for recording up to 8 simultaneous artists.

Tony & Gaynor
Suffolk Lodge, 3 Heathview Gardens, Putney Heath, London SW15 3SZ
tel 020-8780 5570 *fax* 020-8780 5571
email studio@tonyandgaynor.com
website www.tonyandgaynor.com
Composers Tony and Gaynor Sadler

Established in 1984. Caters for all areas of musical composition from orchestral scores to sound design for film, TV and radio. Recent clients include: WCRS, HTW, BBC and Lambie Nairn. Works within a 24 track analogue recording studio with grand piano. Pay rates in accordance with PCAM.

Tsunami Sounds
Muscott House, Meadow, Godalming, Surrey GU7 3HL
tel (01483) 410100
email info@tsunami.co.uk
website www.tsunami.co.uk

Founded in 2000. Composes music for media, i.e. TV and adverts. Clients include: Warner Bros, Fox, BBC and Endemol UK.

Welsh Media Music
Gorwelion, Llanfynydd, Carmarthen, Dyfed SA32 7TG
tel (01538) 668525
email dpierce@fsmail.net
Proprietor Dave Pierce

Founded in 1976. Provides music for regional TV alongside speech recording and sound FX. Clients include: BBC Wales and S4C. Works with an 88 channel digital/analogue console and portable kit.

Mastering

10th Planet

40-44 Newman Street, London W1T 1QJ
tel 020-7637 9500 *fax* 020-7637 9599
email sales@10pdm.com
website www.10pdm.com

Established in 1996. Services include long-run CD-R/DVD-R duplication, media encoding, CD mastering, recordable media, print and packaging, and design services. Can duplicate 1000 disks per hour with cutting-edge production-line technology and error-checked through the Clover Systems CD analyser.

360 Mastering Ltd

18A Farm Lane Trading Centre, 101 Farm Lane, London SW6 1QJ
tel 020-7385 6161 *fax* 020-7386 0473
email info@360mastering.co.uk
website www.360mastering.co.uk
Studio Manager Dick Beetham

Services include magnetic and optical duplication, mastering and post production. Studio comprises a selection of post-production and mastering equipment, including Maselec custom mastering console, graphic equalisers and compressors/limiters by Maselec, Fairman, Summit, Weiss. 'No noise' audio cleaning and remastering service available.

Abbey Road Studios

3 Abbey Road, London NW8 9AY
tel 020-7266 7000 *fax* 020-7266 7250
email bookings@abbeyroad.com
website www.abbeyroad.com
Studio Manager Colette Barber

Opened in 1931. Became famous for its large orchestral recording sessions. Hosts technically advanced recording and mixing, stereo and surround mastering and remastering, interactive design and digital video services.

AGR Manufacturing

Melville House, High Street, Great Dunmow, Essex CM6 2AF
tel (01371) 859393 *fax* (01371) 859375
email martyn@agrm.co.uk – general quotations and pricing info; ed@agrm.co.uk – production and artwork
website www.agrm.co.uk
Studio Manager Martyn

Services include all aspects of vinyl record manufacture including 7", 12", picture disks, white labels, promos and sleeve production. CD and DVD replication and duplication, including video CD, enhanced CD, CD albums and singles. Mastering service for both vinyl and CD offering a choice of engineers to oversee the project.

Ape Studios

15 Quayside, Little Neston, Neston, Cheshire CH64 0TB
tel 0151-336 1098
email info@apestudios.com
website www.apestudios.com
Studio Manager Coz Littler

A vintage analogue studio that aims to bring out the classic, big-sounding production of the past. Mastering equipment includes Neumann mastering console with PEV Eq, Studer C37 2trk mastering, Ampex 350 2trk 1\2" mastering, Revox B77 mastering and digital mastering with Pro Tools HD 24 96.

Ascape Studios

Unit E, The Clan Works, 1A Howard Rd, Bromley, Kent BR1 3QJ
tel 020-8460 0048
email info@ascapestudios.com
website www.ascapestudios.com
Key Engineer Cesar Gimeno Lavin

Modern, well-equipped studio offering all aspects of mastering and post-production services. The following equipment is available: Digidesign Pro Tools, Digidesign Control 24, Yamaha and Genelec monitors, Manley, Empirical Labs, and API outboard.

AudioPlexus

10 Manhattan, Fairfield Road, London E3 2UJ
tel 020-8980 8947 *mobile* (07940) 791739
website www.audioplexus.co.uk

Services include mastering and post production for singles and albums using an extensive selection of studio equipment, including: Adam, PMC, Dynaudio and Yamaha Monitors – Avalon, Manley, Behringer and Drawmer Tubes and Valves, Motu, Drawmer, Panasonic and Tascam AD/DA converter and clocks and Prism, Alesis, Behringer and Lexicon Solid State and Digital Processors. Modern air-conditioned and comfortable studio.

B and B Studios

280 Park Avenue, Kingston Upon Hull, East Yorkshire HU5 4DA
mobile (07092) 087573
email info@bandb-group.com
website www.bandb-group.com
Contact Dave Bradfield

Offers post production and mastering of audio tracks with a self-contained duplicating factory, duplicating CD and vinyl.

Creekside Studios

Units C102 & C104 Faircharm Trading Estate, 8-12 Creekside, London SE8 3DX

tel 020-694 9484 *fax* 020-8694 9466
email studio@creeksidestudios.co.uk
Studio Manager Steve Unterberger

Services include digital editing, mastering of DAT, CDR, Wav, Aif, MP3, Minidisc and CD copying, cross fading in or out and digital editing within a well-equipped studio using: TC Electronic Finalizer Plus, 5 band parametric EQ, delay processor, compressor, limiter, expander, Noise Gate, pitch control de-click/de-noise and Red Book CD writing.

Cyclone Music Productions
tel (01634) 714522
email sales@cyclonemusic.co.uk
website www.cyclonemusic.co.uk

Offers professional mastering service to DDP with test CD for approval. Also provides glass mastering, jewel cases, colour booklets and UK Mainland delivery. Equipment includes Sadie Series5 and Cedar de-noise.

eMasters
website www.emasters.co.uk

Offers professional mastering online for CD and vinyl. Also provides opportunity for 1GB library space to share and manage tracks.

Fairview
Cavewood Grange Farm, Common Lane, North Cave, Brough, North Humberside HU15 2PE
tel (01430) 425546 *fax* (01430) 425547
email info@fairviewstudios.co.uk
website www.fairviewrecording.co.uk
Contact Andrew Newlove

Established in 1966 and one of the oldest premier recording facilities in the North of England. Self-contained duplication facility offering audio mastering and post-production services. Equipment includes: Otari Radar II 24 track recorder, Soundcraft 2400 series mixing console, JBL 4350 monitors, Alesis midiverbs and other effects units, and Drawmer compressors.

Finesplice
1 Summerhouse Lane, Harmondsworth, West Drayton, Middlesex UB7 0AT
tel 020-8564 7839 *fax* 020-8759 9629
email info@finesplice.co.uk
website www.finesplice.co.uk

Finesplice has over 20 years' experience in studio mastering and post-production work in the classical, pop, jazz and world genres and in an all-digital environment. Many restoration tools. Analogue and older digital formats also catered for.

Flow Mastering
83 Brixton Water Lane, London SW2 1PH
tel 020-7733 8088 *fax* 020-7326 4016
email brethes@mac.com
website www.wolfstudio.co.uk
Owner Dominique Brethes

Flow Mastering is the mastering branch of Wolf Studios – **see page 183**.

Flying Ace Productions
Walders, Oldbury Lane, Ightham, Sevenoaks TN15 9DD
tel (01732) 887056 *mobile* (07778) 165931

Specialist services in audio post production, CD mastering and general sound design. Deals largely with spoken-word production (i.e. documentaries/education) including location recording. Equipment used: Mac-based Digi-design, Pro Tools, Logic, Waves and Sadie 5 software.

Heathmans Mastering
19 Heathmans Road, Parsons Green, Fulham, London SW6 4TJ
tel 020-7371 0978 *fax* 020-7371 9360
website www.heathmans.co.uk
Studio Manager Susana Martinez

Established in 1989 to provide complete post-production facilities over 6 studios. Services include: vinyl disk cutting, CD mastering and audio restoration, and duplication of watermarked CD-Rs and Mini CDs. Equipment includes SADIE workstations (analogue and digital processing); Pioneer and Technics equipment to compile DJ mix CDs; and VMS 80 Vinyl Lathes cutting either master lacquers or acetates.

Hilton Grove Ltd
The Studios, Hiltongrove Business Centre, Hatherley Mews, London E17 4QP
tel 020-8509 2244 *fax* 020-8509 1155
email dave@hiltongrovemastering.com
website www.hiltongrovemastering.com
Managing Director Dave Blackman *Studio Manager* Kat Smith *Key Engineers* Dave Blackman, Matt Pople

Specialises in audio mastering and vinyl cutting. Recent clients include: EMI, Universal, Fierce Panda and Cooking Vinyl. Equipment includes Sadie 3 workstation, hi-end digital and analogue processors, B&W 801 monitoring and Newmann VMJ80 cutting lathe.

HRH Mastering
Hush Recording Studio (Mastering), Unit B3, Little Heath Industrial Estate, Old Church Road, Coventry CV6 7ND
tel 0870-930 2263
website www.hrsmastering.co.uk
Mastering Engineer Daz Wood

Services include high-end audio digital mastering and editing. Prospective tracks can be uploaded to an online FTP site to give fast turnaround of mastering and editing work.

Ideal Mastering Ltd
Shop, 696 Holloway Road, London N19 3NL
tel 020-7263 3346 *fax* 020-7263 3396

email mark@idealmastering.co.uk
website www.idealmastering.co.uk
Director Mark Saunders *Key Producer/Engineer* Jeff Mortimer

Founded in 1999. Aims to provide a quality mastering service at a price that makes it accessible for unsigned bands as well as more established acts. Also provides a 15bp CD/DVD production facility for converting audio and artwork ideas into a quality finished product. Equipment includes Pyramix HD mastering system and PMC mastering/quad amp.

Rates: £35 per hour plus VAT.

Iguana Studios
Unit 1, 88A Acre Lane, Brixton, London SW2 5QN
tel 020-7924 0496 or (07966) 665349
email info@iguanastudio.co.uk
website www.iguanastudio.co.uk
Contact Andrea or Tom

Offers post-production, mastering, recompilation and duplication services.

JTS Studio
73 Digby Road, London E9 6HX
tel 020-8985 3000 *fax* 0870-762 3019

Studio offering the following: vinyl mastering of 7", 10", 12" master and dubs, vinyl manufacture, CD mastering, transferring, compiling, editing, declicking and noise reduction. Equipment includes Neuman lathes and cutting electronics, and full-production professional CD master facilities.

Liquid Mastering
6Q Atlas Business Centre, Oxgate Lane, London NW2 7HU
tel 020-8452 2255 *fax* 020-8452 4242
email bob@liquidmastering.co.uk
website www.liquidmastering.co.uk
Director Bob Kane *Key Producer/Engineer* Nick Bennett

Works with the mastering and manufacture of vinyl records. Equipment includes: Newman VMS10 Lathe, Massemburg EQ and valve compressors.

The Masteroom/777 Productions
66 Paddenswick Road, London W6 OUB
tel 020-8743 8585 *fax* 020-8743 6633
email masterroom@btconnect.com
Director Howard Grey *Key Producers/Engineers* Jeremy Cooper, Neil Devine

Founded in 1978. Specialists in vinyl cutting and editing/arrangement. Clients include: Green Day, New Order, Shapeshifters, and KT Tunstall. Equipment includes Newmann VMS 80 cutting lathe, Manley Compression, Sadie and Pro Tools. Call for rates details.

Metropolis Mastering
Metropolis Group Ltd, The Power House, 70 Chiswick High Road, London W4 1SY
tel 020-8742 1111 *fax* 020-8742 2626
email mastering@metropolis-group.co.uk
website www.metropolis-group.co.uk
Key Contact Michele Conroy

Part of the Metropolis recording group. Contains 5 studios offering stereo or surround mastering across all currently available music formats including CD, DVD, vinyl, SA-CD and cassette. Utilises PMC monitoring, electronic transmission facilities with dedicated data line and a variety of high-quality digital and analogue EQ. Also provides an exclusive 1/2 speed vinyl paradigm process, i-mastering, music video production and an in-house creative design agency.

Powermaster
30A Glenthorne Road, London N11 3HJ
tel 020-8368 3080 or (07732) 847843
email postproduction@hotmail.com
website http://mysite.wanadoo-members.co.uk/powermaster/
Contact Dave Hewitt

Independent post-production and CD mastering facility offering the following services: audio clean-up, restoration, mastering, PQ encoding, audio editing. The following is also available: Nuendo editing programme, Red Book CD standard and 24 bit processing.

RMS Studios
43-45 Clifton Road, London SE25 6PX
tel 020-8653 4965
email studiosrms@aol.com
website www.rms-studios.co.uk

Over 25 years' experience. Equipment includes: Sadie 5 editing with Cedar Denoise and Retouch/TC Finaliser. Provides low-cost short-run CDR duplication with colour copying. Also offers cassette copying.

RPM
6 Grand Union Centre, West Row, London W10 5AS
tel 020-8960 7222
email www.rpmuk.com

Established for more than 18 years in CD mastering and duplication services. Offers copy masters, editing, barcodes and disc testing. Also provides graphic design with booklet and inlay. Pricess are approx. £600 for 1000 CDs (including booklet and inlay).

Sanctuary Mastering
150 Goldhawk Road, London W12 8HH
tel 020-8932 3200 *fax* 020-8932 3209
email mastering@sanctuarystudios.co.uk
website www.sanctuarygroup.com
Contact Sophie Nathan

Well-established studio – part of Sanctuary group. Mastering facilities comprise 5 suites housing 10 mastering engineers. Services offered include digital editing, mastering, restoration, declicking, denoising, sound analysis, 5.1 surround sound mastering. CD, cassette, PCMD, DAT and Mini Disc duplication with in-house graphic design.

Sound Discs Ltd

Unit 5, Barley Shotts Business Park,
off St Ervans Road, London W10 5YG
tel 020-8968 7080 *fax* 020-8968 7475
email sound.discs@virgin.net
website www.sound-discs.co.uk
Contact Peter Bullick

Provides in-house mastering and digital editing studio with 24 track ADAT mixing and voice-over facility, Avid editing suite, glass mastering, CD EP/CD/LP duplication, cassette supply and duplication, music video service, art and design service. The studio uses an array of post-production equipment including Sound Designer II digit editing system, Masterlist CD PQ encoding system, Tascam DA20 professional DAT machine, Drawmer DL221 dual compressor and limiter, Alesis Quadraverb programmable multi-effects processor, Tascam M-2524 MIDI-programmable mixing console.

Sound Recording Technology

Audio House, Edison Road, St Ives,
Cambridgeshire PE27 3LF
London: *tel* 020-8446 3218
Cambridge: *tel* (01480) 461880 *fax* (01480) 496100
email sales@soundrecordingtechnology.co.uk
website www.soundrecordingtechnology.com

Offers high-end mastering within a 6-studio complex. Provides sonic solutions restoration and all analogue and digital formats. Also offers authoring and design services. Provides 24-hour online quotes.

Sounds Good Ltd

12 Chiltern Enterprise Centre, Station Road, Theale,
Berkshire RG7 4AA
tel 0118-930 1700 *fax* 0118-930 1709
email sales-info@sounds-good.co.uk
website www.sounds-good.co.uk
Manager/Engineer Henry Smithson

Founded in 1989. CD mastering and digital editing service. Recent clients include: The Johnsons, Emma-Jane Thommen and PAMA International. Equipment includes Sadie and Sequoia editing systems, TC finaliser, DBX quantum, focusrite analogue mastering processors and ATC monitoring. Also provides CD/DVD pressing and duplication and DVD authoring service.

Rates: Start at £55 (plus VAT) per hour with £135 (plus VAT) 3-hour package deal available.

Transition Studios

Kemble House, Kemble Road, London SE23 2DJ
tel 020-8699 7888 *fax* 020-8699 9441
email info@transition-studios.co.uk
website www.transition-studios.com
Manager Karen Andrews *Key Producers/Engineers* Jason Goz, Leon Day

Post-production company specialising in vinyl and CD mastering. Works with a wide variety of independents and majors including Sony BMG, EMI, V Recordings and BBC1 XTRA. Equipment includes: Manley (specially commissioned), Newmann (vintage), Phillips (vintage), Prism, Sadie, TC Electronic, Urei and Waves. Contact for rates information.

Setting up your desktop studio

Nic Rowley points out that there has been a revolution in the world of desktop recording over the past five years. It is now possible for anyone with musical ideas (and a few hundred pounds to spend) to create tracks of broadcast quality at home – but there are a number of issues to consider when setting up a desktop studio. In this article, we look at the choices facing the desktop musician who wants to purchase a cost-effective home recording system.

What equipment will I need to purchase?

The essential components of the desktop studio are:

- A suitable private space in which to set up.
- A good-sized desk or workstation unit on which to arrange your equipment. You will find cheap, flexible and sturdy examples in low-cost furniture stores such as IKEA – but you may also want to consider purpose-built equipment stands (available from major music stores). You will, of course, need a comfortable chair in which to work, and good lighting for your workspace.
- A recording device suitable for the type of music you produce. Decide between a computer (with audio interface) running a standard sequencer package, a standalone hard-disk recorder, and a workstation keyboard.
- The means to create and capture musical performances (keyboards, guitars, decks, microphones, etc.), plus a library of samples and loops (and/or the necessary software and hardware to create your own).
- Nearfield monitor speakers and/or professional quality headphones, to monitor your recordings when tracking and mixing.
- A way of transferring your finished recordings onto CD, DVD or other media.
- A way of backing up and archiving your recordings.
- A reliable power supply, plus all necessary mains, extension, audio and MIDI cables.

How do I know what equipment is right for me?

This depends upon a number of factors:

- *Are you an experienced computer user?* If you are, you will find it very easy to adapt to using music software packages such as sequencers and samplers, and you should definitely base your desktop studio around a computer DAW (digital audio workstation). If you intend to buy a computer especially for music recording, you will need to decide whether a Mac or a PC is the more suitable for your needs. In essence, both are capable of producing excellent results, and if you are experienced on one platform then there is nothing to be gained from changing to the other. Macs are still the computers of choice in most professional studios, but Apple's move to Intel processors may change this situation over the next few years.
- *What experience do you have using analogue recording equipment?* If you are used to using traditional mixing consoles and analogue 'outboard' processors (compressors, noise gates, equalisers, etc.) then you may find the lack of hands-on control in a computer-based recording set-up frustrating or restricting. Most modern recording software borrows from (and in many cases mimics) the operation of a hardware studio; but using a mouse and keyboard to control functions and enter parameters can lead to using the eyes more than

the ears – to the detriment of the music. There are several excellent hardware 'control surfaces' that allow music software to be manipulated with knobs, faders and buttons, but many are expensive, and few replace the mouse entirely in the software-based studio. So if you are a fan of analogue recording, but still want a compact desktop set-up, you could consider buying one of the excellent all-in-one hard disk recorders manufactured by Yamaha, Korg or Roland. These are capable of producing top-class professional recordings with minimum complication and clutter (though at the expense of some flexibility and ease of use when it comes to the editing of individual tracks).

● *Do you already own a computer?* If you own a reasonably up-to-date computer (desktop or laptop), it may well be possible to use it as the basis for your desktop studio. You may need to add extra RAM (as much as you can afford) and an additional high-capacity, fast hard disk drive (160GB plus and 7200 rpm) to enable it to cope with the demands of music recording. Many musicians prefer to separate their music from their day-to-day computing by creating a 'dual-boot' system in which all musical activities take place on a dedicated music 'partition'. This helps to avoid wasting processor power on non-musical background computing activities, and reduces the risk of accidental damage to music-related files. Information on optimising a computer for music use is widely available on the Internet, and in music technology magazines.

● *What musical equipment do you already own?* Most of the musical equipment you already own will find a role in your desktop studio. MIDI-equipped keyboards can be used to control software instruments, as well as acting as sound sources in their own right. Stompbox and rack effects units from live rigs can also be pressed into service to add variety and colour to your recordings – and dynamic stage mics (such as Shure's SM57 and 58) can be used to produce high-class vocal and instrumental recordings.

● *What style(s) and genre(s) of music will you be recording, and will you be making extensive use of loops and samples?* There has been a convergence of functionality in music software, which means that nearly all the music production packages currently available can be adapted to most working methods and styles of music. It is fair to say, however, that the 'Big Five' – Logic Audio, Cubase/Nuendo, Sonar, Digital Performer and Pro Tools – tend to suit those who think of the desktop studio as a virtual, digital version of the conventional studio. Those with a background in contemporary dance music, or those new to production, may find packages such as Ableton Live, Propellerhead Reason, Mackie Traction and Sony Acid more intuitive and more spontaneous to use.

● *Will you routinely be recording a vocalist or any acoustic instruments, and do you yourself play an instrument or instruments?* If you are going to be recording vocals or acoustic instruments, you will need to invest in a large diaphragm condenser microphone (plus stand, pop shield and shockmount). There are now many excellent studio condenser mics available from companies such as SE, Studio Projects, Rode, Samson, Audio Technica, AKG and ADK, for under £100, capable of producing high-quality recordings from a variety of sound sources. Most, however, require phantom power – so make sure your audio interface (or hard disk recorder) is equipped with suitable pre-amps, offering 48-volt phantom power. If you sing or play an instrument yourself, you may consider buying a remote control system for your set-up (preferably wireless), such as Frontier Design's 'Tranzport'. This enables you to operate your digital audio workstation without running back and forth from your desk to the recording position.

- *Do you understand and use music notation?* If you routinely score out your compositions, you will find the ability to edit your work using an on-screen score editor invaluable. Most of the major sequencing packages (except Pro Tools) offer this functionality, but there are also specialist notation programmes (such as Sibelius, Finale and Overture) which can be used to notate and audition your compositions.

How should I arrange my recording space?

The ideal recording space is asymmetrical in shape. This helps to avoid the production of room nodes (resonances that make some frequencies in the music appear too loud, and others too soft). Some floor carpet, soft furniture and heavy curtains should also be used to tame room reverberations. Acoustic treatment panels and foam (when fitted according to the manufacturer's instructions) are an excellent investment, and there are a number of companies now producing low-cost acoustic treatments, suitable for use in the home studio. If these are not an option, then consider choosing smaller monitors, which produce less energy at low frequencies.

Monitors should be placed away from side and back walls, with the distance from the speakers to the back walls being different from the distance to the side walls. These monitors should be placed on purpose-built stands, arranged symmetrically at head height (relative to your seating position) and about a metre apart and a metre or so away from you – angled in towards you at 30 degrees to the centre line. If possible, arrange your set-up along the longer dimension of the room, so that the speakers are kept away from the side walls.

For vocal and instrumental recording, you can improvise an effective 'vocal booth' – using thick duvets suspended from curtain rails, or placed over room dividers. When using a cardioid condenser microphone, it is most important that the singer has a duvet *behind* them, since room reflections that might colour the sound will be reflected from the wall or surface facing the microphone.

What other points should I bear in mind when setting up my desktop studio?

- Try out the different DAW software packages by downloading online demos. When you find one you like, compare the feature sets of the various available versions. A light/express version may offer all the functionality you need, and will cost considerably less than the top-of-the-range programme.
- Try to avoid clutter. Keep cables as short as possible, and avoid piles of black spaghetti under your work desk.
- Any equipment or instruments that you don't use regularly should be removed from your studio space and stored elsewhere.
- Supply all the mains power to your studio equipment from one mains socket. Plug an extension board into a convenient socket, and then plug sufficient further extension boards into it to provide enough sockets for all your gear. The power consumption of a typical desktop studio is quite low, and this arrangement will help avoid hums and ground loops. Consider using a surge protector on the main socket, and – if you are worried about the possibility of power cuts during critical recordings – an uninterruptible power supply.
- Make sure there is a comfortable chair or sofa in the workspace in which you can relax (and in which other musicians and guests can relax!). Efficient studio work requires periods of rest and reflection.

- Think about ergonomics, and arrange audio interfaces, keyboards, controllers, etc. in a way that suits your working methods.
- Buy the best microphones and monitors you can afford: software equalisers and effects will not salvage a fundamentally poor recording, and you can only be sure that your music will be heard as you intend, if your monitors are accurate. While it is possible to produce reasonable results using headphones for monitoring, most musicians agree that hearing the music 'live and breathe' in three dimensions is the best way to make decisions about volume, tone, balance and stereo imaging.
- Consider purchasing a 'monitor controller' so that you can easily adjust your monitoring level (and mute the monitors when recording vocals or instruments in the same room).
- Make sure that your digital music system is capable of recording at 24-bit resolution, but don't worry too much about being able to record at high sample rates. The subjective improvement in sound-quality of files recorded at 96kHz and above, in the home or project studio environment, is small at best (and usually negligible). Attention to room acoustics, good microphones and good monitors are the things most likely to improve the quality of your desktop recordings.

Conclusion

Once you have set up your desktop studio, remember to devote time and resources to its maintenance. A clean, dust-free environment prolongs the life and preserves the quality of studio equipment; making sure that you are running up-to-date versions of software with current hardware drivers helps ensure enjoyable, crash-free recording sessions. If your finances allow, a small development budget will help you to adjust the system to your needs over time, but the point of a desktop studio is to make music: once your set-up is enabling you to do this comfortably and effectively, there is usually little need for extra expenditure.

However small or large your budget (and whatever recording gear you choose), remember that the music you make is more important than the equipment you possess. High-end technology will not turn poorly crafted, badly played songs into masterpieces; but even the simplest of set-ups – used wisely – can capture music of quality and originality. Your desktop studio should encourage you to make music, but it should not keep you awake at night wondering if it is time to upgrade your kit! It is much more important to get the equipment you need, and learn how to use it well, than to hanker after the latest releases, upgrades and updates which are regularly on offer in music technology magazines.

During his 30 years as a keyboard player, arranger and musical director, **Nic Rowley** has worked on countless record, television and film sessions. He has also conducted three West End musicals and toured widely as a bandleader with artists such as Lulu, The Supremes, and The Three Degrees. As a composer he has written countless advertising jingles, 12 theatre scores and more than 50 signature tunes/scores for TV (including *Not the Nine o'Clock News*, *Dame Edna Everage*, and *The Two Ronnies*), plus on-screen logo packages for ITV.

Glossary of terms used in desktop music

AAC: Advanced Audio Coding.

Additive synthesis: A type of synthesis that uses multiple waveforms added together to create a different waveform.

ADSR: Attack, Decay, Sustain and Release. This is referred to as an 'Envelope', and is generally used in synthesis for level or filtering effect. Attack is how long a note takes to fade in; Decay is how long it takes to reduce to the Sustain level – at which it stays, then fades out at the rate determined by Release.

After touch: Some controller keyboards have the function to vary the amount of pressure on a key, after it has been pressed and held down. For example, this could be used to add a vibrato effect to a held note.

AIFF: Audio Interchange File Format. Initially, the standard file format for transferring audio between Macs and PCs.

Algorithm: A mathematical calculation, most commonly relating to how a plugin or other effect works.

All notes off: A MIDI message which tells all notes to stop on any connected MIDI synthesisers. Useful if you get notes 'hanging' after they should have stopped.

Amplitude: The level or volume of a signal when considering it at sample magnification.

Analogue: 'Constantly changing', as opposed to digital, which has a definite value at any point in time.

Apple: The manufacturer of Macintosh (Mac) computers and iPods.

Arpeggiater: A device that plays all the notes in a defined chord sequentially.

Attack: How long a sound takes to get from minimum to maximum level.

Bank: A collection of programs or sounds in a synthesiser.

Binary: A numerical system that consists of only two values – 0 and 1. This is used in digital systems, as it is simple for the system to detect whether the electricity is OFF (0) or ON (1).

Bit: Abbreviation for 'Binary Digit', and relating to either a 0 or a 1 in Binary.

Byte: 8 Bits (see above) together form a Data Word known as a Byte.

Buffer: A temporary storage area, which slows down the amount of time a piece of data takes to get from output to input, while ensuring that the speed of the data is constant. Commonly found on hard disks, CD writers, and in DAWs.

Central processing unit (CPU): The 'brain' of a computer.

Channels: There are 16 MIDI channels that can be used simultaneously in a standard General MIDI system: 16 different paths of note information that do not necessarily relate to each other.

Continuous controller: A MIDI message that relates to a control, which can be constantly changing.

Controller: An instruction that can be sent down a MIDI cable alongside note information. MIDI controllers can relate to Volume, Pan, Modulation, Cutoff Frequency, program changes, and much more. They can also relate to a physical knob or fader.

Decibel: The measurement of sound level. A high number of decibels means a sound is quite loud compared to the reference level.

Decay: How long a sound takes to reduce from the peak level, after its initial attack, to its sustaining level.

Default: An initial state, or 'normal' setting.

Delay: An echo effect, or the amount of time it takes for some data to be processed.

Digital synthesis: A simulation of analogue synthesis, using digital technology to create waveforms artificially.

DIN plug: A MIDI connector (5 Pins).

DSP (Digital Signal Processing): Using a form of computer system to affect data a certain way: for example, adding reverb using a plugin.

Envelope: See ADSR.

Error correction: A system for correcting corrupted or missing data.

Equalisation (EQ): Used to change the tonal balance of a sound. Bass and Treble are the most basic forms (generally found on home Hifis). Mixing desks can have much more complex EQ – capable of adjusting several different specified frequencies of a signal at the same time. This may be used to correct problems when recording or mixing, or used for special effect to make a sound seem like it is in a certain location, or from a different source. EQ can, for example, be used to make a normally recorded voice sound like it is coming through a megaphone.

Fade: Raising or lowering the volume of a signal over time.

Fader: The part of a mixing desk that controls the output level of a channel. Simulated in most computer music software packages in the 'Mix' window.

Filter: A type of equaliser that removes certain frequencies, depending on the type of filter.

Frequency: How often something repeats in one second. In sound terms, the higher the frequency of a sound wave, the higher the pitch that we hear.

Gigabyte: 1024 Megabytes – a measurement of storage space in a digital system.

Hertz: The unit of frequency per second.

Keyboard split: Dividing the keyboard into different 'zones' that can each trigger a different sound or program.

LCD: Liquid Crystal Display.

LFO: Low Frequency Oscillator. Much slower than the oscillator used to generate a sound, and most commonly used to affect an existing sound with a filter or volume controller.

Local: Can be set to ON or OFF on a controller keyboard with built-in sounds, which will determine whether the internal sounds are triggered by pressing a key.

Loop: A section of music or sound that plays over and over repeatedly, such as a 1-bar drum 'loop', which can be repeated to make it seem like the drummer is playing constantly.

Metronome: A device that helps us keep time. Traditionally, a metronome makes a clicking sound at a user-defined tempo.

MIDI: Musical Instrument Digital Interface. The standard communication protocol for digital musical instuments since the early 1980s.

MIDI clock: A standard system used to synchronise different MIDI devices.

MIDI interface: Adds MIDI functionality to a computer system, normally as an external box connected by USB.

MIDI merge: Combines two or more MIDI cables into one, so as to connect multiple controllers to a single destination device.

MIDI ports: Either MIDI In (receives data), MIDI Out (sends data) or MIDI Thru (duplicates what is arriving at the MIDI In).

MIDI time code (MTC): A time reference for synchronisation of MIDI devices.

Modulation: Affecting an existing signal; for example, adding vibrato, tremolo, or chorus effects.

Mono: One channel that can be heard equally by both ears.

Multitimbral: A feature of a device that can produce many different sounds simultaneously.

Note On: A MIDI command that instructs a note to play. It will have a specific pitch and velocity attached to it.

Note Off: A MIDI command that instructs a specific note to stop.

Nyquist theorem: The theory that the sample rate of a system should be at least twice the highest frequency we can hear. Theoretically, we can hear up to 20KHz; therefore, we should sample in excess of 40KHz (hence CD quality being 44.1KHz).

Octave: A difference in pitch of 12 semitones.

Oscillator: A device that creates a repeating waveform, either to create a sound, or to affect another sound in some way.

Pan: Used to position the sound in a channel at a variable point between the left and right speakers. There is normally a detent at the dead-centre position.

Parameters: Values that can be changed by the user.

Patch: A specific type of sound from a synthesier, otherwise known as a Program.

Pitch Bend: A MIDI controller that can vary the pitch of a note within a semitone. Most controller keyboards have a built-in Pitch Bend Wheel on the left-hand side of the keys.

Polyphonic: A feature of a device that allows multiple notes to be played simultaneously.

Presets: The standard set of sounds when a device comes 'from the factory', without anyone editing them.

Program: See Patch.

Program Change Message: A MIDI command which instructs a synthesiser to change to a particular patch.

Quantisation: Affecting the timing of a performance by making the notes snap to a pre-defined musical grid (by using crotchets, or semiquavers, for example).

RAM: Random Access Memory. A set of chips in a computer that store data temporarily, until the computer is turned off.

Real time: Something happening in time that corresponds to our real lives, rather than 'Offline' (i.e. calculated separately).

ROM: Read Only Memory. Similar to RAM, but cannot be written to, and still remains when the computer is powered down. Presets are a type of ROM.

Sampler: A device that can record short phrases of audio, which can then be triggered by a MIDI note on message.

Sampling: The process of recording a short phrase or 'hit' of audio.

Sampling rate: Relates to the quality of the audio sample (i.e. how many measurements per second are taken of the analogue waveform as it is converted to digital).

Sequencer: A piece of software or hardware that records 'sequences' of MIDI data for overdubbing and playback.

SMPTE: A timing reference used to synchronise different devices in a studio. Stands for Society of Motion Picture and Television Engineers.

Step Time: Recording a performance in the order the notes come without a timing reference, as opposed to recording a performance in 'Real Time'.

Standard MIDI file: A common format of MIDI file that can be read by all MIDI sequencers, and should play back almost identically regardless of the system.

Sustain (pedal): A type of MIDI controller used to simulate the sustain pedal of an acoustic piano.

System Exclusive Message: MIDI data that is sent to a specific device to give it an instruction that may not be possible on other MIDI devices.

Tempo: The speed of a piece of music, generally codified in Beats Per Minute (BPM).

Timbre: The tone of a sound.

Velocity: How hard a MIDI controller key is pressed, and normally controlling how loud the note will sound, relative to others.

Waveform: What sound 'looks' like – when plotted on a graph, as sound pressure over time.

Courses

Academy of Contemporary Music

Rodboro Buildings, Bridge Street, Guildford,
Surrey GU1 4SB
tel (01483) 500800 *fax* (01483) 500801
email enquiries@acm.ac.uk
website www.acm.ac.uk
Principal Chris Hayne

Established in 1996, ACM is now at the forefront of
contemporary popular music education. The
information technology, sound and production
courses are taught in the custom-built production
suite and 3 recording studios, both of which offer
industry-standard facilities. Students also have access
to several pre/post studios, 2 music IT suites lined
with iMacs, and industry-specialist staff. Offers
production courses at Diploma, Higher Diploma and
Degree; the training includes modules in Studio
Recording, Composition and Arranging, Music IT,
Digital Audio Techniques and Post Production.

Qualifications: Diploma in Contemporary Popular
Music (Music Production); Higher Diploma in
Contemporary Popular Music (Music Production);
BA (Hons) Degree in Contemporary Popular Music
(Technology); BA (Hons) Degree in Creative Sound
Design.

Alchemea College of Audio Engineering

The Windsor Centre, Windsor Street,
London N1 8QG
tel 020-7359 3986
email info@alchemea.com
website www.alchemea.com
Lecturer Neil Pickles

Founded in 1992. Aims to provide graduates with the
knowledge, experience, commitment and real-world
know-how needed to develop and maintain a
successful career in the professional sound recording
industry.

The practical ethic is seen in the Diploma course,
which requires practical submissions to include the
following: Speech and Music Edit Using Pro Tools,
Practice Mixing Projects (Dry & Wet), Sampling and
Synthesis Project, Cubase SL MIDI/Audio Exercise,
Logic Pro 7 MIDI/Audio Exercise, Live Recordings
and Multitrack Recordings. Study also involves
aspects of music theory, post production for film and
TV, and music business.

Qualifications: Diploma in Audio Engineering. See
website for details of other part-time and weekend
courses.

Audiocourses.com

2 Eliot Drive, Marlow, Bucks
tel 020-7871 4760
email support@audiocourses.com
website www.audiocourses.com
Managing Director Chris Hambly

Audio recording school specialising in sound
engineering and music production with bases in
London and Milan. Areas of study include: advanced
recording techniques, digital audio operations, basic
audio recording, broadcast audio and sound theory.
Potential applicants should visit the website for
application details.

Qualifications: City and Guilds Sound Engineering
Part 3, and in-house certification.

Ayr College

Dam Park, Ayr KA8 0EU
tel (01292) 293503 *fax* (01292) 263889
email m.mchugh.ayrcoll.ac.uk
website www.ayrcoll.ac.uk/digidesign/index.asp
Editor Curriculum Manager Michael McHugh

Established in 1998. One of the leading training
centres for Sound Production in Scotland. Facilities
include 3 recording studios with 5.1 surround sound
mixing, 2 MIDI computer labs with 16 PCs in each,
and a full PA system with mobile recording facility.
Also a Digidesign Certified Training Location,
offering specialist short courses in Protools software.
Initial applications online or directly by post. NC,
NQ, HNC and HND are all subject to interview.

Qualifications: NC Music Technology; NQ Music
Foundation; HNC/D Sound Production; Protools
101, 110, 201 and 210 certificates.

Bath Spa University

Department of Music, Newton Park, Bath BA2 9BN
tel (01225) 875875 *fax* (01225) 875505
email www.bathspamusic.com
website http://performance.bathspa.ac.uk or
www.myspace.com/bathspamusic

Established in 1992 and now with 350 full-time music
students. The department operates 5 on-site
recording studios, including 'MusicLab', a
professional studio created as part of its 'Centre of
Excellence In Teaching & Learning' status. All
Commercial Music and Creative Music Technology
undergraduate students study music production. The
department has more than 50 Apple Mac
workstations, and all students in the department
study Pro Tools. Bath Spa is an accredited Apple
training provider (Logic Pro/Final Cut Pro) and a
Digidesign approved school (Pro Tools). It also
validates a Foundation Degree (FdA) in Music
Production, taught at local partner colleges. Music
technology and multimedia specialisms are offered as
part of the MA in Creative Music Technology; this

programme is composition-based and spans commercial and Sonic Art styles with an overall focus on a creative and experimental approach. Application through UCAS for undergraduate programmes, or direct to the University for Masters' programmes.

Qualifications: BA (Hons) Music Technology; BA (Hons) Commercial Music; MA in Creative Music Technology (main campus); FdA Music Production (at local partner colleges).

Bournemouth and Poole College

Knighton Heath Music Centre, 855 Ringwood Road, Bournemouth BH11 8NE
tel (01202) 582192 *fax* (01202) 582192
email jacobsj@bpc.ac.uk or skinnerh@bpc.ac.uk
website www.thecollege.co.uk
Head of Music Martin Outhwaite

Established in delivering music courses for 15 years. Aims to create a well-resourced and professional environment. Specialises in Creative Music Technology. Potential students should phone for application pack.

Qualifications: ND and NC Music Technology.

Bournemouth University – Media School

Weymouth House, Talbot Campus, Fern Barrow, Poole, Dorset BH12 5BB
tel (01202) 965745 *fax* (01202) 965875
email rchater@bournemouth.ac.uk
website www.media.bournemouth.ac.uk
Programme Adminstrator Robin Chater

Founded in 1992. The Bournemouth Media School aims to combine the pursuit of academic excellence with thriving professional enterprise in an attempt to illuminate and enrich academic understanding. The 1-year full-time (or 2-year part-time) Masters in 'Post Production: Sound Design' studies the art of taking the entire responsibility for the post-production soundtrack of a film or television programme, including the ability to work with composers, directors and others to ensure the best technical and artistic outcome. The programme comprises the following units: Production – Sound Design, Principles of Post Production, Theory, Professional Studies, Collaborative Projects, Masters Project or Dissertation. Background experience is preferable, but the most important prerequisite is a keen interest and a demonstratable potential in sound design. (May consider applicants without a Degree.) Application forms can be downloaded from the website.

Qualifications: MA Post Production: Sound Design.

Brighton Institute of Modern Music

7 Rock Place, Brighton, East Sussex BN2 1PF
tel (01273) 626666
email info@bimm.co.uk
website www.bimm.co.uk
Co-founder Sarah Clayman

Specialises in contemporary popular genres. Aims to provide the facility for students to train to become the recording artists, songwriters, music teachers and session players of tomorrow. The recording and production course is centred on live sound; includes modules on the Studio Production Process and Events Management.

Qualifications: Diploma in Sound Engineering and Tour Management.

The Brit School for Performing Arts and Technology

60 The Crescent, Croydon CR0 2HN
tel 020-8665 5242 *fax* 020-8665 8676
website www.brit.croydon.sch.uk
Principal Nick Williams

The UK's only non-fee-paying school for performing arts. Predominantly deals with contemporary popular styles. Specialises in recording, songwriting and performance with a very practical emphasis. Application details can be found on the website. Initial selection process on basic aptitude; successful applicants invited to audition.

Qualifications: GCSE Music; BTEC First Diploma in Music (years 10 and 11); BTEC National Diploma in Music Practice (years 12 and 13); AS/A2 Music (Edexcel).

City Literary Institute

Keeley Street, Covent Garden, London WC2B 4BA
tel 020-7492 2630 *fax* 020-7492 2735
email music@citylit.ac.uk
website www.citylit.ac.uk
Head of Music Janet Obi-Keller

Established in 1919. Provides part-time courses for adults in Central London from beginner to professional levels. Specialist technology training available, including tuition in the use of sequencing packages such as Logic and hard-disc recording including Ableton Live. Contains newly fitted music technology studio. See website for application process.

Qualifications: ATCL; LTCL; Music Foundation Levels 1, 2 and 3.

City of Westminster College

Paddington Centre, 25 Paddington Green, London W2 1NB
tel 020-7258 2745
email steve.hepworth@cwc.ac.uk
website www.cwc.ac.uk
Head of School Steve Hepworth

Founded in 1980. Offers a range of courses that cover sound engineering, recording technology, music business, digital audio, live and broadcast sound. See **www.cwc.ac.uk/sound** for more course information. Application through completion of form, followed by January interviews for successful candidates.

Qualifications: Basic Sound Level 1/2; City and Guilds Sound Engineering Level 2/3 and 4; BTEC National in Music Technology Level 3; HNC Music Production Level 4; Foundation Degree in Music Technology Level 4/5.

Clydebank College

Kilbowie Road, Clydebank G81 2AA
tel 0141-952 7771
email raymondrashid@hotmail.com
website www.clydebank.ac.uk
Lecturer Raymond Rashid

Originally opened as a technical college in 1965. The new campus opens in 2007 as a striking 3-storey building on a 6-acre site overlooking the River Clyde. The full-time Electronic Music and Recording course contains a blend of practical and theoretical work supported by lectures, tutorials and visits. Modules include: Music Composition; Stereo Recording; Multi-track Recording; Group and Solo Instrument Studies; and Communication Web Design/Video Project. Successful completion of all the modules on the programme will equip students for entry onto the Higher National Certificate/Diploma programmes in EMR and related subjects. Past students have gone directly from the NC into programmes at James Watt College, North Glasgow College, Stow College, and Perth College. Potential applicants will need to participate in a 20-minute audition and must be over 16 years of age. Application forms can be downloaded from the 'Application' section of the website or by calling 0141-951 2122.

Qualifications: National Certificate in Electronic Music and Recording.

Coatbridge College

Kildonian Street, Coatbridge,
North Lanarkshire ML5 3L5
tel (01236) 436000 or (01236) 422316
fax (01236) 440266
email admissions@coatbridge.ac.uk
website www.coatbridge.ac.uk
Senior Lecturer in Music and Sound Production Martin Dewar

Has been delivering music technology courses since 1989. Current activities include a research project in conjunction with Glasgow Caledonian University, and joint developments with Riverside Studios, Glasgow. Students are also given access to the college theatre for live sound training. Units covered include: multitrack recording and mixing, audio and MIDI sequencing (Pro Tools/Cubase), digital audio workstations, electronic music systems and acoustics. Contact admissions by phone for more information on how to apply.

Qualifications: NQ Music Technology and HNC/D Sound Production. HND offers direct entry into the 3rd year of audio technology with multimedia degree at Glasgow Caledonian University.

Colaiste Stiofain Naofa

College of Further Education, Tramore Road,
Cork City, Ireland
tel/fax +353 4961020/4961029
email info@csn.ie
website www.csn.ie
Principal Tim Kelleher *Deputy Principal* William McAuliffe

Provides hands-on training in all aspects of the music business as part of 'Music, Management and Sound' course. Specialises in musicianship, press and promotion, music contracts, PA set-up, digital and analogue recording, songwriting, live performance and voice training. Potential students will be required to be present for live audition.

Qualifications: FETAC – Certificate; BTEC – Higher National Diploma; Rockschool – Graded Exams; Associated Board – Graded exams.

Confetti School of Recording Technology

6-10 Convent Street, Nottingham NG1 3LL
tel 0115-952 2075
website www.confettistudios.com
Student Adviser Cate Johnson

A custom-designed facility, housing a progressive learning institute alongside commercial recording studios and a film company. Aims to create a modern, influential learning environment, inspirational staff and creative, vocational courses in order to allow students a headstart in the creative industries, as well as developing invaluable life skills, gaining in confidence and thinking positively about their future.

Qualifications: Level 1 Introduction to Music Technology; Level 2 BTEC First Diploma in Music (Technology); Level 2 BTEC First Diploma in Media (Technology); NCFE Level 2 Certificate in Music Technology; NCFE Level 2 Certificate in Music Technology (Mix DJ Skills); Level 3 BTEC National Diploma in Music Technology; Level 4 FdSc in Music Technology in conjunction with De Montfort University; Level 4 FdSc Digital Video and Broadcast Production in conjunction with De Montfort University; BSc Hons Degree in Audio and Recording Technology in conjunction with De Montfort University; and Level 1 and 2 Part Time Short Courses.

Coventry University

Priory Street, Coventry CV1 5FB
tel 024-7688 7688
email info.rao@coventry.ac.uk
website www.coventry.ac.uk

Music at Coventry aims to encourage experimentation, curiosity and investigation alongside a flexible and entrepreneurial approach. Within the Music Technology Degree, students study principles of sound and acoustics, recording, studio design and specification, composition/production, recording technology and techniques, IT systems for music technology, software use and development, musical analysis and live sound. Music business units are also incorporated to equip students with the latest 'real world' knowledge.

Qualifications: Music Technology BSc Honours Degree.

Cumbernauld College

Tryst Road, Town Centre, Cumbernauld G67 1HU
tel (01236) 731811 *fax* (01236) 723416
email info@cumbernauld.ac.uk
website www.cumbernauld.ac.uk
Curriculum Manager Ronnie Gilmour

Established in 1978 and significantly expanded in 2006. Provides an extensive range of programmes from NQ to BA degree level over 2 sites in North Lanarkshire and East Dunbartonshire. Full-time and part-time modes of delivery available.

Qualifications: Access to Music Production; NQ Music Technology; HNC Sound Production; HND Sound Production.

Doncaster College

Waterdale, Doncaster DN1 3EX
tel (01302) 553553 *fax* (01302) 553559
email infocentre@don.ac.uk or
david.collins@don.ac.uk
website www.don.ac.uk
Head of Intermedia and Performance Arts Dr David Collins

Recognised successful Institute of Further and Higher Education. Aims to nurture a reputation for giving individual attention to students' needs, while developing close links with industry. Undergraduate opportunities include Music and Digital New Media – the application of new innovative and experimental technologies to music practice in both performance and composition; and Creative Music Technology – including study of sound recording, composition for media, multimedia and broadcasting.

Qualifications: BA (Hons) Music and Digital Media; BA (Hons) Creative Music Technology.

Farnborough College of Technology

Boundary Road, Farnborough, Hampshire GU14 6SB
tel (01252) 407270 *fax* (01252) 407289
email m.coslett@farn-ct.ac.uk
website www.farn-ct.ac.uk
Course Leader Martin Coslett

Founded in 1957. Aims to train students for work in the media and creative arts industries. Specialisms include studio recording and sound design/composition. Applicants should apply through UCAS for Foundation Degree and directly through the college for National Diploma.

Qualifications: Foundation Degree in Music Production (validated by the University of Surrey); National Diploma in Music Technology.

Gateway School of Recording

Kingston Hill Centre, Kingston-upon-Thames, Surrey KT2 7LB
tel 020-8549 0014 *fax* 020-8547 7337
email gatewayeducation@kingston.ac.uk
website www.gsr.org.uk
Music Administrator Sarah Winter *Admissions Tutor* Tim Ewers

Founded in 1976. Offers professional facilities including 4 recording/mixing studios with corresponding live rooms (and a mixture of digital and analogue equipment), 2 large programming suites, 3 Pro Tools TDM mastering rooms, and multimedia and sound-to-picture facilities. The BA course (3 years) is designed to cover the theory, practical techniques and creative practices employed in the audio industry. Also a DigiDesign Certified Training Centre for Pro Tools courses 101, 201 and 210.

Qualifications: BA Hons Audio Technology and Music Industry Studies.

Havering College

Ardleigh Green Road, Hornchurch, Essex RM11 2LL
tel (01708) 455011
email information@havering-college.ac.uk
website www.havering-college.ac.uk
Curriculum Manager (ND) Nigel Hooper *Curriculum Manager (HE)* David Wood

Offers a Diploma-level music technology course incorporating units in Sound Recording, Studio Production and MIDI sequencing, and HNC and HND courses with a sound creation and computer music production emphasis. The BA (Hons) in Music Practice and Technology combines study of music technology with composition and performance; the Media and Music Degree course offers study of music production with relation to video and radio production, multimedia and performance.

Qualifications: Level 3 National Diploma in Music Technology; Level 4 Higher Diploma Certificate in Music Production; Higher National Diploma in Music Production; BA (Hons) in Music Practice and Technology; BA (Hons) in Media and Music.

The Institute of Music and Technology

Hurricane Studios, 17 Deptford Broadway, Deptford, London SE8 4PA
tel 020-8691 1900 *fax* 020-8691 1688
email info@hurricane.org
website www.imthurricane.org
Director Phil McDonnell

Founded in 1989. Provides vocational training for careers within the music and multimedia industries. Specialises in sound engineering, music technology and multimedia. The delivery and assessment of all qualifications aims to emphasise the development of practical transferable skills.

The Sound Engineering Foundation course covers all the basic skills required for work in recording studios and live sound. The Sound Engineering Advanced provides more of a technical background and contains more project-based work with opportunity to use a wide range of applications. The Music Technoogy course teaches theoretical and practical instruction in the use of programmes such as Logic, Pro Tools, Cubase and Reason.

The Multimedia qualification aims to teach the concepts required for creating multimedia projects and delivering them over networks. Study includes learning how to digitise and optimise a sound, edit video, and integrate audio into a multimedia authoring application. Also offers a New Deal for Musicians course/open learning mentoring programme (between 13 and 36 weeks) which is designed to help students prepare for a sustainable financially self-supporting career in the music industry.

Qualifications: City and Guilds in Music Technology; City and Guilds in Sound Engineering Foundation; City and Guilds in Sound Engineering Advanced; City and Guilds in Multimedia.

Jewel and Esk Valley College
24 Milton Road East, Edinburgh EH15 2PP
tel 0131-660 1010 *fax* 0131-657 2276
email info@jevc.ac.uk
website www.jevc.ac.uk
Curriculum Leader (Sound Engineering and Music Technology) Jon Buglass

Music production specialisms available, with study including MIDI sequencing, dance music, multitrack mixing and recording, DJ skills and sound engineering.

Qualifications: NQ Access Level, NQ Higher Level (SQA) Certificate Programmes and HNC/D Sound Production. All validated by SQA.

Keele University
Keele, Staffordshire ST5 5BG
tel (01782) 583295 *fax* (01782) 583295
email a.jackson@mus.keele.ac.uk
website www.keele.ac.uk
Director of Music Dr Diego Garro

Aims to provide a lively musical environment, within and beyond the academic curriculum. The Music Technology degree course offers artistic and technical training, encouraging experimentation and critical thinking. Optional specialisms in Sonic Art Composition, Sound Recording, Sound Design, Interactive Music, Audiovisual Work and Music Software Development. Digital Arts are also studied within their historical, social, aesthetic and technical contexts. Seven studio areas are available 24/7. Music Technology must be combined with another principal study as part of Keele's distinctive double-honours scheme.

Qualifications: BA (Dual Hons) Music Technology (a range of combined subjects available, including Music).

Kylemore College MTC
Kylemore Road, Ballyfermot, Dublin 1
tel 00-353-1-6265901 *fax* 00-353-1-680710
email terry.hackett@kylemore.cdvec.ie
website www.kylemorecollegemtc.ie
Head of PLC Courses Terry Hackett

Founded in 1990. Offers 2x 1-year full-time courses. Courses specialise in music technology or music performance; aspects of music theory, business studies, music IT and electronics are covered. Selection process through interview and/or audition.

Qualifications: FETAC Level 5 Award in Music.

Leeds College of Music
3 Quarry Hill, Leeds LS2 7PD
tel 0113-222 3400 *fax* 0113-243 8798
email enquiries@lcm.ac.uk or d.perkins at lcm.ac.uk
website www.lcm.ac.uk
Assistant Head of Music Technology Dale Perkins

The UK's largest specialist music college provides a creative and stimulating environment for study. Foundation and further education study of Music Technology offers units including Sound Recording Techniques, MIDI sequencing and Software, and The Music Industry. The Degree programme focuses on study of the latest digital recording techniques, computer-based synthesis, sampling and MIDI production techniques, with the opportunity to create a major studio-based specialised project in the final year. Postgraduates are encouraged to create a challenging and innovative portfolio of recordings and are given opportunities to work with musicians across all LCM programmes.

Qualifications: Music Foundation Programme (Music Technology); BTEC National Diploma/Certificate in Music Technology; BA (Hons) Music Production; Foundation Degree in Music Production for Film and Television; MA Music Production.

Liverpool Institute for Performing Arts
Mount Street, Liverpool L1 9HF
tel 0151-330 3000 *fax* 0151-330 3131
email reception@lipa.ac.uk
website www.lipa.ac.uk
Principal Mark Featherstone-Witty

All LIPA qualifications work on the basis that to enjoy a long-term career in the contemporary and popular music field, musicians need to be versatile and to possess a wide range of abilities. The Diploma course in Popular Music and Sound Technology is aimed at students who wish to learn more about the technology of modern music production and recording, and can serve as a foundation level for the degree programme. The degree combines high levels of theory, intensive practical tuition and the opportunity to put these into practice at professional levels in a wide range of disciplines. Facilities include: 6 recording studios with Protool systems and Audient (ASP8024 24 channel and 36 channel), Yamaha (2 x 02R, DM2000), Soundcraft (Ghost) and Amek (Galileo) technology.

Qualifications: LIPA Diploma in Popular Music and Sound Technology; BA (Hons) in Sound Technology.

The London Music School
41 Spelman Street, London E1 5LQ
tel 020-7247 1311
email jo@londonmusicschool.com
website www.tlms.co.uk
General Manager Jo Kemp

Provides a range of 6-month and 1-year courses in music performance and production. Production courses specialise in audio recording and midi sequencing and are taught by industry professional engineers. Courses are available to all from 16 years upwards – no audition process. Enrolment form available for download from website.

Manchester MIDI School
Bexley Chambers, 1 Bexley Square M36DB
tel 0161-833 4722
email mail@midischool.com
website www.midischool.com
Course Manager Jonny Miller

Founded in 1997. The Diploma course specialises in practical and creative methods, allowing room for students to experiment. The 2nd stage of the Diploma allows students to improve their recording and mixing skills by working with bands in the studio. Specialist study of dance music is available as part of the Dance Music Production course, where each student works at mixing a track by using the ideas and samples that inspire them.

Qualifications: MMS Diploma Module One and Diploma Module Two.

Miskin Music
North West Kent College, Oakfield Lane,
Kent DA1 2JT
tel (01322) 629561 *fax* (01322) 629400
email miskinrecords@yahoo.co.uk
website www.miskintheatre.co.uk or
www.myspace.com/miskinrecords
Head Producer Matt Power

Founded in 1992. Aims to provide a springboard for those interested either pursuing a career within the music industry, or in furthering their knowledge at university. Areas of focus for production include: Studio Recording, Computer-Based Music

Production and Live Sound. Supports a practical and career-focused approach through the provision of industry professional staff and facilities. Facilities are run as a commercial venture outside of college hours. Recently gained a 4th grade 1 in OFSTED inspection. Applicants will be required to audition and/or interview. To receive a prospectus and/or application form, please contact by phone.

Qualifications: BTEC National Diploma in Music Technology; BTEC National Award in Acoustics; BTEC National Award in Music for Media; BTEC Level 5 Professional Diploma in Music Production and Audio Recording.

North Down and Ards Institute of Further Education
Castle Park Road, Bangor, Co Down,
N Ireland BT20 4TF
tel 028-9127 6600 *fax* 028-9127 6601
email gcaffrey@ndai.ac.uk
website www.ndai.ac.uk
Senior Lecturer Dr Greg Caffrey

Leading educational establishment in N Ireland for the delivery of BTEC qualifications. Currently has approximately 250 music and performing arts students. The music department aims to deliver its variety of qualifications in a very practical environment. Make contact by phone for an application form.

Qualifications: First Diploma Performing Arts (Music Technology); National Diploma Music Technology; Higher National Diploma Music Production; DJ Skills (BTEC short course); and National Award Music Technology (Music for Media).

North Glasgow College
110 Flemington Street, Glasgow G21 4BX
tel 0141-558 9001 *fax* 0141-558 9905
email cowens@north-gla.ac.uk
website www.north-gla.ac.uk
Senior Lecturer Campbell Owens

FE college offering a range of courses. Application online or by post.

Qualifications: NQ Sound Production; HND Sound and Media.

Perth College
Admissions Office, Perth College, Freepost,
Perth PH1 2BR
tel 0845-270 1177 or (01738) 877001
email pc.admissions@perth.uhi.ac.uk
website www.perth.ac.uk
Course Leader Lorenz Cairns

Leading Scottish HE institution providing a variety of popular music courses (established the UK's first full-time rock course in 1985). Provides specialist music production courses taught in studios designed and installed by Eastlake Audio and with professional equipment from Amek, Digidesign, MTA, Steinberg, Apple, Tascam, MCI, Quested and Neve.

The NQ in Sound Engineering Studies provides basic training in subjects such as multitrack and stereo recording and MIDI sequencing. The HNC in Audio Engineering provides options for students considering a career in studio, television and radio production, live theatre and concert work. The HND is an opportunity to build on skills from HNC level and includes units in digital and analogue recording, digital editing techniques, MIDI sequencing and video production. Also provides aspects of music production study within the Rock Music Studies, HNC and HND in Music and Popular Music Performance BA.

Qualifications: NQ Sound Engineering Studies; NQ Rock Music Studies; HNC and HND in Audio Engineering; HNC and HND in Music and BA in Popular Music Performance. (Students successfully competing the HND course may be able to progress directly to the 3rd year of the Degree course.)

The Recording Workshop

Unit 10, Buspace Studios, Conlan Street, London W10 5AP
tel 020-8968 8222 *fax* 020-7460 3164
email recordingworks@btconnect.com
website www.therecordingworkshop.co.uk
Course Leader Jose Gross

Founded in 1989. Provides full- and part-time courses on all aspects of Music Technology, Music Production and Sound Engineering. Focuses on practical, 'hands-on' study with emphasis on digital and analogue multitrack recording, digital editing, MIDI sequencer techniques, sound synthesis, microphone techniques and live recording. Caters for beginners alongside the more experienced with a maximum of 5 per class. Students have progressed to work for highly renowned companies such as Mayfair, Sphere and Metropolis studios and the BBC, and as DJs and artists. A&R personnel from labels such as EMI Parlophone, Warner Music, Polygram and Jive Records have taken part in the course. See website for more details of the range of available courses.

Reid Kerr College

Renfrew Road, Paisley PA3 4DR
tel 0141-581 2222
website www.reidkerr.ac.uk
Senior Lecturer Finlay MacDonald

Offers courses in music law, management, marketing and sound production. Potential applicants should visit website for application details.

Qualifications: HND in Music; HNC in Sound Production.

Sandwell College

Smethwick College, Crocketts Lane, Smethwick, West Midlands B66 3BU

tel 0121-556 6000
email andy.hubble@sandwell.ac.uk
website www.sandwell.ac.uk
Music Technology Lecturer Andy Hubble

Provides music technology training in the Lakeside Recording Studios at Smethwick campus. Facilities include: 1 x SSL console and 3 x O2R Consoles in 4 x controlrooms, with 2 live rooms and 6 rooms dedicated to running Logic on Macs.

Qualifications: BTEC HND in Music Production and Performance; BTEC ND in Music Technology; NOCN Logic Pro Training Award. Apply directly to college for ND and NOCN and through UCAS for HND.

School of Audio Engineering Institute

SAE Institute, United House, North Road, Islington, London M7 9DP
tel 020-7409 2653 *fax* 020-7609 6944
email saelondon@sae.edu
website www.saeuk.com
Founder Tom Misner

Founded in 1976; runs courses in sites across the world. Specialises in providing Music Production courses.

The Electronic Music Certificate is a 6-month programme aimed at beginners and encourages practical expermimentation and creativity. The Diploma programme (1 year) studies all aspects of audio engineering and includes work with Pro Tools and Neve consoles. Work assignments feature band recording, post production and mixing.

The Degree courses include units such as Industry Perspectives, Issues and Research Techniques, Business and Legal Studies and Cultural Perspectives alongside the core study of production which involves units such as Live Engineering, Digital Audio and Synchronisation. See website for details of other UK SAE sites (including Liverpool and Glasgow) and application information.

Qualifications: Electronic Music Production Certificate; Audio Engineering Diploma; BA (Hons)/ Masters Recording Arts Degrees.

School of Sound Recording

65-69 Downing Street, Manchester M1 7JE
tel 0161-276 2100 (General) or 0161-276 2111 (Admissions) *fax* 0161-272 7242
email enquiries@s-s-r.com
website www.s-s-r.com

Aims to be one of the most dynamic, industry-focused and networked training organisations in the world, delivering training from basic to Degree level. Prides itself on being Europe's first Authorised Digidesign Pro School, and still the largest; offers a comprehensive range of training in ProTools, either as stand-alone modules or intergrated within broader programmes. Provides tuition in Audio Engineering,

Live Sound, Sound Post Production, Electronic Music Production, Remixing and DJ Skills.

Technics DJ Academy is the DJ arm of SSR. The DJ Courses offer a comprehensive range of learning from the basics of DJ skills to advanced technique, for mixers, for scratchers and for the digital DJ. They also offer training in promotions and events, electronic music production, Reason, CDJs, Serato and Ableton.

Sound Training Centre

3rd Floor, Temple Bar Music Centre, Curved Street, Temple Bar, Dublin 2
tel 00353 16709033 *fax* 00353 16709042
email soundtrainingcentre@gmail.com
website www.soundtraining.com

Established in 1986. Provides training in SSL and Neve-technology-based studios.

*Qualifications:*City and Guilds Sound and Music Technology Diploma – 7503, Levels 1, 2 and 3 and STC Diploma.

South Thames College

Wandsworth High Street, Wandsworth, London SW18 2PP
tel 020-8918 7189 *fax* 020-8918 7777
email tonybiola@south-thames.ac.uk
Course Leader Tony Biola

Supports more than 20,000 students. Provides study of music technology as part of a range of FE courses aiming to give students a deeper understanding of modern music production and insight into the workings of the music industry. Also runs a Degree foundation course in music technology in association with Thames Valley university, including study of analogue and digital recording, sequencing, sampling and programming as well as a focus in convergence technology. The Degree course contains emphasis on industry-relevant practical skills with study through practical assignments, including producing a professional CD of own work, producing live acts, making a promotional music video and writing and setting up ringtones. Facilities include fully equipped rehearsal, music studios and music technology suites.

Qualifications: BTEC First Diploma in Music Technology (Level 2); National Award in Music Technology (Level 3); National Certificate in Music Technology (Level 3); Diploma Music Production and Performance Diploma (Level 3); Music Production National Award (Level 3); Foundation Degree in Music Technology.

Thames Valley University

St Mary's Road, Ealing, London W5 5RF
tel 020-8231 2677
email music@tvu.ac.uk
website www.tvu.ac.uk
Head of Academic Studies Peter Rudnick

Founded in 1860 and with campuses in Ealing, Slough and Reading, TVU now runs music courses

previously provided by the London College of Music and Media. The Music Technology department aims to enable students to acquire skills appropriate to contemporary sound and music pre- and post-production. The 2-year diploma-level course includes study of units such as Audio Theory, Introduction to Video Introduction, Sound Studio Techniques, and Introduction to Multimedia Music Technology (MIDI & Synthesis).

The 3-year degree-level course focuses on the practical application of audio and MIDI technology from a creative base. Students will be expected to operate and control complex recording sessions in high-performance environments. Units studied include Creative Sound, Music in Industry, Live Sound and Recording Techniques and Digital Recording. It is possible to combine study of Music Technology with a range of subjects at degree level including Digital Arts, Advertising and Multimedia Computing.

Postgraduate students will study a gamut of recording styles, encompassing multimedia (including DVD authoring), contextual studies and human-computer interface elements. Graduates from the MA will benefit from an enhanced grasp of issues of change within the industry and will be equipped with an augmented and competitive skillset.

Qualifications: DipHE in Music Technology Specialist; BA (Hons) in Music Technology Specialist; MA in Audio Technology.

University of Derby (School of Engineering)

Music Department, Kedleston Road, Derby DE22 1GB
tel (01332) 591763
email d.werner@derby.ac.uk
website www.derby.ac.uk
Programme Leader Duncan Werner

Established in 1994. Units include: Music Technology, Audio Systems, Popular Music, Multimedia Technology and Music Production. Application through UCAS.

Qualifications: BSc and BA (both with honours).

University of Salford

School of Media, Music and Performance, University of Salford, Salford, Greater Manchester M5 4WT
tel 0161-295 5000 *fax* 0161-295 4704
email n.spelman@salford.ac.uk
website www.smmp.salford.ac.uk
Course Leader Nichola Spelman

Provides facility for more than 400 students to study on 4 specialist degree music courses. Music Technology is incorporated into the BA (Hons) Music programme alongside study in Performance, Jazz, Analytical and Historial Studies and

Composition. The Popular Music and Recording degree offers a 'Studio Producer' pathway and focuses on popular music and technology with emphasis on music business and the recording industry. Facilities include: 24/48-track recording studios, video edit suites, music workshops, electro-acoustic, television and radio studios.

Qualifications: BA (Hons) Music; BA (Hons) Popular Music and Recording.

University of Westminster

Admissions Enquiries and Student Finance Office, 35 Marylebone Road, London NW1 5LS
tel 020-7911 5000 (Music Management Co-ordinator:
020-7911 5000 ext 4573) *fax* 020-7911 5858
email admissions@wmin.ac.uk or gross@wmin.ac.uk
website www.wmin.ac.uk
Programme Director Sally Gross

Founded in 1838 as Britain's first polytechnic. Aims to be imaginative in recognising new needs and developing appropriate offerings in many target markets. The Media courses were ranked in the top 5 as part of the last 3 annual surveys of university media courses by the *Guardian* newspaper.

The MA in Audio Production endeavours to provide an innovative education programme. Aims to develop each student's abilities in audio across music, sound design, radio, television, film, and multimedia to a professional level.

Qualifications: MA in Audio Production (1 year full time, 2 years part time).

University of York

Department of Music, Sir Jack Lyons Concert Hall, University of York, Heslington, York YO16 5DD
tel (01904) 432446 *fax* (01904) 432450
email music@york.ac.uk
website www.music.york.ac.uk
Head of Department Professor R Marsh *Admissions Tutor* Dr J Eato

– see University of York.

Westminster Kingsway College

Regents Park Centre, Longford Street, London NW1 3HB
tel 020-7391 6456
email sheila.maloney@westking.ac.uk
website www.westking.ac.uk
Key Personnel Sheila Maconey, Charlie Round-Turner

Large FE college in central London running a range of performing arts courses. Specialises in popular music and music technology. Refer to website for details of application process and open evenings. All prospective applicants are expected to attend an interview or audition.

Qualifications: First Diploma in Music, Level 2 and 3; National Diploma in Music Technology/Popular Music.

Recording and production agreements

Recording and production agreements have a great deal in common: indeed, a production agreement is a type of recording agreement. While both are based on the exploitation of copyrights, there is a big difference as to how they are exploited. Music lawyer, **Len Bendel**, explains.

Copyright in the UK is primarily governed by the Copyright Designs and Patents Act 1988, and can subsist in 'original literary, musical or artistic works' (and the copyright in a song consists both of *a literary work* in the lyrics, and of *a musical work* in the music). Importantly, copyright can also subsist in 'sound recordings'.

So there is a distinction between the copyright in a song as an entity in itself, and the copyright in the recording of that song. The copyright in a song belongs, in the first instance, to the initial author/s of the song – and the associated 'publishing rights' in the song belong to the copyright owners (no matter who records the song). The copyright in a sound recording belongs, in the first instance, to the owner of the sound recording: this is usually the producer (i.e. the person – or company – who makes the arrangements for the recording to happen, and generally the person who pays for the recordings). The copyright in a sound recording lasts for a period of 50 years from the year of first release of that recording.

The Copyright Act gives copyright-holders six distinct and exclusive rights:

- to copy the work;
- to issue copies of the work to the public;
- to rent or lend the work to the public;
- to perform, show or play the work in public;
- to communicate the work to the public;
- to make adaptations of the work, or do any of the above in relation to an adaptation.

Copyright holders can license or assign these exclusive rights to third parties in order for them to 'exploit' them – and, as such, the copyright in a sound recording is an asset that can be used to generate income over an extended period of time.

Income from sound recordings

Sound recordings can generate income for the copyright-holder in several ways. Money can be earned from sales of recordings (both physical sales and downloads), from radio and TV broadcasts of those recordings (collected through specialist collection societies – such as PPL in the UK), and also from licensing the recordings to others. Such licensing can lead to significant income generation from 'synchronisation' – where the music is synchronised with a visual picture, and included in a TV programme or film, or even adverts and video games. Quite often, sound recordings are licensed to other record companies, for use in compilations (music from various sources and copyright owners).

The licensing of sound recordings from one body to another constitutes the main difference between a 'Recording Agreement' and a 'Production Agreement'.

Recording agreements

Recording agreements can themselves be classified into two main types. In the first, the artist owns his or her recordings and licenses them to a record label (this is known as a 'Licence Deal'). The artist can restrict the licence to a specific length of time, and release the recordings only in particular territories; there will commonly be different record labels, or other companies licensing and releasing the same recordings across the world under different labels. In the second type of recording agreement, the record label will own the copyright in the recordings.

A production agreement could be said to be a cross between the above two types of recording agreement. In both, the record label or production company generally funds the production of the sound recordings, and will own the copyright in them for the full period of copyright. The major difference is that a production company will then look to license the recordings to a record label – to market and release the recordings to the public.

The production company will get involved with an artist at an early stage, and work with him or her not only to develop recordings, but also to work on a marketing plan. The general idea is that the record label can very easily market, distribute and sell the artist, with much of the groundwork having already been done by the production company. There is then less of a cost and risk to the record label than there would be in developing an artist from scratch.

The contracts

The contracts presented to an artist for either a recording or production deal will contain a number of similar terms, but with some important differences. In both, the main clauses will deal with:

Exclusivity

Both deals will require from the artist an assignment of their exclusive recording – or recording and audiovisual – rights. This means that during the term of the contract, the artist will not be allowed to record for any other companies.

Term

What will be the duration of the agreement? Will it be measured by time, or by the fulfilment of a number of recordings, or a mixture of both (for example, a four-album deal – but in any event not to exceed a period of ten years)? The record label or production company are likely to require 'options' to extend the term: very often a 'four-album deal' means that the record label *may* release four albums; they will often commit to releasing one or perhaps two albums, and then, depending on the commercial success of those, will have an option to release a further album, and then another option for the fourth album. If they choose not to take up an option, the deal will come to an end and the artist will be free to sign another deal with another company.

There will often be a clause in the production agreement stating that if the third-party record label who will eventually be releasing the recordings requires a longer term than is provided for in the agreement, then the artist will agree to extend the term of that agreement to match the term required by the label.

Territory

To what territories or countries will the contract relate? Most production and recording agreements will seek the worldwide rights, whereas if a production company or artist is licensing recordings to a third-party company, they will commonly license the recordings to different companies in different countries. A record label who owns the copyright in recordings may themselves look to exploit the recordings in different countries, by licensing them to different companies within those territories.

Royalties

How will the record label and production company account? Most record labels generally pay artists (or a production company) on one of two bases: either a 'Net Receipts' basis (where the label shares the profits from a recording once its costs have been recouped – most commonly shared 50/50), or else on a 'Percentage' basis (where the label pays a fixed percentage of the 'dealer price' – usually between 15 and 22 per cent). The dealer price (or wholesale price) is the price at which a record gets sold to shops. Percentage deals are often subject to deductions – such as 'packaging deductions', or reduced rates for budget releases or during a TV advertising campaign. It is also very important in a net receipts deal to agree what allowable expenses should be recouped from a recording (for example, recording and marketing costs, but not office overheads).

Traditionally (but not strictly), indie labels and production companies pay on a net receipts basis, and major labels pay on a percentage basis. Most production deals pay the artist on a net receipts basis. If however, an artist has signed to a production company on a 50/50 net receipts split, and the production company then licenses recordings to a record label on an 18 per cent royalty, the artist will actually only receive a royalty of 9 per cent, with the production company also receiving 9 per cent. Bands who are offered production agreements take heed – 50/50 may not be sufficient!

Advances

What advances are on offer in the contract? An advance is a sum of money that should (ideally) sustain the artist through the recording period and manufacture of an album, and through the recouping of costs, until royalties start to flow. There should be a new advance with each album or option, and in increasing amounts. Advances will have to be recouped by the label or company through income from exploiting the recordings, but the artist should not have to pay anyone back should the recordings fail to recoup. Advances are often paid in instalments: for example, one-third on signature of the agreement, one-third on commencing recording, and one-third on completion (or release).

Accounting

So when will royalties be paid? Generally, record labels and production companies account either two or four times a year, and (if costs and advances have been recouped) pay royalties 30-90 days after accounting. If you sign a production agreement, try to ensure that the production company pays as soon as practicable after receiving royalties from the record label. A lawyer will also ensure that the contract provides the artist wih rights of audit: that is, the right to send an accountant to check and challenge the royalty statements.

The above are only a selection of some of the most important clauses in a recording or production agreement. There will be a number of other clauses – dealing with warranties and obligations by the artist and companies, indemnities, termination clauses and other matters. Such contracts will often be tens of pages long. It is essential that the artist seek specialist legal advice when offered either a recording or production agreement; indeed, a production company or record label should also seek legal advice. Where possible, an artist signing to a production agreement should also try to have approvals over the terms in any agreement a production company signs with a record label: you don't want to sign a good production agreement with a company which then signs a poor deal with a record label!

Len Bendel is a music lawyer and bass player. He advises such clients as performing artists, record labels, and management companies. He also lectures on music law.

Societies

Association of Independent Music (AIM)
Lamb House, Church Street, Chiswick,
London W4 2PD
tel 020-8994 5599 *fax* 020-8994 5222
email info@musicindie.com
website www.musicindie.com
Chief Executive Alison Wenham

Founded in 1998. A non-profit-making trade organisation representing both large and small UK-based independent record companies and distributors. Over 850 members represent a variety of styles and receive business advice and support through seminars and networking opportunities. Collective deals are negotiated on behalf of members alongside political representation and a range of other support services. Joining fee typically £100 plus subscription of 12% of PPL income. A £120 annual membership fee is payable quarterly from the 2nd year. AIM guidebook and seminar tickets available to non-members. Online application form available.

Association of Professional Recording Services (APRS)
PO Box 22, Totnes, Devon TQ9 7YZ
tel (01803) 868600 *fax* (01803) 868444
email info@aprs.co.uk
website www.aprs.co.uk
Executive Director Peter Filleul

Established in 1947. Trade association for the UK Professional Sound Industry comprising recording and post-production facilities, suppliers of equipment and services, record producers and engineers, providers of audio training, mastering, duplication and authoring services. Membership ranges from £75 – £550 (plus VAT) and includes networking, technical e-groups, business support helpline, quarterly bulletin, active website, terms and conditions/booking form, representation at trade exhibitions, and lobbying.

Bandname.com
website www.bandname.com
– see page 104.

The British Phonographic Industry
Riverside Building, County Hall,
Westminster Bridge Road, London SE1 7JA
tel 020-7803 1300 *fax* 020-7803 1310
email general@bpi.co.uk
website www.bpi.co.uk

The British record industry's trade association. Membership comprises of hundreds of music companies, including all 4 major record companies, associate members such as manufacturers and distributors, and many independent music companies representing thousands of labels. Membership costs independent labels an annual fee of £75 + 5% of PPL revenue. Joint membership with Association of Independent Music (AIM) is encouraged. Also provides membership options for companies who do not own sound recordings. Phone for application form.

International Federation of Phonographic Industry (IFPI)
IFPI Secretariat, 54 Regent Street, London W1B 5RE
tel 020-7878 7900 *fax* 020-7878 7950
email info@ifpi.org
website www.ifpi.org

Represents the recording industry worldwide, with over 1450 members in 75 countries and affiliated industry associations in 48 countries. Aims to fight music piracy; to promote fair market access and adequate copyright laws; and to help develop the legal conditions and the technologies for the recording industry to prosper in the digital era. Also promotes the value of music in the development of economies, as well as in social and cultural life. Any company, firm or person producing sound recordings or music videos which are made available to the public in reasonable quantities is eligible for membership.

Membership includes 5 subscription categories: 'A' – major producers of phonograms or music videos (around £2800); 'B' – medium-sized producers of phonograms or music videos (£1400); 'C' – small producers of phonograms or music videos (£350); 'D' – producers of phonograms or music videos in the early period of their existence or in a developing country (£175); 'E' – producers of phonograms or music videos who are members of a National Group of IFPI or an affiliated organisation which recommends their admission in this category (£40). Online application form available.

Mechanical-Copyright Protection Society (MCPS) and Performing Rights Society (PRS) Alliance
Copyright House, 29-33 Berners Street,
London W1T 3AB
website www.mcps-prs-alliance.co.uk
– see page 48.

Music Producers' Guild (MPG)
71 Avenue Gardens, London W3 8HB
tel 020-3110 0060

email office@mpg.org.uk
website www.mpg.org.uk
Office Administrator Mike Howlett

A professional organisation promoting and representing individuals working in the fields of music production and recording. Membership includes producers, engineers, mixers, re-mixers, programmers, students and trainees, those involved in multimedia, and any other individuals involved in the creative process. Within the MPG there exist Special Interest Groups: Technical, Education and MPG Live. Full membership fee is around £75 each year, with a discounted rate for students (£37.50). Online application form available.

New Music In Scotland (NEMIS)
2nd Floor, 22 Jamaica Street, Glasgow G1 4QD
tel 0141-221 6660 *fax* 0141-427 5755
email alec@nemis.org
website www.nemis.org
New Music Development Officer Alec Downie

Founded in 1999 as a music network for Scottish artists, labels, businesses, media, recording studios, venues, radio, other professional services, and creators of music. Aims to help promote and develop music in Scotland.

Offers advice to anyone involved in any area of the music business, and assists with marketing and promotion through the showcasing of bands regionally, nationally and internationally. Produces compilation CDs to promote independent Scottish music of all genres, and provides music industry workshops and seminars throughout Scotland as a facility where people can have the opportunity to network with like-minded industry individuals. Participation is available for those active in the Scottish contemporary music scene – contact by phone for more info.

Phonographic Performance Ltd
1 Upper James Street, London W1F 9DE
tel 020-7534 1000 *fax* 020-7534 1111
email info@ppluk.com
website www.ppluk.com

A not-for-profit UK music industry service company which licenses recorded music on behalf of over 3500 record companies and 40,000 performers. Collects domestic and international broadcast/new media

revenues and public performance income, which is then distributed and paid to the company's record company and performer members. These include featured artists as well as all session musicians – ranging from orchestral players to percussionists and singers. The company also licenses clubs, shops, pubs, restaurants, bars and grills and thousands of other music users who play sound recordings in public. Processes more than 18 million tracks per year; revenue now exceeds £85 million a year, which makes PPL the largest collector of this type of income in the world today, with these revenues becoming increasingly important to both record companies and performers. There is no joining fee or administration charge.

Society for Producers and Composers of Applied Music (PCAM)
Birchwood Hall, Storridge, Malvern,
Worcs WR14 5EZ
tel (01886) 884204 or 0906-895 0908 (Helpline)
fax (01886) 884204
email bobfromer@onetel.com
website www.pcam.co.uk
– see page 49.

Video Performance Ltd (VPL)
1 Upper James Street, London W1F 9DE
email info@vpluk.com
website www.vpluk.com

Collection society that aims to ensure payments are received when music videos are used by broadcasters or within the public performance sector. Each video has a unique ISRC (International Standard Numbering Code), which enables VPL to track the usage and ownership of music videos.

Administers the right to broadcast and publicly to perform music videos, and the right to dub music videos for both of these purposes. Provides a searchable online catalogue, and an online enquiry form in order to obtain a quote for a licence. Any company or individual who owns the UK audiovisual copyright in 'short-form' music videos is eligible to join. In most cases, copyright owners are record companies, but can also be production companies or individual artists. No membership fee. Online application form available.

Duplication

A1 CDs

Oasis 139 High Road, Islington, Kings Lynn,
Norfolk PE34 3BH
tel (01553) 617546 *fax* (01553) 617645
email merv@a1cds.co.uk
website www.a1cds.co.uk
Director Merv Futter

A variety of services offered, including CD and DVD
pressing and replication from glass master over large
runs and duplication for smaller numbers, full-colour
printing on discs and printed CD/DVD sleeves.
Competitive packages and a UK delivery service also
available.

A1 Duplication Ltd

2nd Floor, 2 Albion Place, Hammersmith,
London W6 0QT
tel 020-8748 0440 *fax* 020-8748 0412
email sales@a1duplication.co.uk
website www.a1duplication.co.uk

Offers client-tailored services, including design of
packaging, package and disc printing and a fast turnaround service. Duplication of DVD-Rs/CD-Rs is
laser written rather than manufactured, which
increases the speed of orders up to a 1000 units. Glass
master replication on high-volume orders of 1000 to
1,000,000. High-quality inkjet printing of discs. Also
offers diskette, VHS duplication, mastering and video
conversion.

Adaptive Conversions

Unit 2, Bell Industrial Estate, Cunnington Street,
Chiswick W4 5HB
tel 0845-108 0413 *fax* 0870-458 2659
email sales@adaptiveconversions.co.uk
website www.adaptiveconversions.co.uk

Offers 14 years of experience in the duplication of
various kinds of media, and the ability to ensure that
masters are properly set up for duplication. Handles
small runs through to large-scale runs. Print and
package design, a nationwide/international
distribution service and video conversion and
encoding services also available.

AGRM

The Stables, 44 Stortford Road, Great Dunmow,
Essex CM6 1DL
tel (01371) 859393 *fax* (01731) 859375
email martyn@agrm.co.uk
website www.agrm.co.uk

Offers many years' experience with the independent
music industry. Services are strongly based on the
requirements of an independent label, and offer: CD
manufacture, CD replication, CD duplication, CD

packaging design and supply, and a print and
reproduction service including sleeve artwork.
Supplies and presses vinyl records in the following
formats: 7", 10", 12". Also offers coloured vinyl and
picture discs.

Alliance Multimedia Ltd

1 Lister Place, Hillington Park, Glasgow,
Scotland G52 4HZ
tel (01418) 104664 *fax* (01418) 104774
email info@alliancemultimedia.com
website www.alliancemultimedia.com

Offers technical services including high-quality DVD/
CD duplication and replication from glass master,
DVD authoring and full digital media services. Also
offers CD encoding, CD mastering and batch testing
and CD master repair. A fully equipped print house
provides: black thermal print, colour thermal print,
digital matt thermal print, digital gloss thermal print,
screen print and offset printing. Packaging design and
supply in a vast array of formats also available.

Alpha Duplication Ltd

Unit 2 Halifax Road, Cressex Business Park,
High Wycombe, Bucks HP12 3SD
tel (01494) 536646
email info@alpha-duplication.com
website www.alpha-duplication.com

Offers high-scale CD/DVD replication in all formats,
pressed from a glass master and finished with a
professional quality silk screen or offset printed
finish. Litho printing is offered on CD and DVD
booklets, case inserts, wallets and software cartons as
well as packaging design and supply. Also offers
media assembly and shirnk-wrapping/over-wrapping
so that the finished product is ready to distribute.

Amarok Multimedia Ltd

3 Anthony Court, Largs, Ayrshire,
Scotland KA30 8TA
tel (01475) 689096
website www.amarok.uk.com
Director Eric Letton

Specialises in CD and DVD duplication including
pressing and print. Clients have included: Al Stewart,
Little Panic and Jamie Marshall.

Amstore CD Production Ltd

Block J, Tower Bridge Business Complex,
100 Clements Road, London SE16 4DG
tel 020-7232 5820
email sales@amstore.co.uk
website www.amstore.co.uk

Provides full-colour CDs from 1 to 500 units for
duplication, and 500-plus for replication. Offers a 24-

hour order line and a range of packaging services, from plastic sleeves and bulk packaging to jewel and slim cases. Email logan@amstore.co.uk for free sample CD.

Brandedmedia Ltd

Unit A, Lutyens Industrial Centre, Bilton Road, Basingstoke, Hampshire RG24 8LJ
tel (01256) 355533 *fax* (01256) 812668
email sales@brandedmedia.net
website www.brandedmedia.net

Over 14 years' industry experience and host to production outlets in both the UK and Sweden. Many services are offered, ranging from CD/DVD replication/duplication and printing, video duplication, electronic business card replication, packaging solutions and full creative design. Offers a 24-hour fast track turnaround, online quotations and UK and international distribution.

Bump Studios

8 Kremlin Drive, Liverpool L13 7BY
tel 0151-259 9406 *fax* 0870-133 0957
email info@bumpstudios.co.uk
website www.bumpstudios.co.uk
Manager Kris Kristiansen

Founded in 2001. Aims to help musicians and artists gain positive exposure by offering a professional and efficient service. Clients have included: Jet Harris, Green Peace, Polar Print and 21st Sentry. Works with automated CD and DVD duplicators and printers, a high-output photo-quality digital copier, and a graphic design and audio mastering suite. Rates start from £20 an hour. Instant online quotes available for CD and DVD products.

CD-Writer.com

Unit 15, Greenwich Centre Business Park, 53 Norman Road, London SE10 9QF
tel (08707) 605737 *fax* 020-8293 0666
email sales@cd-writer.com
website www.cd-writer.com

Offers a variety of deals on bulk replication of CDs/ DVDs and smaller duplication runs, including a full professional printing service and a professional in-house design service. Also offers a fast copy service, packaging design and print, CD/DVD insert printing and on-line design templates. Supplies bulk CDs/ DVDs and duplication machine consumables to the trade and public.

CD Team

Team House, 1 Fairview Estate, Reading Road, Henley on Thames, Oxfordshire RG9 1HE
tel (01491) 636373 *fax* (01491) 636374
email info@cdteam.co.uk
website www.cdteam.co.uk

Supplies a variety of duplication requirements from a minimum of 2 copies to larger projects duplicating

thousands. Provides packing and despatching services to multiple addresses nationally and internationally.

Cluny Studios

36 Lime Street, Newcastle Upon Tyne NE1 2PQ
tel 0191-232 3934
email enquiries@clunystudios.co.uk
website www.clunystudios.co.uk

Established in 1980. Offers graphic design, multimedia design, mastering and pre-mastering, disc production, printing and packaging services. CDs are Grade A media printed directly onto CD at 2400 x 1200 dpi. Supplies jewel, single cases and card wallets amongst other packaging options. Prices start at £1.25 per disc including design, CDR, duplication and PVC sleeve.

CVB Duplication

179A Bilton Road, Perival, Middlesex UB6 7HQ
tel 020-8991 2610 *fax* 020-8997 0180
email sales@cvbduplication.co.uk
website www.cvbduplication.co.uk
Sales Manager Adrian Tubman

Established in 1982. Deals with CD, DVD, VHS and audio cassette duplication. Also provides packaging and printing services. Recents clients include: MOD, Vodafone, Ford, Audi and the BBC.

dbMasters Ltd

9 Waterside Close, Upper Brents, Faversham, Kent ME13 7AU
tel (01795) 597755 *fax* (01795) 597766
email info@dBMasters.co.uk
website www.dbmasters.co.uk

Offers optical disc duplication, replication and printing services. Only uses high-quality A-grade discs. Also provides a variety of packaging options including clear plastic wallets, jewel cases, laser-printed or litho-printed paper-parts and spindles.

Digital Disc Duplication Ltd

Digital House, 25 Huntingfield Road, Bury St Edmunds, Suffolk IP33 2JA
tel (01284) 700773
email sales@digitaldiscduplication.com
website www.digitaldiscduplication.co.uk

Operated by musicians for musicans – aims to create a high-quality replication service. Also provides mastering, design, printing and packaging services. Online quotes available via website.

Disc Manufacturing Services Ltd

Grosvenor House, Belgrave Lane, Plymouth PL4 7DA
tel (01752) 201275
email info@discmanufacturingservices.com
website www.pmc.uk.net

Works with both replication from glass master for large runs and duplication from CDR for smaller orders. Offers solutions for audio creation, mastering, printing and package design. Also provides a complete range of DVD services ranging from duplication, replication and authoring.

Disc Wizards
3 Oakleigh Court, Edgware, London HA8 5JB
tel 0845-045 4550 *tel* 020-8931 0001
email info@discwizards.com
website www.discwizards.com

Suppliers of glass mastered, stamped and pressed CDs starting from 500 up to hundreds of thousands. Professional design and printing service available. Offers a comprehensive range of CD and DVD packaging – including jewel cases, card cases and special muti-packs. Provides a quick turnaround on orders and website hosts an easy ordering service. Other services include mastering and post production and DVD authoring.

Discburner
Woodside Road, Chiddingfold, Surrey GU8 4UH
tel (01428) 681434
email info@discburner.co.uk
website www.discburner.co.uk
Owner Mr David L Biggs

Founded in 1999. Aims to provide an unrivalled level of personal service and attention to detail for all clients. Offers an in-house audiovisual media service providing a fast turnaround and competitive rates. Low-volume clients include local small businesses, solo artists and bands. High volume clients are Honda, Academy Of Contemporary Music, Waitrose and Royal Mail. Works with high-quality CD and DVD duplication machines, full-colour in-house printing facilities, in-house finishing and assembly, video editing/media authoring, digital recording and production facilities. Low minimum order requirement of 25 units – ideal for gigging bands on a budget. Discounts for high-volume runs.

Dischromatics Ltd
Unit 20, Prince of Wales Industrial Estate, Abercam, Newport, South Wales NP11 5AR
tel (01495) 243222 *fax* (01495) 243777
email sales@dischromatics.co.uk
website www.dischromatics.co.uk
Sales Director Gareth Spencer *Sales Manager* Alex Spencer *Technical Manager* Kayle Garkut

Sony DADC broker with ISO9001 and ISO14001 accreditation. Specialises in CD and DVD duplication and replication. Offers high-quality CDs, DVDs and Blu-Ray discs (8-12cm) alongside more innovative products such as vinyl effect CDs and a variety of packaging solutions. Clients have included: The Guns, Scottish Widows, Woolworths, and Unison. Utilises 6 X CD/DVD duplicators and thermal inkjet printers.

Dupe.co.uk
Fradley Junction, Alrewas,
Burton-on-Trent DE13 7DN
tel (01283) 791008 or 0870-622 1723
email info@dupe.co.uk
website www.dupe.co.uk
Account Manager Simon Asbury *Sales Assistant* Barbara Blazkova

Provides replication and duplication services. Clients include: De Montfort University, Thames Valley University and Safety Media Ltd.

DVD-and-Media.com
Unit 9A, 4 Carcroft Enterprise Park, Station Road, Carcroft, Doncaster DN6 8DD
tel (01302) 330333 *fax* (01302) 338888
email sales@dvd-and-media.com
website www.dvd-and-media.com

Large-scale company offering professional CD and DVD replication services, including a variety of CD and DVD bespoke packages tailored to suit a variety of requirements. Packaging and printing services backed with a very fast turnaround and exceptional quality. Also large-scale providers of all CD/DVD consumables to the trade and public.

Fairview Studios
Cavewood Grange Farm, Common Lane, North Cave, East Yorkshire HU15 2PE
tel 0800-018 1482 or (01430) 425546
fax (01430) 425547
email info@fairviewstudios.co.uk
website www.fairviewstudios.co.uk
Duplication Manager Jackie Herd

Recording studio and duplication service. Clients include: *Sound on Sound* Magazine, Mercury Records and Sincere Management. Equipment includes a Radar II and Soundcraft Seris desk.

Gillies Audio
Albert Lodge, Barry Road, Carnoustie DD7 7QR
tel/fax (01241) 853935
email info@gilliesaudio.com
website www.gilliesaudio.com
Office Manager Stuart Gillies

Provides a large variety of different products, from glass mastered replication to burned duplicated discs. Uses a wide range of different printing systems and methods, from inkjet/thermal inkjet and screen printing to digital laser printing. Operates a no-minimum-order policy and a flexible price structure aiming to ensure that clients can receive the product they desire at a price that suits. Recent clients include: Rockaction Records, Phacilitate UK, Shoeshine Records and Say Dirty Records.

Grade A Media
11 Lanfrey Place, London W14 9PY
tel 0870-199 6112 *mobile* (07092) 844686
email enquiries@gradeamedia.co.uk
website www.gradeamedia.co.uk

Offers a quick turnaround on short-run DVD and CD duplication with a fully integrated service for replication of run numbers. Offers full artwork design and printing (including CD/DVD, package and insert design) and the large-scale supply of blank CD/DVD, PVC wallets and jewel cases. See website for ordering service and special offers.

HDC Optical Media Group

Bracken House, Broad Lane, Bradford,
West Yorkshire BD4 8PA
tel (01274) 656565 *fax* (01274) 656575
email info@hdc.uk.com
website www.hdc.uk.com

Offers a one-stop service for CD and DVD duplication. Deals with all elements from the initial design through to the finished package. Prints with inkjet, screen print, offset lithographic and digitally. Also offers funky and retro vinyl CDs. Specialises in being enviromentally friendly.

Hip2duplicate Ltd

10 Hadleigh Court, Harpenden,
Hertfordshire AL5 1SX
tel 0845-229 7760 *fax* 0845-229 7761
email sales@hip2duplicate.co.uk
website www.hip2duplicate.co.uk
Sales Director Toby Russell *Sales Manager* Christopher Mills

Specialises in CD and DVD manufacture. Caters for any project size, from small promotional runs to large retail quality products. No minimum order up to a maximum of 100,000 units. Typical clients include both signed and unsigned artists. Also provides replication, printed parts and packaging (including a design and artwork service).

Labute

Cambridge Printing Park, Milton,
Cambridge CB24 6AZ
tel (01223) 42000 *fax* (01223) 420783
email sales@labute.co.uk
website www.labute.co.uk

Established in 1978 as a print design house that has now grown into an expert provider of CD and DVD duplication, replication and printing. Numbers produced range from 1 to 1000s, with the availability of 4-colour printing onto disc and complete packaging creation and provision. Total project management and express delivery available.

Lemon Media

The Hub, Warne Road,
Weston-super-Mare BS23 3UU
tel (01934) 423023 *fax* (01934) 645834
email info@lemonmedia.co.uk
website www.lemonmedia.co.uk

Offers small and large-scale CD/DVD duplication and replication for pre-recorded music and software. Bit to Bit verification is carried out to ensure exact quality of copies. Full-package services are available,

including: in-house design and reprographics' disc printing (6-colour screen and offset); CD mastering and authoring; cassette and VHS duplication; and package design, print and creation.

The Little Bazaar

Marlborough House, 159 High Street,
Harrow HA3 5DX
tel 0845-658 6550
email info@littlebazaar.co.uk
website www.littlebazaar.co.uk
Director/Chief Engineer Paul Egan

Offers a wide range of services including audio mastering, CD/DVD duplication, graphic design and cassette to CD transfers. Recent clients have included: Balfour and Beauty, Gumball 3000, Islington Council, and Children in Need. Instant quotes available from website.

Live Wire Duplication

The Office, Tamarind, Copthorne Common Road,
Copthorne, West Sussex RH10 3LF
tel (01342) 714183
email sales@livewire-cds.com
website www.livewire-cds.com
Partner Kevin Beattie

Established in 1988. Aims to offer high-quality CD and DVD duplication and printing products with excellent customer service. Utilises digital Xerox and Rimage printing. Clients have included: Raymond Froggatt, Jane McDonald and TMC records. Provides online quote service.

Media Heaven Ltd

12 Castleton Close, Leeds LS12 2DS
tel 0113-244 3550 *fax* 0113-244 3994
email info@mediaheaven.co.uk
website www.mediaheaven.co.uk
Director Paul Lines

Offers full service optical media service. Specialises in CD and DVD duplication and creative packaging. Clients include: Virgin Cosmetics, Leeds City Council, and Regatta. Offers package deal of: 1000 CDs in full colour; full replication; jewel case packed; 4PP booklet 4/4; and traycard 4/0 for 55p per unit (excl. VAT).

Media Hut

9 Churchhill Park, Colwick, Nottingham NG4 2HF
tel 0115-987 3777 *fax* 0115-987 4181
email sales@cdreplication.co.uk
website www.cdreplication.co.uk

Provides fast turnaround replication service and quality inkjet printing. Minimum order of 500. Also offers bespoke design, a large variety of packaging options, and alternative CD styles including unusually shaped and scented CDs.

ODS BD Swindon

Frankland Road, Balgrove, Swindon SN5 8YG
tel (01793) 421300

email media.replication@ods-businessservices.com
website www.ods-businessservices.com
– see ODS BS London.

ODS BS Glasgow
4 Woodside Terrace, Glasgow G3 7UY
tel 0141-354 0050
email media.replication@ods-businessservices.com
website www.ods-businessservices.com
– see ODS BS London.

ODS BS London
Hatfield House, 52-54 Stamford Street,
London SE1 9LX
tel 020-7960 4100
email media.replication@ods-businessservices.com
website www.ods-businessservices.com

Established for more than 16 years. Provides services for duplication and disc printing of DVDs and CDs. Member of the International Disc Duplicating Association. Services offered include: DVD-R duplication, DL-DVD+R duplication, USB loading, VHS duplication, mini CD duplication, disc colour thermal printing, audio copy protection, data encryption, cassette duplication, and CD-R card duplication.

Riviera Multimedia Ltd
Unit 2C Redbrook Business Park, Barnsley S75 1JN
tel (01226) 730606 *fax* (01226) 732112
website www.rivierapublishing.co.uk

Offers a variety of CD and DVD duplication and packaging services. Provides options for fast 24-hour turnaround. Minimum order of 50 units.

Samron Technologies
88 Canberra Road, Marton in Cleveland,
Middlesbrough TS7 8ER
tel (01642) 312929
email query@samron-tech.com
website www.samron-tech.com

Offers retail-ready packages and specialises in Duplicate on Demand service, where discs are created, printed, packaged and shipped on order-demand direct from customers. Other services include: edge-to-edge digital colour printing, master disc creation and authoring.

Sounds Good Ltd
12 Chiltern Enterprises Centre, Station Road, Theale,
Berkshire RG7 4AA
tel 0118-930 1700 *fax* 0118-930 1709
email sales-info@sounds-good.co.uk
website www.sounds-good.co.uk

A company with a vast experience of CD/DVD pressing and duplication, CD mastering, cassette duplication, DVD authoring, video encoding and transfer, and VHS duplication. Free glass mastering

on bulk orders of 1000 CDs or over. Discs can be screenprinted up to 4 colours; litho printing can be offered for an extra charge. Package deals are available to musicians. Also offers multimedia, web design and graphic design services.

Syonica Ltd CD-UK
Alder House, High Road, Rayleigh, Essex SS6 7SA
tel (01268) 765674 *fax* (01268) 763316
email sales@cd-uk.org
website www.cd-uk.co.uk

Offers full-colour CD duplication. Specialises in package deals including mastering, production, packing and online distribution. See website for easy-to-use quotation service.

Testa Rossa
tel 0845-603 0237
email andy@testa-rossa.com
website www.testa-rossa.com

Offers a large selection of bespoke packages for CD/DVD replication and duplication, with very fast turnaround times for shorter runs. Specialist in-house printing is available for discs, inserts, card cases and other media. Also offers audio mastering, audio editing, CD mastering and CD text services. Web-based ordering service available.

TVV Productions Ltd
Suite 310, Wingrove House, Ponteland Road,
Newcastle Upon Tyne NE5 3DP
tel 0191-286 9800
email studio@tvv.co.uk
website www.tvv.co.uk

Provides low- and high-volume CD/DVD production, packaging and printing at competitive prices. High-resolution, full-colour printing available on discs, including up to 5-colour silk screen printing. Various CD formats are supported (CD-DA, CD-ROM, Mixed Mode CD, VCD and Mini CD). Fast turnaround on CD duplication of low volumes between 10 to 1000 units.

Vinyl Factory Group
The Basement Studio, 45 Foubert's Place,
London W1F 7QH
tel 020-7725 1381 *fax* 020-7287 4912
email antony.hill@vinylfactory.co.uk
website www.vinylfactory.co.uk
Manager Antony Hill

Presses records for a vast number of labels; offers bespoke solutions for clients. An annual production of over 7 million records. Has 2 offices and pressing factories – 1 in London and 1 in Sydney. Offers vinyl pressings in any quantity or format (7", 10", 12", etc). Packages are offered for cutting, pressing and print. Also publishes *FACT* magazine and website as a bimonthly review of Vinyl music and events listings.

WEBS Ltd Media House

Media House, 19 Dorking Road, Bookham,
Surrey KT23 4PU
tel 0845-638 4214 *fax* 0845-638 4215
email sales@cdrom-businesscard.co.uk
website www.cdrom-businesscard.co.uk
Managing Director Justin Williams

Founded in 1998. Specialises in low-volume CD-R
and DVD-R duplication and printing. Operates a 24-
hour turnaround for many jobs, working with 4 x
Auto Everest II thermal process printers. Also
provides high-volume CD and DVD replication
services using silkscreen and offset litho printing
units. Recent clients have included: Alianz Cornhill,
MOD, Qinetic, Lloyds Bank, Landrover and HTFRL.
To receive an exclusive 5% discount, use the
following code at checkout: MSY_U20547.

Wizbit Internet Services Ltd

Corhampton Lane Farm, Corhampton,
Hampshire SO32 3NB
tel (01489) 872980 *fax* (01489) 878396
email info@wizbit.net
website www.wizbit.net
Creative Director Paul Martin

Specialises in the production of business card and
circular 8cm and 12cm CDs and DVDs. Works with
quantities from 50 discs upwards. Recent clients have
included: Unilever, EMI Publishing, Universal
Studios, BBC World Service, and Nissan. Prices begin
from £0.19 per disc depending on quantities.

XPRESSCDS Ltd

The Converted Barn, Widehurst Farm,
Thorne Road, Marden, Tonbridge, Kent TN12 9LN
tel (01622) 832302
email info@xpresscds.co.uk
website www.xpresscds.co.uk

Provides CD replication services with packages
available combining printing, 4-page booklet, jewel
case and delivery at a discounted overall price. Also
has in-house graphic design service.

Setting up a studio: business considerations

JoJo Gould considers a range of important commercial aspects for those who are thinking of converting the jumble of studio equipment in their loft or spare room into a small, viable enterprise.

Benefits of studio ownership

In the 19th century, social and political thinker Karl Marx highlighted the value and power of owning the means of production. Had he been talking about the modern music industry, he couldn't have been more accurate! Owning a studio can be greatly beneficial for the artistic development of bands, songwriters and record producers, who can flourish through having regular access to recording technologies. Studio ownership can also greatly increase the bargaining power of individuals such as artist managers.

If you can cover your costs, then there are many potential benefits to be gained from the freedom, independence and dedicated space that a studio can bring. Where viable, hiring out your facility on a commercial basis will help you to cover these costs; alternatively, you may wish to set up a private studio, purely for your own personal development.

Your market

Becoming a self-employed studio owner is, of course, a major leap forward from being a bedroom music-technology enthusiast. One key element in such a transition is first of all to identify your role in the marketplace: are you opening a commercial facility, or are you simply hiring premises for your own band to work in? Will you provide rehearsal facilities, or recording facilities, or both? Note that some studios also perform business-to-business roles – such as recording advertising jingles, audio books or other spoken-word products. Many bands grow tired of paying hire fees for commercial rehearsal rooms.

Depending on where you are in the country, you may be able to access a small business unit on which you can secure a commercial lease, and then be able to practise 24 hours a day. If you do take out a lease, then it is unlikely that you will be in there all of the time, and so you may enter into the market of becoming a rehearsal-room operator yourself. Many recording studio owners started out as rehearsal-room operators, and then gradually expanded the scope of their work into the business of recording 'demos'.

If you do wish to take this step up, then making the move from a simple rehearsal room to a recording facility will require significant investment in equipment, not to mention other factors such as improved soundproofing (to mask, for example, the sound of trains thundering over your roof, or the noise from the workshop through the wall!). As well as acoustics, also think carefully about aesthetics – the layout, design, lighting, furniture and other general accommodation – and don't forget to consider additional 'comfort' facilities for your paying customers, who may be spending long days on your premises. Reputation means a great deal among musicians and in recording circles, so it is imperative that you aim to deliver a quality product and service at affordable and competitive prices. Much business will depend on word of mouth, so the customer experience is vital.

Red tape

There are a number of regulations which anyone starting up their own business should consider. Matters such as Health & Safety laws, noise pollution, public liability insurance, a fire certificate, data protection for records, an annual tax return and even recent laws regarding smoking in public should be taken into account. If you plan to employ someone, then you will also be entering into the vast arena of rules pertaining to employment law. Additionally, you should think about the legal status of your firm – is it a sole trader, a partnership, or will you formalise it into a limited company? Setting up a registered limited company may be cheaper than you think: company registration agents can be found in the phone book.

Owning a studio is, to an extent, like running any other business. If you are hiring out studio time on a commercial basis, then you will normally need to register with the tax authorities within three months of commencing trading. You should be able to charge your expenses (such as rent and the purchase of capital items such as PA systems) against your income, thus reducing your overall tax burden. Do remember to file safely all relevant receipts and invoices, or it will be your word against the taxman's – and there can only be one winner if you don't keep the evidence!

Operations

Think carefully about the monthly overheads involved in running your studio. When you step out of the home environment, your costs will rise significantly. Take time to negotiate the best deals that are right for your business plan. What length of lease will suit you? Do you have permission to make alterations to the premises? Remember that very few buildings are custom-built for studio purposes, so will generally require some adaptation. And will you need planning permission from the local authority if you are intending to make any major changes to a building? As well as rent bills, also consider factors such as your electricity provider and charges for business rates (work hard to secure the best deal).

There may be a number of competitors in your region, so you should do some market research and find out the going rates for hiring out their premises. Also find out about the equipment your rivals have to offer in order to lure in customers. When you know the market rates, think about your pricing strategy: will you offer discounted prices for unpopular times of the day? What about discounts for block-booking?

Security is a major issue – you don't want to see your prized assets disappear in the middle of the night. Therefore think carefully about any practical measures you can take in this regard. Spending adequately on security could be money well spent. Also think about the location, as cheaper premises in areas that aren't exactly salubrious may be false economy if you're unsure how safe things will actually be. Likewise, fires are a hazard from which many businesses never actually recover, so take out adequate insurance, implement fire safety precautions, and maintain an accurate log and undertake regular checks of all your equipment.

As well as financial records, you should seek to maintain detailed records of bookings. Double bookings are commonplace in unprofessionally run studios, and do little for customer relations or reputation. If you run a rehearsal facility, then your goal will be to secure as many block-bookings as possible. These will steady your cash flow, build business confidence, and give you a basis on which to expand or invest more. Be careful, though: ensure that you have trustworthy customers. Accommodating those who repeatedly default on payments, always seek credit from you or abuse the facilities should, of course, be avoided as another false economy.

Maintaining your equipment is a paramount concern. (Block-bookings will quickly disappear if the quality of your studio deteriorates due to a lack of investment.) So expect to have to make allowance for upgrades of speakers, amplifiers and other equipment, above and beyond your initial start-up costs. Do also ensure that your equipment is regularly serviced for any electrical hazards.

Promotion

You will need to consider how to market your studio. Beyond word of mouth, you will probably use traditional methods such as advertisements at strategic locations (which may include local musical equipment retail outlets), and/or you may decide to create a website. Think carefully about your name and corporate identity, and remember that credits (even on demo tapes) are part of your 'marketing mix', so do encourage this. You may want to think big and develop promotional tie-ins with a local radio station or magazine, such as, 'Competition winners receive two days' free recording'. This may be worthwhile in order to raise your profile among your target customers – particularly if yours is a brand new venture.

Remember that your potential customers will also consider practical logistics, such as transport links and the availability of car parking. Any strength in this regard should also be highlighted.

Your team

Running a studio can be a time-consuming business, so it is common for several people to be involved in such a new venture. If you are going into business with others, then be very careful about the choices you make. Consider your business structure and format, and the individuals with whom you will be working. Beware of false friends, and remember that many solid friendships have foundered on the rocks of personal rivalries and badly managed business ventures.

Assistance

The government is generally keen to encourage entrepreneurial flair and small enterprise. As a result, many business-support services exist. You should take advantage of these (especially their free advice) and try not to be overcome by any sense of being burdened by red tape.

You may also wish to consider joining industry organisations such as the Association of Professional Recording Services (APRS) or the Music Producers' Guild (MPG). Likewise, some geographical areas have local music development bodies that may be able to offer friendly advice. Examples would include 'Generator' in the North of England, and in Wales the 'Welsh Music Foundation'.

Anyone seeking financial assistance with start-up costs from banks or local enterprise agencies will need to prepare a formal business plan. If you are serious about setting up a studio, then do seek legal and financial advice from qualified professionals.

Expanding the business

Owning a studio can be an exciting prospect. If you are successful, you may consider expansion – both in terms of premises and your activities. This may mean moving to a larger facility, and targeting new markets. As your enterprise grows, your business plan may evolve and you may wish to consider potential synergies and new opportunities.

Such opportunities can open a whole new gateway for you. For example, you may want to consider managing bands (who are often attracted by the lure of someone who owns a rehearsal/recording facility), or you may wish to consider moving into studio production, or even setting up a small record company. Recording costs are a significant burden for small labels, so if you can absorb these costs, then you will have a much more solid foundation on which to build an independent label. More funds may then be available for the marketing and promotion of your releases.

Summary

Setting up a new studio is a challenging and expensive task, so be clear about your future direction and how you see a studio fitting into your overall business plan. Remember that many small businesses do not turn a profit within the first few years, and that commercial success is sometimes forged on the anvil of failure! Try to think for the long-term, and consider how you can contribute some 'added value' to your local music industry infrastructure. There are a number of possibilities, but all require you taking those important first, serious steps into music business enterprise, being prepared to work hard, and – with luck – developing personally and professionally while enjoying the journey along the way.

Useful websites

Association of Professional Recording Services – **www.aprs.co.uk**
Business Link – **www.businesslink.gov.uk**
Music Producers' Guild (UK) – **www.mpg.org.uk**

JoJo Gould is a UK-based lecturer, and was for five years joint Managing Editor of *Music Business Journal*. He lectures and consults on the European Degree in International Music Management, and holds a Master of Science degree in Business IT Systems. He was a co-founder and first Chairman of New Music in Scotland, and was previously Senior Lecturer in Music Industry Management at Buckinghamshire Chilterns University College.

Recording acoustic instruments

Now that 'the secret is out', and anyone, it seems, can learn to use the latest technology to produce, mix and release their own music, it's worth examining the various recording processes involved in successfully recording any newly created piece of music – as **Adi Winman** explains.

The vast majority of young independent musicians and artists are today using their own recording equipment with the aim of exploiting their material for some sort of commercial gain. The past ten years or so have slowly seen the demise of the traditional recording studio, and the rise of home studio set-ups. The availability of relatively cheap recording hardware and software has aided this process. Whether you are a truly independent artist, group, collective, or songwriter – or even if you employ the skills of a sound engineer, producer or remixer – the chances are either that you or your 'hired help' will now have access to your own equipment.

Where do I start?

With the exception of many sample-based and instrumental recordings, the majority of modern recordings usually include at least one acoustic instrument of some description (in which may be included the vocals). This fact obviously requires the use of at least one microphone, a microphone amplifier, and some sort of recording device. Although this simple set-up will certainly get you started, it can be somewhat limiting, and can have an adverse affect on the overall quality of the recording. Investing in some additional 'choice' hardware and software can vastly improve your chances of creating a dynamic, layered and professional sounding recording. This, along with some 'old school' production and miking techniques, can help ensure that your recordings sound as good as possible.

Investing in a good microphone collection, and learning appropriate microphone technique, is a good place to start, and should ensure that your original recording will require less 'fixing in the mix' – or hours of additional tweaking, at a later stage. As previously mentioned, one microphone is very limiting. Although not preventing you from recording multiple source instruments – such as drum kits, live band recordings, musical ensembles and the like – it will certainly limit the amount of control you have at the mixing stage. All acoustic instruments have very specific and often complicated timbres that require several microphones to emulate successfully all of their nuances. Using multiple microphones is also something to consider when recording individual instruments, such as acoustic guitars, percussion, bass, and so on.

Microphone technique

At their simplest, microphones fall into two main categories: Dynamic and Condenser, with other specific microphone types also worth considering at some later stage (such as Ribbon, Valve and PZM). The more robust dynamic microphones tend to be better at dealing with higher SPLs (Sound Pressure Levels) and are very good for placing closer to instruments with very loud levels and fast attack such as drums, percussion and guitar amps. However, combining them with other types of dynamic microphones or condenser microphones can yield better results. Setting up two distinct microphones with different characteristics (either equidistant from a sound source, or using one as a separate ambient mic) will enable you to blend the two together to create a 'fuller' sound. As condenser mics are more sensitive, have a better frequency response at the lower and top ends of the frequency spectrum, and can pick out more detail, they can complement more 'middley' sounds.

Multiple miking of a single source has to be thought out properly, as it can cause adverse affects. For example, if you decide to use two microphones to record an acoustic guitar, the mics need to be placed in such a way so that there are no 'phase' problems. Phase problems occur when the signal reaches the microphones at different times, and this tends to cause comb-filtering effects that can 'thin out' or 'hollow' the combined signals. If you follow the '3-to-1' rule – where the second mic is three times the distance away from the first – the problem will be alleviated, and it will also help with mono compatibility. This rule can be implemented when using a second microphone as an 'ambient' or room microphone, and is a technique that is often used in professional recordings. Another popular recording technique is to use a matched pair of microphones to record in true stereo.

Stereo microphone techniques

There are a plethora of microphone techniques, but many of them (particularly stereo ones) are all derived from the same initial experiments done in the 1930s by such recording legends as Alan Blumlein and Dr Harvey Fletcher (in the UK and US respectively). These techniques have been used by both the music and film industries for decades, and have contributed to the production of some great-sounding albums and movies throughout the years.

The music industry, in particular, can use very many microphones and a mixed bag of techniques. Take just the drum kit, for example: depending on the style of music being recorded, each part of the kit may require a microphone (or group of microphones) in order to reproduce individual sounds, all of which are mixed together to create an (ideally) 'phase coherent', beautifully natural, ambient, stereo drum kit sound! For instance, there could be two microphones on the kick drum, three microphones for the toms, two snare mics (top and bottom), two overheads, two ambients, and the list goes on. It's not unheard of to use 14 tracks just for drums! If you take the trouble to do all this, then ask yourself if you shouldn't go to the same trouble to record guitar sounds, or percussion, or ambient background noises. Even if you don't think it's worth taking quite that much trouble, you might still considering using some 'old school' stereo miking techniques to give you a head start when it comes to creating a professional recording.

The three main stereo techniques

There are essentially three main types of stereo microphone techniques. They are: Co-incident Pairs, Near-Coincident Pairs, and Spaced Arrays (with many other options such as Baffled Omni Pairs, and Dummy Head – or Binaural – techniques, and so on). Each type has its own advantages and disadvantages. The Coincident Pair technique (or XY) is a really good starting point for stereo recording, and is based on the level differences between the pair of cardioid microphones as sound passes over each of the microphone diaphragms.

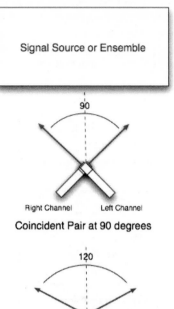

Coincident Pair at 90 degrees

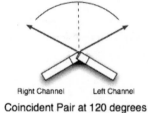

Coincident Pair at 120 degrees

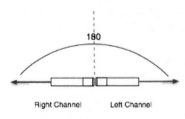

Coincident Pair at 180 degrees

The microphones are angled at anything up to 180°, and the capsules are usually placed directly above each other for a 'phase-coherent' signal that is 'sharp' – and very mono compatible. This is quite helpful for sound quality, where Left and Right signals can be combined to make one 'fuller' sound in Mono without any comb filtering problems, or left as is for traditional stereo use.

The Near-Coincident technique helps with the relatively restricted image width of a coincident pair, using two directional microphones both angled *and* spaced apart. In this case, if the spacing of the mics is increased, then the stereo spread also increases, and vice versa. Near-Coincident techniques are said to add depth and 'air' to the sound. One such technique is the ORTF (Office de Radiodiffusion Television Française) technique that uses two cardioid mics at 110 degrees, while being spaced (17 cm) apart on the horizontal plane. The ORTF technique is supposed to have accurate localisation, but is not as mono compatible as the coincident pair technique. Additional flanking 'omni' (omni-directional) microphones can also be used to increase spaciousness.

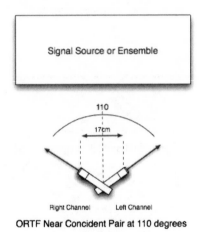

ORTF Near Concident Pair at 110 degrees

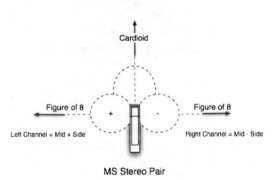

MS Stereo Pair

The slightly more unusual 'M-S' ('mid-side') technique again uses two microphones, except this time it utilises one cardioid microphone facing the source, and another figure of eight facing outwards on the same plane. The figure-of-eight signal is essentially split into two signals, with one side being 'phase reversed': these two signals are then panned left and right to produce the stereo signal that surrounds the mono cardioid signal. Using a mixing console or MS matrix decoder, the balance between the mono and stereo signal can be adjusted between wide and narrow. Mono compatibility is excellent; in fact, this method is often used as a field recording method, to source sound effects.

Spaced microphone techniques usually use two (but sometimes three) omni-directional microphones at various distances, depending on the source width, room acoustics and desired perspective. Due to the 'time-of-arrival cues' (or time differences) of spaced microphones, they are said to possess more 'spaciousness' and 'warmth', which is why many classical recordings use this method. As classical recordings are almost always issued in stereo, the lack of mono compatibility is not a concern. Bringing the microphones closer together can restrict the width substantially; but if the microphones are spaced too far apart an undesirable 'hole in the middle' appears. To overcome the 'hole in the middle' problem, a third microphone can be used to 'fill' the gap (supplying the deficient centre image).

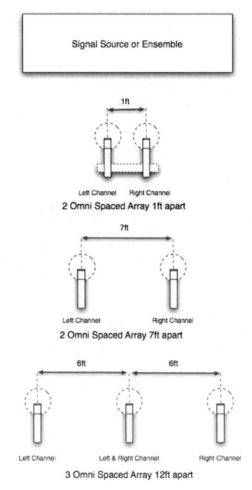

Probably the most famous three-microphone technique is the Decca Tree, which uses a third omni-microphone placed centrally, although further forward than the main two microphones. This signal is then blended with the original stereo signal, and panned in the centre to bolster the centre image. A special bar or holding device may be required to house the microphones, which can be positioned above or just in front of the source. For classical recordings, the Decca Tree is often placed just above and behind the conductor. The Decca Tree also preserves excellent imaging and separation when employed with the various matrix-encoding systems used to distribute film soundtracks.

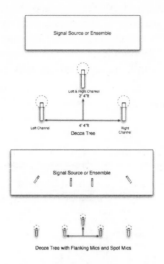

Decca Tree with Flanking Mics and Spot Mics

All of the aforementioned techniques can also benefit from the use of spot microphones to accent the signals being recorded. This is done by placing additional microphones closer to individual sections within, or near to, the signal source. Using spot mics can offer greater control over the balance between ambient and direct sources, while also giving you more options when you mix. Conversely, in surround recording techniques, additional microphones representing the centre channel, the left and right surrounds, and even the '.1' channel, can be added to conventional microphone techniques to help to achieve true surround immersion.

What sort of microphones and other equipment do I need?

Ideally, the equipment you purchase should reflect the type of recording that you are going to undertake. A large microphone collection is unnecessary if you only intend to record an acoustic guitar and some vocals. But if you are serious about recording a full band, ensemble, or multiple sound sources, then a good selection is essential. For a simple set-up, you should consider purchasing at least one matched pair of reasonable quality condensers – as they can be used in stereo for anything from drum overheads, room ambience, and acoustic guitar, to stereo group vocals and orchestral recordings. You can complement this pair with a varied selection of dynamic microphones, which can be used for various purposes. A drum microphone package is very useful. Typically, a drum mic package will come with various mics designed to be used for individual drums or cymbals. There will be a kick-drum mic, for example, and tom-tom mics – but these can also be useful as 'all round' mics in almost all recording situations. If you have a bigger budget, then you may want to consider microphones that also have polar pattern switches, pads and filters on them. This will give you even more flexibility when it comes to your microphone techniques.

A good-quality microphone pre-amp can be very expensive, but with a little shopping around you can find some reasonably priced high-quality ones. Again, if you are only recording very straightforwardly, then one or two channels are all you are going to need, and many audio interfaces for computers include a couple of mic 'pre's' on their inputs.

As the majority of home studios usually incorporate multi-track Digital Audio Workstations (DAW's) – such as Logic, Cubase or ProTools – then this would seem like the obvious approach. However, with just two inputs, you are limited in the amount of control that you have. Using a device with eight or more mic pre's on the input will give the control and flexibility to record multiple instruments at once onto separate tracks, but these can be quite expensive. Another approach would be to use a small mixing desk with anything from 8 to 32 mic inputs, then sub-mix them down to feed them through your audio interface. This will not only give you separation, but also enable you to mix multiple mic sources together before they are recorded.

The choice of recording device is up to you, but as the majority of computer-based DAW's offer so much flexibility, track count, processors and mixing capabilities, programs such as Logic, ProTools and Cubase will be hard to resist. Other options include 'stand-alone' digital recorders – that usually also include a mixing desk with EQ, processing and mic inputs as standard. These devices are an 'all-in-one' solution that can also be very portable, but for many, the user interface and mixing options can be a bit cumbersome and fiddly.

EQ and compression

From a purist's perspective, the use of EQ and Compression when recording is almost always a 'no-no', but a subtle use of both, along with a good initial recording using the right microphone technique, can further improve the sound. Typically, instruments such as bass, vocals and acoustic guitar can be recorded with a little compression to iron out any peaks in the dynamics; but used as an actual processor rather than a tool, a compressor can help 'shape' the sound. Compressors can add depth, warmth and punch to certain sounds at source, but obviously if they are overused the audio can sound too 'squashed', 'pinched', or (worse) distorted. A little compression added to help with the initial sound may seem like a risk (as you can't undo it once it's recorded), but if you take the risk – being confident in the sound – then it is usually worth it!

EQ is also something that you shouldn't really reach for, if it doesn't sound right at source. But once you have got a sound that is 'almost there', a touch of EQ to eradicate unwanted frequencies, or to add a bit of 'colour', should not be a problem. If you have to add substantial EQ to a signal, then there is obviously something wrong: try another mic, another mic position, another room, or maybe tune the instrument. If all else fails, get another musician (or use a sample)!

Adi Winman was Assistant Engineer at Pink Floyd's Britannia Row Studios, where he worked with engineers, producers and artists including Pulp, Suede, Chemical Bros (and Pink Floyd themselves) before moving on to Great Linford Manor Studios as 'in-house' engineer – working on many projects including Skunk Anansie, Jamiroquai, Rocket From The Crypt, Supergrass, and Shed Seven. He holds a Masters degree in Audio Engineering from Westminster University, and is now Creative Director and Audio Consultant at Dilute Recordings – which provides audio services for the games, music and multimedia industries. See **www.diluterecordings.com**.

The A&R department

JoJo Gould points out that in the UK, more than 100 acts are usually signed every year by the major record labels and large independents. The A&R (Artiste and Repertoire) department is generally the first point of contact with a record company for any aspiring new artist. Attracting the interest of these relatively powerful individuals is perhaps the most difficult task for the new manager of a new artist; therefore, a well-connected, knowledgeable and resourceful manager is a significant initial advantage.

Chasing the dream

It is often said that A&R representatives are looking for something special in their signings. This concept is an intangible one, but it generally relates to an image and ability that exceeds the norm in terms of potential commercial appeal. So how do you come to the attention of an A&R rep? Unfortunately, submitting unsolicited demo tapes to A&R departments usually represents a waste of time and money. Indeed, some record companies (especially in the USA) will simply return them unopened unless they are passed on by means of a 'recognised channel', such as an established manager or lawyer.

Unsigned bands and solo artists may wish to consider the following factors when seeking record company interest (and indeed music publishing interest, if also an original songwriter):

- Create a local profile first – e.g. through newspapers, venue operators and radio stations.
- Record a maximum of three songs as professionally as can be afforded (always place your best song first, on any demo).
- Co-ordinate your image, and your sonic style (do not confuse the general public and A&R representatives with vastly different musical styles).
- Plan a co-ordinated diary of live performances, in careful sequence.
- Create an informative biography.
- Obtain professionally produced photographs.
- Build a database of fans by distributing and collecting contact sheets at live performances and through your website.
- Consider self-financing an independent single release incorporating a small tour, a promotional media campaign and independent distribution.
- Seek out participation at industry showcase events (such as *In The City*, an event which is held every September).
- Above all, find a capable manager who is willing to act as a third party and sell the artist and their 'message' to A&R departments.

Note that music publishing companies (not just record companies) have A&R representatives, too. Such individuals in publishing perform similar roles to record company representatives; however, their key interest lies in the commercial exploitation of songs, as opposed to records. New artists who are also songwriters may perhaps choose to target these A&R publishers (many of whom are friendly with record company A&R staff, and communicate with each other on a regular basis with regard to interesting new acts).

Indeed, some artists receive music publishing deals first (this is becoming increasingly common). If the songwriter is also a performing artist, then the publisher will help their new signing to achieve a record deal (in this way the music publisher can then tap into 'exploitation income' – such as mechanical royalties from the manufacturing process, broadcasting royalties from airplay, public performance income from public area licensing, and synchronisation income from the placement of the works in films, TV and multimedia products). An established publisher will usually provide an advance, which may allow the songwriter to pursue their craft full-time. They may also pay for equipment, and quality studio time for demo-making purposes.

As music is a core entertainment industry product, do bear in mind that record company A&R departments are looking for 'acts'. An act should have clearly discernible qualities, such as:

- performance skills (stagecraft)
- character
- personality
- image
- presence
- media skills
- and, of course, talent!

These skills can help provide the basis for a Promotions Department to 'spin doctor' stories effectively, which can then generate wider media interest.

Most signed artists will have spent several formative years chasing a record deal. Hence, the first album release by an artist usually represents the culmination of many years of songwriting and hard work. While many signed artists fail to live up to expectations after the first promising album, and do not pass the test of the critical second album, others illustrate their true depth and excel with their second album.

Even after signing, it can sometimes take several years for a record label to release the first record. During this time, an elaborate A&R development process can take place, before the artist is considered to be 'ready' for the marketplace. The signed artist must be patient, and should liaise closely with the A&R department. Meanwhile, the manager should maximise the act's priority on the label's roster at this development stage. Unfortunately, few artists these days with poor sales for a first album are likely to be commissioned to record a second album. Likewise, over 80 per cent of signed artists never sell enough product actually to see a royalty cheque from their record company.

Classic mistakes by artists seeking record deals

The following common mistakes made by new artists when seeking a record deal should be noted:

- submitting unsolicited demos to A&R Departments;
- sending in demos to A&R departments with no contact details on them;
- not putting their best song first on the demo (as they will be fortunate to get past the first 20 seconds of the first song);
- performing high-profile gigs, such as A&R showcases, before they are technically competent enough to do so;
- playing their new songs at A&R showcases – as opposed to their *best* songs (you may be bored by playing the same songs on your set for a couple of years ... but remember that the Rolling Stones, for example, have been playing 'Satisfaction' at concerts now for over 40 years!).

A&R structure

Some inside knowledge of the workings of an A&R department may help to establish a strategy to attract their attention. A&R departments are broadly similar to R&D (Research and Development) departments in other companies, in that they look to find and develop new raw 'product', which can then be successfully marketed within a commercial environment.

The major labels, on average, may spend a double-digit figure of their annual budget on their A&R departments. This is a comparatively large amount, and represents a huge investment in the industry. (In other lines of business, the average R&D budget is often only around 6 per cent of the annual budget.)

In terms of staff, A&R departments are very small (even within major labels), and may be structured in the following way:

- Directors
- Managers
- Talent Scouts
- Administration

It is sometimes suggested that every employee of a record company is actually a 'talent scout', in that they should always have their ear to the ground with regard to discovering exciting new artists. In this way, some personnel manage to switch from, for example, administrative duties, to joining the A&R department on the basis of proving that they have a 'good ear' for a hit record. A&R personnel are usually recruited by the department itself. They generally do not advertise these vacancies through the usual channels. Interestingly, most A&R personnel do not have backgrounds as musicians; instead, their backgrounds are usually diverse: some are university graduates, while others are experienced in other aspects of the music business (such as artist management).

Joining an A&R department is therefore very difficult, and may involve years of cultivating existing A&R representatives, attending gigs, and building a network of contacts and a reputation among the industry decision-makers.

Working conditions

Talent scouts are employed to seek out 'buzz' acts across the country, to listen to the many demos posted in (or online), and generally to build up a network of useful contacts for future reference. These individuals are often young (teens to mid 20s) and usually chase up information on what other A&R talent scouts at other labels have been investigating. Quite often, a great deal of their practical working day is actually spent in transit.

The hours for most A&R personnel are very long – from perhaps 10am or 11am to the small hours of the next day. It is, undoubtedly, very much a vocation rather than a conventional job! A love of music and a keen knowledge of the practical workings of the music business should therefore be apparent.

Wages for talent scouts are relatively low, and their real practical 'signing power' is very limited; however, they could strongly recommend an act to their A&R managers and directors, who will then give the artist a fairer hearing, and make a decision on whether or not to sign.

It could be argued that, due to the relative lack of job security in A&R, many representatives become guilty of only wanting to sign acts that other labels are also chasing, instead of actually following their own intuition and signing the acts they really believe could be a success. This may perhaps be the reason why an artist being offered a recording contract is sometimes also offered contracts by other competitor labels around the same time.

In fairness, it is also the case that A&R personnel generally socialise with their contemporaries at other labels anyway (they see the same people at gigs night after night), so it is inevitable that some kind of collective understanding may develop towards high-profile unsigned acts – especially at annual industry events such as *In The City*, *MIDEM* or *South By South West*. Indeed, A&R departments are always particularly pleased to sign an act their rivals haven't even heard of!

Talent scouts who do impress may then move into A&R management. This brings the added responsibility of nurturing and developing artists who have already been signed.

A&R directors are the most senior members of the A&R team. These individuals have usually established themselves as experienced and capable A&R managers with a proven track record in identifying commercially viable acts, and seeing the process through to the release of commercially viable 'product'. Directors are often very well paid by record companies, as they perform a key executive role within the most important department of the organisation. A&R directors within major record companies must also maintain good working relations with the corporate management structure of the company. Record companies, like any other business, operate in a political climate. This is also a 'people-based' environment, and so is one in which the chemistry between individuals can be a key underlying factor in the decision-making process.

A&R managers and directors are usually well-connected with industry professionals across the country, and especially at strategic population centres (e.g. Manchester, Liverpool, Newcastle, Glasgow and Cardiff in the UK). Local artist managers, venue owners and rehearsal/recording studio operators are particularly useful sources of information for them.

Regardless of the A&R level, all personnel must travel extensively. Senior members usually venture overseas for international meetings, corporate strategies and conferences. Job security is a luxury for many A&R personnel: the fortunate ones – those who are usually headhunted, or already have a good track record with the company – may receive a time-limited employment contract, which at least provides some stability.

Working with signed artists

A&R managers and directors, in conjunction with the Business Affairs department, decide at what level to bid for a new artist to join their label. After the signing process (which can take several months to finalise), they then carry out a number of key developmental activities. Such activities might embrace a degree of involvement in the following:

- establishing a recording budget;
- establishing a recording schedule;
- identifying a recording studio;
- identifying an appropriate and available producer;
- finding appropriate songs and songwriters (for non-songwriting acts);
- identifying a video producer;
- establishing a video budget;
- establishing a release schedule;
- deciding which recorded tracks to include on an album;
- deciding which tracks will be singles;
- commissioning remixes;
- deciding on bonus tracks.

A&R managers will also liaise with the artist's manager with regard to touring schedules, promotional schedules and international release strategies.

To achieve these tasks, the A&R department will process its artists through all other departments within the record company: marketing, promotions, business affairs, finance, legal, and so on. A&R therefore provides a useful centralised link to the other departments, and to the senior management of the company; its personnel will often become close friends with the artist and their manager. A&R managers and directors spend the majority of their time with signed artist projects. This explodes the myth of the A&R representative as someone who spends all day listening to demos, and all night at live performances!

Some A&R executives are also proactive in the studio, and in the production process. Those who make a significant contribution to an artist's recorded output may sometimes even be granted an 'Executive Producer' credit.

A record company, like any other business, must prioritise its activities within a limited annual budget. Artist managers must seek to receive a tangible level of backing and support from their A&R representative. A potential danger occurs, of course, when the A&R representative who signs a new artist then subsequently leaves the label. This sometimes results in the artist being marginalised compared to the others on the roster. Many artists are dropped by their label in this situation, as enthusiasm for the 'project' can be lost. Note, then, that A&R departments often decide who to *drop* from the roster, as well as who to add!

The real A&R objective

The challenge in finding and developing commercially viable new acts should not be underestimated. To take what is essentially an idea, and then to mould it into a product with appeal to the consumer, is a difficult task.

A&R is also a 'people-business', and, as we have seen, success can often depend on the chemistry between the people involved in the internal processes!

An increasing trend in A&R has been towards the 'off the shelf' licence agreements with independent labels and production companies. In this way, major labels can sign licensing agreements to manufacture, market and distribute relatively successful artists, who could benefit from the resources and input of a major record company. Profits generated can then be shared, risk can be minimised, and the A&R process can, in effect, be short-circuited and simplified (in this way, the independent sector often acts as a *de facto* A&R filter).

It is worth remembering at this stage that very few signed artists ever receive a record company royalty cheque – as they do not recoup the substantial investment required to break an act in the modern marketplace. Indeed, it is generally agreed that only around 15 per cent or so of signed acts ever 'recoup'. Therefore, most record companies primarily rely on a small number of hugely successful international-level artists to generate sustainable income into the company, over many years, through 'back catalogue' album sales from the likes of, for example: Eminem, Bruce Springsteen, Pink Floyd, Dire Straits, Eagles, Garth Brooks, Bee Gees, Queen, Michael Jackson, David Bowie, Abba, REM, Bob Dylan, Frank Sinatra, Led Zeppelin, Prince, Rolling Stones, Bon Jovi, George Michael, Oasis, The Beatles, Eric Clapton, The Doors, Fleetwood Mac, The Who, Elton John, Enya, Whitney Houston, U2, Madonna and Elvis Presley. Such established artists can be said to help support a record label's substantial A&R budget – with the aim of discovering the next generation's talent.

Indeed, finding and developing potential artists of real international stature is the main target of most A&R managers and directors. To find just one act at this level may well constitute a successful A&R career!

However, identifying great acts, and then encouraging and managing this potential, is an exceptionally difficult, and often underestimated, task.

JoJo Gould is a UK-based lecturer, and was for five years joint Managing Editor of *Music Business Journal*. He lectures and consults on the European Degree in International Music Management, and holds a Master of Science degree in Business IT Systems. He was a co-founder and first Chairman of New Music in Scotland, and was previously Senior Lecturer in Music Industry Management at Buckinghamshire Chilterns University College.

The role of the record producer

The producer plays a vital role in the development of an artist's recorded output. Some producers, such as Dr Dre, Phil Spector, Trevor Horn, and Stock, Aitken & Waterman have been hugely successful, and enjoyed as much acclaim as the artists with whom they have worked. **JoJo Gould** tells us more.

The importance of the producer

Regardless of the style of music, producers can be instrumental in achieving a particular sound or determining an arrangement for a track, or even for a whole album or series of albums. Therefore, it is often the case that what the consumer ultimately hears in the form of an 'end product' has usually been significantly rearranged and restructured by the producer, and not solely by the artist.

Availability is a major concern when trying to secure a producer – as most of the popular ones have busy order books, sometimes for many years in advance. When you consider that an album will often take several months to make, it is not difficult to see how this situation can arise. Appropriate producers are normally identified by the A&R representative, or manager, who will work in conjunction with the artist. This process varies, however, as some artists have pre-defined ideas about the producer with whom they would like to work in the recording studio, while others are sometimes assigned a complete stranger by the record company (based on their competence, their availability, and how expensive they are)! Note that record companies can normally use legally binding clauses in recording contracts, which, if necessary, will allow them to control the creative process and the choice of appropriate personnel. Record company staff members – such as A&R representatives – are also sometimes credited as 'Executive Producer' on the sleeve of a record. This is due to their contribution (or perceived contribution) to the creative process in the studio, and in putting an album together.

Skills and qualities

Many record producers are knowledgeable and proficient in the use of studio technologies. Those seeking to carve out a career in production should endeavour to master the features and capabilities of such technologies. Gaining such knowledge sometimes involves much trial and error, and will probably initially require the amassing of various items of equipment in your spare room! Technology is an ever-evolving area of the industry and so a substantial investment in equipment and infrastructure may be required. It could be argued that a resourceful producer should be able to generate a good end-product, even with minimal technology. Consider, for example, that *Sergeant Pepper's Lonely Hearts Club Band* by The Beatles was recorded using a only four-track tape recorder (the appropriate technology of the day). A good record cannot be 'bought' simply by using a good studio; instead (provided that the performances and instruments are satisfactory) the skills of the producer are often what make the difference between a successful and unsuccessful recording. And record producers continue to develop new recording methods, as well as generally being on the look out for new ideas and technologies.

Of course, there is a practical difference between being a recording engineer or studio programmer, and being a record producer – the latter will also involve having a creative ear for making music and being a 'good ideas' person. Songwriting and instrumental abilities often go with the territory as well. Remember that it makes sense to own the means of production and, in practice, that involves investing in equipment and possibly setting up your own recording facility. It is possible to incorporate a working studio into your house; this, however, may have legal implications for your mortgage or tenancy agreement, as well as there being insurance considerations – so examine the regulations thoroughly. You should remember your neighbours, too, if you want to avoid receiving complaints from the local council about noise pollution! A good general knowledge of the record industry, and an analytical ear for how sound recordings are put together, is also helpful.

Producers are often risk-takers, and very good at networking – not only with artists, but also with ancillary personnel in the industry, such as A&R representatives, managers, other studio owners and songwriters. The ability to turn a song into a record can be a difficult, arduous and sometimes a tense business. It involves dealing with creative people for a long period of time within an enclosed space. Throw in time constraints, budget constraints, commercial pressures and different opinions about where a record should be progressing 'sonically', and it is easy to see why this socio-economic cocktail can sometimes constitute quite a strained environment in which to make music.

At the mixing desk, some producers are more 'hands-on' than others. And some have a penchant for unorthodox methods. Every producer has their own unique style, and these idiosyncrasies with respect to working methods (and associated ideas) can make interacting with a producer an interesting part of the business. Despite any such eccentricities, bands often enjoy working with a respected third party in the studio, and positive personal chemistry can influence the end result. A producer may even become a regular feature with a certain artist, and build up a solid working relationship with them over several albums (consider, for example, George Martin's association with The Beatles, Stephen Street with Blur, Brian Eno with U2, Nigel Godrich with Radiohead, Guy Chambers with Robbie Williams, and Quincy Jones's work with Michael Jackson).

Responsibilities

The songwriting artist will usually approach the producer with the fundamental outline of a song (usually in 'demo' form). This is often literally arranged and rearranged at the pre-production stage, and then carefully crafted into the recorded, edited, mixed and mastered version with which we become familiar. If you ever get the chance to hear demo versions of popular records, you will notice that some are very close to the finished article, although the majority are significantly altered and developed in the studio.

As recording budgets are strictly controlled, the producer should also assist in meeting the targets of the agreed time schedule, and costs for the recording process. Schedules and budgets are usually discussed in conjunction with the record company's Business Affairs department and/or A&R department. Consequently, producers are allocated a significant element of general operational control when working in the studio with an artist. Such latitude includes making practical decisions (including the need – or not – to hire session musicians and backing vocalists).

The three key elements of a good record are the *song*, the *performance* and the *production*. The producer should therefore strive to get the best possible performance from their artist in the studio. This may entail encouraging them and perhaps making them feel as comfortable as possible, and 'finessing' all aspects of their musicianship and vocals in order to obtain a great final 'cut'. Making subjective decisions is a necessary role for the producer as s/he oversees the whole creative process.

Despite the current abundance of studio gadgetry, producers normally seek to exploit technology without 'overproducing' (often following the mantra that *production is the art of reduction*), and they also have an element of responsibility for ensuring that any samples which have been used have full copyright clearance (from the music publisher if re-recordings, and from the publisher and appropriate record label if taken from an existing record). They must therefore ensure that no copyright infringements are included in any recorded output.

Remuneration

A record producer's remuneration is market-driven, and will depend on his/her current popularity and reputation. Financial rewards usually take the form of a fee and/or a percentage royalty from the artist's royalties (perhaps between two and four points, although producers who are in exceptional demand at a given time may command a higher royalty and/or a greater advance). It is important to bear in mind that although these rewards may appear to be substantial, the producer of a recorded song has usually played a key role in shaping and structuring the final version of the song in the studio, yet usually receives no claim on the worldwide music publishing (i.e. the songwriting royalties).

Some producers choose to specialise in 'remix' work; hence they will receive tracks from the record company with the specific remit of remixing a bonus track, or perhaps a 12" vinyl dance mix of a particular song. Due to the relatively low sales of remix tracks, a producer may charge a set fee for this service, as opposed to taking a percentage royalty from sales. The label may pay half of the producer's fee up-front, with the remainder settled on delivery of an acceptable product. Any advances would be charged against the producer's royalty first if s/he has chosen a 'points' deal.

If, in the process of making a commercially released record, a producer actually performs on it (as a session musician, for example), it would be advisable to make sure that s/he is a member of the UK Performer Services division of Phonographic Performance Limited (PPL). Membership is free and, through their monitoring systems, they will collect any royalties that may accrue as a qualifying performer, for airplay or public performance of the sound recordings. This may also include royalties from some overseas territories. (PPL – a not-for-profit organisation – will deduct a small percentage from these royalties, in order to cover its operating costs.)

Professional support

In addition to the numerous music production and recording courses currently available at colleges and universities around the country, the UK also has the Music Producers' Guild (MPG), which helps support new producers. The MPG – a membership-based organisation – exists to promote, inform and enhance the interests of this sector of the industry. The benefits of joining include: networking opportunities, equipment demonstrations, professional advice, regular news, and a collective voice for all producer-related matters. The MPG also has a number of educational aspects to its activities, and welcomes the aspiring and ambitious.

Many producers also have professional managers, who assist them in developing their career. These managers help to look after the producer's financial and legal affairs, create and update their showreel, and, vitally, help their client to obtain a busy 'order book' – usually with a rising scale of royalty entitlements as that producer's popularity grows. An example of one such successful company is SBM in London.

Moving up

As well as spending a number of years learning their craft, many producers are music industry entrepreneurs who have invested much capital in equipment and premises. Owning a recording facility also provides an income stream from studio booking fees (a useful guaranteed sum) and the possibility of expanding your activities into an integrated production house that may offer recording, production and even a small record company imprint (thus potentially opening the doors to entering into licensing agreements with larger labels). This lucrative step will require significant knowledge, business acumen and industry savvy on the part of the producer/manager, but has been made somewhat easier by the affordability of small business recording technologies.

A way of life

Producers spend a great deal of time at the 'coalface' of the music industry (the studio mixing desk), and irregular hours are a key feature of the role. This will also mean additional hours, long after the band has left the studio. So, if you don't like working for a long period of time in an enclosed environment (often with no windows, yesterday's fast food wrappers and a well-worn sofa), then studio production is probably not the career move for you.

Becoming a producer requires much time, dedication and (probably) significant expense. It will also involve developing a resilient attitude, building up your name over a period of time, and working with a number of artists en route. One fast way to make a reputation is to produce a successful new act before their star ascends, and to continue working with them as they progress towards some sort of fame (and, ideally, fortune). So, make sure that you are properly credited for your work. In addition, the aspiring producer should consider the musical genres with which they may wish to be associated. (As a producer, you may be able to 'specialise' in one or more areas – classical, pop, jazz, etc.) In practice, many successful producers have found that their role evolved literally from fiddling with a box of wires, then through an 'extensive record collection in the loft' stage, and finally on to the setting up of their own studio facility. This last major entrepreneurial step – along with an expanding showreel and good networking skills – can (if blessed by that ever-essential ingredient, good fortune) propel the skilful and talented individual towards great things.

Useful websites

Music Producers' Guild (UK) – **www.mpg.org.uk**
SBM – **www.record-producers.com**
PPL – **www.ppluk.com**

JoJo Gould is a UK-based lecturer, and was for five years joint Managing Editor of *Music Business Journal*. He lectures and consults on the European Degree in International Music Management, and holds a Master of Science degree in Business IT Systems. He was a co-founder and first Chairman of New Music in Scotland, and was previously Senior Lecturer in Music Industry Management at Buckinghamshire Chilterns University College.

Resources

BOOKS

The A to Z of Record Labels

Author Brian Southall
Publisher Sanctuary Publishing, 2003
ISBN 1860744923

Inexpensive guide which includes a foreword by Chris Wright – founder of Chrysalis Records. Overview provided of many of the most successful and well-known record companies in a straightforward A to Z format (incorporating 200 labels, from A&M Records to the Zomba Music Group). The recording industry featured leans towards popular music – especially established independent labels and those affiliated to the corporate groups. Entries are also provided for influential labels which had an impact in the past, but are no longer active. Logos are included, and statistics are provided for each entry, giving cumulative totals for No.1 singles and albums in both the US and UK markets. An informative reference book, and one which includes much valuable detail with regard to the (sometimes obscure) origins of well-known record companies, and which may also prove of inspiration to entrepreneurs.

A Century of Recorded Music: Listening to Musical History

Author Timothy Day
Publisher Yale University Press, 2002
ISBN 0300094019

Written by the curator of Western art music at the Sound Archive of the British Library, London, this text explains how our experience of music has been deeply affected by the impact of a century of recording technology. It discusses how our listening habits, and musical performances themselves, have been influenced by innovations in recorded music. Likewise, how a century of recorded music has had its impact upon the images of the artists to which we are exposed, the choice of programming in concert halls and opera houses, and the work of contemporary composers. The role played by famous recording engineer-impresarios such as Fred Gaisberg and Walter Legge is described, as well as the place of conductors, orchestras, and soloists in the evolution of recorded music history. There is also a section on the development of the great classical recording labels.

This text, with its focus on classical music, is a useful addition to the canon of books describing recorded music history, most of which focus on popular music.

Creative Recording I – Effects and Processors (2nd edn)

Author Paul White
Publisher Sanctuary, 2003
ISBN 1860744567

One of the 'Bibles' of music recording, this clear text aims to help lead the reader to an understanding of how to use studio effects and signal processors in the most creative and practical ways in the recording environment. Includes sections on software plug-ins, virtual mixers, and surround-sound technology.

Creative Recording II – Microphones, Acoustics, Soundproofing and Monitoring (2nd edn)

Author Paul White
Publisher Sanctuary, 2003
ISBN 184492002X

Companion volume to that listed above, covering the further topics described in its title.

Creative Recording III – Recording on the Move

Author Paul White
Publisher Sanctuary, 2004
ISBN 1844920674

Companion volume to the 2 listed above.

Creative Sequencing Techniques for Music Production: A Practical Guide for Logic, Digital Performer, Cubase and Pro Tools

Author Andrea Pejrolo
Publisher Focal Press, 2005
ISBN 0240519604

Extremely clear and logical presentation of the subject of music sequencing, with many helpful diagrams. Intended to explain how to get the most out of the 4 leading audio sequencers, the text uses real-life examples to demonstrate a wide range of creative techniques. Begins with the basics and gradually leads to some advanced concepts, and so is suitable for music students as well as acoustic and MIDI composers. Includes a CD-ROM containing loops, templates and audio examples, together with advice on troubleshooting and how to overcome common mistakes.

Directory of BPI Members

Editor Christopher Green
Publisher British Phonographic Industry Limited (Annual)
ISBN No ISBN – see www.bpi.co.uk

A directory of all record labels that are current members of the British Phonographic Industry. Lists their full contact details, specialist music categories and contains a brief summary of each label with particular points of which to be aware. It also contains a useful index by category. Available direct from the BPI.

How to Make and Sell Your Own Recording: The Complete Guide to Independent Recording (Rev. 5th edn)
Author Diane Rapaport (Foreword by Loreena McKennitt)
Publisher Prentice Hall, 1999
ISBN 0139239472

Well structured, and including many pointed illustrations, this title has been through several editions and is acknowledged as vital reading for anyone who wants to understand the whole process of making and selling their own recordings. It is orientated towards the US industry, but readers from other countries should still find it very useful.

The Live Sound Manual
Author Ben Duncan
Publisher Backbeat Books, 2002
ISBN 0879306998

A comprehensive introductory handbook written for sound engineers, musicians and DJs, and including a technical glossary. Covers setting up and using microphones, DI boxes, mixers, EQ, compressors, crossovers, power amps and speakers. With tips on mic placement, EQ-ing, stopping feedback, plus monitoring, troubleshooting and equipment maintenance.

MIDI for the Technophobe (2nd edn)
Author Paul White
Publisher Sanctuary Publishing/Sound on Sound Publications, 2002
ISBN 1860744443

Eminently readable explanation of the important role MIDI plays in contemporary music production, concentrating on its practical use rather than delving into explanations on the nature of the complex technology itself. Includes sections on software instruments and MIDI automation.

Record Label Marketing
Authors Tom Hutchison, Amy Macy, Paul Allen
Publisher Focal Press, 2006
ISBN 0240807871

A US-centred publication, also valuable for UK readers for its comprehensive coverage of theoretical marketing aspects (marketing mix, market segmentation and consumer behaviour), as well as applied corporate marketing processes, recorded music project budgeting, publicity, advertising, retail distribution, marketing research, video production, promotional touring, and the use of special products to build revenue. Includes figures, tables, graphs and glossaries.

Recording and Production Techniques (2nd edn)
Author Paul White
Publisher Sanctuary, 2002
ISBN 1860744435

Readable, large-format book by the editor of *Sound on Sound*. Explains how the role of the producer and studio technology has changed rapidly in the last few years, and focuses on the equipment currently used. Begins with how to plan a recording session and moves on to present a variety of recording techniques, including how to coax the best performance from musicians, and all the stages leading up to mastering and final release. Includes a helpful glossary.

Sound and Recording: An Introduction (5th edn)
Authors Francis Rumsey, Tim McCormick
Publisher Focal Press, 2005
ISBN 0240519965

A comprehensive, easy-to-read reference manual for those at the outset of their careers. Covers basic acoustics, auditory perception, mixing console layout and functions, mixer automation, analogue and digital recording, noise reduction, MIDI, timecode synchronisation, microphone principles and loudspeaker systems. Highly regarded.

MAGAZINES

Computer Music
Editor Ronan Macdonald
Publisher Future Publishing

Monthly magazine which aims to help create music on either PC or Mac. Includes easy-to-follow tutorials for all sorts of music software, reviews of the latest products, and answers to technical questions. The accompanying DVD-ROM often includes free samples, reader demos and other useful software. See **www.computermusic.co.uk**.

Future Music
Editor Oz Owen
Publisher Future Publishing

Monthly magazine from the Future Music stable; presents the latest in music technology with an explanation of its possible and likely uses. Includes reviews, tutorials, advice and interviews, and a DVD-ROM of royalty-free samples and other software.

MusicTech
Editor Neil Worley
Publisher Anthem Publishing
ISSN 1479-4187

A highly regarded magazine for producers, engineers and recording musicians, which includes a DVD-

ROM of royalty-free samples. See
www.musictechmag.co.uk.

Sound on Sound

Editor Paul White
Publisher SOS Publications
ISSN 0951-6816

The leading monthly magazine in the field of
recording, edited by Paul White – well-respected
author of numerous books on music recording and
related subjects. Includes supporting DVD-ROM.
Many back-issue annual article collections are
available on CD, and may be purchased through the
comprehensive SOS website at
www.soundonsound.com.

Labels and distribution
Introduction

At the turn of the millennium, some music industry commentators were predicting the death of the traditional record industry. It was said that music would finally come 'out of its containers' (making CDs redundant, for instance), so that every single piece of music ever written would be held electronically in some great 'celestial jukebox' in the sky (or more likely, within a computer server or across a computer network). All consumers would have instant access to this great pool of digitally stored music, from which they could – on demand – select all the music they wanted. And as music would then become available anywhere, anytime, no-one need 'possess' music any longer.

Certainly, it took time for the major record companies to follow where budding entrepreneurs and innovative new-media companies were heading, but today all the major record companies have important new-media divisions, and – to date – most people still want to 'own' the music that they especially like. With the introduction of new technologies, the likelihood is that record companies of all kinds will have more, not less, opportunity for sales of their music – and by an increasing variety of means. One of the many ways in which the record industry is certainly unique lies in the fact that its product is often given to you 'for free' (when it is broadcast on the radio, for instance, or over the Internet). Then, if you really like it, you can choose to buy it in some form (held on a CD, or as a download for your MP3 player, etc.). With most other products, you are required to purchase the product *before*, not *after*, you've initially 'consumed' it.

Of course, like the share market, the recorded music market has seen many peaks and troughs over the past few decades. But although the value of CD sales seems currently to be on the wane in the developed world, there is no reason to think that new-media technologies won't soon open up new markets and embrace new customers – once such technology can be fully harnessed and made to pay its way. The recording industry was, in fact, founded on the notion of selling 'sound carriers' – a concept still exemplified by traditional recording contracts. It has been a challenge for many in the industry to accept that this situation may at last be set to change.

Yet irrespective of whether music is possessed in physical carriers or accessed electronically, the essential conundrum for musicians, songwriters, composers, publishers and record labels has never changed: it is centred on the problem of how to make potential consumers *aware* of your music ... and, then, how to target precisely these customers and sell them your particular musical product (while keeping costs as low as possible, for these costs are often substantial).

It should, therefore, come as no surprise that each record label usually represents a very particular musical genre or 'niche market'. The artist/composer needs to find a label that is a perfect fit for them, and the label in turn needs to find customers who perfectly fit its music. This is the real challenge for any new artist, and there are no easy answers as to how this can be done: knowledge and perseverance will help, though the effort required, and the obstacles to be overcome, may sometimes seem like choosing voluntarily to undertake all the labours of Hercules at once! At least the goal will rarely change, and this should stay permanently fixed in your mind: it lies in finding the ideal record label for your musical style, and being persuaded that this label has such efficient means of distribution – through traditional physical and/or electronic means – that any consumer who wants your music (anywhere in the world) can easily pay for, and receive it – whether by means of a celestial jukebox or not!

MUSIC CURRY

"The A&R man switched off the stereo, and swung to face me in his black leather office lounger. (Picture Jeremy Clarkson at his most quizzical.)

'It puts me in mind of a ... curry,' he said.

'A curry?' I asked.

'Yeah, you know – it's a hot, spicy dish, often served in Indian restaurants.'

'Yes, yes,' I spluttered, 'but what on earth has that got to do with the song I just played you?'

He hit the hook without blinking. 'The overall effect's not too bad, but if you really examine the ingredients, the quality just ain't there.'

Wow, A&R dagger straight to the heart, Batman!

Nowadays, I'd probably counter with something bullish like, 'Great! Curry's just replaced fish and chips as the national favourite, so it's bound to do well.' But I was younger then, and was still heard muttering ineffective excuses as I was ushered out of the building, and into the freezing London drizzle.

The moral? Cruel rejection is a reality of life for the writer/composer, but you must not let it put you off your stride. Cole Porter suffered enormous disappointments during his illustrious career – and wrote more than 1000 songs, for his 30-ish worldwide standards. So my advice? 'Keep it coming!'"

Dominic King's hits include 'Modern Girl', 'My Simple Heart' and 'Music Sounds Better With You'. See **www.thesongguru.org** for details of songwriting seminars.

Record labels

3 Beat Music Ltd

3 Beat Records, 5 Slater Street, Liverpool L1 4BW
tel 0151-709 3355 *fax* 0151-703 0503
email sales@3beat.co.uk
website www.threebeatrecords.co.uk

Liverpool-based dance music label offering online downloads.

14th Floor Records

Electric Lighting Station, 46 Kensington Court,
London W8 5DA
tel 020-7938 5500 *fax* 020-7368 4928
email firstname.lastname@warnermusic.com
website www.14thfloorrecords.com
A&R Manager Alex Gilbert

Home to artists such as Ray LaMontagne, Nerina Pallot, The Wombats and Damien Rice. Potential acts should make contact via the website.

Additive Records

EMI House, 43 Brook Green, London W6 7EF
tel 020-7605 5000 *fax* 020-7605 5050
email firstname.lastname@emimusic.com
website www.additiverecords.co.uk
A&R Manager Ben Cherrill

Founded in 1996 by Positiva to represent the underground club scene and experimental music, in order to provide crossover successes – **see Positiva.**

Asylum Records

PO Box 121, Hove, East Sussex BN3 4YY
tel (01273) 774468
email Asylum2006@gmail.com
website www.asylumrecords.com

Originally founded as a rock label by David Geffen in 1971, changing to a country label. Now dedicated to hip hop recording and part of Warner's Independent Label group.

Atlantic Records

Electric Lighting Station, 46 Kensington Court,
London W8 5DA
tel 020-7938 5500
email info@atlanticrecords.co.uk
website www.atlanticrecords.co.uk
Managing Director Max Lousada

Founded in 1947 as a jazz and R&B label and now part of Warner's Atlantic Records group. Artists include: Notorius BIG, Jewel, James Blunt, and Sean Paul.

Bedrock Records

Reverb House, Bennett Street, London W4 2AH
tel 020-8742 7670 *fax* 020-8994 8617
email info@bedrock.uk.net
website www.bedrock.uk.net
Label Manager Nick Bates

Deals with progressive house/breaks. Recent releases include: Bedrock – 'Heaven Scent'; Lemon 9 – 'Lose Control'; and Guy Gerber – 'Stoppage Time'. Potential clients should email for more information.

Beggars Banquet Records

17-19 Alma Road, London SW18 1AA
email beggars@beggars.com
website www.beggars.com

Founded circa 1981. Originally an independent punk label. Artists signed have included: The Ramones, The Fall, The Prodigy, Badly Drawn Boy and Tindersticks. Potential acts should post demos on CD, vinyl or cassette to the A&R department at the above address. Please see the website for requirements. No submissions via email.

Candid Productions Ltd

16 Castelnau, London SW13 9RU
tel 020-8741 3608 *fax* 020-8563 0013
email info@candidrecords.com
website www.candidrecords.com
Managing Director Alan Bates

Independent label founded in New York in 1960. Specialises in modern and mainstream jazz, world jazz, blues and latin. Back catalogue includes recordings by artists such as Charles Mingus, Booker Little and Eric Dolphy. Developing artists include Jamie Cullum, Terell Stafford, Jessica Williams and Hector Martignon.

Caritas Records

Achmore, Moss Road, Ullapool,
Ross & Cromarty IV26 2TF
tel/fax (01854) 612938
email caritas-records@caritas-music.co.uk
website www.caritas-music.co.uk
Managing Director James Douglas

Founded in 1986. A classical record company with labels including Caritas, Caritas Classics, Caritas Media and Caritas Live. Recent output includes: 'Caritas Live No. 9' and 'Caritas Live No. 10' by James Douglas. Also provides a music production library for TV, film, video and DVD. Does not accept unsolicited material.

Chandos Records

Chandos House, 1 Commerce Park,
Commerce Way, Colchester, Essex CO2 8HX
tel (01206) 225200 *fax* (01206) 225201
email enquiries@chandos.net
website www.chandos.net
Sales Contact Dave Martin

One of the world's premier classical music record companies, best known for searching out 'neglected gems'. The company has pioneered the idea of the 'series' and proudly includes series from composers such as Prokofiev, Tchaikovsky, Haydn and Walton – with ongoing series of Berkeley, Bridge and Yoshimatsu. The catalogue contains over 1500 titles, and includes recordings of music, ancient and modern, by composers from around the globe.

Columbia Records

Bedford House, 67-69 Fulham High Street, London SW6 3JW
tel 020-7384 7500
email info@columbia.co.uk
website www.columbia.co.uk
Managing Director Mike Smith

Part of the Sony BMG group. Acts include: Jamiroquai, Incubus, Editors and Matisyahu.

Concrete Recordings

35 Beech Road, Chorlton, Manchester M21 8BX
tel 0161-881 2332 *fax* 0161-860 7283
email sarah@concreterecordings.co.uk
website www.concreterecordings.co.uk
Director Sarah Purcell

Established in 2004. Deals with a wide variety of music genres. Releases include: 'Glastonbury Unsigned Bands' 2004 and 2005, and music by The Deadbeats. Potential clients should forward demos to the above address. Also provides press service and promotional services.

Crash Records

PO Box 13, Chinnor, Oxon OX39 4Q6
tel (01844) 353154
email info@crash-records.co.uk
website www.crash-records.co.uk
Head of A&R Michele

Founded in 2001. Aims to help new and emerging talent reach their potential. Works within rock, pop, punk and metal genres. Clients include: Hedroom, Simple Reason, Andensum, Tim Matthews, John Leyton, Guessworks and Soverin. Also provides management, agency, recording studio, PR and marketing, digital distribution and gig promotion services.

DB Records

PO Box 19318, Bath BA1 6ZS
tel (01225) 782322
email demo@dbrecords.co.uk
website www.dbrecords.co.uk
A&R Representatives David Bates, Chris Hughes

Founded in 1998. Aims to discover, promote and assist young artists. Interested in a range of genres including pop, rock, electronica, world and ethnic. Recent clients include: Tom McRae, Psychid, and High and Lonesome. Accepts submissions by post,

but email, postal and telephone contact must be supplied by sender. Will contact all senders if email is provided, but note 6-week backlog. Also provides independent A&R and production.

Decca Music Group

Universal Classics & Jazz (UK),
364-366 Kensington High Street, London W14 8NS
tel 020-7747 4000 *fax* 020-7747 4599
website www.deccaclassics.com
Managing Director Bill Holland

Division of Universal Classics and Jazz (UK).

Decca UK

Universal Classics & Jazz (UK),
364-366 Kensington High St, London W14 8NS
tel 020-7471 5000 *fax* 020-7471 5001
website www.deccaclassics.com
Managing Director Dickon Stainer

Division of Universal Classics also known as Decca Music Group. Previously signed Louis Armstrong, Billie Holiday and Judy Garland. Current acts include a variety of singers, instrumentatlists, conductors, composers, ensembles and crossover artists. Roster includes: Andrea Bocelli, Jose Carreras, Hayley Westenra and Ludovico Einaudi.

Democracy Records

Upper York Street, Earlsdon, Coventry, Warwickshire CV1 3GQ
tel 024-7622 9341 *fax* 024-7622 9341
email admin@glasshouseproductions.co.uk
website www.democracymusic.co.uk
Director Amos Anderson

Founded in 1979. Aims to promote, develop and deliver viable quality products into the music industry mainstream. Markets locally, nationally and internationally. Deals with a range of genres, including reggae, ragga, hiphop, R&B, house, pop and rock. Recent releases include: 'Zero Time' – Selector; 'Remember me' – Shirzell; 'How' – Robbie G; 'On a Mission' – D-Dubs; and 'Stretch is on His Way' – Stretch. Potential clients should submit package with 3-5 tracks (with lyrics), biography and giglist (past and future) via post. Also offers recording studio, training and publishing.

Deutsche Grammophon

Universal Classics & Jazz (UK),
364-366 Kensington High Street, London W14 8NS
tel 020-7471 5000 *fax* 020-7471 5001
email info@umusic.com
website www.universalclassics.com
Managing Director Bill Holland

Division of Universal Classics and Jazz (UK). Current signings include: Bryn Terfel, Elvis Costello, Andre Previn and Leonard Bernstein.

Digimix Records

Sovereign House, 12 Trewartha Road, Praa Sands, Penzance, Cornwall TR20 9ST

tel (01736) 762826 *fax* (01736) 763328
email panamus@aol.com
website www.digimixrecords.com
Managing Director Roderick Jones

Founded in 1989. Works with songwriters, composers, singer/songwriters, bands, musicians, singers, DJs, remixers, MCs and producers across all styles of music. Deals with publishing in-house as part of the Panama Music Group of Companies (see **www.panamamusic.co.uk**). Interested to hear from acts both established and up-and-coming. See website for submission details.

Dilute Recordings

The Lodge, St Martha's Priory, Halfpenny Lane, Guildford GU4 8PZ
tel/fax (01483) 449852
email adi@diluterecordings.com
website www.diluterecordings.com
Label Manager Adi Winman

Founded in 2005. Deals in popular and classical recordings, sound effects and music for computer games.

Distinctive Records

The Heals Building, A3 Third Floor, 22-24 Torrington Place, London WC1E 7HJ
tel 020-7240 1399
email info@distinctiverecords.com
website www.distinctiverecords.com

Dance label hosting big-name acts and remixers such as Hybrid. Potential acts should submit all material for the attention of the A&R department at the above address.

DOR

PO Box 1797, London E1 4TZ
tel 020-7702 7842
email info@dor.co.uk
website www.dor.co.uk
Label Manager Martin Parker

Aims to be a catalyst and sponsor of new musical forms. Often deals with multimedia form including video, interactive enhanced CDs and artwork created by the musicians themselves.

Drowned in Sound Recordings

1 Chilworth Mews, London W2 3RG
tel 020-7087 8880 *fax* 020-7087 8899
email info@disrecords.com
website www.drownedinsound.com

Hip indie/alternative label with roster including releases from Martha Wainwright and Brett Anderson.

EMI Catalogue

43 Brook Green, London W6 7EF
tel 020-7605 5000
email info@emimusic.com
website www.nowmusic.com or www.emicatalogue.com

Catalogue of releases from EMI and associated companies. Releases include box sets, classic album re-issues and 'Best of's'.

EMI Classics UK

43 Brook Green, London W6 7EF
tel 020-7605 5000 *fax* 020-7605 5050
email firstname.lastname@emic.co.uk
website www.emiclassics.com
Managing Director Thomas Kaurich

Founded in 1990. Historical re-issues include landmark achievements by artists such as Vladmir Horowitz, Jacqueline du Pre and Pablo Casals. The Debut series aims to support artists at the beginning of international careers.

EMI Gold

43 Brook Green, London W6 7EF
tel 020-7605 5000
email info@emimusic.com
website www.emirecordedmusic.com
Co MDs, EMI Marketing Steve Pritchard, Peter Duckworth

Founded in 1996. Contains EMI back catalogue including original studio albums and hits collections. Acts featured include: Frank Sinatra, Cliff Richard, Blondie and UB40.

EMI Group plc (Headquarters)

27 Wrights Lane, London W8 5SW
tel 020-7795 7000 *fax* 020-7795 7001
email info@emimusic.com
website www.emigroup.com
Chairman Eric Nicoli

EMI Group comprises EMI Music and EMI Music Publishing. Largest independent music company in the world. Represents more than 1000 artists worldwide and is home to 6000 employees, with reported profits of £125 million in 2005.

EMI Liberty

43 Brook Green, London W6 7EF
tel 020-7605 5000
email info@emimusic.com
website www.emimusic.co.uk or www.emicatalogue.com

Founded in 2001. Releases material from both new and established artists. Aims to embrace unique and lateral marketing opportunities.

EMI Music UK and Ireland

43 Brook Green, London W6 7EF
tel 020-7605 5000 *fax* 020-7605 5050
email info@emimusic.com
website www.emimusic.co.uk
Chairman and CEO Tony Wadsworth

EMI Music UK and Ireland is the regional operating company for EMI Music – the largest successful independent music company worldwide and dating back to 1897. EMI Music UK consists of Capitol Music (containing Parlophone and EMI Records labels) and Virgin Music (containing Virgin Records and Innocent Labels). It also has a number of affiliated labels that exist as separate business units. These include EMI Classics, Heavenly Records and Positiva.

EMI Records

EMI House, 43 Brook Green, London W6 7EF
tel 020-7605 5000 *fax* 020-7605 5050
email info@emimusic.com
website www.emirecords.co.uk
Senior A&R Manager George Tyekiff

Part of EMI Music. Acts affiliated include: Pink Floyd, Iron Maiden, Kate Bush and Robbie Williams. Partnerships with Heavenly Recordings and Positiva.

Freeport Records

324 Beaux Arts Building, 10-18 Manor Gardens, London N7 6JW
tel (07796) 950406
email harry@freeportrecords.com
website www.freeportrecords.com
Managing Director Harry Leckstein

Founded in 2003. Independent record label, consultancy and artist management company. Creates unique youth music projects for local and national governments such as 'London Urban Collective' and 'Get Heard'. Recent releases include: Pink Punk 'Zoo Politics', London Urban Collective I, II and III, and Luminous Frenzy 'Violence Ambience'. Potential clients can view projects and artist on the website, **www.freeportrecords.com**.

Futureproof Music

PO Box 31631, London W11 1UA
tel 020-7221 6520 *fax* 020-7221 3694
email info@futureproofmusic.com
website www.futureproofrecords.com
Managing Director Phil Legg

Founded in 2003. Output includes urban, hip hop, reggae, D&B, breakbeat and dance genres. Potential acts may submit material with a press release/artist profile to the above address. Also provides marketing and promotion, consultancy, distribution and events services.

Global Warming

PO Box 5192, Hatfield Peveral, Chelmsford, Essex CM3 2QH
email trevglobalwarming@supalife.com
website www.globalwarmingrecords.com
Director Trevor Holden

Founded in 1997. Recent releases include: Liam Lynch – 'United States of Whatever'; Helene – 'Postcard'; and Smother – 'Great White Hoax'. Covers all genres from singer/songwriter to rock with the exception of dance. Potential clients should submit a clearly labelled demo.

Gronland Records

9-10 Domingo Street, London EC1Y 0TA
tel 020-7553 9166 *fax* 020-7553 9198
email thebear@groenland.com
website www.groenland.com or
www.myspace.com/gronlandrecords
Managing Director Rene Renner

Aims to keep music and craft at its heart. Deals with all genres including pop, rock, R&B, hip hop, electronica and dance. Potential artists should submit a demo CD by post.

Handspun Records

64 Harbour Street, Whitstable, Kent CT5 1AG
email handspun@haveaniceday.ws
Director Anthony Cooper

Specialises in developing 'enviromental and lifestyle' pop. 'Don't do the Dodo' is amongst recent releases. Potential clients should make contact via email. Currently actively looking for tracks.

Heavenly Recordings

47 Frith Street, London W1D 4SE
tel 020-7494 2998 *fax* 020-7437 3317
email info@heavenlyrecordings.com
website www.heavenly100.com

Endeavours to deliver the finest quality records in any genre. Acts include: Doves, Ed Harcourt, The Magic Numbers, The Little Ones and Cherry Ghost.

Holier Than Thou Records

46 Rother Street, Stratford on Avon, Warwickshire CV37 6LTT
tel (01789) 268661
email David@HolierThanThouRecords.com
website www.holierthanthourecords.com
Label Manager David Begg

Rock, indie, alternative, punk and metal label. Targets university and independent radio, clubs venues, rock press, online and printed zines with new releases. Reports back to an artist at least 2 x per month with updates on reactions. Potential acts should post demos to the above address.

Hope Recordings

Hope Music Group, Loft 5, The Tobacco Factory, Raleigh Road, Southville, Bristol BS1 5JA
tel 0117-953 5566
email luke@hoperecordings.com
website www.hoperecordings.co.uk
Label Manager Luke Allen

Dance label with roster including Starecase, Jaytech and Parallel Sound.

Hyperion Records Ltd

PO Box 25, London SE9 1AX
tel 020-8318 1234 *fax* 020-8463 1230
email info@hyperion-records.co.uk
website www.hyperion-records.co.uk

Independent British classical label founded in 1890. Specialises in the recording of sacred, choral, solo, vocal, orchestral, chamber and instrumental music from all periods of early and classical movements. Multi-award-winning, notably the 1996 'Best Label' by MIDEM at the Cannes Classiques Awards.

Independent Records Ltd
PO Box 30884, London W12 9AX
tel 020-8746 7461 *fax* 020-8749 7441
email info@independentrecordsltd.com
website www.irl.org.uk
Director Tom Haxell

Founded in 2003. Works within the pop, rock, folk and world music genres. Roster includes: Damien Dempsey, The Wonder Stuff, Royseven, The Bellagios, Priya Thomas and Miles Hunt. Typically offers 50/50 deals or licensing. For postal submissions, include a stamped addressed envelope if you wish your work to be returned. Email submissions also possible – include a link to your site.

Independiente Ltd
website www.independiente.co.uk
Founder Andy MacDonald

Established in 1997. Responsible for signings such as Travis, Embrace, Gomez and The Tears.

Innerground Records Ltd
8 Roland Mews, Stepney Green, London E1 3JT
tel 020-7929 3333 *fax* 020-7929 3222
email oliver@bulldozermedia.com
website www.innergroundrecords.com
Managing Director Oliver Brown

Releases a range of dance, D&B, techno and house. Potential clients should send demos by post on CD or vinyl.

Innocent Records
Kensal House, 553-579 Harrow Road,
London W10 4RH
tel 020-8962 5800 *fax* 020-8962 5801
email info@virginmusic.com
website www.the-raft.com

Formed in 1998 as a Virgin Records imprint. Specialises in pop releases. Successes have included 2 No.1 singles from Billie Piper, and Martine McCutcheon's No. 1, 'Perfect Moment'.

Island Records
22 St Peter's Square, London W6 9NW
tel 020-8910 3333 *fax* 020-8748 1998
email info@umusic.com
website www.islandrecords.co.uk
Managing Director Nick Gatfield

Originally established as a Jamaican label in 1959 and now part of the Universal group. Responsible for many major signings, including Bob Marley, U2 and Frankie Goes to Hollywood; more recently,

Sugababes, Amy Winehouse and Mika. Potential acts should post demos for the attention of the A&R manager.

Kickin' Music Ltd
282 Westbourne Park Road, Notting Hill,
London W11 1EH
tel 020-7985 0700 *fax* 020-7985 0701
email christian@kickinmusic.com
website www.kickinmusic.com
Head of A&R Christian Larsson

Founded in 1990. Comprises 3 independent record labels based in-house (Slip n' Slide), dance/crossover/trance (Kickin' Records) and D&B (Hard Leaders). Releases have included: DeLacy – 'Hideaway 2005'; King Britt – 'Our Time'; and Tiger Stripes – 'Vem Sambar'. Potential clients should submit material via CDR, links or MP3s. Also provides publishing through Haripa Music Publishing and a Phonographic Performance Royalties Collection Service – 'Music Data Tracking'.

Kitchenware Records
7 The Stables, Saint Thomas Street,
Newcastle Upon Tyne NE1 4LE
tel 0191-230 1970 *fax* 0191-232 0262
email info@kitchenwarerecords.com
website www.kitchenwarerecords.com
Managing Director Keith Armstrong

Established in 1982. Roster includes: Editors, The Changes and Sirens. Currently accepting submissions in all genres; potential artists should email a link to a myspace page.

Matador Records
17-19 Alma Road, London SW18 1AA
tel 020-8875 6202 *fax* 020-8969 6633
email info@matadorrecords.com
website www.matadorrecords.com
Managing Director Mike Houldsworth

Founded in 1989. Diverse international indie label. Signings include: Yo La Tengo, Mogwai, Pavement, and Belle and Sebastian. Does not accept unsolicited demo submissions.

Matchbox Recordings Ltd
3 Gilt Edge House, 33 Bath Street, Abingdon,
Oxon OX14 3RH
tel (01235) 559800
email info@matchboxrecordings.co.uk
website www.matchboxrecordings.co.uk
Head of A&R/Director Dale Olivier *A&R Manager* Will Sherman

Founded in 2000. Specialises in releasing new music compilations featuring brand new independent bands and artists. Also offers radio plugging, CD manufacturing, Internet distribution service and runs own radio station – Matchbox Radio 24. Works with indie, rock and pop artists and bands. Recent compilation releases include: 'Spotlight On', 'Recovery' and 'Groovycide'. Potential clients should post a CD demo or an MP3 demo to demos@matchboxrecordings.co.uk.

Mate Recordings International

PO Box 4149, Manchester M60 1ZH
email info@materecordings.com
website www.materecordings.com

Aims to celebrate the irregular and international underground modern movements in electronic arts and music. Deals with mainly electronic music – see current roster for more info. Potential artists should post a demo CD.

Mercury Records

364-366 Kensington High Street, London W14 8NS
tel 020-7471 5000 *fax* 020-7471 5001
email firstname.lastname@umusic.com
website www.mercuryrecords.co.uk
Marketing Director Richard Marshall

Part of the Universal group. Acts have included: Just Jack, Fall Out Boy, Lucie Silvas and The Killers. Potential acts should post 3 track demos to the above address.

Mohock Records

Sovereign House, 12 Trewartha Road, Praa Sands, Penzance, Cornwall TR20 9ST
tel (01736) 762826 *fax* (01736) 763328
email panamus@aol.com
website www.panamamusic.co.uk
Managing Director Roderick Jones

Founded in 1987. Works with folk and roots artists. Album releases include: Pete Arnold – *The Drums of Childhood Dreams*; Frank – *A Band Called Frank*; and Willow – *Folk & Country*. Potential acts and artists should post clearly labelled CD submissions with biographies, photos and sae.

MOMT Records

13 Chesterfield Road, Newbury, Berkshire RG14 7QB
tel (07887) 547731
email contact@momt.co.uk
website www.momt.co.uk
Director Ian Proudfoot

Founded in 2003. Specialises in left-field electronic music, covering such genres as electronica, IDM, techno, industrial and ambient. Recent releases include: Holon – 'Some Kind of Order'; and Shinis Yamashita – 'Kanashmi'. Welcomes emails from potential clients (without attachment initially). No group emails – see website for more details.

Mook Records

PO Box 155, Leeds, West Yorkshire LS72XN
tel 0113-230 4008 *fax* 0113-230 2008
email mail@mookhouse.ndo.co.uk
website www.mookhouse.ndo.co.uk
Label Manager Phil Mayne

Established in 2000 as a small independent record label. Resident in its own studio and rehearsal-room complex. Current artists include: Percy, Rudolph Rocker and Pop Threat.

Neon Records

19 Marine Crescent, Glasgow G51 IHD
tel 0141-429 6366 *fax* 0141-429 637
email Mail@go2neon.com
website www.go2neon.com
Key Contact Stephanie Pordage

Founded in 2000. Specialises in young acoustic/roots performers and songwriters. Recent releases include: Karine Polwart, The Cellers, Rab Noakes and Faultlines. Potential acts should email prior to submission.

Parlophone Records

43 Brook Green, London W6 7EF
tel 020-7605 5438
email nathan.thompson@emimusic.com
A&R Manager Nathan Thompson

Became part of the EMI group in 1931. Famously signed The Beatles in 1962 and went on to sign well-established acts such as Queen, Coldplay, Kylie Minogue and Gorillaz. Potential clients should submit material by post or email, or enquire by phone.

Philips Music Group

Universal Classics & Jazz (UK),
364-366 Kensington High Street, London W14 8NS
tel 020-7471 5000 *fax* 020-7471 5001
email firstname.lastname@umusic.com
website www.universalclassics.com
Managing Director Bill Holland

Division of Universal Classics and Jazz (UK). Current signings include: Jose Carreras, Donny Osmond, John Williams, Hans Zimmer and Julian Lloyd Webber.

Planet Records

11 New Market Street, Colne, Lancashire BB8 9BJ
tel (01282) 866317
email info@pendlehawkmusic.co.uk
website www.pendlehawkmusic.co.uk
Managing Director Adrian Melling

Founded in 1982. Distributes to UK retail shops (including mixed media retail, i.e. bookshops) and online worldwide. Deals mainly with folk, blues, jazz and country genres. Clients have included: Planet Records, Slam, Leo, and Old Bridge. Also provides a booking and promotions service for UK tours, Planet Records (label) and contains an in-house 24-track recording studio.

Polydor UK

Black Lion House, 72-80 Black Lion Lane, London W6 9BE
tel 020-8910 4800 *fax* 020-8910 4801

email info@umusic.com
website www.polydor.co.uk
Joint MDs David Joseph, Colin Barlow

Part of the Universal group. Acts include: Black Eyed Peas, Guillemots, Kaiser Chiefs and Snow Patrol. Potential acts should post 3 track demos to the above address.

Positiva

43 Brook Green, London W6 7EF
tel 020-7605 5157 *fax* 020-7605 5186
website www.positivarecords.com
Director Jason Ellis

Respected commercial house label founded by EMI Records in 1993. Deals with booking, promoting and disitributing. Clients have included: The Source, feat. Candi Staton ('You Got the Love'); Deep Dish, feat. Stevie Nicks ('Dreams'); and Shapeshifters ('Incredible'). Also contains the Additive imprint. Potential artists should post material to the above address.

Priory Records Ltd

3 Eden Court, Leighton Buzzard, Beds LU7 4FY
tel (01525) 377566 *fax* (01525) 371477
email sales@priory.org.uk
website www.priory.org.uk
Managing Director Neil Collier

Choral and organ music label. Recent output includes: Gillian Weir and 'Complete New English Hymnal', consisting of texts and history of 542 hymns sung by 23 different choirs. Potential clients may submit material via email, fax or by post. Also provides a label distribution service.

Pure Gold Records

Sovereign House, 12 Trewartha Road, Praa Sands, Penzance, Cornwall TR20 9ST
tel (01736) 762826 *fax* (01736) 763328
email panamus@aol.com
website www.panamamusic.co.uk
Managing Director Roderick Jones

Founded in 1988. Works with country, easy listening and pop (nostalgia) genres including re-issues. Album releases include: PJ Proby – *Thanks*; Cadillacs – *Johnny Remember Me*; and Willow – *Memories*. Potential acts and artists should post clearly labelled CD submissions with biographies, photos and sae.

Rainy Day Records

Sovereign House, 12 Trewartha Road, Praa Sands, Penzance, Cornwall TR20 9ST
tel (01736) 762826 *fax* (01736) 763328
email panamamus@aol.com
website www.panamamusic.co.uk
Managing Director Roderick Jones

Founded in 1986. Specialises in working with unsigned acts, songwriters and composers, promoting no-gain licensing and publishing deals and shopping

artists to record companies. Works with all genres of music. Releases include a 4-part series of 'Songwriters and Artistes Showcase' albums. Potential clients should send audio/visual material with biog, photos, giglists, info on any previous contracts and sae for return contact. Also provides studio facilities and consultancy service.

RCA Label Group

Bedford House, 67-69 Fulham High Street, London SW6 3JW
tel 020-7384 7500
email info@rca-records.co.uk
website www.rca-records.co.uk

Part of the Sony BMG group. Acts include: Britney Spears, Justin Timberlake, Jennifer Lopez and Natalie Imbruglia.

Regal Recordings

EMI House, 43 Brook Green, London W6 7EF
tel 020-7605 5000 *fax* 020-7605 5050
email info@emimusic.com
website www.regal.co.uk

Affiliated to the EMI group. Aims to release fresh and interesting music across a range of genres.

Relentless Records

Kensal House, 553-579 Harrow Road, London W10 4RH
tel 020-8964 6720 *fax* 020-8964 6720
email firstname@mvillage.co.uk
website www.relentless-records.net

Established in 1999. Aims to represent the best British urban music. Acts have included: So Solid Crew, Pied Piper, Joss Stone, and Masters of Ceremonies.

Sanctuary Records Group

Sanctuary House, 45-53 Sinclair Road, London W14 0NS
tel 020-7602 6351 *fax* 020-7603 5941
email info@sanctuaryclassics.com
website www.sanctuaryrecordsgroup.co.uk
CEO Joe Cokell

Formed in 1976 and now a major independent record label looking after around 120 acts. Endeavours to sign artists with long-term appeal. Catalogue includes: Dokken, Morrissey, New York Dolls, and The Charlatans.

Series 8

PO Box 5192, Hatfield Peverel, Chelmsford, Essex CM3 2QH
email series8@supalife.com
website www.series8records.co.uk or www.myspace.com/series8

Founded in 2005. Deals with all genres from singer/ songwriter to rock. Recent releases include: Helene – 'Routines'; Magoo – 'All Electric ...'; and Oom – 'Dead Analogue'.

Skint/Loaded Records

PO Box 174, Brighton BN1 4BA
tel (01273) 738527 *fax* (01273) 208766
email mail@skint.net
website www.skint.net or
www.myspace.com/skintrecords
Label Manager Damian Harris

Eclectic young record label with a varied selection of clients. Roster includes: Ralfe Band, Fatboy Slim, Midfield General and Space Raiders. Demos should be sent to the above contact for consideration.

Solarise Records

PO Box 31104, London E16 4UE
tel (07980) 453628
email info@solariserecords.co.uk
website www.solariserecords.co.uk
Owner Paul Fackerell

Established in 2003. Aims to showcase, promote, release and sell all genres of independent unsigned music online. Caters for all music genres. Recent releases include: 'Light Years Ahead' (various), and 'Autumn Acoustics' (acoustic). Potential clients should submit material via email with an online link to samples, or by post. Also provdes an MP3 and CD shop including ringtones.

Some Bizzare

14 Tottenham Court Road, London W1T 1JY
tel 020-7836 9995 *fax* 020-8348 2526
email info@somebizzare.com
website www.somebizzare.com
Label Manager Stephen John Pearce

Founded in 1980. Mainstream terroristic pioneering dance label. Clients include: MFF, Meka, Soft Cell and Dark Poets. Potential clients should submit material to the above address.

Sonic 360

33 Riding House Street, London W1W 7DZ
tel 020-7636 3939 *fax* 020-7636 0033
email zen@sonic360.com
website www.sonic360.com
Label Manager Zen Grisdale

Founded in 2000. An eclectic label covering a variety of genres but specialising in latin and rock. Recent output includes: Kayip – 'Kayip'; Tammy – 'Amor de Computadora'; and Almeida Girl and Descarga – 'Llanita'. Potential clients should submit demos by post.

Sony BMG Music Entertainment UK and Ireland

Bedford House, 67-69 Fulham High Street, London SW6 3JW
tel 020-7384 7500 *fax* 020 7371 9298
email info@sonybmg.com
website www.sonybmgmusic.co.uk
Chairman Tim Bowen

A major 'Big 4' record company founded in 2004 as a result of a joint venture between Sony Music Entertainment and BMG Entertainment. Includes labels such as Arista Records, Columbia Records, Epic Records, Jive Records, RCA Victor, RCA Records and Sonic Wave America. Potential acts should send a 3-track demo to the above address.

Sony Classical

Bedford House, 67-69 Fulham High Street, London SW6 3JW
tel 020-7384 7500 *fax* 020-7371 9298
email firstname.lastname@sonybmg.com
website www.sonybmgmasterworks.com
Chairman Tim Bowen

Part of the Sony BMG group overseeing and promoting its artists to the classical market.

Spin Out Records Ltd

Global House, Bridge Street, Guildford GU1 4SB
tel (01483) 501211 *fax* (01483) 501201
email info@spinoutrecords.co.uk
website www.spinoutrecords.co.uk or
www.myspace.com/spinoutrecords
Label Manager Audrey Kocharoff

House and breaks label based in Guildford, working with artists such as Meat Katie, Switch, Atomic Hooligan, Dylan Rhymes, Rich Dinsdale, Shafunkers, Metric and Vandal. Running for 3 years. Unique in its commitment to releasing at least 1 house and 1 breaks mix on each vinyl. This approach has earned plaudits from some of the scene's biggest players, such as Fergie, Annie Nightingale, Sasha, Timo Maas and Steve Lawler; No.1 in the Beatport download charts and regular 5-star reviews in *DJmag* and *IDJ*. For more info on Spin Out, check out **www.spinoutrecords.co.uk**, **www.myspace.com/ spinoutrecords** or **www.dontstayin.com/parties/ spin-out-records**.

Splank! Records

3rd Floor, 24-26 Lever Street, Manchester M1 1DZ
tel (07748) 643170
email info@splankrecords.co.uk
website www.splankrecords.co.uk
Label Manager Chris Hughes

Established in 2003. Works primarily with breaks and dance. Aims to deliver funky and fun breaks with 1970s/1980s funk and disco influence. Has attracted remixes from Drumattic Twins and Scissorkicks, alongside releases by Groove Allegiance, Sgt Rock, Myagi and Simon Paul. Potential clients should post completed material. Contact accepted via email but no emailed MP3s. Please see website to ensure that material is of a relevant style. Also provides DJ agency, remix work and compilation licensing services.

Sunday Best Recordings

Studio 11 (3rd Floor), 25 Denmark Street, London WC2H 8NJ

tel 020-7379 3133 *fax* 0870-420 4392
email info@sundaybest.net or julian@sundaybest.net
website www.sundaybest.net
Product Manager Julian Peck

Established in 1995. Genres covered include house, techno, indie, pop and rock. Grand National – 'Playing in the distance'; Kompis – 'In Somebody's Spot'; and Kish Mauve EP are among recent releases. Potential clients should make contact via email or submit material by post.

Supercharged/Against The Grain
2nd Floor, 29 Kensington Gardens,
Brighton BN1 4AL
tel (01273) 628181 *fax* (01278) 670444
email lloyd@superchargedmusic.com
website www.superchargedmusic.com
Label Manager Lloyd Seymour

Founded in 2001. Specialises in breakbeats. Recent output features: Freestylers – 'Ran as F**k'; 'Push Up'; and Krafty Kuts – 'Freakshow'. Potential clients should submit a CD by post. Also provides a clubnight promotions and TV licensing service.

Tru Thoughts
PO Box 2818, Brighton BN1 4RL
fax (01273) 694589
email mail@tru-thoughts.co.uk
website www.tru-thoughts.co.uk
A&R Manager Robert Luis *Label Manager* Paul Jonas

Founded in 1999. Releases a diversity of styles with a particular orientation towards jazz, breaks, hip hop, soul and funk. Releases include: 'My Favourite Letters' – Alice Russell; and 'When Shapes Come Together' – a trilogy of compilations. Accepts material via CD. Advises potential clients to visit website to ensure suitability of style, and to ensure that material is clearly labelled with email given.

Universal Classics and Jazz (UK)
364-366 Kensington High Street, London W14 8NS
tel 020-7471 5000 *fax* 020-7471 5001
email info@umusic.com
website www.universalclassics.com
Managing Director Bill Holland

Part of the Universal group. Holding site for labels including Decca, Phillips and Deutsche Grammophon.

Universal Music International (Headquarters)
364-366 Kensington High Street, London W14 8NS
tel 020-7471 5000 *fax* 020-7471 5001
email info@umusic.com
website www.universalclassics.com
Chariman and CEO Lucian Grainge

The international global offices of one of the biggest major record companies in the industry, hosting some of the world's biggest artists including Eminem, U2, Luciano Pavarotti and Kanye West. This particular office handles artists and acts outside of North America. The parent company oversees an amalgam of sub-labels.

Universal Music (UK) Ltd
364-366 Kensington High Street, London W14 8NS
tel 020-7471 5000 *fax* 020-7471 5001
email info@umusic.com
website www.universalclassics.com
CEO & Chairman Lucian Grainge

Holding company for UMG labels including Polydor, Island and Mercury.

V2
website www.v2music.com or www.myspace/v2music

Roster includes: The Stereophonics, Elbow, Paul Weller, and The Rakes.

The Viper Label
PO Box 48, Liverpool L17 7JE
website www.the-viper-label.co.uk
Partner Paul Hemmings

Founded in 1999. Independent label aiming to release interesting and exciting archive and contemporary material worldwide. See complete discography online. Potential clients should post demos.

Virgin Records
Crown House, 72 Hammersmith Road,
London W14 8UD
tel 020-7605 5000 *fax* 020-7605 5050
email firstname.lastname@emimusic.com
website www.the-raft.com
Managing Director Ferdy Unger-Hamilton

Founded in 1972; became part of the EMI group in 1992. Covers a wide range of genres including pop, urban, dance and rock. Artists include: Beverley Knight, The Vines, Graham Coxon, and Placebo.

Visible Noise
231 Portobello Road, London W11 1LT
tel 020-7792 9791 *fax* 020-7792 9871
email info@visiblenoise.com
website www.visiblenoise.com
A&R Director Julie Weir

Founded in 1998. Aims to nurture and expand the careers of up-and-coming artists. Works within the rock, metal, hardcore and guitar-based contemporary music genres. Clients include: The Lostprophets, Bullet for my Valentine, and Fireapple Red. Potential artists should submit material on CD with a good-quality photo and biog (no emailed submissions please).

Warner Bros Records
12 Lancer Square, London W8 4EH
tel 020-7368 3500 *fax* 020 -7368 3760

email info@warnermusic.com
website www.warnerbrosrecords.com
Managing Director Korda Marshall

Long-established label launched in 1958 through the success of the Warner Bros Film Empire. Secured one of the first ever million-dollar contracts by signing the Everly Brothers. The label has had a history of successful clients and has been home to acts such as Madonna, Green Day, Red Hot Chili Peppers, REM, and Alanis Morissette.

Warner Classics

The Electric Lighting Station, 46 Kensington Court, London W8 5DA
tel 020-7938 5500 *fax* 020-7368 4903
email info@warnermusic.com
website www.warnerclassics.com
Director Matthew Cosgrove

Deals with both re-issues and new classical recordings. Artists have included: Susan Graham, Boris Berezovsky, Nikolai Lugansky, and Pierre-Laurent Aimard. The City of Birmingham Symphony Orchestra, the Chamber Orchestra of Europe and Concentus Musicus Wien are among recording orchestras.

Warner Music International (Headquarters)

28 Kensington Church Street, London W8 4EP
tel 020-7368 2500 *fax* 020-7368 2734
email info@warnermusic.com
website www.wmg.com
Chairman/CEO Edgar Bronfman Jnr

Parent company of a range of successful record labels including Asylum, Atlantic, Bad Boy, Cordless, East West, Elektra, Lava, Maverick, Nonesuch, Reprise, Rhino, Sire, Warner Bros and Word. Also contains Warner Chappell Music.

Warner Music Ireland

Alexandra House, Earlsfort Centre, Earlsfort Terrace, Dublin 2, Ireland

tel +353 1 676 2022 *fax* +353 1 676 2602
email firstname.lastname@warnermusic.com
website www.warnermusic.com
Managing Director Dennis Woods

Board member of the Irish Record Music Association representing Irish artists' publicity and recording.

Warner Music UK

The Warner Building, 28A Kensington Church, London W8 4EP
tel 020-7368 2500 *fax* 020-7368 2770
email info@warnermusic.com
website www.warnermusic.co.uk
Chairman Nick Phillips

Has hosted a range of well-established artists. Newer signings include: The Streets, Muse, and Ash.

Warp Records

PO Box 25387, London NW5 1GL
tel 020-7284 8350 *fax* 020-7284 8360
email info@warprecords.com
website www.warprecords.com

Specialises in interesting electronic dance music. Artists have included: Aphex Twin, Boards Of Canada, Autechre, Squarepusher, Plaid and Vincent Gallo.

Worst Case Scenario Records

Global House, Bridge Street, Guildford GU1 4SB
tel (01483) 500800 *fax* (01483) 501201
email info@wcsrecords.com
website www.wcsrecords.com
Head of Label Mark Bounds

First release was January 2006 with a split 7" single of The Coronation c/w Midnight Juggernauts. Releases music on 7" and through Universal's digital partners such as iTunes and Napster. Perceived as a tastemaker label for up-and-coming bands for one-off-single releases. Recent signing, SixNationState, has just been signed to Jeepster for a full album deal.

Music piracy

Piracy may be illegal, but some perpetrators continue to find it rewarding. Like any legitimate businessman, a pirate has to decide whether the return on the investment provides a sufficient reward – given the risks involved for that class of business (fines and imprisonment). **Keith Lowde** explains.

Let's be clear: music industry piracy is not a new phenomenon. Indeed, unauthorised copying of a creator's work was considered by some early music publishers to be doing the writer a great service (by popularising the writer's works) – for which the publisher sought approbation, and even praise!

When publishers May and Hedgebutt published – without permission – the complete music and libretto of Henry Purcell's opera, *The Indian Queen*, around 1695, they went so far as to claim that it was in the public's interest for people to be able to purchase their unauthorised version of Purcell's songs, in the same way people could buy the popular (and usually anonymous) ballads of the day. The publishers further argued their case by stating that such a 'modest' composer as Purcell might never otherwise see this work in print.

In other words, prefaced by an elegant justification, they stole the composer's music. Copying and publishing the music of others without permission was not then against the law, and there wasn't anything a composer could do about it.

In the UK, the right to make a copy of an author's work was first enshrined in the Statute of Anne, of 1710. From that date, unauthorised copying of an author's work was illegal, provided that the work was registered at Stationers' Hall – a process that cost the author sixpence.

These days, registration is no longer necessary to prove copyright ownership, and a work is in copyright as soon as it exists in some *material form*. However, without the benefit of statutory registration, proving copyright ownership can be a problem.

Lawyers representing infringers will certainly seek proof of ownership before embarking on a defence, and writers will need to be able to demonstrate the date on which they wrote a work, backing up that assertion with evidence to support their claim of ownership.

Sending a copy of the work to yourself by the Post Office's Special Delivery or International Signed For services, and storing it unopened, is not proof of ownership – but the certificate provided by the Post Office can be used as dating evidence to support a claim for ownership. The letter, when received, should be filed away together with any other documentary evidence which may possibly later be needed to support a claim in court.

Pirates and sound recordings

Today, while there is some unauthorised copying of sheet music, both publishers and the writers they represent suffer more from piracy of sound recordings (which aurally embody their creative musical works).

Digital technology has given the pirate an opportunity to make an absolutely perfect copy of any sound recording at a fraction of the cost of the original. This enables the pirate to sell his or her product at a quarter of the price of the legitimate CD and still achieve a significant profit. With this price advantage, pirates probably sell as many illegal CDs as those sold legitimately.

Copying packaging is a little more expensive – and some pirates recognise that counterfeiting is a more serious crime than merely making perfect copies of the content and delivering it in an alternative form of packaging. They therefore use cheap packaging that does not try to emulate the original – a useful defence against a charge of counterfeiting. The consumer may, of course, consider that the content of the recording is no better than its dodgy packaging, and refuse to buy the product. The pirate's dilemma is thus one of choosing between credibility of content, or cheap packaging.

Of course, if piracy were eliminated, not every illegal CD sold would translate to a legitimate sale. Nevertheless, a large number would, and there is a real financial loss to the writing and publishing communities as a result of such piracy.

Perhaps the greatest loss is suffered by the record labels, however. The record pirate operates with the enormous benefit of not having to invest in artist development, and can pick and choose the products that are already achieving legitimate success. The pirate has made no contribution towards that success, which has been bought through a significant marketing investment by the record label.

Different scales of piracy

There are two distinct levels of piracy: making to order from the bedroom; or operating large-scale commercial duplication (and feeding a distribution network).

The bedroom operator needs copying equipment and a willing community of consumers. CD duplication at 48 x real time is a standard facility on domestic PCs costing just a few hundred pounds – and the cost of a blank CD is a mere few pence. The club, the school, and the workplace are all potential outlets, and a bedroom operator will find a ready market if the price is right and delivery reasonably rapid. Games are probably most profitable, and DVDs produced in advance of a film's release can command a premium price – but music provides a steady bread-and-butter income for this illegal cottage industry.

Car boot sales and market stalls are more likely to be fed by the larger-scale operator. The pirate prefers no traceable connection between the outlet to the customer and the duplicator. While this reduces the risk of being caught, it also reduces the control of the distribution network. Those at the sharp end are not always honest in passing the cash back down the line, so a pirate supplying a distribution network will probably want hard cash upfront for each delivery network being fed.

Large-scale piracy often involves duplication in countries where there is less concern for the issue of piracy. The Balkans and China have, in recent years, proved capable of supplying very cheap but high-quality goods.

Distribution to the UK is not difficult, as there is always someone involved in international logistics that is willing to transport goods, without asking too many awkward questions. One container can hold millions of CDs. While Customs & Excise can sniff out trafficking in people and drugs, there is no sniffer-dog equivalent for finding CDs! More importantly, the penalties for being caught with illegal CDs hardly match those for bringing in illegal immigrants or a few pounds of cocaine.

The penalties of being caught

Migrating from the bedroom to operating on an international scale does have its risks. The heavy guys from the mafias and tongs do not appreciate competition, and an enterprising new face runs the risk of being taken aside by the mafia for some harsh off-the-record interrogation, often resulting in 'serious personal modification'! This punishment is far worse (and consequently much more effective) than anything meted out by those who wish to uphold the law: probation for a first offence; maybe a fine for the second; and, if appearing in court a third time, a short jail sentence. As a deterrent, these comparatively small irritations hardly match the mafia's preferred method of surgical redistribution of the self.

In truth, most law enforcement agencies are not overly enthusiastic at being asked to divert manpower to deal with illegal copying and distribution of CDs: it's not usually high on their agenda. With most illegal products flying out of car boot sales and market stalls at weekends, Trading Standards Officers would have to work overtime to get meaningfully involved. Again, it's difficult to argue for overtime payments for dealing with CD piracy when there are many other social issues with which to deal.

In reality, it is the music industry trade bodies that have to take on the burden of protecting their copyright-owning members from piracy. The British Phonographic Industry (BPI) does this for the record industry, and the Mechanical-Copyright Protection Society (MCPS) does the same for music publishers and composers: both have active and overstretched investigative teams, working flat out to bring pirates before the courts and to make life more difficult for those who help them ply their trade. No wonder, then, that by 2005 the BPI put high on its list of priorities a willingness to lobby for new laws to make car boot sale organisers responsible for any counterfeit goods on sale at their markets.

The future – digital distribution

It can be argued that the music industry made a huge blunder in failing to see downloads and streaming of music as an opportunity; and, in the late 1990s, digital distribution seemed to have been hijacked by Peer-to-Peer (P2P) file sharing. In 2005, the International Federation of the Phonographic Industry (IFPI) was reporting: "Third party research shows that illegal file-sharing has been a key factor in the recording industry's 22% worldwide decline between 1999 and 2004." This was certainly piracy, but without the pirate taking a cut!

Illegal P2P was as annoying for the pirate as for the legitimate record industry – since it created the impression among some consumers that music is, or should be, free. Free P2P particularly appealed to those customers who had previously been comfortable buying from the pirate. If you were able to overcome the moral and legal issues of ripping off the legitimate music industry, then why pay £3 for a CD from a pirate, when you could download it for free? Ironically, the pirates needed the legitimate industry to crack down on free P2P.

For the legitimate industry, the cost of fighting illegal P2P has been expensive and, on occasions, their legal action has been counterproductive and attracted bad press. Much was made of the US and UK record industries' attempts to sue their own 'customers' – some of whom were young teenagers.

The most successful way of combating illegal P2P was to support a legitimate and reasonably priced download service; then, in 2003, Apple exploded onto the scene with iPod – and its associated iTunes.

With Apple closely followed in 2004 by Napster (and others), the legitimate download market is growing at a significant rate. In a press release dated 19th January 2006, the

International Federation of Phonographic Industries declared that: "Record company revenues (trade revenues) *from digital distribution* reached $US 1.1 billion in 2005, showing a threefold increase on 2004 ($US 380 million)."

With growth like this, some industry forecasters have suggested that legal downloading will account for 25 per cent of industry sales by the end of the decade. Microsoft's Bill Gates goes further, and predicts the death of the physical carrier as a means of distributing entertainment, by 2010.

Both the legitimate music industry and the pirates are having to consider how this new phenomenon will impact on their respective operations in future years. Can the physical pirate enjoy success in the virtual world – where transactions and their sources are so easily capable of being monitored? Will the record industry succeed in controlling and monetising P2P? Or will the streetwise kid be transferring music files using mobile phones, and bluetooth technology?

One scenario now emerging leads to the possibility that digital distribution – once considered a threat by the record industry – could, in fact, lead to the demise of the commercial pirate.

Keith R D Lowde, FCA, is a former Deputy Chairman of the UK's Mechanical-Copyright Protection Society (MCPS). Today he runs his own company, which offers business solutions to the music, media and entertainment industries.

Distributors

Absolute Marketing and Distribution Ltd
The Old Lampworks, Rodney Place,
London SW19 2LQ
tel 020-8540 4242 *fax* 020-8540 6056
email info@absolutemarketing.co.uk
website www.absolutemarketing.co.uk
General Manager Simon Wills

Founded in 2000. A fully managed sales, marketing, administration, distribution and rights management company based in London. Looks after a range of independent labels, from the traditional label through to labels that focus on only one artist. Takes care all aspects of a release. Clients include: Ocean Colour Scene, Marillion, Shirley Bassey, Imogen Heap, and The Editors.

Amato Distribution
4 Minerva Business Centre, 58-60 Minerva Road,
London NW10 6HJ
tel 020-8838 8350 *fax* 020-8838 8331
email info@amatodistribution.co.uk
website www.amatodistribution.co.uk
Head of Label Management Graham Kelly

Established in 1992. Aims to be the world's premier distributor. Works in all genres. Clients include: Renaissance, Waterfall Home Entertainment, Media Records, and a range of independent labels. Supplies the majority of major and indie high-street outlets and online digital sites.

Backs Distribution
St Mary's Works, St Mary's Plain, Norwich,
Norfolk NR3 3AF
tel (01603) 626221 *fax* (01603) 619999
Distribution Manager Derek Chapman

Founded in 1979. Provides a distribution service for independent labels. Works with both online and traditional methods.

Cargo Records
17 Heathman's Road, Parson's Green,
London SW6 4TJ
tel 020-7731 5125 *fax* 020-7731 3866
email info@cargorecords.co.uk
website www.cargorecords.co.uk
Contact Craig Gogay

Founded in 1992. Distributes independent records to UK retailers and distributors worldwide. Has dealt with acts such as Blink 182, The White Stripes and Devendra Banhardt. Distributes manually and online. See website (under contact) for more details on suitability.

Classical International Ltd
3rd Floor, 82-84 Clerkenwell Road,
London EC1M 5RF
tel 020-7689 1080 *fax* 020-7689 1180
email info@classical.com
website www.classical.com
VP Content and Business Roger Press

Well-established digital classical distributor.

CM Distribution
North Works, Hook Stone Park, Harrogate HG2 7DB
tel (01423) 888979 *fax* (01423) 885761
website www.celtic-music.co.uk
Contact D R Bulmer

Founded in the 1970s as a media-based mail-order company and distributor. Distributes the following labels: Georgian Recordings, Lyrichord Discs, Red Sky Records, and Springthyme Records.

Copperplate Distribution
68 Belleville Road, London SW11 6PP
tel 020-7585 0357
email copperplate2000@yahoo.com
website www.copperplatedistribution.com
Contact Alan O'Leary

Established in 1999. Specialises in the distribution of Irish music; provides a PR service to Irish traditional musicians, bands and Irish labels. Distributes for Viva Voce, Clo iar Chonnachta and Shanachie.

Devilfish Distribution Ltd
GH Cooper House, 2 Michael Road,
London SW6 2AD
tel 020-7384 1524
email info@devil-fish.com
website www.devil-fish.com
Label Manager Mark MacDonald

Deals mainly with small independent labels including Vino, Prototype and Metro in the dance, D&B and world genres. Works with traditional distribution methods including export and UK key accounts.

Direct Dance Distribution
Unit F34 Park Hall Trading Estate, 40 Martell Road,
Dulwich, London SE21 8EN
tel 020-8670 9433 *fax* 020-8670 8452
email steve@directdance.co.uk
Managing Director Steve Bradley

Founded in 1999. Aims to provide sales, promotion and distribution in all territories worldwide. Works with all labels, both major and indies, in a variety of genres.

EMI Distribution
Hermes Close, Tachbrook Park, Leamington Spa,
Warwickshire CV34 6RP

tel (01926) 466300 *fax* (01926) 466332
email John.williams@emimusic.com
website www.emimusic.com
Contact John Williams

Part of EMI Music. Labels distributed include:
Classics for Pleasure, EMI, HMV Classics, Virgin
Classics and Virgin Records.

Entertainment UK
234 Blyth Road, Hayes, Middlesex UB3 1DN
email enquiries@entuk.co.uk
website www.entuk.com
Contact Lloyd Wigglesworth

A leading wholesale distributor of home
entertainment products, supplying many well-known
stores (e-tailers and retailers). Currently distributing
approximately a quarter of the UK's music and video
industry's entire output.

Essential Direct Ltd
Brewmaster House, 91 Brick Lane, London E1 6QL
tel 020-7375 2332 *fax* 020-7375 2442
email info@essentialdirect.co.uk
website www.essentialdirect.co.uk
Contact Gary Dedman

Formed in 1996 and specialising in the distribution of
garage and house music in 12" vinyl format both
nationally and internationally.

Harmonia Mundi
45 Vyner Street, London E2 9DQ
tel 020-8709 9509 *fax* 020-8709 9501
email info.uk@harmoniamundi.com
website www.harmoniamundi.com
Managing Director Serge Rousset

Classical distributor dealing with labels such as
Cantaloupe Music, Stradivarius, Unicorn-Kanchana
and Vanguard.

Kudos Records Ltd
77 Fortress Road, Kentish Town, London NW5 1AG
tel 020-7482 4555 *fax* 020-7482 4551
email rosie@kudosrecords.co.uk
website www.kudosrecords.co.uk
Founder Danny Ryan

Founded in 1991. Endeavours to provide efficient
distribution services to new and rising independent
record labels.

Lasgo Chrysalis
Unit 2 Chapmans Business Park Industrial Estate,
378-388 High Road, Willesden, London NW10 2DY
tel 020-8459 8800 *fax* 020-8451 5555
email info@lasgo.co.uk
website www.lasgo.co.uk
Contact Paul Burrows

Wholesale distributor of music CDs, DVDs, vinyl and
books nationally and internationally. A company

created from the merger of Chrysalis and Lasgo
Exports.

Media UK Distribution
Sovereign House, 12 Trewartha Road, Praa Sands,
Penzance, Cornwall TR20 9ST
tel (01736) 762826 *fax* (01736) 763328
email panamamus@aol.com
website www.panamamusic.co.uk
Managing Director Roderick Jones

Established in 1986. Distributors of audio and
audiovisual product worldwide. Covers all genres.
Clients include: Mohock Records, Rainy Day
Records, and Pure Gold Records. Deals with both
traditional and online distribution. Also provides a
media promotions and consultancy service.

Nervous Records
5 Sussex Crescent, Northolt UB5 4DL
tel 020-8423 7373 *fax* 020-8423 7773
website www.nervous.co.uk
Managing Director Roy Williams

Founded in 1978. Distributes physically and online to
mainly independent labels including Fury, Nervous
and MCDP. Deals mainly with rockabilly and
psychobilly. Also houses record label and publisher.

Nova Sales and Distribution (UK) Ltd
22 Isabel House, 46 Victoria Road, Surbiton,
Surrey K26 4JL
tel 020-8390 3322 *fax* 020-8390 3338
email info@novadist.net
website www.novadist.net
Managing Director Wilf Mann

Founded in 2001. Distributes in UK and Ireland to a
range of independent audio and DVD labels
including Chrome Dreams, Prestige and Rotator.
Works with a variety of genres from rock to world
music. Deals with Pinnalle and online via Aggregator
Parfner.

Nu Urban Music
Unit 3 Rivermead Industrial Estate, Pipersway,
Thatcham, Berkshire RG19 4EP, UK
tel (01635) 587900 *fax* (01635) 292314
email shop@nu-urbanmusic.co.uk
website www.nu-urbanmusic.co.uk
Contact Tobie Scapes

Dedicated to the distribution of urban artists and
acts, with offices and production based both in the
UK and the USA.

On Demand Distribution
OD2 Limited, Bush House, 72 Prince Street,
Bristol BS1 4QD UK
tel 0117-910 0150 *fax* 0117-910 0151
email info@od2.com
website www.od2.com
Co-founder Peter Gabriel

Founded in 1999. Offers business-to-business digital media solutions including the supply of white-label digital music platforms and downloadable/streaming music media to PCs across Europe.

Pendle Hawk Music
11 New Market Street, Colne, Lancashire BB8 9BJ
tel (01282) 866317
email info@pendlehawkmusic.co.uk
website www.pendlehawkmusic.co.uk
Managing Director Adrian Melling

Founded in 1982. Distributes to UK retail shops (including mixed-media retail, i.e. bookshops) and online worldwide. Deals mainly with folk, blues, jazz and country genres. Clients have included: Planet Records, Slam, Leo, and Old Bridge. Also provides a booking and promotions service for UK tours, Planet Records (label) and contains an in-house 24-track recording studio.

Pinnacle Records
Heather Court, 6 Maidstone Road, Sidcup, Kent DA14 5HH
tel 020-8309 3600 *fax* 020-83093892
email Susan.rush@pinnaclerecords.co.uk
website www.pinnacle-entertainment.co.uk

One of the UK's largest independent distributors, distributing over 400 labels including Colosseum, Pure Classics, Sanctuary and Snapper Music.

Plastic Head Music Distribution Ltd
Avtech House, Hithercroft Road, Wallingford, Oxfordshire OX10 9DA
tel (01491) 825029 *fax* (01491) 826320
email info@plastichead.com
website www.plastichead.com
Managing Director Steve Beatty

Founded in 1991. International distributors dealing with physical and online distribution. Works with a range of styles with an emphasis on metal and dance genres. Clients have included: HMV, Virgin, **play.com** and **amazon.com**. Also provides tour merchandise for bands including online and postal mail order.

Savoy Strict Tempo Distributors
PO Box 271, Coulsdon, Surrey CR5 3TR
tel (01737) 554739 *fax* (01737) 556737
email admin@savoymusic.com
website www.savoymusic.com
Director Wendy Smith

The successor of the 'Dancetime Record Company' formed in 1959. Specialises in the manufacture and distribution of Old Time Dance and Sequence Dance music. Also the main distributor worldwide for all British dance music labels, including Savoy, Dance and Listen, Dulcima, Grasmere, Melody, Maestro, Tema and President.

Select Music and Video Distribution Ltd
3 Wells Place, Redhill, Surrey RH1 3SL
tel (01737) 645600 *fax* (01737) 644065

email cds@selectmusic.co.uk
website www.selectmusic.co.uk

Founded in 1991. Specialises in the distribution of classical labels. Labels distributed include: Chandos, First Edition Recordings, Hyperion, and Naxos.

Shellshock Distribution
23A Collingwood Road, London N15 4LD
tel 020-8800 8110 *fax* 020-8800 8140
email info@shellshock.co.uk
website www.shellshock.co.uk
Contact Gareth Ryan

Independent national distributor dealing with all major UK music retailers. Also offers planning, placement and marketing services.

Silverword Music Group (Silverword Distribution)
16 Limetrees, Llangattock, Crickhowell, Powys NP8 1LB
tel (01873) 810142 *fax* (01873) 811557
email smgdistribution@aol.com
website www.silverword.co.uk
Proprietor Kevin King

Established in 1983. Deals mostly with small independent labels in a range of genres. Distributes both physically and online. Also contains 'Promo UK' – a promotional service for the distributed product.

Stern's African Record Centre
74 Warren Street, London W1T 5PF
tel 020-7387 5550 *fax* 020-7388 5533
email sales@sternsmusic.com
website www.sternsmusic.com
Sales Manager Ian Thomas

Founded in 1987. Provides distribution services for a range of African and world music clients including Sharpwood and Sense World Records. Distributes mainly within the UK but also has US offices and will export worldwide. Also deals with website sales including negotiable download facility.

Ten (The Entertainment Network)
Rabans Lane, Aylesbury, Bucks HP19 7TS
tel (01296) 426151 *fax* (01296) 481009
email info@ten-distribution.com
website www.ten-net.com
Contact Shaun Plunkett

Currently distributes on behalf of nearly 20 clients to around 18,000 audio, video and games outlets. Products distributed include CDs, cassettes, vinyl and mini discs. Labels distributed include: Atlantic Records, Atrium Records, Finlandia, Nonesuch and Warner Music UK.

Timewarp Distribution
GFM House, Cox Lane, Chessington, Surrey KT9 1SD

tel 020-8397 4466 *fax* 020-8397 1950
email info@timewarpdis.com
website www.timewarpdis.com
Contact Bill Shannon

The distribution arm of Gentle Fire Music group, offering worldwide distribution through a series of partners across the globe. Other services include a Marketing & Promotions division.

Tuned Distribution Ltd

Unit 26 Acklam Workshops, 10 Acklam Road, London W10 5QZ
tel 020-8964 1355
email lee@tuned-distribution.co.uk
website www.tuned-distribution.co.uk
Managing Director Lee Muspratt

Established in 2000. Deals primarily with dance music labels and independent stores. Distributes for Tripoli Trax, Volkswagon, YO5, Impact Short Circuit and many small independent record labels, white labels and limited promos. Means of distribution is physical, via DHL next-day delivery.

Unique Records and Distribution

Unit 12 Lodge Bank Industrial Estate, Off Crown Lane, Horwich, Bolton BL6 5HY
tel (01204) 67550 *fax* (01204) 479005
email hi@uniquedist.co.uk
website www.uniquedist.co.uk
Contact Alan Smith

Specialises in distributing a wide range of dance label material, particularly vinyl records, to wholesaler retailers.

Vital Distribution

338A Ladbroke Grove, London W10 5AH
tel 020-8324 2400 *fax* 020-8324 0001
email kelly.renda@vitaluk.com
website www.vitaluk.com
PA to General Manager Kelly Renda

Provides exclusive sales, marketing and distribution to more than 75 labels. Works within a large international and export department. Also specialists in professionalised digital distribution.

ZYX Records

11 Cambridge Court, 210 Shepherds Bush Road, London W6 7NJ
tel 020-7371 6969 *fax* 020-7371-6688
email lauren.lorenzo@zyxrecords.freeserve.co.uk
website www.zyxmusic.co.uk
General Manager Lauren Lorenzo

Founded in 1975. Distributes both online and physically to labels across Europe and the US, including Mobeatz, KTown, Fonky and Sniper. Deals with a range of styles including dance, rock, rap, blues and country.

Digital distribution

When Richard Branson announced in the early 1980s that Virgin had discovered a revolutionary way to distribute high-quality music by telephone, the industry took a collective intake of breath. **Keith Lowde** tells us why.

The announcement had been made in *Music Week*, on 1st April - and there were many sighs of relief when the magazine subsequently reported the spoof. The industry had a good laugh at its own expense, and assumed that the matter would never return. The traditional model of selling physical products at retail was safe ... for now. The World Wide Web did not then exist, and there was no e-commerce to worry about. The telephone line was not a threat.

Fifteen years later, and the threat *was* being discussed – but the Internet and e-commerce at that time merely provided another channel to market physical recordings. The 'hybrid' – sales of CDs and tapes through online outlets – was not considered a threat to artists, writers, publishers or labels. However, high street retailers were getting concerned. Should they invest in websites? Would the hybrid produce new money? Could you make a profit from hybrids, given the thin margins available to pay for warehousing, and the overheads for picking, packing and posting one-off products?

Hybrid sales met the needs of customers who could not get satisfaction through traditional retail outlets. For the first time, it was possible to browse a vast catalogue of product without first finding the right shelf and fingering through unwanted product, or asking an often indifferent assistant for help. The search engine took away these tasks, and did so without bombarding the consumer with in-store music chosen by someone with very different music tastes.

Not surprisingly, the search engine particularly satisfied demand for items from back catalogue. For the industry, it provided a welcome opportunity to revive sales of records that had been, or were, becoming candidates for deletion from the catalogue. For the e-retailer, the 80 per cent sales of a wide variety of back catalogue was a problem. A traditional retailer enjoyed 80 per cent chart-only sales, and it is much easier to make a profit from high-volume sales of fewer products.

If hybrid sales were embryonic in the mid 1990s, then downloading music still represented a far distant possibility in the industry's collective mind. But almost unnoticed, a number of new developments were gathering pace, which would conspire to make true April fools of most industry executives.

MP3 and Napster

MP3 compression technology had been available even before the CD had been adopted by the industry as the favoured format, in the early 1980s. However, no killer application had been available to take advantage of its 1:10 compression advantage over CDs. The launch of Napster – the first significant Peer-to-Peer (P2P) service in 1999 – and the availability of a reasonably priced MP3 player (the Rio), was to change the whole face of the music industry.

Initially, the record industry was bent on stopping Napster. Incredibly, Napster endeavoured to fight the music industry through the courts rather than work towards a mutual solution. Having said that, it must be stated that the industry was not then looking for a partner like Napster. In fact, it was looking to make an example of Napster by closing it down – and to stop other similar sites starting up.

Napster's defence was flawed, and it suffered a significant problem insofar as the service relied on a central server through which all Peer-to-Peer transactions took place. To comply with a US court's decision, Napster had to remove from its files any reference to copyright material owned by the major record companies. This effectively killed off the service, since the majors represent such a massive market share of all recorded music currently in copyright.

Even so, since being founded in 1999, Napster's growth had been startling. Within two years of establishing itself, it claimed to have 50 million members worldwide swapping up to 1.3 billion music files every month. The fact that it was a free service was clearly a significant factor in Napster's success, but this level of transaction shocked the industry to its core. The major record companies were clear: Napster had to be closed down – but unfortunately there was no plan to satisfy the now well-established needs of the Web music consumer. Large numbers of such consumers wanted a download service.

By not offering, or at least not encouraging, a legal downloading service to consumers after they succeeded in shutting down Napster, the record industry effectively invited others to fill the vacuum. Where there is a demand, someone will try to satisfy it – and so several Napster clones and mutants entered the field, and enjoyed over three years of activity and growth without effective competition from legal downloading services.

Crucially, these alternative P2P systems no longer relied on a central server, but permitted direct relationships between the up-loader and the down-loader. The industry now had to police millions of individual transactions conducted by hundreds of thousands of illegal file swappers. The Record Industry Association of America (RIAA) started to pursue the most significant abusers in the US, with only limited success in the courts.

The development of legal download services

The record industry has often been criticised for not devising and offering a legal downloading service immediately upon the closure of Napster. However, providing such a service is not without difficulty and cost. The process requires:

- licences from record labels for the copyright in the sound recording;
- licences from publishers for the music content;
- digitised product delivered in a format suitable for downloading Metadata and tagging – the product and contributor identifying data;
- hefty investment in computer and communications equipment;
- new marketing strategies and different pricing policies to attract customers;
- customers willing to use the service payment systems which deal with micro-billing (small transaction values);
- Digital Rights Management (DRM) tracking systems.

To have developed such a system would have required considerable co-operation throughout an industry noted more for its in-fighting than its ability to formulate common strategies to integrate new technology. The record industry is, at its best, competing to create sound recordings for sale through physical retail outlets – not mixing it with hi-tech communications companies.

Legal downloading services had been available in the US even before Napster had broken the mould in 1999, but these had suffered from the lack of an attractive catalogue of recordings. To be successful, it would be necessary for a downloading service to attract the catalogue of the major record companies, and it was the computer hardware company, Apple, that managed to put together a package that at last met all the processing requirements – and offered the majors sufficient revenues per track to bring them on board.

Consumer take-up of Apple's iTunes service was as swift, if not as startling, as Napster's free service five years previously. Sales of the iPod – the essential portable kit to play iTunes – immediately outstripped supply. Apple's business model was to offer downloads at a price that made them little if any money, but generated highly profitable iPod sales. Apple's shareholders were naturally ecstatic at the success of this business campaign.

With Apple in the lead, the Napster brand was revived – but this time with industry backing. From villain to hero, Napster now offered a subscription-based alternative, and its downloads were playable on a variety of hardware. Interoperability became a buzz word as the industry wondered which kind of service would win the battle for domination of the Internet: track by track sales, or as much as you like for a monthly fee. Would Apple permit its downloads to be played on non-iPod players? Would they license other manufacturers?

By the end of 2004, legal downloads had carved out over 1 per cent share of the market for sound recordings. And according to the record industry body, IFPI, digital distribution in all its forms provided the record industry worldwide with over US$1 billion of trade revenues in 2005 – a threefold increase during the year. Again, like the hybrid, some downloads sales represent new money, as consumers take advantage of the opportunity to buy just the one track they want to hear – at a price which is significantly less than that of a physical single.

The charts

Sales of singles have, at best, been volatile in the UK in the last decade; at worst, the sales trend shows serious decline. Except for chart toppers selling hundreds of thousands of units, the single has not been a profit-spinner for the industry. However, it *has* proved to be a useful marketing tool. Releasing and promoting a single can measure whether a new band or act will find favour with the consumer. If the single sells well, then it is probably worth the cost of releasing an album. If the single bombs, then the act can be sidelined in favour of a more profitable investment.

In April 2005, the UK Official Chart Company (OCC) – co-owned by the record labels' representative organisation, BPI, and the retailers' organisation, BARD – decided to bring downloads into the singles chart. By this time, downloads were matching single sales, and the logic of adding the two together was clear. However, the independent record label organisation, AIM (the Association of Independent Music) was livid, since many of its members had not yet offered their products to service providers in the virtual space. AIM felt their members would be disadvantaged by this move, and complained to the Office of Fair Trading.

The complaint was not followed through, but it is clear that independent labels recognised the significance of the change to the charts. Adding downloads to the Singles chart has changed the relative position of every title in the chart. Many radio stations inform their playlist decisions by reference to the chart position of a title. Since radio play can influence record sales, some labels in the independent sector may have lost income because their physical releases had been some way down the chart, and consequently achieved a lower priority in the playlists.

Compounding the problem was the later decision by OCC to include downloads to mobile phones – a new channel to market, which was set to explode in 2005.

Mobile phones

The mobile phone industry has achieved worldwide penetration at an alarming rate, and is constantly seeking new services to offer their consumers in order to raise profitability. The primary measure of success is ARPU – the Average Revenue Per User. Content such as music, films and games is not only expected to provide the next growth stage for mobile telephony, but should also increase ARPU significantly.

There is much to support this proposition. Mobile ringtones have been a success story for music publishers. New ring-back services are being developed, and already have experienced significant uptake. Record companies have largely missed out on these sales, as their sound recordings were not capable of being used on monophonic phones. The new mobile phones now provide photography, video, music, Internet access, barcode reading, broadcast reception, and no doubt many more services in the future.

Mobile telephony has a number of advantages over the Internet. It can provide a service to almost anywhere in the world, without landlines. The equipment is robust and truly mobile, and can easily be enhanced to store content in compressed formats; there is already in place a micro-billing system, which can be adapted to interface with the music industry's Digital Rights Management (DRM) systems (for obtaining copyright clearance).

Content suppliers can produce the same suitably metatagged and digitised content that is required for landline downloads, so there is no great additional cost for migrating to this new distribution system. The new generation of telephones offer MP3 storage capability, and will shortly interface with other amplification hardware, such as home entertainment systems and in-car stereo.

Try before you buy

Another strength of the mobile is its ability to interact using Bluetooth wireless technology. This is giving rise to some intriguing new marketing concepts for the music industry to consider.

Napster's founder, Shaun Fanning, is now delivering a product whereby mobile phone users can swap music files with a DRM system, which determines how many free plays the recipient of a file can have, before being asked to dial up for a subscription.

This 'Try before you buy' option effectively makes the consumer a distributor, and the Digital Rights System provides for a financial incentive to be paid to the distributing partner, by returning a percentage of the new subscription. With young children now taking the mobile phone as a first step towards maturity, this offers the music industry an opportunity to win back the younger customer.

The future

So will mobile music be the future? *Mobile Music (3rd Edn)* – from researchers Informa Telecoms & Media – predicts that over US$11 billion will be generated by all forms of mobile music by 2010. That is a massive figure – and the equivalent of around a quarter of all record sales in 2004. Some of it will be incremental money, but clearly some will be 'substitutional' (taking ground from traditional product income). In March 2005, EMI's Executive Vice President for strategy and development, Adam Klein, said: "EMI believes digital will drive future market growth and could represent up to 25 per cent of total music sales in five years." Are the two forecasts compatible? Probably not. But what is certain is that the music industry has now embraced Digital Distribution wholeheartedly, and the growth rate is and is likely to remain significant. We will have to wait and see if the mobile phone is going to replace the landline.

Yet share and size of market are not the only questions. Does digital distribution and its new marketing opportunities complement a change in consumer behaviour? The answer is, very probably. The younger generation is more likely than its elders to want to listen to music through a hand-held device; seniors are still wedded to their radios and hi-fi systems. The once-revered quality of digitally recorded CD may be giving way to an acceptable quality MP3 – or perhaps something even more compressed?

Could we also be witnessing a change in the concept of 'ownership'? The CD and its product-based precedents gave a real sense of ownership to the consumer, even though the intellectual rights remained beyond their reach.

A download is as intangible as the intellectual property rights that permit its playback. Does the young consumer believe in ownership, when the product has been replaced by a service? Probably not. The concept of access to a service is more likely to replace ownership of a product.

And this gives rise to a further question: if access is all-important, then why the need to download music at all? 'Streaming' would seem to be a reasonable alternative for someone who has no preconceptions about ownership. In which case, music distribution not only moves from product to service, but what was 'collectable' now becomes simply 'consumable'.

The impact of digital distribution on the creators of music

The Crazy Frog ringtone phenomenon has already shown how marketing can take advantage of new technology; and no doubt the writers of the associated music were writing specifically for the 'format'.

The 'format' is an important factor in writing music. It is useful to recall that the duration of a piece of recorded music was originally founded on, and determined by:
a) the practicality of a needle's ability to vibrate in a groove of plastic;
b) the length of the groove, as determined by the acceptable size of the package; and
c) the sound quality that the consumer expected to hear.
For the first two-thirds of the last century, these features determined that a song's duration should be around three minutes. When vinyl replaced plastic in the late 1950s, the 30+-minute album provided a new opportunity to extend the duration of a song, or to package together a number of separate songs, into a collection. Writers were now writing for a new format: the album.

So maybe in the future, writers will be looking merely to pen a single piece of music for a specific download, rather than delivering sufficient music for an album. If so, we have gone full circle in around 50 years – and the single becomes king again! Will there be a new form of album in 20 years' time?

And what will Branson be saying next April? How about 'Virgin Satellite Music' – the world's repertoire streamed from the Universal Jukebox, providing immediate access with minute-by-minute billing, or low monthly subscription rates? Whatever the future holds exactly, we are undoubtedly moving nearer the day when we can listen to the music of our choice, or browse our celebrity selections, wherever we are in the world.

Keith R D Lowde, FCA, is a widely experienced Chartered Accountant, and offers business solutions to the music, media and entertainment industries. He is also Head of the Business School at the Academy of Contemporary Music.

The evolution of record contracts in the digital era

"When I started out in the music business, it was possible to see a clear pattern as to how deals were done. First came the record deal, followed closely by a publishing deal. The record deal would usually be with one of the established five or six major record companies, or with one of the raft of bigger independent labels. It would be an exclusive deal, for potentially five or six albums (slightly fewer with the independents).

However, merger mania amongst the majors has meant that there are now only four major record companies – with possibly a further merger of WEA and EMI resulting in only three by the end of 2007. This reduction in access to the budgets of major record companies has inevitably led to a search for other means of getting your music heard. The indie sector has, however, also been hit to the extent that there are very few labels that command anything like the level of success of labels like Creation, Mute, Nude or Independiente in the 1990s. Domino and B-Unique are among the honourable exceptions, but even they have to look for some funding from the majors, or at least assistance in overseas distribution and marketing.

In order to fill the remaining gap, much smaller labels (often home-grown) are using local recording facilities or their own studio to establish a label with relatively little money, with which to record an album. Usually these are done on a basis where the studio/label and artist are in a kind of partnership, where they split the profits 50/50, after all the costs have been paid back. They either distribute themselves through independent distributors, or online from their website, or through Internet aggregators like The Orchard and services like i-Tunes – or, they seek bigger companies to fund this stage (on a licence basis) once the album is finished.

Major record company deals do of course, still exist, but the majors are also realising that they have to tap into the digital download and online marketing world if they are to have any hope of making profits and keeping the shareholders happy.

The biggest change of all is, however, this shift from major to home studio and one-man labels, which has been facilitated by the relatively low entry-level of access to a worldwide distribution network, in the form of the Internet. The bigger record companies have seen their role reduced in many cases to a marketing and overseas distribution role – and even that role is not secure. A&R does still have a rightful place, but finding fine musicians and good tunes is only a small part of the whole process. It is more than ever an issue of how you rise above the noise and how your marketing gets you heard. We have seen the first 'digital only' No.1; we have seen the phenomenon that was the Arctic Monkeys' rise to fame; and we have seen 'digital only' deals from companies like Universal.

Record contracts are evolving, and the major labels as well as the independents are experimenting with business models that involve them sharing in other sources of revenue – such as merchandising and live ticket sales. It is certainly an era of new possibilities."

Ann Harrison is Managing Director of Harrisons Entertainment Law Ltd, and author of *Music: The Business – The Essential Guide to the Law and the Deals* (Virgin). A widely respected independent legal consultant, she offers advice to both new and established artists, as well as to managers, record labels, entrepreneurs, executives, producers and publishers.

Marketing, management and finance
Introduction

All musicians owe it to themselves to develop some knowledge of the business side of the music industry – not least because it may help them to clarify the various ways in which income can be generated (indeed, multiple income sources are not uncommon in the music industry). Business skills also help you to know how to present yourself, and how to go about marketing your particular skills.

Very few people in the musical world have a '9 to 5' job: a large proportion are classified as part-time, and many are self-employed or work in small companies where flexibility regarding working practices is the norm. Therefore, even the many jobs related to the management, business and financial aspects of the industry may not fall into a regular pattern of set working hours.

Such facts demand of most industry personnel – from musicians to managers – a degree of multi-skilling, a super-efficient diary/booking/scheduling capacity, financial 'nous', and an astute sense of how to seize and benefit from a passing opportunity (or more often than not, being able to create your own opportunities through clear-sighted, entrepreneurial, goal-orientated plans). It is, therefore, a complete myth that musicians can afford to be slovenly, disorganised and unreliable! Most music industry personnel work long and often unsociable hours.

Counterbalancing all the hard work is the excitement of working in a fast-changing industry where new, creative projects can be developed within a matter of weeks, days, or even hours. Those with a flair for the business side of the industry should try to understand thoroughly the basic psychological and financial needs of the artists, songwriters, DJs and producers with whom they find themselves working – for it is this level of commitment and depth of knowledge which is the foundation of long-lasting industry relationships, and a fundamental key to success.

Despite the fact that today many songwriters/composers have access to more industry professionals and specialist advisers than ever before (publishers, publicists, agents, etc.), a number of music creators and performers still complain that up to 50 per cent of their time can be spent on 'business' aspects – usually liaising with various industry people, but more often than not lobbying for new work. Good lawyers, accountants, publishers or agents will bear the worst of such administrative burdens for you, and make them man-ageable. Successful business personnel will, over time, have developed the skill to build (quickly) a solid rapport with other professionals with whom they work – becoming experts at 'networking' – and always dealing with their clients in an unobtrusive and clear manner (like the most discreet and reliable of butlers!).

The musical world – like the entertainment industry in general – still thrives on the concept of 'who you know', as much as 'what you know'. Skill and talent by themselves are rarely enough, but this need not make your future progress too difficult. It has, in fact, been pointed out that no person in the music industry is ever more than two steps away. If you don't know the right person, the likelihood is that an acquaintance of yours does know how to contact that vital 'someone else' with whom you may need to work next, in order that your career may continue to grow and flourish.

Music marketing and promotion

Commercial success in the music industry is dependent upon engaging the hearts and minds of the consumer. Generating product awareness is a key aspect of this challenge, and is an activity which has been greatly facilitated by modern methods of communication – as **JoJo Gould** explains.

As the music business has developed over the years, the mechanisms for achieving exposure have become ever more sophisticated. As well as traditional advertising methods – such as billboards and live performances – today's music industry can now harness promotional opportunities through television, radio, videos, mobile phone technologies, computer games, and the online environment.

The music business has continually had to adapt to technological change, with the result today that promotional activity now varies from finding creative ways of utilising an unsigned band's small database of fans, right up to dealing with multimillion-pound video productions and international tours for established acts. Regardless of scale, the core promotional principle has remained the same: to increase consumer awareness, and – ultimately – to encourage the public to part with their hard-earned cash.

When discussing marketing and promotion, it is important to distinguish between these two separate but related activities. Marketing is more conceptual in nature (deciding, for example, on the line-up of a band, the look of an album cover, and when the market is ripe for releases). Promotion is very practical and hands-on. It involves a diverse range of tasks, such as putting up posters, travelling around the country doing interviews and in-store performances, and hiring pluggers to seek airplay (by visiting radio stations well in advance of a record's release).

Media promotion

In the 1920s and 30s, when the industry we recognise today was in its former reincarnation, radio was an important new medium. Ironically, in today's market it is generally agreed that radio remains the most important mechanism for promoting a new record (as the potential buyer has to hear it first, before s/he can make a judgement on it).

Media promotion has benefited from the opportunities made available by new technologies, and can now look to a range of broadcasters and publications for coverage. A media promoter will design a strategy which involves targeting the most appropriate media formats for a particular act. Promotion costs money, and performers will also be expected to allocate a substantial amount of their time to participating in interviews and other media activities – especially when touring or publicising a new release.

Above the line and below the line

These expressions mean respectively, 'paid for' and 'not paid for' promotion in the media. For example, if you see an advert for a new album on TV, or on a poster by a tube escalator, then it has been paid for (it is 'above the line'). If you see a band perform as a feature in a TV show, then you wouldn't expect them to pay for this privilege: instead, the act should be there on merit ('below the line'). Below-the-line advertising also includes methods such as direct mail shots and sponsorship.

Pluggers

These individuals visit radio stations and other media outlets, literally to 'plug' new releases in advance of their release. They have the task of convincing programme directors and playlist committees of the merits of each record. For established acts, of course, this is somewhat easier than for new or unknown acts. Pluggers spend much time on the road, but can build useful working relationships with significant figures within the broadcasting industry. Some industry commentators have argued that records are now plugged too far in advance of their actual release – thereby creating a lengthy lead-time between the consumer hearing the record, and being able to purchase it at retail.

Live promotion

Touring is a key aspect of promotion for performing acts. Depending on the stage of a successful band's development, touring may vary in scale from a circuit of small clubs, up to football stadia or national arenas. Live concerts are rare opportunities for the music fan to interface directly with their idols, and this sector remains very substantial in monetary terms. The live music industry is a highly specialised area: you can even study for a degree in this particular market sector. It is essentially a blending of logistics (getting man and machine to the right place at the right time!) combined with promotional know-how.

With regard to live music, it is important not to confuse the roles of agents and promoters: the former represent their clients (bands) and sell them on to promoters; promoters then put the nuts and bolts of a show together, organising everything from security and ticketing, to sanitation and advertising.

Independent promoters

A look through a music industry directory will usually bring a number of media promoters to your attention. These companies often specialise in certain fields, such as print media or broadcast media. Others may be regional, or even genre-specific – as with the promotion of dance music through nightclubs and targeted DJ mailing lists. Independent promoters are often paid monthly retainers from the budgets of signed bands.

But why go independent? The internal promotions staff, even at a major record company, would find it difficult to promote properly all of their artists on an 'in-house' basis. Independent promoters therefore serve the purpose of filling this gap. Some acts also prefer a distinction between their label and their promotional 'svengalis'. Many independent promoters also have experience of working for the major record labels – usually networking and developing substantial contacts, before setting up privately in business.

Marketing

As mentioned, marketing is more conceptual in nature than promotion, and involves a consideration of record formats, compilations, release dates, and such like. At a strategic level, it requires marketing personnel to be proactive: indeed, other record company departments respond to the decisions of the marketers. The 'marketing mix' is a term often used to capture a number of ingredients, which come together to connect a new product to the marketplace – commonly referred to in business courses across the world as the 4 Ps: product, price, place and promotion. So as you can see, promotion is a reactive activity, and an element of the overall marketing mix (not a stand-alone activity).

The unsigned act

The unsigned act should appreciate the value of self-promotion. If you are lucky enough to pick up a recording deal, then your promotional activity will be co-ordinated and resourced. In the meantime, you should work hard at raising your own profile. This can be achieved through initiatives such as setting up a mailing list of fans, running your own website, preparing a proper press pack (containing a biography, demo, photograph, any other press coverage, forthcoming gig dates and contact details), and liaising with local journalists, radio stations and venue owners. Biographies should be interesting and stylish: try to find an angle for your band, so that you stand out from the crowd.

Remember that the long-standing, key method of self-promotion is, of course, through live performances and the distribution of a demo (usually a 3-track CD, recorded to the highest standards that your skills and budget will allow). Your demo should be packaged properly and targeted at the right kind of record labels and music publishers (if containing original compositions), as well as artist managers, broadcasters, print media and venues. Demos can also be sold at gigs; if you do so, be sure to include a contact return sheet (for your mailing list).

It is highly uncommon for an unsigned band to pick up a record deal through an unsolicited demo tape; therefore, in the first instance, use this promotional device as a means of raising your local profile. Your promotional plan should be bold and ambitious, and is often more effective if channelled through a third-party representative – such as an aspiring manager, or even a streetwise friend (who is a good communicator).

The digital era

During the dot.com boom of the late 1990s, many commentators felt that the Internet would liberate promotion, and create a more level playing field between those with financial clout and those without. Beyond a few isolated success stories, this has not been the experience of the music industry. In reality, an avalanche of unsigned bands continue to struggle to achieve an online profile, while those with the resources, skills and established reputation have harnessed the Internet as a component and intrinsic feature of a much broader promotional strategy.

As a quick information source, the Internet is a world-beater (for updates on a band's news, or to find out what's happening in their angst-ridden tour diary, for example). However, as a promotional panacea for the unknown band, it usually is not!

The contribution of the media

The music industry depends on the modern media to peddle its wares to the masses. In return, it provides broadcasters and publishers with popular content. Before the advent of radio, TV, videos, the Internet and mobile phones, society tended to look down upon musicians – live performances and occasional sheet music sales being their main means of scraping a living. Now, in sharp contrast, entertainers are commonly referred to within our society as 'stars'. This ascending profile has mainly been achieved through clever promotional interplay between the media and the entertainment industries – a symbiotic relationship which has generated household names, together with great success for the music industry.

JoJo Gould is a UK-based lecturer, and was for five years joint Managing Editor of *Music Business Journal*. He lectures and consults on the European Degree in International Music Management, and holds a Master of Science degree in Business IT Systems. He was a co-founder and first Chairman of New Music in Scotland, and was previously Senior Lecturer in Music Industry Management at Buckinghamshire Chilterns University College.

THREE CHORDS AND A BROADBAND MODEM

"In 1977, *Sniffing Glue* fanzine claimed that to form a band, all you needed were three chords and a guitar. Today all you need is three chords and a broadband modem. The true essence of Punk Rock (embodying the DIY ethic) is now finally attainable.

In recent years, the music industry pretty much ignored rapid changes in technology and the effect the Internet might have on sales – at the same time that the cost of signing new acts to record labels was becoming prohibitive. But this is good news for someone starting out today. The Web enables any artist to be completely autonomous, and creatively free. You can define your own release schedule, and communicate directly with fans.

An artist's website can be a one-stop shop for merchandise, as well as for music. Online distribution of your songs worldwide also provides the opportunity to collect details of everyone who buys an album. This means that, where viable, you can plan tours around the city location of every purchaser. You'd never get that from HMV!

Everything can be achieved inside a box – from recording your album to processing credit-card orders, or emailing your fan base for assistance with your online record label. In the long-term, this investment of time and energy will bring in a steady stream of revenue, and a large back catalogue – a luxury not afforded to acts that become victims of the short-termism of some record labels. Music is the universal language: now add html to that."

Jake Shillingford, songwriter and artist, is the founder member of cult orchestral Britpop band, My Life Story. He now runs the highly successful music Internet site, ExileInside. For further information, see **www.exileinside.co.uk**.

PR companies

Absolute PR
Hazlehurst Barn, Valley Road, Derbyshire SK22 2JP
tel (01663) 747970 *mobile* (07768) 652899
fax (01663) 747970
email neil@absolutepr.demon.co.uk
website www.absolutepr.demon.co.uk
Key Contact Neil Cossar

Established in 2000 as a niche public relations agency offering the following services: media relations, copywriting, launches, event management and media training.

Alchemy PR
212A The Bridge, 12-16 Clerkenwell Road,
London EC1M 5PQ
tel 020-7324 6260 *fax* 020-7324 6001
email info@alchemypr.com
website www.alchemypr.com
Director Matt Learmouth

Founded in 2002. Works with promotion through national and regional music PR and press. Deals mainly with dance, pop and mainstream genres. Also provides a consultancy and events management service.

All About Promotions
27A King's Gardens, West End Lane,
London NW6 4PX
tel 020-7328 4836 *fax* 020-7372 3331
email info@allaboutpromo.com
Proprietor Amanda Beel

Founded in 2004. Promotes a wide range of music artistes, across all genres, to radio and television in the UK. Deals with national, and some regional, radio and television stations. Clients include: Tom Waits, Katie Melua, Panic! At the Disco, Joe Jackson, and The Frames. Also offers general music business consultancy.

All Press
Unit 13 Acklam Workspace, 10 Acklam Road,
London W10 5QZ
tel 020-8969 3636
email alex.barfield@all-press.co.uk or
Nienke.Klop@all-press.co.uk
website www.all-press.co.uk
Director of Press Nienke Klop *Junior Press Officer* Alex Barfield

Founded in 2004. Works with musicians of all genres in national, regional and online campaigns. Fees are negotiated on a campaign-to-campaign basis.

Big Blue Star
Gatehouse, Kippen, Stirlingshire FK8 3EL
tel (01786) 870910

email paulgoodwin@bigbluestar.co.uk
website www.bigbluestar.co.uk
Managing Director Paul Goodwin

Founded in 1997. Marketing agency working with record labels, artist development and design. Potential clients should make contact via post or email.

The Big Group
91 Princedale Road, London W11 4NS
tel 020-7229 8827 *fax* 020-7243 1462
email info@biggroup.co.uk
website www.biggroup.co.uk

Bloc Media
61 Charlotte Road, London EC2A 3QT
tel 020-7739 1718 *fax* 020-7739 9494
email hello@blocmedia.com
website www.blocmedia.com
New Business Information Alex Powell

Creative agency specialising in youth-orientated marketing and delivering award-winning digital campaigns. Services include web design, email marketing, online advertising and digital marketing.

Blurb PR
7 Tower Mansions, 136 West End Lane,
West Hampstead, London NW6 1SB
tel 020-7419 1221
email hello@blurbpr.com
website www.blurbpr.com or
www.myspace.com/BlurbPR
Managing Director Mike Plumley *Director of Public Relations* Michael Eccleshall

Founded in 1997. Typically signs new bands that are either unsigned, or signed to a small independent label. Works with PR, marketing, radio press, college media and online marketing. Aims to help break new and interesting acts into the mainstream by providing the media for a more diverse selection of musical talents. Specialises in heavy radio and press coverage across Great Britain and Southern Ireland. Typical fees range from £500 – £1500 a month (based on a campaign-to-campaign basis). Also provides a selection of production and distribution management for international artists.

Copperplate Consultants
68 Belleville Road, London SW11 6PP
tel/fax 020-7585 0357
email coppeprlate2000@yahoo.com
website www.copperplateconsultants.com
CEO Alan O'Leary

Founded in 1990. Works mainly with the promotion of unsigned indie Irish trad/folk artists. Deals with press and radio in the UK, Europe and USA.

Diffusion PR

Unit 16 Talina Centre, Bagleys Lane, Chelsea,
London SW6 2BW
tel 020-7384 3200 fax 020-7384 2999
email jodie@music2mix.com
website www.music2mix.com
Director of Promotions Jodie Stewart

Founded in 2006. Aims to promote Dance/Urban
music online to radio DJs worldwide through a free
download service. Costed at £150 per campaign over
3-4 months.

DWL (Dave Woolf Ltd)

53 Goodge Street, London W1T 1TG
tel 020-7436 5529 fax 020-7637 8776
email info@dwl.uk.net
website www.dwl.uk.net
Director Dave Woolf

Founded in 1996. Clients include: Joss Stone,
Jamiroquai and KT Tunstall. Works with a range of
national print media.

Emms Publicity

100 Aberdeen House, 22-24 Highbury Grove,
London N5 2E
tel 020-7226 0990 fax 020-7354 8600
email info@emmspublicity.com
website www.emmspublicity.com
Owner Stephen Emms

Founded in 2001. Aims to provide a creative,
passionate, detailed and well-communicated service.
Typical clients include indie guitar bands and dance
labels. Deals with national and regional print plus full
online PR and marketing. Also provides third-party
services including stylists and photographers plus
marketing and brand consultancy. Fee information
available on request.

Frank PR

3rd Floor, Centro 4, 20-23 Mandela Street,
London NW1 0DU
tel 020-7693 6999 fax 020-7693 6998
email contactus@frankpr.it
website www.frankpr.it

Creative general media PR and marketing company.

Frontier Promotions/Jigsaw Music

The Grange, Cockley Cley Road, Hillborough,
Thetford, Norfolk IP26 5BT
tel (01760) 756394 fax (01760) 756398
email frontieruk@btconnect.com
Managing Director Sue Williams

Founded in 1972. Independent press and radio
promotion company working within the country,
blues, roots and some mainstream genres. Deals with
press, radio and TV, including tour promotion, on a
national and regional level.

Greenroom Digital

87A Worship Street, London EC2A 2BE
tel 020-7426 5700

email will@greenroom-digital.com
website www.greenroom-digital.com
A&R Representative Will Scongal Head of Music Glen
Dormienx

Founded in 1999. Main areas of work include online
PR, aggregation, mobile, web design, viral marketing
and record labels. Works nationally and deals with
the web, TV and print. Also provides a video
production and creative consultancy service.

Hall or Nothing

11 Poplar Mews, Uxbridge Road, London W12 7JS
tel 020-8740 6288 fax 020-8749 5982
email press@hallornothing.com
website www.hallornothing.com
Key Contact Gillian Porter

Established in 1986 as an independent publicity
company. Co-ordinates print media publicity within
the UK for a vast roster of clients including Muse,
Oasis, Elbow and Feeder – 3 x winner of the Music
Week PR Award.

HardZone PR

Jackie Davidson Management, The Business Village,
3 Broomhill Road, London SW18 4JQ
tel 020-8870 8744 fax 020-8874 1578
email davinia@hardzone.co.uk
website www.hardzone.co.uk or
www.myspace.com/hardzonestreetteam
New Accounts Executive Davinia

Specialises in 'direct marketing' – aims to design the
campaign specifically to clients' requirements, with
an unusual yet effective approach in order to ensure
that campaigns gain all possible exposure. Recent
clients have included: Dr Martins, McCain, Lemar,
Beyonce, and Nintendo. Utilises promo events,
branding companies, e-marketing, artist promotion,
music promo and street and e-teaming. Deals with
London and regional coverage.

Hero PR

3 Tennyson Road, Thatcham, Berks RG18 3FR
tel (01635) 868385 fax (01635) 868385
email owen@heropr.com
website www.heropr.com
Founder Owen Packard

Founded in 2002. Specialises in promoting rock/
metal bands. Deals with national press, specialist
radio and TV. Fees are decided on a case-by-case
basis.

HPS-PR Ltd

Park House, Desborough Park Road,
High Wycombe, Bucks HP12 3DJ
tel (01628) 894700
email letstalk@hpsgroup.co.uk
website www.hpsgroup.co.uk

Broad-ranging PR, advertising and marketing
consultancy firm.

Impressive PR

9 Jeffrey's Place, Camden, London NW1 9PP
tel 020-7284 3444 *fax* 020-7284 1840
email mel@impressivepr.com
website www.impressivepr.com
Director Mel Brown

Founded in 1998. Aims to provide a proactive approach to press, and total commitment to artists represented. Works enthusiastically utilising a wide range of contacts – from publications such as *The Sunday Times* and *NME* to TV and radio, including *Jonathan Ross TV* and the *Radio 2 Show*. National, regional, student, fanzine and Internet press are covered. Also offers advice on photographers, stylists and hair and make-up artists.

Infected

18 Eddison Court, 253 Sussex Way,
London N19 4DW
tel 020-7272 9620
email mike.infected000@btclick.com
Manager Mike Gourlay

Works with both signed and unsigned acts promoting through regional press, online, fanzine, ezine and student press. Arcade Fire, Coldplay, Gossip, Razorlight and Richard Ashcroft are among a wide variety of clients. Fees are relative to artist requirements.

Katherine Howard PR

Eastwick Farm, Clay Lane, Braiseworth,
Suffolk IP23 7DZ
tel (01379) 678811
email info@katherinehoward.co.uk
website www.katherinehoward.co.uk or
www.eastwickarts.co.uk
Managing Director Katherine Howard

Founded in 1998. International arts and media communications company. Typical clients include record companies, festivals and education. Specialises in classical, jazz and soundtracks. Deals with national and regional press, radio and TV.

Material

36 Washington Street, Glasgow G3 8AZ
tel 0141-204 7970 *fax* 0141-248 5743
email info@materialmc.co.uk
website www.materialmc.co.uk
Key Contact Colin Spence

Creative established agency offering small- or large-scale brand management and bespoke services, etc. Clients include: T in the Park and MTV.

Momentum PR

83 Great Titchfield Street, London W1W 6RH
tel 020-7323 9789 *fax* 020-7436 9347
email mandy@momentumpr.co.uk
Director of Press/Proprietor Mandy Crompton

Founded in 2002. Aims to build awareness of acts through regional press, i.e. all newspapers and magazines outside of London. Specialises in indie, alternative and rock acts. Fees judged on a case-by-case basis.

Mosquito Media

PO Box 33790, 19 Chelsea Manor Street,
London SW3 6WF
tel 020-7286 0503 *fax* 020-7286 0503
email mosquitomedia@aol.com
website www.mosquito-media.co.uk
Key Contact Richard Abbott

Works primarily with the music industry as a sales and marketing company. Endeavours to assist the growth and development of independent fledgling talents – providing marketing, promotion, sales and distribution.

Noble PR

1 Mercers Mews, London N19 4PL
tel 020-7272 7772 *fax* 020-7272 2227
email suzanne@noblepr.co.uk
website www.noblepr.co.uk
Key Contact Suzanne Noble

Established in 1993. Offers a communications and reputation management consultancy. Holds strong connections with the entertainment, leisure and media industries.

The Outside Organisation Ltd

Butler House, 177-178 Tottenham Court Road,
London W1T 7NY
tel 020-7436 3633 *fax* 020-7436 3632
email info@outside-org.co.uk
website www.outside-org.co.uk

Established in the mid-1990s. Offers strategic planning of public-relation campaigns with the aim of increasing profiles for artists and clients in the entertainment industry.

Paddy Forwood PR

The Studio, Manor Farmhouse, Stubhampton,
Blandford, Dorset DT11 8JS
tel/fax (01258) 830014
email pad.forwood@virgin.net
Director Paddy Forwood

Founded in 2000. Aims to provide wide-ranging and effective press coverage at highly competitive rates. Past and present clients include: Track and Field, Sub Pop, Yep Roc, and Secretly Canadian. Genres are typically alternative country, singer/songwriter and indie rock. Promotes through national print and webzines. Fees are tailored to individual projects.

Piranha PR

Flat 7, 51 The Gardens, London SE22 9QQ
tel 020-8299 1928 *mobile* (07956) 460372
email rosie@piranha-pr.co.uk
website www.piranha-pr.co.uk
Key Contact Rosie Wilby

Established in 2004. Specialises in national and regional press releases for singer/songwriters, indie and rock acts. Clients include: Trashcan Sinatras, Cousteau, and Zillionaire.

Renegade
Music House Group, Host Europe House, Kendal Avenue, London W3 0TT
tel 020-8896 8200 *fax* 020-8896 8201
email renegade@music-house.co.uk
website www.music-house.co.uk
Key Contact Chris Smith

Established in 1992 as a division of the Music House Ltd group of companies. Specialises in student/college promotion. Music House Ltd is one of the fastest-growing independent companies in the music industry.

Republic Media Ltd
Studio 202, Westbourne Studios, 242 Acklam Road, London W10 5JJ
tel 020-8960 7449 *fax* 020-8960 7524
email info@republicmedia.net
website www.republicmedia.net
Director Sue Harris

Founded in 1999. Clients range from mainstream pop to crossover jazz. Specialises in PR through both national and regional print.

Sainted PR
Suite 35, Pall Mall Deposit, 124-128 Barlby Road, London W10 6BL
tel 020-8962 5700 *fax* 020-8962 5701
email info@saintedpr.com
website www.saintedpr.com
Managing Director Heather Finlay *Senior Account Director* Amanda Freeman

Established in 1998. Aims to deliver high-profile and effective press campaigns for artists. Works across all musical genres. Clients have included: Massive Attack, Air, Travis, and Embrace. Deals with printed media and online PR.

Scruffy Bird
The Nest, 205 Victoria Street, London SW1E 5NE
tel 020-7931 7990 *fax* 020-7900 1557
email info@scruffybird.com
website www.scruffybird.com

Handles a range of public relations tools for press, radio and television promotion and artist management. Clients include: Bjork, Wolfmother, The Young Knives, and The Stanton Warriors.

Seesaw PR
Lower Ground Floor, 22 Tower Street, London WC2H 9TW
tel 020-7539 8203 *fax* 020-7836 1167
email firstname@seesawpr.net
website www.seesawpr.net
Director Sam Wright

Founded in 2001. Specialises in providing national bespoke promotion for projects that require unique TV attention. Clients consist largely of mainstream acts including Ronan Keating, Jamie Cullum and Meat Loaf.

Serious Press & PR/Serious Management
The Old Paper Shop, North Street, Langport, Somerset TA10 9RQ
tel (01458) 250266 *mobile* (07968) 450839
email jane@seriouspress.co.uk
Manager/Owner Jane Osborne

Founded in 1994. Deals with publicity and promotional management for press and marketing campaigns. Also works with event management and personal appearances. Works with all genres but particularly R&B, easy listening, jazz, world, roots and new country. Deals with print, radio, TV and web within the south-west (including radio plugging) but also takes national and international projects. Fees negotiable.

Singsong Entertainment Publicity
14 Market Square, Winslow, Bucks MK18 3AF
tel (01296) 715228
email peter@singsongs.biz
website www.singsongs.biz
Managing Director Peter Muir

Founded in 2001. Aims to successfullly raise profiles in order to build careers. Works with all clients but typically within the jazz, rock, blues, and singer/songwriter genres. Deals with all media regionally, nationally and in some parts of Europe, USA, Ireland and Australasia. Also provides related new release and touring marketing services. Fees are scaled according to project.

Slidingdoors PR
PO Box 21469, Highgate, London N6 4ZG
tel 020-8340 3412
email james@slidingdoors.biz
website www.slidingdoors.biz
Managing Director James Hamilton

Established in 2005. Aims to provide a high-quality PR service across all media in order to create and exploit positive opportunities on behalf of clients. Clients include: Roger Sanchez, Judge Jules, UMTV and Mainifesto labels, and bands such as Moco and Marlowe. Fee information given on application.

Terrie Doherty Promotions
40 Princess Street, Manchester M1 6DE
tel 0161-234-0044
email terriedoherty@zoo.co.uk
Director Terrie Doherty

Founded in 1998. Promotes acts through regional radio and TV. Clients have included: Katie Melua and Whitney Houston. Works within UK and Northern Ireland. Fees negotiable.

Traffic Marketing

6 Stucley Place, London NW1 8NS
tel 020-7485 7400 *fax* 020-7267 5151
email info@trafficmarketing.co.uk
website www.trafficmarketing.co.uk or
www.trafficonline.net
Managing Director Lisa Paulon

Specialises in regional and national tour, online and
street-team marketing for the music and
entertainment industry. Also deals with online viral
campaigns and fanbase development. Typically
clients include records labels, management and
artists.

Use Your Ears

PO Box 52808, London SW11 2YU
tel 020-7223 7472 *mobile* (07931) 350121
email via website
website www.useyourears.co.uk

Founded in 2000 as a music portal and networking
platform for musicians and music industry
professionals. Also provides music consultancy and
services including: project management for
independent releases covering print and online PR;
marketing; TV and radio promotion; Internet;
distribution and manufacturing.

Vision

22 Upper Grosvenor Street, London W1K 7PE
tel 020-7499 8024 *fax* 020-7499 8032
email vision@visionmusic.co.uk
website www.visionmusic.co.uk
Head of Promotions Rob Dallison

Founded in 1998. Works with a wide variety of
clients from Unkle and Moby to bedroom producers
and small labels. Covers press, radio and digital
management. Fees are tailored to suit project. Other
services include organising licensing for ringtones
and download sites.

Managing a band

JoJo Gould provides an overview of artist management and the relationship between a band and its manager.

The music manager is a key figure in the development of the artist. Traditionally maligned as an exploitative 'Mr 20 per cent', today's artist manager requires a sophisticated set of business and personal qualities in order to elevate their artist to full potential.

Artist management is a learning curve, and like many other ventures it can be driven in the first instance by enthusiasm and friendship. A friend who drives the band's van may, for example, become their *de facto* manager. Indeed, third-party representation is generally considered to be advantageous when negotiating gigs or media coverage – even at the earliest stages of your career.

Historically, some managers gained significant celebrity – such as Malcolm McLaren (the Sex Pistols), Brian Epstein (the Beatles), Andrew Loog Oldham (the Rolling Stones) and Colonel Tom Parker (Elvis Presley). However, the vast majority of those who provide this important business service are movers and shakers who work quietly behind the scenes.

Attributes and goals

The core objective of the manager is to guide and maximise their artist's career opportunities, and this can manifest itself in many forms. As a result, there is no one-stop manual for band management – instead, every manager can bring his or her own style, values and qualities to the task.

An aspiring manager must acknowledge that the music industry is people-based. Contacts with an array of industry personnel should therefore be formed and cultivated over time. Securing a recording contract by overcoming the 'barbed wire' of the record company's A&R department is usually the most difficult aspect of the work of a new manager of an unsigned act. Where successful, this is generally achieved through hard work, an ascending local profile, a very thick skin, and an element of good fortune!

Industry knowledge is also vital. If the act is a songwriter, then the manager will require an understanding of the dynamics and income-stream opportunities arising from the activity of music publishing. If the artist is a live performer, then knowledge of gigs, venues, touring, agents and promoters will be necessary. Underpinning legal knowledge of typical music industry contracts and the entrepreneurial know-how to set up companies on the artist's behalf are also useful vocational skills for the manager.

The manager's role can be summarised as follows: to strategise, motivate, represent, guide, advise, negotiate and schedule, while maximising earning potential and celebrity. In some cases, and particularly for a new artist, the manager may help to finance the project. Like any business venture, an element of risk may therefore be involved in artist management – and this, of course, will include a significant investment of time and energy as well. The manager should have belief in their artist, and a clear vision. Ideally, their organisational, motivational, communication and numeric skills can combine with business acumen, industry knowledge and current market awareness, to enrich and enhance the band's prospects in the competitive marketplace that is the modern music business.

When seeking a manager, such personal qualities are important; however, the artist should also consider integrity and the honesty of the individual who will, in effect, be directing their career.

The logistical role of artist management will differ depending upon the stage of the band's development. The manager of a new act will be concerned with booking rehearsals, securing gigs, cultivating those all-important first contacts with the local media, and making a demo tape. Creating a local 'buzz' first is always preferable to the uncertainties of sending unsolicited demo tapes to record companies. The manager should also strive to protect their artist from premature exposure to live audiences and A&R representatives.

In sharp contrast, the manager of an internationally successful act will find that their role shifts from hands-on activities to the delegation of tasks through a multitude of industry individuals – such as agents, promoters, studio producers, video directors, tour managers, media pluggers and A&R managers. This gradual path developing from operational to strategic matters will naturally occur as an act successfully matures.

Income streams

The band's manager has an important responsibility to ensure that appropriate royalties and other incomes are collected and distributed properly. Money, and its proper handling, is a key element of the *fiduciary* relationship that is considered to exist between a band and their manager (i.e. a relationship based on trust).

An unsigned act may rely on gigs and limited merchandising among a developing fan base for income. More likely than not, a band at this stage will have more outlays than income. A signed act, though – which sells records, writes songs, and tours – will require regular and rigorous assistance from professionals. Bands at such levels may generate income streams from such diverse activities as:

- recording advances;
- recording royalties;
- music publishing advances;
- music publishing royalties;
- performers' royalties;
- merchandising;
- sponsorship;
- touring;
- media engagements;
- fan clubs;
- online activities.

The band's manager has an obligation to see that all relevant monies are channelled properly. In doing so, they should also encourage all band members to join the appropriate industry collection societies.

Legalities

Contracts are increasingly recognised as essential in today's complex music industry; it is therefore advisable for the manager to have a written agreement with the band. This formal document will usually have a duration of between one and five years, and may be performance-related, with options. It will outline the manager's commission: usually around 20 per cent, although this can be negotiable (e.g. 15 per cent on music publishing monies, but 25 per cent on merchandising income). The artist should be careful to specify that the manager is remunerated on net receipts and not on gross receipts. The typical artist-management agreement usually covers *all* territories, and includes clauses on exclusivity, activities, expenses, duties of both parties, indemnities, warranties, termination, commission, post-termination commission, accounting procedures, and governing laws.

Note that the post-termination commission clause is particularly contentious. If this clause is written to cover 'the duration of the copyright', then you, as an artist, will be paying commission to your manager for 50 years on each sound-recording income stream, and for the full lifetime of the band's songwriters – plus an additional 70 years – on all songwriting income! It is common practice therefore, to limit the manager's commission on expiry of the contract. Again, this is negotiable, and may be as little as a few years following the end of the agreement, or based on a declining scale over a defined period of time.

Having an artist-management agreement is not, however, a legal requirement. Some managers have long and flourishing careers with their artists without the need to write any specifics of this relationship down on paper (most famously, Peter Grant, who managed Led Zeppelin). In today's more litigious era, though, it is considered good practice for all parties to have such a document.

Managers can also implement good practice by encouraging the band to have their own internal 'band agreement'. This partnership agreement can be written to cover potentially divisive issues such as arrangements for leaving members and joining members, and the agreed split of songwriting income between the band members.

Before signing any legal document, all parties should have access to independent legal advice.

Trading structure

As the music industry is a business, the band's manager should construct a formal trading relationship through which the band and the manager can interact. The manager will be required to set up and operate his or her own firm. On a day-to-day level, this will be financed at their own expense. Through this firm, the manager can invoice the band (who should also operate as a legal trading entity).

As a result, knowledge of company formation and statutory obligations – such as tax and accounting requirements – will be necessary at some stage on the manager's part. Again, these issues can be delegated to appropriately qualified professionals.

Industry support

The music business has become quite sophisticated, and managers, like many other industry practitioners, now have their own trade body. In the UK, this is known as the Music Managers Forum (MMF), and is affiliated to the International Managers Forum. The MMF has as its central objective that of raising professional standards in music management. Managers of unsigned acts can join as associate members at discounted rates. Benefits include regular workshops, contract advice, networking opportunities, social events, and a united voice on issues that affect the everyday activities of music managers.

Summary

Artist management is a challenging activity and a key element of music business service provision. Due to its multi-faceted nature, and comparatively vulnerable legal position, it is often cited as the most difficult job in the music industry. However, the task can be an exciting journey, and may sometimes be as close to performing as many talented music business individuals ever get.

A hardworking and visionary manager can make a significant contribution to a band's development, and he or she will probably represent the single most important personal and business relationship in the career of the aspiring artist.

JoJo Gould is a UK-based lecturer, and was for five years joint Managing Editor of *Music Business Journal*. He lectures and consults on the European Degree in International Music Management, and holds a Master of Science degree in Business IT Systems. He was a co-founder and first Chairman of New Music in Scotland, and was previously Senior Lecturer in Music Industry Management at Buckinghamshire Chilterns University College.

GET THE RIGHT ADVICE

"When you are about to sign a deal, and someone blurts out, 'They aren't concerned about the contract, just show them the money,' then be very wary of the deal. The music business can be relatively superficial, and my advice to you would be, 'Don't chase the money!' Royalties will be generated regardless of the size of the advance, so the quicker you recoup in the first place, the better chance you have of getting a more favourable deal the next time round.

Furthermore, it is crucial that you obtain an enthusiastic professional manager, as well as hire a respected lawyer. Try to learn about the general flow of income – things such as advances, royalty streams and recoupment. Most importantly, make sure you understand what you are signing. Don't be afraid to ask questions if you are not certain about something. Your songs are your bread and butter (and, with luck, your pension), so don't be casual with your future.

Finally, use the people that are available around you to help. There are many organisations out there which can give you excellent, quality advice – such as the Musicians' Union, the British Academy of Composers and Songwriters, and British Music Rights. Call them all and get clued up."

Jay Mistry, former Royalty Tracker Manager for BMG, runs a successful royalty tracking company called Musical Sleuth Ltd. See **www.musicalsleuth.com**.

Management companies

19 Management
33 Ransome's Dock, 35-37 Parkgate Road,
London SW11 4NP
tel 020-7801 1919 *fax* 020-7801 1920
email reception@19.co.uk
website www.19.co.uk
Contact Simon Fuller

Major management company with roster including
high-profile acts such as Will Young, Kelly Clarkson,
Rachel Stevens and Emma Bunton. Specialises in
integrating brands with entertainment properties.

ACA Music Management
7 North Parade, Bath, Somerset BA2 4DD
tel (01225) 428284 *fax* (01225) 400090
email aca_aba@freenet.co.uk
Owner Harry Finegold

Founded in 1995. Represents performers, composers,
songwriters and festivals mainly in the jazz, rock and
pop genres. Potential clients should submit DVD or
CD and photos via post. Commission typically
charged at 10-15%. Also runs own studio.

Adventures in Music Management
4 Mill Lane, Wallingford, Oxon OX10 0DH
tel (01491) 832183
email paul@adventuresin-music.com
website www.adventure-records.com
Paul Conroy Managing Director

Independent management company.

Alliance Artist Management
PO Box 388, Bristol
tel (212) 304-3538 *fax* (212) 304-3538
email rob@allianceartistmanagement.com
website www.allianceartistmanagement.com
Contact Rob Robbins

Established to offer artist management and
representation to vocal ensembles, string quartets,
chamber groups, jazz and world music attractions
worldwide. Dedicated to enhancing the promotion of
these artists and recognising the importance of
educating listeners to the best that this genre of music
has to offer.

Amber
PO Box 1, Chipping Ongar, Essex CM5 9HZ
tel (01277) 365046
email management@amberartists.com
website www.amberartists.com
Founder Paul Tage

Established in 1997. Works mainly within the pop,
jazz and soul genres. Artists on roster include Bridget
Metcalfe. Potential clients should make contact by
phone before submitting a 3-track CD.

Ambush Artist Management
32 Ransome's Dock, 35-37 Parkgate Road,
London SW11 4NP
tel 020-7801 1919 *fax* 020-7738 1819
email ambush.native@19.co.uk
website www.ambushgroup.co.uk
Managing Director Alister Jamieson

Works with performers, songwriters, composers and
producers in the fields of pop, dance and MOR.
Potential clients should make contact through
showreel submission.

ASM Damage Ltd
42 City Business Centre, Lower Road,
London SE16 2XB
tel 020-7740 1600 *fax* 020-7740 1700
email asm@missioncontrol.net
website www.asmanagement.co.uk
Contact David Samuel

Works mainly in dance, pop and urban genres.
Clients include: Leo The Lion, Amanda Wilson(from
freemasons), Si Hulbert (producer, songwriter, remixer), and Harry Brooks (singer/songwriter).

Big Blue Music
Windy Ridge, 39-41 Buck Lane, London NW9 OAP
tel/fax 020-8205 2990
email info@bigbluemusic.biz
website www.bigbluemusic.biz
Manager/Producer Steve Ancliffe

Founded in 1999. Aims to develop and market new
talent across all music genres. Clients include
performers, songwriters and composers. Potential
clients should post a showreel or CD – please do not
send tracks via email.

Bulldozer Management
8 Roland Mews, Stepney Green, London E1 3JT
tel 020-7929 3333 *fax* 020-7929 3222
email oliver@bulldozermedia.com
website www.bulldozermedia.com
Managing Director Oliver Brown

Founded in 1998. Represents a range of artists
working in the dance, D&B, techno and house
genres. Artists represented include: DJ Marky,
Anderson Noise, and DJ Patife. Potential clients
should send demos by post on CD or vinyl. Also
provides sponsorship and brand consultancy,
promotion and project development services.

Conception Artist Management
36 Percy Street, London W1T 2DH
tel 020-7580 4424 *fax* 020-7323 1695
email info@conception.gb.com
website www.conception.gb.com
Managing Director Jean-Nicol Chelmiah

Works within the fields of pop, rock, dance, indie, hip hop, R&B and electronic music. Typical clients include performers and songwriters. Commission is artist-specific. Potential clients should submit a showreel or demo and website details.

Cool Music Media
1A Fishers Lane, Chiswick, London W4 1RX
tel 020-8995 7766 *fax* 020-8987 8996
email enquiries@coolmusicltd.com
website www.coolmusicltd.com

Represents composers for film and TV.

Creative World Entertainment
The Croft, Deans Lane Farm, Clay Pit Lane, Lichfield, Staffs WS14 0AG
tel (01543) 253576 *fax* (01543) 255184
email info@creative-world-entertainment.co.uk
website www.creative-world-entertainment.co.uk
Managing Director Mervyn Spence

Founded in 2001. Specialises in pop, rock and dance; is particularly interested in working with artists with quality songs, focus and direction. Material to be submitted via CD or MP3.

Cultural Foundation
Rosedale, North Yorkshire TO18 8R
tel (08454) 584699
email info@cultfound.org
website www.cultfound.org
Director Peter Bell

Founded in 2000. Works only with North East UK/ North Yorkshire-based musicians in the rock, blues, jazz, world and indie genres. Clients include: Back Door, Manfat Voodoo, and 3 Foot Ninja. Bases commission on a co-operative work practice. Potential clients should email in the first instance (do not email MP3s).

Deluxxe Management
PO Box 373, Teddington TW11 8QZ
tel 020-8755 3630 *fax* 020-8404 7771
email info@deluxxe.co.uk
website www.deluxxe.co.uk or www.myspace.com/deluxxemanagement
Managing Director Diane Wagg *General Manager* Sam Cooke

Founded in 2001. Provides international music management and consultancy services. Works with a variety of genres including pop, rock, dance and alternative. Clients include: Lily Fraser, Captain Wilberforce, Scouting for Girls, and Elektralux. Also provides professional coaching – see **www.dianewagg.com** for more details.

Eaton Music Ltd
Eaton House, 39 Lower Richmond Road, Putney, London SW15 1ET
tel 020-8788 4557 *fax* 020-8780 9711
email info@eatonmusic.com
website www.eatonmusic.com
Director Mandy Oates

Founded in 1975. Mainly represents film and TV composers including George Fenton and David Mackey. Potential clients should submit material by post or email.

Empire Artist Management
36 Uxbridge Street, London W8 7TN
tel 020-7221 1133 *fax* 020-7243 1585
email info@empire-management.co.uk
website www.empire-management.co.uk

High-profile artist management company, currently representing Daniel Bedingfield, Natasha Bedingfield and The Feeling.

F & G Management
Unit 101, The Saga Centre, 326 Kensal Road, London W10 5BZ
tel 020-8964 1917 *fax* 020-8960 9971
email gavino@btclick.com
Director Gavino Prunas

Works to represent artists and bands in a wide variety of genres. Potential clients should make contact by post, sending demos and biography.

First Time Management
Sovereign House, 12 Trewartha Road, Praa Sands, Penzance, Cornwall TR20 9ST
tel (01736) 762826 *fax* (01736) 763328
email panamamus@aol.com
website www.panamamusic.co.uk
Managing Director Roderick Jones

Established in 1987. Management and promotions company working with songwriters, composers and all categories of performing artists in a range of genres. Clients have included: Kevin Kendle, Pete Arnold, and Wendy Patrick. Commission is subject to negotiation. Potential clients should send CD, biogs, photos, gig listing, previous contracts and any other necessary information in order to create interest. Will attend showcases.

Fox Records (Management)
62 Lake Rise, Romford, Essex RM1 4EE
tel (01708) 760544 *fax* (01708) 760563
email foxrecords@talk21.com
website www.foxrecordsltd.co.uk
Directors Colin Brewer, Linda Ryle

Established in 1996. Represents mainly young performers in the pop, rock and dance industries. Commission charged at 15–20%. Potential clients should post CD with biog, pictures and DVD if available.

Georgina Ivor Associates
28 Old Devonshire Road, London SW12 9RB
tel 020-8673 7179 *fax* 020-8675 8058
email info@giamanagement.com
website www.giamanagement.com

Highly focused artist management agency created for the development of classical musicians throughout the world, and with over 30 years' experience within the classical music industry. The company is a member of the Association Europeene des Agents Artistiques (AEAA). Current musicians include: Nikolai Demidenko, Marc-Andre Hamelin, Piers Lane and Leonid Gorokhov.

Heavenly Management
47 Frith Street, London W1D 4SE
tel 020-7494 2998 *fax* 020-7437 3317
email andrew@heavenlymanagement.com
Managing Director Martin Kelly

Founded in 1998. Represents artists and bands mainly in rock and pop genres. Clients include: Starsailor, Saint Etienne, Duke Spirit, and Soulsavers. Commission charged at 20%. Potential clients should post a demo CD and picture.

ie:music
111 Frithville Gardens, London W12 7JG
tel 020-8600 3400 *fax* 020-8600 3401
email info@iemusic.co.uk
website www.iemusic.co.uk
Directors Tim Clark, David Enthoven

Founded in 1994. Works with performers, composers and songwriters in all genres. Roster includes: Robbie Williams and Craig Armstrong. Potential clients should post demos.

Intermusica Artists' Management Ltd
16 Duncan Terrace, London N1 8BZ
tel 020-7278 5455 *fax* 020-72788434
email mail@intermusica.co.uk
website www.intermusica.co.uk

Leading international music agency geared around the classical music genre and representing renowned conductors, instrumentalists, singers, composers and orchestras from around the world. Instrumental in representation, promotion and putting together festivals, special tours, projects and concerts.

Intuition Music
1 Devonport Mews, London W12 8NG
email big@intuitionmusic.com
Director Bernie Griffiths

Founded in 1999. Aims to develop, promote and expose music of quality and integrity from all genres. Currently looking for new clients to represent in the fields of rock, pop and dance. Potential applicants should posts CDs or email MP3s.

Jackie Davidson Management
The Business Village, 3 Broomhill Road,
London SW18 4JQ
tel 020-8870 8744 *fax* 020-8874 1578
email firstname@jdmanagement.co.uk
website www.jdmanagement.co.uk
Managing Director Jackie Davidson

Represents a number of artists, songwriters and producers, including: Mickey P (Neneh Cherry,

Yousson N'Dour), Wayne Hector (Il Divo, Westlife, Rascal Flatts, Charlotte Church, James Morrison, Black Eyed Peas), and Ali Lorne Tennant (Lemar, Blue, *Pop Idol*).

JBM Management
15 Berlin Road, Edgeley, Stockport SK3 9QD
tel 0161-474 0204
email jbmmanagement@aol.com
Managing Director Jason Brierley

Works within the pop, rock, dance, hip hop and indie genres. Commission taken at 15% of net earnings. Potential clients should send promo pack by post. Please give 2 weeks' notice for any showcases.

Jive Entertainments
PO Box 5865, Corby, Northamptonshire NN17 6ZT
tel (01536) 743366 *fax* (01536) 460591
email hojive@aol.com
Managing Director Dave Bartrum *Personal Assistant* Sue Carr

Established in 1987. Managment agency working mainly with pop and rock genres. Clients include: Showaddywaddy and Suzi Quatro. Fee scale is variable. Contact via email followed by CD or publicity pack.

John Waller Management & Marketing
The Old Truman Brewery, 91 Brick Lane,
London E1 6QL
tel 020-7247 1057
email john.waller@dial.pipex.com
Owner John Waller

Founded in 1998. Artist management and marketing consultancy service. Works within the singer/ songwriter, pop, latino house and alternative country/folk rock genres. Clients include: The Storys, The Zombies, Melanie C, Cathy Burton and Paul Carrack. Potential clients should ring, email or post demo CD and biography information. Commission charged at 20%.

Madrigal Music
Guy Hall Awre, Gloucestershire GL14 1EL
tel (01594) 510512 *fax* (01594) 510512
email artists@madrigalmusic.co.uk
website www.madrigalmusic.co.uk
Managing Director Nick Ford

Founded in 1972. Offers a range of services for bands and musicans worldwide in a range of genres including rock, indie and pop. Represents artists at major international industry events, including Midem and Popkomm. Clients include: Tony McPhee, Freefall, and Klasshaus. Members of the Music Managers Worldwide Forum (MMF). Potential clients should make contact via post, email or phone. Unsolicited material is accepted but requires CD, biography and photo. Will attend showcases. Commission charged at around 20%.

Memnon Entertainment (UK)
Habib House, 3rd Floor, 9 Stevenson Square,
Piccadilly, Manchester M1 1DB
tel 0161-238 8516 *fax* 0161-237 6717
email info@memnonentertainment.com
website www.memnonentertainment.comm
Key Contact Rudi Kidd

Founded in August 2000. Deals with all genres.
Recent clients have included Dan Askew – Spooks,
H-Town and Laine Norbury. Potential clients should
submit 3-song CD with biog by post. Also provides
management services.

Mighty Music Management
2 Stucley Place, Camden, London NW1 8NS
tel 020-7482 6660 *fax* 020-7482 6606
email jo@mainmastery.co.uk
Co-director Jo Mirowski

Founded in 1995. Works with performers,
songwriters and composers in the pop and rock
genres. Commission charged at 20% across all clients.
Potential clients should make contact with preferably
3-or 4-track demos, biog and photos.

Modest! Management
91 Peterborough Road, London SW6 3BU
tel 020-7384 6410 *fax* 020-7384 6411
email info@modestmanagement.com
website www.modestmanagment.com

London-based music management company run by
Richard Griffiths and Harry Magee, who have over 55
years' combined music industry knowledge and
experience. Currently in the process of expanding out
of the UK to create an Australian office. Current
roster includes: Delta Goodrem, Brian McFadden,
Lemar, and The Webb Sisters.

The Modest Music Group
The Hat Factory, 65-67 Bute Street, Luton,
Bedfordshire
tel (01582) 508726
email info@themodestmusicgroup.com
website www.themodestmusicgroup.com

An independent music company incorporating artist
management, promotion and consultancy. Welcomes
enquiries from both new and developing artists.
Other services include courses in music management,
and songwriting; can also offer festival management
and security.

Native Management
32 Ransome's Dock, 35-37 Parkgate Road,
London SW11 4NP
tel 020-7801 1919 *fax* 020-7738 1819
email info@nativemanagement.com
website www.nativemanagement.com
Managing Director Peter Evans

High-profile producer/songwriter management
company with roster including Paulo Nutini, Gwen
Stefani and James Blunt.

Northern Music Company
Cheapside Chambers, 43 Cheapside, Bradford,
West Yorks BD1 4HP
tel (01274) 300301 *fax* (01274) 730097
email info@northernmusic.co.uk
website www.northernmusic.co.uk
Managing Director Andy Farrow

Founded in 1987. Represents performers, songwriters
and producers, typically in the rock music genre.
Charges up to 20% commission. Potential clients
should make contact by post with CD, biog and
photo.

Positive Management
41 West Ella Road, London NW10 9PT
tel 020-8961 6257 *fax* 020-8963 1974
email Meira@positive-mgmt.co.uk
website www.positive-mgmt.co.uk
Managing Director Meira Shore

Supports a rich and varied roster, including artists
such as Terry Callier and Tina Grace.

Robin Morton Consultancy
22 Herbert Street, Glasgow G20 6NB
tel 0141-560 2748 *fax* 0141-357 0655
email robin@robinmorton.com
Managers Robin and Neil Morton

Founded in 1995. Works within the pop and rock
fields. Aims to work with personally preferred artists
and develop their careers while building teams of
like-minded experts around them. Clients
represented include: The Trashcan Sinatras, Jo
Mango, and Old Solar. Commission charged at 20%.
Potential clients should make contact via email.

Rough Trade Artist Management
66 Golborne Road, London W10 5PS
tel 020-8960 9888 *fax* 020-8968 6715
email kelly.kiley@roughtraderecords.com
website www.roughtraderecords.com
A&R Mog Yoshihara

Offers an artist and producer management service.
Roster has included: Bernard Butler, Graham Sutton,
Cerys Matthews, McAlmont & Butler, and Pulp.

Safe Management
St Ann's House, Guildford Road, Lightwater,
Surrey GU18 5RA
tel (01274) 476676 *fax* (01276) 451109
email alex@safemanagement.co.uk
website www.safemanagement.co.uk or
www.myspace.com/safemanagement
Director Chris Herbert

Founded in 1994. Works with bands, solo artists,
writers and producers within pop music. Clients
include: Kym Marsh, Sparx, and Alexis Strum.
Charges 20% commission. Potential clients should
submit full info pack including showreel, biog, photo
and/or video.

Sanctuary Artists Management

Sanctuary House, 45-53 Sinclair Road,
London W14 0NS
tel 020-7602 6351 *fax* 020-7603 5941
email info@sanctuarygroup.com
website www.sanctuarygroup.com
CEO Joe Cokell

Major management company with a roster that
includes Groove Armada, Slayer, Slipknot and Super
Furry Animals.

SGO Music Management Ltd

PO Box 2015, Salisbury, Wiltshire UK
tel (01264) 811154 *fax* (01264) 811172
email sgomusic@sgomusic.com
website www.sgomusic.com
Managing Director Stuart Orgley

Founded in 1991. Primarily works with pop, rock and
world music genres. Clients include: Chris Eaton
(songwriter), Lunasa (band), and Eric Bibb (artist).
Contact through personal recommendation only.

SMA Talent

SMA Talent Ltd, The Cottage, Church Street,
Fressingfield, Suffolk IP21 5PA
tel (01379) 586734 *fax* (01379) 586131
email carolynne@smatalent.com
website www.smatalent.com
Agents Carolynne Wyper, Olav Wyper, Iain Rousham

Represents a number of composers and music
producers. Clients include: John Altman (*Little Voice,
Titanic, The Roman Spring of Mrs Stone*); Tim Atack
(*Much Ado About Nothing, Elephant Juice, Among
Giants*); Alan Parker (*Fallen Angel, Walking With
Cavemen, Rhodes*); Paul Leonard-Morgan (*Spooks,
Galapagos, Silent Witness*).

Spirit Music & Media

PO Box 30884, London W12 9AX
tel 020-8746 7461 *fax* 020-8749 7441
email info@spiritmm.com
Director Tom Haxell

Founded in 2000. Works within the pop, rock, folk
and world music genres. Roster includes Damien
Dempsey, The Wonder Stuff, We Start Fires, The
Bellagios and Miles Hunt. Commission charged at
20%.

For postal submissions include a stamped
addressed envelope if you wish your work to be
returned. Email submissions also possible - send a
link to your site.

Steve Draper Entertainments

2 The Coppice, Beardwood Manor, Blackburn,
Lancashire BB2 7BQ
tel (01254) 679005 *fax* (01254) 679005
email steve@stevedraperents.fsbusiness.co.uk
website www.stevedraperents.org.uk
Directors Steve Draper, Tracy Kendall

Founded in 1972. Provides management service for
musicians working within pop, rock and dance
genres. Potential clients may submit material via
email, or send CD.

Top Banana Management

Monomark House, 27 Gloucester Street,
London WC1N 3XX
tel 020-7419 5026
email garry@topbananaman.com or
david@topbananaman.com
website www.topbananaman.com
Artist Manager Garry Kemp *Head of A&R* David
Vaughen Roberts

Founded in 2001. Aims to provide the most
professional service possible in a trustworthy manner
in order to support and nurture new talent. Deals
with performers, producers and engineers working in
the rock, pop and R&B genres. Commission charged
at 20% for artists; producers negotiable. Potential
clients should post CDs to David.

Wild West Management

Argentum, 2 Queen Caroline Street,
London W6 9DX
tel 020-8323 8013 *fax* 020-8323 8080
email ela@ela.co.uk
website http://www.ela.co.uk/wildwest/home.htm
Managing Director John Giacobbi

Deals with artist management, business affairs and
management consultancy. Clients have included: Eyes
Wide Open, Christiansilva and Mirima.

The Yukon Management

91 Saffron Hill, London EC1N 8PT
tel 020-7242 8408 *fax* 020-7242 8408
email music@theyukonmusic.com
Proprietor Andrew Maurice

Founded in 1998. Represents a range of artists,
songwriters and producers in a variety of genres.
Clients also include record labels and publishers for
sychronisation purposes. Potential clients should
send CD or showcase invitations. Commission varies
between 15 and 20%.

Z Management

The Palm House, PO Box 19734,
London SW15 2WU
tel 020-8874 3337 *fax* 020-8874 3599
email office@zman.co.uk
MCQ/MD Zita Wadwa *General Manager* Holly
Lintell

Works within the fields of pop, rock, dance and
classical music. Clients include: Chris Potter, James
Sangler, and Jony Rockstar. Commission charged at
20%. Potential clients should post showreels/CVs.

Lawyers

Addleshaw Goddard
150 Aldersgate Street, London EC1A 4EJ
tel 020-7880 5653
email david.engel@addleshawgoddard.com
website www.addleshawgoddard.com

A firm with specialist knowledge in media and the Internet, with particular expertise that includes: defamation on the web; recovery of domain names; illegal downloads; and unauthorised use of copyright material on websites.

Angel & Co
1 Green Street, Mayfair, London W1K 6RG
tel 020-7495 0555 fax 020-7495 7550
email mail@legalangel-uk.com
Director Nigel Angel

Founded in 1993. Specialises in media contracts.

Baxter McKay Schoenfeld LLP
Suite 208 Panther House, 38 Mount Pleasant, London WC1X OAN
tel 020-7833 9191 fax 020-7833 9494
email gba@bmsllp.co.uk
Senior Partner Gillian Baxter

Founded in 2002. Media and entertainment specialists with particular orientation towards composers and musicians. Will advise on all company law matters, employment and freelance. Has 2 published works: *Music Copyright in Film and TV* and *Industry Agreements*. Initial interview free, happy to negotiate.

Benedicts (Solicitors) LLP
Hope House, 40 St Peters Road, London W6 9BD
tel 020-8741 6020 fax 020-8741 8362
website www.benedicts.biz
Partners Serena and John Benedict

Established in 1987. Aims to provide a high-level professional service and practical commercial expertise to meet needs on a cost-effective basis. Specialises in working with music industry clients including: record labels; publishers; artists; writers; managers; sponsorship; merchandising; live events and producers. Work is charged at hourly rates but can sometimes be discussed and pre-agreed on the basis of what is involved.

Brabners Chaffe Street
1 Dale Street, Liverpool L2 2ET
tel 0151-600 3000 fax 0151-600 3009
email frances.mcentegart@brabnerscs.com
website www.brabnerschaffestreet.com
Associate/Barrister Francis McEntegart

Established in 1790. Recently placed in the top category of the Legal 500. Offers a full range of services for the commercial sector. Clients are typically artists, management, songwriters, publishers, labels and venues.

Briffa
Business Design Centre, Upper Street, Islington, London N1 0QH
tel 020-7288 6003 fax 020-7288 6004
email alexp@briffa.com
website www.briffa.com
Solicitor Alex Papkyriacou

Founded in 1995. A well-established intellectual property law firm. Typically, clients include independent labels, artists, publishing companies and songwriters. These can range from multinational and global companies to individuals with a good idea. Operates a successful Design Protect Insurance Scheme and gives a free half-hour consultation to all new clients.

Brookstreet Des Roches
25 Milton Park Road, Oxford OX14 4SH
mobile (07885) 498800
email charlie.seaward@bsdr.com
website www.bsdr.com
Partner Charlie Seaward

Founded in 1994. Offers advice on commercial law. Clients include recording artists, publishing companies and record labels.

Calvert Solicitors
77 Weston Street, London Bridge, London SE1 3RS
tel 020-7234 0707
email mail@calvertsolicitors.co.uk
website www.calvertsolicitors.co.uk
Senior Partner Nigel Calvert

Established in 1996. Provides specialist advice in the fields of copyright design and artistic invention, dealing with both commercial exploitation and protection. Typical clients include producers, composers and performers. Fees are either hourly or fixed on a case-by-case basis.

Clintons
55 Drury Lane, London WC2B 5RZ
tel 020-7379 6080 fax 020-7240 9310
email info@clintons.co.uk
website www.clintons.co.uk
Partner Peter Button

Founded in 1956. Works with groups and solo artists in all genres of music. Other typical clients include record companies, music publishers, managers and agents.

Colins Long Solicitors
24 Pepper Street, London SE1 0EB
tel 020-7401 9800 fax 020-7401 9850

email info@collinslong.com
website www.collinslong.com
Director Simon Long

Founded in 2000. Specialises in music law aiming to provide a personal service and independent ethos. Typically works with writers, producers and artists. Offers a free initial consultation.

Collyer-Bristow

4 Bedford Row, London WC1R 4DF
tel 020-7468 7233 *fax* 020-7468 7338
email nick.kanaar@collyerbristow.com
website www.collyerbristow.com
Consultant Solicitor Nick Kanaar

Established in 1880. Aims to advise across the whole spectrum of media law business. Typically works with creative and independent clients.

David Wineman Solicitors

Craven House, 121 Kingsway, London WC2B 6NX
tel 020-7400 7800 *fax* 020-7400 7890
email irving.david@davidwineman.co.uk
website www.davidwineman.co.uk
Co-Senior Partner Irving David

Established in 1981. Specialist commercial and media practice holding the prestigious practice management quality mark – Lexcel. Has dealt with an impressive array of artist clients such as Sir George Martin, Ozzy Osbourne, Black Sabbath and Luciano Pavarotti. Also provides services for a variety of singer/songwriters, independent music publishers, record labels and producers – including those just starting out in the industry. Fees are based on an hourly rate and will not be exceeded without a client's consent.

Engel Monjack

16-18 Berners Street, London W1T 3LN
tel 020-7291 3838 *fax* 020-7291 3839
email info@engelmonjack.com
website www.engelmonjack.com
Partner Jonathan Monjack

Specialises in working with songwriters, recording artists, producers and publishing companies.

Gray & Co

Habib House, 3rd Floor, 9 Stevenson Square, Piccadilly, Manchester M1 1DB
tel 0161-236 6717 *fax* 0161-236 6717
email grayco@grayand.co.uk
website www.grayand.co.uk
Partner Rudi Kidd

Established in 1995. An entertainment and law practice that provides legal services in all areas of the entertainment industry. Represents artists and both record and publishing companies. Provides a half-hour free consultation for new clients.

GSC Solicitors

31-32 Ely Place, London EC1N 6TD
tel 020-7822 2222 *fax* 020-7822 2211

email info@gscsolicitors.com
website www.gscsolicitors.com
Partner Saleem Sheikh

Founded in 1972. An innovative City law firm with expertise in media and intellectual property, commercial property and corporate and international work. Main areas of work include: recording contracts, film and video contracts, licensing, publishing, management and promotion, merchandising agreements and royalty disputes. Specialisms include the protection of intellectual property rights in the courts, and specialist tribunals.

Howell-Jones LLP

Flint House, 52 High Street, Leatherhead, Surrey KT22 8AJ
tel (01372) 860650 *fax* (01372) 860660
email peter.scott@hjplaw.co.uk
website www.hjplaw.co.uk
Entertainment Partner Peter Scott

Founded in 1977. Deals with all legal services and contract negotiation. Typical clients include music companies, artists and composers. First consultation is free without obligation.

Iain Adam

2 Whitmore Gardens, London NW10 5HH
tel 020-869 5243 *fax* 020-8960 2128
Solicitor Iain Adam

Established in 1975. Specialises in all issues connected with the music business. Welcomes independently minded people in particular.

James Rubenstein & Co

149 Chomley Gardens, Mill Lane, London NW6 1AB
tel 020-7431 5500 *fax* 020-7431 5600
email help@jamesrubenstein.co.uk
Founding Partner James Rubenstein

Founded in 1992. Legal and business affairs consultants to the music industry. Aims to provide a specialised and cost-effective personal service.

James Ware LLP

6 Gray's Inn Square, London WC1R 5AX
tel 020-7269 9022 *fax* 020-7404 7275
email james.ware@jamesware.co.uk
Director James Ware

Founded in 2005. Specialises in copyright, commercial regulations and contracts relating to rights, structuring ownership and licensing of rights. Typical clients include composers and songwriters, composers' estates, and music publishers (both popular and classical). Also deals with asset and estate planning and wills and trusts. Fixed-price quotation for most transactions.

Jayes & Page

Universal House, 251 Tottenham Court Road, London W1T 7JY

tel 020-7291 9111 *fax* 020-7291 9119
email enquiries@jayesandpage.com
website www.jayesandpage.com
Partners Anthony Jayes, Bob Page

Founded in 2001. Specialist music and media solicitors experienced in undertaking non-contentious and contentious work for corporate and individual clients. Typical clients include: recording artists, songwriters, producers, managers, independent record labels and music publishers.

John Ireland & Co
57 Elgin Crescent, London W11 2JU
tel 020-7792 1666
email john@johnirelandco.net
website www.johnirelandandco.net
Director John Ireland

Founded in 2001. Music, entertainment and media lawyer offering legal and business advice to companies, executives and artistes.

Lee & Thompson
Greengarden House, 15-22 St Christophers Place, London W1U 1NL
tel 020-7935 4665 *fax* 020-7563 4949
email mikebrookes@leeandthompson.com
website www.leeandthompson.com
Partners Mike Brookes, Andrew Thompson

Founded in 1983. Provides commercial and legal advice to a broad range of entertainment and media clients, including many famous recording artists and celebrities. Largely represents the talent sector, but also acts for a substantial number of industry corporate clients. Holds particular expertise in the negotiation of contracts and a full range of litigation and mediation services.

Leonard Lowy & Co
500 Chiswick High Road, London W4 5RG
tel 020-8956 2785 *fax* 020-8956 2786
email lowy@leonardlowy.co.uk
website www.leonardlowy.co.uk
Principal Leonard Lowy

Established in 1998. Aims to provide a personal, friendly, reliable and economical service. Deals mainly with artists, record labels, publishers, managers, composers and producers. Free initial meeting.

Maclay, Murray & Spens
151 St Vincent Street, Glasgow G2 5NJ
tel 020-7606 6130 *mobile* (07803) 160320
email magnus.swanson''mms.co.uk
website www.mms.co.uk
Consultant Solicitor Murray Buchanan

Well-established law firm working primarily with songwriters, composers, recording artists, performers, producers and DJs. Aims to provide friendly practical advice on a range of legal issues including all

contracts, music publishing, licensing and engagements.

Magrath & Co
66-67 Newman Street, London W1T 3EQ
tel 020-7495 3003 *fax* 020-7317 6766
email alexis.grower@magrath.co.uk
website www.magrath.co.uk
Consultant Alexis Grower

Founded in 1990. London-based lawyers working within the field of music law.

Marriott Harrison
12 Great James Street, London WC1N 3DR
tel 020-7209 2093 *fax* 020-7209 2001
email tony-morris@marriottharrison.co.uk
website www.marriottharrison.com
Partner/Head of Media Tony Morris

Founded in 1985. Corporate and media lawyers dealing with all aspects of media and entertainment industries – corporate finance, mergers and acquisitions, public company work, litigation and dispute resolutions, and property and employment law. Clients vary across a wide range of media-related professionals including music publishers, artists, managers and songwriters. Intial half-hour free consultation for potential clients.

MC Kirton & Co
83 St Albans Avenue, London W4 5JS
tel 020-8987 8880 *fax* 020-8932 7908
email michael@mckirton.com
Director Michael Kirton

Established in 1997. Specialises in working with artists, writers, producers, managers and publishers. Deals mainly with brands/rights management and merchandising.

Michael Simkins LLP
45-51 Whitfield Street, London W1T 4HB
tel 020-7907 3000 *fax* 020-7907 3111
email paddy.graftongreen@simkins.com
website www.simkins.co.uk
Senior Member Paddy Grafton-Green

Established in 2005. Full-service West End law firm advising clients in all sectors, with a particular focus on the creative industries – especially media and entertainment. Typical clients include record companies, publishers and high-profile musicians.

Nicolau Solicitors
The Barn Studios, Burnt Farm Ride, Goffs Oak, Herts EN7 5JA
tel (01707) 877707 *fax* (01707) 877708
email nicolaou@tiscali.co.uk
Solicitor Constantina Nicolau

Founded in 1992. Music industry and entertainment specialists. Provides advice and documents both efficiently and accessibly.

Northrop McNaughtan Deller

18C Pindock Mews, Little Venice, London W9 2PY
tel 020-7289 7300 *fax* 020-7286 9555
email nmd@nmdsolicitors.com
website www.nmdsolicitors.com
Partners Martin Deller, Tim Northrop, Christy
McNaughtan

Founded in 2004. Contains a non-contentious
department (largely contract negotiation) and a
litigation department (disputes). Represents singers,
songwriters, musicians, managers, producers and
small labels across the music business. Offers an
initial 15- to 30-minute consultation free of charge.

Peter Last

75 Holland Road, Kensington, London W14 8HL
tel 020-7603 4245
email prlast@aol.com
Barrister Peter Last

Established in 1995. Specialises in advising on music
contracts, including negotiation.

Sally Bevan

14 Birchlands Avenue, London SW12 8ND
tel 020-8675 5747 *fax* 020-8675 9101
email sally@legalside.co.uk
Director Sally Bevan

Specialises in music law.

Schillings

Royalty House, 72-74 Dean Street, London W1D 3TL
tel 020-7453 2500 *fax* 020-7453 2600
email legal@schillings.co.uk
website www.schillings.co.uk

Seddons

5 Portman Square, London W1H 6NT
tel 020-7725 8000 *fax* 020-7725 5235
email media@seddons.co.uk
website www.seddons.co.uk
Head of Media & Entertainment David Kent

Established in 1980. Advises on contentious and non-
contentious matters in the fields of media and
entertainment, including commercial contract
negotiation and intellectual property rights. Deals
with a range of clients including: individual artists
(including musicians, songwriters, composers,
producers), bands, managers, record companies,
recording and television production companies and
publishing companies. Discounted rates for initial
meeting with new clients.

Swan Turton

68A Neal Street, Covent Garden, London WC2H 9PA
tel 020-7520 9555 *fax* 020-7520 9556

email julian.turton@swanturton.com or
julian.bentley@swanturton.com
website www.swanturton.com
Founding Partners Julian Turton, Julian Bentley

Founded in 2005. Aims to provide high-quality,
competitively priced advice to creative businesses and
individuals in all fields of media and entertainment.
Typical clients include record companies, music
publishers, recording artists, composers, producers
and music industry associations.

Taylor Wessing

50 Victoria Embankment, London EC4Y 0DX
tel 020-7300 7000 *fax* 020-7300 7100
email p.mitchell@taylorwessing.com
website www.taylorwessing.com
Partner Paul Mitchell

Established in 1800. Specialises in working with
performers, composers, publishers, collecting
societies, merchandisers, online publishers and
Internet service providers, among others. Deals with a
range of music-industry-related issues including
copyright and publishing/recording deals.

Tods Murray LLP

Edinburgh Quay, 133 Fountainbridge,
Edinburgh EH3 9AG
tel 0131-656 2000 *fax* 0131-656 2023
email richard.findlay@todsmurray.com
website www.todsmurray.com
Entertainment and Media Law Partner Richard
Findlay

Founded in 1750 and offering a full client service on
a wide range of subjects. Specialises in entertainment
and media law for musicians, composers, producers,
managers and publishers.

Web Sheriff

Argentum, 2 Queen Caroline Street,
London W6 9DX
tel 020-8323 8013 *fax* 020-8323 8080
email ela@ela.co.uk
website www.ela.co.uk
Managing Director John Giacobbi

Founded in 1992. Specialists in protecting online
rights. Clients typically include artists and record
labels.

The name game: registering a band name

Music lawyer **Ben Challis** explains the importance of band names, and how the law can protect a band's name, brand and image.

The band as a brand – the importance of a name

Never underestimate the value of a band's or artist's name. Bands as diverse as Westlife, Suede, Liberty X and Blue have all been involved in legal actions over their names. Westlife started their career as Westside, until an American band of the same name objected; in the USA, Suede are called the 'London Suede' – again after it was found that an American artist had the same name. Even Celine Dion had to change the name of her Las Vegas show, when the British rock band Muse objected to her trying to call her own show 'Muse'.

Band names are important in the modern music industry because they immediately connect a band with its audience – and that name has the potential to become a long-term 'brand'. Indeed, a name is a vital signifier when selling records, merchandise, concert tickets and even when setting up a website. Choosing and protecting your band name is one of the music industry essentials; there are laws in place to protect band names.

Choosing your name

Once you think you've selected the perfect name, it is really sensible to check it out thoroughly before you start using it. For a start, try your local telephone directory, and see if anyone else is using a similar name in business. After that, try putting the name you've chosen into a search engine like Google, and see what comes up. If someone else is using the same – or a similar name – it is probably wise to think again.

As a domain name will probably be important to a band or performer at some point, stick 'www' in the front of the name, and add obvious endings like .com or .co.uk and see what comes up. If you have access to a music industry guide (such as *International Showcase*), then have a look at the names of bands listed in that: *International Showcase* has an 80-page artist index, listing thousands of band names. These searches will at least tell you if there is a band already using the name you might want to use. And at this stage it is probably worth checking the online band registers – not least to see if there are people outside the United Kingdom using the name you want. While these are not official registers, they do show who is using what names. Two you may like to use are **www.bandname.com** and **www.bandreg.com**. The latter site (the Band Register) states that it has 370,000 band names registered.

Trademarks

If you are convinced that you have a brilliant new name that no-one else is using, then the best way to protect this is to register it. You can register the name with either of the two band name registries (listed above), but neither gives you any formal legal protection – although they do at least prove when you started using the name. The phrase you have probably heard of is 'trademark' – and this really is the holy grail of protecting a band name (and logo).

First, it is important to make sure that no-one else has a trademark identical – or even similar – to the name (or logo design) you want to use. The best place to start is the trademark search page at the website **http://webdb4.patent.gov.uk/tm/text/**. This also searches the Companies House database for any similarly named companies. If someone else has the name you want to use, and they operate in any area in which you may be trading (such as concert performing, selling records, selling clothes and other merchandise), they will probably be able to stop you using the name you've chosen – so think again! It is not fatal if someone in an unconnected area is using the same name (think of Oasis – a band, a drink, sports clubs, a clothes range), but if someone else connected to music has that name, you will have an uphill battle to protect it. Recently, Westlife lost the right to register their name as a trademark across Europe, because the cigarette company West already operated in certain areas of merchandising that the band wanted to operate in (clothing, for example).

Registering a trademark

To register a trademark you need to have a word, series of words, or logo. These may consist of a device, name, signature, word, letter, numeral, or any combination of these. Sometimes a word itself may not be registerable, but a logo containing the word may be. The mark needs to be distinctive of the business, recognisable as such by the public, and capable of graphic representation. Sounds and smells cannot be registered!

Trademarks in the UK are registered at the Patent Office. There is a period during which the mark you want to use is publicised, and other people can object to your registration. There is also a new Community Trade Mark which gives Europe-wide protection for your name and logo. Either way, to obtain the registration, you are going to need to use a solicitor or a trademark attorney, so put some money aside for this. There are minimum filing fees which are in the low hundreds of pounds, as well as legal fees, which can quickly mount up. And you will probably need to register your name in a number of classes (to cover, say, the sale of CDs, posters, tickets, clothing, and Internet sales): there is an additional charge for each class. European-wide protection in a number of classes can therefore cost thousands of pounds. Further protection (for example, in the USA) will cost even more. However, the end result of a registered trademark, if successful, is well worth it. It is much easier to protect your band's name using trademark law. A trademark will begin from the date of a successful application for registration, and will last for as long as it is renewed.

Passing-off

Passing-off is what is called a 'common law' action, and usually comes into play if you haven't registered your band name as a trademark. This action can be used to protect an established band name, if that band can prove that someone else's use of the same, or a very similar name, would cause confusion in the minds of customers: for example, where customers wouldn't know which band they were going to see at a show, or would be confused as to whether the band on a certain CD was really the one they wanted to hear. Liberty X had to change their name from simply Liberty, after a band already called Liberty (who had had a reasonably successful career and had released a couple of records) used the action of passing-off to protect their established name. However, with passing-off, you do have to prove that someone else is trading on your reputation – and that isn't always as simple as it sounds. The best way of preventing others from using the same name as yours, or a confusingly similar name, is to register it as a trademark.

Image rights

Image rights are the commercial rights to someone's name, image and personality. While this is an accepted right in the US, this area of law is not very well developed in the UK – although by using a mixture of trademark law and passing-off, celebrities can still go some way towards protecting their commercial 'brand'. (The racing driver Eddie Irvine, for example, prevented a radio station from using an unauthorised photo to support the station's advertising.) And image rights have also been extended to cartoon characters and plastic figurines of pop stars. In a world where celebrity endorsement and sponsorship provide huge financial rewards, image rights are a very important new area of legal protection.

Domain names

These are now very important for businesses and artists. The registration of domain names is still done on a first come, first served basis, but there are now rules governing who can own what name on the Internet. Robbie Williams, Julia Roberts and the Glastonbury Festival have all regained control of domain names based on their names, even though those names had already been registered by other people. Registrars of top-level domain names (suffixes such as .com or .net) are governed by certain rules, and supervised by ICANN (the Internet Corporation for Assigned Names and Numbers). Parties wishing to register domain names submit to ICANN rules, which are enforced by appointed regulatory bodies, such as WIPO (the World Intellectual Property Organisation). UK names such as .co.uk are supervised by Nominet in a similar manner. Registrars and registrants (the people who ask to register the names) are bound to comply with the decisions of the regulatory body concerned. Most often, complaints are about requests to set aside unlawful domain name registrations – such as copycat registrations, or registrations made in bad faith (where the complainant may ask the regulator to transfer to the complainant the offending domain name, or ask that the domain name be cancelled).

So names are important. Make sure you pick an original name, and make sure you do everything you can to protect it.

Ben Challis is a UK-based music lawyer, with the Glastonbury Festival among his top clients. He is a visiting lecturer at Buckinghamshire Chilterns University College, and a writer on music and entertainment industry law. Reference: *International Showcase* (see latest annual edition), Hollis Publishing.

Accountants

Addis & Co
Emery House, 192 Heaton Moor Road, Stockport,
Cheshire SK4 4DU
tel 0161-432 3307 *fax* 0161-432 3376
email enquiries@a-addis.co.uk
website www.a-addis.co.uk
Proprietor Anthony Addis

Founded in 1983. Typically deals with musicians,
entertainers and music-industry-associated
businesses.

Backoffice Babies
380 Longbanks, Harlow, Essex CM18 7PG
tel (07939) 261577
email info@backofficebabies.com
website www.backofficebabies.com
Managing Partners John Weston, Paul Harvey

Founded in 2005. Royalty administration and audit
company that focuses on investigating and collecting
current, future and outstanding royalty payments.
Typical clients include artists, bands, songwriters,
managers and producers. All fees work on a
percentile and audits are undertaken on a no win, no
fee basis.

M Barnfather & Co
15 Birley Street, Blackpool FY1 1DU
tel (01253) 622519 *fax* (01253) 294179
email mike@mikebarnfather.co.uk
Accountant Michael Barnfather

Bettersounds Consultancy
Little Orchards, Sandyhurst Lane, Ashford,
Kent TN25 4NT
tel (01233) 643325
email bettersounds@btconnect.com
Director Bernard Symonds

Founded in 2001. Over 25 years of record and
publishing finance experience. Works with both small
and large record companies with all-round
accounting. Specialises in royalty-based projects.

Bevis & Co
Apex House, 6 West Street, Epsom, Surrey KT18 7RG
tel (01372) 840280 *fax* (01372) 840282
email chris@bevisandco.co.uk
website www.bevisandco.co.uk
Director Chris Bevis

Founded in 1988. Commercially experienced
accountants specialising in the music industry and
dealing with royalty audits, catalogue valuations,
statutory audits and management accounts.
Distributors, artists, writers, copyright societies and
record companies are amongst typical clients. Also

deals with computer games companies, book
publishers and other owners of intellectual property.

BKL LLP
35 Ballards Lane, London N1 3XW
tel 020-8922 9335 *fax* 020-7681 4487
email lesley.alexander@bkl.co.uk
website www.bkl.co.uk
Principal Lesley Alexander

Aims to provide a personal accounting service for a
range of music-based clients including artists,
producers, agents, record companies and publishing
companies.

Conroy & Company
27 Beaumont Avenue, St Albans,
Hertfordshire AL1 4TL
tel (01727) 858589
email conroyandcompany@btconnect.com
Key Contact Arnold Conroy

Founded in 1966. Specialises in accounts, returns, tax
advice and finance. Typically works with music-
industry-based clients.

De La Haye Royalty Services
76 High Street, Stony, Stratford, Bucks MK11 1AH
tel (01908) 568800 *fax* (01908) 568890
email royalties@delahaye.co.uk
website www.delahaye.co.uk
Director Roger La Haye

Founded in 1998. Accountancy service specialising in
royalty auditing.

Deloitte
180 Strand, London WC2R 1BL
tel 020-7007 0833 *fax* 020-7303 4786
email cbradbrook@deloitte.co.uk
website www.deloitte.co.uk
Partner Charles Bradbrook

Provides tax planning (UK and international),
accounting and business support services.
Experienced in acquisitions, disposal and licensing of
intellectual property rights. Typically, clients are both
new and established artists and creative businesses.
Operates a 'Brass in Pocket' scheme for new artists,
providing an all-round tax and accounting service.

Dunbar & Co
70 South Lambeth Road, London SW8 1RL
tel 020-7820 0082 *fax* 020-7820 0806
email mason@equitax.co.uk
Accountants Nick Mason (Senior Partner), Bob Long

EMTACS (Entertainers & Musicians Tax & Accountancy)
69 Loughborough Road, West Bridgford,
Nottingham NG2 7LA

tel 0115-981-5001 *fax* 0115-981-5005
email emtacs@aol.com
website www.emtacs.com
Senior Partner Geoff Challinger

Founded in 1984. Specialises in dealing with self-employed musicians.

Ernst & Young

Becket House, 1 Lambeth Palace Road,
London SE1 7EU
tel 020-7951 6394 *fax* 020-7951 1345
email rreespulley@uk.ey.com
website www.ey.com/uk
Partner Richard Rees-Pulley

Offers tax advice and accounting support to musicians.

Guy Rippon Organisation

21 Bedford Square, London WC1B 3HH
tel 020-7637 4444 *fax* 020-7323 2857
email admin@fspg.co.uk
website www.fspg.co.uk
Key Contacts Jon Glasner, Guy Rippon

Specialises in advising clients on running their business in the most efficient and tax-effective manner. Typical clients include artists, managers, promotors, record companies and producers.

Harris & Trotter

65 New Cavendish Street, London W1G 7LS
tel 020-7467 6300 *fax* 020-7467 6363
email mail@harrisandtrotter.co.uk
website www.harrisandtrotter.co.uk
Partners Ronnie Harris, Russell Selwyn, Jason Boas

Founded in 1940. Aims to assist new writing, performing and producing talent alongside taking care of established artists. Clients have included: Mark Knopfler, Tom Jones, and Bryan Ferry. Free initial consultation.

HW Fisher & Company Chartered Accountants

Acre House, 11-15 William Road, London NW1 3ER
tel 020-7388 7000 *fax* 020-7380 4900
email info@hwfisher.co.uk
website www.hwfisher.co.uk
Partner Martin Taylor

Founded in 1933. Aims to provide clients with a high level of expertise and comprehensive experience within the music and media sectors, while maintaining a personal service and giving value for money. In addition to tax advice, clients are also advised of royalty and licensing issues, ensuring that full revenue is received from intellectual property. Clients typically represent a wide range of individuals and businesses in the music industry, including performers and composers.

Ivan Sopher & Co

5 Elstree Gate, Elstree Way. Borehamwood,
Herts WD6 1JD

tel 020-8207 0602 *fax* 020-8207 6758
email accountants@ivansopher.co.uk
website www.ivansopher.co.uk
Director Ivan Sopher

Founded in 1974. Offers a wide range of services including authoring, accounting, tax and VAT work and payroll for sole traders, companies and partnerships in the music industry.

Johnsons Chartered Accountants

2nd Floor, 109 Uxbridge Road, London W5 5TL
tel 020-8567 3451 *fax* 020-840 6823
email mail@johnsonsca.com
website www.johnsonsca.com
Partner Shaukat Murad

Founded in 1980. Aims to provide a personalised service to members of the music industry. Specialises in consultancy and royalty auditing services. Typical clients include artists, musicians, songwriters, management companies, PR companies and publishers. Also provides a comprehensive tax planning service. First visit is free of charge.

Leigh Philip & Partners

1-6 Clay Street, London W1U 6DA
email mail@pplondon.couk
Partner Leigh Genis

Founded in 1985. Specialises in working with music-industry-based clients.

Lloyd Piggott

Wellington House, 1st Floor, 39/41 Piccadilly,
Manchester M1 1LQ
tel 0161-236 7677 *fax* 0161-236 7678
email info@lloydpiggott.co.uk
website www.lloydpiggott.co.uk
Tax Associate Paula Abbott

Founded in 1898. General practice with clients ranging from sole traders to large corporate clients. Niche market in music/performing arts with around 300 clients in this sector. Aims to provide a personal and professional service to all clients. Offers all clients a book in order to help keep income and expenditure records. For larger companies, offers a full accountancy and tax planning service. Supplies a fixed fee quotation.

Martin Greene Ravden

55 Loudoun Road, St John's Wood,
London NW8 0DL
tel 020-7625 4545 *fax* 020-7625 5265
email justine.gannon@mgr.co.uk
website www.mgr.co.uk
Head of Business Development and Marketing Justine Gannon

Founded in 1980. Works with a cross-section of both corporate and personal clients in the 'Media' sector. Advisory services cover financial planning, tax, business management and touring services.

Specialises in a reliable music-industry knowledge in order to ensure that clients are able to fully mitigate their liabilities and capitalise on opportunities. Also provides a free confidential consultation in order to help provide a bespoke service.

Music Business Associates Ltd

Apex House, 6 West Street, Epsom, Surrey KT18 7RG
tel (01372) 840281 *fax* (01372) 840282
email paulk@musicbusinessassociates.com
website www.musicbusinessassociates.com
Royalty and Accounts Manager Paul Kerslake

Founded in 1999. Offers a range of accounting, tour accounting, licensing, and royalty services to the music industry. Artists, writers, performers and record companies are typically amongst clients.

MWM Chartered Accountants & Business Advisors

11 Great George Street, Bristol BS1 5RR
tel 0117-929 2393 *fax* 0117-929 2696
email office@mwmuk.com
Director Craig Williams

Founded in 1999. Entertainment and media specialists aiming to provide a personal 'hands-on' service. Typically works with artists, composers, record companies and publishers. Services include tax and VAT planning/compliance, tax enquiries, royalty audit and business management. Free initial interview.

Newman & Co

Regent House, 1 Pratt Mews, London NW1 OAD
tel 020-7554 4840 *fax* 020-7267 9643
email partners@newmanandco.com
website www.newmanandco.com
Partner Colin Newman

Founded in 1978. Accountancy service working typically within the music, media and entertainment sectors.

Note for Note

15 Marroway, Weston Turville, Aylesbury, Bucks HP22 5TQ
tel (01296) 614966 *fax* (01296) 614651
email chris@note-for-note.co.uk
Proprietor Chris Turner

Founded in 1992. Provides accounting service for musicians, producers, record companies and journalists.

Positive Accounting Solutions

29 Langley Park, London NW7 2AA
tel 020-8906 2343 *fax* 020-8906 2343
email simon@positiveaccounting.co.uk
Accountant Simon Durban

Founded in 2002. Aims to provide affordable accounting services to music industry clients.

Specialises in royalty accounting and MCPS. Clients include: Wall of Sound Recordings, CR2 Records, Underwater Records, and Orient Recordings.

PricewaterhouseCoopers LLP

1 Embankment Place, London WC2 6RH
tel 020-7583-5000 *fax* 020-7822-4652
email info@uk.pwc.com
website www.pwc.com/uk/e&m
Head of UK Entertainment & Media Phil Stokes

Leading professional services organisation for the Entertainment & Media industry, providing industry-focused assurance, tax and advisory services to help clients manage risk, maximise shareholder value and support merger and acquisition activities. Offers a deep and diverse industry-dedicated team of professionals, working together to provide solutions for critical issues facing companies in the sector. The Entertainment & Media practice also addresses business strategies to leverage digital technology; marketplace positioning in industries characterised by consolidation and convergence; and identifying new sources of financing.

RCO (Royalty Compliance Organisation)

4 Crescent Stables, 139 Upper Richmond Road, London SW15 2TN
tel 020-8789 6444 *fax* 020-8785 1960
email ask@therco.co.uk
website www.rcoonline.com
Partner Mike Skeet

Founded in 1999. Specialises in royalty auditing to ensure that clients receive full entitlement of royalties. Also provides a royalty accounting service. Typical clients include artists, writers and producers.

Ryan & Co

4F Shirland Mews, London W9 3DY
email ryan@ryanandco.com
Chartered Accountant Cliff Ryan

Founded in 1993. Specialises in the intricacies of the music industry and making sense of them to the client. Typical clients include musicians, songwriters, bands, producers and small record and publishing companies. Also carries out royalty audits and offers a free initial consultation.

Sedley Richard Laurence Voulters

Kendal House, 1 Conduit Street, London W1S 2XA
tel 020-7287 8595 *fax* 020-7287 9696
email general@srlv.co.uk
website www.srlv.co.uk
Senior Partner Richard Rosenberg *Partner* Steve Jeffrey

Founded in 1988. Specialises in working with music-industry-based clients.

Sloane & Co

36-38 Westbourne Grove, Newton Road, London W2 5SH

tel 020-7221 3292 *fax* 020-7229 4810
email mail@sloane.co.uk
website www.sloane.co.uk
Partners David Sloane, Mark Allen

A specialist firm of chartered certified accountants dealing in the music and entertainment industries. Specialises in working with songwriters, publishers, recording artists and record companies in all areas including royalty tracking and auditing. Also deals with tax, payroll, bookkeeping and company formation as well as a range of other financial services.

Thomas Harris Chartered Accountants

1929 Building, Merton Abbey Mills, Wimbledon, London SW19 2RD
tel 020-8542 4262 *fax* 020-8545 0662
email ct@thomasharris.co.uk
Senior Partner Chris Thomas

Founded in 1980. Offers a personal service helping to keep financial services in order. Works with artists from major record companies. Provides a free initial consultation and financial appraisal carried out at clients' premises with no obligation.

William Evans Partners

20 Harcourt Street, London W1H 4HG
tel 020-7563 8390 *fax* 020-7569 8700
email wep@williamevans.co.uk
Partners Stephen Evans, Sanjay Shah

Founded in 1980. Specialises in accountancy and taxation for composers, performers and management companies, alongside a range of other music-industry-based clients.

Yellocello

49 Windmill Road, London W4 1RN
tel 020-8742 2001
email info@yellocello.com
website www.yellocello.com
ACA Charlie Carne

Accountancy, VAT, PAYE and business management specialists for the media industries. Income tax and corporate tax compliance and consultancy. Offers fixed-rate fees, agreed in advance. Charlie Carne is a director of the Music Managers Forum and a Chartered Accountant.

Setting up as self-employed in the music industry – and the basics of budgeting

JoJo Gould provides an overview of how to start your own music business, and considers various legal and financial issues for the prospective entrepreneur.

The music industry offers a number of enterprise opportunities. Beyond the possibility of becoming a full-time professional musician, this could take the form of running your own independent record label, rehearsal facility, recording studio, promotions company or management company.

Most jobs in the music industry are actually based on self-employment. As a result, an understanding of the basics of running a small business can be advantageous when carving out your own niche in the music world.

The entrepreneur

Starting your own business represents a leap of faith for any individual. It can be a time of adventure, but also one of great uncertainty, risk and challenge. Being self-employed means managing your own working hours, dealing with non-routine workloads, and enjoying greater freedom. On the downside, however, entrepreneurs usually have no regular income or holiday entitlement, and often work in isolation.

Business start-ups require innovation, resources, and a positive mind-set. Many of the largest and most successful music-industry companies started out as small-business ideas which developed and gained momentum over a period of time – such as Richard Branson's Virgin Group, Simon Fuller's 19 Group, and Berry Gordy's legendary Motown Records.

The key challenge for the entrepreneur is to develop a product or service, and successfully take this to market for a sustained period of time. In order to succeed, enterprising individuals require a focused business strategy, a strong work ethic, and high levels of intrinsic motivation.

The business plan

A useful starting point for anyone setting up their own enterprise is to identify their precise business idea, target market, competitors, sources of funding, and early accounting projections. These proposed objectives can be outlined in a formal business plan. There is no legal requirement to draw up a business plan – although potential funders such as banks or local business support agencies will request this document. For the uninitiated, most high street banks will be happy to supply you with a business plan template, and advice on how to complete this.

Your business plan should be concise, properly structured, and credible. It should cover a timeframe of several years, and provide succinct answers to a series of basic questions about your business proposal: Who? What? Why? Where? When and How?

Sources of funding

Access to start-up capital, and funds to provide a decent standard of living, are common problems for entrepreneurs. Finance may be sourced from family and friends, your own savings, business support organisations, lending institutions such as banks, or third-party individuals who may wish to invest in your company (but not necessarily be involved in the day-to-day running of it). At a more advanced level, venture capital firms are sometimes involved in high-level business proposals.

The entrepreneur should be realistic, and may need to continue working in another job while developing a particular music-industry idea – until s/he gradually transforms the plan into a viable full-time enterprise.

New business formats

Choosing your business structure is a key initial requirement. Most new firms fall into one of the following three categories: sole trader, partnership or limited company. A sole trader – the most popular small-business format in the UK – is the easiest to establish; the newly self-employed person should inform the Inland Revenue and Contributions Agency of the enterprise by completing a CWF1 form. This must be submitted within three months of commencing trading. The sole trader benefits from greater freedom and flexibility, and less red tape, than do the other two categories; however, the individual and the enterprise are legally considered to be the same entity – meaning that the sole trader operates under the risk of potential unlimited liability. Creditors may thus seek personal assets – not just business assets – in the event of any non-payment of debts.

Partnerships also have potential unlimited liability – although it is now possible to establish a Limited Liability Partnership. Partners are advised to engage a solicitor to draw up a formal deed on their behalf, known as a 'Partnership Agreement'. This written agreement is a form of good practice, as it outlines important issues such as the roles and obligations of the partners, ownership of the business assets, the sharing of profits, and operational matters such as banking arrangements, working hours and holiday entitlements.

Limited companies, as the name suggests, are incorporated legal entities which can protect their owners (the shareholders) from unlimited personal liability. This company format is more regulated, and involves compliance with a number of legal requirements – such as the provision of shareholders, directors and a company secretary, the filing of annual returns, and the drawing-up of constitutional documents (e.g. Memorandum of Association; Articles of Association). Limited companies are issued with a formal registration number by Companies House, and can be formed 'off the shelf' from existing firms, or as brand new entities. This formation process is usually undertaken through the services of a lawyer, or company registration agent.

Financial requirements

In order to establish tax liability, the music industry – like any other business sector – has a legal requirement for regular accounting. All companies are therefore required to submit annual accounts. Sole traders and partnerships may file these through the Inland Revenue's Self-Assessment scheme. Failure to submit accounts by the end of January for the preceding financial year can result in a penalty. Like any other individual, sole traders and partners can claim personal tax allowances (the actual amount depends on their circumstances); they are also able to offset legitimate business expenses against their turnover – in effect reducing their tax liabilities. Professional advice should be sought in this area from a qualified accountant.

In addition, the self-employed person must normally pay two classes of national insurance: the flat-rate Class 2 contribution, and the profit-related Class 4 contribution. You may be exempt from Class 2 contributions if your net earnings are low. Class 4 contributions will be determined on the basis of your taxable profits, as outlined in your annual Self-Assessment return.

Music companies with a certain annual turnover (amended every year in the budget) must also register with Customs & Excise for VAT (Value Added Tax). Low-turnover firms can undertake voluntary VAT registration, although there are advantages and disadvantages to doing this. VAT registration means that the firm must charge an additional levy on its goods and services (taxable supplies). Note that a record-company advance, for example, may instantly propel a small firm over the defined VAT threshold.

Limited-company accounts are normally submitted to Companies House within ten months of the close of the firm's financial year, and are then made available for public inspection (which includes your competitors!) on request. These accounts must be in the correct format, and failure to deliver on time can result in proceedings against the company's directors. Company directors should also be careful not to trade while insolvent, and should generally exercise 'due care and attention' with regard to general management of the firm.

Rates, allowances, National Insurance contributions and VAT thresholds usually change on an annual basis. Current levels can be obtained from your local business advisory service, government websites or qualified professionals.

Your business plan will also include financial information. This document is not legally binding, but the usefulness of having a cash flow, balance sheet and profit/loss statement will be clearly evident in terms of firm financial planning, monitoring and control. All small music businesses should implement a robust record-keeping system. Receipts, invoices and bank statements should be maintained for a minimum five-year period, as these may be requested on demand by the relevant authorities (it is, in fact, advisable to keep these records *in perpetuity*).

Advice and support

Starting a new business can be a daunting experience. The combination of financial risk, irregular working hours and bureaucratic regulations can all serve to put people off. In an effort to encourage the development of an enterprise culture, local agencies and central government provide a number of services for entrepreneurs; these usually include free advice booklets, access to personal business advisers, and sometimes financial assistance (the latter depending on individual circumstances, such as locality, age and gender).

Depending on the particular sector of the music industry in which you are working, you may be able to join a trade association and benefit from their advice, experience and networking opportunities. AIM (the Association of Independent Music) provides a useful range of services for independent record labels. The MU (Musicians' Union), MPG (Music Producers' Guild), MMF (Music Managers' Forum) and MPA (Music Publishers' Association) also provide useful support functions and services for their members.

Summary

Never forget that today's music industry has in fact been shaped by the entrepreneurial flair and vision of scores of uniquely talented and hard-working individuals. Starting a new business is indeed a formidable challenge, and clearly should not be entered into lightly. The potential benefits of doing so, however, can be hugely rewarding to the individual; and, of course, successful businesses are essential to the development of a vibrant music scene, as well as beneficial to the economy at large.

JoJo Gould is a UK-based lecturer, and was for five years joint Managing Editor of *Music Business Journal*. He lectures and consults on the European Degree in International Music Management, and holds a Master of Science degree in Business IT Systems. He was a co-founder and first Chairman of New Music in Scotland, and was previously Senior Lecturer in Music Industry Management at Buckinghamshire Chilterns University College.

NB: Independent professional advice should be sought when starting and operating a new business. See **www.businesslink.gov.uk**.

Courses

Academy of Contemporary Music
Rodboro Buildings, Bridge Street,
Guildford GU1 4SB
tel (01483) 500800 *fax* (01483) 500801
email enquiries@acm.ac.uk
website www.acm.ac.uk

Established in 1996, ACM is at the forefront of contemporary popular music education. Music Business is an integral part of all full-time courses, so students are well equipped to fully understand the industry. Also offers a BA (Hons) degree in Music Business, which gives an extensive and practical insight into the music industry. The courses includes units such as: Business and Artist Management, Record Company Structure and Management, Music Publishing, Research Methods, Music Law and Contracts, Entrepreneurial Practice, Music Marketing and Media, and Cultural and Critical Perspectives.

In addition, ACM has a Business Development Centre, the aim of which is proactively to assist students with all aspects of career progression. The BDC holds auditions and showcases for record labels and management companies on an ongoing basis, as well as offering A&R advice, music industry placements and personal promotional assistance.

Qualifications: Diploma in Contemporary Popular Music (Music Performance/Music Production); Higher Diploma in Contemporary Popular Music (Music Performance/Music Production); BA (Hons) Degree in Contemporary Popular Music (Business).

Buckinghamshire Chilterns University College
Chalfont Campus, Gorelands Lane,
Chalfont St Giles, Buckinghamshire HP8 4AD
tel (01494) 522141 *fax* (01494) 871954
email online form
website www.bcuc.ac.uk

Established in 1893 and aiming to sustain a friendly, professional and caring environment through creating constructive personal relationships between our staff and students. The Music Management Degree course is also available in combination with other courses such as Live Production and Marketing.

The main programme is designed to give students a broad overview of a range of music and entertainment industry activity. It includes investigation of the social and cultural factors that have an impact on the production and consumption of popular music. Units include: Music & Entertainment Business Enterprise, Negotiation and Communication, Music Marketing and the Media, and Event Theory & Management.

Qualifications: BA (Hons) Music Industry Management (3 years).

City College Manchester
Whitworth Street, Manchester M1 3HB
tel 0161-614 8000
email admissions@ccm.ac.uk
website www.ccm.ac.uk

Established in 2001. Welcomes around 25,000 students on a variety of full- and part-time courses over 4 sites.

The FDSc is aimed at those working towards a career in the business sector of the music industry. Provides students with essential skills and knowledge in key areas of the music business – largely through project work. Hands-on experience is encouraged, with students taking part in the running of the university record labels (**www.rfrecords.com**) and visiting international conferences such as MIDEM and SXSW. Modules include: Music and Production Analysis, Artist Development, Music and New Media Industry Studies, Entrepreneurship in the Arts, Music and New Media Technology, Management, Music Legal Affairs, and Professional Practice/Work Experience.

Applicants should have gained a range of GCSE passes at Grade C and above, and possess at least 3 GCE A levels (2 at C or above) or BTEC National Diploma (MDD profile) or GNVQ Advanced (Merit or above).

Qualifications: Foundation Degree Music and New Media Management (FDSc – 2 years).

City University London
Music Department, City University London,
Northampton Square, London EC1V 0HB
tel 020-7040 8284 *fax* 020-7040 8576
email music@city.ac.uk
website www.city.ac.uk/music
Departmental Administrator Louise Gordon

– see City University London.

Cumbernauld College
Tryst Road, Town Centre, Cumbernauld G67 1HU
tel (01236) 731811 *fax* (01236) 723416
email info@cumbernauld.ac.uk
website www.cumbernauld.ac.uk
Curriculum Manager Ronnie Gilmour

Established in 1978 and significantly expanded in 2006. Provides an extensive range of programmes from NQ to BA degree level over 2 sites in North Lanarkshire and East Dunbartonshire. Full- and part-time modes of delivery available.

Qualifications: Access to Music Production; NQ Music Technology; HNC Sound Production; HND Sound Production.

Jewel and Esk Valley College
24 Milton Road East, Edinburgh EH15 2PP
tel 0131-660 1010 *fax* 0131-657 2276
email info@jevc.ac.uk
website www.jevc.ac.uk
Curriculum Leader (Business) Iain Bruce

The Business courses focus on event management, law, marketing and artist development. Application through interview.

Qualifications: NQ Access Level, NQ Higher Level (SQA) Certificate Programmes, and HNC/D Music Business. All validated by SQA.

New College Durham
Framwellgate Moor, Durham DH1 5ES
tel (01913) 754565 *fax* (01913) 754223
email andy.wain@newdur.ac.uk
website www.newdur.ac.uk
Programme Leader Andy Wain

With more than 400 graduates from its precursor – the HND in Music Industry Management (started in 1985) – the relatively new Foundation Degree in Music Management covers areas such as live performance management, music retail and distribution, music law and artist management. Graduates are guaranteed a place on the BA (Hons) in Business top-up (1 year). Entry requirements are 1 A level or equivalent and some experience within the music industry.

North Glasgow College
110 Flemington Street, Glasgow G21 4BX
tel 0141-558 9001 *fax* 0141-558 9905

email cowens@north-gla.ac.uk
website www.north-gla.ac.uk
Senior Lecturer Campbell Owens

FE College offering a range of courses. Application online or by post.

Qualifications: HND Music Business.

University of Westminster
Admissions Enquiries & Student Finance Office, 35 Marylebone Road, London NW1 5LS
tel 020-7911 5000 or Music Management Co-ordinator: 020-7911 5000 ext 4573 *fax* 020-7911 5858
email admissions@wmin.ac.uk or grosss@wmin.ac.uk
website www.wmin.ac.uk
Programme Director Sally Gross

Founded in 1838 as Britain's first polytechnic. Aims to be imaginative in recognising new needs, and in developing appropriate offerings in many target markets. The Media courses were ranked in the top 5 as part of the last 3 annual surveys of university media courses by the *Guardian* newspaper.

The MA MBM is designed to equip students for management careers in the music industry. Works with music industry leaders and organisations to develop a unique curriculum that combines a strong underpinning of key business skills with essential music industry management knowledge. Units include: Intellectual Property and Copyright Management, Music Business Finance, Music Marketing Management, Leadership and Organisational Management, and Innovation and Technology Management.

Qualifications: MA Music Business Management.

Financing new music-business ventures

In the following *aide memoire*, **Jonathan Little** outlines some of the practicalities that need to be addressed regarding the financial aspects of new and growing businesses.

There may be said to be *three key considerations* when proposing a new music-business venture (or indeed, any new business venture).

1. **A thorough business plan needs to be prepared.** Make sure that you yourself are satisfied with your business plan – not just your investors or potential investors. Prepare your figures on a 'worst case' scenario (*and* have a Plan B ready, just in case it all goes wrong). A watertight business plan may take 6-12 months to prepare and revise properly; expect to go through literally dozens of both major and minor amendments to your document over the long course of its development. To test your ideas, questionnaires may be sent out to a specially selected focus group of music industry experts – or specialists in your field. However, you should be very careful to whom you show your business plan – in full, and even in part. (Refer to the reading list below for one useful book explaining the typical format of business plans; many banks today will help you to formulate and refine one. This text deals mainly with general principles and financial considerations.)

2. **Investors need to be convinced that your business has good management.** Can you provide evidence that your management team has relevant experience in the sector in which they intend to operate? Have you chosen the right 'horses for courses'; is your team willing and able to adapt to change if need be? You must have all your staff and resources prepared and ready to go prior to the launch of your venture.

3. **Determine how and when any investors will be paid back.** How soon can any investors exit if they wish to do so, without damaging the business?

Some important initial points

● If you cannot integrate concisely all of the essential information into your business plan, supply relevant supporting material in an Appendix.

● From the outset, be clear about the period of your cash-flow forecast – i.e. is it quarterly, half-yearly, or annually?

● It may help to summarise your proposal – or even parts of your proposal – on one-page Fact Sheets, written in straightforward language (avoiding the sort of jargon and acronyms to which the music industry is particularly prone). If necessary, provide a few clear examples of what you propose; these could be supported, in outline, by income flow charts.

● Define exactly when payments will come in. If relevant, show (in simple terms) how and when 'intangibles' – such as copyright assets – can be expected to generate income. (NB: Non-music-industry investors often have trouble understanding the flow of music-industry income from intangibles. Likewise, the role played by the various music-collection societies can be a mystery to new investors, so try to be clear.)

● In some cases, it may help to select a similar business (a successful one!) to provide a concrete illustration of what you propose, especially if you intend to start up a non-traditional or other new type of business (e.g. Internet-based, or a business utilising new technology). Where possible, provide the earnings history of this company as a comparable example. Depending on your business, you may not necessarily have to pitch it as a music-industry-specific product. A magazine that discusses music, for example, is best pitched in traditional publishing terms, irrespective of its musical content. Investors sometimes perceive the music industry as relatively high risk; therefore anything you can do to lessen potential investors' fears will certainly help your case.

● Always put your proposal in context: don't be afraid to mention competitors (be honest, because by wearing blinkers you could end up jeopardising your business). But explain why you will do what you do better than, or differently from, the competition. Emphasise in particular your *unique selling point* (USP). In other words, stand out from the crowd.

● Can either you, or your staff, show evidence of a track record of successful business management? If not, 'organic growth' (using small loans from family and friends, or using your own savings) is in the first instance, for many people, the only way of demonstrating that there is some potential in your business: it is Step One on the road to finding serious finance for start-up music businesses (unless, of course, you are lucky enough to attract investment from someone already in the music business).

● Try to identify investors with an interest in the creative industries – today, there are more such individuals and companies than ever before, and it is easier to explain your proposal to like-minded people. Similarly, there is now a plethora of advisers specific to the music industry prepared to assist new music entrepreneurs (though always be sure to check out their credentials and experience thoroughly first). Some governments are giving incentives to investors in the creative industries: in the UK, for example, the EIS (Enterprise Investment Scheme) provides tax relief of up to 20 per cent for investors in certain music, film and other entertainment businesses.

More on business plans

● Learn to talk the same language as accountants and bankers if you wish to have any chance of persuading them of the value of your proposal. Make sure that you understand your profit and loss spreadsheets, and be able to justify *every single number.*

● Push each individual number to breaking point, and cover this in your 'Risks and Opportunities' section – showing how you are prepared for, and will overcome, any potential difficulties.

● Include the Curriculum Vitae of each member of your management team (adapted, as relevant, to the nature of the business), so that people reviewing your proposal know who you all are and can be persuaded of your experience and expertise. (CVs could appear in an Appendix to your business plan.)

● Ally yourself to top-quality professionals who are able to nit-pick through drafts of your business plan, and who will challenge your assumptions. Encourage such people to play 'devil's advocate', and make sure you can counter all of their negative arguments with solid facts and figures.

● Research, research, and research your market! Who exactly is your target audience? Clarify this point at the outset. Use someone else's research (provided that it is freely available) if it supports your case (e.g. if you are starting a genre-specific record label, integrate relevant BPI, RIAA, or other annual national record-industry statistics).

● Can you provide any banker's security? If not, you may need to look to music-industry investor networks, or approach organisations consisting of 'Music Business Angels' (music-industry investors of high individual net worth, who back musical projects wherever they see real potential). By such methods, it is sometimes possible to raise anywhere between £100,000 to around £2.5 million (or possibly more), but you must usually have an outstanding business track record to justify such investment.

● Preface your entire business plan with a two-page Executive Summary. This summary needs to be very punchy and concise. Ideally, the rest of your business plan should also be concise. Relegate intricate details or explanations to the Appendices.

● Know when you've sold your business plan to potential investors, and then stop talking! (Many a good business plan has been unsold again by overdoing it.)

● Your business plan should not 'end' once finance has been raised. Every six months or so, it should be reviewed, and new plans, forecasts and targets set.

Further general considerations

● Always try to deal with people and companies you understand well (if at all possible).

● The music industry is still a people business: keep networking and continue to build up confidence in yourself and your business.

● Investor exit strategies need to be considered carefully. Many investors will expect to be able to exit their investment after three to five years, taking with them their initial investment plus a return of 20-30 per cent per annum. After five years, for example, if the initial investors need to exit, you may need to turn to a Venture Capitalist (VC), or other investor, to renew or extend your finance. Anticipate this well in advance. And keep communicating with your investors (but only if they require this), providing them with regular updates and information. Many investors will be genuinely interested in the growth and development of your business – so keep them involved and on your side.

Development capital (after your business has successfully passed its early stages)

● Despite what you may think, the banking and finance communities do tend to be more realistic than many over-enthusiastic new-music entrepreneurs. So listen seriously to their advice, and take it into account in your plans.

● In financing your business, a split between equity and debt is likely, and the balance between these two factors is often critical. (NB: Any valuation of your business only ever applies to the equity part!)

● Domestic banks rarely ask for shares (equity) in a company, except as a last resort. Such banks usually seek regular term payments – at around 2-4 per cent above the normal base rate. Raising finance by this means (if you are able to) is generally only useful when short-term cash flow is required.

● Independent Public Offerings (IPOs) – issuing shares to institutions and the public – can, paradoxically, often be the easiest way of raising finance. However, it is more likely that you will seek help from Venture Capitalists (VCs), or other private equity investors (sometimes referred to Individual Private Investors, or IPIs). These people are looking for a high return on what is often a high-risk investment, with less security, and one in which banks are frequently reluctant to get involved. Venture Capitalists, nevertheless, vet potential investments carefully. They want to see that you have: a proven business model and stable ongoing business plan; a continuing track record of growth; a well-developed business with solid management; a good profit margin; and an exit strategy over three to five years. In short, they will ask if this is a business that has already proven its place. Instead of pursuing security, like banks, IPIs and VCs will prefer to scrutinise all aspects of the business and its revenue. The whole financial infrastructure of the company will be examined, as will how focused the management team seems to be. Such funders will look at cash flow, and consider if there are fairly predictable revenue streams. Thus for music publishers, a steady flow of income from back catalogue is an advantage. (There may well be ways of leveraging against back catalogue income for relatively small loans.) It needs to be said that certain Venture Capitalists are not likely to be interested in investing less £5-15 million: because of the sums involved, record companies may well be required to insure the lives of any major artists on whom they rely for income – especially if such artists have been advanced a significant amount of money!

- With IPIs and VCs, spend some time getting the 'Heads of Terms' right from the outset. This will prevent painful and drawn-out renegotiations later on.
- The investment terms may deal with many different and complex types of shares. So learn the vocabulary relating to various equities, and seek financial advice where necessary.
- Consider if you will allot any shares to your key staff. Also consider how you will be able to retain majority control of your company in different scenarios, under any agreed allocation of shares.
- Due to the special nature of some music industry businesses, it may be best to show investors the revenue gained per project, and not necessarily from financial year to financial year. This is because music industry investment – as, for example, with an artist – may occur all at once, perhaps just before the end of the financial year. Returns, on the other hand, may not commence until the next financial year (e.g. on record release).
- The criteria for qualifying for investment capital – and inevitably the paperwork, too – is getting stricter. Be prepared for this fact.

Final points

Ask yourself if your business is under-exploited (e.g. are there other territories into which you can sell your product?). When examining this question, you may find that there are ways of generating significant revenue from various sources you may not initially have contemplated. Then ask yourself whether the company brand you have created is worth more than competing brands, because of the particular market that it represents. If your brand appears to be worth more, then you have reason to think that you have built a successful new business with a clear and valuable identity.

Former Principal of the Academy of Contemporary Music, **Dr Jonathan Little** also worked as lecturer at Buckinghamshire University College on its innovative Music Industry Management course (the first such degree course in Europe), where he specialised in the workings of the British and international recording industry, and taught songwriting analysis. For the Hudson Institute's *American Outlook* magazine, he wrote an important series of articles assessing the state of contemporary songwriting, the phenomenon of the 'celestial jukebox', and the implications of the rise of digital cinema.

Recommended reading

Barrow, Colin & Paul, and Brown, Robert (2005), *The Business Plan Workbook* (5th edn). London: Kogan Page. ISBN 0749443464

Roberts, Dennis (2000), *How to Form a Company*. London: ICSA Publishing (includes CD-ROM). ISBN 1860721001

Web and graphic design

ANCDesign.com
Unit 25,
Gainsborough Waterfront Enterprise Centre,
Gainsborough DN21 1LX
tel (01427) 619561
email sales@ancdesign.com
website www.ancdesign.com

Offers 1-page advert sites through to full e-commerce sites, with a starting package from around £250. Services offered, on top of standard design and development, are content management systems, feedback forms, message boards/forums, e-commerce and photo galleries.

Arpey Internet
2 Rose Yard, Maidstone, Kent ME14 1HN
tel (01622) 755286 or 0871-236 1610
email info@arpey.co.uk
website www.arpey.co.uk

Provides 'one-stop' website design and creation. Offers website hosting, domain names, search engine optimisation, multi-media effects, secure e-commerce, PDF production, logo creation, copywriting and marketing strategy. High-quality web design with competitive pricing.

Band-Space Sites
Fuzed Design, 99 Eggbuckland Road,
Higher Compton, Plymouth, Devon PL3 5JR
email mail@band-space.com
website www.band-space.com

Offers fully customised and conceptually designed band and artist websites of a few static pages through to a larger presence offering newsfeeds, gig information and MP3 downloads.

Beatwax
91 Berwick Street, Soho, London W1F 0NE
tel 020-7292 8330 *fax* 020-7292 8333
email info@beatwax.com
website www.beatwax.com

Offers a range of graphic design and media services including marketing solutions and bespoke branding.

Cake Group Ltd
9-11 North End Road, Olympia, London W14 8ST
tel 020-7471 6666 *fax* 020-7471 6677
email adrian@cakemedia.com
website www.cakegroup.com

Website creators offering highly developed concept packages giving user interaction and combining rich visual and audio combinations. A variety of packages are available to suit any budget. Also offers multimedia brand advertising, developing high-level digital promotional launches over the globe. Other services include PR, live event promotion, brand design and digital and viral marketing.

CreativeJar
The Old Bakehouse, 26 High Street, Twyford,
Berkshire RG10 9AG
tel 0118-934 4069 *fax* 0118-934 3066
email info@creative-jar.com
website www.creative-jar.com

Offers strong and creative web designs to a vast range of potential clients in many sectors of industry. A fully bespoke service available to deliver all facets of modern design from simple static pages, dynamic interactive applications and content management.

Darkhorse Multimedia
35 Almorah Road, Victoria Park, Bristol BS3 4QQ
tel 0117-907 6954
email info@darkhousemultimedia.com
website www.darkhousemultimedia.com

Graphic and web design specialists, offering assistance with small- or large-scale website design. Allows users content management of own website with Content Management System software. Domain name registration, web hosting and a choice of a few page static websites through to large dynamic data-driven web applications. Also offers music composition and audio design and production and Podcast creation.

EasySpace
Iomart Ltd, Lister Pavilion, Kelvin Campus,
West of Scotland Science Park, Glasgow G20 0SP
tel 0870-755 5088
website www.easyspace.com

One of the first ever domain and web hosting companies – set up in the UK in 1997. Aims to make web design and creation as easy as possible for the client, with content management and 24-hour support, in-house design, email and web security with professional certified partners at a sensible, cost-effective price.

The Image Group
Barton Hall, Hardy Street, Eccles,
Manchester M30 7NB
tel 0800-389 9898 *fax* 0800-389 0479
email enquiries@imagegroupuk.com
website www.imagegroupuk.com

Graphic design specialists, providing printed media and display and promotional media such as backdrops, exhibition stands, graphics and banners.

Integralvision
3 Station Yard, Chuley Road, Ashburton,
Devon TQ13 7EF

tel (01364) 653788 *fax* (01364) 654561
email admin@integralvision.co.uk
website www.integralvision.co.uk
Owner David Townsend

Established in 1997. Specialises in the development of creative websites, e-commerce solutions and multimedia projects. Aims to offer a website tailored to the specific needs of the client whilst being highly functional, eye-catching and optimised to the top search engine positions.

Provides a wide range of web design, flash animation and multimedia services to companies and organisations situated in Devon, Cornwall and Somerset as well as throughout the UK and Europe.

Interactive Web Solutions
10 Parker Court, Dyson Way,
Staffordshire Technology Park, Stafford ST18 0WP
tel (01785) 279920 *fax* (01785) 223514
email services@iwebsolutions.co.u
website www.iwebsolutions.co.uk

Graphic design and web entity creation specialising in providing e-commerce websites with secure checkout and credit-card-handling facilities. Aims to offer fluid design and ease of use, with full content management and reporting tools. Providers of E-recordshop, a tailored secure online music shopping package for use by retailers and record labels.

JellyMedia
The White House, 6 Queens Square,
Poulton-Le-Fylde, Lancashire FY6 7BN
tel 0870-750 6070 *fax* 0870-750 4040
email info@jellymedia.com
website www.jellymedia.com

Established in 1999. Offers complete web creation from simple pages through to corporate make-overs. Aims to carefully consider the effects of marketing, design, advertising and Internet applications in the process. Services also offered include web and email hosting and search-engine registration and optimisation.

Logo Design and Marketing Ltd
Engine House, The Flete Estate, Ivybridge,
Devon PL21 9NX
tel (01752) 830000 *fax* (01752) 830529
email enquiries@logodesign.co.uk
website www.logodesign.co.uk

Established in designing corporate identities since 1977 in a range of different markets. Offers a starter package website with the ability to pick and choose options from email forms, online shopping and news feeds. Search-engine optimisation and full content management of websites also offered. Other services include: media promotion and design, web applications, logos and packaging.

me company
14 Apollo Studios, Charlton Kings Road,
London NW5 2SB

tel 020-7482 4262 *fax* 020-7284 0402
email jonathan@mecompany.com
website www.mecompany.com
Web Designer Jonathan Tobin

Founded in 1985. Specialises in global brand development and in delivering strong and creative web entities and marketing strategies. Offices based in UK, Japan and Berlin.

Metacosm Ltd
Suite 107, Hiltongrove Business Centre,
Hatherley Mews, London E17 4QP
tel 020-8521 7272 *fax* 020-8521 6600
email info@metacosm.net
website www.metacosm.net
Senior Designer/Director Jason Lennick

Founded in 2000. Aims to create state-of-the-art, accessible and unique websites and stunning graphic design while providing the highest standards of client service. Deals with web, print and multimedia. Clients include: small businesses, arts, music industry, media, financial services and the non-profit sector. National and international client base. Websites from £1500+ vat. Logo design from £400+ vat. CDROM design POA. Also offers search engine optimisation and consultancy, audio/video streaming & Flash animation. Content management and database-driven systems.

Mologo
website www.mologo.co.uk
Director David Foster

Offers creative and innovative web design packages with special offers for musicians. Contact via website for more information and example designs.

MusicProfiles.co.uk
15 St Brendans Road, North Manchester M20 3FE
email info@musicprofiles.co.uk
website www.musicprofiles.co.uk

Organised by **www.musicteachers.co.uk** to help give musicians a no-fuss professional solution to making their presence felt on the Internet.

Pipedream Design & Communications
Durham House, Durham House Street,
London WC2N 6HG
tel 0870-803 2293
email sales@pipedreamdesign.co.uk
website www.pipedreamdesign.co.uk

Specialises in 'no frills' web design. Works with a variety of styles including: single home web page; multipages; online catalogue; shopping cart; search facility; animated web pages; data-base driven sites; and start-up sites. Prices start from around £399.

QR8 Design
Sheffield Technology Park, Arundel Street,
Sheffield S1 2NS

tel 0114-2211 818 or 0870-133 8957
email info@qr8.co.uk
website www.qr8.co.uk

Graphic and web design company offering complete web design service, from small-scale static websites through to global projects. Offers search engine optimisation to ensure a good search engine rating and a strong web presence. Total project management of process from graphic design, brand identity through to the final web creation. Also offers a professional photography studio available for third-party hire.

Rehabstudio Ltd

1st Floor, 101 Redchurch Street, London E2 7DL
tel 020-3222 0080
email london@rehabstudio.com
website www.rehabstudio.com

Specialists in graphic design and the development of creative concepts through a range of media – including digital communication. Offers very strong global web identity and design packages.

Research Studios

94 Islington High Street, London N1 8EG
tel 020-7704 2445 fax 020-7704 2447
email info@researchstudios.com
website wwwresearchingstudios.com
Studio Manager Juliana Tramontana

Chiefly concerned with the creation of strong visual communications and marketing as web-based entities.

ripe media

Suite 2, 67/73 Park Street,
Camberley Surrey GU15 3PE
tel (01276) 28663
email info@ripe-media.co.uk
website www.ripe-media.co.uk

Design and development of visually stimulating media for all aspects of business and marketing, from web and logo creation through to print work. Web design services range from improving site ranking within search engines to delivering website hosting and secure e-commerce solutions. Domain registration and full content and site management catered for. Offers website creation for small sites through to large corporate sites.

Simbiotic Ltd

Mercat House, 1103 Argyle Street, Glasgow G3 8ND
tel 0141-243 2439 fax 0141-243 2449
email sales@simbiotic.co.uk
website www.simbiotic.co.uk

Offers strong website development and web application integration such as online ticketing and content management solutions. Creative web solutions offered, from small-scale websites of a few pages through to large integrated global entities.

SK-Designs Ltd

2 Miles's Buildings, George Street, Bath BA1 2Q
tel (01225) 462997
email info@sk-designs.co.uk
website www.sk-designs.co.uk
Studio Director Stuart Killops

Founded in 2004. A full-service design group attempting to cater for all budgets. Typical clients include: artists, retailers, galleries, corporate, estate agencies and property developers. Committed to applying great design into commercial environments and always presenting a company or products to maximum effect. Main areas of work include: web design, graphic design, Flash and motion graphics. Works both nationally and internationally. Fixed-price design and/or day-rate studio time. Also offers web hosting and domain registration services.

Smart Designers

1A Grey Friars, Chester CH1 2NW
tel (01244) 346600
email solutions@smartdesigners.co.uk
website www.smartdesigners.co.uk

Aims to create websites that are easy-to-use yet informative and visually attractive. See website for a range of example sites.

Stylorouge

57-60 Charlotte Road, London ECZA 3QT
tel 020-7729 1005 fax 020-7739 7124
email mail@stylorouge.co.uk
website www.stylorouge.co.uk
Head of Production Jamie Gibson

Founded in 1981. Aims to produce work with personality, originality and integrity. Specialises in working with the music industry. Deals with press, video, TV and internet worldwide.

Tmedia Ltd

32 Scale Lane, Hull HU1 1LF
tel (01482) 327230
email info@tmedia.co.uk
website www.tmedia.co.uk
Director George Griggs

Specialises in offering high-impact, low-cost tailored media solutions – overseeing all phases of a project. Adept at delivering small-scale solutions or large corporate media campaigns. Services range from small static websites of a few pages through to dynamic, feature-rich web entities. Offers domain hosting and domain registration services and also delivers secure e-commerce sites with shopping basket, checkout and card payment facilites.

Toucher Web Design

32 Beaton Road, Balloch, Alexandria,
West Dunbartonshire G83 8QQ
tel (01389) 758245 fax 0871-733 4005
email info@toucher.co.uk
website www.toucher.co.uk
Web Designer Bryan Weir

Founded in 2001. Works with small and medium enterprises including freelance individuals such as consultants, musicians and photographers. Aims to be easily accessible by all, and provides assistance and information on all processes linked to web design. Operates throughout the UK and beyond.

Search-engine-optimised online brochure websites typically priced between £400 – £800, with larger sites priced according to the work involved. Also deals with website redesign, Internet consultancy and search-engine optimisation.

Twisted Reality Studios

12 Clayton Court, Nottingham NG7 3HU
tel 0800-977 4909
email intouch@twistedreality.co.uk
website www.twistedreality.co.uk

Media developers specialising in delivering advertising media and offering comprehensive and affordable complete web packages that can be tailored to suit. Offers an all-inclusive price and service. Web packages start from around £99. Also offers music and video feeds on websites, creating high-impact multimedia web presence.

Web Sheriff

Argentum, 2 Queen Caroline Street,
London W6 9DX
tel 020-8323 8013 *fax* 020-8323 8080
email websheriff@websheriff.com
website www.websheriff.com
Managing Director John Giacobbi

Established in 2003. Works globally to protect rights on the Internet. Typical clients include: record labels, celebrities and national newspapers.

WebCreation UK

tel 0845-054 0060
email info@webcreationuk.com
website www.webcreationuk.com

Bespoke developers of complete websites from personal to corporate entities. Tailored packages include total or partial design, including free secure hosting, free email and free content-managed page that can be updated by the client, support and free search-engine optimisation.

FAQs: The management of songs

Why is music publishing generally less understood than the work of record companies?

Music publishers normally work behind the scenes. Their products – song copyrights – are usually incorporated into other 'end-user' products, such as records, films, computer games, and TV adverts. Don't forget, though, that music publishers have been around much longer than record companies, as the printing press was invented hundreds of years before the first sound recordings!

Why do we call it music 'publishing'?
The concept of 'publishing' derives from the original role of the music publisher, which involved physically pressing and printing *sheet music*. Before CDs, tapes, vinyl or MP3s were even invented, this was the only way the consumer could purchase music. Music publishers still produce sheet music today – but it is now a marginal activity compared to their other income streams.

What is the basic core competency of the music publisher?
It's all about owning and controlling the use of song copyrights. This has its basis in intellectual property law.

Songs can be copyrighted separately from sound recordings, and one song could be recorded by a hundred different artists – with each contributing to the music publishing royalties. Copyright laws provide songwriters with certain rights, such as manufacturing rights (called 'mechanical' rights), performance and broadcasting rights, and moral rights. Such rights can be assigned to music publishers.

What are the main roles of a music publisher?
The music publisher's main activities can be categorised into several distinct functions:
- the administrator
- the developer
- the financier
- the promoter
- the protector

As **administrator** the music publisher completes all necessary paperwork, including official forms for granting manufacturing rights and printing rights, and synchronisation agreements with third parties. The publisher must register their copyright works with the relevant collection societies. As administrator, the publisher may oversee sub-publishing agreements (such as those with other publishers in foreign territories). The administration role also involves overseeing all contractual relationships with songwriters, as well as documenting the songs in manuscript form.

In the UK, the publisher will usually be a member of MCPS, PRS and the MPA (Music Publishers' Association), and will complete all necessary documentation for these purposes. Additionally, the publisher will necessarily deal with enquiries and liaise with accountants and lawyers.

Some publishers are also happy to administrate the catalogue of smaller publishers. In return for this service, they will take a lower royalty rate as commission. It is common for the major corporate publishers to provide this kind of service to smaller third parties.

As **developer** the music publisher will seek out new songwriters and aim to cultivate and enhance their creative skills. The development role may take the form of purchasing instruments and equipment, financing studio time and perhaps linking up the songwriter with other like-minded songwriters – sometimes forming partnerships. This support role means facilitating, mentoring, and generally encouraging the creative process!

As **financier** the music publisher takes a risk by paying advances to songwriters. The publisher also acts as a collecting house for the receipt of income such as MCPS manufacturing royalties, PRS broadcasting and public performance royalties, sheet music royalties and synchronisation fees. Royalty administration is sometimes undertaken using information technology such as the popular Counterpoint system. The publisher also produces regular accounts which contain details of royalty statements and sums paid to the songwriter. Internal issues such as VAT returns to Customs and Excise should also be accounted for in annual financial planning.

As **promoter** the music publisher actively uses contacts and initiative to seek out commercial opportunities for their songs – 'exploiting' works by placing them, for example, in films, in TV programmes and advertisements, and in multimedia and online programmes. Such 'placements' are achieved by interfacing with media production companies, and other music and associated entertainment industry networks.

Music publishers also plug songs to recording artists, A&R staff, artist managers and producers, in the hope that they will be recorded and released (thus triggering royalty payments). This latter role is also useful when helping songwriting artists secure a recording agreement. A performing artist in this situation is much more likely to secure a record deal if a publisher is actively touting them around record company A&R departments, and has already invested and demonstrated commercial faith in them. A number of bands – such as Travis – were first spotted by A&R staff at music publishers.

As **protector** the music publisher acts to counter any illegal exploitation or inappropriate moral use of the composer's, songwriter's or lyricist's works. The publisher will also ensure that activities such as the foreign-language translations of lyrics are agreed and paid for. Likewise, permission for samples, cover versions, partial revisions, or the reproduction of lyrics on the sleeves of records will be required. They therefore keep a watchful eye on the worldwide use of their song catalogue. Sometimes this can result in court action under copyright legislation.

Note that some publishers will perform these various roles more efficiently, and/or to different degrees, than others. In pursuing all these roles, the music publisher will have a duty to keep 'good faith' with their songwriting or lyricist client (known as a *fiduciary* relationship). Publishers should also inform their clients of sub-publishing arrangements, synchronisation use, and any likely takeovers or mergers. In practice, however, this may not always happen. As in the recording industry, there are various types of music publishers, and they have diverse working methods.

Is there still a role for the stand-alone songwriter?

Very much so. The industry depends on new songs for its lifeblood. Look at prolific US-songwriter Diane Warren, for example, who has penned successful hits for a range of different artists, including: Aretha Franklin, Britney Spears, Aerosmith, Whitney Houston, Elton John, Celine Dion, Toni Braxton, LeAnn Rimes and Christina Aguilera.

Surely, there's more potential income to be gained if you're a performing artist who can also write your own material?

Yes, correct. If you can both write and perform, then you might secure a record contract and a music publishing contract – and, consequently, have more income streams. Songwriting is difficult, though, and some performing artists prefer to source their material from elsewhere.

What is the main copyright law in the UK?

The Copyright, Designs and Patents Act (1988) – or CDPA. Britain's first real copyright law was the Statute of Anne (1710) and there have been numerous revisions since. In fact, the Statute of Anne was the first copyright law in the English-speaking world.

Why do we bother with copyright?

Copyright is generally considered to provide commercial incentives for producing artistic work by encouraging and rewarding creativity. There are now EU-wide laws and international treaties which try to provide copyright control throughout the world.

How do you actually go about copyrighting a song in the UK?

It's tricky to be definitive about this. First of all, the song must be 'tangible' (i.e. held in some kind of physical form, and not an idea in your head). It has then to be 'placed' somewhere – perhaps posted to yourself (recorded delivery and left unopened), or, better still, deposited with a lawyer, manager, or other secure third party.

Why don't we have an official place to copyright our songs?

The UK government hasn't felt the need to go about doing this (although it was once compulsory in Britain to register books with Stationer's Hall). Some countries, such as the USA, have a Copyright Office where songs can be formally 'deposited'. A US-songwriter (or an American publisher, if you have one) will do this at the Library of Congress, in Washington DC, for a standard fee.

Legally, do songs and records enjoy the same copyright durations in the UK?

Absolutely not! In fact, this is a sore point for the record companies! A song is under copyright protection until the end of the 70th year after the death of the songwriter. Recordings, however, are only under copyright for a fixed period of 50 years from the end of the year of their release.

What if there is more than one songwriter for a particular song?

In the case of their being more than one songwriter, the song would be under copyright control until the end of the 70th year after the death of the *last remaining songwriter*. That is, potentially, quite a long time!

Where do the royalties go for the 70 years after the songwriter's demise?

Any royalties generated in this period become part of the late songwriter's 'estate' – and usually go to their next of kin (unless otherwise indicated in their will). Successful songwriters should, therefore draw up a will! The law was framed so that a songwriter's dependents would benefit from the income generated by their creative works for a fixed period after the songwriter's death.

Why do music publishers pay much better royalty rates than record companies?

Publishers generally pay better rates because record companies undertake a much higher-risk activity. The vast majority of records don't make a profit. Music publishers also have much lower running costs than record companies. (Note that music publishing royalties should never be used to recoup record company debts. Such practice is called cross-collateralisation, and should always be avoided.)

What are the main sources of income for the music publisher?
Publishers have largely moved away from depending primarily on sheet music sales. In our era, they receive income from diverse sources, which may include the manufacturing of all manner of products: CDs, DVDs, birthday cards, film reels, mobile phone ringtones, and computer games. They also collect royalties for live performances, for the public performance of music in places such as nightclubs and sports arenas, from general broadcasting, and even from the reprinting of lyrics.

What do we mean by 'mechanical royalties', and how is this income collected?
A copyright song can only be manufactured into a physical product (a CD, for example) by securing a 'mechanical licence', and on payment of a mechanical royalty. To simplify this process, standard royalty rates are used, and collection agencies are assigned the task of collecting and distributing these royalties on behalf of their members. In the UK, the current standard mechanical royalty rate is 8.5 per cent of the published dealer price of the record. This sum is collected in the first instance by the MCPS (Mechanical-Copyright Protection Society) and then distributed to relevant copyright owners after the deduction of commission (to cover society operating costs).

Do other countries follow the same practice?
In the developed world, yes they do. Other 'territories' have their own mechanical royalty collection societies, and these include AMCOS (for Australia & New Zealand), CMRRA (Canada), JASRAC (Japan), GEMA (Germany), the Harry Fox Agency (USA), and STEMRA (Netherlands).

What are synchronisation fees?
These relate to permission to use copyrighted songs within films, TV shows, and indeed any other format where moving images are synchronised to sound. Synchronisation licences are negotiable, and will depend on a number of factors, ranging from how well-connected the music publisher is, to the size of the viewing audience and the exact terms of the contract. Songwriters are asked if they object to their material being used in conjunction or association with particular films or advertised products. Some publishers are more proactive than others at securing synchronisation income.

Do music publishers require the use of legal contracts?
Yes, a proper legal contract is required in order to assign the song copyrights from the songwriter to the publisher. An advance may be used as a financial incentive, and a royalty rate will be agreed. The contract should grant a minimum of 50 per cent to the songwriter. Some well-known songwriters receive between 60 and 80 per cent of the royalties generated. Most songwriters acknowledge that sharing royalties with a publisher is worthwhile, as the income pool generated is generally higher when backed by a competent publisher. The publisher will wish to recoup any advance, however, before paying such royalties.

Publishing contracts tend to differ from record contracts in terms of duration, as the song copyrights often revert back to the songwriter after a limited period of time. This means that the songwriter may sign a second publishing deal, upon expiry of the first. In some cases, songs may revert back sooner due to the inclusion in the contract of a 'reversion clause' (triggered if the publisher fails to 'exploit' the songs, or goes into liquidation). By contrast, many record companies will seek to own the rights to their 'masters' for the full phonographic copyright period.

A music publishing contract should be vetted by an experienced music industry lawyer. Key clauses will normally cover the assignment of copyright, the duration (an initial song-writing period and a longer retention period during which the publisher controls the rights to the songs), applicable territories, advances, royalties, accounting procedures, sub-publishing arrangements, warranties, and a 'governing laws' clause.

Not all music publishing agreements involve a transfer of copyright. Some contracts are 'administration deals' – where the publisher will receive a percentage of the income generated by the song catalogue for undertaking certain necessary tasks such as administration, registration, monitoring and royalty collection.

Is the songwriter usually the richest member of the band?

Yes! And it is common for band members to fall out due to the distribution of music publishing income, as inequality can cause friction and internal resentment. As a result, some songwriters agree to share some of their music publishing income with their colleagues.

Artist managers often help to resolve any potential conflict, and a band may be encouraged to draw up and sign a partnership agreement. Note that most managers will also seek a small share of their songwriting artist's income.

Any tips for going it alone, and setting up your own music publishing company?

Publishing can be a time-consuming activity, but if you are seriously thinking about it, then:

- Seek legal and financial advice from qualified professionals.
- Set up a limited company. Copyrights can often lead to legal wrangling, and you might prefer to be incorporated. Build up your 'catalogue'. You will have to secure the rights to songs through publishing agreements with songwriters. So, consider legal advice, representation and official documentation (such as an in-house 'Publishing Agreement' template).
- Build up your industry contacts, and network with industry associations. Seek their advice, news and information. Join the MCPS and PRS, and be aware of how to register your works with them. Also build up contacts with non-musical companies in order to help 'place' your songs as widely as possible (start with advertising, TV, film and multimedia production companies).
- Set up efficient administration systems. Acquire a Data Protection licence.
- Set up royalty tracking and accounting systems. Software is available on the market for this purpose. Consider obtaining specialised software for converting your works into sheet music format.
- Try to set aside a budget to make demo recordings for promotional purposes.
- If you want to go global, then consider attending industry conventions such as MIDEM, held in France every January (the music industry's equivalent of the Cannes Film Festival). Do your homework before you go, and seek out new opportunities!

Useful websites

MCPS-PRS Alliance – **www.mcps-prs-alliance.co.uk**
Music Publishers' Association – **www.mpaonline.org.uk**

JoJo Gould is a UK-based lecturer, and was for five years joint Managing Editor of *Music Business Journal*. He lectures and consults on the European Degree in International Music Management, and holds a Master of Science degree in Business IT Systems. He was a co-founder and first Chairman of New Music in Scotland, and was previously Senior Lecturer in Music Industry Management at Buckinghamshire Chilterns University College.

Resources

BOOKS

Bagehot on Music Business Agreements (2nd edn)
Author Nicolas Kanaar
Publisher Sweet and Maxwell, 1998
ISBN 0421624507

Long the only book of its type to deal comprehensively with British music business agreements, this 2nd edition is currently the legal 'Agreements Bible' for industry professionals. It includes specimen agreements and case reviews, and should prove relevant not only to lawyers, but also to artists, their agents, managers and promoters – all of whom may need to understand, in detail, the meaning of modern music industry contracts.

The Billboard Guide to Billboard Publicity (Rev. edn)
Author Jim Pettigrew
Publisher Billboard Books, 1997
ISBN 0823076261

Chapter 4 of this text – on 'Press Kit Components' – is essentially the main focus and starting point for a detailed analysis, in following chapters, of all the various components that go to make up the modern music press pack. Aimed at anyone involved in music industry press or publicity (with examples drawn from the US market), this guide outlines the essential facts to impart when compiling an artist's biography, and shows how to write a concise but information-rich fact sheet. It also speaks about the best methods of assembling press clippings, and how to impart the right 'feel' to publicity photos. The chapter on press releases and pitch letters is also a useful starting point for anyone new to the subject. The book's fundamentals certainly need to be appreciated before embarking on any music press campaign. Subtitled as: 'Techniques and Tools of the Professional Publicist for Musicians, Managers, Publicists, Promoters, Record Companies'.

BPI Statistical Handbook
Editor Christopher Green
Publisher British Phonographic Industry Limited (Annual)

A guide to all aspects of British record industry and related sales, including statistics on trade deliveries, singles, albums, artists' nationality, classical, music video, market share, music retailing, music buyers, press and advertising, radio and television, audio hardware, piracy and worldwide sales. See **www.bpi.co.uk**.

The Business of Music: The Definitive Guide to the Music Industry (9th edn)
Authors M William Krasilovsky, Sidney Shemel
Publisher Billboard Books, 2003
ISBN 0823077284

In its latest incarnation, this tome has to be the 'Bible' of US music business texts. It is extremely detailed, comprehensive, and contains a wealth of sample contracts and other documents. Recommended for anyone who needs to learn about the American music business. Includes CD-ROM of Copyright Office Documents, sample contracts, and articles and bulletins from the major US performing right societies.

The Business of Music Marketing and Promotion (2nd edn)
Author Tad Lathrop
Publisher Billboard Books, 2003
ISBN 0823077292

This US-focused book, which largely revolves around the record business, illustrates general principles relevant to all those involved in some way in marketing and promoting music. Its early chapters cover traditional record- and publishing-company marketing procedures, but it is most valuable for its subsequent chapters illustrating core products and their potential audiences, pricing policies, packaging and various distribution methods. The final chapters on Internet marketing, although now dated, do promulgate solid basic principles which still hold good. An informative and rounded introduction to music marketing.

Copinger and Skone James on Copyright (14th edn, 3 vols)
Authors Kevin Garnett, Jonathan Rayner James, Gillian Davies
Publisher Sweet and Maxwell, 1999
ISBN 0421589108

Comprehensive and (necessarily) very detailed description of UK Copyright Law (first published as *The Law of Copyright* in 1870). Elucidates the intricacies of copyright and 11 other separate, but related, rights. The 14th edition is built around 4 fundamental rights: copyright; moral rights; rights performance; and rights in design. It contains chapters on industry exploitation of rights, collecting societies, and control of rights.

Copyright and Public Performance of Music
Author Stanley Rothenberg, AB, LLB, LLD
Publisher Martinus Nijhoff, 1954

Useful for appreciating not only the history of copyright, but also the development of performing rights (and other royalty collection) societies throughout America and Europe – especially in Britain, France and the Netherlands. It includes information on the development of ASCAP, BMI, CISAC, the PRS, PPL, and SACEM, and is supported by full appendices containing a list of works cited, tables of the various statutes and conventions cited, while also covering important test cases. Now out of print, it is worth obtaining secondhand if not available through a library.

The Dictionary of Music Business Terms
Author Tim Whitsett, *Editor* Sarah Jones
Publisher Mix Books, 1998
ISBN 0872886840

Comprehensive guide to the terminology used in today's music industry. While many of the 3000+ entries in this book betray the fact that the US is its primary focus, there are enough references to the worldwide music industry to make it a valuable resource for most industry practitioners and educators. A helpful book, though now in need of updating.

How to Make It in the Music Business (3rd edn)
Author Sian Pattenden
Publisher Virgin, 2004
ISBN 0753509032

Written by an experienced music industry journalist, this guide provides an entertaining and rather anecdotal insight into available career opportunities within the music business. A summary is provided for a range of positions – such as record company managing director, tour manager, booking agent and artist manager. Each section contains a glossary, a summary of skills required and a series of related Internet addresses. Augmented by interviews with contemporary music industry professionals, this text is aimed at young people seeking to embark on a career in the music industry.

How to Succeed in the Music Business
Authors Allan Dann, John Underwood
Publisher Omnibus Press, 2002
ISBN 0711994331

Following a straightforward 'Question and Answer' format, this book provides information for songwriters, performers and recording artists, and is aimed at newcomers to the industry. Geared towards the UK market, the authors have also provided information on many record labels, music publishers and other useful organisations – such as press, lawyers, accountants, TV firms and industry regulators. Other topics covered are sample recording, publishing, management and live

engagement contracts – as well as an 'Instant Guide to Royalties' and a glossary.

The Illustrated Story of Copyright
Author Edward Samuels
Publisher Griffin, 2002
ISBN 0312289014

Clearly presented history of copyright, complete with many relevant illustrations and diagrams. Explains the purpose of copyright and how it has changed over the years, while also covering what copyright protects, how to determine what is original, and the rights of copyright holders (and how they can be enforced).

The IMF Handbook 2000: A Guide to Professional Band Management
Authors Andrew Thompson, et al
Publisher Sanctuary Publishing, 1999
ISBN 1860742572

Among few books of its type focusing solely on the UK market, this text includes sections on management, record, artist and producer contracts, as well as explaining the role of agents, the factors involved in live performing, dealing with press, PR, and how to manage merchandising. Compiled by the International Managers Forum, the emphasis is on the legalities of relationships between artists/ songwriters and record companies, music publishers, managers and agents. Worth obtaining secondhand if it goes out of print.

Music, Money and Success: The Insider's Guide to Making Money in the Music Industry (4th edn)
Authors Jeffrey Brabec, Todd Brabec
Publisher Schirmer, 2004
ISBN 0825673267

Written by 2 US entertainment law attorneys (and former recording artists), this book describes all the possible sources from which music creators can derive income – and then explains related fine detail such as how much money one should expect to earn from the use of music in commercials, movies, TV, on the stage, and for foreign uses (even for karaoke!). Its financial details and computations are almost impossible to find elsewhere. It also includes bargaining tips, and dissects the terms found in standard contracts, again pointing out their financial implications.

Music: The Business – The Essential Guide to the Law and the Deals (3rd edn)
Author Ann Harrison
Publisher Virgin, 2005
ISBN 978-1852272593

Affordable, popular UK music industry book – written by a leading London-based entertainment lawyer specialising in copyright and contract law – which covers a comprehensive range of music industry activities, and has legal considerations always to the fore. It is structured into 15 chapters with appendices; the definitions (and typefaces) are clear, and the text embraces new media and e-commerce issues. The role of industry framework organisations is covered, standard features of contracts are explained, and some 'how-to' information is provided for those at various levels in the industry. Also outlines key elements of case law which have helped to shape the development and operation of current UK music industry law.

Music Industry Management and Promotion

Author Chris Kemp
Publisher Elm Publishing, 2001
ISBN 1854502859

The great strength of this neat, concise text is its section on venue management, which is the author's area of specialist expertise. It benefits from Kemp's practical experience of running live shows, and covers many aspects of staging and promoting live music events.

The Music Management Bible

Authors Music Managers Forum
Publisher Sanctuary, 2003
ISBN 978-1844920259

A resource of particular use to anyone with an interest in artist management. Areas covered include the various types of management contract, contract lengths, expected fees and trial periods – all discussed in more depth than in many other music business books, while always keeping technical detail accessible to the lay reader.

The Recording Industry in Numbers

Publisher IFPI (London Secretariat) (Annual)

Summarising sales in recorded music markets in many countries and territories throughout the world, this is an invaluable (but expensive) statistical guide which may be available in selected libraries. Also see your national recording industry's website to obtain detailed national music industry statistics. In some cases, such statistics may be summarised online, and/ or available for purchase in booklet form – with the British Phonographic Industry's BPI Statistical Handbook. See **www.ifpi.org**.

Running a Band as a Business

Authors Ian Edwards, Bruce Dickinson, Phil Brookes
Publisher Cimino Publishing Group, 1999; PC Publishing, 2000

ISBN 1878427768 (US edition); 1870775627 (UK edition)

Affordable, slim volume which exists in both US and UK editions, although the many lessons contained between its covers apply equally the world over. From naming your band, to how to deal with success (or the lack of it!), from touring to T-shirts, concerts to contracts – almost everything a newly formed band may need to know is discussed in a logical and concise way, besides being illustrated with dozens of apt music industry stories. Importantly, the focus remains throughout on a band's long-term commercial viability. Structured in easily digestible sections and packed with sensible advice.

A User's Guide to Copyright (6th edn)

Authors Michael F Flint, Nicholas Fitzpatrick, Clive Thorne
Publisher Tottel Publishing, 2006
ISBN I1845920686

Covering not only music, but indeed all aspects of UK intellectual property law, this book is acknowledged as the leading introductory text in its field. The latest, updated edition takes into account recent EC Directives and emendations to the Copyright, Designs & Patents Act (CDPA) 1988. Useful to specialists and laymen alike, it describes the nature and scope of copyright, while also embracing such topics as rights in performances, collection societies, industrial designs, EU law and copyright, and much more. It contains sections on different forms of media, computer software, and piracy, and also includes appendices describing countries party to different copyright conventions, a full list of EU and EEA member states, a contact list of relevant organisations, and a useful table on copyright duration. Exemplary for its clarity, it contains an extensive cross-referencing system which is extraordinarily useful.

MAGAZINES

Music Week

Editor Martin Talbot
Publisher CMP Information: United Business Media
ISSN 0265-1548

The UK's main music business weekly and invaluable to those involved or interested in the business side of the music industry. Contains current news, technology and business developments, and chart information. See **www.musicweek.com**.

Appendices
History of copyright: a chronology in relation to music

(**As applicable in Britain, unless otherwise stated.**)

Copyright is not a new idea. Even scholars in Ancient Greece and Rome had to insist upon their right to be recognised as the authors of their works (the 'right of paternity') in an era when plagiarism was no crime. However, these Classical scholars certainly had no automatic, legal right to income from their works (the 'economic right'). In the Middle Ages – a time when most of the population was illiterate, and manuscripts laboriously copied by hand and available only to the privileged few – copyright was not a major issue. Gutenberg and Caxton changed all that with the introduction of mechanical printing, and the subsequent viability of commercial publishing.

Yet even by the 18th century, the transfer of copyrights for economic gain was still primarily made through outright sale of a manuscript (with no royalties payable for subsequent commercial 'exploitation'). Only in the 19th century did the law grant 'lifetime' copyright protection to composers, who were becoming more economically independent. Royalty contracts emerged as standard, ensuring that payment was due for repeat performances. Then, in the 20th century, rights were broadened, and 'multi-channel' exploitation of musical works became possible – with structures developing to cope with collecting monies from multifarious sources (whether from any format of recorded music, or from films, advertising, and 'broadcasts' of all types).

Half a millennium after Gutenberg, the Internet (and digital technology) have further revolutionised and added complexity to the situation, because they permit virtually unlimited duplication of documents, often at a single key-stroke. In the 1990s, Jim Griffin, former Director of Technology at Geffen Records, characterised the digital age as the era of the 'friction-free Gutenberg'. (Timeline compiled by **Jonathan Little**.)

1455 Johannes Gutenberg is the first in the Western world to print using movable type. In about 1455, in Mainz, he produces his famous Bible, the first complete typeset book extant in the West. (If Gutenberg's process revolutionises the dissemination of the printed word, the Internet will go a vital step further at the end of the 20th century.)

1476 William Caxton introduces the printing press into England, establishing himself at Westminster after returning from several years working on the Continent. Between 1477 and his death (ca. 1492) he is said to have issued around 96 different printed books in various quantities.

1557 Queen Mary I gives control of all printing and bookselling to a single guild, the *Stationer's Company*.

1662 The *Licensing Act* establishes a register of licensed books, as well as requiring a copy of a licensed book to be deposited with the *Stationer's Company*, who are given powers to seize books suspected of being hostile to Church or Government.

1681 The *Licensing Act* is repealed, but the *Stationer's Company* has now passed a by-law establishing rights of ownership for books registered to its members, so the Company is able to continue regulating the printing trade.

1707 Following the political union between Scotland and England on 1st May 1707, laws passed by the London Parliament now became generally applicable throughout Great Britain.

1709/10 The *Statute of Anne* is enacted in 1709, which becomes effective on 10th April 1710. Copyright in books and other writings now has the protection of an Act of Parliament. Prior to this, disputes over the rights to the publishing of books could be enforced by common law. The *Statute of Anne* (being a law passed during the reign of Queen Anne) is the first modern copyright law in England, and the first in the English-speaking world. Writers are given control of their works for a limited period of 14 years (with the option of renewing for another 14 years).

1765 Influential English jurist William Blackstone provides a definition of literary property which draws a close analogy between it and real property, the right to such *"property"* being claimed *"in total exclusion of the right of any other individual in the universe"*.

1774 The House of Lords declares that authors and publishers have no *absolute* property rights over their works – meaning that they must still seek confirmation of rights of ownership by recourse to law, and enforce such rights through the powers of the state.

1777 Music (in the form of printed notation – as 'sheet music' – and not necessarily that solely published or included in 'book' form) is confirmed as copyrightable subject matter embraced by the *Statute of Anne*.

1787 The United States Constitution recognises the concept of Intellectual Property.

1790 Like the *Statute of Anne* in Britain, the *US Copyright Act* of 1790 gives writers of books, maps, and charts a 14-year copyright, with the option of renewing for a similar period. Major revisions to the Act are undertaken in 1831, 1870, 1909 and 1976.

1791/93 French revolutionary governments pass author laws which emphasise *post mortem auctoris* terms (see below). The laws specify that works may not be performed in public without the consent of a living author or composer (and, importantly, these laws also conferred such rights on the heirs of authors and composers for a period of five years after their death). In 1791 – inspired by these new laws – the dramatist (and musician) Beaumarchais founds the first copyright collecting society for composers, but the venture is not a success.

1831 Any *"musical compositions in traditional notation"* are affirmed as protected under revised US copyright laws.

1833 In the reign of William IV, the *Dramatic Copyright Act* is enacted. It is commonly known as '*Bulwer-Lytton's Act*' – after the prolific writer, poet and dramatist, Edward George Bulwer-Lytton, who promoted this seminal statute concerned with stage works. This is effectively the first British Act to protect performing rights in dramatic works, though only for a limited number of years. (The performing right is defined as the *"sole right of representation or performance"*.) After this Act, many other copyright measures are passed, most of which are repealed on the passing of the great codifying Act of 1911.

1837 The most comprehensive and advanced copyright law of its time, the *Prussian Act* (11th June) emphasises *post mortem auctoris* terms. It is fully titled, *"Gesetz zum Schutze des Eigenthums an Werken der Wissenschaft und Kunst in Nachdruck und Nachbildung"* (*"Law to protect ownership of scientific and artistic works against reproduction and copying"*).

1842 The *Literary Copyright Act* of 1842 in the UK ('*Talfourd's Act*' – subsequent to the 1833 *Dramatic Copyright Act*); authors are granted 'lifetime' property rights in their own work. This Act grants copyright for 42 years from the date of publication, or the life of the author plus seven years, whichever is the greater. But the Act fails to cover performances of dramatisation of non-dramatic works. Unless an author dramatises his or her own literary works, stage productions are not copyright-protected. Further, if a play is published before being produced, the performing right is usually lost. As a consequence, some authors employ actors to give a single *"copyright performance"* – of a stage dramatisation of one of their works (a novel, or narrative poem, for instance) – *"in a place of public entertainment"*, in order to establish dramatic copyright.

1842 Copyright legislation is extended to protect music produced overseas, though at this stage is aimed mainly at publishers of sheet music in France and in some German states.

1847 The Paris Concert Café Ambassadeurs is successfully sued by popular music composers Ernest Bourget, Victor Parizot and Paul Henrion. The exclusive right of the author to approve public performances – although established in France in 1791– did not thus become a reality until over 50 years after the law's enactment.

1849 Following the Ambassadeurs Case (1847), the Cour d'Appel de Paris on 26th April orders the owner of Ambassadeurs Café to pay 'compensation' (effectively 'royalties') to composer Ernest Bourget for unauthorised use of his music. This, in turn, leads to publisher Jules Colombier joining forces with the three composers involved in the case, and setting up an 'Agence Centrale' (the predecessor of SACEM), for the administration of performing rights in their musical works.

1851 On 28th February, SACEM – the world's first copyright collecting society for musical works (specifically for performing rights) – is established in France (Société des Auteurs et Compositeurs et Editeurs de Musique).

1873 The need for international protection of intellectual creations becomes clear when many foreign exhibitors boycott *The International Exhibition of Inventions* in Vienna. They fear, as has previously occurred, that their ideas will be stolen and commercially exploited in other countries.

1875 A Royal Commission in Britain suggests that present copyright-related Acts be improved and codified, and recommends that the government enter a bilateral copyright agreement with the United States of America.

1883/84 The *Paris Convention for the Protection of Industrial Property* is signed by 14 European member states, and comes into force in 1884.

1884 The Society of Authors is founded for *"the maintenance, definition, and defence of Literary Property"*. The Society's first objective is to obtain copyright protection for English authors in the United States. Among its other aims, it also lobbies for a *Bill for the Registration of Titles*.

1886/87 The seminal *Berne Convention for the Protection of Literary and Artistic Works* is signed (in Berne, Switzerland). It intends to give international copyright protection to the creative works of the citizens of European member state signatories. Works protected include: *novels, short stories, poems and plays; songs, operas, musicals, sonatas and symphonies; drawings, paintings, sculptures and architectural works*. In the *International Copyright Act* of 1886, Great Britain gives assent to the obligations of the *Berne Convention*. This Act abolishes the requirement to register foreign works, and introduces an exclusive right to import or produce translations. The UK ratifies the *Berne Convention* with effect from 5th December 1887. The US, however, remains governed by its 1790 *Copyright Act*, and is not subject to the *Berne Convention*. Longstanding US literary and musical piracy of works by European authors and composers (and vice-versa) continues to be an accepted way of life for publishers, until finally brought to an end by the establishment of separate bilateral copyright agreements with the US. The *Berne Convention* is revised in 1908 and 1928. The *Berlin Act* of 1908 extends the duration of copyright to the life of the author plus 50 years, takes account of new technologies, and declares that formal registration is unnecessary in order to hold a copyright. The *Rome Act* of 1928 is the first to codify the moral rights of authors and artists.

1908 The *Berlin Convention* adds *photography, film and sound recordings* to the list of works protected under the *Berne Convention*.

1909 A major third revision to the *US Copyright Act* is completed. More categories of protected works are included than ever before (effectively, *all* works of authorship). The renewal term is also extended from 14 years to 28, taking the total possible period of protection to 56 years. With respect to music, Congress declares: *"The main object to be desired in expanding copyright protection afforded to music has been to give the composer an adequate return for the value of his composition ..."* The law also prohibits *"unauthorised mechanical reproduction of musical compositions"*.

1911/12 The great codifying *Copyright Act, 1911*, comes into force in Britain on 1st July 1912. For the first time, all provisions on copyright are unified in one Act. The Act adds to the composer's rights that of controlling reproductions of his work by *any mechanical means*, and his right to authorise performances. Sound recordings are now protected (as are works of architecture). The Act abolishes the requirement to register copyright with *Stationer's Hall*, and abolishes common law copyright protection in unpublished works, apart from unpublished drawings and photographs. Copyright duration is extended: it is granted for the life of the holder plus 50 years after his death. This new Act gives the copyright holder three principal rights:

● to print and sell copies of his work [largely via publishers];
● to reproduce his work by means of mechanical contrivances, such as gramophone records and perforated piano rolls [thus the necessity of establishing what became the MCPS (see: 1924)];
● to perform works in public, and to authorise these acts [thus the necessity of establishing the PRS (see: 1914)].

Each of these rights can be separately exercised.

1914 First meeting of the UK's newly formed Performing Right Society (PRS), on 1st April. The US equivalent – the American Society of Composers, Authors and Publishers (ASCAP) – is founded in the same year (13th February).

1924 Founding of the Mechanical-Copyright Protection Society (MCPS).

1934 Following a test case brought by the Gramophone Company against a coffee shop [Gramophone Company Ltd v Stephen Cawardine & Co], the British courts now recognise that owners of sound recordings should be paid for the broadcasting and public performance of their copyrights (songwriters were already being remunerated for these activities by virtue of their membership of the Performing Right Society). This acknowledgement of a separate right (from songwriters' rights), led to the establishment of a new collection society – *PPL (Phonographic Performance Limited)* – with a specific remit to collect and distribute broadcasting and public performance royalties on behalf of UK sound-recording owners.

1956/57 The *Copyright Act, 1956*, comes into force on 1st June 1957. It takes into account further amendments to the *Berne Convention*, and also the *Universal Copyright Convention*, to which the UK is a signatory. Films and broadcasts are now protected in their own right. The Performing Right Tribunal, predecessor of the Copyright Tribunal, is established.

1961 The *Rome Convention for the Protection of Performers, Producers of Phonograms and Broadcasting Organisations* is signed. This proves important to the recording industry, and assists in the prevention of recorded music piracy (further strengthened by the later *Geneva Convention* – see: 1971).

1967/70 The United Nations Convention establishing the World Intellectual Property Organisation is signed (of which the international bureaus set up to administer the *Paris* and *Berne Conventions*, almost a century earlier, were forerunners). (WIPO, as an international copyright umbrella organisation, commences operations in 1970.)

1971 The *Convention for the Protection of Producers of Phonograms Against Unauthorised Duplication of Their Phonograms* is adopted in Geneva on 29th October (sometimes referred to as the *Geneva Convention*).

1976 In the fourth major revision of the *US Copyright Act*, fair use and first sale doctrines are codified for the first time, and copyright is extended to unpublished works. In anticipation of becoming a Berne signatory, this statute is framed to bring the US more into line with international copyright law.

1982 The introduction of MIDI technology (Musical Instrument Digital Interface) begins to revolutionise music production.

1982 The introduction of the CD (Compact Disc) constitutes the first mass consumer product (or sound carrier) which holds music in digitised form.

1984 Richard Stallman, working at MIT, founds the Free Software Foundation, which is believed to be the first anti-copyright organisation of the digital era.

1988 The United States finally becomes a signatory to the *Berne Convention*.

1988/89 The *Copyright, Designs and Patents Act (CDPA), 1988,* supersedes the various amendments to the *Copyright Act, 1956*. The 1988 Act comes into force on 1st August 1989. In addition to *economic rights*, this Act introduces the concept of *moral rights* for the first time (The Right of Paternity and The Right of Integrity). (This present Act continues to be amended, and now incorporates various European Directives.)

1990 The *US Copyright Act* is amended in order to prohibit the commercial lending of computer software.

1993 Issue of United Nations Report on the *Study of the Protection of the Cultural and Intellectual Property of Indigenous Peoples*. (Final report issued in 1995.)

1994 The WTO (World Trade Organisation) *TRIPS Agreement* (Agreement on Trade Related Aspects of Intellectual Property) extends the principles established by the 1886 *Berne Convention* to all countries in the global free trade area. While reinforcing creator's rights ('author's life' terms), it also emphasises the concept of transferable property rights – in order to give economic stimulus to the exchange of 'cultural productions'.

1994 Emergence of the MP3 compression standard for music.

1994 John Perry Barlow (a former lyric writer for The Grateful Dead, and co- founder of the Electronic Frontier Foundation) declares, in a widely read manifesto, that intellectual property law *"cannot be patched, retrofitted, or expanded to contain digitised expression"*.

1995/96 The period of copyright is extended, in Europe and then America, to the life of the author plus 70 years *pma* (*post mortem auctoris*) for most printed works. (Sound recordings remain at 50 years.) (See the actual amendments to the 1988 *CDPA* for various details and exceptions, and dates of applicability. In the UK, works created on/after 1st January 1996 become 70-years *pma.*)

1996 In the US, the *TRIPS Agreement* restores, from 1st January, copyright protection to many works of foreign origin which are already in the public domain in the United States.

1996 On 1st December, the UK formally adopts European Union Directive 92/100/EEC, which was concerned with rental, lending and neighbouring rights matters. This meant that those featured artists and session performers who performed on sound recordings broadcast or performed in public after 1st December 1996 in the UK now had a legal right to receive "equitable remuneration" for this use of the copyright. As well as *PPL (Phonographic Performance Limited)*, the legislation subsequently led to the need for further collection societies in the UK – namely, *PAMRA (Performing Artists' Media Rights Association)* and *AURA (Association of United Recording Artists)*. Fees are paid by the user of the sound recording (e.g. radio station or nightclub, etc.) and are collected at source by PPL. Half of this income is paid by PPL to the owners of the sound recordings (record companies). The remainder is distributed to the featured artists and session performers through their individual membership of either PPL, PAMRA or AURA.

1996 WIPO issues its *Performances and Phonograms Treaty*.

1998 In the US, the *Copyright Term Extension Act* is enacted on 27th October (also known as the *Sonny Bono Copyright Term Extension Act*, and pejoratively as the *Mickey Mouse Protection Act*). This Act extends the period of copyright in the United States by 20 years (from *pma +50 years* to *pma +70 years*). The Act does not revive copyrights that have already expired.

1998 The *Digital Millennium Copyright Act (DMCA)* is enacted in the United States. It is soon criticised as being already out of date in respect of new Internet and other technological developments. The Internet music-file swap site, Napster, when sued by all the major record companies, uses the Act to argue (unsuccessfully) in court that Napster is merely a 'dumb pipe' – a conductor of digitised information – and therefore is not liable for users' copyright infringements (which Napster facilitates). Around this time a general concern emerges in the music industry that the potential removal of long-existing copyright 'intermediary' structures will reduce or otherwise permanently alter the infrastructure and the bargaining power, or relationship, between creators and consumers. The concept of 'disintermediation' – in relation to music distribution – is increasingly promulgated.

2001 *The European Copyright Directive* (Directive 2001/29/EC), which harmonises certain aspects of copyright across the 15 member states, is approved by the European Parliament and the European Council (22nd May).

2002 Effective from 1st January, the German *Bundestag* (Parliament) introduces a new law to provide for collective bargaining between organisations representing creators and exploiters of intellectual property, aimed at encouraging fairer remuneration for creators – including the statutory right for creators to ask for payment reviews and audits of companies involved in such exploitation.

2006 In the UK (in December), the *Gowers Review of Intellectual Property* recommends that the 50-year copyright protection term on sound recordings and performers' rights is not extended – as many music creators and record companies had wished (having argued for an extension of a further 45 years).

Recommended reading:

Ehrlich, Cyril (1989). *Harmonious Alliance: A History of the Performing Right Society*. Oxford & New York: Oxford University Press. ISBN 978-0193119246

Goldstein, Paul (2003). *Copyright's Highway: From Gutenberg to the Celestial Jukebox*. Palo Alto, California: Stanford University Press. ISBN 978-0804747486

Lessig, Lawrence (2001). *The Future of Ideas: The Fate of the Commons in a Connected World*. New York: Random House. ISBN 978-0375505782

Moser, David J (2002). *Music Copyright for the New Millennium*. Vallejo, California: ProMusic Press. ISBN 978-1931140164

Samuels, Edward (2000). *The Illustrated Story of Copyright*. New York: St. Martin's Press. ISBN 978-0312261764

Vaidhyanathan, Siva (2001). *Copyrights and Copywrongs: The Rise of Intellectual Property and How It Threatens Creativity*. New York: New York University Press. ISBN 978-0814788066

Further references:
www.wipo.org
www.caslon.com.au/ipchronology.htm

Glossary of UK music industry (and related) acronyms

Compiled by Lucy Weston, Policy Co-ordinator, British Academy of Composers and Songwriters.

AACP: Alliance Against Counterfeiting and Piracy
ACE: Arts Council for England
AIM: Association of Independent Music
AMIA: Association of Music Industry Accountants
APRS: Association of Professional Recording Services
APU: Anti-Piracy Unit
ASCAP: American Society of Composers, Authors and Publishers
AURA: Association of United Recording Artists
BAC&S: British Academy of Composers and Songwriters
BARN: British Academy Regional Network (through British Academy of Composers & Songwriters)
BCC: British Copyright Council
BETA: Broadcasting and Entertainment Trade Alliance
BMI: Broadcast Music Incorporated
BMIC: British Music Information Centre
BMR: British Music Rights
BPI: British Phonographic Industry
CCISSC: Creative and Cultural Industries Sector Skills Council
CIIPWG: Creative Industries [Taskforce] Intellectual Property Working Group
CLA: Copyright Licensing Agency
CLIP: Common Law Institute of Intellectual Property
COMA: Contemporary Music Making for Amateurs
CPA: Concert Promoters' Association
CRA: Creator's Rights Alliance
DCF: Digital Content Forum
DMC: Dance Music Community
EMO: European Music Office
ERA: Educational Recording Agency Ltd
ERA: Entertainment Retailers' Association
FACT: Federation Against Copyright Theft
IAEL: International Association of Entertainment Lawyers
IAPU: International Anti-Piracy Tool, 'Songbird'
IFPI: International Federation of the Phonographic Industry
IMRO: Irish Music Rights Organisation
IPI: Intellectual Property Institute
IRMA: Irish Recorded Music Association
ISCM: International Society for Contemporary Music

ISM: Incorporated Society of Musicians
ISRC: International Standard Recording Code
ISWC: International Standard Work Code
MBF: Music Business Forum
MBF: Musicians' Benevolent Fund
MCRG: Music Copyright Reform Group
MCPS: Mechanical-Copyright Protection Society
MEC: Music Education Council
MIA: Music Industries' Association
MMF: Music Managers' Forum
MPA: Music Publishers' Association
MPG: Music Producers' Guild
MU: Musicians' Union
NBR: National Band Register
NFMS: National Federation of Music Societies/'Making Music'
NIMIC: Northern Ireland Music
NMC: National Music Council
NMPA: National Music Publishers' Association
OCC: Official Chart Company
PAMRA: Performing Artists' Media Rights Association
PCAM: Society for Producers and Composers of Applied Music
PPL: Phonographic Performance Ltd
PRS: Performing Right Society
PRSF–PRS: Foundation for New Music
RCO: Royalty Compliance Organisation
RPS: Royal Philharmonic Society
RSM: Royal Society of Musicians
SDMI: Secure Digital Music Initiative
SMC: Scottish Music Centre
SMIA: Scottish Music Industry Association
SPARS: The Society of Professional Audio Recording Services
SPNM: Society for the Promotion of New Music
VPL: Video Performance Ltd
WIPO: World Intellectual Property Organisation
WMF: Welsh Music Foundation
WMIC: Welsh Music Information Centre

Lucy Weston provides the British Academy Board and Executive Committees with support in all administrative matters relating to the Academy's interaction with government and music industry organisations. She is also Administrator for the Creator's Rights Alliance – an informal confederation of 'creator' trade unions and associations.

Index